WYCLIFFE'S NEW TESTAMENT

Translated by
JOHN WYCLIFFE
and JOHN PURVEY

*A modern-spelling edition
of their 14ᵀᴴ century Middle English translation,
the first complete English vernacular version,
with an Introduction by*

TERENCE P. NOBLE

My thanks to
QUYNH M. DANG

in memory of
LOUIS

Original Edition ©August 2001 by Terence P. Noble
Revised Edition ©November 2011 & ©September 2015 by Terence P. Noble

Library and Archives Canada Cataloguing in Publication

Bible. N.T. English (Middle English). Wycliffe. 2011
    Wycliffe's New Testament : translated by John Wycliffe and John
Purvey : a modern-spelling edition of their 14th century Middle English
translation, the first complete English vernacular version / with an
introduction by Terence P. Noble, editor and publisher. – Rev. ed.

 Includes bibliographical references.
 ISBN 978-1-467-99493-4

    I. Wycliffe, John, d. 1384. II. Purvey, John, 1353?-1428? III. Noble,
Terry, 1954- IV. Bible. N.T. English (Middle English). Wycliffe. 2011.
V. Title.

BS2035 2011   225.5'201   C2011-906546-0

For more information, contact Terry Noble at:

terry@smartt.com

Table of Contents

Introduction

Then Jesus spake to the people....

By the sea or on a hilltop, in the Temple or at the well, to individuals and to multitudes alike, when Jesus walked the earth, he spoke to people in words they could understand.

Paul's actual letters were written in Greek, the everyday language of those to whom they were sent. Thirty years later, the same would be true of the original Gospels.

1300 years later, in England, the Word of Truth was written only in Latin, a foreign language to 99% of that society. Indeed, Latin was only understood by some of the clergy and the well-off, and the relatively few who were university-educated. As well, the Church's "Divine Commission" – to preach the Word and to save souls – had been transformed into a more temporal undertaking: the all-consuming drive to wield authority over every aspect of life and, in the process, to accumulate ever-greater wealth.

John Wycliffe, an Oxford professor and theologian, was one of those few who had read the Latin Bible. Though a scholar living a life of privilege, he nevertheless felt a special empathy for the poor and the uneducated, those multitudes in feudal servitude whose lives were "short, nasty, and brutish". He challenged the princes of the Church to face their hypocrisy and widespread corruption – and to repent. He railed that the Church was no longer worthy to be The Keeper of the Word of Truth. And he proposed a truly revolutionary idea:

"The Scriptures," Wycliffe stated, "are the property of the people and one which no party should be allowed to wrest from them...Christ and his apostles converted much people by uncovering of scripture, and this in the tongue which was most known to them. Why then may not the modern disciples of Christ gather up the fragments of the same bread? The faith of Christ ought therefore to be recounted to the people in both languages, Latin and English."

Wycliffe believed that with the Word of Truth literally in hand, each individual could work out his or her own salvation, with no need for any human or institutional intermediary.

And so John Wycliffe and his followers, most notably John Purvey, his secretary and close friend, translated Jerome's *Vulgate*, the "Latin Bible", into the first English Bible. Their literal and respectful translation was hand-printed around 1382. Historians refer to this as the "Early Version" of the "Wycliffe Bible".

The Church princes, long before having anointed themselves sole (soul?) arbitrator between God and man, condemned this monumental achievement as heretical – and worse:

"This pestilent and wretched John Wycliffe, that son of the old serpent...endeavour[ing] by every means to attack the very faith and sacred doctrine of Holy Church, translated from Latin into English the Gospel that Christ gave to the clergy and doctors of the Church. So that by his means it

v

Introduction

has become vulgar and more open to laymen and women who can read than it usually is to quite learned clergy of good intelligence. And so the pearl of the Gospel is scattered abroad and trodden underfoot by swine."

(*Church Chronicle*, 1395)

The Church princes decreed that Wycliffe be removed from his professorship at Oxford University, and it was done. Two years later, his health broken, he died.

In the decade following John Wycliffe's death, his friend John Purvey revised their Bible. The complete text, including Purvey's "Great Prologue", appeared by 1395. But portions of that revision, in particular the Gospels and other books of the New Testament, were likely circulated as early as 1388.

Historians refer to this as the "Later Version" of the "Wycliffe Bible". This vernacular version retained most, though not all, of the theological insight and poetry of language found in the earlier, more literal effort. But it was easier to read and understand, and quickly gained a grateful and loyal following. Each copy had to be hand-written (Gutenberg's printing press would not be invented for more than half a century), but this did not deter widespread distribution. The book you now hold in your hands is that Bible's New Testament (*with modern spelling*).

For his efforts, the Church princes ordered John Purvey arrested and delivered to the dungeon. He would not see freedom until he recanted of his "sin" – writing the English Bible. His spirit ultimately broken, he eventually did recant. Upon release, he was watched, hounded at every step, the Church princes determined that he would tow the party line. His life made a living hell, eventually the co-author of the first English Bible disappeared into obscurity and died unknown.

But the fury of the Church princes was unrelenting. Edicts flew. John Wycliffe's bones were dug up – and burned. Wycliffe's writings were gathered up – and burned. All unauthorized Bibles – that is, those in the English language – were banned. All confiscated copies were burned. Those who copied out these Bibles were imprisoned. Those who distributed these Bibles were imprisoned. Those who owned an English Bible, or, as has been documented, "traded a cart-load of hay" for part of one, were imprisoned. And those faithful souls, who refused to "repent" the "evil" that they had committed, were burned at the stake, the "noxious" books they had penned hung about their necks to be consumed by the same flames. In all, thousands were imprisoned and many hundreds executed. Merry olde England was engulfed in a reign of terror. All because of an English Bible. This Bible.

But the spark that John Wycliffe, John Purvey, and their followers had ignited would not, could not, be extinguished. The Word of Truth was copied, again, and again, and again. The Word of Truth was shared, from hand, to hand, to hand. The Word of Truth was spoken, and read, and heard by the common people in their own language for the first time in over 1300 years. At long last, the Word of Truth had been returned to simple folk who were willing to lose everything to gain all.

And so the pearl of the Gospel was spread abroad and planted in their hearts by the servants of God....

Introduction

216 years after Purvey's revision appeared, somewhat less than a century after Martin Luther proclaimed his theses (sparking the Protestant Reformation), and Henry VIII proclaimed his divorce (thereby creating the Church of England), what would become the most famous, enduring, beloved and revered translation of the Bible, the *"Authorized"* or *King James Version* (*KJV*), was published in 1611.

In their preface, "The Translators to the Reader", in the 1ˢᵗ edition of the *KJV*, the 54 translators detail many sources utilized, and arduous efforts undertaken, to achieve their supreme accomplishment. Interestingly enough, they make scant mention of even the existence of earlier, unnamed English versions. And they make no specific reference to the work of John Wycliffe and John Purvey. It is not my desire or intention here to speculate on the political and ecclesiastical reasons for this omission, simply to state its fact.

From 1611 until today, historians of the English Bible have uniformly followed the lead of the *KJV* translators, and have either ignored, dismissed or denigrated John Wycliffe's and John Purvey's contributions to, and influences upon, that ultimate translation, the *KJV*. To wit:

"The Bible which permeated the minds of later generations shows no direct descent from the Wycliffite versions; at most a few phrases from the later version seem to have found their way into the Tudor translations...Tyndale's return to the original languages meant that translations based on the intermediate Latin of the *Vulgate* would soon be out of date."
(*Cambridge History of the Bible,* Vol. 2, p. 414.)

When you finish reading this present volume, you may reach a different conclusion.

Regarding *Wycliffe's New Testament*

Wycliffe's New Testament comprises the New Testament found in extant copies of the "Later Version" of the "Wycliffe Bible", with modernized spelling. For more than 99% of *Wycliffe's New Testament*, word order, verb forms, words in *italics*, and punctuation are as they appear in the "Later Version". In addition, words, phrases and verses, found only in the "Early Version" are presented within square brackets, "[ ]", to provide more examples of Wycliffe's and Purvey's groundbreaking scholarship, as well as to often aid reader comprehension and improve passage flow (more on this below).

Because mortal danger was a very real possibility and personal glory was of no consequence to either man, neither Wycliffe nor Purvey signed any extant copy of either version, attesting to authorship. This omission has allowed some historians to debate the matter. *Wycliffe's New Testament* is unambiguously credited: "Translated by John Wycliffe and John Purvey". The evidence supports this stand and there is absolutely no doubt about the essential role that each man played in the effort to bring the English Bible to the English people.

Introduction

Middle English

The "Wycliffe Bible" was written in Middle English in the last three decades of the 14TH century. "Middle English" is the designation of language spoken and written in England between 1150 and 1450. The year 1300 is used to divide the period into "Early Middle English" and "Late Middle English". During the time of Late Middle English, there were 5 regional dialects in England (with London itself eventually developing a sixth distinct dialect). Elements of at least three dialects can be found in the "Later Version" of the "Wycliffe Bible".

What does one encounter reading the "Later Version"? An alphabet with a widely used 27TH letter, "ȝ". A myriad of words which today are obsolete ("disparple": "to scatter"), archaic ("culver": "dove"), or at best, strangely spelled ("vpsedoun": "upside-down"). Spelling and verb forms that are not standardized because they are phonetic to different dialects: the word "saw" is spelled a dozen ways, and differently for singular and plural nouns, similarly the word "say"; "have take" and "have taken" are found in the same sentence, as are "had know" and "had known"; and so forth. Prepositions and pronouns that often seem misplaced and incorrectly used: "in", "of", "to", "what", "which", and "who" again and again seem wrongly situated; "themself" and "themselves", and "youself" and "yourselves", regularly appear in the same sentence; etc. Capitalization, punctuation, and other grammatical conventions that are rudimentary by today's standards and vary greatly from sentence to sentence: for example, *past tenses* are made by adding nothing to the present tense, or an "e", "en", "id", "ede", and still other suffixes. One encounters, in short, a seemingly incomprehensible challenge within (what will become) a single verse of scripture.

And so the reason for *Wycliffe's New Testament*. *Wycliffe's New Testament* is the New Testament of the "Later Version" of the "Wycliffe Bible" with irregular spelling deciphered, verb forms comprehended and made consistent, and numerous grammatical variations standardized. *Wycliffe's New Testament* is the key that unlocks the amazing secrets found within the "Wycliffe Bible".

Three Types of Words: Obsolete, Archaic and Precursors

As indicated above, when the spelling is modernized, three types of words are found in the "Later Version": **obsolete** ("dead", unknown and unused for centuries), **archaic** (old-fashioned, now chiefly used poetically), and, the vast majority, **"precursors"**, that is, strangely spelled forerunners of words that we use today. To comprehend the text, each group of words must be dealt with in a particular way.

Obsolete Words

Approximately 5% of the words in the "Later Version" are "dead" words that are neither presently used, nor found in current dictionaries. To fully understand the text, these obsolete words must be replaced. (In a handful of instances, the *KJV* follows the "Later Version" in the use of an obsolete or an archaic word – words

Introduction

such as "holden":"held"; "washen":"washed"; "wot":"know"; "wist":"knew"; "anon":"at once"; and "let":"to hinder" – and *Wycliffe's New Testament* follows suit. In most other instances, the obsolete words have been replaced.)

Fortunately for our purposes, the "Wycliffe Bible" was created at an exciting time of transition, just as the nascent language was beginning to blossom into the English that we know today. So, frequently, a modern equivalent of an obsolete word is present in the "Later Version", already in use alongside its soon to be discarded doublet. These "in-house" replacement words include "know", "follow", "praise", "with", "scatter", "lying", "harm", "commandment", "reckon", "ignorance", "ignorant", "offence", "ascend", "again", and many others (including even "that" and "those", derived from either "the"+"ilk" or "thilke"). More than half of the obsolete words in the "Later Version" were replaced with these "in-house" substitutions. Somewhat surprisingly, a number of the equivalent modern words were found only in the "Early Version" of the "Wycliffe Bible". In these instances, which are not infrequent, it is the "Later Version" that utilizes only the older, soon-to-be defunct, term.

For the remaining obsolete words, reference works were consulted and the appropriate word chosen and utilized. Older words, in use as close in time to the "Later Version" as possible, were favored over more recent words. And, as often as possible, when selecting a replacement word not already found in the text, one different from that used in the *KJV* was chosen, so as not to artificially produce similar phraseology. Sometimes, however, the only appropriate replacement word was that which the *KJV* also used.

When an obsolete word was replaced, the effort was made to use the same replacement word as often as possible to reflect word usage in the "Later Version". However, words often have more than one meaning and readability itself sometimes required multiple renderings. So, a word usually rendered "suitable", also became "opportune"; one rendered "grumble", also became "grudge"; one rendered "of kind" or "by kind", occasionally became "naturally"; one rendered "part" (i.e., "to divide"), also became "separate"; one rendered "cause to stumble", also became "offend"; one rendered "rush", also became "force"; one rendered "household", also became "family" and "members"; and so on.

In all, approximately 240 replacement words (and their various forms) were utilized. Some replacement words ("parched", "wrenched", "physician", etc.) were used infrequently; other replacement words ("call", "ascend", "promise", etc.) were used repeatedly.

Archaic Words

More than 10% of the words used in the "Later Version" are today considered "archaic", that is, not presently or widely used, but still found in good, current dictionaries. Words in this category include "youngling" (young person), "ween" (suppose), "trow" (trust/believe), "swevens" (dreams), "strand" (stream), "querne" (hand-mill), "repromission" (promise), "principat" (principality), "comeling" (stranger/new-comer), "livelode"/"lifelode" (livelihood), "knitches" (bundles), "anon" (at once), "culver" (dove), "soothly" (truly), and "forsooth" (for truth). Once understood, these words are valid, vital, and provide a sense of the times and atmosphere in which the "Later Version" was written. Most archaic words have been retained. For definitions, refer to the Glossary at the back of the book, or to the *KJV*, or to your own dictionary.

In numerous instances within the "Later Version", archaic words also have their own more modern equivalents. So within *Wycliffe's New Testament*, following the "Later Version", you will find both "again-rising" and "resurrection"; "again-buying" and "redemption"; "gobbets" and "pieces"; "meed" and "reward"; "volatiles" and "birds"; "wem" and "spot"; "virtue" and "power"; "leaveful" and "lawful"; "maumet" and "idol"; "simulacra" and "idols"; "comprehend" and "apprehend" (i.e., to physically catch, lay hold of, or to grasp); and numerous other doublets of archaic and "modern" words.

Precursors

But the vast majority of words in the "Later Version", 85% or more, though often spelled quite differently, are nevertheless the direct precursors of words that we use today. Their spelling modernized, they are comprehensible – with a few caveats.

Within *Wycliffe's New Testament*, you will encounter familiar words in unfamiliar settings: "health" in place of "salvation"; "enhance" in place of "exalt"; "clarity" and "clearness" in place of "glory"; "deem" in place of "judge"; "doom" in place of "judgment"; "defoul" in place of "defile"; "virtue" in place of "power"; "dread" in place of "fear"; "either" in place of "or"; "charity" in place of "love"; "take" in place of "receive"; "and" in place of "also"; and so forth. Consult a dictionary. Even as defined in the year 2001, these words remain relevant in their particular context. Their use in favorite and well-known passages breathes new life into these verses and can bring fresh insight and illumination.

In some instances, however, words that we recognize have significantly changed definition in the intervening six centuries. Confusion would result if these words were retained in *Wycliffe's New Testament*. So they were replaced. Words in this category include "wood" (meaning "mad"); "behest" (meaning "promise"): "let" (meaning "to hinder"); "cheer" (meaning "face"); "anon" (meaning "at once" or "immediately", not the more modern "by and by"); "sick" (meaning "weak" or "frail"); "sad" (meaning "firm"); "cloth" (meaning "cloak"; it is also the singular of "clothes", and as such, "a garment"); "lose" (meaning "to destroy", active sense); "lost" (meaning "destroyed", active sense); "leech" (meaning "physician"); "leave" (meaning "dismiss" or "send away"); "left" (meaning "dismissed" or "sent away"); " drench" (meaning "to drown"); and so forth. About twenty words comprise this group and about half of their replacements were found already in the "Later Version". For more information regarding these words, consult the Glossary, which follows the text of *Wycliffe's New Testament*.

To aid comprehension and readability, two separate words in the "Later Version" are often joined together in *Wycliffe's New Testament*. Examples include

Introduction

"in+to", "-+self", "-+selves", "no+thing", and a few others. Conversely, many unfamiliar compound nouns found in the "Later Version" are hyphenated in *Wycliffe's New Testament*. So, for example, "aȝenrisynge" became "again-rising" ("resurrection"). For added comprehension, it is sometimes beneficial to reverse the order of hyphenated words, so "against-stand" can be read "stand against", "against-said" can be read "said against", and so on.

Occasionally an appropriate prefix or suffix was added to a familiar root word to aid understanding. These include "en" to make "engender" and "enclose", "sur" to make "surpassingly", "ac" to make "acknowledge", "re" to make "restrained" and "requite", "de" to make "deprived", "ap" to make "approved", and "ly" to make "mostly". All of the prefixes and suffixes used were already found in abundance in the "Later Version". Sometimes a comma was inserted to aid readability. Words not found in the original text that were added to aid reader comprehension and passage flow are placed in parentheses "( )", and are regular font. Most are inconsequential prepositions ("the", "a", "which", "that" or "for"), or are nouns such as "self" and "selves". None are integral or determinate.

To summarize: More than 95% of the words that you will read in *Wycliffe's New Testament* are modernized spellings of the original words (or their contemporary equivalents) found in the 14TH century manuscripts. Less than 5% of the words are "replacement" words, that is, appropriate words chosen to replace obsolete or "dead" words. Of this small group – less than 240 individual words and their various forms – about half are already found in the original text and half are my selections as replacements.

Ultimately, the presence of each word in *Wycliffe's New Testament* was decided by its fidelity to the source texts, as well as its aid to reader comprehension and passage flow.

Use of the *KJV*

In transforming the "Later Version" into *Wycliffe's New Testament*, the *KJV* was followed in three aspects: Verse number, book order, and proper names.

Verses are not found in either version of the "Wycliffe Bible". Each chapter consists of one unbroken block of text. There are not even paragraphs. In creating *Wycliffe's New Testament*, the "Later Version" New Testament was defined, word by word. Then, the *KJV* was placed alongside and used to divide each chapter into the traditional verses. (Verse divisions were established and numbered in the middle of the 16TH century, 60 years before the *KJV* was printed. The *KJV* translators copied what was already established.) As the blocks were broken up, there were many moments of astonishment, for time after time, John Wycliffe and John Purvey had written it first, written it right, more than two centuries before the *KJV* translators.

New Testament book order to which we are accustomed long pre-dates the *KJV*: it appeared at least as early as the 5TH century in some Latin Bibles, and was established as the accepted order at the same time the verse divisions were made, as stated, 60 years before the *KJV* was printed. The "Wycliffe Bible" follows that order with one exception: "Deeds of (the) Apostles", (in some copies of both versions of the "Wycliffe Bible" entitled "Actus Apostolorum", Latin for "Acts of the Apostles"), is placed after Hebrews and before James. In *Wycliffe's New Testament*, "Deeds"/"Actus" is returned to its more familiar position between The Gospel of John and The Epistle of Paul to the Romans.

(As indicated, New Testament book names vary among copies of the "Wycliffe Bible". But overall, they are more basic, and less formal, than those found in the *KJV*. To wit: "The Gospel of Luke" rather than "The Gospel according to Saint Luke"; "The Epistle of Paul to the Colossians" rather than "The Epistle of Paul the Apostle to the Colossians"; and so forth. *Wycliffe's New Testament* follows the simplicity of the "Wycliffe Bible", rather than the more ecclesiastical *KJV*, in this regard.)

Proper names have been modernized in *Wycliffe's New Testament* to conform to those in the *KJV* and so aid in comparison purposes. However, where a name in the "Later Version" is significantly different from its counterpart in the *KJV*, it was not changed in *Wycliffe's New Testament*.

Names of God are a special circumstance. In the "Wycliffe Bible" (both versions), "God", "Jesus", "Christ", and the "Holy Ghost" are always capitalized, while the "Father", the "Son" (of God, or of man), the "Spirit", "Lord", and "Saviour" are only sometimes capitalized. For consistency's sake, all have been capitalized in *Wycliffe's New Testament*. Other appellations and adjectives for God and Jesus, such as "the word", "the lamb", "shepherd", "master", "prince", "king", "holy" and "just" are not capitalized in the "Wycliffe Bible", and remain not capitalized in *Wycliffe's New Testament*. "christian" is not capitalized in the "Wycliffe Bible" nor in *Wycliffe's New Testament*. As always, the goal was to achieve a workable balance between comprehension on the one hand and an honest representation of the original texts on the other.

With *Wycliffe's New Testament* and the *KJV* side-by-side, you can readily compare one text to the other. Sometimes first reading *Wycliffe's New Testament*, then the *KJV*, you will see how the *KJV* grew out of the "Wycliffe Bible". Sometimes the *KJV* will help you to understand a difficult passage in *Wycliffe's New Testament*. Sometimes the two are different, but related; sometimes just different. But often, you will find these two texts very similar or even identical.

Words in *italics* are as found in both the "Wycliffe Bible" and the *KJV*, and in each case signify words added by their respective translators to aid the reader's understanding. The *KJV* contains many more words in *italics* than does the "Later Version", but less words in *italics* than the "Early Version".

A Word Regarding the Primary Source

Both versions of the "Wycliffe Bible" contain prologues (introductions to each book, mostly taken from Jerome), and marginal glosses (explanations of the text by the translators). These have not been reproduced in *Wycliffe's New Testament*. If of interest, the reader is encouraged to locate a copy of the present volume's primary source, Forshall & Madden's *The Holy Bible, Made from the Latin Vulgate By John Wycliffe and His Followers, Vol. IV* (most likely found in a university library).

Introduction

Twenty years in the making, this magnificent 4-volume opus is a monumental work of scholarship from the mid-19ᵀᴴ century. In it, The Rev. Josiah Forshall and Sir Frederic Madden correlate 160 extant hand-written copies of the two versions of the "Wycliffe Bible" into two master texts. There are over 90,000 footnotes, more than 25,000 of them pertaining to the New Testament alone (both versions). These footnotes delineate textual divergence – copy errors, omissions, and insertions – between the master text and each hand-written copy of the "Wycliffe Bible". (A footnote can refer to a single copy or to multiple copies.) Close reading of these footnotes indicates that many times when a copy of either the "Early" or "Later" version was made, the source texts were also consulted. For time and again, words added to, or changed, in one phrase or another, produce a more accurate rendering of the original Greek. In creating *Wycliffe's New Testament*, many of these footnotes were utilized to provide the most precise translation of the New Testament found within all extant copies of the "Wycliffe Bible". Footnotes were also used when a change created a more satisfying (i.e., balanced, rhythmic) read. However, with regard to the "Later Version", no footnote was simply used to produce greater consistency with the *KJV*, nor were two footnotes combined within the same phrase ("between the commas") for that purpose. With regard to the "Early Version", noteworthy phrasing from two (or more) footnotes were often combined due to space limitations and to avoid needless repetition. These excerpts are marked with a plus sign in superscript, "+"; all other "Early Version" passages are from a single source. A forward slash, "/", separates different renderings of the same phrase from two sources. It is significant to note that many textual variances indicated by footnotes for the "Early Version" appear within the *KJV*. This strongly suggests that the *KJV* translators consulted a variety of copies of the "Wycliffe Bible" as they accomplished their work (more on this below).

In creating *Wycliffe's New Testament*, textual errors that were found in the "Later Version" were not corrected (they are also part of the reality of this book); none are major, see which ones you can find. A handful of printing errors – reversed letters or misread vowels of prepositions, pronouns and adverbs – appear to have been discovered. They were confirmed by referring to the "Early Version", which in each case agreed with the Greek and not the "Later Version". In these instances, the "Early Version" phrases have been provided for comparison purposes.

Use of the "Early Version"

The "Later Version" is the foundation upon which *Wycliffe's New Testament*, like the *KJV* itself, was built. Strictly speaking, *Wycliffe's New Testament* is not a composite of the "Early" and "Later" versions. However, as has already been touched upon, and now will be further delineated, the "Early Version" was utilized in a number of ways.

First, the "Early Version" was used to help define unknown words found in the "Later Version". For, as was stated above, often a modern equivalent of a "dead" word was found only in the "Early Version". Similarly, and again surprisingly, modern verb forms were quite often found only in passages of the "Early Version".

Introduction

Their presence there aided immeasurably in attaining a consistency of verb forms throughout *Wycliffe's New Testament*. Finally, irregular spelling sometimes made even the simplest words difficult to decipher. Many times the "Early Version" served as a reference source of another, more recognizable spelling of the same word, and so helped make those words comprehensible.

Second, the "Early Version" served as a source of "missing" or "dropped" words and phrases. A limited number of times, a textually significant word or partial phrase not found in the "Later Version", but present in the "Early Version" (following the Greek and found also in the *KJV*), was inserted into *Wycliffe's New Testament* to enhance its accuracy, reader comprehension, and/or the flow of the passage. Seven significant examples include Deeds 6:3, 13:20, 17:10, 18:21, Ephesians 6:21, and Apocalypse 16:4-5 and 17:16. Countless more times, less consequential "missing" words – in many cases prepositions perhaps inadvertently "dropped" by weary or distracted copyists – were extracted from the same passage in the "Early Version" and added to *Wycliffe's New Testament*. All of these "missing" words, significant or otherwise, are contained in square brackets, "[ ]".

Third, the "Early Version" served as a source of "alternate" words and phrases. When the "Early Version", the "Later Version" and the *KJV* are compared side-by-side, one quickly discovers innumerable instances where the *KJV* follows not the "Later Version", but, instead, the "Early Version". Sometimes it is a single word, sometimes it is a phrase, and sometimes it is the order of several phrases within a verse. In many of the examples presented in *Wycliffe's New Testament*, the "Early Version" more closely follows the Greek than does the "Later Version", and the *KJV* deviates from following the "Later Version" and, to a greater or lesser degree, mirrors the "Early Version". These "alternate" words and phrases are also contained in square brackets, "[ ]".

Fourth, a subset of category three, the "Early Version" served as a source of "interesting" words, perhaps no more accurate than what is found in the "Later Version", and many not utilized by the *KJV*, but nonetheless fascinating, and so presented in *Wycliffe's New Testament*. Words such as "experiment", "prescience", "copious", and "litigious", to name but a few. These excerpts are also placed in square brackets, "[ ]".

To sum up: All of the words in *Wycliffe's New Testament* contained in square brackets, "[ ]", are from the "Early Version" of the "Wycliffe Bible". Some words are missing from the same passage in the "Later Version" and have been added to aid textual accuracy, reader comprehension, and/or passage flow. Some words are "alternate" words from the "Early Version", that are closer to both the original Greek and what is found in the *KJV*; other words are simply interesting variations demonstrating the rich and historic vocabulary found in the "Wycliffe Bible".

For the Revised Edition, the number of "Early Version" verses in square brackets have been dramatically reduced in an effort to reduce clutter on the page, and so to improve readability. However, not wanting to short-change the reader of many of the insights and fascinating alternatives found in the "Early Version", notable excerpts were taken from these verses, and placed in square brackets "[ ]". For more details on this, see 'Regarding the Revised Edition' that follows this Introduction.

Introduction

All of the foregoing understood, it needs to be stated that *Wycliffe's New Testament* can be read and readily comprehended without reference to any of the words or phrases found within the square brackets or the parentheses. The "Later Version" – as represented by *Wycliffe's New Testament* – can and does stand on its own. The inclusion of the words in square brackets simply provides an additional dimension of this seminal work in the English translation of the New Testament; the words in parentheses simply help to improve sentence flow. (For more discussion of "Early Version" highlights and insights, see 'Endnote: Regarding the "Early Version"', at the back of this book.)

A Final Note

With the spelling up-dated, and the obsolete words replaced, the document you now hold in your hands is a fair and accurate representation of John Wycliffe's and John Purvey's 14TH century translation of the very first English vernacular New Testament. This *is* their New Testament *with modern spelling* – not some 21ST century variation on a medieval theme. The melodies and harmonies are distinctly Wycliffe's and Purvey's. Only now, they are sung with words that we all can understand. Six centuries later, you can now read what those common folk were themselves at long last able to read (or, more likely, have read to them). Simple, direct words, with their own charm and rhythm, their own humble, cogent beauty. Sophisticated and graceful words, their originality and newness making the well-known and the fondly remembered fresh and alive once again. All because John Wycliffe, and John Purvey, and their compeers, cared so deeply, and sacrificed so dearly.

Today there are over 100 modern translations of the New Testament in English, available at bookstores, the public library, and on the Internet. But once, there was just one. This one. Try to imagine the impact upon hearing, or reading, these words for the very first time:

Oure fadir that art in heuenes,	Our Father that art in heavens,
halewid be thi name;	hallowed be thy name;
thi kingdoom come to;	thy kingdom come to;
be thi will don in erthe	be thy will done in earth
as it is in heuene;	as it is in heaven;
ȝyue to vs this dai oure ech	give to us this day our each
dayes breed;	day's bread;
and forȝyue to vs oure dettis,	and forgive to us our debts,
as we forȝyuen to oure dettouris;	as we forgive to our debtors;
and lede vs not in to temptacioun,	and lead us not into temptation,
but delyuere vs fro yuel. Amen.	but deliver us from evil. Amen.
"Later Version", MATTHEW, Chapter 6,	MATTHEW 6:9-13,
The Holy Bible, 1395, unaltered.	*Wycliffe's New Testament*, 2011.

Regarding the Revised Edition

When I first published *Wycliffe's New Testament*, a modern-spelling edition of the "Later Version" of the "Wycliffe Bible" in 2001, I included thousands of words from the "Early Version" of the "Wycliffe Bible" as well, phrases and verses printed within square brackets, "[ ]". My original intention was to have the Wycliffe New Testament side-by-side with the "King James Version", to demonstrate the profound influence both Wycliffe versions had on the translators of the KJV. That plan proved impractical, and so only the Wycliffe New Testament was printed, but still including the "Early Version" phrases and verses. I believe these "Early Version" words helped many readers to better understand the text of the "Later Version". But all those words in square brackets possibly gave the pages a busy look, and disrupted the passage flow. And so, when the opportunity arose, I decided to revise *Wycliffe's New Testament*, and remove many of the words in the square brackets. (For those interested in all the "Early Version" words, and in the side-by-side comparison with the KJV, various sites around the Internet host these efiles, including www.ibiblio.com, and a printed version is available at www.biblereadersmuseum.com.)

Originally, this revision was going to be a "pure" "Later Version", with no words in square brackets or in parentheses (the latter are my added words, usually "a" or "the", to improve passage flow, or my reordering of the original words, to aid comprehension), just the best of the "Later Version", the master text and footnote variations, as found in Forshall and Madden's magnificent work. However, in the end, I was not willing to part with many of the insights and interesting alternatives found in the "Early Version". And so while most of the complete "Early Version" verses have been removed, numerous notable words and phrases were taken from these "Early Version" verses and placed in square brackets, "[ ]", in the same "Later Version" verses. Now the reader has the best of the "Early Version", still present to aid understanding, but in a form easier to read.

However, as stated in the Introduction, all of the words in square brackets, and those in parentheses as well, can be ignored – the "Later Version" of the "Wycliffe Bible" can stand on its own – and one will still experience the genius and the majesty of what Wycliffe and Purvey produced more than 600 years ago, at tremendous personal cost, and of inestimable value.

Terence Noble
Vancouver Canada
September 2015

Wycliffe's
New Testament

MATTHEW

CHAPTER 1

1   The book of the generation of Jesus Christ, the son of David, the son of Abraham.

2   Abraham begat Isaac. Isaac begat Jacob. Jacob begat Judas and his brethren.

3   Judas begat Phares and Zara, of Thamar. Phares begat Esrom. Esrom begat Aram.

4   Aram begat Aminadab. Aminadab begat Naasson. Naasson begat Salmon.

5   Salmon begat Booz, of Rachab. Booz begat Obed, of Ruth. Obed begat Jesse.

6   Jesse begat David the king. David the king begat Solomon, of her that was Urias' *wife*.

7   Solomon begat Roboam. Roboam begat Abia. Abia begat Asa.

8   Asa begat Josaphat. Josaphat begat Joram. Joram begat Ozias.

9   Ozias begat Joatham. Joatham begat Achaz. Achaz begat Ezekias.

10   Ezekias begat Manasses. Manasses begat Amon. Amon begat Josias.

11   Josias begat Jechonias and his brethren, into the transmigration of Babylon (or until the exile to Babylon).

12   And after the transmigration of Babylon (or And after the exile to Babylon), Jechonias begat Salathiel. Salathiel begat Zorobabel.

13   Zorobabel begat Abiud. Abiud begat Eliakim. Eliakim begat Azor.

14   Azor begat Sadoc. Sadoc begat Achim. Achim begat Eliud.

15   Eliud begat Eleazar. Eleazar begat Matthan. Matthan begat Jacob.

16   Jacob begat Joseph, the husband of Mary, of whom Jesus was born, that is called Christ (or who is called the Messiah).

17   And so all the generations from Abraham to David *be* fourteen generations, and from David to the transmigration of Babylon *be* fourteen generations, and from the transmigration of Babylon to Christ *be* fourteen generations. (And so all the generations from Abraham to David *be* fourteen generations, and from David to the exile to Babylon *be* fourteen generations, and from the exile to Babylon to the Messiah *be* fourteen generations.)

18   But the generation of Christ was thus (or But the birth of the Messiah was thus). When Mary, the mother of Jesus, was espoused to Joseph, before that they came together, she was found having of the Holy Ghost in the womb, [or she was found having in the womb of the Holy Ghost], (or she was found being with child by the Holy Spirit).

19   And Joseph, her husband, for he was rightful [or when he was a just man], and would not publish her, he would privily have left her. (And her husband Joseph, for he was a good man, and would not make her public, he wanted to privately let her go.)

20   But while he thought (on) these things, lo! the angel of the Lord appeared to him in sleep, and said, Joseph, the son of David, do not thou dread to take Mary, (to be) thy wife; for that thing that is born in her is of the Holy Ghost. (But while he thought on these things, behold, the angel of the Lord appeared to him in sleep, and said, Joseph, the son of David, do not fear to take Mary to be thy wife; for that which is born in her is by the Holy Spirit.)

21   And she shall bear a son, and thou shalt call his name Jesus; for he shall make his people safe from their sins (or for he shall save his people from their sins).

22   For all this thing was done, that it should be fulfilled, that was said of the Lord by a prophet, saying,

23   Lo! a virgin shall have in [the] womb, and she shall bear a son, and they shall call his name Emmanuel, that is to say, God with us.

24   And Joseph rose [up] from sleep, and did as the angel of the Lord commanded him, and took *Mary*, (to be) his wife;

25 and he knew her not, till she had born her first begotten son, and he called his name Jesus.

CHAPTER 2

1 Therefore when Jesus was born in Bethlehem of Judea, in the days of king Herod, lo! astronomers, (or behold, astrologers), [or lo! kings, *or wise men*], came from the east to Jerusalem,

2 and said, Where is he, that is born [the] king of (the) Jews? for we have seen his star in the east, and we have come to worship him.

3 But king Herod heard, and was troubled, and all Jerusalem with him.

4 And he gathered together all the princes of (the) priests, and scribes of the people, and inquired of them, where Christ should be born. (And he gathered together all the high priests, and the scribes of the people, and inquired of them, where the Messiah would be born.)

5 And they said to him, In Bethlehem of Judea; for so it is written by a prophet,

6 And thou, Bethlehem, the land of Judah, art not the least among the princes of Judah; for of thee a duke shall go out, that shall govern my people Israel.

7 Then Herod called privily the astronomers, [or the kings], and learned busily of them the time of the star that appeared to them. (Then Herod privately called the astrologers/called the kings, and diligently learned from them the time of the star that appeared to them.)

8 And he sent them into Bethlehem, and said, Go ye, and ask ye busily of the child, (or Go, and diligently ask about the child), and when ye have found (him), tell ye *it* to me, (so) that I also come, and worship him.

9 And when they had heard the king, they went forth. And lo! the star, that they saw in the east, went before them, till it came, and stood above, where the child was.

10 And they saw the star, and joyed with a full great joy.

11 And they entered into the house, and found the child with Mary, his mother; and they felled down, and worshipped him. And when they had opened their treasures, they offered to him gifts, gold, incense, and myrrh.

12 And when they had taken an answer in sleep, that they should not turn again to Herod, they turned again by another way into their [own] country. (And when they had received a warning in their sleep, that they should not return to Herod, they returned by another way to their own country.)

13 And when they were gone, lo! the angel of the Lord appeared to Joseph in sleep, and said, Rise up, and take the child and his mother, and flee into Egypt, and be thou there, till that I say to thee; for it is to come, that Herod seek the child, to destroy him.

14 And Joseph rose [up], and took the child and his mother by night, and went into Egypt,

15 and he was there till the death of Herod; that it should be fulfilled, that was said of the Lord by the prophet, (or so that it would be fulfilled, what was said by the Lord through the prophet), saying, From Egypt I have called my son.

16 Then Herod seeing that he was scorned, *either deceived*, of the astronomers, [or of the kings], was full wroth; and he sent, and slew all the children, that were in Bethlehem, and in all the coasts thereof, from two years (of) age and within, after the time that he had inquired of the astronomers, [or after the time that he had sought out of the kings]. (Then Herod seeing that he was scorned, *or deceived*, by the astrologers/by the kings, was enraged; and he sent his soldiers, and killed all the children, who were in Bethlehem, and in all its coasts, from two years of age and under, after the time that he had learned of from the astrologers/from the kings.)

17 Then it was fulfilled, that was said by Jeremy, the prophet, saying, (Then it was

fulfilled, what was said by the prophet Jeremiah, saying,)

18 A voice was heard on high, weeping and much wailing, Rachel beweeping her sons, and she would not be comforted, for they be nought [or for they be not].

19 But when Herod was dead, lo! the angel of the Lord appeared to Joseph in sleep in Egypt,

20 and said, Rise up, and take the child and his mother, and go into the land of Israel; for they that sought the life of the child be dead.

21 Joseph rose [up], and took the child and his mother, and came into the land of Israel.

22 And he heard that Archelaus reigned in Judea for Herod, his father, and dreaded to go thither (or and he feared to go there). And he was warned in sleep, and went into the parts of Galilee;

23 and [he] came, and dwelt in a city, that is called Nazareth, that it should be fulfilled, that was said by prophets, (or so that it would be fulfilled, what was said by the prophets), For he shall be called a Nazarene.

CHAPTER 3

1 In those days John (the) Baptist came, and preached in the desert of Judea,

2 and said, Do ye penance, for the kingdom of heaven shall [come] nigh. (and said, Repent, for the Kingdom of Heaven is near.)

3 For this is he, of whom it is said by Esaias, the prophet, saying, (or For it is he, of whom it was said by the prophet Isaiah, saying), A voice of a crier in (the) desert, [or A voice of a man crying in (the) desert], Make ye ready the ways of the Lord; make ye right the paths of him.

4 And this John had clothing [or a cloth] of camel's hairs, and a girdle of skin about his loins; and his meat was honeysuckles [or locusts], and honey of the wood. (And this John had a cloak of camel's hair, and a girdle of skin about his loins; and his food was locusts, and

honey from the woods.)

5 Then Jerusalem went out to him, and all Judea, and all the country(side) about (the) Jordan (River);

6 and they were washed of him [or and they were christened of him] in (the) Jordan, (or and they were baptized by him in the Jordan River), acknowledging their sins.

7 But he saw many of the Pharisees and of (the) Sadducees coming to his baptism, and said to them, Generation of adders (or Children of snakes), who showed to you to flee from the wrath that is to come?

8 Therefore do ye worthy fruits of penance, (And so do worthy fruits of repentance,)

9 and do not ye say within you(rselves), We have Abraham to our father [or We have the father Abraham]; for I say to you, that God is mighty to raise up (out) of these stones the sons of Abraham. (and do not say within yourselves, We have Abraham for our father; for I tell you, that God is mighty enough to raise up the sons of Abraham from these stones.)

10 And now the ax is put to the root of the tree; therefore every tree that maketh not good fruit, shall be cut down, and shall be cast into the fire.

11 I wash you in water, into penance (or for repentance); but he that shall come after me is stronger than I, whose shoes I am not worthy to bear; he shall baptize you in the Holy Ghost, and (in) fire, [⁺or he shall christen you in the Holy Ghost, and in fire], (or he shall baptize you with the Holy Spirit, and with fire).

12 Whose winnowing cloth, [or tool, *or fan*], *is* in his hand, and he shall fully cleanse his cornfloor, (or and he shall completely cleanse his grain floor, or his threshing floor), and shall gather his wheat into his barn; but the chaff he shall burn with (the) fire that may not be quenched [or that is unquenchable].

13 Then Jesus came from Galilee into (the) Jordan to John, to be baptized of him. (Then Jesus came from Galilee to the Jordan River to

John, to be baptized by him.)

14   And John forbade him, and said, I owe to be baptized of thee (or I ought to be baptized by thee), and thou comest to me?

15   But Jesus answered, and said to him, Suffer now (or Allow this), for thus it falleth to us to fulfill all rightwiseness. Then *John* suffered him [or Then *John* let him].

16   And when Jesus was baptized, anon (or at once) he went up from the water; and lo! (the) heavens were opened to him, and he saw the Spirit of God coming down as a dove, and coming (or lighting) on him;

17   and lo! a voice from heaven, saying, This is my [be]loved Son, in which I have well pleased to me (or in whom I am well pleased).

CHAPTER 4

1   Then Jesus was led of a spirit into desert, to be tempted of the fiend [or of the devil]. (Then Jesus was led by the Spirit into the desert, to be tested by the Devil.)

2   And when he had fasted forty days and forty nights, afterward he hungered.

3   And the tempter came nigh (or And the Tester came near), and said to him, If thou be God's Son [or If thou art the Son of God], say that these stones be made (into) loaves.

4   Which answered, and said to him, It is written, Not only in bread liveth man, but in each word that cometh forth of God's mouth. [The which answering said to him, It is written, A man liveth not in bread alone, but in every word that cometh forth from the mouth of God.]

5   Then the fiend [or the devil] took him into the holy city, and setted him on the pinnacle of the temple,

6   and said to him, If thou art God's Son, send thee adown, [or If thou art the Son of God, send thee down]; for it is written, That to his angels he commanded of thee, and they shall take thee in (their) hands, lest peradventure

thou hurt thy foot at a stone.

7   Again Jesus said to him, It is written, Thou shalt not tempt thy Lord God, [or Thou shalt not tempt the Lord thy God], (or Thou shalt not test the Lord thy God).

8   Again the fiend [or the devil] took him [up] into a full high hill, and showed to him all the realms of the world, and the joy [or the glory] of them; (And the Devil took him up onto a very high hill, or onto a mountain, and showed him all the kingdoms of the world, and their glory;)

9   and said to him, All these I shall give to thee, if thou fall down and worship me.

10   Then Jesus said to him, Go, Satan; for it is written, Thou shalt worship thy Lord God [or Thou shalt worship the Lord thy God], and to him alone thou shalt serve.

11   Then the fiend [or the devil] left him; and lo! angels came nigh, and served to him (or and ministered to him).

12   But when Jesus had heard that John was taken (captive), he went into Galilee.

13   And he left the city of Nazareth, and came, and dwelt in the city of Capernaum, beside the sea, in the coasts of Zabulon and Nephthalim (or of Zebulun and Naphtali),

14   that it should be fulfilled, that was said by Esaias, the prophet, saying, (so that it would be fulfilled, what was said by the prophet Isaiah, saying,)

15   The land of Zabulon and the land of Nephthalim, the way of the sea over (the) Jordan (River), of Galilee of heathen men (or in Galilee of the Gentiles),

16   the people that walked [or that dwelt] in darknesses saw (a) great light (or the people who lived in darkness saw a great light), and while men sat in the country of [the] shadow of death, light arose to them.

17   From that time Jesus began to preach, and [to] say, Do ye penance, for the kingdom of heavens shall come nigh, [or Do ye penance, for the realm of heaven hath nighed], (or

Repent, for the Kingdom of Heaven is near).

18 And Jesus walked beside the sea of Galilee, and saw two brethren, Simon, that is called Peter, and Andrew, his brother, casting nets into the sea; for they were fishers. (And Jesus walked beside Lake Galilee, and saw two brothers, Simon, that is called Peter, and Andrew, his brother, throwing their nets into the lake; for they were fishermen.)

19 And he said to them, Come ye after me, and I shall make you to be made fishers of men.

20 And anon they left their nets, and (pur)sued him. (And at once they left their nets, and followed him.)

21 And he went forth from that place, and saw twain other brethren, James of Zebedee, and John, his brother, in a ship with Zebedee, their father, amending their nets, and he called them.

22 And anon they left the nets and the father, and (pur)sued him. (And at once they left their nets and their father, and followed him.)

23 And Jesus went about all Galilee, teaching in the synagogues of them, and preaching the gospel of the kingdom, and healing every languor, [or all sorrow, or ache], and each sickness among the people. (And Jesus went about all Galilee, teaching in their synagogues, and preaching the Gospel, or the Good News, of the Kingdom, and healing every languor, or every sorrow, or ache, and every sickness among the people.)

24 And his fame went into all (of) Syria; and they brought to him all that were at mal-ease, and that were taken with diverse languors [or sorrows], and torments, and them that had fiends [or devils], (or and those who had demons), and lunatic men, and men (sick) in [the] palsy, and he healed them.

25 And there (pur)sued him much people of Galilee, and of Decapolis, and of Jerusalem, and of Judea, and of beyond (the) Jordan. (And many people followed him from Galilee, and from Decapolis, and from Jerusalem, and from Judea, and from over the Jordan River.)

CHAPTER 5

1 And Jesus, seeing the people, went up into the hill (or went up onto a hill); and when he was set, his disciples came to him. [†Jesus forsooth, seeing the companies, went up into an hill; and when he had sat, his disciples came nigh to him.]

2 And he opened his mouth, and taught them, and said,

3 Blessed be poor men in spirit, for the kingdom of heavens is theirs. [Blessed be the poor in spirit, for the kingdom of heaven is theirs.]

4 Blessed be mild men, for they shall wield the earth. (Blessed be the meek, or the humble, for they shall possess the earth.)

5 Blessed be they that mourn, for they shall be comforted.

6 Blessed be they that hunger and thirst (for) rightwiseness, for they shall be fulfilled.

7 Blessed be merciful men [or Blessed (be) the merciful], for they shall get mercy.

8 Blessed be they that be of clean heart, for they shall see God.

9 Blessed be peaceable men, for they shall be called God's children. [Blessed (be) the peaceable, for they shall be called the sons of God.]

10 Blessed be they that suffer persecution for rightwiseness, for the kingdom of heavens is theirs [or for the kingdom of heaven is theirs].

11 Blessed be ye, when men shall curse you, and shall pursue you (or shall persecute you), and shall say all evil against you lying, for me.

12 Joy ye, and be ye glad, for your meed is plenteous in heavens; for so they have pursued also (the) prophets that were before you. (Rejoice, and be glad, for your reward in heaven is great; for in like manner they have persecuted the prophets who were before you.)

13 Ye be (the) salt of the earth; (so) that if the

salt vanish away, wherein shall it be salted? To nothing it is worth over, [no] but that it be cast out, and be defouled of men, (or Then it is good for nothing, except that it be thrown away, and be defiled, or trodden upon, by people).

14 Ye be [the] light of the world; a city set on an hill may not be hid (or a city set on a hill cannot be hidden);

15 nor men tendeth a lantern, and putteth it under a bushel, but on a candlestick, (so) that it give light to all that be in the house.

16 So shine your light before men, (so) that they see your good works, and glorify your Father that is in heavens (or and glorify your Father who is in heaven).

17 Do not ye deem, [or guess], (or Do not think), that I came to undo [or to destroy] the law, or the prophets; I came not to undo [or to destroy] the law, but to fulfill (it).

18 Forsooth I say to you, till heaven and earth pass (away), one letter [or one i, *that is, the least letter*], or one tittle shall not pass (away) from the law, till all things be done.

19 Therefore he that breaketh one of these least commandments, and teacheth thus men, shall be called the least in the realm of heavens (or shall be called the least in the Kingdom of Heaven); but he that doeth (them), and teacheth (them), shall be called great in the kingdom of heavens.

20 And I say to you, that but your rightwiseness be more plenteous than (that) of scribes and of Pharisees (or that unless your righteousness be more plentiful than that of the scribes and of the Pharisees), ye shall not enter into the kingdom of heavens.

21 Ye have heard that it was said to old men, Thou shalt not slay; and he that slayeth, shall be guilty to the doom. (Ye have heard that it was said to men of old, Thou shalt not kill; and he who killeth, shall be brought to judgement, or Thou shalt not murder; and he who murdereth, shall be brought to the court.)

22 But I say to you, that each man that is wroth to his brother, shall be guilty to (the) doom (or shall be brought to judgement); and he that saith to his brother, Fie!, [*that is, a word of scorn*], shall be guilty to the council; but he that saith Fool, [*that is, a word of despising*], shall be guilty to the fire of hell.

23 Therefore if thou offerest thy gift at the altar, and there thou bethinkest (or and there thou rememberest), that thy brother hath somewhat [or hath something] against thee,

24 leave there thy gift before the altar, and go first to be reconciled to thy brother, and then thou shalt come, and shalt offer thy gift.

25 Be thou consenting to thine adversary soon, while thou art in the way with him (or while thou art on the way with him), lest peradventure thine adversary take thee to the doomsman [or to the judge], and the doomsman take thee to the minister, and thou be sent into prison.

26 Truly I say to thee (or I tell you the truth), Thou shalt not go out from thence, till thou yield the last farthing.

27 Ye have heard that it was said to old men, Thou shalt not do lechery. (Ye have heard that it was said to men of old, Thou shalt not do adultery.)

28 But I say to you, that every man that seeth a woman [for] to covet her, hath now done lechery by her in his heart (or hath now done adultery with her in his heart).

29 (So) That if thy right eye cause thee to stumble, pull it out, and cast *it* from thee; for it speedeth to thee (or for it is more expedient for thee), that one of thy members perish, than that all thy body go into hell.

30 And if thy right hand cause thee to stumble, cut it away, and cast [it] from thee; for it speedeth to thee (or for it is more expedient for thee), that one of thy members perish, than that all thy body go into hell.

31 And it hath been said, Whoever leaveth his wife, give he to her a libel [or a little book]

of forsaking, (or give her a bill of divorce, or a notice of his leaving).

32 But I say to you, that every man that leaveth his wife, except (for) [the] cause of fornication, maketh her to do lechery (or maketh her to do adultery), and he that weddeth the forsaken *wife*, doeth adultery.

33 Again ye have heard, that it was said to old men (or that it was said to men of old), Thou shalt not forswear, but thou shalt yield thine oaths to the Lord.

34 But I say to you, that ye swear not for anything (or that ye do not swear by anything); neither by heaven, for it is the throne of God;

35 neither by the earth, for it is the stool of his feet; neither by Jerusalem, for it is the city of a great king [or for it is the city of the great king];

36 neither thou shalt swear by thine head, for thou mayest not make one hair white, or black;

37 but be your word, Yea, yea; Nay, nay; and that that is more than these, is of evil. (but let your words be, Yes, yes; No, no; and anything more than this, cometh from the Evil One.)

38 Ye have heard that it hath been said, Eye for eye, and tooth for tooth.

39 But I say to you, that ye against-stand not an evil *man*, [or But I say to you, to not against-stand evil]; but if any smite thee in the right cheek, show to him [or give to him] also the other; (But I tell you, that ye should not stand against an evil *person*; but if anyone strike thee on the right cheek, give to him also the other cheek;)

40 and to him that will strive with thee in doom, and take away thy coat, leave thou to him also thy mantle [or thine over-cloth]; (and to him who will fight with thee in court, to take away thy coat, give to him also thine overcoat;)

41 and whoever constraineth thee (to go) a thousand paces, go thou with him (an)other twain.

42 Give thou to him that asketh of thee, and turn thou not away from him that will borrow

of thee. (Give to him who asketh of thee, and do not turn away from him who desireth to borrow from thee.)

43 Ye have heard that it was said, Thou shalt love thy neighbour, and hate thine enemy.

44 But I say to you, love ye your enemies, do ye well to them that hate you, and pray ye for them that pursue, and slander you; (But I tell you, love your enemies, do good to those who hate you, and pray for those who persecute, and slander you;)

45 that ye be the sons of your Father that is in heavens, that maketh his sun to rise upon good and evil men, and raineth on just men and unjust (men). (so that ye be the sons of your Father who is in heaven, who maketh his sun to rise upon the good and the evil, and raineth upon the just and the unjust.)

46 For if ye love them that love you, what meed shall ye have? whether [the] publicans do not (do) this thing? (Because if ye love those who love you, what reward should ye get? do not the tax-collectors also do this?)

47 And if ye greet your brethren only, what shall ye do more[over]? do not heathen men, [or (the) pagans], (do) this? (or do not the Gentiles do this?)

48 Therefore be ye perfect, as your heavenly Father is perfect.

CHAPTER 6

1 Take heed, that ye do not your rightwiseness before men, to be seen of them, else ye shall have no meed at your Father that is in heavens. (Take heed, that ye do not do your righteousness before men, to be seen by them, or else ye shall have no reward with your Father, who is in heaven.)

2 Therefore when thou doest alms, do not thou trumpet before thee, as (the) hypocrites do in (the) synagogues and (in the) streets, that they be worshipped of men; soothly I say to you, they have received their meed. (And so when

thou givest charity, do not thou make a noise or a public show about it, like the hypocrites do in the synagogues and in the streets, so that they find honour with men; I tell you the truth, they have received their reward.)

3   But when thou doest alms, know not thy left hand what thy right hand doeth,

4   that thine alms be in huddles, and thy Father that seeth in huddles, shall requite to thee [or shall yield to thee]. (so that thy charity be given in secret, and thy Father who seeth in secret, shall reward thee.)

5   And when ye pray, ye shall not be as (the) hypocrites, that love to pray standing in (the) synagogues and [in] (the) corners of (the) streets, to be seen of men, [or that they be seen of men], (or so that they be seen by men); truly I say to you, they have received their meed, (or I tell you the truth, they have received their reward).

6   But when thou shalt pray, enter into thy couch (or enter into thy bedchamber), and when the door is shut, pray (to) thy Father in huddles, (or pray to thy Father in secret, or in private), and thy Father that seeth in huddles, shall yield to thee.

7   But in praying do not ye speak much, as heathen men do (or as the Gentiles do), for they guess that they be heard in their much speech.

8   Therefore do not ye be made like to them, for your Father knoweth what is need[ful] to you, before that ye ask him.

9   And thus ye shall pray, Our Father that art in heavens (or Our Father who art in heaven), hallowed be thy name;

10   thy kingdom come to (or thy kingdom come); be thy will done in earth as it is in heaven [or thy will be done as in heaven and in earth];

11   give to us this day our each day's bread;

12   and forgive to us our debts, as we forgive to our debtors;

13   and lead us not into temptation (or and do not bring us to the test), but deliver us from evil. Amen.

14   For if ye forgive to men their sins, your heavenly Father shall forgive to you your trespasses [or your sins].

15   Soothly if ye forgive not to men [the sins of them], neither your Father shall forgive to you your sins.

16   But when ye fast, do not ye be made as (the) hypocrites (be, looking) sorrowful, for they deface themselves, [or they put their faces out of *kindly* (or natural) terms], to seem fasting to men; truly I say to you, they have received their meed, (or I tell you the truth, they have received their reward).

17   But when thou fastest, anoint thine head, and wash thy face,

18   that thou be not seen fasting to men, but (only) to thy Father that is in huddles, (or so that thou not be seen to be fasting by men, but only by thy Father who is in secret), and thy Father that seeth in privy, [or in huddles], (or in secret), shall yield to thee.

19   Do not ye treasure to you(rselves) treasures [here] in (or on the) earth, where rust and moth destroyeth (it), and where thieves delve (it) out, and steal (it), (or and where thieves dig it up, and steal it);

20   but gather ye to you(rselves) treasures in heaven, where neither rust nor moth destroyeth (it), and where thieves delve not (it) out, nor steal (it), (or and where thieves cannot dig it up, nor can steal it).

21   For where thy treasure is, there also thine heart is.

22   The lantern of thy body is thine eye; if thine eye be simple, (or if thine eye is single, or if it is sound), all thy body shall be light-full;

23   but if thine eye be wayward, all thy body shall be dark[-full]. If then the light that is in thee be darknesses, how great shall those darknesses be?

24   No man may serve two lords, for either he shall hate the one, and love the tother; either he shall sustain the one, and despise the other. Ye

may not serve God and riches (or Ye cannot serve God and money, or wealth).

25 Therefore I say to you, that ye be not busy to your life, what ye shall eat; nor to your body, with what ye shall be clothed. Whether life is not more than meat, and the body more than the cloth? (And so I tell you, do not be concerned about your life, what ye shall eat; nor about your body, with what ye shall be clothed. Is not life more than food, and the body more than a cloak?)

26 Behold ye the fowls of the air (or Look at the birds of the air), for they sow not, neither reap, neither gather into barns; and your Father of heaven feedeth them. Whether ye be not more worthy than they?

27 But who of you (by) thinking may put [or may add] to his stature one cubit?

28 And of clothing what be ye busy? Behold the lilies of the field, how they wax. They travail not, neither they spin; (And why be concerned about clothing? Look at the lilies of the field, how they grow. They do not labour, nor do they spin;)

29 and I say to you, that Solomon in all his glory was not covered as one of these.

30 And if God clotheth thus the hay of the field, that today is, and tomorrow is cast into an oven [or is sent into the furnace], (then) how much more you of little faith?

31 Therefore do not ye be busy (or And so do not be concerned), saying, What shall we eat? or, What shall we drink? or, With what thing shall we be covered?

32 For heathen men seek all these things; and your Father knoweth, that ye have need to all these things. (For the Gentiles seek all these things; and your Father knoweth, that ye have need of all these things.)

33 Therefore seek ye first the kingdom of God, and his rightwiseness, and all these things shall be cast to you. (And so seek first the Kingdom of God, and his righteousness, and all these other things shall be thrown, or shall come, unto you.)

34 Therefore do not ye be busy into the morrow, for the morrow shall be busy (un)to itself; for it sufficeth to the day his own malice. (And so do not be concerned about tomorrow, for tomorrow shall have its own concerns; for each day sufficeth with its own malice, or its own problems.)

CHAPTER 7

1 Do not ye deem, that ye be not deemed; (Do not judge, so that ye be not judged;)

2 for in what doom ye deem, ye shall be deemed, and in what measure ye mete, it shall be meted again to you. (for with what judgement ye judge, ye shall be judged, and by what measure ye measure, it shall be measured unto you.)

3 But what seest thou a little mote in the eye of thy brother (or And why seest thou a little speck in thy brother's eye), and seest not a beam in thine own eye?

4 Or how sayest thou to thy brother, Brother, suffer [that] I shall do out a mote from thine eye, and lo! a beam is in thine own eye? (or Brother, allow me to take out the speck from thine eye, and behold, a beam is in thine own eye?)

5 Hypocrite, first do out the beam of thine eye/do thou out first the beam of thine own eye, and then thou shalt see to do out the mote of the eye of thy brother.

6 Do not ye give holy thing(s) to hounds, neither cast ye your margarites before swine, (or throw your pearls to the hogs, or to the pigs), lest peradventure they defoul them with their feet, and *the hounds* be turned, and tear you all to pieces.

7 Ask ye, and it shall be given to you; seek ye, and ye shall find; knock ye, and it shall be opened to you.

8 For each that asketh, taketh, (or For each one who asketh, receiveth); and he that

seeketh, findeth; and it shall be opened to him, that knocketh.

9 What man of you is, that if his son ask him (for some) bread, whether he will take to him a stone? (or will he give him a stone?)

10 Or if he ask (for) [a] fish, whether he will give [to] him an adder? (or will he give him a snake?)

11 Therefore if ye, when ye be evil men, know how to give good gifts to your sons, how much more your Father that is in heavens shall give good things to men that ask him?

12 Therefore all things, whatever things ye will that men do to you, do ye to them, for this is the law and the prophets. (And so everything, whatever ye want or desire people to do for you, do that for them, for this is the Law and the Prophets.)

13 Enter ye by the strait gate (or Enter by the narrow gate); for the gate that leadeth to perdition, [or to damnation], is large, and the way is broad, and there be many that enter by it.

14 How strait (or narrow) is the gate, and narrow the way, that leadeth to life, and there be few that find it.

15 Be ye ware of false prophets, that come to you in clothings of sheep, but withinforth they be wolves of raven [or but within they be ravishing (or snatching) wolves];

16 of their fruits ye shall know them. Whether men gather grapes of thorns, or figs of briers? (by their fruits ye shall know them. Do people gather grapes from thorns, or figs from briars?)

17 So every good tree maketh good fruits; but an evil tree maketh evil fruits.

18 A good tree may not make evil fruits, neither an evil tree [may] make good fruits. (A good tree cannot make bad fruits, nor can a bad tree make good fruits.)

19 Every tree that maketh not good fruit, shall be cut down, and shall be cast into the fire (or and shall be thrown into the fire).

20 Therefore of (or by) their fruits ye shall know them.

21 Not every man that saith to me, Lord, Lord, shall enter into the kingdom of heavens; but he that doeth the will of my Father that is in heavens, he shall enter into the kingdom of heavens.

22 Many shall say to me in that day, Lord, Lord, whether we have not prophesied in thy name, and have cast out fiends [or devils] in thy name, and have done many virtues in thy name? (Many shall say to me on that day, Lord, Lord, have we not prophesied in thy name, and have thrown out demons in thy name, and have done many works of power, or miracles, in thy name?)

23 And then I shall acknowledge to them, That I knew you never; depart away from me, ye that work wickedness.

24 Therefore every man that heareth these my words, and doeth them, shall be made like to a wise man, that hath builded his house on a stone.

25 And rain came down, and floods came, and winds blew, and rushed into that house; and it felled not down, for it was founded on a stone.

26 And every man that heareth these my words, and doeth them not, is like a fool, that hath builded his house on gravel [or on sand].

27 And rain came down, and floods came, and winds blew, and hurled against that house; and it felled down, and the falling down thereof was great.

28 And it was done, when Jesus had ended these words, the people wondered on his teaching;

29 for he taught them, as he that had power, and not as the scribes and the Pharisees.

CHAPTER 8

1 But when Jesus was come down from the hill, much people (pur)sued him [or many

companies followed him].

2　And lo! a leprous man came, and worshipped him, and said, Lord, if thou wilt, thou mayest make me clean. (And behold, a leprous man came, and honoured him, and said, Lord, if thou desirest it, or if thou wantest to do it, thou can make me clean.)

3　And Jesus held forth the hand, and touched him, and said, I will, be thou made clean. And anon the leprosy of him was cleansed. (And Jesus held forth his hand, and touched him, and said, I will, be thou made clean. And at once he was cleansed of the leprosy.)

4　And Jesus said to him, See, say thou to no man; but go, show thee to the priests, and offer the gift that Moses commanded, in witnessing to them (or as a testimony to them).

5　And when he had entered into Capernaum, the centurion nighed to him, and prayed him, (And when he entered into Capernaum, a centurion came up to him, and beseeched him,)

6　and said, Lord, my child lieth in the house sick on the palsy [or sick in the palsy], and is evil tormented. (and said, Lord, my servant lieth in the house sick with palsy, and is greatly tormented.)

7　And Jesus said to him, I shall come, and shall heal him.

8　And the centurion answered, and said to him, Lord, I am not worthy, that thou enter under my roof; but only say thou by (a) word, and my child shall be healed, (or but only say the word, and my servant shall be healed).

9　For why I am a man ordained under power, and have knights under me (or and have soldiers under me); and I say to this (one), Go, and he goeth; and to another, Come, and he cometh; and to my servant, Do this, and he doeth it.

10　And Jesus heard these things, and wondered, and said to (the) men that (pur)sued him, Truly I say to you, I found not so great faith in Israel. (And Jesus heard these things, and wondered, and said to the people who followed him, I tell you the truth, I have not found such great faith in all of Israel.)

11　And I say to you, that many shall come from the east and the west, and shall rest with Abraham and Isaac and Jacob in the kingdom of heavens;

12　but the sons of the realm shall be cast out into outer-more [or uttermost] darknesses; there shall be weeping, and grinding of teeth.

13　And Jesus said to the centurion, Go, and as thou hast believed, be it done to thee. And the child was healed from that hour, (or And the servant was healed from that hour, or at that moment).

14　And when Jesus was come into the house of Simon Peter, he saw his wife's mother lying (down), and shaken [or shaking] with fevers.

15　And he touched her hand, and the fever left her; and she rose, and served them.

16　And when it was even(ing), they brought to him many that had devils, and he casted out (the) spirits by (a) word, and healed all that were evil-at-ease [or having sickness];

17　that it were fulfilled, that was said by Esaias, the prophet, saying, (or so that it was fulfilled, what was said by the prophet Isaiah, saying), He took our infirmities, and bare our sicknesses.

18　And Jesus saw much people about him, and bade [or commanded] *his disciples* [to] go over the water.

19　And a scribe nighed, and said to him, Master, I shall (pur)sue thee, whither ever thou shalt go. (And a scribe approached, and said to him, Teacher, I shall follow thee, wherever thou shalt go.)

20　And Jesus said to him, Foxes have dens [or burrows], and birds of the air *have* nests, but man's Son hath not wherein to rest his head [or but man's Son hath not where he shall rest his head].

21　Another of his disciples said to him, Lord,

suffer me to go first, and bury my father, (or Lord, first allow me to go, and bury my father).

22   But Jesus said to him, (Pur)Sue thou me, and let the dead men bury their dead men, (or Follow me, and let the dead bury their dead).

23   And when he was gone up into a little ship, his disciples (pur)sued him (or his disciples followed him).

24   And lo! a great stirring was made in the sea, so that the ship was covered with waves; but he slept.

25   And his disciples came to him, and raised him, and said, Lord, save us; (for) we perish.

26   And Jesus said to them, What be ye of little faith aghast [or afeared]? (or Why be so afraid, ye of little faith?) Then he rose [up], and commanded to the winds and the sea, and a great peaceableness was made.

27   And (the) men wondered, and said, What manner *man* is this, for the winds and the sea obey to him?

28   And when he was come over the water into the country of (the) men of Gergesenes, two men met him, that had devils (or who had demons), and came out of (the) graves (or from the tombs), full mad, [or going out from (the) burials, full fierce, *or wicked*], so that no man might go by that way.

29   And lo! they cried, and said, What to us and to thee, Jesus, the Son of God? art thou come hither before the time to torment us?

30   And not far from them was a flock of many swine [or a drove of many hogs] pasturing. (And not far from them was a herd of many pigs at pasture.)

31   And the devils prayed him, and said, If thou castest out us from hence, send us into the drove of swine [or into the drove of hogs]. (And the demons beseeched him, and said, If thou throwest us out of here, then send us into that herd of pigs.)

32   And he said to them, Go ye. And they went out, and went into the swine [or into the hogs]; and lo! in a great rush all the drove went headlong into the sea, and they were dead in the waters. (And he said to them, Go! And they went out, and went into the pigs; and behold, in a great rush the whole herd went headlong into the lake, and they were dead in the water.)

33   And the herders fled away, and came into the city, and told all these things, and of them that had the fiends, [or the devils], (or and about them who had the demons).

34   And lo! all the city went out to meet Jesus; and when they had seen him, they prayed [*him*], that he would pass from their coasts, (or they beseeched *him*, that he would go away from their coasts).

CHAPTER 9

1   And Jesus went up into a boat, and passed over the water, and came into his city.

2   And lo! they brought to him a man sick in (the) palsy, lying in a bed. And Jesus saw the faith of them, and said to the man sick in (the) palsy, Son, have thou trust; thy sins be forgiven to thee.

3   And lo! some of the scribes said within themselves, This blasphemeth.

4   And when Jesus had seen their thoughts, he said, Whereto think ye evil things in your hearts? (And when Jesus had perceived their thoughts, he said, Why think ye such evil things in your hearts?)

5   What is lighter to say (or What is easier to say), Thy sins be forgiven to thee, either to say, Rise thou, and walk?

6   But (so) that ye know that man's Son hath power to forgive sins in (or on the) earth, then he said to the sick man in (the) palsy [or then he said to the man sick in (the) palsy], Rise up; take thy bed, and go into thine house.

7   And he rose, and went into his house.

8   And the people seeing dreaded, and glorified God, that gave such power to men. (And the people seeing this were filled with fearful reverence, and glorified God, who gave

such power to men.)

9   And when Jesus passed from thence, he saw a man, Matthew by name, sitting in a tollbooth. And he said to him, (Pur)Sue thou me (or Follow me). And he rose, and followed him.

10   And it was done, while he sat at the meat in the house, lo! many publicans and sinful men came, and sat at the meat with Jesus and his disciples. (And it was done, while he sat at a meal in the house, behold, many tax-collectors and sinners came, and sat at the meal with Jesus and his disciples.)

11   And the Pharisees saw, and said to his disciples, Why eateth your master with publicans and sinful men? (or Why is your teacher eating with tax-collectors and sinners?)

12   And Jesus heard, and said, A leech is not needful to men that fare well, but to men that be evil-at-ease [or having evil]. (And Jesus heard them, and said, A physician is not needed by men who be well, but by men who be sick.)

13   But go ye, and learn what it is, I will mercy, (or I want mercy, or kindness), and not sacrifice; for I came, not to call rightful [or rightwise] men, but sinful men *to penance* (or but sinners *to repentance*).

14   Then the disciples of John came to him, and said, Why we and the Pharisees fast oft, but thy disciples fast not?

15   And Jesus said to them, Whether the sons of the spouse may mourn [or may wail] as long as the spouse is with them? But (the) days shall come, when the spouse shall be taken away from them, and then they shall fast.

16   And no man putteth a patch of rough cloth, [or of rude, *or new*, cloth], into an old clothing; for it doeth away [or it taketh away] the fullness of the cloth, and a worse breaking is made. (And no one putteth a patch of new cloth onto an old piece of clothing; for it doeth away the fullness of the cloak, and a bigger hole is made.)

17   Neither men put new wine into old

bottles, else the bottles be broken, and destroyed, and the wine shed out. But men put new wine into new bottles, and both be kept. [Neither men send new wine into old wine vessels, else the wine vessels be broken, and the wine is shed out, and the wine vessels perish. But men send new wine into new wine vessels, and both be kept.]

18   Whiles that Jesus spake these things to them, lo! a prince came, and worshipped him, (or behold, a leader (of a synagogue) came, and honoured him), and said, Lord, my daughter is now dead; but come thou, and put thine hand on her, and she shall live (again).

19   And Jesus rose, and his disciples, and (pur)sued him (or and followed him).

20   And lo! a woman, that had a bloody flux, [or that suffered the running of blood], (for) twelve years, nighed behind, and touched the hem of his cloth. (And behold, a woman, who had suffered a flow, or an issue, of blood for twelve years, approached behind him, and touched the hem of his cloak.)

21   For she said within herself, If I touch only the cloth of him, I shall be safe. (For she said within herself, If I only touch his cloak, then I shall be saved, or I shall be healed.)

22   And Jesus turned, and saw her, and said, Daughter, have thou trust; thy faith hath made thee safe, (or thy faith hath saved thee, or hath healed thee). And the woman was [made] whole from that hour (or at that moment).

23   And when Jesus came into the house of the prince, and saw (the) minstrels, and the people making noise, (And when Jesus came into the house of the leader (of the synagogue), and saw the musicians, and the people making a commotion,)

24   he said, Go ye away, for the damsel is not dead, but sleepeth. And they scorned him.

25   And when the folk was put out (or And when the people were put out), he went in, and held her hand; and the damsel rose [up].

26   And this fame, (or this story, or this

telling), went out into all that land.

27   And when Jesus passed from thence, two blind men crying (pur)sued him, and said, Thou son of David, have mercy on us. [And Jesus passing from thence, two blind men (pur)sued him, crying, and saying, Thou son of David, have mercy on us.] (And when Jesus went away from there, two blind men followed him, and crying out, they said, O Son of David, have mercy on us.)

28   And when he came into the house, the blind men came to him; and Jesus said to them, What will ye, that I do to you? (or What do you desire that I do for you? or What do you want me to do for you?) And they said, Lord, that our eyes be opened. And Jesus said, Believe ye, that I may do this thing to you? [or Believe ye, that I may do this thing?] (or Believe ye, that I can do this for you?) They said to him, Yea, Lord.

29   Then he touched their eyes, and said, After your faith be it done to you.

30   And the eyes of them were opened. And Jesus threatened them, and said, See ye, that no man know.

31   But they went out, and famed him through(out) all that land.

32   And when they were gone out, lo! they brought to him a dumb man, having a devil, (or they brought to him a man who could not speak, because he had a demon).

33   And when the devil was cast out, the dumb man spake. And the people wondered, and said, It hath not been seen thus in Israel [or It appeared never so in Israel].

34   But the Pharisees said, In the prince of devils he casteth out devils (or By the Prince of demons he throweth out demons).

35   And Jesus went about all the cities and castles, teaching in the synagogues of them, and preaching the gospel of the kingdom, and healing every languor [or all ache], and every sickness. (And Jesus went about all the cities and villages, teaching in their synagogues, and preaching the Gospel, or the Good News, of the Kingdom, and healing every languor, or every ache and sorrow, and every sickness.)

36   And he saw the people, and had ruth on them; for they were travailed, and lying as sheep not having a shepherd. (And he saw the people, and had compassion for them; for they were troubled, and living like sheep not having a shepherd.)

37   Then he said to his disciples, Soothly *there is* much ripe corn (or Truly *there is* a great harvest to be gotten), but few workmen.

38   Therefore pray ye the Lord of the ripe corn, that he send workmen into his ripe corn. (And so pray to the Lord of the harvest, that he send workers to gather in his harvest.)

CHAPTER 10

1   And when his twelve disciples were called together, he gave to them power of unclean spirits (or he gave to them power over unclean spirits), to cast them out *of men*, and to heal every languor [or all ache], and [all] sickness.

2   And these be the names of the twelve apostles; the first, Simon, that is called Peter, and Andrew, his brother; James of Zebedee, and John, his brother;

3   Philip, and Bartholomew; Thomas, and Matthew, (a) publican (or a tax-collector); and James [*of*] Alphaeus, and Thaddaeus;

4   Simon Canaanite, and Judas Iscariot, that betrayed Christ, [or which betrayed him], (or who betrayed the Messiah).

5   Jesus sent these twelve, and commanded [to] them, and said, Go ye not into the way of heathen men (or Go not on the way to the Gentiles), and enter ye not into the cities of (the) Samaritans;

6   but rather go ye to the sheep of the house of Israel, that have perished.

7   And go ye, and preach ye, and say, that the kingdom of heavens shall nigh; (And go, and preach, and say, that the Kingdom of

Heaven is near;)

8 heal ye sick men, raise ye dead men, cleanse ye mesels [or leprous men], cast ye out devils; freely ye have taken, freely give ye. (heal the sick, raise the dead, cleanse the lepers, throw out the demons; freely ye have received, freely give.)

9 Do not ye wield (or possess) gold, nor silver, nor money in your girdles,

10 not a scrip in the way, neither two coats, neither shoes, nor a staff [or a rod]; for a workman is worthy (of) his meat, (or for a workman is worthy of his food, or hath earned his keep).

11 Into whatever city, or castle, ye shall enter (or Whatever city, or village, ye shall enter into), ask ye who therein is worthy, and there dwell ye, till ye go out.

12 And when ye go into an house, greet ye it, and say, Peace to this house.

13 And if that house be worthy, your peace shall come on it; but if that house be not worthy, your peace shall turn again to you (or your peace shall return to you).

14 And whoever receiveth not you, nor heareth your words, go ye forth from that house or city, and sprinkle off the dust of your feet, [or (and) smite away the dust from your feet], (or and shake off the dust from your feet).

15 Truly I say to you, it shall be more sufferable to the land of (the) men of Sodom and of Gomorrha in the day of judgement, than to that city. (I tell you the truth, it shall be more bearable for the land of the men of Sodom and Gomorrah on the Day of Judgement, than for that city.)

16 Lo! I send you as sheep in the middle [or into the midst] of wolves; therefore be ye sly, [or prudent, or wary, *or wise*], as serpents, and (as) simple as doves.

17 But be ye ware of men, for they shall take you in (to) councils, and they shall beat you in their synagogues;

18 and to mayors, *or to presidents*, and to

kings, ye shall be led (in) for me, in witnessing to them, and to heathen men. (and to mayors, *or to governors*, and to kings, ye shall be led in for me, to give a testimony to them, and to the Gentiles.)

19 But when they take (hold of) you, do not ye think, how or what thing ye shall speak, for it shall be given to you in that hour, what ye shall speak;

20 for it be not ye that speak, but the Spirit of your Father, that speaketh in (or through) you.

21 And the brother shall betake the brother into death (or And a brother shall deliver, or shall betray, a brother unto death), and the father the son, and sons shall rise against [their] father and mother, and shall torment them by death [or to the death].

22 And ye shall be in hate [or in hatred] to all men for my name; but he that shall dwell still [or shall continue] into the end, shall be made safe. (And ye shall be hated by everyone for my name; but he who shall continue unto the end, shall be saved.)

23 And when they pursue you in this city, flee ye into another (or And when they persecute you in this city, flee to another). Truly I say to you (or I tell you the truth), ye shall not end the cities of Israel, before that man's Son come.

24 The disciple is not above the master, [or The disciple is not above his master], (or The student is not above the teacher), nor the servant above his lord;

25 it is enough to the disciple, that he be as his master, and to the servant as his lord, (or it is enough for the student, that he be like his teacher, and for the servant, that he be like his lord). If they have called the husbandman, [or the father of the household], Beelzebub, (then) how much more his household members?

26 Therefore dread ye not them; for nothing is hid [or is covered], that shall not be showed; and nothing is privy, that shall not be known. (And so do not fear them; for nothing is hidden,

that shall not be shown, or brought out into the open; and nothing is private, or is secret, that shall not be made known.)

27 That thing that I say to you in (the) darknesses, say ye in the light; and preach ye on houses [or upon roofs], that thing that ye hear in the ear.

28 And do not ye dread them that slay the body; for they may not slay the soul; but rather dread ye him, that may lose both soul and body into hell. (And do not fear those who can kill the body; for they cannot kill the soul; but rather fear him, who can destroy both body and soul in hell.)

29 Whether two sparrows be not sold for an halfpenny? and one of them shall not fall on the earth without your Father. (Be not two sparrows sold for half a penny? and not one of them shall fall to the ground without your Father knowing about it, or allowing it.)

30 And all the hairs of your head be numbered.

31 Therefore do not ye dread (or And so do not fear); ye be better than many sparrows.

32 Therefore every man that shall acknowledge me before men, I shall acknowledge him before my Father that is in heavens.

33 But he that shall deny me before men, I shall deny him before my Father that is in heavens.

34 Do not ye deem (or guess) that I came to send peace into [the] earth; I came not to send peace, but (the) sword.

35 For I came to part a man against his father (or For I came to set a man against his father), and the daughter against her mother, and the son's wife against the husband's mother;

36 and the enemies of a man be they, that be at home with him.

37 He that loveth father or mother more than me, is not worthy to me/is not worthy of me. And he that loveth son or daughter more than me, is not worthy to me [or is not worthy of

me].

38 And he that taketh not (up) his cross, and (pur)sueth me (or and followeth me), is not worthy to me [or is not worthy of me].

39 He that findeth his life, shall lose it; and he that loseth his life for me, shall find it.

40 He that receiveth you, receiveth me; and he that receiveth me, receiveth him that sent me.

41 He that receiveth a prophet in the name of a prophet, shall take [or shall receive] the meed (or the reward) of a prophet. And he that receiveth a just man in the name of a just man, shall take [or shall receive] the meed, (or the reward), of a just man.

42 And whoever giveth drink to one of these least, a cup of cold water only, in the name of a disciple, truly I say to you, he shall not lose his meed. (And whoever giveth drink to one of these least ones, even just a cup of cold water, because he is my student, or my follower, I tell you the truth, he shall not lose his reward.)

CHAPTER 11

1 And it was done, when Jesus had ended (these words), he commanded to his twelve disciples, and passed from thence to teach and preach in the cities of them.

2 But when John in bonds had heard (of) the works of Christ (or But when John in prison had heard of the works of the Messiah), he sent two of his disciples,

3 and said to him, Art thou he that shall come, or we abide another?

4 And Jesus answered, and said to them, Go ye, and tell again to John those things that ye have heard and seen.

5 Blind men see, crooked men go, mesels be made clean, deaf men hear, dead men rise again, poor men be taken to preaching of the gospel. (The blind see, the lame walk, the lepers be cleansed, the deaf hear, the dead rise again, the poor be taken to the preaching of the

Gospel or the Good News.)

6 And he is blessed, that shall not be caused to stumble in me. (And he is blessed, who shall not be caused to stumble because of me.)

7 And when they were gone away, Jesus began to say of John to the people, What thing went ye out into (the) desert to see? a reed waved with the wind?

8 Or what thing went ye out to see? a man clothed with soft clothes? Lo! they that be clothed with soft clothes be in the houses of kings.

9 But what thing went ye out to see? a prophet? Yea, I say to you, and more than a prophet.

10 For this is he, of whom it is written, Lo! I send mine angel before thy face, that shall make ready thy way before thee (or who shall prepare thy way before thee).

11 Truly I say to you (or I tell you the truth), there rose none more [or none greater] than John (the) Baptist among the children of women; but he that is less [or that is the least] in the kingdom of heavens, is more than he.

12 And from the days of John (the) Baptist till now the kingdom of heavens suffereth violence, and violent men ravish it, (or seize it, or snatch it).

13 For all [the] prophets and the law till John prophesied;

14 and if ye will receive (it), he is Elias, that is to come. (and if ye will receive it, he is Elijah, who was to come.)

15 He that hath ears of hearing, hear he.

16 But to whom shall I guess this generation like? It is like to children sitting in the chapping (or at the market), that cry to their peers,

17 and say, We have sung to you, and ye have not danced; we have mourned to you, and ye have not wailed.

18 For John came neither eating nor drinking, and they say, He hath a devil.

19 The Son of man came eating and drinking, and they say, Lo! a man a glutton, and a drinker of wine, and a friend of publicans and of sinful men. And wisdom is justified of her sons (or And wisdom is proved right by its results).

20 Then Jesus began to say reproof to (the) cities, in which full many virtues of him were done, for they did not penance. (Then Jesus began to rebuke the cities, in which a great many works of power, or miracles, were done by him, because they did not repent.)

21 Woe to thee! Chorazin, woe to thee! Bethsaida; for if the virtues that be done in you had been done in Tyre and Sidon, sometime they had done penance in haircloth and ashes. (Woe to thee, Chorazin! woe to thee, Bethsaida! for if the works of power, or the miracles, that had been done in you had been done in Tyre and Sidon, they would have repented in sackcloth and ashes long ago.)

22 Nevertheless I say to you, it shall be less pain(ful) to Tyre and Sidon in the day of doom (or on the Day of Judgement), than to you.

23 And thou, Capernaum, whether thou shalt be araised up into heaven? Thou shalt go down into hell. For if the virtues that be done in thee had been done in Sodom (or For if the works of power, or the miracles, that had been done in thee had been done in Sodom), peradventure they should have dwelled till into this day.

24 Nevertheless I say to you, that to the land of Sodom it shall be less pain(ful) in the day of doom (or on the Day of Judgement), than to thee.

25 In that time Jesus answered, and said, I acknowledge to thee, Father, Lord of heaven and of earth, for thou hast hid these things from wise men, and ready, [or wary, or prudent, or sly], (or for thou hast hidden these things from the wise and the prudent), and hast showed them to little children;

26 so, Father, for so it was pleasing before thee.

27 All things be given to me of my Father (or Everything is given to me by my Father); and no man knew the Son, but the Father, neither any

man knew the Father, but the Son, and to whom the Son would show (him). [All things be given to me of my father; and no man knoweth the son, no but the father, neither any man knoweth the father, no but the son, and to whom the son would show (him).]

28   All ye that travail, and be charged (or All ye who labour, and be burdened), come to me, and I shall fulfill you [or and I shall refresh you].

29   Take ye my yoke on you, and learn ye of me, for I am mild and meek in heart; and ye shall find rest to your souls. (Take my yoke upon you, and learn from me, for I am gentle and humble in heart; and ye shall find rest for your souls.)

30   For my yoke is soft, and my charge (or my burden) *is* light. [For my yoke is sweet, and my charge *is* easy.]

CHAPTER 12

1   In that time Jesus went by (some) corns in the sabbath day [or on the sabbath day]; and his disciples hungered, and began to pluck the ears of corn, and to eat (them).

2   And the Pharisees, seeing, said to him, Lo! thy disciples do that thing that is not leaveful to them to do in [the] sabbaths. (And the Pharisees, seeing that, said to him, Behold, thy disciples do what is not lawful for them to do on the Sabbath.)

3   And he said to them, Whether ye have not read, what David did, when he hungered, and they that were with him?

4   how he entered into the house of God, and ate (the) loaves of proposition, [*either of setting forth*], which *loaves* it was not leaveful to him to eat, neither to them that were with him, [no] but to (the) priests alone? (or which *bread* it was not lawful for him to eat, nor for those who were with him, but only the priests?)

5   Or whether ye have not read in the law, that in (or on) the sabbaths (the) priests in the temple defoul the sabbaths (or defile the

Sabbath), and they be without blame?

6   And I say to you, that here is a greater than the temple. (And I tell you, that here is something greater than the Temple.)

7   And if ye knew, what it is, I will mercy, and not sacrifice, ye should never have condemned innocents. (And if ye only knew, what is meant by, I want mercy, or kindness, and not sacrifice, ye would never have condemned the innocent.)

8   For man's Son is Lord, yea, of the sabbath.

9   And when he passed from thence, he came into the synagogue of them.

10   And lo! a man that had a dry hand. And they asked him, and said, Whether it be leaveful to heal in the sabbath? that they should accuse him. (And behold, a man who had a withered hand. And they asked him, and said, Is it lawful to heal on the Sabbath? so that they could accuse him.)

11   And he said to them, What man of you shall there be, that hath one sheep, and if it fall into a ditch in (or on) the sabbaths, whether he shall not (take) hold (of it), and lift it up?

12   How much more is a man better than a sheep? Therefore it is leaveful to do good in the sabbaths, [or And so it is leaveful to do good in the sabbath], (or And so it is lawful to do good on the Sabbath).

13   Then he said to the man, Stretch forth thine hand. And he stretched (it) forth; and it was restored to health as the other.

14   And the Pharisees went out, and made a counsel (or a plan) against him, (as to) how they should destroy him.

15   And Jesus knew it, and went away from thence; and many (pur)sued him (or and many followed him), and he healed them all.

16   And he commanded to them, that they should not make him known;

17   that that thing were fulfilled, that was said by Esaias, the prophet, saying, (so that it was fulfilled, which was said by the prophet Isaiah, saying,)

18 Lo! my child, whom I have chosen, my darling, in whom it hath well pleased to my soul; I shall put my Spirit on him, and he shall tell doom to (the) heathen men (or and he shall tell out judgement to the Gentiles).

19 He shall not strive, nor cry, neither any man shall hear his voice in (the) streets.

20 A bruised reed he shall not break [or He shall not break (al)together a shaken reed], and he shall not quench smoking flax, till he cast out doom (or judgement), (un)to victory;

21 and heathen men shall (have) hope in his name. (and the Gentiles shall have hope in his name.)

22 Then a man blind and dumb, that had a fiend [or a devil], was brought to him; and he healed him, so that he spake, and saw.

23 And all the people wondered, and said, Whether this be the son of David?

24 But the Pharisees heard, and said, He this (man) casteth not out fiends, (no) but in Beelzebub, (the) prince of (the) fiends. [⁺But the Pharisees hearing, said, This (man) casteth not out fiends, no but in Beelzebub, prince of devils]. (But the Pharisees heard, and said, He throweth out demons by Beelzebub, the Prince of demons.)

25 And Jesus, witting their thoughts, said to them, Each kingdom parted against itself, shall be desolated, [or shall be desolate], (or Each kingdom divided against itself, shall be destroyed), and each city, or house, parted against itself, shall not stand.

26 And if Satan casteth out Satan, he is parted against himself, (or And if Satan throweth out Satan, he is divided against himself); therefore how shall his kingdom stand?

27 And if I in Beelzebub cast out devils, in whom, [or by whose might], (do) your sons cast (them) out? Therefore they shall be your doomsmen (or And so they shall be your judges).

28 But if I in the Spirit of God cast out fiends, then the kingdom of God is come into you [or is come among you]. (But if I by the Spirit of God throw out devils and demons, then the kingdom of God is come unto you.)

29 Either how may any man enter into the house of a strong man, and take away his vessels, [no] but he first bind the strong man, and then he shall spoil his house? (Or how can any man enter into the house of a strong man, and take away his things? first he must bind up the strong man, and then he can rob his house.)

30 He that is not with me, is against me; and he that gathereth not together with me, scattereth abroad.

31 Therefore I say to you, all sin and blasphemy shall be forgiven to men, but [the] blasphemy of the Spirit shall not be forgiven (or but blasphemy against the Holy Spirit shall not be forgiven).

32 And whoever saith a word against man's Son, it shall be forgiven to him; but who that saith a word against the Holy Ghost (or but who that saith a word against the Holy Spirit), it shall not be forgiven to him, neither in this world, nor in the tother.

33 Either make ye the tree good, and his fruit good; either make ye the tree evil and his fruit evil; for a tree is known of his fruit (or for a tree is known by its fruit).

34 Ye generation of adders, how may ye speak good things, when ye be evil? (or Ye children of snakes, how can ye say anything good, when ye yourselves be evil?) For the mouth speaketh (out) of the plenty [or (out) of the great abundance] of the heart.

35 A good man bringeth forth good things of good treasure, and an evil man bringeth forth evil things of evil treasure.

36 And I say to you, that of every idle word, that men speak, they shall yield reason thereof in the day of doom; (And I tell you, that for every idle word, that men speak, they shall have to give a reason for it on the Day of Judgement;)

37 for of thy words thou shalt be justified,

and of thy words thou shalt be condemned.

38　Then some of the scribes and the Pharisees answered to him, and said, Master, we will see a token of thee, (or Teacher, we desire to see a sign from thee).

39　Which answered, and said to them, An evil kindred and a spouse-breaker seeketh a token [or An evil generation and adulterous seeketh a token], and a token shall not be given to it, [no] but the token of Jonas, the prophet. (And he answered, and said to them, An evil and adulterous generation seeketh a sign, and no sign shall be given to it, except for the sign of the prophet Jonah.)

40　For as Jonas was in the womb of a whale three days and three nights (or For as Jonah was in the belly of a whale for three days and three nights), so man's Son shall be in the heart of the earth three days and three nights.

41　Men of Nineveh shall rise in (the) doom with this generation, and shall condemn it; for they did penance in the preaching of Jonas, and lo! here [is] a greater (man) than Jonas. (Men of Nineveh shall rise at the Judgement with this generation, and they shall condemn it; for they repented after the preaching of Jonah, and behold, here is something greater than Jonah.)

42　The queen of the south shall rise in doom with this generation, and (she) shall condemn it; for she came from the ends of the earth to hear the wisdom of Solomon, and lo! here [is] a greater (man) than Solomon. (The Queen of the South shall rise at the Judgement with this generation, and she shall condemn it; for she came from the ends of the earth to hear the wisdom of Solomon, and behold, here is something greater than Solomon.)

43　When an unclean spirit goeth out from a man, he goeth by dry places, seeking rest, and findeth not [or and he findeth none].

44　Then he saith, I shall turn again into mine house, from whence I went out. And he cometh, and findeth it void, and cleansed with besoms, and made fair. (Then he saith, I shall

return to my house, from where I went out. And he cometh, and findeth it empty, and swept clean, and made neat and tidy.)

45　Then he goeth (out), and taketh (back) with him seven other spirits worse than himself; and they enter [in], and dwell there. And the last things of that man be made worse than the former. So it shall be to this worst generation, (or And so the last things of that man be made worse than the first things. So it shall be with this evil generation).

46　Yet while he spake to the people, lo! his mother and his brethren stood withoutforth, seeking to speak with him.

47　And a man said to him, Lo! thy mother and thy brethren stand withoutforth, seeking thee.

48　And he answered to the man, that spake to him, and said, Who is my mother? and who be my brethren?

49　And he held forth his hand into his disciples, and said, Lo! my mother and my brethren;

50　for whoever doeth the will of my Father that is in heavens, he is my brother, and sister, and mother.

CHAPTER 13

1　In that day Jesus went out of the house, and sat beside the sea.

2　And much people was gathered to him, so that he went up into a boat, and sat; and all the people stood on the brink (or and all the people stood on the shore).

3　And he spake to them many things in parables, and said, Lo! he that soweth, went out to sow his seed.

4　And while he soweth, some *seeds* felled beside the way, and (the) birds of the air came, and ate them.

5　But other *seeds* felled into stony places, where they had not much earth; and anon they sprung up (or and at once they sprouted), for they had not (any) deepness of earth.

6   But when the sun was risen, they sweltered, [or they burned for the heat], (or they were parched), and for they had not root, they dried up.

7   And other *seeds* felled among thorns; and the thorns waxed up (or and the thorns grew up), and strangled them.

8   But other *seeds* felled into good land, and gave fruit; some an hundredfold, another sixtyfold, another thirtyfold.

9   He that hath ears of hearing, hear he.

10   And the disciples came nigh, and said to him, Why speakest thou in parables to them?

11   And he answered, and said to them, For to you it is given to know the privates [or the mysteries] of the kingdom of heavens, (or For to you it is given to know the secrets of the Kingdom of Heaven); but it is not given to them.

12   For it shall be given to him that hath, and he shall have plenty; but if a man hath not, also that thing that he hath shall be taken away from him.

13   Therefore I speak to them in parables, for they seeing see not, and they hearing hear not, neither understand;

14   that the prophecy of Esaias' saying be fulfilled in them (or so that the prophecy of Isaiah's saying be fulfilled in them), With hearing ye shall hear, and ye shall not understand; and ye seeing shall see, and ye shall not see;

15   for the heart of this people is greatly fatted, and they heard heavily with (their) ears, and they have closed their eyes, lest sometime they see with eyes, and with ears hear, and understand in heart, and they be converted, and I heal them.

16   But your eyes that see *be* blessed, and your ears that hear.

17   Forsooth I say to you, that many prophets and just men coveted to see those things that ye see, and they saw not, and to hear those things

that ye hear, and they heard not.

18   Therefore hear ye the parable of the sower.

19   Each that heareth the word of the realm, and understandeth (it) not, the evil spirit cometh, and ravisheth (or snatcheth up) that that is sown in his heart; this it is [or this is he], that is sown beside the way.

20   But this that is sown on the stony land, this it is, that heareth the word of God, and anon with joy taketh it (or and at once receiveth it with joy). [Forsooth he that is sown in stony land, is this, that heareth the word of God, and anon with joy taketh it.]

21   And he hath not root in himself, but is temporal. For when tribulation and persecution is made for the word, anon he is slandered. (But it hath no root in him, and is but temporary. For when tribulation and persecution cometh because of this word, at once he is caused to stumble.)

22   But he that is sown in thorns, is this that heareth the word, and the busyness (or the concerns) of this world, and the fallacy [or the falseness] of riches strangleth the word, and it is made without fruit.

23   But he that is sown into good land, is this that heareth the word, and understandeth (it), and bringeth forth fruit. And some maketh an hundredfold, truly another sixtyfold and another thirtyfold.

24   Another parable Jesus put forth to them, and said, The kingdom of heavens is made like to a man, that sowed good seed in his field.

25   And when men slept, his enemy came, and sowed above tares in the middle of (the) wheat, [⁺or and sowed above darnels, *or cockles*, in the midst of the wheat], and (then) went away.

26   But when the herb was grown, and made fruit, then the tares, [or the darnels, *or* (the) *cockles*], appeared.

27   And the servants of the husbandman came, and said to him, Lord, whether hast thou

not sown good seed in thy field? whereof then hath it tares, [or darnels, *or cockles*]?

28   And he said to them, An enemy hath done this thing. And the servants said to him, Wilt thou that we go, and gather them?

29   And he said, Nay, lest peradventure ye in gathering (the) tares, [or the darnels, *or* (the) *cockles*], draw up with them [also] the wheat by the root.

30   Suffer ye them both to wax into reaping time; and in the time of ripe corn, I shall say to the reapers, (or Allow them both to grow until harvest time; and at harvest time, I shall say to the harvesters), First gather ye together the tares, [or the darnels, *or* (the) *cockles*], and bind them together in knitches, [*or small bundles*], to be burnt, but gather ye the wheat into my barn.

31   Another parable Jesus put forth to them, and said, The kingdom of heavens is like to a corn of sinapi, which a man took, and sowed in his field. (Jesus put forth another parable to them, and said, The Kingdom of Heaven is like a kernel, or a grain, of mustard seed, which a man took, and sowed in his field.)

32   Which [truly] is the least of all seeds, but when it hath waxen, it is the most of all worts, (or but when it hath grown, it is the largest of all herbs, or all plants), and is made (into) a tree; so that [the] birds of the air come, and dwell in the boughs [or in the branches] thereof.

33   Another parable *Jesus* spake to them [or He spake another parable to them], The kingdom of heavens is like to sourdough (or is like yeast), which a woman took, and hid in three measures of meal, till it were all soured (or until it was all leavened).

34   Jesus spake all these things in parables to the people, and he spake not to them without parables,

35   (so) that it should be fulfilled, that is said by the prophet, saying, I shall open my mouth in parables; I shall tell out hid things [or things hid] from the making of the world (or I shall tell out hidden things from the creation of the world).

36   Then he left the people (or Then he dismissed the people, or let them go), and came into an house; and his disciples came to him, and said, Expound to us the parable of the tares, [or the darnels, *or* (the) *cockles*], of the field.

37   Which answered, and said, He that soweth good seed is man's Son;

38   the field is the world; but the good seed, these be the sons of the kingdom, but (the) tares, these be (the) evil children, [or forsooth (the) darnels, *or* (the) *cockles*, these be (the) sons of the wicked (one)];

39   the enemy that soweth them is the fiend [or the devil]; and the ripe corn (or the harvest) is the ending of the world, the reapers be (the) angels.

40   Therefore as (the) tares, [or (the) darnels, *or* (the) *cockles*], be gathered together, and be burnt in [the] fire, so it shall be in the ending of the world.

41   Man's Son shall send his angels, and they shall gather from his realm all causes of stumbling, and them that do wickedness;

42   and they shall send them into the chimney of fire; there shall be weeping, and beating together of teeth (or and grinding of teeth).

43   Then just men shall shine as the sun, in the realm of their Father (or in their Father's Kingdom). He that hath ears of hearing, hear he.

44   The kingdom of heavens is like to (a) treasure hid in a field (or The Kingdom of Heaven is like a treasure hidden in a field), which a man that findeth, hideth; and for (the) joy of it he goeth, and selleth all (the) things that he hath, and buyeth that field.

45   Again the kingdom of heavens is like to a merchant, that seeketh good margarites [or good pearls];

46   but when he hath found one precious margarite (or one precious pearl), he went, and sold all (the) things that he had, and bought it.

47   Again the kingdom of heavens is like to a net cast into the sea, and that gathereth together of all kinds of fishes;

48   which when it was full, they drew it up, and sat by the brink, and chose the good into their vessels, but the evil they cast out. (which when it was full, they drew it up, and sat on the shore, and chose the good ones for their pails, or their baskets, but the bad ones they threw away.)

49   So it shall be in the end(ing) of the world. Angels shall go out, and shall separate evil men from the middle [or from the midst] of just men.

50   And they shall send them into the chimney of fire; there shall be weeping, and grinding of teeth.

51   Have ye understood all these things? They say to him, Yea.

52   He saith to them, Therefore every wise man of [the] law [taught] in the kingdom of heavens, is like to an husbandman, that bringeth forth of his treasure new things and old.

53   And it was done, when Jesus had ended these parables, he passed from thence (or he went away from there).

54   And he came into his country, and taught them in their synagogues, so that they wondered, and said, From whence this wisdom and virtues, (or works of power, or miracles), *came* to this? [or Whereof to him this wisdom and virtues?] (or From where did he get such wisdom and power to work such miracles?)

55   Whether this is not the son of a carpenter? Whether his mother be not said Mary? (or Is not his mother called Mary?), and his brethren, James, and Joseph, and Simon, and Judas?

56   and his sisters, whether they all be not among us? From whence then all these things *come or came* to this? [and his sisters, whether they be not all among us? Therefore whereof to him all these things?]

57   And so they were offended in him. But Jesus said to them, A prophet is not without honour, [no] but in his own country, and in his own house. (And so they were offended by him, or they were contemptuous of him. And Jesus said to them, A prophet is not without honour, except in his own hometown, and among his own family.)

58   And he did not there many virtues, for the unbelief of them. (And he did not do many works of power, or miracles, there, because of their unbelief.)

CHAPTER 14

1   In that time Herod tetrarch, [*that is*, (the) *prince of the fourth part*], heard (of) the fame of Jesus;

2   and said to his children, This is John (the) Baptist, he is risen from death [or he hath risen from (the) dead], and therefore virtues work in him, (or and that is why works of power, or miracles, can be done by him).

3   For Herod had (taken) hold (of) John, and bound him, and putted him in prison for Herodias, the wife of his brother.

4   For John said to him, It is not leaveful to thee to have her. (For John said to him, It is not lawful for thee to have her as your wife.)

5   And he willing to slay him, dreaded the people; for they had him as a prophet. (And he wanted to kill him, but he feared the people; for they said that he was a prophet.)

6   But in the day of Herod's birth (or But on Herod's birthday), the daughter of Herodias danced in the middle, and pleased Herod.

7   Wherefore with an oath he promised to give to her, whatever thing she asked of him.

8   And she before-warned of her mother, said, [or And she before-admonished of her mother, saith], (or And having earlier been admonished by her mother, she answered), Give thou to me here the head of John (the) Baptist in a dish.

9   And the king was sorrowful, but for the oath, and for them that sat together at the meat,

(or but because of his promise, or his oath, and because of those who sat together with him at the meal), he commanded (it) to be given (to her).

10 And he sent (word), and beheaded John in the prison.

11 And his head was brought in a dish, and it was given to the damsel, and she bare it to her mother (or and she carried it to her mother).

12 And his disciples came, and took his body, and buried it; and they came, and told to Jesus.

13 And when Jesus had heard (about) this thing, he went from thence in a boat, into a desert place beside. And when the people had heard, they followed him on their feet from (the) cities.

14 And Jesus went out, and saw a great people [or a great multitude], and had ruth on them (or and had compassion for them), and he healed the sick men (and women and children) of them.

15 But when eventide was come, his disciples came to him, and said, The place is (a) desert, and the time is now passed; let the people go into (the) towns, to buy them(selves) meat (or to buy some food for themselves).

16 Jesus said to them, They have not need to go [or They have no need to go]; give ye them somewhat to eat (or you give them something to eat).

17 They answered, We have not here, [no] but five loaves and two fishes.

18 And he said to them, Bring ye them hither to me (or Bring them here to me).

19 And when he had commanded the people to sit to [the] meat on the hay (or And when he had commanded the people to sit down on the hay for the meal), he took (the) five loaves and (the) two fishes, and he beheld into heaven, and blessed (or and gave thanks), and brake (them), and gave [(the) loaves] to his disciples; and the disciples gave (them) to the people.

20 And all ate, and were fulfilled, [or And all ate, and were filled]. And they took the remnants of broken gobbets, twelve coffins full, (or And they gathered up the remaining pieces of food, twelve baskets full).

21 And the number of men that ate was five thousand of men, without (the) women and (the) little children.

22 And anon (or at once) Jesus compelled the disciples to go up into a boat, and [to] go before him over the sea, while he left the people, (or while he dismissed the people, or let them go).

23 And when the people was left, he ascended alone into an hill to pray, (or And after the people were dismissed, or let go, he went up alone onto a hill to pray). But when the evening was come, he was there alone.

24 And the boat in the middle of the sea was shogged with (the) waves, for the wind was contrary to them. [+Forsooth the boat in the midst of the sea was thrown with (the) waves, for the wind was contrary to them.]

25 But in the fourth waking of the night, he came to them walking on the sea. (But about the fourth watch of the night, he came to them walking on the lake.)

26 And they, seeing him walking on the sea, were disturbed [or were distroubled], and said, That it is a phantom; and for dread they cried (or and they cried out in fear).

27 And anon Jesus spake to them, and said, Have ye trust, I am (he); do not ye dread. (And at once Jesus spoke to them, and said, Have trust, it is me; do not fear.)

28 And Peter answered, and said, Lord, if thou art (thee), (or if it is thee), command me to come to thee on the waters.

29 And he said, Come thou. And Peter went down from the boat, and walked on the waters to come to Jesus.

30 But he saw the wind strong, and was afeared; and when he began to drench, he cried, and said, Lord, make me safe. (But when he saw the strength of the wind, he was afraid; and when he began to drown, he cried, and

said, Lord, save me.)

31 And anon (or at once) Jesus held forth his hand, and took *Peter* [or (and) caught him], and said to him, Thou of little faith, why hast thou doubted?

32 And when he had ascended into the boat, the wind ceased. (And when he had gone up into the boat, the wind ceased.)

33 And they, that were in the boat, came, and worshipped him, and said, Verily, thou art God's Son (or Truly, thou art the Son of God).

34 And when they had passed over the sea, they came into the land of Gennesaret.

35 And when men of that place had known him, they sent into all that country(side), (or they sent word throughout all that region); and they brought to him all that had sicknesses [or and they brought to him all having evil].

36 And they prayed him, that they should touch the hem of his clothing; and whoever touched (it) were made safe (or and whoever touched it were healed).

CHAPTER 15

1 Then the scribes and the Pharisees came to him from Jerusalem, and said,

2 Why break thy disciples the traditions of (the) elder men? [or Why (do) thy disciples break the traditions, *either the teachings*, of (the) elder men?] (or Why do thy disciples break the traditions of the elders?) for they wash not their hands, when they eat bread.

3 He answered, and said to them, Why break ye the commandment of God for your tradition?

4 For God said, Honour thy father and thy mother, and he that curseth father or mother, die he by death.

5 But ye say, Whoever saith to father or mother, Whatever gift is of me, it shall profit to thee, (or Whatever gift is for me, it shall profit thee);

6 and he hath not worshipped [or hath not honoured] his father or his mother; and ye have made the commandment of God void (or empty) for your tradition.

7 Hypocrites, Esaias the prophet, prophesied well of you, and said, (Hypocrites, the prophet Isaiah prophesied well about you, and said,)

8 This people honoureth me with lips, but their heart is far from me;

9 and they worship me without cause, [or truly they worship me without cause], (or and they worship me for no good reason, or in vain), (while) teaching the doctrines and the commandments of men.

10 And when the people were called together to him, he said to them, Hear ye, and understand ye.

11 That thing that entereth into the mouth, defouleth not a man; but that thing that cometh out of the mouth, defouleth a man. (That which entereth into the mouth, defileth not a person; but that which cometh out of the mouth, defileth a person.)

12 Then his disciples came, and said to him, Thou knowest [or Knowest thou], that, if this word be heard, the Pharisees be offended?

13 And he answered, and said, Every planting, that my Father of heaven hath not planted, shall be drawn up by the root.

14 Suffer ye them (or But allow them); (for) they be blind, and (the) leaders of blind men. And if a blind man lead a blind man, both fall into the ditch.

15 Peter answered, and said to him, Expound to us this parable.

16 And he said, Yet be ye also without understanding?/Yet ye be without understanding?

17 Understand ye not, that all thing that entereth into the mouth, goeth into the womb (or goeth into the belly), and is sent out into the going away?

18 But those things that come forth from the mouth, go out from the heart, and those things

defoul the man (or and those things defile the person).

19 For of the heart go out evil thoughts [or For out of the heart cometh evil thoughts], manslayings, adulteries, fornications, thefts, false witnessings (or false testimonies), blasphemies.

20 These things it be that defoul a man; but to eat with hands not washed, defouleth not a man. (These be the things which defile a person; but to eat with hands not washed, defileth not a person.)

21 And Jesus went out from thence, and went into the coasts of Tyre and Sidon.

22 And lo! a woman of Canaan went out of those coasts, and cried, and said to him, Lord, the son of David, have mercy on me; my daughter is evil travailed of a fiend [or of a devil]. (And behold, a Canaanite woman from those parts cried to him, and said, Lord, the Son of David, have mercy on me; my daughter is greatly troubled and tormented by a demon.)

23 And he answered not to her a word. And his disciples came, and prayed him, and said, Leave thou her, (or Let her go, or Send her away), for she crieth after us.

24 He answered, and said, I am not sent, but to the sheep of the house of Israel that have perished.

25 And she came, and worshipped him, and said, Lord, help me. (And she came, and honoured him, and said, Lord, help me.)

26 Which answered, and said, It is not good to take the bread of children, and cast [it] to (the) hounds.

27 And she said, Yes, Lord; for [the] whelps eat of the crumbs, that fall down from the board of their lords. (And she said, Yes, Lord; but even the pups can eat the crumbs, that fall down from their masters' table.)

28 Then Jesus answered, and said to her, A! woman, thy faith is great; be it done to thee, as thou wilt. And her daughter was healed from that hour (or at that moment).

29 And when Jesus had passed from thence, he came beside the sea of Galilee. And he went up into an hill, and sat there. (And when Jesus had left there, he came beside Lake Galilee. And he went up onto a hill, and sat there.)

30 And much people came to him, and had with them dumb men and crooked [men], (or and lame men), feeble and blind, and many others; and they casted down them at his feet, [or and they cast them down at his feet], (or and they set them down at his feet). And he healed them,

31 so that the people wondered, seeing dumb men speaking, and crooked [men] going, (or and lame men walking), blind men seeing; and they magnified (the) God of Israel.

32 And Jesus, when his disciples were called together, said to them, I have ruth of the people, for they have abided now three days with me, and have nothing to eat; and I will not leave them fasting, lest they fail in the way. (And Jesus, when his disciples were called together, said to them, I have compassion for the people, for now they have been here three days with me, and have nothing to eat; and I will not let them go away fasting, lest they faint on the way home.)

33 And the disciples say to him, Whereof then so many loaves among us in (the) desert, to fulfill so great a people? [And the disciples say to him, Therefore whereof so many loaves to us in (the) desert, (so) that we (can) fill so great a company of people?]

34 And Jesus said to them, How many loaves have ye? And they said, Seven, and a few small fishes [or and a few little fishes].

35 And he commanded to the people, to sit to [the] meat on the earth. (And he commanded the people, to sit down on the ground for the meal.)

36 And he took the seven loaves and (he) five fishes, and did thankings (or and gave thanks), and brake them, and gave (them) to his

disciples; and the disciples gave (them) to the people.

37 And all ate, and were fulfilled, [or And all ate, and were filled], and they took (up) that that was left of [the] remnants (or and they gathered up the remaining pieces of food that were left), seven baskets full.

38 And they that ate were four thousand of men, without (the) little children and (the) women.

39 And when he had left the people (or And when he had let the people go), he went up into a boat, and came into the coasts of Magdala.

CHAPTER 16

1 And the Pharisees and the Sadducees came to him tempting [him], and prayed him to show them a token from heaven. (And the Pharisees and the Sadducees came to him to test him, and beseeched him to show them a sign from heaven.)

2 And he answered, and said to them, When the eventide is come, ye say, It shall be clear, for heaven is ruddy [or for the heaven is red]; (And he answered, and said to them, When the evening hath come, ye say, It shall be clear, for the heavens, or the sky, is red;)

3 and the morrowtide, Today tempest, for (the) heaven(s) shineth heavily. Then ye know how to deem [wisely] the face of heaven, but ye may not know the tokens of (the) times. (and in the morning, Today there shall be a storm, for the sky is dark. So ye wisely know how to judge the face of the heavens, but ye cannot discern the signs of the times./but can ye not understand the signs of the times?)

4 An evil generation and adulterous seeketh a token; and a token shall not be given to it, but the token of Jonas, the prophet, (or An evil and adulterous generation seeketh a sign; and a sign shall not be given to it, except the sign of the prophet Jonah). And when he had left them, he went forth [or he went away].

5 And when his disciples came over the sea, they forgot to take loaves.

6 And he said to them, Behold ye, and beware of the sourdough of (the) Pharisees and of (the) Sadducees. (And he said to them, Behold, and beware of the yeast, or the leaven, of the Pharisees and the Sadducees.)

7 And they thought among them[selves], and said, For we have not taken loaves (or Because we have not brought any bread).

8 But Jesus witting said to them, What think ye among you of little faith, for ye have not taken loaves? (But Jesus, knowing what they were saying, said to them, Why think ye among yourselves, because we have not brought any bread? O ye of little faith!)

9 Yet ye understand not, neither have mind, of five loaves into five thousand of men, and how many coffins ye took (up)? (Yet ye understand not, nor remember, the five loaves for the five thousand men, and how many baskets did ye fill up?)

10 neither of seven loaves into four thousand of men, and how many baskets ye took (up)? (nor the seven loaves for the four thousand men, and how many baskets did ye fill up?)

11 Why understand ye not, for I said not to you of bread, Be ye ware of the sourdough of (the) Pharisees and of (the) Sadducees? (Why do ye not understand, that I did not speak to you about bread when I said, Beware of the yeast, or the leaven, of the Pharisees and the Sadducees?)

12 Then they understood, that he said not to beware of [the] sourdough of loaves, but of the teaching of (the) Pharisees and of (the) Sadducees. (Then they understood, that he did not say to beware of the yeast, or the leaven, of bread, but of the teaching of the Pharisees and of the Sadducees.)

13 And Jesus came into the parts of Caesarea of Philippi, and asked his disciples, and said, Whom say men to be man's Son?

14   And they said, Some John (the) Baptist; others Elias (or Elijah); and others Jeremy (or Jeremiah), or one of the prophets.

15   Jesus said to them, But whom say ye me to be?

16   Simon Peter answered, and said, Thou art Christ, the Son of God living [or the son of (the) quick God]. (Simon Peter answered, Thou art the Messiah, the Son of the living God.)

17   Jesus answered, and said to him, Blessed art thou, Simon Barjona; for flesh and blood showed not to thee, but my Father that is in heavens.

18   And I say to thee, that thou art Peter, and on this stone I shall build my church, and the gates of hell shall not have might or power, [or strength], against it.

19   And to thee I shall give the keys of the kingdom of heavens; and whatever thou shalt bind on earth, shall be bound also in heavens; and whatever thou shalt unbind on earth, shall be unbound also in heavens.

20   Then he commanded to his disciples, that they should say to no man, that he was Jesus Christ.

21   From that time Jesus began to show to his disciples, that it behooved him to go to Jerusalem, and suffer many things, of the elder men [or of the elders], and of the scribes, and of (the) princes of (the) priests, (or and suffer many things, from the elders, and from the scribes, and from the high priests); and be slain, and the third day to rise again.

22   And Peter took (hold of) him, and began to blame him (or and began to rebuke him), and said, Far be it from thee, Lord; this shall not be to thee.

23   And he turned, and said to Peter, Satan, go thou after me; thou art a cause of stumbling to me; for thou savourest not [or thou understandest not] those things that be of God, but (only) those things that be of men.

24   Then Jesus said to his disciples, If any man will come after me, deny he himself, and take (up) his cross, and (pur)sue me (or and follow me);

25   for he that will make his life safe, shall lose it; and he that shall lose his life for me, shall find it.

26   For what profiteth it to a man [or Soothly what profiteth to a man], if he win all the world, and suffer impairing of his soul? or what (ex)changing shall a man give for his soul?

27   For man's Son shall come in the glory of his Father, with his angels, and then he shall yield to every man after his works.

28   Truly I say to you (or I tell you the truth), there be some of them that stand here (today), which shall not taste death, till they see man's Son coming in his kingdom.

CHAPTER 17

1   And after six days Jesus took Peter, and James, and John, his brother, and led them aside into an high hill, (or and led only them up onto a high hill, or a mountain),

2   and was transfigured, [or turned], into another likeness before them. And his face shone as the sun; and his clothes were made (as) white as snow.

3   And lo! Moses and Elias appeared to them, and spake with him. (And behold, Moses and Elijah appeared to them, and spoke with him.)

4   And Peter answered, and said to Jesus, Lord, it is good (for) us to be here. If thou wilt, make we here three tabernacles; to thee one, to Moses one, and one to Elias. (And Peter answered, and said to Jesus, Lord, it is good for us to be here. If thou desirest, we shall make three tents, or three tabernacles, here; one for thee, one for Moses, and one for Elijah.)

5   Yet while he spake, lo! a bright cloud overshadowed them; and lo! a voice out of the cloud, that said, This is my dearworthy Son, in whom I have well pleased to me; hear ye him, (or This is my beloved Son, in whom I am well

pleased; listen to him).

6 And the disciples heard, and felled down on their faces, and dreaded greatly (or and greatly feared).

7 And Jesus came, and touched them, and said to them, Rise up, and do not ye dread (or and do not fear).

8 And they lifted up their eyes, and saw no man, but Jesus alone.

9 And as they came down of the hill [or down from the mountain], Jesus commanded to them, and said, Say ye to no man the vision, till man's Son rise again from death [or till man's Son rise again from (the) dead].

10 And his disciples asked him, and said, What then say the scribes, that it behooveth that Elias come first? (And his disciples asked him, Why then do the scribes say, that it behooveth that Elijah must come first?)

11 He answered, and said to them, Elias shall come (or Elijah shall come), and he shall restore all things.

12 And I say to you, that Elias is now come, and they knew him not, but they did in him whatever things they would; and so man's Son shall suffer of them. (And I tell you, that Elijah hath now come, and they knew him not, but they did to him whatever things they wanted to do; and so man's Son shall also suffer by them.)

13 Then the disciples understood, that he said to them of John the Baptist.

14 And when he came to the people, a man came to him, and felled down on *his* knees before him, and said,

15 Lord, have mercy on my son; for he is (a) lunatic, and suffereth evil, for oft times he falleth into the fire, and oft times into the water.

16 And I brought him to thy disciples, and they might not heal him (or but they could not heal him).

17 Jesus answered, and said, A! thou generation unbelieveful [or out of the faith] and wayward, (or O thou unfaithful and wayward generation!); how long shall I be with you? how

long shall I suffer you? Bring ye him hither to me.

18 And Jesus blamed him, and the devil went out from him; and the child was healed from that hour. (And Jesus rebuked the demon, and he went out of him; and the child was healed at that moment.)

19 Then the disciples came to Jesus privily, and said to him, Why might not we cast him out? (Then the disciples came privately to Jesus, and asked him, Why could we not throw him out?)

20 Jesus saith to them, For your unbelief. Truly I say to you, if ye have faith, as a corn of sinapi, ye shall say to this hill, Pass thou, [from] hence, and it shall pass (away); and nothing shall be impossible to you; (Jesus said to them, Because of your lack of faith. I tell you the truth, if ye have faith, like a kernel, or a grain, of mustard seed, ye shall say to this mountain, Go away from here, and it shall go away; and nothing shall be impossible for you;)

21 but this kind is not cast out, [no] but by prayer and fasting.

22 And whiles they were abiding together in Galilee, Jesus said to them, Man's Son shall be betrayed into the hands of men;

23 and they shall slay him, and the third day he shall rise again to life. And they were [made] full sorry, [or And they were sorrowful greatly], (or And they were greatly grieved).

24 And when they came to Capernaum, they that took tribute, came to Peter, and said to him, Your master payeth not tribute? (And when they came to Capernaum, those who collected the Temple tax, came to Peter, and said to him, Your teacher payeth no tax?)

25 And he said, Yes. And when he was come into the house, Jesus came before him, and said, Simon, what seemeth to thee? Kings of the earth, of whom take they tribute? of their sons, either of aliens? (or Kings of the earth, from whom do they collect tolls or taxes? from their own people, or from strangers, or

foreigners?)

26   And he said, Of aliens (or From foreigners). Jesus said to him, Then (the) sons be free.

27   But that we offend them not, go thou to the sea, and cast an hook, and take that fish that first cometh up; and, when his mouth is opened, thou shalt find a stater, [*that is, a certain* (kind) *of money*]; take it, and give (it) [to them] for thee and for me.

CHAPTER 18

1   In that hour the disciples came to Jesus, and said, Who, guessest thou, is [the] greater in the kingdom of heavens? (At that time the disciples came to Jesus, and asked, Who, thinkest thou, is the greatest in the Kingdom of Heaven?)

2   And Jesus called (for) a little child, and put him in the middle [or in the midst] of them;

3   and said, I say truth to you [or Truly I say to you], [no] but ye be turned, and [be] made as little children, ye shall not enter into the kingdom of heavens. (and said, I tell you the truth, unless ye be changed, and be made like little children, ye shall not enter into the Kingdom of Heaven.)

4   Therefore whoever meeketh him[self] as this little child, he is (the) greater in the kingdom of heavens. (And so whoever humbleth himself, like this little child, he is the greatest in the Kingdom of Heaven.)

5   And he that receiveth one such little child in my name, receiveth me.

6   But whoso causeth to stumble one of these small (ones), [or these little (ones)], that believe in me, it speedeth to him, that a millstone of asses be hanged in his neck, and he be drenched in the deepness of the sea. (But whosoever causeth to stumble one of these little ones, who believe in me, it is more expedient for him, that a donkey's millstone be hung about his neck, and he be drowned in the depth of the sea.)

7   Woe to the world, for causes of stumbling; for it is need(ful), (or it is necessary), that causes of stumbling come; nevertheless woe to that man by whom a cause of stumbling cometh.

8   And if thine hand or thy foot cause thee to stumble, cut it off, and cast *it* away from thee. It is better to thee to enter [in]to life feeble, either crooked, (or It is better for thee to enter into (eternal) life maimed, or lame), than having twain hands or two feet to be sent into (the) everlasting fire.

9   And if thine eye cause thee to stumble, pull it out, and cast *it* away from thee. It is better to thee, with one eye to enter into life, (or It is better for thee to enter into (eternal) life with one eye), than having twain eyes to be sent into the fire of hell [or into hellfire].

10   See ye, that ye despise not one of these little (ones). For I say to you [or Truly I say to you], that the angels of them in heavens see (for)evermore the face of my Father that is in heavens, (or For I tell you the truth, that their guardian angels in heaven always see the face of my Father who is in heaven).

11   For man's Son came to save that thing that perished.

12   What seemeth to you? If there were to a man an hundred sheep, and one of them hath erred, whether he shall not leave (the) ninety and nine in (the) desert [or in the hills], and shall go to seek that that erred? (What seemeth to you? If a man hath a hundred sheep, and one of them hath wandered off, shall he not leave the ninety-nine on the hills, and go to seek the one which hath wandered off?)

13   And if it fall that he find it, truly I say to you (or I tell you the truth), that he shall have joy thereof, [or for he shall joy thereon], more than on (the) ninety and nine that erred not.

14   So it is not the will of your Father that is in heavens [or that is in heaven], that one of these little (ones) perish.

15   But if thy brother sinneth against thee, go thou, and reprove him, betwixt thee and him

alone, (or And if thy brother sinneth against thee, go, and rebuke him, between thee and him alone); if he heareth thee, thou hast won thy brother.

16 And if he heareth thee not, take with thee one or twain, (so) that every word stand in the mouth of twain or three witnesses.

17 And if he heareth not them, say thou to the church. But if he heareth not the church, be he as an heathen and (as) a publican to thee, [or be he to thee as an heathen man and a publican], (or be he like a Gentile and a tax-collector to thee).

18 I say to you truly, (or Truly I say to you, or I tell you the truth), whatever things ye bind on earth, those shall be bound also in heaven; and whatever things ye unbind on earth, those shall be unbound also in heaven.

19 Again I say to you, that if twain of you consent on earth, of everything whatever they ask, it shall be done to them of my Father that is in heavens. (Again I tell you, that if two of you consent, or agree, on the earth, about anything, whatever they ask, it shall be done for them by my Father who is in heaven.)

20 For where twain or three be gathered in my name, there I am in the middle of them. [For where two or three be gathered in my name, there I am in the midst of them.]

21 Then Peter came to him, and said, Lord, how oft shall my brother sin against me, and I shall forgive him? Whether till seven times?

22 Jesus saith to him, I say not to thee, till seven times; but till seventy times seven times.

23 Therefore the kingdom of heavens is likened to a king, that would reckon with his servants.

24 And when he began to reckon, one that owed to him ten thousand talents, was brought to him. [+And when he began to put reason, one was brought to him, that owed to him ten thousand bezants, *or talents*.]

25 And when he had not whereof to yield, his lord commanded him to be sold, and his wife, and children, and all things that he had, and (so) to be paid.

26 But that servant felled down, and prayed him, and said, Have patience in me (or Have patience with me), and I shall yield to thee all things.

27 And the lord had mercy on that servant, and suffered him to go, (or and allowed him to go), [or (and) delivered him, (or let him go)], and forgave him the debt.

28 But that servant went out, and found one of his even-servants, that owed him an hundred pence, (or But that servant went out, and found one of his fellow servants, who owed him a hundred pennies); and he held him, and strangled him, and said, Yield that that thou owest.

29 And his even-servant fell down, and prayed him, and said, Have patience in me, and I shall requite all things to thee. (And his fellow servant fell down at his feet, and beseeched him, and said, Have patience with me, and I shall repay everything to thee.)

30 But he would not; but went out, and put him [or sent him] into prison, till he paid all the debt.

31 And his even-servants, seeing the things that were done, sorrowed greatly, (or And his fellow servants, seeing what was done, greatly sorrowed). And they came, and told to their lord all the things that were done.

32 Then his lord called him, and said to him, Wicked servant, I forgave to thee all the debt, for thou prayedest me.

33 Therefore whether it behooved not also thee to have mercy on thine even-servant, as I had mercy on thee? (And so did it not also behoove thee to have mercy on thy fellow servant, like I had mercy on thee?)

34 And his lord was wroth, and took him to tormentors, till he paid all the debt.

35 So my Father of heaven shall do to you, if ye forgive not every man to his brother, of your hearts. (So shall my Father in heaven do to you,

if any of you do not forgive his brother, from your heart.)

CHAPTER 19

1   And it was done, when Jesus had ended these words, he passed from Galilee (or he went forth from Galilee), and came into the coasts of Judea over (the) Jordan (River).

2   And much people (pur)sued him (or And many people followed him), and he healed them there.

3   And the Pharisees came to him, tempting him, and said, Whether it be leaveful to a man to leave his wife, for any cause? [⁺or Whether it is leaveful for a man to leave, *or forsake*, his wife, for whatever cause?] (And the Pharisees came to him, to test him, and said, Is it lawful for a man to leave his wife, for any reason?)

4   Which answered, and said to them, Have ye not read, for he that made men at the beginning, made them male and female?

5   And he said, For this thing a man shall leave (his) father and mother, and he shall draw [or shall cleave] to his wife; and they shall be twain in one flesh.

6   And so they be not now twain, but one flesh. Therefore man separate not that thing that God hath joined [or Therefore a man part not that thing that God enjoined, *or knit together*].

7   They say to him, What then commanded Moses, to give a libel [or a little book] of forsaking, and (then) to leave of [or to forsake]? (And they said to him, Then why did Moses command us, to write a bill of forsaking, or a notice of divorce, and then we be able to leave, or to forsake, a woman?)

8   And he said to them, For Moses, for the hardness of your heart(s), suffered you to leave your wives, (or It was because of the hardness of your hearts, that Moses allowed you to leave your wives); but from the beginning it was not so.

9   And I say to you, that whoever leaveth his

wife, [no] but for fornication, and weddeth another, doeth lechery [or doeth adultery]; and he that weddeth the forsaken *wife*, doeth lechery [or doeth adultery].

10   His disciples say to him, If the cause of a man with his wife is so, it speedeth not to be wedded (or it is more expedient not to be married).

11   And he said to them, Not all men take this word; (no) but *they* to which it is given. (And he said to them, Everyone cannot receive this word; only those to whom it is given.)

12   For there be geldings, which be so born of the mother's womb [or which be thus born of their mother's womb]; and there be geldings, that be made of men; and there be geldings, that have gelded themselves, for the kingdom of heavens. He that may take, take he, (or He who can receive this word, receive it).

13   Then little children were brought to him, that he should put [his] hands to them, and pray (for them). And the disciples blamed them. (Then little children were brought to him, so that he would lay his hands on them, and pray for them. And the disciples rebuked them.)

14   But Jesus said to them, Suffer ye that (the) little children come to me [or Suffer ye (the) little children (to) come to me], and do not ye forbid them; for of such is the kingdom of heavens. (But Jesus said to them, Allow the little children to come to me, and do not forbid them; for of such is the Kingdom of Heaven.)

15   And when he had put to them (his) hands, he went from thence. (And after he had laid his hands on them, he went away from there.)

16   And lo! one came, and said to him, Good master, what good [thing] shall I do, that I have everlasting life? (And behold, one came, and said to him, Good Teacher, what good thing should I do, so that I can have, or so that I can get, eternal life?)

17   Which saith to him, What askest thou me of good thing(s)? (or Why askest me about good things, or about what is good?) There is one

good God. But if thou wilt enter into life, keep the commandments.

18 He saith to him, Which? And Jesus said, Thou shalt not do manslaying, thou shalt not do adultery, thou shalt not do theft, thou shalt not say false witnessing, (or thou shalt not give false testimony, or thou shalt not lie);

19 worship thy father and thy mother [or honour thou thy father and thy mother], and, thou shalt love thy neighbour as thyself.

20 The young man saith to him, I have kept all these things from my youth, what yet faileth to me?

21 Jesus saith to him, If thou wilt be perfect, go, and sell all (the) things that thou hast, and give (the proceeds) to poor men (or to the poor), and (then) thou shalt have treasure in heaven; and come, and (pur)sue me (or and follow me).

22 And when the young man had heard these words, he went away sorrowful, for he had many possessions.

23 And Jesus said to his disciples, I say to you truth, [or Truly I say to you], (or I tell you the truth), for a rich man of hard shall enter into the kingdom of heavens.

24 And again I say to you, it is lighter (for) a camel to pass through a needle's eye, [or it is easier (for) a camel to pass through the hole of a needle], than (for) a rich man to enter into the kingdom of heavens.

25 When these things were heard, the disciples wondered greatly, and said, Who then may be safe? (or Then who can be saved?)

26 Jesus beheld (them), and said to them, With men this thing is impossible; but with God all things be possible.

27 Then Peter answered, and said to him, Lo! we have forsaken all things, and we have (pur)sued thee; what then shall be to us? (Then Peter answered, and said to him, Behold, we have forsaken everything, and we have followed thee; then what shall be for us?)

28 And Jesus said to them, Truly I say to you, that ye that have forsaken all things, and have (pur)sued me, in the regeneration when man's Son shall sit in the seat of his majesty, [also] ye shall sit on twelve seats, deeming the twelve kindreds of Israel. (And Jesus said to them, I tell you the truth, that ye who have forsaken everything, and have followed me, in the regeneration when man's Son shall sit on the throne of his majesty, ye shall also sit on twelve thrones, judging the twelve tribes of Israel.)

29 And every man that forsaketh house, [or] brethren or sisters, [or] father or mother, [or] wife or children, or fields, for my name, he shall take an hundredfold, and shall wield everlasting life, (or he shall receive a hundred times as much, and shall gain, or possess, eternal life).

30 But many shall be, the first the last, and the last the first.

CHAPTER 20

1 The kingdom of heavens is like to an husbandman, that went out first by the morrow [or early], to hire workmen into his vineyard. (The Kingdom of Heaven is like a farmer, who went out early in the morning, to hire workmen for his vineyard.)

2 And when the covenant was made with the workmen, of a penny for the day, he sent them into his vineyard.

3 And he went out about the third hour (or about nine o'clock in the morning), and saw others standing idle in the market.

4 And he said to them, Go ye also into mine vineyard, and that that shall be rightful, I shall give to you. And they went forth.

5 Again he went out about the sixth hour, and the ninth, and did in like manner.

6 But about the eleventh hour he went out, and found others standing (there); and said to them, What stand ye idle here all day? [or What stand ye here idle all day?] (or Why stand ye here idle all day?)

7   They say to him, For no man hath hired us. He saith to them, Go ye also into my vineyard.

8   And when (the) evening was come, the lord of the vineyard saith to his procurator, Call the workmen, and yield to them their hire, (or Call the workmen, and pay them their wages), and begin thou at the last till to the first.

9   And so when they were come, that came about the eleventh hour, also they took every each (one) of them a penny, [or also they took even-pence, *that is, every man a penny*], (or each one of them received a penny).

10   But (then) the first came, and deemed (or judged), that they should take more, but they (also) took each one by themselves a penny; [Truly and the first coming deemed, that they were worthy to take more, but also they took even-pence.] (But then the first came, and thought that they should receive more, but each one of them also received a penny;)

11   and in the taking, they grudged against the husbandman, (and upon receiving it, they grumbled against the farmer,)

12   and said, These last wrought one hour, and thou hast made them even to us, that have borne the charge of the day, and [the] heat? (and said, These last men have worked only one hour, and thou hast made them equal to us, or and thou hast paid them equal to us, we who have borne the burden all day long, and the heat?)

13   And he answered to one of them, and said, Friend, I do thee none wrong, [or Friend, I do thee no wrong]; whether thou hast not accorded with me for a penny? (or did thou not agree to work for me for a penny?)

14   Take thou that that is thine, and go; for I will give to this last *man*, as to thee.

15   Whether it is not leaveful to me to do that that I will? (or Is it not lawful for me to do what I desire, or what I want, with my own money?) Whether thine eye is wicked, for I am good?

16   So the last shall be the first, and the first [shall be] the last; for many be called, but few *be* chosen.

17   And Jesus went up to Jerusalem, and took his twelve disciples in private, and said to them,

18   Lo! we go up to Jerusalem, and man's Son shall be betaken to (the) princes of (the) priests, and to (the) scribes, (or and man's Son shall be delivered, or given over, to the high priests, and the scribes); and they shall condemn him to death.

19   And they shall betake him to (the) heathen men, for to be scorned, and scourged, and crucified, (or And they shall deliver him unto the Gentiles, to be scorned, and scourged, and crucified); and the third day he shall rise again *to life*.

20   Then the mother of the sons of Zebedee came to him with her sons, honouring [or worshipping], and asking something of him.

21   And he said to her, What wilt thou? She saith to him, Say that these two my sons sit [or Say that these my two sons sit], one at thy right half, and one at thy left half, in thy kingdom. (And he said to her, What desirest thou? or What do you want? She said to him, Say that these my two sons sit one at thy right hand, or on thy right side, and one at thy left hand, or on thy left side, in thy Kingdom.)

22   Jesus answered, and said, Ye know not what ye ask. May ye drink of the cup that I shall drink of? [or May ye drink the cup that I am to drink?] They say to him, We may. (Jesus answered, and said, Ye do not know what ye ask. Can ye drink from the cup that I shall drink from? They said to him, We can.)

23   He saith to them, Ye shall drink my cup; but to sit at my right half or [at my] left half, is not mine to give to you; but to whom it is made ready of my Father. (He said to them, Ye shall drink from my cup; but to sit at my right hand or at my left hand, is not mine to give to you; but for whom it is prepared by my Father.)

24   And the ten hearing, had indignation of

the two brethren. (And the other ten hearing this, felt indignation toward the two brothers.)

25 But Jesus called them to him, and said, Ye know, that [the] princes of heathen men be lords of them, and they that be [the] greater [or (the) more], use power on them. (And Jesus called them to him, and said, Ye know, that the leaders of the Gentiles be their lords, and they who be the greater ones have power over the others.)

26 It shall not be so among you; but whoever will be made [the] greater [or (the) more] among you, be he your minister (or he will be your servant);

27 and whoever among you will be the first, (yea), he shall be your servant.

28 As man's Son came not to be served, but to serve, and to give his life (as a) redemption for many.

29 And when they went out of Jericho, much people (pur)sued him. (And when they left Jericho, many people followed him.)

30 And lo! two blind men sat beside the way, and heard that Jesus passed (by); and they cried, and said, Lord, the son of David, have mercy on us.

31 And the people blamed them, that they should be still, (or And the people rebuked them, so that they would be quiet); and they cried the more, and said, Lord, the son of David, have mercy on us.

32 And Jesus stood, and called them, and said, What will ye, that I do to you? (or What desire ye, that I do for you? or What do ye want me to do for you?)

33 They say to him, Lord, that our eyes be opened.

34 And Jesus had mercy on them, and touched their eyes; and anon they saw, and (pur)sued him (or and at once they saw, and followed him).

CHAPTER 21

1 And when Jesus came nigh to Jerusalem, and came to Bethphage, at the mount of Olives, then sent he his two disciples, [And when Jesus came nigh to Jerusalem, and came to Bethphage, to the mount of Olives, then Jesus sent his two disciples,]

2 and said to them, Go ye into the castle that is against you, and anon ye shall find an ass tied (up), and a colt with her; untie ye, and bring (them) to me. (and said to them, Go ye into the village that is opposite you, and at once ye shall find a donkey tied up, and a colt with her; untie them, and bring them to me.)

3 And if any man say to you anything, say ye, that the Lord hath need to them; and anon he shall leave them. (And if anyone say anything to you, say, that the Lord hath need of them; and then at once, he shall let them go, or come here.)

4 All this was done, that that thing should be fulfilled, that was said by the prophet, saying,

5 Say ye to the daughter of Sion (or Say to the daughter of Zion), Lo! thy king cometh to thee, meek, sitting on an ass, and a foal [or a colt] of *an ass* under yoke.

6 And the disciples went, and did as Jesus commanded [to] them.

7 And they brought an ass, and the foal [or the colt], and laid their clothes on them, and made him [to] sit above. (And they brought the donkey, and the colt, and laid their clothes on them, and had him sit upon the donkey.)

8 And full much people spreaded their clothes in the way; others cutted branches of (the) trees, and strewed in the way. (And many people spread their clothes on the way, or on the road; others cut off branches from the trees, and strew them on the way.)

9 And the people that went before, and that (pur)sued (or who followed), cried, and said, Hosanna to the son of David; blessed *is* he that cometh in the name of the Lord; Hosanna in high things, [or Hosanna in the highest things], (or Hosanna in the highest).

10 And when he was entered into Jerusalem, all the city was stirred, and said, Who is this?

11 But the people said, This is Jesus, the prophet, of Nazareth of Galilee.

12 And Jesus entered into the temple of God, and cast out of the temple all that bought and sold; and he turned upside-down the boards of (the) (money-)changers, and the chairs of men that sold culvers. (And Jesus entered into the Temple of God, and threw out of the Temple all who bought and sold; and he turned upside-down the tables of the money-changers, and the chairs of men who sold doves and pigeons.)

13 And he said to them, It is written, Mine house shall be called an house of prayer (or My House shall be called a House of Prayer); but ye have made it (into) a den of thieves.

14 And (the) blind and (the) crooked came to him in the temple, and he healed them. (And the blind and the lame came to him in the Temple, and he healed them.)

15 But the princes of (the) priests, and the scribes, (or But the high priests, and the scribes), seeing the marvelous [or the wonderful] things that he did, and the children crying in the temple, and saying, Hosanna to the son of David, they had indignation [or disdain],

16 and said to him, Hearest thou what these say? And Jesus said to them, Yea; whether ye have never read, That (out) of the mouth(s) of young children, and of suckling children, thou hast made perfect praising?

17 And when he had left them, he went forth out of the city, into Bethany; and there he dwelt, and taught them of the kingdom of God.

18 But on the morrow, he, turning again into the city, hungered. (But the next morning, as he returned to the city, he was hungry.)

19 And he saw a fig tree beside the way, and came to it, and found nothing therein [or nothing thereon], [no] but leaves only. And he said to it, Never fruit come forth of thee [or Never be fruit born of thee], into without end.

And anon the fig tree was dried up (or And at once the fig tree dried up).

20 And the disciples saw, and wondered, saying, How anon it dried, [or How it dried up anon], (or How at once, or so quickly, it dried up).

21 And Jesus answered, and said to them, Truly I say to you (or I tell you the truth), if ye have faith, and doubt not, not only ye shall do of the fig tree, but also if ye say to this hill, Take [away thee], and cast thee into the sea, (or Go away, and throw thyself into the sea), it shall be done so [or it shall be done].

22 And all things whatever ye believing shall ask (for) in prayer, ye shall take (or ye shall receive them).

23 And when he came into the temple, the princes of (the) priests, and (the) elder men of the people, (or the high priests, and the elders of the people), came to him that taught, [or came to him (while he was) teaching], and said, In what power doest thou these things? and who gave [to] thee this power?

24 Jesus answered, and said to them, And I shall ask you one word (or And I shall ask you one question), the which if ye tell me, I shall say to you, in what power I do these things.

25 Of whence was the baptism of John; of heaven, or of men? And they thought within themselves, saying, If we say of heaven, he shall say to us, Why then believe ye not to him? (From where was the baptism of John; from heaven, or from men? And they thought within themselves, saying, If we say from heaven, he shall say to us, Then why did ye not believe him?)

26 If we say of men, we dread the people, for all had John as a prophet. (If we say from men, we fear the people, for everyone believed that John was a prophet.)

27 And they answered to Jesus, and said, We know not. And he said to them, Neither I say to you, in what power I do these things.

28 But what seemeth to you? A man had two

sons; and he came to the first, and said, Son, go work this day in my vineyard.

29 And he answered, and said, I will not; but afterward he forthought, and went forth, [or but afterward he stirred by penance, *or forthinking*, (or repenting), went], (or but later he repented, and went, and worked).

30 But he came to the other, and said in like manner. And he answered, and said, Lord, I go; and he went not (or but he did not go).

31 Who of the twain did the father's will? They say to him, The first. Jesus saith to them, Truly I say to you, for publicans and whores shall go before you into the kingdom of God. (Which of the two did the father's will? They said to him, The first one. Then Jesus said to them, I tell you the truth, tax-collectors and prostitutes now go ahead of you into the Kingdom of God.)

32 For John came to you in the way of rightwiseness, and ye believed not to him; but publicans and whores believed to him. But ye saw, and had no forthinking after, that ye believed to him, [or But ye seeing, had not penance afterward, that ye should believe to him]. (For John came to you by the way of righteousness, and ye did not believe him; but tax-collectors and prostitutes believed him. Yes, ye saw this, but ye had no repenting later, so that ye believed him.)

33 Hear ye another parable. There was an husbandman, that planted a vineyard, and hedged it about, and delved a presser therein, and builded a tower, and hired it to earth-tillers, and went far (away) in pilgrimage. (Listen to another parable. There was a landowner, who planted a vineyard, and hedged it about, and dug a hole for a winepress in it, and built a look-out tower, and rented the land to farmers, and then went on a journey.)

34 And when the time of fruits nighed, he sent his servants to the earth-tillers, to take (the) fruits of it. (And when the time of fruits approached, he sent his servants to the farmers, to receive some of its fruits.)

35 And the earth-tillers took his servants, and they beat one, they slew another, and stoned another.

36 Again he sent other servants, more than the first, and in like manner they did to them [or and they did to them in like manner].

37 And at the last he sent his son to them, and said, They shall dread my son. (And finally he sent his son to them, and said, They shall fear my son, or They shall show reverence, or respect, for my son.)

38 But the earth-tillers, seeing the son, said within themselves, This is the heir; come ye, slay we him, and we shall have his heritage. (But the farmers, seeing the son, said to each other, He is the heir; come, let us kill him, and then we shall get his inheritance.)

39 And they took him, and casted him out of the vineyard, and slew *him*. (And they took him, and threw him out of the vineyard, and killed *him*.)

40 Therefore when the lord of the vineyard shall come, what shall he do to those earth-tillers?

41 They say to him, He shall lose evil (or He shall destroy evil), (yea), the evil men, and he shall set to hire his vineyard to other earth-tillers, which shall yield to him (the) fruit in their times.

42 Jesus saith to them, Read ye never in (the) scriptures, The stone which the builders reproved, this is made into the head of the corner? Of the Lord this thing is done, and it is marvelous [or it is wonderful] in our eyes.

43 Therefore I say to you, that the kingdom of God shall be taken from you, and [it] shall be given to a folk doing [the] fruits of it. (And so I tell you, that the Kingdom of God shall be taken away from you, and it shall be given to a nation and a people bringing forth its proper fruits.)

44 And he that shall fall on this stone, shall be broken; but on whom it shall fall, it shall

bruise him [or it shall pound him] all to pieces.

45 And when the princes of (the) priests, and [the] Pharisees had heard his parables, they knew that he said of them. (And when the high priests, and the Pharisees had heard his parables, they knew that he had spoken about them.)

46 And they sought to (take) hold (of) him, but they dreaded the people (or but they feared the people), for they had him as a prophet.

CHAPTER 22

1 And Jesus answered, and spake again in parables to them, and said,

2 The kingdom of heavens is made like to a king that made weddings to his son. (The Kingdom of Heaven is like a king who gave a wedding for his son.)

3 And he sent his servants to call men that were bidden to the weddings, and they would not come.

4 Again he sent other servants, and said, Say to the men that be bidden to the feast, Lo! I have made ready my meat, (or Behold, I have prepared my food), my bulls and my volatiles, [or my fat beasts], be slain, and all things be ready; come ye to the weddings.

5 But they despised, and went forth, one into his town, another to his merchandise. [Soothly they despised, or reckoned not, and they went away, one into his vineyard, forsooth another to his merchandise.]

6 But others held his servants, and tormented them, and slew [them].

7 But the king, when he had heard, was wroth; and he sent his hosts, and destroyed those man-quellers, and burnt their city. (But the king, when he had heard, was enraged; and he sent his army, or his soldiers, and destroyed those murderers, and burned down their city.)

8 Then he said to his servants, The weddings be ready, but they that were called to the feast, were not worthy.

9 Therefore go ye into the ends of ways, and whomever ye find, call ye to the weddings.

10 And his servants went out into the ways, and gathered together all that they found, good and evil; and the bridal was [or the weddings be] full-filled with men sitting at the meat (or and the wedding feast was filled full with people come for the meal).

11 And the king entered, to see men sitting at the meat (or to see those who had come for the meal); and he saw there a man not clothed with bride clothes [or and he saw there a man not clothed with bridal clothes].

12 And he said to him, Friend, how enteredest thou hither without bride clothes? And he was dumb (or And he did not answer).

13 Then the king bade his ministers, [or Then the king said to his ministers], (or Then the king said to his servants), Bind him both hands and feet, and send ye him into outer-more [or uttermore] darknesses; there shall be weeping, and grinding of teeth.

14 For many be called, but few be chosen.

15 Then (the) Pharisees went away, and took a counsel [or took counsel] to take Jesus in word. (Then the Pharisees went away, and made a plan to catch Jesus with his own words.)

16 And they send to him their disciples, with (the) Herodians, and said, Master, we know, that thou art soothfast, and thou teachest in truth the way of God, and thou chargest [or care(st)] not of (or for) any man('s opinion), for thou beholdest not the person of men.

17 Therefore say to us, what seemeth to thee. Is it leaveful that tribute be given to the emperor, either nay? [†or Is it leaveful that tribute be given to Caesar, rent, (yea) or nay?] (or Is it lawful to pay taxes to Caesar, yes or no?)

18 And when Jesus had known the wickedness of them, he said, Hypocrites, what tempt ye me? (And when Jesus had perceived their malice, he said, Hypocrites, why do you

test me? or why do you try to trap me?)

19　Show ye to me the print of the money. And they brought to him a penny.

20　And Jesus said to them, Whose is this image, and the writing above? (or Whose image is this, and the writing upon it?)

21　They say to him, The emperor's. Then he said to them, Therefore yield ye to the emperor those things that be the emperor's, and to God those things that be of God. [+They say to him, Of Caesar. Then he saith to them, Therefore yield ye to Caesar those things that be of Caesar/those things that be Caesar's, and to God those things that be of God.]

22　And they heard, and wondered; and they left him, and went away.

23　In that day (some) Sadducees, that say there is no rising again *to life* (or who say that there is no resurrection), came to him, and asked him,

24　and said, Master, (or Teacher), Moses said, if any man is dead, not having a son, that his brother wed his wife, and raise seed to his brother.

25　And there were seven brethren to us; and the first wedded a wife, and is dead. And he had no seed, and left his wife to his brother;

26　also the second, and the third, till to the seventh.

27　But the last of all, [also] the woman is dead.

28　Also [or Therefore] in the rising again *to life* (or And so in the resurrection), whose wife of the seven shall she be? for all had her.

29　Jesus answered, and said to them, Ye err, not knowing the scriptures, nor the virtue of God. (Jesus answered, and said to them, Ye err, not knowing the Scriptures, nor the power of God.)

30　For in the rising again *to life* (or For in the resurrection *to life*), neither they shall wed, neither shall be wedded; but they be as the angels of God in heaven.

31　And of the rising again of dead men (or And about the resurrection of the dead), have ye not read, that [it] is said of the Lord, that saith to you,

32　I am God of Abraham, and God of Isaac, and God of Jacob? he is not (the) God of dead men, but of living men, (or he is not the God of the dead, but of the living).

33　And the people hearing, wondered on his teaching.

34　And the Pharisees heard that he had put silence to (the) Sadducees, and came together (to him).

35　And one of them, a teacher of the law, asked Jesus, and tempted him, (or and tested him, or and tried to trap him),

36　Master, which is a great commandment in the law? (Teacher, which is the greatest, or the most important, commandment in the Law?)

37　Jesus said to him, Thou shalt love thy Lord God [or Thou shalt love the Lord thy God], of all thine heart, and in all thy soul, and in all thy mind. (Jesus said to him, Thou shalt love the Lord thy God, with all thine heart, and with all thy soul, and with all thy mind.)

38　This is the first and the most (important) commandment. (This is the first and the greatest commandment.)

39　And the second is like to this; Thou shalt love thy neighbour as thyself.

40　In these two commandments hangeth all the law and the prophets.

41　And when the Pharisees were gathered together, Jesus asked them,

42　and said, What seemeth to you of Christ (or What seemeth to you regarding the Messiah), whose son is he? They say to him, Of David.

43　He saith to them, How then David in spirit calleth him Lord, and saith, (He said to them, How then did David by the Holy Spirit call him Lord, and say,)

44　The Lord said to my Lord, Sit [thou] on my right half, till I put thine enemies a stool of thy feet? (The Lord said to my Lord, Sit at my right hand, or on my right side, until I make thine enemies thy footstool?)

45   Then if David calleth him Lord, how (then) is he his son?

46   And no man might answer a word to him, neither any man was hardy from that day (on), (or nor was any man bold enough from that day on), to ask him (anything) more.

CHAPTER 23

1   Then Jesus spake to the people, and to his disciples,

2   and said, On the chair of Moses, scribes and Pharisees have sat.

3   Therefore keep ye, and do ye all (the) things, whatever things they say to you. But do not ye do after their works; for they say, and do not. (And so obey ye them, and do everything, whatever they tell you to do. But do not do, or follow, after their works; for they say to do something, but they do not do it themselves.)

4   And they bind grievous charges (or heavy burdens), and that may not be borne, and put (them) on [the] shoulders of men; but with their (own) finger they will not move them (or but with their own finger they will not even touch them).

5   Therefore they do all their works to be seen of men (or And so they do all their works to be seen by men); for they draw abroad their phylacteries, and magnify [their] hems.

6   And they love the first sitting places in suppers [or at suppers], and the first chairs in synagogues;

7   and salutations in [the] chapping, and to be called of men, master. (and respectful greetings at the market, and to be called by men, Teacher, or Rabbi.)

8   But do not ye be called master; for one is your master, and all ye be brethren. (But do not ye be called Rabbi; for there is only one Teacher, and all of ye be brothers.)

9   And do not ye call to you(rselves) a father on earth, for one is your Father, that is in heavens, (or for there is only one Father, who is in heaven).

10   Neither be ye called masters, for one is your master, Christ. (Nor be ye called teachers, for there is only one Teacher, the Messiah.)

11   He that is (the) greatest among you, shall be your minister. (He who is the greatest among you, shall be your servant.)

12   For he that higheth himself, shall be meeked; and he that meeketh himself, shall be enhanced. (For he who maketh himself high, shall be humbled; and he who maketh himself humble, shall be exalted.)

13   But woe to you, scribes and Pharisees, hypocrites, that close (the door of) the kingdom of heavens before men [or for ye close (the door of) the realm of heaven before men]; and ye enter not, neither suffer other men entering to enter. (But woe to you, scribes and Pharisees, hypocrites, who shut the door of the Kingdom of Heaven in front of people; and ye enter not, nor allow others entering to enter.)

14   Woe to you, scribes and Pharisees, hypocrites, that eat (up) the houses of widows, and pray by long prayer; for this thing ye shall take the more doom (or ye shall receive the greater, or the harsher, judgement).

15   Woe to you, scribes and Pharisees, hypocrites, that go about the sea and the land, to make one proselyte; and when he is made, ye make him (to be) a son of hell, double more than ye *be*.

16   Woe to you, blind leaders, that say, Whoever sweareth by the temple of God, it is nothing; but he that sweareth in the gold of the temple (or but he who sweareth by the gold of the Temple), is (a) debtor [or oweth].

17   Ye fools and blind (or Ye blind fools), for what is greater, the gold, or the temple that halloweth the gold?

18   And whoever sweareth in the altar, it is nothing; but he that sweareth in the gift that is

on the altar, oweth [or is a debtor]. (And whoever sweareth by the altar, it is nothing; but he who sweareth by the gift that is on the altar, is a debtor.)

19 Blind men, for what is more, the gift, or the altar that halloweth the gift?

20 Therefore he that sweareth in the altar, sweareth in it, and in all things that be thereon. (And so he who sweareth by the altar, sweareth by it, and by all the things that be on it.)

21 And he that sweareth in the temple, sweareth in it, and in him that dwelleth in the temple. (And he who sweareth by the Temple, sweareth by it, and by Him who dwelleth in the Temple.)

22 And he that sweareth in heaven, sweareth in the throne of God, and in him that sitteth thereon. (And he who sweareth by heaven, sweareth by the throne of God, and by Him who sitteth on it.)

23 Woe to you, scribes and Pharisees, hypocrites, that tithe mint, anise, and cummin, and have left those things that be of more charge of the law (or that be of greater importance in the Law), (yea), doom (or judgement), and mercy, and faith. And it behooved [or needed] to do these things, and not to leave (undone) those (other things).

24 Blind leaders, cleansing a gnat, but swallowing a camel.

25 Woe to you, scribes and Pharisees, hypocrites, that cleanse the cup and the platter withoutforth; but within ye be full of raven, and uncleanness, (or but within ye be full of the spoils gotten from robberies, and uncleanness).

26 Thou blind Pharisee, cleanse first the cup and the platter withinforth, (so) that [also] that that is withoutforth be made clean.

27 Woe to you, scribes and Pharisees, hypocrites, that be like to sepulchres whited [or made white], which withoutforth seem fair to men, (or who be like white tombs, which on the outside look beautiful to men); but within they be full of (the) bones of dead men, and of all filth.

28 So ye withoutforth seem just [or rightful] to men; but within ye be full of hypocrisy and wickedness.

29 Woe to you, scribes and Pharisees, hypocrites, that build [the] sepulchres of (the) prophets, and make fair the burials of just men, (Woe to you, scribes and Pharisees, hypocrites, who build the tombs of the prophets, and make the tombs of the righteous beautiful,)

30 and say, If we had been in the days of our fathers, we should not have been their fellows in (spilling) the blood of (the) prophets. (and say, If we had lived in the days of our fathers, we would not have been their partners in spilling the blood of the prophets.)

31 And so ye be in[to] witnessing to yourselves, that ye be the sons of them that slew the prophets. (And so ye testify about yourselves, that ye be the sons of those who killed the prophets.)

32 And (so) full-fill ye (then) the measure of your fathers. [And (so) fill ye (full) the measure of your fathers.]

33 Ye adders, and adders' brood [or (the) fruits of adders], how shall ye flee from the doom of hell? (Ye snakes, and children of snakes, how shall ye flee from the judgement of hell, or from being condemned to hell?)

34 Therefore lo! I send to you prophets, and wise men, and scribes [or writers]; and of them ye shall slay and crucify, and of them ye shall scourge in your synagogues, and shall pursue from city into city, [or and shall pursue from city to city], (or and shall persecute them from city to city);

35 that all the just blood come on you, that was shed on the earth, from the blood of just Abel to the blood of Zacharias, the son of Barachias, whom ye slew betwixt the temple and the altar. (so that all the righteous or innocent blood come upon you, that was shed upon the earth, from the blood of innocent Abel to the blood of Zechariah, the son of

Barachiah, whom ye killed between the Temple and the altar.)

36 Truly I say to you (or I tell you the truth), all these things shall come on this generation.

37 Jerusalem, Jerusalem, that slayest prophets, and stonest them that be sent to thee, how oft would I gather together thy children, as an hen gathereth together her chickens under her wings, and thou wouldest not (or but thou would not let me).

38 Lo! your house shall be left to you desert(ed), [or forsaken].

39 And I say to you, ye shall not see me from henceforth, till ye say, Blessed *is he*, that cometh in the name of the Lord.

CHAPTER 24

1 And Jesus went out of the temple; and his disciples came to him, to show him the buildings of the temple.

2 But he answered, and said to them, See ye all these things? Truly I say to you (or I tell you the truth), a stone shall not be left on a stone/a stone shall not be left here on one stone, that not it shall be destroyed [or which shall not be destroyed].

3 And when he sat on the mount of Olives, his disciples came to him privily (or in private), and said, Say to us, when these things shall be, and what (is the) token (or the sign) of thy coming, and of the ending of the world.

4 And Jesus answered, and said to them, Look ye [or See ye], that no man deceive you.

5 For many shall come in my name, and shall say, I am Christ (or I am the Messiah); and they shall deceive many.

6 For ye shall hear battles, and opinions of battles; see ye that ye be not disturbed [or that ye be not distroubled]; for it behooveth these things to be done, but not yet is the end.

7 For folk shall rise together against folk, and realm against realm, and pestilences, and hungers, and earth-movings shall be by places;

(For nation shall rise against nation, and kingdom against kingdom, and plagues, and famines, and earthquakes shall be in places;)

8 and all these be (but the) beginnings of (the) sorrows.

9 Then men shall betake you into tribulation, and shall slay you, and ye shall be in hate [or in hatred] to all folks for my name. (Then men shall deliver you unto trials and troubles, and shall kill you, and ye shall be hated by all the nations and all the peoples, for my name's sake.)

10 And then many shall be caused to stumble, and betray each other, and they shall hate each other.

11 And many false prophets shall rise, and deceive many.

12 And for wickedness shall be plenteous, the charity of many shall wax cold (or the love of many shall grow cold);

13 but he that shall dwell still [or steadfast] into the end, shall be safe. (but he who shall endure unto the end, shall be saved.)

14 And this gospel of the kingdom shall be preached in all the world, in[to] witnessing to all folks; and then the end shall come. (And this Gospel, or Good News, of the Kingdom shall be preached in all the world, as a testimony to all the nations and all the peoples; and then the end shall come.)

15 Therefore when ye see the abomination of discomfort, that is said of (or by) Daniel, the prophet, standing in the holy place; he that readeth (this), understand he;

16 then they that be in Judea, flee to the mountains;

17 and he that *is* in the house roof (or and he who *is* on the roof of the house), come not down to take anything (out) of his house;

18 and he that *is* in the field, turn not again to take his coat (or do not return to get his coat).

19 But woe to them that be with child, and nourishing [or nursing] in those days.

20 Pray ye, that your flying be not made in

winter, or in the sabbath. (Pray ye, that your fleeing be not made in winter, or on the Sabbath.)

21 For then shall be great tribulation, what manner was not from the beginning of the world to now [till now], neither shall be made.

22 And but those days had been abridged (or shortened), each flesh, [or all flesh, *that is, mankind*], should not be made safe (or none of mankind could be saved); but those days shall be made short, for the chosen men.

23 Then if any man say to you, Lo! here is Christ, or there, do not ye believe (him). (Then if anyone say to you, Behold, here is the Messiah, or there, do not believe them.)

24 For false Christs and false prophets shall rise (up), (or For false Messiahs and false prophets shall rise up), and they shall give great tokens [or great signs] and wonders; so that also the chosen be led into error, if it may be done.

25 Lo! I have before-said to you.

26 Therefore if they say to you, Lo! he is in (the) desert, do not ye go out; lo! *he is* in privy places, (or behold, *he is* in private, or secret, places), do not ye believe (them).

27 For as lightning goeth out from the east, and appeareth into the west, so shall be also the coming of man's Son.

28 Wherever the body shall be, also the eagles shall be gathered thither.

29 And anon (or at once) after the tribulation of those days, the sun shall be made dark, and the moon shall not give her light, and the stars shall fall from (the) heaven(s), and the virtues (or the powers) of (the) heavens shall be moved [or shall be stirred].

30 And then the token of man's Son shall appear in (the) heaven(s), and then all the kindreds, [or all the lineages], (or all the tribes), of the earth shall wail; and they shall see man's Son coming in the clouds of (the) heaven(s), with much virtue, and majesty. (And then the sign of man's Son shall appear in the heavens, and then all the peoples of the earth shall wail;

and they shall see man's Son coming on the clouds of the heavens, with great power, and majesty.)

31 And he shall send (out) his angels with a trumpet, and a great voice (or and a great blast); and they shall gather his chosen from (the) four winds, from the highest things of heaven (un)to the ends of them.

32 And learn ye the parable of the fig tree. When his branch is now tender, and the leaves be sprung, ye know that summer is nigh, (or When its branch is now tender, and the leaves be sprung out, ye know that summer is near);

33 and so ye when ye shall see all these things, know ye that it is nigh, (yea), in the gates, (or know that it is near, yes, even at the door).

34 Truly I say to you (or I tell you the truth), for this generation shall not pass (away), till all (these) things be done;

35 heaven and earth shall pass (away), but my words shall not pass (away).

36 But of that day and hour no man knoweth, neither [the] angels of heaven, [no] but the Father alone (or but only the Father).

37 But as it was in the days of Noe (or Noah), so shall be the coming of man's Son.

38 For as in the days before the great flood, they were eating and drinking, wedding and taking to wedding, till that day, that Noe (or Noah) entered into the ship;

39 and they knew not, till the great flood came, and took (away) all men, so shall be the coming of man's Son.

40 Then twain shall be in a field, one shall be taken, and the other left;

41 two *women* shall be grinding in a quern [or (at a) mill], one shall be taken, and the other left; twain in a bed, the one shall be taken, and the other left.

42 Therefore wake ye, (or And so be on watch, or stay awake), for ye know not in what hour the Lord shall come.

43 But know ye this, that if the husbandman

knew in what hour the thief were to come, certainly he would wake, and suffer not his house to be undermined (or and would not allow his house to be robbed).

44   And therefore be ye ready, for in what hour ye guess not, man's Son shall come.

45   Who guessest thou is a true [or is a faithful] servant and prudent, whom his lord ordained on his household, to give them meat in (its) time? (Then who thinkest thou, is a faithful and a wise servant, whom his lord hath ordained upon, or over, his household, to give them their food at the proper time?)

46   Blessed *is* that servant, whom his lord, when he shall come, shall find so doing.

47   Truly I say to you, for on all his goods he shall ordain him. (I tell you the truth, that he shall put him in charge over all of his property.)

48   But if that evil servant say in his heart, My lord tarrieth to come,

49   and beginneth to smite his even-servants, and to eat, and drink with drunken men;

50   the lord of that servant shall come in the day [in] which he hopeth not, and in the hour that he knoweth not,

51   and shall part him (or and shall divide him in pieces), and put his part with (the) hypocrites; there shall be weeping, and grinding of teeth.

CHAPTER 25

1   Then the kingdom of heavens shall be like to ten virgins, which took their lamps, and went out to meet the husband and the wife;

2   and five of them were fools, and five (of them were) prudent.

3   But the five fools took their lamps, and took not oil with them;

4   but the prudent (ones) took oil in their vessels with the lamps.

5   And whiles the husband tarried, all they napped and slept [or all napped and slept].

6   But at midnight a cry was made, Lo! the spouse cometh, go ye out to meet with him [or go ye out to meet him].

7   Then all those virgins rose up, and arrayed their lamps.

8   And the fools said to the wise (ones), Give ye to us (some) of your oil, for our lamps be quenched.

9   The prudent (ones) answered, and said, Lest peradventure it suffice not to us and to you, go ye rather to men that sell (it), and buy to you (or and buy some for yourselves).

10   And while they went to buy (some), the spouse came; and those that were ready, entered [in] with him to the weddings; and the gate was shut.

11   And at the last the other virgins came, and said, Lord, lord, open to us.

12   And he answered, and said, Truly I say to you, I know you not. (And he answered, and said, I tell you the truth, I do not know you.)

13   Therefore wake ye, for ye know not the day nor the hour. (And so be on watch, or stay awake, for you do not know the day or the hour.)

14   For as a man that goeth [far] in pilgrimage, called his servants, and betook to them his goods (or and gave his substance, or his assets, to them);

15   and to one he gave five bezants or five talents, to another twain, and to another one, to each after his own virtue; and he went forth anon. (and to one he gave five talents, to another two, and to another one, to each according to his own power, or his own ability; and then he went forth at once.)

16   And he that had (received) five bezants [or five talents] went forth, and wrought in them, and won (an)other five. (And he who had received five talents went forth, and worked with them, and earned another five.)

17   Also and he that had taken twain, won (an)other twain (or earned another two).

18   But he that had taken one, went forth, and delved in the earth (or and dug in the ground),

and hid the money of his lord.

19 But after (a) long time, the lord of those servants came, and reckoned with them.

20 And he that had taken five bezants, came, and brought (an)other five, and said, Lord, thou betookest to me five bezants, lo! I have gotten above five others. [⁺And he that had taken five talents, nighing (or approaching), offered (an)other five, saying, Lord, thou betookest to me five talents, lo! I have gotten over (an)other five.] (And he who had received five talents, came, and brought another five, and said, Lord, thou gavest to me five talents, behold, I have earned another five.)

21 His lord said to him, Well be thou, good servant and faithful, (or Well done, good and faithful servant); for on few things thou hast been true, [or thou hast been faithful], (now) I shall ordain thee on many things; enter thou into the joy of thy lord.

22 And he that had taken two bezants, *or two talents*, came, and said, Lord, thou betookest to me two bezants; lo! I have won over (an)other twain. [⁺Forsooth he that had taken two talents, nighed (or approached), and said, Lord, thou betookest to me two talents, lo! I have gotten over (an)other two.] (And he who had received two talents, came, and said, Lord, thou gavest to me two talents; behold, I have earned another two.)

23 His lord said to him, Well be thou, good servant and true [or good servant and faithful], (or Well done, good and faithful servant); for on few things thou hast been true, [or thou hast been faithful], (now) I shall ordain thee on many things; enter thou into the joy of thy lord.

24 But he that had taken one bezant [or one talent], came, and said, Lord, I know that thou art an hard man; thou reapest where thou hast not sown, and thou gatherest together where thou hast not spread abroad; (But he who had received one talent, came, and said, Lord, I know that thou art a hard man; thou harvestest where thou hast not sown, and thou gatherest

together where thou hast not spread abroad;)

25 and I dreading (or and I greatly fearing thee), went, and hid thy bezant [or thy talent] in the earth; lo! thou hast that that is thine.

26 His lord answered, and said to him, Evil servant and slow, knewest thou that I reap where I sowed not, and gather together where I spreaded not abroad? (His master answered, and said to him, Wicked and lazy servant, knewest thou that I harvest where I did not sow, and gather together where I did not spread abroad?)

27 Therefore it behooved thee to betake my money to (money-)changers, that when I came, I should have received that that is mine with usuries. (And so it behooved thee to give my money to the money-changers, so that when I came back, I could have received what was mine with interest.)

28 Therefore take away from him the bezant, and give to him that hath ten bezants. [And so take away the talent from him, and give ye it to him that hath ten talents.]

29 For to every man that hath me shall give, and he shall increase [⁺or For to every man having it shall be given, and he shall have plenty, *or increase*]; but from him that hath not, also that that he seemeth to have, shall be taken away from him.

30 And cast ye out the unprofitable servant into outer-more [or uttermore] darknesses; there shall be weeping, and grinding of teeth.

31 When man's Son shall come in his majesty, and all his angels with him, then he shall sit on the seat (or on the throne) of his majesty;

32 and all folks shall be gathered before him (or and all the nations and all the peoples shall be gathered before him), and he shall separate them [or he shall part them] atwain, as a shepherd separateth [or parteth] sheep from kids;

33 and he shall set the sheep on his right half, and the kids on the left half [or and the

kids forsooth on his left half]. (and he shall set the sheep on his right side, and the goats on his left side.)

34   Then the king shall say to them, that shall be on his right half, Come ye, the blessed of my Father, take ye in possession the kingdom made ready to you from the making [or from the beginning] of the world. (Then the King shall say to those, who shall be on his right side, Come, the blessed of my Father, take into possession the Kingdom prepared for you from the creation of the world.)

35   For I hungered [or Forsooth I was hungry], and ye gave me (something) to eat; I thirsted, and ye gave me (something) to drink; I was harbourless, and ye harboured me;

36   naked, and ye covered me; sick, and ye visited me; I was in prison, and ye came to me.

37   Then just men shall answer to him, and say (or Then the righteous shall say to him), Lord, when saw we thee hungry, and we fed thee; thirsty, and we gave to thee, [or and we gave thee], (something to) drink?

38   and when saw we thee harbourless, and we harboured thee, [or when forsooth saw we thee harbourless, and we gathered thee to harbour]; or naked, and we covered thee?

39   or when saw we thee sick, or in prison, and we came to thee?

40   And the king answering shall say to them, Truly I say to you (or I tell you the truth), as long as ye did (it) to one of these my least brethren, ye did (it) to me.

41   Then the king shall say also to them, that shall be on his left half, Depart from me, ye cursed, into (the) everlasting fire, that is made ready to the devil and his angels. (Then the King shall say to those, who shall be on his left side, Go away from me, ye cursed, into the eternal fire, which is prepared for the Devil and his angels.)

42   For I hungered, and ye gave not me (anything) to eat; I thirsted, and ye gave not me (anything) to drink; [⁺For I hungered, and ye

gave not to me (anything) to eat; I thirsted, and ye gave not to me (anything) to drink;]

43   I was harbourless, and ye harboured not me, [or I was harbourless, and ye gathered not me to harbour]; naked, and ye covered not me; sick, and in prison, and ye visited not me.

44   Then and they shall answer to him, and shall say, Lord, when saw we thee hungering, or thirsting, or harbourless, or naked, or sick, or in prison, and we served not to thee?

45   Then he shall answer to them, and say, Truly I say to you (or I tell you the truth), as long as ye did (it) not to one of these least (ones), neither ye did (it) to me [or ye did (it) not to me].

46   And these shall go into everlasting torment; but the just men shall go into everlasting life. (And they shall go into eternal torment; but the righteous shall go into eternal life.)

CHAPTER 26

1   And it was done, when Jesus had ended all these words, he said to his disciples,

2   Ye know, that after two days pask shall be made, and man's Son shall be betaken to be crucified. (Ye know, that in two days it shall be Passover, and man's Son shall be delivered, or shall be given over, to be crucified.)

3   Then the princes of (the) priests, and the elder men of the people were gathered into the hall of the prince of (the) priests, that was said Caiaphas, (Then the high priests, and the elders of the people were gathered together in the hall of the High Priest, who was called Caiaphas,)

4   and made a counsel to (take) hold (of) Jesus with guile, and slay him; [and made a counsel, that they should (take) hold (of) Jesus with guile, and slay *him*;] (and made a plan to take hold of Jesus by treachery, and kill him;)

5   but they said, Not in the holiday, [or Not in the feast day], (or Not on the Feast Day), lest peradventure noise (or a commotion) were

made in the people.

6 And when Jesus was in Bethany, in the house of Simon the leprous,

7 a woman that had a box of alabaster of precious ointment, came to him, and shedded *it* out on the head of him resting (or and poured *it* out upon his head while he was resting).

8 And the disciples seeing (this) had disdain, and said, Whereto *is* this loss?

9 for it might be sold for much [or for this might have been sold for much], and be given to poor men.

10 But Jesus knew, and said to them, What be ye heavy to this woman? (or Why be so harsh with this woman?) for she hath wrought in me a good work [or (for) she hath wrought a good work in me].

11 For ye shall ever[more] have poor men with you, but ye shall not always have me.

12 For this woman sending this ointment into my body, did (it) [for] to bury me. (For this woman poured this ointment upon my body, in preparation for my burial.)

13 Truly I say to you (or I tell you the truth), wherever this gospel shall be preached in all the world, it shall be said, that she did this, in mind of him (or in remembrance of him).

14 Then one of the twelve, that was called Judas Iscariot, went forth to the princes of (the) priests, [or went to the princes of (the) priests], (or went to the high priests),

15 and said to them, What will ye give to me, and I shall betake him to you? (or What will ye give to me, if I shall deliver him, or shall betray him, to you?) And they ordained to him thirty pieces of silver.

16 And from that time he sought opportunity, to betray him.

17 And in the first day of therf loaves the disciples came to Jesus, and said, Where wilt thou [that] we make ready to thee, [for] to eat (the) pask? (And on the first day of Unleavened Bread the disciples came to Jesus, and said, Where desirest thou that we prepare for thee,

for to eat the Passover?)

18 Jesus said, Go ye into the city to a man, and say to him, The master saith, My time is nigh; at thee I make (the) pask with my disciples. (Jesus said, Go into the city to a man, and say to him, The Teacher said, My time is near; I shall keep, or I shall eat, the Passover with my disciples at thine house.)

19 And the disciples did, as Jesus commanded to them; and they made the pask ready (or and they prepared the Passover).

20 And when the eventide was come, he sat to (the) meat, [or he sat at the meat], (or he sat down for the meal), with his twelve disciples.

21 And he said to them, as they ate, Truly I say to you (or I tell you the truth), that one of you shall betray me.

22 And they full sorry, [or And they made sorrowful greatly], (or And they greatly grieved), began each by himself to say, Lord, whether I am *he*?

23 And he answered, and said, He that putteth with me his hand in the platter, shall betray me. (And he said, He who putteth his hand in the platter with me, shall betray me.)

24 Forsooth man's Son goeth, as it is written of him; but woe to that man, by whom man's Son shall be betrayed; it were good to him (or it would be better for him), if that man had not been born.

25 But Judas that betrayed him, answered, saying, Master, (or Teacher), whether I am *he*? Jesus said to him, Thou hast said (it).

26 And while they supped, Jesus took bread, and blessed [it], (or and gave thanks), and brake (it), and gave (it) to his disciples, and said, Take ye, and eat; this is my body.

27 And he took the cup, and did thankings (or and gave thanks), and gave to them, and said, Drink ye all thereof;

28 this is my blood of the new testament (or this is my blood of the new covenant), which shall be shed for many, into remission of sins.

29 And I say to you, I shall not drink from

this time, of this fruit of the vine, into that day when I shall drink it (a)new with you, in the kingdom of my Father.

30 And when the hymn was said, they went out into the mount of Olives. (And after the hymn was sung, they went out to the Mount of Olives.)

31 Then Jesus said to them, All ye shall suffer cause of stumbling in me, in this night; for it is written, I shall smite the shepherd, and the sheep of the flock shall be scattered.

32 But after that I shall rise again (or But after that I am resurrected), I shall go before you into Galilee.

33 Peter answered, and said to him, Though all [men] shall be caused to stumble in thee, I shall never be caused to stumble.

34 Jesus said to him, Truly I say to thee (or I tell you the truth), for in this night before the cock crow, thrice thou shalt deny me.

35 Peter said to him, Yea, though it behooveth that I die with thee, I shall not deny thee. Also all the disciples said (the same thing).

36 Then Jesus came with them into a town, that is said Gethsemane (or Then Jesus came with them to a place, that is called Gethsemane). And he said to his disciples, Sit ye here, while I go thither, and pray.

37 And when he had taken Peter, and (the) two sons of Zebedee, he began to be heavy and sorry [or he began to be sorrowful and heavy in heart].

38 Then he said to them, My soul is sorrowful (un)to the death; abide ye here, and wake ye with me (or wait here, and keep watch, or and stay awake, with me).

39 And he went forth a little, and felled down on his face, praying, and saying, My Father, if it is possible, pass this cup from me, [or My Father, if it is possible, (let) this cup pass from me]; nevertheless not as I will, but as thou *wilt*, (or nevertheless not what I desire, or what I want, but what thou *desirest*, or what thou

wantest to be done).

40 And he came to his disciples, and found them sleeping. And he said to Peter, So, whether ye might not one hour wake with me? [or So, might ye not one hour wake with me?] (or So, could ye not keep watch with me, or could ye not stay awake with me, for one hour?)

41 Wake ye, and pray ye, that ye enter not into temptation; for the spirit is ready, but the flesh *is* sick, [*or unstable, or unsteadfast*]. (Be on watch, or Stay awake, and pray, so that ye enter not into the test; for the spirit is ready, but the flesh *is* frail or weak.)

42 Again the second time he went, and prayed, saying, My Father, if this cup may not pass, but I drink it, thy will be done.

43 And again he came, and found them sleeping; for their eyes were heavied.

44 And he left them, and went again, and prayed the third time, and said the same word(s).

45 Then he came to his disciples, and said to them, Sleep ye now, and rest ye; lo! the hour hath nighed, (or behold, the hour hath approached, or the time is now), and man's Son shall be betaken [or shall be betrayed] into the hands of sinners;

46 rise ye, go we; lo! he that shall take (hold of) me, is nigh. (get up, let us go; behold, he who shall take hold of me, is near.)

47 Yet while he spake, lo! Judas, one of the twelve, came, and with him a great company, with swords and bats, [or staves], (or clubs), sent from the princes of (the) priests, and from the elder men of the people, (or sent from the high priests, and from the elders of the people).

48 And he that betrayed him, gave to them a token (or a sign), and said, Whomever I shall kiss, he it is; hold ye (onto) him (or seize him).

49 And anon he came to Jesus, and said, Hail, master; and he kissed him. (And at once he came to Jesus, and said, Good evening, Teacher; and he kissed him.)

50 And Jesus said to him, Friend, whereto art thou come? Then they came nigh, and laid hands on Jesus, and held him (or and seized him).

51 And lo! one of them that were with Jesus, stretched out his hand, and drew out his sword; and he smote the servant of the prince of (the) priests (or and he struck the servant of the High Priest), and cut off his ear.

52 Then Jesus said to him, Turn thy sword into his place (or Return thy sword into its place); for all that take (up a) sword, shall perish by (the) sword.

53 Whether guessest thou, that I may not pray (to) my Father, and he shall give to me now more than twelve legions of angels?

54 How then shall the scriptures be fulfilled? for so it behooveth to be done.

55 In that hour Jesus said to the people, As to a thief ye have gone out, with swords and bats, [or staves], to take (hold of) me; day by day I sat among you, and taught in the temple, and ye held me not. (At that time Jesus said to the people, Ye have gone out like after a thief, with swords and bats, or clubs, to seize me; yet day after day I sat among you, and taught in the Temple, and ye did not seize me then.)

56 But all this thing was done, (so) that the scriptures of (the) prophets should be fulfilled. Then all the disciples fled, and left him.

57 And they held Jesus, and led him to Caiaphas, the prince of (the) priests (or the High Priest), where the scribes and the Pharisees, and the elder men of the people were come together, [or where the scribes and the elder men of the people had come together].

58 But Peter (pur)sued him afar, into the hall of the prince of (the) priests, (or But Peter followed him from afar, into the courtyard of the High Priest); and he went in, and sat (down) with the servants, to see the end.

59 And the prince of (the) priests, and all the council sought false witnessing against Jesus, that they should (be)take him to (the) death;

(And the High Priest, and all the council sought false testimony against Jesus, so that they could deliver him unto death;)

60 and they found not, when many false witnesses were come. But at the last, two false witnesses came,

61 and said, This (man) said, I may destroy the temple of God, and after the third day build it again [or and after three days build it again]. (and said, He said, I shall destroy the Temple of God, and after three days build it up again.)

62 And the prince of (the) priests rose, and said to him, Answerest thou nothing to those things, that these witness against thee? (And the High Priest rose, and said to him, Answerest thou nothing about these things, that they testify against thee?)

63 But Jesus was still. And the prince of (the) priests said to him, I conjure thee by the living God, that thou say to us, if thou art Christ, the Son of God. (But Jesus was silent. And the High Priest said to him, I command thee by the living God, that thou tell us, if thou art the Messiah, the Son of God.)

64 Jesus said to him, Thou hast said (it); nevertheless I say to you, hereafter ye shall see man's Son sitting at the right half of the virtue of God, and coming in the clouds of (the) heaven(s). (Jesus said to him, Thou hast said it; nevertheless I tell you, hereafter ye shall see man's Son sitting at the right hand, or on the right side, of the power of God, and coming on the clouds of the heavens.)

65 Then the prince of (the) priests rent his clothes, and said, He hath blasphemed; what yet have we need to witnesses? lo! now ye have heard blasphemy; (Then the High Priest tore his clothes, and said, He hath blasphemed; why do we need any more witnesses? behold, now ye have heard blasphemy;)

66 what seemeth to you? And they answered, and said, He is guilty of death.

67 Then they spat in his face, and smote him with buffets; and others gave strokes with the

palm of their hands in[to] his face,

68   and said, Thou Christ, declare to us, [or Thou Christ, prophesy to us], who is he that smote thee? (and mockingly said, O Messiah, declare to us, or prophesy for us, who is he that struck thee?)

69   And Peter sat without in the hall (or And Peter sat outside in the courtyard); and a damsel [or an handmaid] came to him, and said, Thou were with Jesus of Galilee.

70   And he denied before all [men], and said, I know not what thou sayest.

71   And when he went out at the gate, another damsel [or another handmaid] saw him, and said to them that were there, And this was with Jesus of Nazareth.

72   And again he denied with an oath, For I knew not the man.

73   And a little after (that), they that stood (there) came, and said to Peter, Truly and thou art [one] of them; for thy speech maketh thee known.

74   Then he began to curse and to swear, that he knew not the man. And anon (or at once) the cock crew.

75   And Peter bethought on the word(s) of Jesus, that he had said, Before the cock crow, thrice thou shalt deny me. And he went out, and wept bitterly.

CHAPTER 27

1   But when the morrowtide was come, all the princes of (the) priests, and the elder men of the people took counsel against Jesus, that they should take him to the death. (But when the morning was come, all the high priests, and the elders of the people made a plan against Jesus, how they would put him, or send him, to death.)

2   And they led him bound, and betook him to Pilate of Pontii, (the) [chief] justice [or the president]. (And they led him bound, and delivered him to Pontius Pilate, the Governor.)

3   Then Judas that betrayed him, saw [or seeing] that he was condemned, he repented, and brought again the thirty pieces [of silver] to the princes of (the) priests, and to the elder men of the people, (or and returned the thirty pieces of silver to the high priests, and to the elders of the people),

4   and said, I have sinned, betraying rightful [or just] blood. And they said, What (is it) to us? busy thee [or see thou]. (and said, I have sinned, betraying righteous blood. And they said, What is that to us? it is thy concern.)

5   And when he had cast forth the [plates (or pieces) of] silver in the temple, he passed forth, and went, and hanged himself with a snare.

6   And the princes of (the) priests took the [plates (or pieces) of] silver, and said, It is not leaveful to put it into the treasury, for it is the price of blood. (And the high priests took the pieces of silver, and said, It is not lawful to put it in the treasury, for it is the payment for blood.)

7   And when they had taken counsel, they bought with it a field of a potter [or they bought with them a field of a potter], into [the] burying of pilgrims. (And when they had made a plan, they bought a potter's field with it, for the burying of visitors.)

8   Therefore that field is called Aceldama, that is, a field of blood, into this day.

9   Then that was fulfilled, that was said by the prophet Jeremy saying, And they have taken thirty pieces [of silver], the price of a man (ap)praised, whom they (ap)praised of the children of Israel; (Then that was fulfilled, that was said by the prophet Jeremiah, saying, And they have taken thirty pieces of silver, the appraised price of a man, whom they of the children of Israel appraised, or put a price upon;)

10   and they gave them into a field of a potter (or and they used it to buy a potter's field), as the Lord hath ordained to me.

11   And Jesus stood before the doomsman (or the judge); and the justice [or the president] asked him, and said, Art thou king of Jews?

Jesus saith to him, Thou sayest (it). (And Jesus stood before the Governor; and the Governor asked him, and said, Art thou the King of the Jews? Jesus saith to him, Thou sayest it.)

12 And when he was accused of the princes of (the) priests, and of the elder men of the people, he answered nothing. (And when he was accused by the high priests, and by the elders of the people, he answered nothing.)

13 Then Pilate saith to him, Hearest thou not, how many things, [or how many witnessings, (or how many testimonies)], they say against thee?

14 And he answered not to him any word, so that the justice [or the president] wondered greatly. (And he did not answer any word to him, so that the Governor greatly wondered.)

15 But for a solemn day the justice [or the president] was wont to deliver to the people one bound, whom they would. (And on the Feast Day, or during the Festival, the Governor had a custom to release one prisoner to the people, whomever they wanted.)

16 And he had then a famous man bound [or Forsooth he had one famous man bound], that was said Barabbas. (And he had then a notorious prisoner, who was called Barabbas.)

17 Therefore Pilate said to them, when they were [gathered] together, Whom will ye, that I deliver to you [or that I leave to you]? whether Barabbas, or Jesus, that is said Christ? (And so Pilate said to them, when they were gathered together, Whom do ye desire, that I release to you? or Whom do ye want, that I let go to you? Barabbas, or Jesus, who is called the Messiah?)

18 For he knew, that by envy they betrayed him [or they betook him]. (For he knew, that they had betrayed him, or that they had delivered him, out of envy.)

19 And while he sat for doomsman [or for judge], his wife sent (word) to him, and said, Nothing to thee and to that just man (or Do not have anything to do with that innocent or righteous man); for I have suffered this day many things for him, by a vision.

20 Forsooth the princes of (the) priests, and the elder men counselled the people, (or But the high priests, and the elders counselled the people), that they should ask (for) Barabbas, but (that) they should (seek to) destroy Jesus.

21 But the justice [or the president] answered, and said to them, Whom of the twain will ye, that be delivered, [or be left (or be let go)], to you? And they said, Barabbas. (But the Governor answered, and said to them, Whom of the two do ye desire to be released, or to be let go, to you? And they said, Barabbas.)

22 Pilate saith to them, What then shall I do of Jesus, that is said Christ? All they say, Be he crucified. (Pilate said to them, Then what should I do with Jesus, who is called the Messiah? And they all cried, Crucify him!)

23 The justice [or The president] saith to them (or The Governor said to them), What evil hath he done? And they cried (the) more, and said, Be he crucified.

24 And Pilate seeing that he profited nothing, but that the more noise was made (or but that only a greater commotion was made), he took water, and washed his hands before the people, and said, I am guiltless of the blood of this rightful man; busy you (or let it be your concern). [Forsooth Pilate seeing that he profited nothing, but (that) the more a noise was made, (after some) water (was) taken, he washed his hands before the people, saying, I am innocent of the blood of this just man; see ye.]

25 And all the people answered, and said, His blood *be* on us, and on our children.

26 Then he delivered, [or he left, (or he let go)], to them Barabbas, but he [be]took to them Jesus scourged, to be crucified. (Then he released, or he let go, Barabbas to them, but he delivered Jesus unto them, after that he had been scourged, to be crucified.)

27 Then [the] knights of the justice [or of the

president] took Jesus in(to) the moot hall, and gathered to him all the company of knights. (Then the soldiers of the Governor took Jesus into the Hall of Judgement, and gathered unto him all the company of soldiers.)

28 And they unclothed him, and did about him a red mantle;

29 and they folded a crown of thorns, and put (it) on his head, and a reed in his right hand; and they kneeled before him, and scorned him, and said, Hail, king of Jews, (or Hail, the King of the Jews).

30 And they spat on him, and took a reed, and smote his head.

31 And after that they had scorned him, they unclothed him of the mantle, and they clothed him with his clothes, and led him (away) to crucify him [or and led him (away) for to be crucified].

32 And as they went out, they found a man of Cyrene coming from the town, Simon by name; they constrained him to take his cross (or and they compelled him to carry his cross).

33 And they came into a place that is called Golgotha [or And they came to a place that is called Golgotha], that is, the place of Calvary.

34 And they gave [to] him to drink wine meddled or mingled with gall (or And they gave him wine to drink mixed with gall); and when he had tasted (it), he would not drink (it).

35 And after that they had crucified him, they parted his clothes, and cast lots, to fulfill that (that) is said by the prophet, saying, They parted to them my clothes, and on my cloth they cast lots. (And after that they had crucified him, they divided up his clothes, and threw dice, to fulfill what is said by the prophet, saying, They divided my clothes among themselves, and for my cloak they threw dice.)

36 And they sat, and kept (watch over) him;

37 and set [or put] above his head his cause (or the charge against him), written (out), This is Jesus of Nazareth, king of Jews, [or This is Jesus, the king of Jews], (or This is Jesus, the King of

the Jews).

38 Then two thieves were crucified with him, one on the right half, and one on the left half, (or one on his right side, and one on his left side).

39 And men that passed forth blasphemed him, moving their heads,

40 and saying, Vath [or Fie] *to thee*, that destroyest the temple of God, and in the third day buildest it again; save thou thyself; if thou art the Son of God, come down of the cross, [or come down off the cross], (or come down from the cross).

41 Also and [the] princes of (the) priests scorning, with scribes and elder men, said, (And also the high priests, with the scribes and the elders, scorned him, and said,)

42 He made other men safe, he may not make himself safe; if he is [the] king of Israel, come he now down from the cross, and we believe to him; (He saved other men, but he cannot save himself; if he is the King of Israel, let him now come down from the cross, and then we shall believe in him;)

43 he trusted in God; deliver he him now, if he will; for he said, That I am God's Son, [or for he said, I am the Son of God].

44 And the thieves, that were crucified with him, upbraided him of the same thing.

45 But from the sixth hour, darknesses were made on all the earth [or upon all the land], till [to] the ninth hour. (But from noon, darkness was made upon all the land, until three o'clock in the afternoon.)

46 And about the ninth hour Jesus cried with a great voice, and said, Eli, Eli, lama sabachthani, that is, My God, my God, why hast thou forsaken me?

47 And some men that stood there, and hearing, said, This calleth Elias. (And some men who stood there, and heard him, said, He calleth Elijah.)

48 And anon (or at once) one of them running, took and filled a sponge with vinegar, and put [it] on a reed, and gave (it) to him to

drink.

49   But others said, Suffer thou; see we whether Elias come to deliver him. (But others said, Wait; let us see if Elijah shall come to save him.)

50   Forsooth Jesus again cried with a great voice, and (then) gave up the ghost [or sent out the spirit].

51   And lo! the veil of the temple was rent in two parts, from the highest to the lowest, (or And behold, the veil of the Temple was torn in two parts, from the top to the bottom). And the earth shook, and the stones were cloven, [or And the earth was moved, and the stones were cleft];

52   and burials were opened, and many bodies of (the) saints that had slept, rose up. (and graves were opened, and many bodies of God's people who had died, rose up.)

53   And they went out of their burials (or And they went out of their graves), and after his resurrection they came into the holy city, and appeared to many.

54   And the centurion and they that were with him keeping (watch over) Jesus, when they saw the earth-shaking, and those things that were done, they dreaded greatly, and said, Verily this was God's Son. (And the centurion and those who were with him keeping watch over Jesus, when they saw the earthquake, and those things that were done, they were greatly afraid, and said, Truly this was the Son of God.)

55   And there were there many women afar [or Forsooth many women were there afar], that (pur)sued Jesus from Galilee, and ministered to him. (And many women were there, watching from afar, who had followed Jesus from Galilee, and served him.)

56   Among which was Mary Magdalene, and Mary, the mother of James, and of Joseph, and the mother of Zebedee's sons.

57   But when the evening was come, there came a rich man of Arimathaea, Joseph by name, and he was a disciple of Jesus.

58   He went to Pilate, and asked (for) the body of Jesus. Then Pilate commanded the body to be given (to him).

59   And when the body was taken (down), Joseph wrapped it in a clean sendal [or in a clean linen cloth],

60   and laid it in his new burial, that he had hewn in a stone; and he wallowed a great stone to the door of the burial, and went away. (and laid it in his new tomb, which he had cut out of the stone; and he rolled a great stone against the door of the tomb, and then he went away.)

61   But Mary Magdalene and another Mary were there, sitting against the sepulchre. (But Mary Magdalene and the other Mary were there, sitting opposite the tomb.)

62   And on the tother day, that is after pask even(ing), the princes of (the) priests and [the] Pharisees came together to Pilate, (And in the morning of the next day, that was after the evening of the Passover, the high priests, and the Pharisees came together to Pilate,)

63   and said, Sir [or Sire], we have mind (or we have remembered), that that beguiler [or that deceiver] said (while) yet living, After three days I shall rise again to life.

64   Therefore command thou, that the sepulchre be kept (or guarded) into the third day; lest his disciples come, and steal him, and say to the people, He hath risen from death [or He is risen from (the) dead]; and the last error shall be worse than the former (or and then the last lie shall be worse than the first lie).

65   Pilate said to them, Ye have the keeping (or Ye have the guarding of it); go ye, keep ye (watch over it) as (sure as) ye can.

66   And they went forth, and kept (watch over) the sepulchre, marking [or sealing] the stone, with [the] keepers. (And so they went there, and kept watch over the tomb, and sealed the stone, with the guards.)

CHAPTER 28

1   But in (the hour after) the eventide of the

sabbath, [or (the) holiday], that beginneth to shine in the first day of the week (or that beginneth to shine on the first day of the week), Mary Magdalene came, and another Mary (or and the other Mary), to see the sepulchre.

2 And lo! there was made a great earth-shaking; for the angel of the Lord came down from heaven, and nighed, and turned away the stone, and sat thereon. (And behold, there was a great earthquake; for the angel of the Lord came down from heaven, and approached, and rolled away the stone, and then sat on it.)

3 And his looking was as lightning, and his clothes (were as) [white] as snow;

4 and for dread of him the keepers were afeared, and they were made as dead men. (and the guards were greatly afraid of him, and they were made like dead men.)

5 But the angel answered, and said to the women, Do not ye dread (or Do not fear), for I know that ye seek Jesus, that was crucified;

6 he is not here, for he is risen, as he said (he would be); come ye, and see ye the place, where the Lord was laid.

7 And (now) go ye soon, and say ye to his disciples, that he is risen. And lo! he shall go before you into Galilee; there ye shall see him. Lo! I have before-said to you.

8 And they went out soon from the burials [or from the sepulchre], with dread, and great joy, running to tell to his disciples. (And they went out quickly from the tomb, with fearful reverence, and great joy, running to tell his disciples.)

9 And lo! Jesus met them, and said, Hail ye. And they nighed [or And they came to (him)], and held his feet, and worshipped him.

10 Then Jesus said to them, Do not ye dread (or Do not fear); go ye, tell ye to my brethren, that they (should) go into Galilee; there they shall see me.

11 And when they were gone, lo! some of the keepers came into the city, and told to the princes of (the) priests all (the) things that were done. (And when they were gone, behold, some of the guards came into the city, and told the high priests all the things that were done, or about everything that had happened.)

12 And when they were gathered together with the elder men, and had taken their counsel, they gave to the knights much money, (And when they were gathered together with the elders, and had made their plan, they gave the soldiers a lot of money,)

13 and said, Say ye, that his disciples came by night, and have stolen him, while ye slept.

14 And if this be heard of the justice [or of the president], we shall counsel him, and make you secure. (And if this be heard by the Governor, we shall talk with him, and keep you safe.)

15 And when the money was taken, they did, as they were taught, (or they did, as they were told). And this word is published among the Jews, till into this day.

16 And the eleven disciples went into Galilee, into an hill (or up onto a hill), where Jesus had ordained to them.

17 And they saw him, and worshipped (him); but some of them doubted.

18 And Jesus came nigh, and spake to them, and said, All power in heaven and in earth is given to me.

19 Therefore go ye, and teach all folks, baptizing them in the name of the Father, and of the Son, and of the Holy Ghost; (And so go, and teach all the nations and all the peoples, baptizing them in the name of the Father, and of the Son, and of the Holy Spirit;)

20 teaching them to keep all (the) things, whatever things I have commanded to you; and lo! I am with you in all days, into the end of the world. (teaching them to obey everything, whatever I have commanded to you; and behold, I am with you always, unto the end of the world.) †

MARK

CHAPTER 1

1 The beginning of the gospel of Jesus Christ, the Son of God. (The beginning of the Gospel, or the Good News, of Jesus Christ, the Son of God.)

2 As it is written in Esaias, the prophet, (or As it is written by the prophet Isaiah), Lo! I send mine angel before thy face, that shall make thy way ready before thee.

3 The voice of a crier in (the) desert, Make ye ready the way of the Lord, make ye his paths right. [The voice of *one* crying in (the) desert, Make ye ready the way of the Lord, make ye his paths rightful.]

4 John was in (the) desert baptizing, and preaching the baptism of penance, into (the) remission of sins. (John was in the desert baptizing, and preaching the baptism of repentance, for the forgiveness of sins.)

5 And all the country of Judea went out to him, and all (the) men of Jerusalem; and they were baptized of him in the flume of Jordan, [or in the flood of Jordan], (or and they were baptized by him in the Jordan River), acknowledging their sins.

6 And John was clothed with hairs of camels, and a girdle of skin *was* about his loins; and he ate honeysuckles, and wild honey, [or and he ate locusts, and honey of the wood],

7 and preached, and said, A stronger than I shall come after me, and I am not worthy to kneel down, and unloose, [or to undo, *or unbind*], [the thong of] his shoes.

8 I have baptized you in water; but he shall baptize you in the Holy Ghost (or but he shall baptize you with the Holy Spirit).

9 And it was done in those days, Jesus came from Nazareth of Galilee, and was baptized of John in (the) Jordan (or and was baptized by John in the Jordan River).

10 And anon he went up (out) of the water, and saw (the) heavens opened, and the Holy Ghost [or the (Holy) Spirit] coming down as a culver, and dwelling on him. (And at once he went up out of the water, and saw the heavens opened, and the Holy Spirit coming down like a dove, and remaining on him.)

11 And a voice was made from (the) heavens, Thou art my (be)loved Son, in thee I am pleased.

12 And anon the Spirit put him forth into (the) desert. (And at once the Spirit led him forth into the desert.)

13 And he was in (the) desert forty days and forty nights, and was tempted of Satan, and he was with beasts, and angels ministered to him. (And he was in the desert for forty days and forty nights, and was tested by Satan, and he was with beasts, and angels served him.)

14 But after that John was taken, Jesus came into Galilee, and preached the gospel of the kingdom of God, (But after that John was taken captive, Jesus came to Galilee, and preached the Gospel, or the Good News, of the Kingdom of God,)

15 and said, That the time is fulfilled, and the kingdom of God shall come nigh; do ye penance [or forthink ye], and believe ye to the gospel. (and said, The time is fulfilled, and the Kingdom of God hath come near; repent, and believe the Gospel or the Good News.)

16 And as he passed beside the sea of Galilee, he saw Simon, and Andrew, his brother, casting their nets into the sea; for they were fishers. (And as he walked beside Lake Galilee, he saw Simon, and Andrew, his brother, throwing their nets into the lake; for they were fishermen.)

17 And Jesus said to them, Come ye after me; I shall make you to be made fishers of men.

18 And anon they left the nets, and (pur)sued him. (And at once they left their nets, and followed him.)

19 And he went forth from thence a little,

and saw James of Zebedee, and John, his brother, in a boat making their nets.

20 And anon (or at once) he called them; and they left Zebedee, their father, in the boat with (the) hired servants, and they (pur)sued him (or and they followed him).

21 And they entered into Capernaum, and anon in the sabbaths (or and at once on the Sabbath), he went into the synagogue, and taught them.

22 And they wondered on his teaching; for he taught them, as he that had power, and not as [the] scribes.

23 And in the synagogue of them was a man in an unclean spirit, and he cried out, (And in their synagogue was a man with an unclean spirit, and he cried out,)

24 and said, What to us and to thee, thou Jesus of Nazareth? hast thou come to destroy us? I know that thou art the holy (One) of God.

25 And Jesus threatened him, and said, Wax [thou] dumb (or Be silent), and go out of the man.

26 And the unclean spirit wrenching him, and crying with a great voice, went out from him.

27 And all men wondered, so that they sought within themselves, and said, (or so that they asked among themselves, and said), What thing is this? what new doctrine is this? for in power he commandeth to unclean spirits, and they obey to him.

28 And the fame, [or the tale, or (the) tiding(s)], of him went forth anon into all the country of Galilee. (And the story about him went forth at once throughout all the province of Galilee.)

29 And anon (or at once) they went out of the synagogue, and came into the house of Simon and of Andrew, with James and John.

30 And the mother of Simon's wife lay sick in the fevers; and anon they say to him of her (or and at once they told him about her).

31 And he came nigh, and areared her [up],

and when he had taken her hand, anon the fever left her (or at once the fever left her), and she served them.

32 But when the eventide was come, and the sun was gone down, they brought to him all that were of mal-ease, and them that had fiends. [Forsooth the evening made, when the sun went down, they brought to him all having evil, and having devils.] (But when the evening had come, and the sun had gone down, they brought to him all who were sick, and those who had demons.)

33 And all the city was gathered at the gate.

34 And he healed many, that had diverse sicknesses, and he cast out many fiends [or devils], and he suffered them not to speak, for they knew him. (And he healed many, who had various sicknesses, and he threw out many demons, and he did not allow them to speak, for they knew who he was.)

35 And he rose full early [or in the morrowing], (or And he rose early in the morning), and went out, and went into a desert place, and prayed there.

36 And Simon (pur)sued him (or And Simon followed him), and they that were with him.

37 And when they had found him, they said to him, That all men seek thee.

38 And he said to them, Go we into the next towns and cities, that I preach also there, for thereto [or to (or for) this thing] I came. (And he said to them, Let us go to the next towns and cities, so that I can also preach there, for I came for this purpose.)

39 And he preached in the synagogues of them, and in all Galilee, and casted out fiends. (And he preached in their synagogues, and throughout all of Galilee, threw out devils and demons.)

40 And a leprous man came to him, and besought [him], kneeling, and said, If thou wilt, thou mayest cleanse me, (or If thou desirest it, or If thou want to do it, thou can cleanse me).

41 And Jesus had mercy on him, and

stretched out his hand, and touched him, and said to him, I will, be thou made clean.

42 And when he had said this, anon (or at once) the leprosy parted away from him [or anon the leprosy went away from him], and he was cleansed.

43 And Jesus threatened him, and anon (or at once) put him out,

44 and said to him, See thou, say to no man; but go, show thee to the prince of (the) priests, and offer for thy cleansing into witnessing to them, those things that Moses bade. (and said to him, See that thou tell no one; but go, show thyself to the priest, and offer for thy cleansing as a testimony to them, those things that Moses commanded.)

45 And he went out, and began to preach, and to publish the word, so that now he might not go openly into the city, but be withoutforth in (the) desert places; and they came to him on all sides.

CHAPTER 2

1 And again he entered into Capernaum, after eight days. And it was heard, that he was in an house,

2 and many came together, so that they might not be in the house, nor at the gate. And he spake to them the word.

3 And there came to him men that brought a man sick in the palsy, which was borne of four [men]. [And there came to him men bringing or bearing a sick man in palsy, the which was borne of four men.] (And there came to him men that brought a man sick with palsy, who was carried by four men.)

4 And when they might not bring him to Jesus for the people, they uncovered the roof where he was, and [they] opened it, and they let down the bed in which the sick man in palsy lay.

5 And when Jesus had seen the faith of them, he said to the sick man in palsy, Son, thy

sins be forgiven to thee.

6 But there were some of the scribes sitting (there), and thinking in their hearts,

7 What speaketh he thus? He blasphemeth; who may forgive sins, [no] but God alone? (Why speaketh he thus? He blasphemeth; for who can forgive sins, except God alone?)

8 And [anon] when Jesus had known this by the Holy Ghost, that they thought so within themselves, he saith to them, What think ye these things in your hearts? (And at once when Jesus had known this by the Holy Spirit, that they thought so within themselves, he said to them, Why think these things in your hearts?)

9 What is lighter (or is easier) to say to the sick man in palsy, Sins be forgiven to thee, or to say, Rise (up), take thy bed, and walk?

10 But (so) that ye know that man's Son hath power in earth (or on the earth) to forgive sins, he said to the sick man in palsy,

11 I say to thee, rise up, take thy bed, and go into thine house.

12 And anon he rose up, and when he had taken the bed, he went before all men, so that all men wondered, and honoured God, and said, For we saw never so. (And at once he rose up, and when he had taken the bed, he went forth before everyone, so that everyone wondered, and worshipped God, and said, For we have never seen anything like this.)

13 And he went out again to the sea, and all the people came to him; and he taught them.

14 And when he passed (by), he saw Levi of Alphaeus sitting at the tollbooth, and he said to him, (Pur)Sue me. And he rose, and (pur)sued him. (And when he passed by, he saw Levi of Alphaeus sitting at the tollbooth, and he said to him, Follow me. And he rose, and followed him.)

15 And it was done, when he sat at the meat in his house, many publicans and sinful men sat together at the meat with Jesus and his disciples; for there were many that followed him. (And it was done, when he sat at a meal in

his house, many tax-collectors and sinners sat there at the meal with Jesus and his disciples; for there were many that followed him.)

16   And (the) scribes and (the) Pharisees seeing, that he ate with publicans and sinful men, said to his disciples, Why eateth and drinketh your master with publicans and sinners? (And the scribes and the Pharisees seeing, that he ate with tax-collectors and sinners, said to his disciples, Why eateth and drinketh your teacher with tax-collectors and sinners?)

17   When this was heard, Jesus said to them, Whole men have no need to a leech, (no) but they that be evil-at-ease (do), [or (no) but they that have evil (do)], (Healthy men have no need for a physician, only those who have sickness); for I came not to call just men, but sinners.

18   And the disciples of John and the Pharisees were fasting; and they came, and said to him, Why *fast* the disciples of John, and the Pharisees fast, but thy disciples fast not?

19   And Jesus said to them, Whether the sons of the spousals [or of the weddings] may fast, as long as the spouse is with them? As long (a) time as they have the spouse with them, they may not fast, (or they cannot fast, or they shall not fast).

20   But (the) days shall come, when the spouse shall be taken away from them, and then they shall fast in those days.

21   No man seweth a patch of new cloth to an old cloth, else he taketh away the new patch from the old, and a more breaking is made. (No one seweth a patch of new cloth onto an old cloak, because the new patch will tear away from the old, and a bigger hole will be made.)

22   And no man putteth new wine into old bottles, else the wine shall burst the bottles, and the wine shall be shed out, and the bottles shall perish. But new wine shall be put into new bottles. [And no man putteth new wine into old wine vessels, else the wine shall burst or shall break the wine vessels, and the wine shall be poured out, and the wine vessels shall perish. But new wine oweth (or ought) to be put into new wine vessels.]

23   And it was done again, when the Lord walked in the sabbaths by the corns (or when the Lord walked through a cornfield on the Sabbath), and his disciples began to pass forth [or to go forth], and [to] pluck (the) ears of the corn.

24   And the Pharisees said to him, Lo! what thy disciples do in the sabbaths, that is not leaveful. (And the Pharisees said to him, Behold, what thy disciples do on the Sabbath, that is not lawful.)

25   And he said to them, Read ye never what David did, when he had need, and he hungered, and they that were with him?

26   How he went into the house of God, under Abiathar, (the) prince of (the) priests, and ate (the) loaves of proposition, [*either of setting forth*], which it was not leaveful to eat, [no] but to (the) priests alone, and he gave to them that were with him. (How he went into the House of God, under the High Priest Abiathar, and ate the loaves of proposition, or the showbread, which it was not lawful to eat, except for the priests, and he gave some to those who were with him.)

27   And he said to them, The sabbath is made for man, and not man for the sabbath;

28   and so man's Son is Lord also of the sabbath.

CHAPTER 3

1   And he entered again into the synagogue, and there was a man having a dry hand.

2   And they espied him, if he healed in the sabbaths (or on the Sabbath), to accuse him.

3   And he said to the man that had a dry hand, Rise [thou] into the middle, (or Stand here in our midst, or Stand before us).

4   And he saith to them, Is it leaveful to do well in the sabbaths, either evil? to make a soul

safe, either to lose? And they were still. (And he said to them, Is it lawful to do good on the Sabbath, or evil? to save a soul or a life, or to destroy it? And they were silent.)

5 And he beheld them about with wrath, and had sorrow on the blindness of their heart(s), and saith to the man, Hold forth thine hand. And he held (it) forth, and his hand was restored to him.

6 Soothly [the] Pharisees went out anon, and made a counsel with (the) Herodians against him, how they should lose him. (And the Pharisees went out at once, and took counsel, or made a plan, with the Herodians against him, how they could destroy him.)

7 But Jesus with his disciples went to the sea; and much people from Galilee and from Judea (pur)sued him (or and many people from Galilee and Judea followed him),

8 and from Jerusalem, and from Idumaea, and from beyond (the) Jordan (River), and they that were about Tyre and Sidon, (yea), a great multitude, hearing the things that he did, came to him.

9 And Jesus said to his disciples, that the boat should serve him, for the people, lest they thrust him [or lest they oppressed him];

10 for he healed many, so that they felled fast to him, to touch him. And how many ever had sicknesses, [or sores, or wounds],

11 and unclean spirits, when they saw him, felled down to him, and cried, saying, Thou art the Son of God.

12 And greatly he menaced them, that they should not make him known. (And he greatly threatened them, so that they would not make him known.)

13 And he went (up) into an hill (or And he went up onto a hill), and called to him whom he would; and they came to him.

14 And he made, that there were twelve with him, to send them (out) to preach.

15 And he gave to them power to heal sicknesses, and to cast out fiends (or and to

throw out devils and demons).

16 And to Simon he gave a name, Peter,

17 and *he called* James of Zebedee and John, the brother of James, and he gave to them (the) names of Boanerges, that is, the sons of thundering [or the sons of thunder].

18 And *he called* Andrew and Philip, and Bartholomew and Matthew, and Thomas, and James [of] Alphaeus, and Thaddaeus, and Simon Canaanite,

19 and Judas Iscariot, that betrayed him. And they came to an house,

20 and the people came together again, so that they might not eat bread. (and so many people came together there, that they could not even eat any food.)

21 And when his *kinsmen* had heard, they went out to (take) hold (of) him; for they said, that he is turned into madness. (And when his *family* had heard, they went out to take hold of him; for people said, that he had gone mad.)

22 And the scribes that came down from Jerusalem, said, That he hath Beelzebub, and that in the prince of devils he casteth out fiends. (And the scribes who came down from Jerusalem, said, He hath Beelzebub, and by the Prince of demons he throweth out demons.)

23 And he called them together, and he said to them in parables, How may Satan cast out Satan? (or How can Satan throw out Satan?)

24 And if a realm be parted against itself, that realm may not stand. (And if a kingdom is divided against itself, that kingdom cannot stand.)

25 And if an house be parted against itself, that house may not stand.

26 And if Satan hath risen against himself, he is parted (or he is divided), and he shall not be able to stand, but hath an end.

27 No man may go into a strong man's house, and take away his vessels, [no] but he bind first the strong man (or unless he first bind the strong man), and then he shall spoil his house, [or he shall ravish, (or he shall rob), his

house].

28 Truly I say to you (or I tell you the truth), that all sins and blasphemies, by which they have blasphemed, shall be forgiven to the sons of men.

29 But he that blasphemeth against the Holy Ghost, hath not remission into without end, but he shall be guilty of everlasting trespass. (But he who blasphemeth against the Holy Spirit, shall never be forgiven, for he shall be guilty of eternal sin.)

30 For they said, He hath an unclean spirit. (For people said, He hath an unclean spirit.)

31 And (so) his mother and his brethren came, and stood withoutforth, and sent to him, and called him.

32 And the people sat about him; and they said to him, Lo! thy mother and thy brethren withoutforth seek thee.

33 And he answered to them, and said, Who is my mother and my brethren?

34 And he beheld them that sat about him, and said, Lo! my mother and my brethren.

35 For who that doeth the will of God, he is my brother, and my sister, and (my) mother.

CHAPTER 4

1 And again Jesus began to teach at the sea; and much people was gathered to him, so that he went into a boat, and sat in the sea, and all the people was about the sea on the land.

2 And he taught them in parables many things. And he said to them in his teaching,

3 Hear ye. Lo! a man sowing goeth out to sow, [or Lo! a sower went out to sow].

4 And while he soweth, some seed felled about the way [or beside the way], and (the) birds of (the) heaven(s), [or the birds of the air], came, and ate it.

5 Other felled down on stony places, where it had not much earth; and anon it sprang up (or and at once it sprouted), for it had not (any) deepness of earth [or for it had no deepness of

earth].

6 And when the sun rose up, it withered for heat, and it dried up, for it had no root(s).

7 And other felled down into thorns, and [the] thorns sprang up, and strangled it, and it gave no fruit.

8 And other felled down into good land, and gave fruit, springing up, and waxing (or growing); and one brought (forth) thirtyfold, and one sixtyfold, and one an hundredfold.

9 And he said, He that hath ears of hearing, hear he. [And he said, He that hath ears to hear, hear.]

10 And when he was by himself, the twelve that were with him asked him to expound the parable.

11 And he said to them, To you it is given to know the private [or the mystery] of the kingdom of God (or To you it is given to know the secret of the Kingdom of God). But to them that be withoutforth, all things be made in parables,

12 (so) that they seeing see, and see not, and they hearing hear, and understand not; lest sometime they be converted, and (their) sins be forgiven to them.

13 And he said to them, Know not ye this parable? and how ye shall know all parables? (And he said to them, Do ye not understand this parable? then how shall ye understand any parable?)

14 He that soweth, soweth a word.

15 But these it be that be about the way, where the word is sown; and when they have heard, anon cometh Satan (or at once Satan cometh), and taketh away the word that is sown in their hearts.

16 And in like manner be these that be sown on stony places, which when they have heard the word, anon they take it with joy (or at once they receive it with joy);

17 and they have not root in themselves, but they be lasting (but) a little time [or but they be temporal]; afterward when tribulation riseth,

and persecution for the word, anon (or at once) they be caused to stumble.

18 And there be others that be sown in thorns; these it be, that hear the word,

19 and dis-ease of the world, and deceit of riches, and other charge of covetousness entereth (or and the burden of envy entereth), and strangleth the word, and it is made without fruit.

20 And these it be that be sown on good land, which hear the word, and take (it), (or and receive it), and make fruit, one thirtyfold, and one sixtyfold, and one an hundredfold.

21 And he said to them, Whether a lantern cometh, that it be put under a bushel, or under a bed? nay, but that it be put on a candlestick?

22 There is nothing hid, that shall not be made open [or that shall not be showed]; neither anything is privy, that shall not come into (the) open. (There is nothing hidden, that shall not be made open or revealed; nor is anything private, or kept secret, that shall not be brought out into the open.)

23 If any man have ears of hearing, hear he.

24 And he said to them, See ye what ye hear. In what measure ye mete, it shall be meted to you again, and *it shall* be cast to you (or By which measure ye measure, it shall be measured unto you again, yea, *it shall* be thrown unto you).

25 For it shall be given to him that hath, and it shall be taken away from him that hath not, also that that he hath. [Forsooth it shall be given to him that hath, and if a man hath not, yea this that he hath shall be taken away from him.]

26 And he said, So the kingdom of God is, as if a man cast seed into the earth,

27 and he sleep, and it rise up night and day, and bring forth seed, and wax fast (or grow fast), while he knoweth not.

28 For the earth [by his own working, or by his own will], (or by its own working, or by its own will), maketh fruit, first the grass, afterward the ear, and after[ward] full fruit in the ear.

29 And when of itself it hath brought forth fruit, anon (or at once) he sendeth a sickle, for reaping time is come.

30 And he said, To what thing shall we liken the kingdom of God? or to what parable shall we comparison it?

31 As a corn of sinapi, (or Like a kernel, or a grain, of mustard seed), which when it is sown in the earth, is less than all (the) seeds that be in the earth;

32 and when it is sprung up, it waxeth into a tree (or it groweth into a tree), and is made greater than all (the) herbs; and it maketh great branches, so that [the] birds of (the) heaven(s) may dwell under the shadow thereof (or so that the birds of the air can live under its shadow).

33 And in many such parables he spake to them the word, as they might hear (or as much as they could understand);

34 and he spake not to them without parable(s). But he expounded to his disciples all things by themselves.

35 And he said to them in that day, when evening was come, Pass we again-ward. (And he said to them on that day, when the evening had come, Let us go over to the other side of Lake Galilee.)

36 And they left the people (or And they let the people go), and took him, so that he was in a boat; and other boats were with him.

37 And a great storm [or a tempest] of wind was made, and cast waves into the boat, so that the boat was full[-filled], (or so that the boat was filled full of water).

38 And he was in the hinder part of the boat, and slept on a pillow. And they raised him, and said to him, Master, (or Teacher), pertaineth it not to thee, that we perish?

39 And he rose up, and menaced the wind (or and threatened the wind), and said to the sea, Be still, wax dumb. And the wind ceased, and great peaceableness was made.

40 And he said to them, What dread ye? (or Why fear ye?) Yet ye have no faith?/Ye have not

faith yet? [or Not yet have ye faith?]

41   And they dreaded with great dread (or And they feared with a great fear), and said to each other, Who, guessest thou, is this? for the wind and the sea obey to him.

CHAPTER 5

1   And they came over the sea into the country of Gadarenes.

2   And after that he was gone out of the boat, anon a man in an unclean spirit ran out of the burials (or out from the graves) to him. (And after that he had gotten out of the boat, at once a man with an unclean spirit ran out from the tombs to him.)

3   Which man had an house in (the) burials [or in (the) graves], and neither with chains now might any man bind him. (And this man lived among the tombs, and now no man could bind or restrain him, not even with chains.)

4   For oft times he was bound in stocks and chains, and he had broken the chains, and had broken the stocks to small gobbets (or and had broken the stocks into small pieces), and no man might make him tame [or and no man might tame him].

5   And (for)evermore, night and day, in (the) burials, and in (the) hills, he was crying and beating himself with stones. (And always, night and day, among the tombs, and in the hills, he was crying and beating himself with stones.)

6   And he saw Jesus afar, and ran, and worshipped him. (And he saw Jesus from afar, and ran over, and honoured him.)

7   And he cried with (a) great voice, and said, What to me and to thee, thou Jesus, the Son of the highest God? I conjure thee (or I adjure thee) by God, that thou torment me not.

8   And Jesus said to him, Thou unclean spirit, go out from the man.

9   And Jesus asked him, What is thy name? And he saith to him, A legion is my name; for we be many.

10   And he prayed Jesus much, that he should not put them out of the country. (And he greatly beseeched Jesus, that he would not send them out of the province.)

11   And there was there about the hill a great flock of swine [or a great drove of hogs] pasturing. (And there was there about the hill a great herd of pigs at pasture.)

12   And the spirits prayed Jesus, and said, Send us into the swine, [or Send us into the hogs], (or Send us into the pigs), (so) that we enter into them.

13   And anon Jesus granted (that) to them. And the unclean spirits went out, and entered into the swine [or (and) into the hogs], and with a great rush the flock was cast headlong into the sea, a two thousand, and they were drenched in the sea. (And at once Jesus granted that to them. And the unclean spirits went out, and entered into the pigs, and with a great rush the herd was thrown headlong into the lake, about two thousand of them, and they were drowned in the lake.)

14   And they that kept (watch over) them, fled [or Soothly they that fed them, fled], and told into the city, and into the fields; and they went out, to see what was done.

15   And they came to Jesus, and saw him that had been travailed of the fiend, sitting clothed, and of whole mind; and they dreaded. (And they came to Jesus, and saw him who had been troubled by the demon, sitting clothed, and being of whole mind; and they had fear, or and they were afraid.)

16   And they that saw, how it was done to him that had a fiend (or how it was done to him who had a demon), and of the swine [or and of the hogs], told to them.

17   And they began to pray him, that he should go away from their coasts. (And they beseeched him, that he would go away from their coasts.)

18   And when he went up into a boat, he that was travailed of the devil, began to pray him,

that he should be with him. (And when he went up into the boat, he who was troubled by the demon, beseeched him, that he would go with him.)

19   But Jesus received him not, but said to him, Go thou into thine house to thine, and tell to them, how great things the Lord hath done to thee, and had mercy of thee. (But Jesus would not take him, but said to him, Go back to thine house or thy family, yea, unto thine, and tell them what great things the Lord hath done for thee, and how he had mercy on thee.)

20   And he went forth, and began to preach in Decapolis, how great things Jesus had done to him (or what great things Jesus had done for him); and all men wondered.

21   And when Jesus had gone up into the boat again over the sea, much people came together to him, and was about (or beside) the sea.

22   And one of the princes of [the] synagogues (or And one of the leaders of one of the synagogues), by name Jairus, came, and saw him, and he fell down at his feet,

23   and prayed him much, and said, My daughter is nigh dead; come thou, put thine hand on her, that she be safe, and live. (and greatly beseeched him, and said, My daughter is near death; come thou, put thine hand on her, so that she can be saved, and live, or so that she can be healed, and live.)

24   And he went forth with him, and much people (pur)sued him, and thrust, *either oppressed*, him. (And he went with him, and many people followed him, and pressed him.)

25   And a woman that had been in the bloody flux (for) twelve years, [And a woman that was in the flux of blood (for) twelve years,] (And a woman who had a flowing, or an issue, of blood for twelve years,)

26   and had received many things of full many leeches, and had spended all her good(s), (or and had received many treatments from a great many physicians, and had spent all her money), and was nothing amended [or and

(had) nothing profited], but was rather the worse,

27   when she had heard of Jesus, she came among the people behind, and touched his cloth (or and touched his cloak).

28   For she said, That if I touch yea his cloth, I shall be safe. (For she said to herself, If I touch even his cloak, then I shall be saved, or I shall be healed.)

29   And anon (or at once) the well of her blood was dried up, and she feeled in *her* body that she was healed of the sickness.

30   And anon Jesus knew in himself the virtue that was gone out of him (or And at once Jesus knew in himself that power had gone out of him), and he turned to the people, and said, Who touched my clothes?

31   And his disciples said to him, Thou seest the people thrusting [or pressing] thee, and sayest, Who touched me?

32   And Jesus looked about to see her that had done this thing.

33   And the woman dreaded, and quaked, (or And the woman was afraid, and shook), witting that it was done in her, and came, and felled down before him, and said to him all the truth. [Forsooth the woman dreading, and trembling, knowing that it was done in her, came, and fell down before him, and said to him all the truth.]

34   And Jesus said to her, Daughter, thy faith hath made thee safe; go in peace, and be thou whole of thy sickness. (And Jesus said to her, Daughter, thy faith hath saved thee, or thy faith hath healed thee; go in peace, and be thou healed of thy sickness.)

35   Yet while he spake, messengers came to the prince of the synagogue (or messengers came to the leader of the synagogue), and said, Thy daughter is dead; what travailest thou the master (or the teacher) further?

36   But when the word was heard that was said, Jesus said to the prince of the synagogue, Do not thou dread, only believe thou. (But when this word was heard that was said, Jesus

said to the leader of the synagogue, Do not fear, only believe.)

37 And he took no man to (pur)sue him (or And he allowed no one to follow him), but Peter, and James, and John, the brother of James.

38 And they came into the house of the prince of the synagogue. And he saw noise, and men weeping and wailing much. (And they came into the house of the leader of the synagogue. And he saw a commotion, with people loudly weeping and wailing.)

39 And he went in, and said to them, What be ye troubled (about), and weep? (or Why be ye troubled, and weep?) The damsel is not dead, but sleepeth.

40 And they scorned him. But when (they) all were put out, he taketh the father and the mother of the damsel, and them that were with him, and they entered, where the damsel lay.

41 And he held the hand of the damsel, and said to her, Talitha, cumi, that is to say, Damsel, I say to thee, arise.

42 And anon the damsel rose (or And at once the young girl rose), and walked; and she was of twelve years. And they were abashed with a great astonishing.

43 And he commanded to them greatly, that no man should know it. And he commanded (them) to give her meat [or And he commanded (them) to give to her (something) to eat].

CHAPTER 6

1 And he went out from thence, and went into his own country; and his disciples followed him.

2 And when the sabbath was come, Jesus began to teach in a synagogue. And many heard him, and wondered in his teaching (or and wondered about his teaching), and said, Of whence *cometh* to this [man] all these things? and what is the wisdom that is given to him, and such virtues, (or such works of power, or

such miracles), which be made by his hands?

3 Whether this is not a carpenter, the son of Mary, the brother of James and of Joseph and of Judas and of Simon? whether his sisters be not here with us? And they were offended in him, (or And they were offended by him, or they were contemptuous of him).

4 And Jesus said to them, That a prophet is not without honour, but in his own country, and among his kin, and in his house. (And Jesus said to them, A prophet is not without honour, except in his own hometown, and among his kin, and his family.)

5 And he might not do there any virtue, save that he healed a few sick men, laying on them his hands. (And he could not do any work of power or miracle there, except that he healed a few sick men, laying his hands on them.)

6 And he wondered for the unbelief of them. And he went about (the) castles on each side, and taught. (And he wondered at their unbelief. And he went about the villages on each side, and taught.)

7 And he called together (the) twelve, and began to send them by two together; and gave to them power of unclean spirits (or and gave them power over unclean spirits),

8 and commanded (to) them, that they should not take anything in the way, (or that they should not take anything on the way, or for the journey), but a staff [or a rod] only, not a scrip, nor bread, neither money in the girdle,

9 but shod with sandals, and that they should not be clothed with two coats.

10 And he said to them, Whither ever ye enter into an house, dwell ye there, till ye go out from thence.

11 And whoever receive you not, nor hear you, go ye out from thence, and shake away the powder from your feet, into witnessing to them. (And whoever will not receive you, or listen to you, go ye out from there, and shake off the dust from your feet, as a testimony against

them.)

12   And they went forth, and preached, that men should do penance (or that men should repent).

13   And they casted out many fiends (or And they threw out many devils and demons), and anointed with oil many sick men, and they were healed.

14   And king Herod heard, for his name was made open, and he said, That John (the) Baptist hath risen again from death, and therefore virtues work in him. (And King Herod heard about this, for Jesus' fame had spread far and wide, and he said, John the Baptist hath risen again from the dead, and so works of power, or miracles, work in him.)

15   Others said, That it is Elias (or He is Elijah); but others said, That it is a prophet, as one of the prophets.

16   And when this thing was heard, Herod said, This is John, whom I have beheaded, he is risen again from death (or he hath risen from the dead).

17   For that Herod sent (for), and held John, and bound him into prison, for Herodias, the wife of Philip, his brother; for he had wedded her.

18   For John said to Herod, It is not leaveful to thee (or It is not lawful for thee), to have the wife of thy brother.

19   And Herodias laid ambush to him, and would slay him, and might not. (And Herodias laid ambush for him, and wanted to kill him, but could find no opportunity to do so.)

20   And Herod dreaded John, and knew him a just man and holy, and kept him, (or And Herod feared John, and knew him to be a just and holy man, and kept him in custody, or And Herod revered John, and knew him to be a just and holy man, and kept him safe). And Herod heard him, and he did many things, and gladly heard him.

21   And when a covenable day was fallen, Herod in his birthday made a supper to the princes, and tribunes, and to the greatest of Galilee. (And when an opportune day had fallen, Herod gave a supper on his birthday for the leaders, or the officials, and the tribunes, and for the greatest of Galilee.)

22   And when the daughter of that Herodias was come in, and danced, and pleased to Herod [or and pleased Herod], and also to (the) men that sat at the meat (or and also the men who sat at the meal), the king said to the damsel, Ask thou of me what thou wilt, and I shall give (it) to thee.

23   And he swore to her, That whatever thou ask, I shall give (it) to thee, though *it be* (even) half of my kingdom.

24   And when she had gone out, she said to her mother, What shall I ask (for)? And she said, The head of John [the] Baptist.

25   And when she was come in anon (or at once) with haste to the king, she asked, and said, I will that anon, (or I desire, or I want, at once), (that) thou give to me in a dish the head of John (the) Baptist.

26   And the king was sorry for the oath, and for (the) men that sat together at the meat, he would not make her sorry [or heavy]; (And the king was sorry for the promise that he had made, or for the oath that he had taken, but because of the men who sat there with him at the meal, he would not make her grieved or disappointed;)

27   but he sent a man-queller and commanded, that John's head were brought in a dish. And (so) he beheaded him in the prison,

28   and brought his head in a dish, and gave it to the damsel, and the damsel gave *it* to her mother.

29   And when this thing was heard, his disciples came, and took his body, and laid it in a burial, (or and laid it in a tomb, or in a grave).

30   And the apostles came together to Jesus, and told to him all (the) things, that they had done, and taught.

31   And he said to them, Come ye by yourselves into a desert place; and rest ye a little. For there were many that came, and went again, and they had not space [for] to eat (or and they had no time even to eat).

32   And they went into a boat, and went into a desert place by themselves.

33   And they saw them go away (or And the people saw them go away), and many knew, and they went afoot from all (the) cities, and ran [together] thither, and came before them.

34   And Jesus went out, and saw much people, and had ruth [or mercy] on them, (or and had compassion for them), for they were as sheep not having a shepherd. And he began to teach them many things.

35   And when it was late in the day, his disciples came to him, and said, This is a desert place, and the time is now passed;

36   let them go into the next towns and villages, to buy them(selves) meat to eat (or to buy themselves some food to eat).

37   And he answered, and said to them, Give ye (something) to them for to eat. And they said to him, Go we, and buy we loaves with two hundred pence, and (then) we shall give (something) to them for to eat.

38   And he saith to them, How many loaves have ye? Go ye, and see. And when they had known, they say, Five, and two fishes.

39   And he commanded to them, that they should make all men sit to meat by companies (or that they should make everyone to sit down for the meal in groups), on [the] green hay.

40   And they sat down by parts [or (in) parties], by hundreds, and by fifties.

41   And when he had taken the five loaves, and two fishes, he beheld into heaven, and blessed (or and gave thanks), and brake [the] loaves, and gave (them) to his disciples, (so) that they should set (them) before them. And he parted (the) two fishes to all (or And he divided the two fish among all the people);

42   and all ate, and were full-filled. [and all ate, and were fulfilled.] (and all ate, and were filled full.)

43   And they took (up) the remnants of broken meats, twelve coffins full, and of the fishes. (And they gathered up the remaining pieces of food, that is, of the bread and the fish, twelve baskets full.)

44   And they that ate, were five thousand of men.

45   And anon he made his disciples to go up into a boat, to pass before him over the sea to Bethsaida, while he left the people. (And at once he made his disciples to go up into a boat, to cross over the lake to Bethsaida ahead of him, while he let the people go, or while he dismissed the people.)

46   And when he had left them, he went into an high hill, to pray. (And when he had dismissed them, or had let them go, he went up onto a high hill, or a mountain, to pray.)

47   And when it was even(ing), the boat was in the middle [or in the midst] of the sea, and he alone in the land (or and he was alone on the land);

48   and he saw them travailing in rowing; for the wind was contrary to them. And about the fourth waking of the night, he wandering on the sea, came to them, and would pass (by) them. (and he saw them labouring, or struggling, with the rowing; for the wind was contrary to them. And about the fourth watch of the night, he came to them, walking on the lake, and would pass by them.)

49   And as they saw him wandering on the sea (or And as they saw him walking on the lake), they guessed that it were a phantom, and cried out;

50   for (they) all saw him, and they were afraid, [or and they were troubled, or disturbed]. And anon he spake with them, and said to them, Trust ye, I am (he); do not ye dread, (or And at once he spoke with them, and said to them, Have trust, it is me; do not fear).

51   And he came up to them into the boat,

and the wind ceased. And they wondered more within themselves;

52 for they understood not of the loaves; for their heart was blinded.

53 And when they were passed over the sea (or And when they had crossed over the lake), they came into the land of Gennesaret, and setted to land.

54 And when they were gone out of the boat, anon (or at once) they knew him.

55 And they ran through all that country(side), and began to bring sick men in beds on each side, where they heard that he was.

56 And whither ever he entered into villages, or into towns, or into cities, they set sick men in (the) streets, and prayed him, that they should touch namely the hem of his cloth; and how(ever) many that touched him, were made safe. (And wherever he entered into villages, or into towns, or into cities, they put their sick people in the streets, and beseeched him, that they could merely touch the hem of his cloak; and however many did touch him, all of them were saved, or were healed.)

CHAPTER 7

1 And the Pharisees and some of the scribes came from Jerusalem together to him.

2 And when they had seen some of his disciples eat bread with unwashen hands, they blamed [them], (or they rebuked them).

3 For the Pharisees and all the Jews eat not, [no] but they wash often their hands, holding the traditions of (the) elder men.

4 And when they turn again from [the] market (or And when they return from the market), they eat not, [no] but they be washed; and many other things there be, that be taken to them to keep (or to obey), as (the) washing of cups, and of water vessels [or of cruets], and of vessels of brass, and of beds.

5 And (the) Pharisees and (the) scribes asked him, and said, Why go not thy disciples after the tradition(s) of (the) elder men, but with unwashen (or unwashed) hands they eat bread?

6 And he answered, and said to them, Esaias prophesied well of you, hypocrites, (or Isaiah prophesied well about you, hypocrites), as it is written, This people worshippeth me with (their) lips [or This people honoureth me with (their) lips], but their heart is far from me;

7 and in vain they worship me, teaching the doctrines and the behests [or the commandments] of men.

8 For ye leave the commandment of God, and hold (fast to) the traditions of men, as [the] washing of water vessels [or of cruets], and of cups; and many other things like these ye do.

9 And he said to them, Well ye have made the commandment of God void (or empty and useless), to keep your tradition.

10 For Moses said, Worship thy father and thy mother [or Honour thou thy father and thy mother]; and he that curseth father or mother, die he by death.

11 But ye say, If a man say to (his) father or mother, Corban, that is, Whatever gift is of me, it shall profit to thee, (or Whatever gift is for me, it shall also profit thee);

12 and over [or further(more)] ye suffer not him [to] do anything to (his) father or mother, (and more than this, ye do not allow him to do anything for his father or mother,)

13 and ye break the word of God by your tradition, that ye have given; and ye do many [other] such things.

14 And he again called the people, and said to them, Ye all hear me, and understand.

15 Nothing that is without a man, that entereth into him, may defoul him (or can defile him); but those things that come forth of a man, those it be that defoul a man.

16 If any man have ears of hearing, hear he. [Forsooth if any man have ears to hear, hear he.]

17 And when he was entered into an house,

from the people, his disciples asked him (about) the parable.

18 And he said to them, Ye be unwise also. Understand ye not, that all thing withoutforth that entereth into a man, may not defoul him? (or Do ye not understand, that everything from outside that entereth into a man, cannot defile him?)

19 for it hath not entered into his heart, but into the womb, and beneath it goeth out, purging all meats (or cleaning out all the food).

20 But he said, The things that go out of a man, those defoul a man (or these defile a person).

21 For from within, of the heart of men come forth evil thoughts, adulteries, fornications, manslayings,

22 thefts, avarices, [or covetousness, *or over-hard keeping of goods*], wickednesses, guile, unchastity, evil eye, blasphemies, pride, folly (or foolishness).

23 All these evils come forth from within, and defoul a man (or and defile a person),

24 And Jesus rose up from thence, and went into the coasts of Tyre and Sidon. And he went into an house, and would that no man knew; and he might not be hid. (And Jesus left there, and went to the coasts of Tyre and Sidon. And he went into a house, and wanted that no one knew that he was there; but he could not stay hidden.)

25 For a woman, anon as she heard of him (or as soon as she heard about him), whose daughter had an unclean spirit, entered, and fell down at his feet.

26 And the woman was (a) heathen, of the generation of Syrophenician. And she prayed him, that he would cast out a devil from her daughter, (or And she beseeched him, that he would throw a demon out of her daughter).

27 And he said to her, Suffer thou (or Allow) that the children be fulfilled first [or Suffer thou that the sons be filled first]; for it is not good to take the bread of children, and give [it] to hounds.

28 And she answered, and said to him, Yes, Lord; for little whelps eat under the board of the crumbs of (the) children. (And she answered him, Yes, Lord; but even little pups can eat the crumbs of the children under the table.)

29 And Jesus said to her, Go thou, for this word the fiend (or the demon) went out of thy daughter.

30 And when she was gone into her house home [or And when she had gone home/And when she had gone into her house], she found the damsel lying on the bed, and the devil gone out from her. (And when she went home, she found the young girl lying on the bed, and the demon had gone out of her.)

31 And again Jesus went out from the coasts of Tyre, and came through Sidon to the sea of Galilee, between the middle of the coasts of Decapolis.

32 And they bring to him a man deaf and dumb, and prayed him to lay his hand/s on him.

33 And he took him aside from the people, and put his fingers into his ears; and he spat, and touched his tongue.

34 And he beheld into heaven, and sorrowed within, and said [to him], Ephphatha, that is, Be thou opened.

35 And anon (or at once) his ears were opened, and the band of his tongue was unbound, and he spake rightly.

36 And he commanded to them, that they should say to no man; but how much he commanded to them, so much the more they preached,

37 and by so much the more they wondered, and said, He did well all things, both he hath made deaf men to hear, and dumb men to speak.

CHAPTER 8

1 In those days, when much people was

with Jesus, and had not what they should eat, when his disciples were called together, he said to them,

2 I have ruth on the people, for lo! now the third day they abide me, and they have not what to eat; (I have compassion for the people, for behold, now it is the third day that they be with me, and they have nothing to eat;)

3 and if I leave them fasting into their houses, they shall fail in the way; for some of them came from (a)far. (and if I let them go fasting unto their houses, they shall faint on the way; for some of them came from afar.)

4 And his disciples answered to him, Whereof shall a man be able to fill them with loaves here in (the) wilderness?

5 And he asked them, How many loaves have ye? Which said, Seven.

6 And he commanded the people to sit down on the earth (or And he commanded the people to sit down on the ground). And he took the seven loaves, and did thankings (or and gave thanks), and brake (them), and gave (them) to his disciples, (so) that they should set (them) forth. And they setted (them) forth to the people.

7 And they had a few small fishes; and he blessed them, and commanded, that they were set forth (also).

8 And they ate, and were fulfilled, [or And they ate, and were filled]; and they took up that that *was* left of [the] remnants, seven baskets (full). (And they ate, and were filled full; and they gathered up the remaining pieces of food that *were* left, seven baskets full.)

9 And they that ate, were as four thousand of men; and he left them. (And those who ate, were four thousand people; and then he dismissed them, or and then he let them go.)

10 And anon (or at once) he went up into a boat, with his disciples, and came into the coasts of Dalmanutha.

11 And the Pharisees went out, and began to dispute with him, and asked a token of him from heaven, and tempted him. (And the Pharisees went out, and began to argue with him, and asked him for a sign from heaven, and tested him.)

12 And he sorrowing within in spirit, said, What seeketh this generation a token, [or a sign, *either* (a) *miracle*]? Truly I say to you, a token [or a sign] shall not be given to this generation. (And he sorrowing within himself, said, Why seeketh this generation a sign? I tell you the truth, a sign shall not be given to this generation.)

13 And he left them, and went up again into a boat, and went over the sea (or and went over the lake).

14 And they forgot to take bread, and they had not with them [no] but one loaf in the boat.

15 And he commanded [to] them, and said, See ye, and beware of the sourdough of the Pharisees, and of the sourdough of Herod. (And he said to them, Watch out, and beware of the yeast, or the leaven, of the Pharisees, and of the yeast, or the leaven, of Herod.)

16 And they thought, and said one to another, For we have not (brought any) loaves [or For we have not (brought any) bread].

17 And when this thing was known, Jesus said to them, What think ye, for ye have not loaves? (or Why do ye think about, or talk about, not having any bread?) Yet ye know not, neither understand; yet ye have your heart(s) blinded.

18 Ye having eyes, see not, and ye having ears, hear not; neither ye have mind (or nor ye remember),

19 when I brake five loaves among five thousand, and how many coffins full of broken meat took ye up? (or and how many baskets full of pieces of food did ye gather up?) They said to him, Twelve.

20 When also seven loaves among four thousand of men, how many baskets [full] of broken meat took ye up? (or how many baskets full of pieces of food did ye gather up?) And they say to him, Seven.

21   And he said to them, How understand ye not yet?

22   And they came to Bethsaida, and they brought to him a blind man, and they prayed him, that he would touch him.

23   And when he had taken the blind man's hand, he led him out of the street (or he led him out of the village), and he spat into his eyes, and set his hands on him; and he asked him, if he saw anything.

24   And he beheld, and said, I see men as trees walking (about).

25   Afterward again he set his hands on his eyes, and he began to see, and he was restored, so that he saw clearly all things (or so that he saw everything clearly).

26   And he sent him into his house, and said, Go into thine house; and if thou goest into the street, say to no man.

27   And Jesus entered [in] and his disciples, into the castles of Caesarea of Philippi. And in the way, he asked his disciples, and said to them, Whom say men that I am? (And Jesus and his disciples went to the villages of Caesarea of Philippi. And on the way, he asked his disciples, Who do people say that I am?)

28   Which answered to him, and said, Some *say*, John (the) Baptist; others *say*, Elias (or Elijah); and others *say*, as one of the prophets.

29   Then he saith to them, But whom say ye that I am? Peter answered, and said to him, Thou art Christ (or Thou art the Messiah).

30   And he charged them, that they should not say of him to any man. (And he commanded them, that they should not say this about him to anyone.)

31   And he began to teach them, that it behooveth man's Son to suffer many things, and to be reproved of the elder men, and of the highest priests, and of the scribes, (or and to be rejected by the elders, and by the high priests, and by the scribes), and to be slain, and after three days, to rise again.

32   And he spake openly the word. And Peter took (hold of) him, and began to blame him [or And Peter taking (hold of) him, began to blame him], and said, Lord, be thou merciful to thee, for this shall not be. (And he openly spoke these words. And Peter took hold of him, and began to rebuke him, and said, Lord, be thou merciful to thyself, do not let this be, or do not let this happen.)

33   And he turned, and saw his disciples, and menaced Peter (or and threatened Peter), and said (to him), Go after me, [thou] Satan; for thou savourest not those things that be of God [or for thou understandest not those things that be of God], (no) but those things that be of men.

34   And when the people was called together, with his disciples, he said to them, If any man will come after me, deny he himself, and take his cross, and (pur)sue he me, [or and (pur)sue me], (or and follow me).

35   For he that will make safe his life, shall lose it, [or Soothly whoso(ever) will make his soul, *that is, his life*, safe, shall lose it]; and he that loseth his life for me, and for the gospel, shall make it safe. (For he who will save his life, shall lose it; and he who loseth his life for me, and for the Gospel or the Good News, shall save it.)

36   For what profiteth it to a man, if he win all the world, and do impairing to his [own] soul?

37   or what (ex)changing shall a man give for his soul?

38   But who that acknowledgeth me and my words, in this generation adulterous and sinful (or in this sinful and adulterous generation), also man's Son shall acknowledge him, when he shall come in the glory of his Father, with his angels.

CHAPTER 9

1   And he said to them, Truly I say to you, that there be some men standing here, which shall not taste death, till they see the realm of God coming in virtue. (And he said to them, I

tell you the truth, that there be some standing here now, who shall not taste death, before they see the Kingdom of God coming in power, or coming with power.)

2 And after six days Jesus took Peter, and James, and John, and led them by themselves alone into an high hill, (or and led only them up onto a high hill, or a mountain); and he was transfigured before them.

3 And his clothes were made full shining and (as) white as snow, which manner white clothes a fuller may not make on (the) earth.

4 And Elias with Moses appeared to them, and they spake with Jesus. (And Elijah and Moses appeared to them, and they spoke with Jesus.)

5 And Peter answered, and said to Jesus, Master, it is good (for) us to be here; and make we here three tabernacles, one to thee, one to Moses, and one to Elias. (And Peter said to Jesus, Teacher, it is good for us to be here; and we shall make here three tents, or three tabernacles, one for thee, one for Moses, and one for Elijah.)

6 For he knew not what he should say; for they were aghast by dread [or for they were afeared by dread].

7 And there was made a cloud overshadowing them; and a voice came out of the cloud, and said, This is my most dearworthy Son, hear ye him (or listen to him).

8 And anon they beheld about, and saw no more any man, [no] but Jesus only with them. (And at once they looked about, and saw no one there, except Jesus with them.)

9 And when they came down from the hill, he commanded them, that they should not tell to any man those things that they had seen, but when (or until) man's Son hath risen again from death, [+or no but when (or until) man's Son hath risen from (the) dead].

10 And they held the word at themselves (or And they held the word within themselves), seeking what *this* should be, when he had risen

again from death [or when he hath risen from (the) dead].

11 And they asked him, and said, What then say [the] Pharisees and [the] scribes, that it behooveth Elias to come first. (And they asked him, Why then do the Pharisees and the scribes say, that it behooveth Elijah to come first.)

12 And he answered, and said to them, When Elias cometh (or When Elijah shall come), he shall first restore all things; and as it is written of man's Son, that he suffer many things, and be despised.

13 And I say to you that Elias is come, and they did to him whatever things they would, as it is written of him. (And I tell you that Elijah hath come, and they did whatever they wanted to do to him, as it is written about him.)

14 And he coming to his disciples, saw a great company about them, and [the] scribes disputing with them.

15 And anon all the people seeing Jesus, was astonied, and they dreaded; and they running [to] (him), greeted him. (And at once all the people seeing Jesus, were astonished, and they had fearful reverence; and running to him, they greeted him.)

16 And he asked them, What (thing) dispute ye among you?

17 And one of the company answered, and said, Master, (or Teacher), I have brought to thee my son, that hath a dumb spirit;

18 and wherever he taketh him, he hurtleth him down, and he foameth, and beateth together with (his) teeth, and waxeth dry (or and then groweth dry). And I said to thy disciples, that they should cast him out, and they might not.

19 And he answered to them, and said, A! thou generation out of belief, [or O! thou generation unbelieveful], (or O thou unbelieving, or unfaithful, generation!), how long shall I be among you, how long shall I suffer you? Bring ye him to me.

20 And they brought him. And when he had

seen him, anon the spirit troubled him (or at once the spirit troubled him); and he was thrown down to the ground, and wallowed, and foamed.

21 And he asked his father, How long is it, since this hath befallen to him? And he said, From childhood;

22 and oft he hath put him into the fire, and into water, to lose him (or to destroy him); but if thou mayest (do) anything, help us, and have mercy on us.

23 And Jesus said to him, If thou mayest believe (or If thou can believe), all things be possible to a man that believeth.

24 And anon (or And at once) the father of the child cried with tears, and said, Lord, I believe; help thou mine unbelief.

25 And when Jesus had seen the people running together, he menaced the unclean spirit (or he threatened the unclean spirit), and said to him, Thou deaf and dumb spirit, I command thee, go out from him, and enter no more into him.

26 And he crying, and much wrenching him, went out from him; and he was made as dead, so that many said, that he was dead.

27 And Jesus held his hand, and lifted him up; and he rose.

28 And when he had entered into an house, his disciples asked him privily, Why might not we cast him out? (And when he had entered into a house, his disciples asked him privately, Why could we not throw him out?)

29 And he said to them, This kind in nothing may go out [or This kind may not go out in anything], [no] but in prayer and fasting. (And he said to them, This kind cannot be made to go out, except by prayer and fasting.)

30 And they went from thence, and went forth into Galilee; and they would not, that any man knew, [or and he would not, that any man know], (or and he did not want, that anyone knew that he was there).

31 And he taught his disciples, and said to them, For man's Son shall be betrayed into the hands of men, and they shall slay him, and he slain shall rise again on the third day.

32 And they knew not the (meaning of the) word(s), and dreaded to ask him (or and feared to ask him).

33 And they came to Capernaum. And when they were in the house, he asked them, What treated ye in the way? (or What did ye discuss on the way?)

34 And they were still; for they disputed among them[selves] in the way, who of them should be [the] greatest. (And they were silent; for they had argued among themselves on the way, who of them was the greatest.)

35 And he sat, and called the twelve, and said to them, If any man will be the first among you, he shall be the last of all, and the minister [or the servant] of all.

36 And he took a child, and set him in the middle [or in the midst] of them; and when he had embraced him, he said to them,

37 Whoever receiveth one of such children in my name, he receiveth me; and whoever receiveth me, he receiveth not me alone, but him that sent me.

38 John answered to him, and said, Master, we saw one casting out fiends in thy name, which (pur)sueth not us, and we have forbidden him. (John answered to him, and said, Teacher, we saw one throwing out devils and demons in thy name, and he followeth not us, and we have forbidden him.)

39 And Jesus said, Do not ye forbid him; for there is no man that doeth virtue in my name, and may soon speak evil of me. (And Jesus said, Do not forbid him; for there is no one who doeth a work of power, or a miracle, in my name, and can soon after speak evil about me.)

40 He that is not against us, is for us.

41 And whoever giveth [to] you (even) a cup of cold water to drink in my name, for ye be of Christ, truly I say to you, he shall not lose his meed. (And whoever giveth to you even just a

cup of cold water to drink in my name, for ye belong to the Messiah, I tell you the truth, he shall receive his reward.)

42 And whoever shall cause to stumble one of these little (ones) that believe in me, it were better to him that a millstone were done about his neck, and he were cast into the sea. (And whoever shall cause one of these little ones who believe in me to stumble, it would be better for him if a millstone was put around his neck, and he was thrown into the sea.)

43 And if thine hand cause thee to stumble, cut it away; it is better to thee to enter feeble into life, (or it is better for thee to enter into (eternal) life weak, or maimed), than (to) have two hands, and (to) go into hell, into the fire that never shall be quenched [or into (the) fire unquenchable],

44 where the worm of them dieth not, and the fire is not quenched.

45 And if thy foot cause thee to stumble, cut it off; it is better to thee to enter crooked into everlasting life, (or it is better for thee to enter into eternal life bent, or lame), than (to) have two feet, and (to) be sent into hell of fire [or into hellfire], that never shall be quenched,

46 where the worm of them dieth not, and the fire is not quenched.

47 That if thine eye cause thee to stumble, cast it out; it is better to thee to enter goggle-eyed into the realm of God (or it is better for thee to enter into the Kingdom of God with one eye), than (to) have two eyes, and (to) be sent into hell of fire, [⁺or than having two eyes, to be sent into hellfire],

48 where the worm of them dieth not, and the fire is not quenched.

49 And every man shall be salted with fire, and every slain sacrifice shall be made savoury with salt. [⁺Forsooth every man shall be made savoury with fire, and every slain sacrifice shall be salted with salt.]

50 Salt is good; if salt be unsavoury, in what thing shall ye make it savoury? Have ye salt among you, and have ye peace among you.

CHAPTER 10

1 And Jesus rose up from thence, and came into the coasts of Judea over (the) Jordan (River), [or And Jesus rising up from thence, came into the ends of Judea beyond (the) Jordan (River)]; and again the people came together to him, and as he was wont, again he taught them.

2 And the Pharisees came [nigh], and asked him, Whether it be leaveful to a man to leave [or to forsake] his wife? and they tempted him. (And the Pharisees came near, and asked him, Is it lawful for a man to leave his wife? and they tested him.)

3 And he answered, and said to them, What commanded Moses to you?

4 And they said, Moses suffered (us) to write a libel of forsaking, and to forsake. (And they said, Moses allowed us to write a bill of forsaking, or a notice of divorce, and then we be able to forsake, or to leave, a woman.)

5 And Jesus answered, and said to them, For the hardness of your heart(s) Moses wrote to you this commandment [or this precept].

6 But from the beginning of creature(s), (or But from the beginning of Creation), God made them male and female;

7 and said, For this thing a man shall leave his father and mother, and shall draw [or shall cleave] to his wife,

8 and they shall be twain in one flesh. And so now they be not twain, but one flesh.

9 Therefore that thing that God hath joined together, no man separate [or part].

10 And again in the house his disciples asked him of the same thing. (And in the house his disciples asked him about this same thing.)

11 And he said to them, Whoever leaveth his wife, and weddeth another, he doeth adultery on her.

12 And if the wife leave her husband, and be

wedded to another, she doeth lechery [or she doeth adultery].

13 And they brought to him little children, (so) that he should touch them; and the disciples threatened the men, that brought them.

14 And when Jesus had seen them, he bare (it) heavy, and said to them, Suffer ye (the) little children to come to me (or Allow the little children to come to me), and forbid ye them not, for of such is the kingdom of God.

15 Truly I say to you (or I tell you the truth), whoever receiveth not the kingdom of God as a little child, he shall not enter into it.

16 And he embraced them, and laid his hands on them, and blessed them.

17 And when Jesus was gone out into the way, a man ran before, and kneeled before him, and prayed him, and said, Good master, what shall I do, that I receive everlasting life? (or and said, Good Teacher, what should I do, so that I can get, or I can receive, eternal life?)

18 And Jesus said to him, What sayest thou that I am good? (or Why sayest thou that I am good?) There is no man good, but God himself, [or None is good, no but God alone].

19 Thou knowest the commandments, do thou none adultery, slay not, steal not, say not false witnessing (or do not give false testimony), do no fraud, worship thy father and thy mother (or honour thy father and thy mother).

20 And he answered, and said to him, Master, (or Teacher), I have kept all these things from my youth.

21 And Jesus beheld him, and loved him, and said to him, One thing faileth to thee; go thou, and sell all (the) things that thou hast, and give (the proceeds) to poor men, and (then) thou shalt have treasure in heaven; and come, (pur)sue thou me (or follow me).

22 And he was full sorry in the word, [or The which made sorrowful in the word], (or And he was greatly grieved by these words), and went away mourning, for he had many possessions.

23 And Jesus beheld about, and said to his disciples, How hard they that have riches [or money] shall enter into the kingdom of God.

24 And the disciples were astonied in his words (or And the disciples were astonished at his words). And Jesus again answered, and said to them, Ye little children [or Little sons], how hard it is for men that trust in riches to enter into the kingdom of God.

25 It is lighter (for) a camel to pass through a needle's eye [or It is easier that a camel pass through a needle's eye], than (for) a rich man to enter into the kingdom of God.

26 And they wondered more, and said among themselves, And who may be saved? (or Then who can be saved?)

27 And Jesus beheld them, and said, With men it is impossible, but not with God; for all things be possible with God.

28 And Peter began to say to him, Lo! we have left all things, and have (pur)sued thee (or and have followed thee).

29 Jesus answered, and said, Truly I say to you (or I tell you the truth), there is no man that leaveth house, or brethren, or sisters, or father, or mother, or children, or fields for me and for the gospel,

30 which shall not take an hundredfold so much now in this time, houses, and brethren, and sisters, and mothers, and children, and fields, with persecutions, and in the world to coming everlasting life [or and in the world to come everlasting life]. (who shall not now receive in this time a hundred times as much, yea, houses, and brothers, and sisters, and mothers, and children, and fields, with persecutions, and in the world to come eternal life.)

31 But many shall be, the first the last, and the last the first.

32 And they were in the way going up to Jerusalem; and Jesus went before them, and they wondered, and followed, and dreaded (or had fear). And again Jesus took the twelve

(aside), and began to say to them, what things were to come to him.

33 For lo! we ascend to Jerusalem, and man's Son shall be betrayed to the princes of (the) priests, and to [the] scribes, and to the elder men; and they shall condemn him by death, and they shall [be]take him to heathen men. (For behold, we go up to Jerusalem, and man's Son shall be betrayed to the high priests, and to the scribes, and to the elders; and they shall condemn him to death, and they shall deliver him to the heathens, or they shall hand him over to the Gentiles.)

34 And they shall scorn him, and bespit him, and beat him; and they shall slay him, and in the third day he shall rise again (or and on the third day he shall rise again).

35 And James and John, Zebedee's sons, came to him, and said, Master, we will, that whatever we ask, thou do to us. (And James and John, Zebedee's sons, came to him, and said, Teacher, we desire, or we want, that whatever we ask, thou do for us.)

36 And he said to them, What will ye that I do to you? (And he said to them, What do ye desire, or want, that I do for you?)

37 And they said, Grant to us, that we sit the one at thy right half, and the other at thy left half, in thy glory. (And they said, Grant unto us, that we sit the one at thy right hand, or on thy right side, and the other at thy left hand, or on thy left side, in thy glory.)

38 And Jesus said to them, Ye know not what ye ask; may ye drink the cup, which I shall drink, (or can ye drink the cup, which I shall drink), or be washed with the baptism, in which I am baptized?

39 And they said to him, We may (or We can). And Jesus said to them, [Truly] Ye shall drink the cup that I drink, and ye shall be washed with the baptism, in which I am baptized;

40 but to sit at my right half or left half is not mine to give to you (or but to sit at my right

hand or my left hand is not mine to give to you), (no) but to whom it is made ready.

41 And the ten heard, and began to have indignation of James and John. (And the other ten heard, and began to feel indignant with James and John.)

42 But Jesus called them, and said to them, Ye know, that they that seem [or that be seen] to have princehood of folks, be (the) lords of them, and the princes of them have power of them. (And Jesus called them, and said to them, Ye know, that they who be seen to have lordship over the nations and the peoples, be their lords, and so their leaders have power over them.)

43 But it is not so among you, but whoever will be made [the] greater, shall be your minister (or shall be your servant);

44 and whoever will be the first among you, shall be (the) servant of all.

45 For why man's Son came not, that it should be ministered to him, but that he should minister, and give his life again-buying [or as a redemption] for many. (For man's Son came not, so that he would be served, but that he would serve, and give his life as a redemption for many.)

46 And they came to Jericho; and when he went forth from Jericho, and his disciples, and a full much people (or a great many people), Bartimaeus, a blind man, the son of Timaeus, sat beside the way, and begged.

47 And when he heard, that it was Jesus of Nazareth, he began to cry, and say, Jesus, the son of David, have mercy on me.

48 And many threatened him, that he should be still; and he cried much the more [or and he cried much more, saying], Jesus, the son of David, have mercy on me.

49 And Jesus stood, and commanded him to be called; and they called the blind man, and said to him, Be thou of better heart, rise up, he calleth thee.

50 And he cast away his cloth (or And he

threw away his cloak), and skipped, and came to him.

51 And Jesus answered, and said to him, What wilt thou, that I shall do to thee? The blind man said to him, Master, that I see. (And Jesus said to him, What desirest thou, that I shall do for thee? The blind man said to him, Teacher, that I see.)

52 Jesus said to him, Go thou, thy faith hath made thee safe. And anon he saw, and (pur)sued him in the way. (Jesus said to him, Go, thy faith hath saved thee, or thy faith hath healed thee. And at once he saw, and followed him on the way.)

CHAPTER 11

1 And when Jesus came nigh to Jerusalem and to Bethany, to the mount of Olives, he sendeth two of his disciples,

2 and saith to them, Go ye into the castle that is against you (or Go into the village that is opposite you); and anon (or at once) as ye enter there ye shall find a colt tied, on which no man hath sat yet; untie ye (it), and bring him (here).

3 And if any man say anything to you, What do ye? say ye, that he is needful to the Lord, and anon, he shall leave him hither. (And if anyone say anything to you, Why do ye that? say, that he is needed by the Lord, and then at once, he shall let him go, or let him come here.)

4 And they went forth, and found a colt tied before the gate withoutforth, in the meeting of two ways; and they untied him.

5 And some of them that stood there said to them, What do ye, untying the colt?

6 And they said to them, as Jesus commanded them; and they left it to them (or and they let it go with them).

7 And they brought the colt to Jesus, and they laid on him their clothes (or and they laid their clothes on him), and Jesus sat on him.

8 And many strewed their clothes in the way, and other men cutted branches [or

boughs] off (the) trees, and strewed (them) in the way. (And many spread their clothes on the way, or on the road, and others cut branches or boughs off the trees, and strew them on the way.)

9 And they that went before, and that (pur)sued (or and who followed), cried, and said, Hosanna, blessed *is* he that cometh in the name of the Lord;

10 blessed *be* the kingdom of our father David that is to come; Hosanna in (the) highest things [or Hosanna in (the) highest].

11 And he entered into Jerusalem, into the temple; and when he had seen all things about, when it was even(ing), he went out into Bethany, with the twelve.

12 And another day (or And the next day), when he went out of Bethany [or when he went out from Bethany], he hungered.

13 And when he had seen a fig tree (from) afar having leaves, he came, if happily he should find anything thereon; and when he came to it, he found nothing, except leaves; for it was not (the) time of figs.

14 And Jesus answered and said to it, Now never eat any man fruit of thee (any) more [or Now no more without end any man eat fruit of thee]. And his disciples heard (him);

15 and they came to Jerusalem. And when he was entered into the temple, he began to cast out sellers and buyers in the temple; and he turned upside-down the boards of (the money-)changers, and the chairs of men that sold culvers; (and they came to Jerusalem. And after he went into the Temple, he began to throw out the sellers and the buyers in the Temple; and he turned upside-down the tables of the money-changers, and the chairs of those who sold doves and pigeons;)

16 and he suffered not, that any man should bear a vessel through the temple. (and he would not allow anyone to carry a vessel through the Temple.)

17 And he taught them, and said, Whether it

is not written, That mine house shall be called the house of praying to all folks? but ye have made it a den of thieves. (And he taught them, and said, Is it not written, My House shall be called the House of Prayer for all the nations and all the peoples? but ye have made it a den of thieves.)

18 And when this thing was heard, the princes of priests, and [the] scribes sought how they should lose him; for they dreaded him, for all the people wondered on his teaching. (And when this was heard, the high priests, and the scribes sought how they could destroy him; for they feared him, for all the people wondered about his teaching.)

19 And when evening was come, he went out of the city.

20 And as they passed forth early (the next day), they saw the fig tree made dry from the roots.

21 And Peter bethought (to) him(self), and said to him, [or And Peter having mind, (or remembering), said to him], Master, (or Teacher), lo! the fig tree, whom thou cursedest, is dried up.

22 And Jesus answered and said to them, Have ye the faith of God;

23 truly I say to you, that whoever saith to this hill, Be thou taken, and cast into the sea; and doubt not in his heart, but believeth, that whatever he say, shall be done, it shall be done to him. (I tell you the truth, that whoever saith to this hill, Be thou taken, and thrown into the sea; and doubt not in his heart, but believeth, that whatever he say, shall be done, it shall be done for him.)

24 Therefore I say to you, all things whatever things ye praying shall ask (for), believe ye that ye shall take (them), (or believe that ye shall receive them), and they shall come to you.

25 And when ye shall stand to pray, forgive ye, if ye have anything against any man, (so) that [also] your Father that is in heavens, forgive to you your sins.

26 And if ye forgive not [or For if ye forgive not], neither your Father that is in heavens, shall forgive to you your sins.

27 And again they came to Jerusalem. And when he walked in the temple, the highest priests, and (the) scribes, and the elder men came to him, (And they came again to Jerusalem. And when he walked in the Temple, the high priests, and the scribes, and the elders came to him,)

28 and said to him, In what power doest thou these things? or who gave to thee this power, that thou do these things?

29 Jesus answered and said to them, And I shall ask you one word (or And I shall ask you something), and answer ye to me, and I shall say to you in what power I do these things.

30 Whether was the baptism of John of heaven, or of men? answer ye to me. (Was the baptism of John from heaven, or from men? answer me.)

31 And they thought within themselves, saying, If we say of heaven, he shall say to us, Why then believe ye not to him; (or If we say from heaven, he shall say to us, Then why did ye not believe him;)

32 if we say of men, we dread the people; for all men had John, that he was verily a prophet. (if we say from men, we fear the people; for everyone believed about John, that he was truly a prophet.)

33 And they answered, and said to Jesus, We know not. And Jesus answered, and said to them, Neither I say to you, in what power I do these things.

CHAPTER 12

1 And Jesus began to speak to them in parables. A man planted a vineyard, and set an hedge about it, and delved a pit, and builded a tower, and hired it (out) to earth-tillers, and went forth in pilgrimage, (or A man planted a vineyard, and set a hedge about it, and dug a

hole for a winepress, and built a look-out tower, and hired it out to farmers, and went forth on a journey).

2 And he sent to the earth-tillers in time a servant, to receive of the earth-tillers of the fruit of the vineyard. (And in time he sent a servant to the farmers, to receive from the farmers some of the fruit from the vineyard.)

3 And they took him, and beat him, and left him void (or and let him go away empty).

4 And again he sent to them another servant, and they wounded him in the head, and tormented him [or and punished him with chidings, *or reprovings*].

5 And again he sent another, and they slew him, and others more, beating some, and slaying others [or soothly they killed others].

6 But yet he had a most dearworthy son, and he sent him last to them, and said, Peradventure they shall dread [with reverence] my son, (or Perhaps they shall fear my son, or Surely they shall revere, or respect, my son).

7 But the earth-tillers said together, [or Forsooth the tenants said to themselves], (or But the tenants said to each other), This is the heir; come ye, slay we him, and the heritage shall be ours. (But the farmers said to each other, He is the heir; come, let us kill him, and then the inheritance shall be ours.)

8 And they took him, and killed him, and casted *him* out without the vineyard (or and threw *him* out of the vineyard).

9 Then what shall the lord of the vineyard do? He shall come, and lose the earth-tillers (or and destroy the farmers), [or He shall come, and lose the tenants (or and destroy the tenants)], and give the vineyard to others.

10 Whether ye have not read this scripture, The stone which the builders have despised, this is made into the head of the corner?

11 This thing is done of the Lord, and *it* is wonderful in our eyes.

12 And they sought to (take) hold (of) him, and they dreaded the people (or but they feared the people); for they knew that to them he (had) said this parable; and (so) they left him, and they went away.

13 And they sent to him some of the Pharisees and (some) of the Herodians, to take him in word (or to catch him with his own words).

14 Which came, and said to him, Master, (or Teacher), we know that thou art soothfast, and reckest not (or takest heed) of any man; for neither thou beholdest into the face of any man, but thou teachest the way of God in truth. Is it leaveful that tribute be given to the emperor, or we shall not give? (or Is it lawful to pay taxes to Caesar, or should we not pay them?)

15 Which witting their privy falseness, said to them, What tempt ye me, [hypocrites]? (or Why do you hypocrites test me?) bring ye to me a penny, (so) that I (can) see (it).

16 And they brought (it) to him. And he said to them, Whose is this image, and the writing above (or upon it)? And they say to him, The emperor's [or Caesar's].

17 And Jesus answered and said to them, Then yield ye to the emperor those things that be the emperor's [or Therefore yield ye to Caesar those things that be of Caesar]; and to God those things that be of God. And they wondered of him (or And they wondered about him).

18 And (some) Sadducees, that say that there is no resurrection, came to him, and asked him, and said,

19 Master, (or Teacher), Moses wrote to us, that if the brother of a man were dead, and left *his* wife, and have no sons, his brother take his wife, and raise up seed to his brother.

20 Then seven brethren there were, [or Therefore seven brethren were], (or And so there were seven brothers); and the first took a wife, and died, and left no seed.

21 And the second took her, and died, and neither he left seed. And the third also.

22 And in like manner the seven took her, and left no seed. And the woman the last of all died.

23 Then in the resurrection, when they shall

rise again, whose wife of these shall she be? for seven had her to wife.

24 And Jesus answered, and said to them, Whether ye err not therefore, that ye know not [the] scriptures, neither the virtue of God? (And Jesus answered, and said to them, And so do ye not err, because ye know not the Scriptures, nor the power of God?)

25 For when they shall rise again from death, neither they shall wed, nor shall be wedded, but they shall be as (the) angels of God in heavens. [+Forsooth when they shall rise again from (the) dead, neither they shall wed, neither shall be wedded, but they shall be as (the) angels of God in heaven.]

26 And of dead men, that they rise again, have ye not read in the book of Moses, on the bush (or in the bush), how God spake to him, and said, I am God of Abraham, and God of Isaac, and God of Jacob?

27 He is not (the) God of dead men, but of living men; therefore ye err much.

28 And one of the scribes, that had heard them disputing together, came nigh, and saw that Jesus had well-answered them, and asked him, [or and seeing that he had answered them well, asked him], which was the first commandment of all (or which is the first, or the most important, commandment of all?).

29 And Jesus answered to him, That the first commandment of all is, Hear thou, Israel, thy Lord God is one God, [or Hear, Israel, the Lord thy God is one God]; (And Jesus answered to him, The first, or the most important, commandment of all is this, Hear O Israel, the Lord thy God is one God;)

30 and thou shalt love thy Lord God of all thine heart, and of all thy soul, and of all thy mind, and of all thy might, [or and thou shalt love the Lord thy God of all thine heart, and of all thy soul, and of all thy mind, and of all thy virtue, *or might, or strength*]. This is the first commandment (or This is the first, or the most important, commandment of all).

31 And the second is like to this, Thou shalt love thy neighbour as thyself. There is none other commandment greater than these.

32 And the scribe said to him, Master, (or Teacher), in truth thou hast well said; for one God is (or for there is but one God), and there is none other, except him;

33 [and] that he be loved of all the heart, and of all the mind, and of all the understanding, and of all the soul, and of all the strength, and to love the neighbour as himself, is greater [or and to love thy neighbour as himself, is more] than all burnt offerings and sacrifices.

34 And Jesus seeing that he had answered wisely, said to him, Thou art not far from the kingdom of God. And then no man durst ask him more anything (or And then no one dared to ask him anything more).

35 And Jesus answered and said, teaching in the temple, How say [the] scribes, that Christ is the son of David? (And Jesus said, teaching in the Temple, How can the scribes say, that the Messiah is the Son of David?)

36 For David himself said in the Holy Ghost, The Lord said to my lord, Sit [thou] on my right half, till I put thine enemies the stool of thy feet. (For David himself said by the Holy Spirit, The Lord said to my Lord, Sit thou at my right hand, or on my right side, until I make thine enemies thy footstool.)

37 Then if David himself calleth him Lord, how then is he his son? And much people gladly heard him.

38 And he said to them in his teaching, Be ye ware of (the) scribes, that will wander [or that will go] (about) in stoles, and be saluted in [the] chapping (or and be respectfully greeted at the market),

39 and sit in synagogues in the first chairs [or and sit in the first chairs in synagogues], and in the first sitting places in suppers;

40 which devour the houses of widows under [the] colour of long prayer; they shall take the longer doom, [*either* (the longer) *damnation*], (or

they shall receive the greater condemnation).

41   And Jesus sitting against (or opposite) the treasury, beheld how the people cast money into the treasury; and many rich men casted many things.

42   But when a poor widow was come, she cast two minutes (or she threw in two mites), that is, a farthing.

43   And he called together his disciples, and said to them, Truly I say to you (or I tell you the truth), that this poor widow cast more than all, that cast into the treasury.

44   For all they cast of that thing that they had plenty of; but this (out) of her poverty cast all things that she had, all her livelode, [or all her lifelode], (or all her livelihood).

CHAPTER 13

1   And when he went out of the temple, one of his disciples said to him, Master, (or Teacher), behold, what manner stones, and what manner buildings.

2   And Jesus answered, and said to him, Seest thou all these great buildings? there shall not be left a stone on a stone, which shall not be destroyed.

3   And when he sat in the mount of Olives against the temple (or And when he sat on the Mount of Olives opposite the Temple), Peter and James and John and Andrew asked him by themselves,

4   Say thou to us, when these things shall be done, and what token [or what sign] shall be, when all these things shall begin to be ended.

5   And Jesus answered, and began to say to them, Look ye [or See ye], that no man deceive you;

6   for many shall come in my name, saying, That I am (he); and they shall deceive many.

7   And when ye hear battles and opinions of battles, dread ye not (or fear not); for it behooveth these things to be done, but not yet anon (or at once) *is* the end, [or for it behooveth

that these things be done, but the end *is* not yet].

8   For folk shall rise on folk, and realm on realm, and earth-movings and hunger shall be by places; these things *shall be* (but the) beginnings of (the) sorrows.

9   But see ye yourselves, for they shall take you in (to) councils, and ye shall be beaten in synagogues; and ye shall stand before kings and doomsmen (or judges) for me, in witnessing to them (or to give a testimony to them).

10   And it behooveth, that the gospel be first preached among all folk. (But it behooveth, that the Gospel or the Good News, first be preached to all the nations and all the peoples.)

11   And when they take you, and lead you forth, do not ye before-think what ye shall speak, but speak ye that thing that shall be given to you in that hour; for ye be not the speakers [or soothly ye be not speaking], but the Holy Ghost (or the Holy Spirit).

12   For the brother shall betake the brother into death [or Forsooth a brother shall betray a brother into death], and the father the son, and sons shall rise together against fathers and mothers, and punish them by death.

13   And ye shall be in hate to all men for my name; but he that lasteth into the end, shall be safe. [+And ye shall be in hatred to all men for my name; but he that shall sustain into the end, shall be safe.] (And ye shall be hated by everyone because of my name; but he who lasteth unto the end, shall be saved.)

14   But when ye shall see the abomination of discomfort, standing where it oweth not (or standing where it ought not to be); he that readeth (this), understand (it); then they that be in Judea, flee to the mountains.

15   And he that is above in the roof (or And he who is above on the roof), come not down into the house, neither enter he, to take anything (out) of his house;

16   and he that shall be in the field, turn not again behind to take his cloth. (and he who is in the field, do not return to get his cloak.)

17 But woe to them that be with child, and nourishing [or nursing] in those days.

18 Therefore pray ye, that those things, [or that your fleeing], (or that your flying), be not done in winter.

19 But those days of tribulation shall be such, (in) which manner were not from the beginning of creature(s), (or in which manner were never so since the beginning of Creation), which God hath made, till now, neither shall be.

20 And but the Lord had abridged those days, all flesh, [or (all) *mankind*], had not be safe, (or And if the Lord had not shortened those days, no one could be saved); but for the chosen which he chose, the Lord hath made short the days.

21 And then if any man say to you, Lo! here is Christ, (or Behold, here is the Messiah), lo! there, believe ye not.

22 For false Christs and false prophets shall rise, and shall give tokens [or signs] and wonders, to deceive, if it may be done, yea, them that be chosen, [or yea, the chosen]. (For false messiahs and false prophets shall arise, and shall make miracles and wonders, to deceive, yes, God's chosen, if it can be done.)

23 Therefore take ye keep, (or And so be on guard, or take heed); lo! I have before-said to you all things.

24 But in those days, after that tribulation, the sun shall be made dark, and the moon shall not give her light,

25 and the stars of heaven shall fall down, and the virtues that be in (the) heavens shall be moved. (and the stars of the heavens shall fall down, and the powers that be in the heavens shall be shaken.)

26 And then they shall see man's Son coming in the clouds of (the) heaven(s), with great virtue (or with great power) and glory.

27 And then he shall send his angels, and shall gather his chosen from the four winds, from the highest thing of earth till to the highest thing of heaven [or from the lowest thing of earth unto the highest thing of heaven].

28 But of the fig tree learn ye the parable. When now his branch is tender, and (its) leaves be sprung out, ye know that summer is nigh.

29 So when ye see these things be done, know ye, that it is nigh in the doors, (or that it is near, right at the door).

30 Truly I say to you (or I tell you the truth), that this generation shall not pass away, till all these things be done.

31 Heaven and earth shall pass (away), but my words shall not pass (away).

32 But of that day or hour no man knoweth, neither (the) angels in heaven, neither the Son, but the Father.

33 See ye, wake ye, and pray ye, (or Look, be on watch, or stay awake, and pray); for ye know not, when the time is.

34 For as a man that is gone far in pilgrimage, left his house, and gave to his servants power of every work, and commanded to the porter, that he [should] wake. (For it is like a man who left his house, and went far away on a journey, and who gave his servants authority to do their work, and commanded to the porter, that he should be on watch or stay awake.)

35 Therefore wake ye, (or And so be on watch, or stay awake), for ye know not, when the lord of the house cometh, in the eventide, or at midnight, or at cock's crowing, or in the morning;

36 lest when he come suddenly, he find you sleeping.

37 Forsooth that that I say to you, I say to all, Wake ye, (or Be on watch, or Stay awake).

CHAPTER 14

1 Pask and the feast of therf loaves was after two days (or Passover and the Feast of Unleavened Bread was two days off). And the high priests and the scribes sought, how they should (take) hold (of) him with guile, and slay [him].

2   But they said, Not in the feast day, lest peradventure a noise were made among the people. (But they said, Not on the Feast Day, lest a commotion was made among the people.)

3   And when he was at Bethany, in the house of Simon leprous, and rested, [or and sat at the meat], (or and sat at the meal), a woman came, that had a box of alabaster of precious ointment spikenard; and when the box of alabaster was broken, she poured it on his head.

4   But there were some that bare it heavily within themselves, and said, Whereto is this loss of ointment made?

5   For this ointment might have been sold for more than three hundred pence, and be given to poor men. And they grudged against her (or And they grumbled against her).

6   But Jesus said, Suffer ye her; what be ye heavy to her? she hath wrought a good work in me. (But Jesus said, Allow her to do this; why be so harsh to her? she hath done a good thing for me.)

7   For evermore ye shall have poor men with you, and when ye will, ye may do well to them; but ye shall not (for)evermore have me. (Ye shall always have the poor with you, and when ye desire, ye can do good things for them; but ye shall not always have me.)

8   She did that that she had (to); she came before to anoint my body into burying (or she came beforehand to anoint my body for burial).

9   Truly I say to you, wherever this gospel shall be preached in all the world, and that that this *woman* hath done, shall be told into mind of him [or shall be told into mind of her]. (I tell you the truth, wherever this gospel shall be preached in all the world, that which this *woman* hath done, shall be told in remembrance of her.)

10   And Judas Iscariot, one of the twelve, went to the high priests, to betray him to them.

11   And they heard, and joyed, and promised to give him money. And he sought how he should betray him covenably (or opportunely).

12   And the first day of therf loaves, when they offered (the) pask, the disciples said to him, Whither wilt thou that we go, and make ready to thee, that thou eat the pask? (And the first Day of Unleavened Bread, when they slew the Passover lambs, the disciples said to him, Where desirest thou that we go, and prepare for thee, so that thou can eat the Passover?)

13   And he sendeth two of his disciples, and saith to them, Go ye into the city, and a man bearing a gallon of water shall meet you; (pur)sue ye him (or follow him).

14   And whither ever he entereth, say ye to the lord of the house, That the master saith, Where is mine eating place, where I shall eat (the) pask with my disciples? (And wherever he entereth, say ye to the master of the house, The Teacher saith, Where is my eating place, where I can eat the Passover with my disciples?)

15   And he shall show to you a great supping place arrayed, and there make ye ready to us (or and there prepare it for us).

16   And his disciples went forth, and came into the city, and found as he had said to them; and they made ready the pask (or and they prepared the Passover).

17   And when the eventide was come, he came with the twelve.

18   And when they sat at the meat, and ate, Jesus said, Truly I say to you, that one of you that eateth with me, shall betray me. (And when they sat at the meal, and ate, Jesus said, I tell you the truth, that one of you who eateth with me, shall betray me.)

19   And they began to be sorry, [or to be sorrowful], (or to be grieved), and to say to him, each by themselves, Whether I?

20   Which said to them, One of the twelve that putteth [in] *his* hand with me in the platter.

21   And soothly man's Son goeth, as it is written of him; but woe to that man, by whom man's Son shall be betrayed. It were good to him (or It would be better for him), if that man had not been born.

22   And while they ate, Jesus took bread, and blessed (or and gave thanks), and brake [it], and gave (it) to them, and said, Take ye; this is my body.

23   And when he had taken the cup, he did thankings (or he gave thanks), and gave (it) to them, and all drank thereof.

24   And he said to them, This is my blood of the new testament (or This is my blood of the new covenant), which shall be shed for many.

25   Truly I say to you (or I tell you the truth), for now I shall not drink of this fruit of the vine, into that day when I shall drink it (a)new in the realm of God.

26   And when the hymn was said, they went out into the hill of Olives. (And after the hymn was sung, they went out to the Mount of Olives.)

27   And Jesus said to them, All ye shall be caused to stumble in me in this night; for it is written, I shall smite the shepherd, and the sheep of the flock shall be scattered.

28   But after that I shall rise again, I shall go before you into Galilee.

29   And Peter said to him, Though all shall be caused to stumble, but not I.

30   And Jesus said to him, Truly I say to thee (or I tell you the truth), that today before that the cock in this night crow twice, thou shalt thrice deny me. [+And Jesus saith to him, Truly I say to thee, for today before that the cock crow twice in this night, thrice thou shalt deny me.]

31   But he said more, Though it behoove, that I die together with thee, I shall not forsake thee, [or And he spake more, Though it shall behoove me to die together with thee, I shall not deny thee]. And in like manner (they) all said (the same thing).

32   And they came into a place, whose name is Gethsemane. And he said to his disciples, Sit ye here, while I pray.

33   And he took Peter and James and John with him, and began to dread, and to be distressed, [or to be heavy], (or and began to have fear, and to be grieved).

34   And he said to them, My soul is sorrowful [till] to the death; abide ye here, and wake ye with me, (or wait here, and keep watch with me, or wait here, and stay awake).

35   And when he was gone forth a little, he felled down on the earth (or he fell down on the ground), and prayed, that if it might be, that the hour should pass from him.

36   And he said, Abba, Father, all things be possible to thee, bear over from me this cup [or turn (away) from me this cup]; but not that I will, but that thou *wilt, be done*, (or but nevertheless not what I desire, or what I want, but what thou *desirest*, or what thou *wantest to be done, be done*).

37   And he came (back), and found them sleeping. And he said to Peter, Simon, sleepest thou? mightest thou not wake with me one hour? (or could thou not keep watch with me, or stay awake with me, for one hour?)

38   Wake ye, and pray ye, that ye enter not into temptation; for the spirit is ready, but the flesh *is* sick. (Be on watch, or Stay awake, and pray, so that ye enter not into the test; for the spirit is ready, but the flesh *is* frail or weak.)

39   And again he went, and prayed, and said the same word(s);

40   and he turned again (or and he returned), and again found them sleeping; for their eyes were heavied. And they knew not, what they should answer to him.

41   And he came the third time, and said to them, Sleep ye now, and rest ye; it sufficeth. The hour is come; lo! man's Son shall be betrayed into the hands of sinful men.

42   Rise ye, go we; lo! he that shall betray me is nigh.

43   And yet while he spake, Judas Iscariot, one of the twelve, came, and with him much people with swords and staves, (or clubs), sent from the high priests, and the scribes, and from the elder men.

44   And his traitor had given to them a token [or a sign], and said, Whomever I kiss, he it is;

hold ye him, and lead ye him (away) warily.

45   And when he came, anon he came to him, and said, Master; and he kissed him. (And when he came, he came up to him at once, and said, Teacher; and he kissed him.)

46   And they laid hands on him, and held him.

47   But one of the men that stood about, drew out a sword, and smote the servant of the highest priest (or and struck the servant of the High Priest), and cut off his ear.

48   And Jesus answered, and said to them, As to a thief ye have gone out with swords and staves, to take (hold of) me? (And Jesus answered, and said to them, Like for a thief ye have gone out with swords and bats, or clubs, to seize me?)

49   Day by day I was among you, and taught in the temple, and ye held not me (or and ye did not seize me then); (no) but that the scriptures be fulfilled.

50   Then all his disciples forsook him, and fled.

51   But a young man, clothed with (a) linen cloth on the bare, (pur)sued him; and they held him. (But a young man, clothed only with a linen cloak, followed him; and they also held onto him.)

52   And he left the linen clothing, and flew naked away from them. [And the linen cloth forsaken, he naked fled away from them.] (And he left the linen cloak, and fled away from them naked.)

53   And they led Jesus to the highest priest (or And they led Jesus to the High Priest). And all the priests and scribes and elder men came together.

54   But Peter (pur)sued him afar into the hall of the highest priest (or But Peter followed him from afar into the courtyard of the High Priest). And he sat with the servants, and warmed him(self) at the fire.

55   And the highest priests, and all the council, sought witnessing against Jesus to (be)take him to the death; but they found not.

(And the high priests, and all the council, sought testimony against Jesus to deliver him unto death; but they could not find any.)

56   For many said false witnessing against him, and the witnessings were not covenable. (For many said false testimony against him, but their testimonies were not suitable, or were not in agreement.)

57   And some rose up, and bare false witnessing against him, and said, (And some rose up, and gave false testimony against him, and said,)

58   For we heard him saying, I shall undo this temple made with hands (or I shall destroy this Temple made with *human* hands), and after the third day [or and by the third day], I shall build another not made with (*human*) hands.

59   And the witnessing of them was not covenable. (But their testimony was not suitable, or was not in agreement.)

60   And the highest priest rose up into the middle [or into the midst], and asked Jesus, and said, Answerest thou nothing to those things that be put against thee of these [men]? (And the High Priest rose up into the midst, and asked Jesus, Answerest thou nothing to those things that be put against thee by these men?)

61   But he was still, and answered nothing. Again the highest priest asked him, and said to him, Art thou Christ, the Son of the blessed God? (or Again the High Priest asked him, Art thou the Messiah, the Son of the blessed God?)

62   And Jesus said to him, I am; and ye shall see man's Son sitting on the right half of the virtue of God, and coming in the clouds of heaven. (And Jesus said to him, I am; and ye shall see man's Son sitting at the right hand, or on the right side, of the power of God, and coming with the clouds of the heavens.)

63   And the highest priest rent his clothes, and said, What yet desire we witnesses? (And the High Priest tore his clothes, and said, Why do we still desire more witnesses?)

64   Ye have heard blasphemy. What seemeth

to you? And they all condemned him to be guilty of death.

65 And some began to bespit him, and to cover his face, and to smite him with buffets, and to say to him, Declare thou, [or And some began to spit on him, and to hide his face, and smite him with buffets, and say to him, Prophesy thou]. And the ministers beat him with strokes (or And the servants beat him with strikes of their hands, or with their fists).

66 And when Peter was in the hall beneath, one of the damsels [or one of the handmaidens] of the highest priest came. (And while Peter was still below in the courtyard, one of the High Priest's handmaids or servantesses came by.)

67 And when she had seen Peter warming him(self), she beheld him, and said, And thou were with Jesus of Nazareth.

68 And he denied, and said, Neither I know, neither I know, what thou sayest. And he went withoutforth before the hall; and anon the cock crew (or And then he went out of the courtyard; and at once the cock crowed).

69 And again when another damsel [or another handmaiden] had seen him, she began to say to men that stood about, That this is of them (or This man is one of them).

70 And he again denied. And after a little, again they that stood nigh, said to Peter, Verily, thou art of them, (or Truly, thou art one of them), for thou art of Galilee also.

71 But he began to curse and to swear, For I know not this man, of whom ye say.

72 And anon again the cock crew (or And at once the cock crowed again). And Peter bethought on the word(s) that Jesus had said to him, Before (that) the cock crow twice, thrice thou shalt deny me. And he began to weep.

CHAPTER 15

1 And anon in the morrowtide the high priests made a counsel with the elder men, and the scribes, and with all the council, and bound Jesus and led, and betook him to Pilate. (And at once when morning came, or early in the morning, the high priests made a plan with the elders, and the scribes, and with all the council, and bound Jesus and led him away, and delivered him to Pilate.)

2 And Pilate asked him, Art thou king of Jews? (or Art thou the King of the Jews?) And Jesus answered, and said to him, Thou sayest.

3 And the high priests accused him in many things. (And the high priests accused him of many things.)

4 But Pilate again asked him (or But Pilate asked him again), and said, Answerest thou nothing? Seest thou in how many things they accuse thee?

5 But Jesus answered no[thing] more, so that Pilate wondered.

6 But by the feast day he was wont to leave to them, one of the men bound [or one of the prisoners], whomever they asked. (But on the Feast Day his custom was to let go, or to release, to them, one of the prisoners, whomever they asked for.)

7 And there was one that was said Barabbas, that was bound with men of dissension, that had done manslaughter in [the] sedition.

8 And when the people was gone up, he began to pray (them), as he (for)evermore did to them. (And when the people had gathered, they began to beseech him, to do as he always did for them.)

9 And Pilate answered to them, and said, Will ye that I leave to you the king of Jews? (And Pilate answered to them, Do ye desire that I let go, or that I release, the King of the Jews to you?)

10 For he knew, that the high priests had taken him by envy.

11 But the bishops stirred [or excited] the people, that he should rather leave to them Barabbas. (But the high priests stirred up, or excited, the people, so that rather he would let go, or release, Barabbas to them.)

12   And again Pilate answered, and said to them, What then will ye that I shall do to the king of Jews? (And again Pilate asked them, Then what do ye want me to do with the King of the Jews?)

13   And they again cried, Crucify him, [*that is, put him on the cross*].

14   But Pilate said to them, What evil hath he done? And they cried the more, Crucify him.

15   And Pilate, willing to make satisfaction to the people, (or desiring to fulfill the will of the people), left to them Barabbas, (or let go, or released, Barabbas to them), and he betook to them Jesus, beaten with scourges, to be crucified.

16   And (the) knights led him withinforth, into the porch of the moot hall. And they called together all the company of (the) knights, (And the soldiers led him outside, into the courtyard of the Hall of Judgement. And they called together all the company of the soldiers,)

17   and they clothed him with purple. And they wreathed a crown of thorns, and put (it) on him.

18   And they began to greet him, *and said,* Hail, king of Jews, (or Hail, King of the Jews).

19   And they smote his head with a reed, and bespat him [or and spat on him]; and (then) they kneeled, and (mockingly) worshipped him.

20   And after that they had scorned him, they unclothed him of the purple, and clothed him with his clothes, and led out him, to crucify him, (or and led him away, to crucify him).

21   And they compelled a man that passed by the way, that came from the town, Simon of Cyrene, the father of Alexander and of Rufus, to bear his cross.

22   And they led him into a place (called) Golgotha [or And they led him into the place of Golgotha], that is to say, the place of Calvary.

23   And they gave to him to drink wine meddled (or mixed) with myrrh [or And they gave him for to drink wine meddled (or mixed) with myrrh], and he took (it) not (or but he would not drink it).

24   And they crucified him, and parted his clothes, and cast lot(s) on those, who should take what. (And they crucified him, and divided his clothes, and threw dice for them, for who should take what.)

25   And it was the third hour (or about nine o'clock in the morning), and they crucified him.

26   And the title of his cause was written, King of Jews. (And the charge against him was written out above him, The King of the Jews.)

27   And they crucified with him two thieves, one at the right half, and one at his left half, [or one on his right half, and one on his left half], (or one on his right side, and one on his left side).

28   And the scripture was fulfilled that saith, And he is ordained with wicked men [or And he is areckoned with wicked men].

29   And as they passed forth, they blasphemed him, moving their heads, and saying, Vath! [or Fie!] thou that destroyest the temple of God, and in three days buildest it again;

30   come adown from the cross, and make thyself safe (or and save thyself).

31   Also the high priests scorned him each to (the) other, with the scribes, and said, He hath made other men safe, (but) he may not save himself. (And the high priests scorned him one to another, along with the scribes, saying, He hath saved other men, but he cannot save himself.)

32   Christ, [the] king of Israel, come down now from the cross, that we see (it), and believe, (or Messiah, King of Israel, come down now from the cross, so that we can see it, and believe). And they that were crucified with him, despised him, [or And they that were crucified with him, put false reproof to him].

33   And when the sixth hour was come, darknesses were made on all the earth, till into the ninth hour. (And when it was almost noon, darkness was made upon all the land, and it

continued until three o'clock.)

34 And in the ninth hour (or And at three o'clock in the afternoon), Jesus cried with a great voice, and said, Eloi, Eloi, lama sabachthani, that is to say, My God, my God, why hast thou forsaken me?

35 And some of the men that stood about heard, and said, Lo! he calleth Elias, (or Behold, he calleth Elijah).

36 And one ran, and filled a sponge with vinegar, and putted (it) about to a reed, and gave (it to) him to drink, and said, Suffer ye, see we, if Elias (or if Elijah) come to do him down.

37 And Jesus gave out a great cry, and died [or sent out the spirit].

38 And the veil of the temple was rent [or was cut], atwo, from the highest to beneath. (And the veil of the Temple was torn in two, from the top to the bottom.)

39 But the centurion that stood over against saw, that he so crying had died, and he said, Verily, this man was God's Son, [or Verily, this man was the Son of God]. (And the centurion, who stood opposite him, saw that after he crying out so had died, and he said, Truly, this man was the Son of God.)

40 And there were also women beholding from afar, among whom was Mary Magdalene, and Mary, the mother of James the less, and of Joseph, and of Salome [or and Salome].

41 And when Jesus was in Galilee, they followed him, and ministered to him (or and served him), and many other *women*, that came up together with him to Jerusalem.

42 And when the eventide was come, for it was the eventide that is before the sabbath, (And when it was evening, and so the day before the Sabbath,)

43 Joseph of Arimathaea, the noble decurion, came, and he abode the realm of God (or and he was waiting for the Kingdom of God); and boldly he entered to Pilate, and asked (for) the body of Jesus.

44 But Pilate wondered, if he were now dead. And when the centurion was called, he asked him, if he were [now] dead; (But Pilate wondered, if he was already dead. And when the centurion was called, he asked him, if he was already dead;)

45 and when he knew of the centurion, he granted the body of Jesus to Joseph [or he gave the body of Jesus to Joseph]. (and when he knew this from the centurion, he gave Joseph permission to take down Jesus' body.)

46 And Joseph bought linen cloth [or (a) sendal], and took him down, and wrapped [him] in the linen cloth, and laid him in a sepulchre that was hewn of a stone [or and put him in a new sepulchre that was hewn in a stone], and wallowed a stone to the door of the sepulchre (or and rolled a stone against the door of the tomb).

47 And Mary Magdalene and Mary of Joseph beheld, where he was laid.

CHAPTER 16

1 And when the sabbath was passed, Mary Magdalene, and Mary of James, and Salome bought sweet smelling ointments, to come and to anoint Jesus.

2 And full early in one in one of the week days (or And very early on the first day of the week), they came to the sepulchre, when the sun was risen.

3 And they said together, Who shall move away to us the stone from the door of the sepulchre? [or Who shall turn away to us the stone from the door of the sepulchre?] (And as they arrived they said to each other, Who shall move away the stone from the door of the tomb for us? For the stone was very large and very heavy.)

4 And they beheld, and saw the stone wallowed away, for it was full great. (But when they looked, they saw that the stone had already been rolled away.)

5 And they went into the sepulchre, and

saw a youngling, covered with a white stole, sitting at the right half; and they were afeared. (And they went into the tomb, and saw a young person, clothed in a white stole, sitting on the right side; and they were afraid.)

6   Which saith to them, Do not ye dread; ye seek Jesus of Nazareth crucified, (or But he said to them, Do not fear; ye seek Jesus of Nazareth who was crucified); he is risen, he is not here; lo! the place where they laid him.

7   But go ye, and say to his disciples, and to Peter, that he shall go before you into Galilee; there ye shall see him, as he said to you.

8   And they went out, and fled from the sepulchre; for dread and quaking had assailed them [or for dread and trembling had assailed them], and to no man they said anything, for they dreaded. (And they went out, and fled from the tomb; for fear and trembling had assailed them, but they said nothing to anyone, for they were afraid.)

9   And Jesus rose early the first day of the week, and appeared first to Mary Magdalene, from whom he had cast out seven devils (or from whom he had thrown out seven demons).

10   And she went, and told to them that had been with him, *which were* (or who were) wailing and weeping [or mourning and weeping].

11   And they hearing that he lived, and was seen of her (or and was seen by her), believed not.

12   But after these things when twain of them wandered (or were walking), he was showed in another likeness to them going into a town. [+Forsooth after these things, he was showed in another likeness, *or figure*, to twain of them walking and going into a town.]

13   And they went, and told to the others, and neither they believed to them.

14   But after(ward) at the last, when the eleven sat at the meat, Jesus appeared to them,

and reproved the unbelief of them, and the hardness of (their) heart(s), for they believed not to them, that had seen that he was risen from death [or that had seen him to have risen from (the) dead]. (But later, when the Eleven sat at a meal, Jesus appeared to them, and rebuked them for their unbelief, and for the hardness or the stubbornness of their hearts, for they did not believe those, who had seen that he was risen from the dead.)

15   And he said to them, Go ye into all the world, and preach the gospel to each creature. (And he said to them, Go into all the world, and preach the Gospel, or the Good News, to all Creation, or to everyone.)

16   Who that believeth, and is baptized, shall be safe (or shall be saved); but he that believeth not, shall be condemned. [+He that shall believe, and shall be christened, shall be saved; soothly he that shall not believe, shall be damned.]

17   And these tokens [or these signs] shall (pur)sue them, that believe. In my name they shall cast out fiends; they shall speak with new tongues; (And these signs shall follow those who believe. In my name they shall throw out devils and demons; they shall speak in new and strange languages;)

18   they shall do away serpents; and if they drink any venom, [*or* (any) *deadly thing*], it shall not annoy (or shall not harm) them. They shall set their hands on sick men, and they shall wax whole, (or They shall put their hands on the sick, and they shall grow whole, or they shall be healed).

19   And the Lord Jesus, after he had spoken to them, was taken up into heaven, and he sitteth on the right half of God (or and he sitteth at the right hand, or on the right side, of God).

20   And they went forth, and preached everywhere, for the Lord wrought [or working] with them, and confirmed the word with signs, [*either miracles*], following. †

LUKE

CHAPTER 1

[1   Forsooth for many men enforced to ordain the telling of things, which be filled in us, (Because many men endeavoured to order the telling of things, which happened among us,)

2   as they that saw at the beginning, and were ministers of the word, betaken, (as they who saw it from the beginning, and were servants of the word, that was delivered,)

3   it is seen also to me, having from the beginning all things diligently by order, to write to thee, thou best Theophilus, (it is seen also by me, having put all things diligently in order from the beginning, to write to thee, O most excellent Theophilus,)

4   (so) that thou know the truth of those words, of which thou art learned.]¹

5   In the days of Herod, (the) king of Judea, there was a priest, Zacharias by name (or called Zechariah), of the sort of Abia, and his wife *was* of the daughters of Aaron, and her name *was* Elisabeth.

6   And both were just before God (or And both were good and righteous before God), going in all the commandments and justifyings of the Lord, without (com)plaint.

7   And they had no child, for Elisabeth was barren, and both were of great age [or had gone far] in their days.

8   And it befell, that when Zacharias should do the office of priesthood, in the order of his course before God, (And it befell, that when Zechariah should do the duties of the priesthood, by the order of his course before God,)

9   after the custom of the priesthood, he went forth by lot, and entered into the temple

[of the Lord], to (offer the) incense.

10   And all the multitude of the people was withoutforth, and prayed in the hour of incensing. (And a great multitude of people were outside, and prayed during the hour of incense.)

11   And an angel of the Lord appeared to him, and stood on the right half of the altar of incense (or and stood on the right side of the altar of incense).

12   And Zacharias seeing (him) was (made) afraid [or was distroubled], and dread fell upon him. (And when Zechariah saw him he was afraid, and fear fell upon him.)

13   And the angel said to him, Zacharias, dread thou not, (or Zechariah, fear not); for thy prayer is heard, and Elisabeth, thy wife, shall bear to thee a son, and his name shall be called John.

14   And joy and gladding shall be to thee; and many shall have joy in his nativity, *or birth*.

15   For he shall be great before the Lord, and he shall not drink wine nor cider, and he shall be full-filled with the Holy Ghost, [or and he shall be filled with the Holy Ghost], (or and he shall be filled with the Holy Spirit), yet from his mother's womb.

16   And he shall convert many of the children of Israel to their Lord God; [And he shall convert many of the sons of Israel to the Lord God of them;]

17   and he shall go before him in the spirit and virtue of Elias (or and he shall go before him in the spirit and in the power of Elijah); and he shall turn the hearts of the fathers into the sons, and men out of belief, [or that believe not], to the prudence of just men (or to the wisdom of the righteous), to make ready a perfect people to the Lord.

18   And Zacharias said to the angel, Whereof shall I know this? for I am old, and my wife hath gone far in her days.

19   And the angel answered, and said to him, For I am Gabriel, that stand nigh before God,

---

¹ These four prefatory verses are only found in two copies of the "Early Version".

(or Yea, I am Gabriel, who standeth near to God); and I am sent to thee to speak, and to evangelize [or to tell] to thee these things.

20   And lo! thou shalt be dumb, and thou shalt not be able to speak till into the day, in which these things shall be done; for thou hast not believed to my words (or for thou hast not believed my words), which shall be fulfilled in their time.

21   And the people was abiding Zacharias (or And the people were waiting for Zechariah), and they wondered, (why) that he tarried (so) in the temple.

22   And he went out, and might not speak to them, and they knew that he had seen a vision in the temple. And he beckoned to them, and dwelled still dumb.

23   And it was done, when the days of his office were fulfilled, he went into his house.

24   And after these days Elisabeth, his wife, conceived, and hid her(self) (for) five months, and said,

25   For so the Lord did to me in the days, in which he beheld, to take away my reproof [or my shame] among men.

26   But in the sixth month the angel Gabriel was sent from God into a city of Galilee, whose name *was* Nazareth,

27   to a maiden [or to a virgin], wedded to a man, whose name was Joseph, of the house of David; and the name of the maiden *was* Mary.

28   And the angel entered to her, and said, Hail, full of grace; the Lord *is* with thee; blessed *be* thou among women.

29   And when she had heard (this), she was troubled in his word (or she was troubled by his words), and thought what manner salutation this was.

30   And the angel said to her, Dread thou not, Mary, (or Fear not, Mary), for thou hast found grace with God.

31   Lo! thou shalt conceive in [the] womb, and shalt bear a son, and thou shalt call his name Jesus.

32   This shall be great [or He shall be great], and he shall be called the Son of the Highest; and the Lord God shall give to him the seat of David, his father, (or and the Lord God shall give him the throne of his father David),

33   and he shall reign in the house of Jacob [into] without end, and of his realm shall be none end (or and there shall be no end to his Kingdom).

34   And Mary said to the angel, On what manner shall this thing be done, for I know not (a) man? or for I know no man?

35   And the angel answered, and said to her, The Holy Ghost shall come from above into thee, and the virtue of the Highest shall overshadow thee, (or The Holy Spirit shall come from above upon thee, and the power of the Highest shall overshadow thee); and therefore that holy thing that shall be born of thee, shall be called the Son of God.

36   And lo! Elisabeth, thy cousin, and she also hath conceived a son in her old (age), and this month is the sixth to her that is called barren;

37   for every word shall not be impossible with God. (for nothing is impossible with God.)

38   And Mary said, Lo! the handmaid of the Lord or Lo! the handmaiden of the Lord; be it done to me after thy word. And the angel departed from her.

39   And Mary rose up in those days, and went with haste into the mountains [or into the hilly places], into a city of Judea.

40   And she entered into the house of Zacharias, and greeted Elisabeth.

41   And it was done, as Elisabeth heard the salutation of Mary, the young child in her womb gladded. And Elisabeth was full-filled with the Holy Ghost, [or And Elisabeth was filled with the Holy Ghost], (or And Elisabeth was filled with the Holy Spirit),

42   and cried with a great voice (or and cried with a loud voice), and said, Blessed *be* thou among women, and blessed *be* the fruit of thy womb.

43 And whereof *is* this thing to me, that the mother of my Lord come to me?

44 For lo! as the voice of thy salutation was made in mine ears, the young child gladded in joy in my womb [or the young child gladded with joy in my womb].

45 And blessed be thou, that hast believed, for those things that be said of the Lord to thee, shall be perfectly done. [And blessed be thou, that hast believed, for those things that be said to thee from the Lord, shall be perfectly done.]

46 And Mary said, My soul magnifieth the Lord,

47 and my spirit hath gladded in God, mine health [or mine health-giver]. (and my spirit hath rejoiced in God, my salvation.)

48 For he hath beheld the meekness of his handmaid or the meekness of his handmaiden. For lo! (because) of this all generations shall say that I am blessed, [or Lo! forsooth of this (or because of this) all generations shall say me blessed].

49 For he that is mighty hath done to me great things, and his name *is* holy.

50 And his mercy is from kindred into kindreds, to men that dread him (or to those who have fearful reverence for him).

51 He made might in his arm, he scattered proud men with the thought of his heart.

52 He put down mighty men from *their* seats, and enhanced meek men. (He brought down the mighty from *their* thrones, and exalted, or raised, up the humble.)

53 He hath full-filled hungry men with goods [or He hath filled hungry men with good things], and he hath left rich men void.

54 He, having mind of his mercy, took Israel, his child; (He, remembering his kindness, helped his servant Israel;)

55 as he hath spoken to our fathers, to Abraham and to his seed, into worlds (or forever).

56 And Mary dwelled with her, as it were three months, and turned again into her house.

(And Mary remained with her for three months, and then returned to her house.)

57 But the time of bearing child was fulfilled to Elisabeth, and she bare a son.

58 And the neighbours and the cousins of her heard, that the Lord had magnified his mercy with her; and they thanked him [or and they together joyed to her, (or with her)].

59 And it was done in the eighth day, they came to circumcise the child; and they called him Zacharias, by the name of his father. (And it was done on the eighth day, they came to circumcise the child; and they called him Zechariah, after his father's name.)

60 And his mother answered, and said, Nay, but he shall be called John.

61 And they said to her, For no man is in thy kindred, that is called [by] this name.

62 And they beckoned to his father, what he would that he were called (or what he wanted him to be called).

63 And he asking (for) a pointel (or And he asking for a stylus), wrote, saying, John is his name. And all men wondered.

64 And anon his mouth was opened, and his tongue, and he spake, and blessed God. (And at once his mouth was opened, and his tongue, and he spoke, and blessed God.)

65 And dread was made on all their neighbours (or And all their neighbours were filled with fearful reverence), and all these words were published on all the mountains [or on all the hilly places] of Judea.

66 And all men that heard putted (it) in their heart(s), and said, What manner child shall this be? For the hand of the Lord was with him.

67 And Zacharias, his father, was full-filled with the Holy Ghost [or was filled with the Holy Ghost], and prophesied, and said, (And his father Zechariah was filled with the Holy Spirit, and he prophesied, and said,)

68 Blessed *be* the Lord God of Israel, for he hath visited, and made redemption of his people (or and made redemption for his

people).

69   And he hath raised to us an horn of health, in the house of David, his child. (He hath raised up for us a Deliverer of salvation, in the house of his servant David.)

70   As he spake by the mouth of his holy prophets, that were from the world. (As he spoke by the mouths of his holy prophets, who lived long ago.)

71   Health from our enemies (or Salvation or Deliverance from our enemies), and from the hand(s) of all (the) men that hated us.

72   To do mercy with our fathers, and to have mind of his holy testament. (To give mercy to our fathers, and to remember his holy covenant.)

73   The great oath that he swore to Abraham, our father,

74   to give himself to us. That we without dread, delivered from the hand of our enemies, serve to him, [to give himself to us. That we delivered from the hand of our enemies, serve to him without dread (or without fear),] (to give himself to us. That we now, without any fear, having been delivered from the hand of our enemies, serve him,)

75   in holiness and rightwiseness before him in all our days.

76   And thou, child, shalt be called the prophet of the Highest; for thou shalt go before the face of the Lord, to make ready his ways (or to prepare his way).

77   To give science of health to his people, into remission of their sins; (To give the knowledge of salvation to his people, by the forgiveness of their sins;)

78   by the inwardness of the mercy of our God, in the which he springing up from on high hath visited us.

79   To give light to them that sit in darknesses, and in the shadow of death; to (ad)dress our feet into the way of peace. (To give light to those who sit in darkness, and in the shadow of death; to direct our feet in the way of peace.)

80   And the child waxed, and was comforted in spirit, and was in desert places unto the day of his showing to Israel. (And the child grew, and was strengthened in spirit, and lived in the desert until the day of his first appearance before Israel.)

CHAPTER 2

1   And it was done in those days, a commandment went out from the emperor Augustus [or a commandment went out from Caesar Augustus], that all the world should be described (or that a census should be taken throughout the Empire).

2   This first describing was made of Cyrenius, (the) justice, [or (the) keeper], of Syria. (This first census was made when Quirinius was the Governor of Syria.)

3   And all men went to make profession, [or acknowledging], each into his own city.

4   And Joseph went up from Galilee, from the city [of] Nazareth, into Judea, into a city of David, that is called Bethlehem, for that he was of the house and of the family of David,

5   (so) that he should acknowledge with Mary, his wife, that was wedded to him, and was great with child.

6   And it was done, while they were there, the days were fulfilled, that she should bear (the) child.

7   And she bare her first-born son, and wrapped him in 'clothes, and laid him in a cratch, for there was no place to him in no chamber. (And she bare her first-born son, and wrapped him in swaddling clothes, and laid him in a feed-trough, for there was no place for him in any room.)

8   And shepherds were in the same country, waking and keeping the watches of the night on their flock. (And shepherds were there in the countryside, awake and keeping the night watch over their flocks.)

9   And lo! the angel of the Lord stood beside

LUKE

them, and the clearness of God shined about them; and they dreaded with great dread. (And behold, the angel of the Lord stood beside them, and the glory of God shone about them; and they feared with a great fear.)

10 And the angel said to them, Do not ye dread; for lo! I preach to you a great joy, that shall be to all people. (And the angel said to them, Do not fear; for behold, I preach to you a great joy, that shall be for all people.)

11 For a Saviour is born today to you, that is Christ the Lord (or who is the Messiah the Lord), in the city of David.

12 And this *is* a token to you; ye shall find a young child wrapped in 'clothes, and laid in a cratch. (And this *is* a sign for you; ye shall find a young child wrapped in swaddling clothes, and laid in a feed-trough.)

13 And suddenly there was made with the angel a multitude of heavenly knighthood, praising God, and saying, (And suddenly there was made with the angel a multitude of heavenly host, praising God, and saying,)

14 Glory *be* in the highest things to God, and in earth peace to men of good will. (Glory *be* to God in the highest place, and on earth peace to men of good will.)

15 And it was done, as the angels passed away from them into heaven, the shepherds spake together, and said, Go we over to Bethlehem, and see we this word that is made, which the Lord hath made, and showed to us.

16 And they hieing came, and found Mary and Joseph, and the young child laid in a cratch (or and the young child laid in a feed-trough).

17 And they seeing, knew of the word that was said to them of this child.

18 And all men that heard wondered, and of these things that were said to them of the shepherds. (And everyone who heard about it, wondered about these things that were told to them by the shepherds.)

19 But Mary kept all these words, bearing (them) together in her heart.

20 And the shepherds turned again, glorifying and praising God in all things that they had heard and seen, as it was said to them. (And the shepherds returned home, glorifying and praising God for all the things which they had heard and seen, as it was said to them.)

21 And after that eight days were ended, that the child should be circumcised, his name was called Jesus, which (name he) was called of the angel (or which name he was called by the angel), before that he was conceived in the womb.

22 And after that the days of the purification of Mary were fulfilled, after Moses' law, they took him into Jerusalem, to offer him to the Lord,

23 as it is written in the law of the Lord, For every male-kind opening the womb, shall be called holy to the Lord;

24 and that they shall give an offering, after that it is said in the law of the Lord, A pair of turtles, or two culver birds, (or A pair of turtledoves, or two young pigeons).

25 And lo! a man was in Jerusalem, whose name *was* Simeon; and this man *was* just, and virtuous [or dread-full], and abode the comfort of Israel; and the Holy Ghost was in him. (And behold, there was a man in Jerusalem, whose name *was* Simeon; and this man *was* righteous, and virtuous, or full of reverence, and awaited the strengthening of Israel; and the Holy Spirit was in him.)

26 And he had taken an answer of the Holy Ghost, that he should not see death, [no] but he saw first the Christ of the Lord. (And he had received an answer from the Holy Spirit, that he would not see death, until he had seen the Messiah of the Lord.)

27 And he came in (the) Spirit into the temple (or And directed by the Spirit he came to the Temple). And when his father and mother led [in] the child Jesus to do after the custom of the law for him,

28 he took him into his arms, and blessed

God, and said,

29   Lord, now thou leavest thy servant after thy word in peace; (Lord, now thou lettest thy servant go or to depart in peace, according to thy word;)

30   for mine eyes have seen thine health, (for my eyes have seen thy salvation or thy deliverance,)

31   which thou hast made ready before the face of all (the) peoples;

32   light to the showing of heathen men, and (the) glory of thy people Israel. (light for the showing to the Gentiles, and glory to thy people Israel.)

33   And his father and his mother were wondering on these things, that were said of him (or that were said about their son).

34   And Simeon blessed them, and said to Mary, his mother, Lo! this (child) is set into the falling down and into the rising again of many men in Israel, and into a token, to whom it shall be against-said, (or and as a sign, to which it shall be said against, or which shall be rejected).

35   And a sword shall pass through thine own soul, (so) that the thoughts be showed of many hearts.

36   And Anna was a prophetess, the daughter of Phanuel, of the lineage of Aser. And she had gone forth in many days, and had lived with her husband seven years from her maidenhood.

37   And this (woman) was a widow to fourscore years and four; and she departed not from the temple, but served *God* night and day in fastings and prayers.

38   And this (woman) came upon them in that hour, and acknowledged to the Lord, and spake of him to all that abided the redemption of Israel. (And she came upon them at that time, and thanked the Lord, and spoke about him to all who waited for Israel's redemption.)

39   And as they had full done all things [or And as they had perfectly done all things], after the law of the Lord, they turned again into Galilee, into their city Nazareth, (or they returned to Galilee, to their city of Nazareth).

40   And the child waxed, and was comforted, full of wisdom, (or And the child grew, and was strengthened, and was full of wisdom); and the grace of God was in him.

41   And his father and mother went each year into Jerusalem, in the solemn day of pask. (And his father and mother went each year to Jerusalem, for the Feast Day, or the Festival, of Passover.)

42   And when Jesus was twelve years old, they went up to Jerusalem, after the custom of the feast day.

43   And when the days were done, they turned again (or they returned home); and the child abode in Jerusalem, and his father and mother knew it not.

44   For they guessing that he had been in the fellowship, came a day's journey, and sought him among his cousins and his acknowledged [or and (his) known].

45   And when they found him not, they turned again into Jerusalem, and sought him. (And when they could not find him, they returned to Jerusalem, and searched for him.)

46   And it befell, that after the third day they found him in the temple, sitting in the middle of the doctors, (or the teachers of the Law), hearing them and asking them.

47   And all men that heard him, wondered on the prudence and the answers of him.

48   And they saw (him), and wondered. And his mother said to him, Son, what hast thou done to us thus? (or Son, why hast thou done this to us?) Lo! thy father and I sorrowing have sought thee.

49   And he said to them, What is it that ye sought me? (or Why is it that ye have searched for me?) knew ye not, that in those things that be of my Father, [or knew ye not, that in those things that be my Father's], it behooveth me to be?

50   And they understood not the word, which

he spake to them.

51   And he came down with them, and came to Nazareth, and was subject to them. And his mother kept together all these words, and bare them in her heart.

52   And Jesus profited in wisdom, age, and grace, with God and men. (And Jesus grew in wisdom, age, and grace, with God and men.)

CHAPTER 3

1   In the fifteen year of the empire of Tiberius, the emperor (or Caesar), when Pilate of Pontii (or Pontius Pilate) governed Judea, and Herod *was* (the) prince of Galilee, and Philip, his brother, *was* (the) prince of Ituraea, and of the country of Trachonitis (or and of the province of Trachonitis), and Lysanias *was* (the) prince of Abilene,

2   under the princes of (the) priests, Annas and Caiaphas, the word of the Lord was made on John, the son of Zacharias, in (the) desert. (under the High Priests, Annas and Caiaphas, the word of the Lord came to John, the son of Zechariah, in the desert.)

3   And he came into all the country of (the) Jordan, and preached baptism of penance into remission of sins. (And he came into all the countryside of the Jordan River, and preached the baptism of repentance for the forgiveness of sins.)

4   As it is written in the book of the words of Esaias, the prophet, (or As it is written in the book of the words of the prophet Isaiah), The voice of a crier in (the) desert, [or The voice of *one* crying in (the) desert], Make ye ready the way of the Lord, make ye his paths right.

5   Each valley shall be full-filled, and every hill and little hill shall be made low; and shrewd things shall be into dressed things, and sharp things into plain ways; [Each valley shall be filled, and each mountain and little hill shall be made low; and shrewd things shall be into dressed things, and sharp things into plain

ways;] (Every valley shall be filled full or filled in, and every mountain and little hill shall be made low; and depraved or crooked things shall be made into aligned or straight things, and rugged or rough ways into smooth or flat ways;)

6   and every flesh [or each man] shall see the health of God. (and everyone shall see God's salvation or deliverance.)

7   Therefore he said to the people, which went out to be baptized of him, Kindlings of adders, who showed to you to flee from the wrath to coming? [Therefore he said to the companies, that went out, (so) that they should be baptized of him, Fruits, *or kindlings*, of adders, who showed to you to flee from the wrath to come?] (And so he said to the people, who went out to be baptized by him, Children of snakes, who showed to you to flee from the wrath to come?)

8   Therefore do ye worthy fruits of penance (or And so do ye worthy fruits of repentance), and begin ye not to say, We have a father Abraham; for I say to you, that God is mighty to raise (up out) of these stones the sons of Abraham.

9   And now an ax is set [or is put] to the root of the tree; and therefore every tree that maketh not good fruit, shall be cut down, and shall be cast into the fire.

10   And the people asked him, and said, What then shall we do? (And the people asked him, Then what should we do?)

11   He answered, and said to them, He that hath two coats, give he to him that hath none; and he that hath meats (or and he who hath some food), do in like manner.

12   And [the] publicans came to be baptized; and they said to him, Master, what shall we do? (And the tax-collectors came to be baptized; and they said to him, Teacher, what should we do?)

13   And he said to them, Do ye nothing more, than that that is ordained to you.

14   And [the] knights asked him, and said, What shall also we do? (or And the soldiers asked him, What should we do?) And he said to them, Smite ye wrongfully no man, neither make ye false challenge, and be ye satisfied with your wages.

15   When all the people guessed, and all men thought in their hearts of John, lest peradventure he were Christ (or that perhaps he was the Messiah),

16   John answered, and said to all men, I baptize you in water; but a stronger (One) than I shall come after me, of whom I am not worthy to unbind the lace [or the thong] of his shoes; he shall baptize you in the Holy Ghost and fire (or he shall baptize you with the Holy Spirit and with fire).

17   Whose winnowing tool, or fan, *is* in his hand, and he shall purge his floor of corn, [or and he shall purge his cornfloor], (or and he shall purge his floor of grain, or his threshing floor), and shall gather the wheat into his barn; but the chaff he shall burn with fire unquenchable.

18   And many other things also he spake, and preached to the people. [Forsooth and he stirring, *or admonishing*, many other things, evangelized to the people.]

19   But Herod [the] tetrarch, when he was blamed of John for Herodias (or after he was rebuked by John for wedding Herodias), the wife of his brother, and for all the evils that Herod did,

20   he increased this over all (or he added something even worse), and shut John in prison.

21   And it was done, when all the people was baptized, and when Jesus was baptized, and prayed, heaven was opened (or the heavens were opened).

22   And the Holy Ghost came down in bodily likeness, as a dove on him; and a voice was made from heaven, Thou art my dearworthy Son, in thee it hath well pleased to me. (And the Holy Spirit came down in bodily likeness, like a dove upon him; and a voice was made from heaven, Thou art my dearworthy Son, I am well pleased with thee.)

23   And Jesus himself was beginning as of thirty years, that he was guessed the son of Joseph, which was of Heli,

24   which was of Matthat, which was of Levi, which was of Melchi, that was of Janna, that was of Joseph,

25   that was of Mattathias, that was of Amos, that was of Naum, that was of Esli, that was of Nagge,

26   that was of Maath, that was of Mattathias, that was of Semei, that was of Joseph, that was of Juda,

27   that was of Joanna, that was of Rhesa, that was of Zorobabel, that was of Salathiel, that was of Neri,

28   that was of Melchi, that was of Addi, that was of Cosam, that was of Elmodam, that was of Er,

29   that was of Jose, that was of Eliezer, that was of Jorim, that was of Matthat, that was of Levi,

30   that was of Simeon, that was of Juda, that was of Joseph, that was of Jonan, that was of Eliakim,

31   that was of Melea, that was of Menan, that was of Mattatha, that was of Nathan, that was of David,

32   that was of Jesse, that was of Obed, that was of Booz, that was of Salmon, that was of Naasson,

33   that was of Aminadab, that was of Aram, that was of Esrom, that was of Phares, that was of Juda(h),

34   that was of Jacob, that was of Isaac, that was of Abraham, that was of Thara, that was of Nachor,

35   that was of Saruch, that was of Ragau, that was of Phalec, that was of Heber, that was of Sala,

36   that was of Cainan, that was of Arphaxad,

that was of Sem, that was of Noe, that was of Lamech,

37　that was of Mathusala, that was of Enoch, that was of Jared, that was of Maleleel, that was of Cainan,

38　that was of Enos, that was of Seth, that was of Adam, that was of God.

CHAPTER 4

1　And Jesus full of the Holy Ghost turned again from (the) Jordan, and was led by the Spirit into (the) desert (And Jesus full of the Holy Spirit returned from the Jordan River, and was led by the Spirit into the desert)

2　(for) forty days, and was tempted of the devil (or and was tested by the Devil), and [he] ate nothing in those days; and when those days were ended, he hungered.

3　And the devil said to him, If thou art God's Son, say to this stone, that it be made (into) bread.

4　And Jesus answered to him, It is written, That a man liveth not in bread alone, but in every word of God. (And Jesus answered him, It is written, A man liveth not by bread alone, but by every word from God.)

5　And the devil led him into an high hill, and showed to him all the realms of the world in a moment of time; (And the Devil led him up onto a high mountain, and showed him all the kingdoms of the world in a moment of time;)

6　and said to him, I shall give to thee all this power, and the glory of them, for to me they be given, and to whom I will, I give them; (and said to him, I shall give thee all this power, and their glory, for they have been given to me, and to whom I desire, I give them;)

7　therefore if thou fall down, and worship before me, all (these) things shall be thine.

8　And Jesus answered, and said to him, It is written, Thou shalt worship thy Lord God [or Thou shalt worship the Lord thy God], and to him alone thou shalt serve.

9　And he led him into Jerusalem, and set him on the pinnacle of the temple, and said to him, If thou art God's Son, send thyself from hence down;

10　for it is written, For he hath commanded to his angels of thee, (or For he hath commanded to his angels about thee), that they keep thee (safe) in all thy ways,

11　and that they shall take thee in (their) hands, lest peradventure thou hurt thy foot at [or on] a stone.

12　And Jesus answered, and said to him, It is said, Thou shalt not tempt thy Lord God, [or It is said, Thou shalt not tempt the Lord thy God], (or Thou shalt not test the Lord thy God).

13　And when every temptation was ended, the fiend [or the devil] went away from him for a time. (And when every test was ended, the Devil went away from him for a while.)

14　And Jesus turned again in the virtue of the Spirit into Galilee, and the fame went forth of him through all the country. (And Jesus returned in the power of the Spirit to Galilee, and the story about him went forth throughout all the land.)

15　And he taught in the synagogues of them, and was magnified of all men. (And he taught in their synagogues, and was praised by everyone.)

16　And he came to Nazareth, where he was nourished (or where he grew up), and he entered after his custom in (or on) the sabbath day into a synagogue [or and he entered after his custom in the sabbath day into the synagogue], and rose to read.

17　And the book of Esaias, the prophet, was taken to him; and as he turned the book, he found a place, where it was written, (And the scroll of the prophet Isaiah was given to him; and as he turned the scroll, he found a place, where it was written,)

18　The Spirit of the Lord *is* [up]on me, for which thing he anointed me; he sent me to preach [or to evangelize] to poor men, to heal contrite men in heart, and to preach remission (or a pardon) to (the) prisoners [or to (the) captives], and sight to blind men, and to deliver broken men into remission (or and to give relief to broken men);

19   to preach the year of the Lord pleasant, and the day of yielding again. [to preach the year of the Lord accepted, *or pleasant*, and the day of retribution, *or yielding again.*] (to proclaim the exceptional year of the Lord, yea, the Day of Reward.)

20   And when he had closed the book, he gave [*it*] again to the minister, and sat, (or And when he had rolled up the scroll, he gave *it* back to the priest, and sat down); and the eyes of all men in the synagogue were beholding into him.

21   And he began to say to them, For in this day this scripture is fulfilled in your ears.

22   And all men gave witnessing to him (or And everyone gave good testimony about him), and wondered in the words of grace, that came forth of [or that came out of] his mouth. And they said, Whether this is not the son of Joseph?

23   And he said to them, Soothly ye shall say to me this likeness, Leech, heal thyself, (or Truly, or Surely, ye shall say to me this proverb, Physician, heal thyself). The Pharisees said to Jesus, How (or What) great things have we heard done in Capernaum, do thou also here in thy country.

24   And he said, Truly I say to you, that no prophet is received [or is accepted] in his own country. (And he said, I tell you the truth, no prophet is accepted in his hometown.)

25   In truth I say to you, that many widows were in the days of Elias, the prophet, in Israel, when heaven was closed three years and six months, when great hunger was made in all the earth [or in every land]; (Truly I say to you, or I tell you the truth, that there were many widows in Israel, in the days of the prophet Elijah, when the heavens were closed up for three years and six months, when great hunger was made in

every land;)

26   and to none of them was Elias sent, (no) but into Sarepta of Sidon, to a woman a widow [or no but to Sarepta of Sidon, to a woman widow]. (and to none of them was Elijah sent, except unto Sarepta of Sidon, yea, to a widow woman.)

27   And many mesels were in Israel, under Eliseus, the prophet, and none of them was cleansed, [no] but Naaman of Syria. (And there were many lepers in Israel, at the time of the prophet Elisha, and none of them were cleansed, except for Naaman of Syria.)

28   And all in the synagogue hearing these things, were filled with wrath.

29   And they rose up, and drove him out without the city, and led him to the top of the hill on which their city was builded, to cast him down (or to throw him down).

30   But Jesus passed (forth), and went through the middle of them; (But Jesus passed forth, and went through their midst;)

31   and he came down into Capernaum, a city of Galilee, and there he taught them in (or on) [the] sabbaths.

32   And they were astonied in his teaching, for his word was in power. (And they were astonished with his teaching, for there was power in his words.)

33   And in their synagogue was a man having an unclean fiend, and he cried with (a) great voice, (And in their synagogue was a man who had a devil, or a demon, yea, an unclean spirit, and he cried with a loud voice,)

34   and said, Suffer, what to us and to thee, thou Jesus of Nazareth? art thou come to lose us? (or art thou come to destroy us?) I know thee, that thou art the holy (One) of God.

35   And Jesus blamed him, and said, Wax dumb, and go out from him. And when the fiend had cast him forth into the middle (of them), he went away from him, and he annoyed him nothing. (And Jesus rebuked him, and said, Be still, and go out of him. And when

the demon had thrown him forth into their midst, he went out of him, and he did him no harm.)

36 And dread was made in all men, and they spake together, and said, What is this word, for in power and virtue he commandeth to unclean spirits, and they go out? (And everyone was filled with fearful reverence, and they spoke together, and said, What be these words of his? for in power and with authority he commandeth to unclean spirits, and they go out!)

37 And the fame was published of him into each place of the country. (And the story about him was told in every part of the land.)

38 And Jesus rose up from the synagogue, and entered into the house of Simon; and the mother of Simon's wife was holden with great fevers, and they prayed him for her (or and they beseeched him for her).

39 And Jesus stood over her, and commanded to the fever, and it left her; and anon she rose up (or and at once she got up), and served them.

40 And when the sun went down, all that had sick men with diverse languors, [or aches], led them to him; and he set his hands on each by themselves, and healed them.

41 And fiends went out from many, and cried, and said, For thou art the Son of God. And he blamed, and suffered them not to speak, for they knew him, that he was Christ. (And devils and demons went out from many, and cried, and said, For thou art the Son of God. And he rebuked them, and did not allow them to speak, for they knew him, that he was the Messiah.)

42 And when the day was come, he went out, and went into a desert place; and the people sought him, and they came to him, and they held (onto) him, that he should not go away from them (or so that he would not go away from them).

43 To whom he said, For also to other cities

it behooveth me to preach [or to evangelize] the kingdom of God, for therefore I am sent [or for thereto I am sent].

44 And (so) he preached in the synagogues of Galilee.

CHAPTER 5

1 And it was done, when the people came fast to Jesus, to hear the word of God, he stood beside the pool [or the water] of Gennesaret, (or he stood by Lake Gennesaret, that is, Lake Galilee),

2 and saw two boats standing beside the pool [or (at the edge of) the water]; and the fishers were gone down, and washed their nets, (or and the fishermen had left them, and were washing their nets).

3 And he went up into a boat, that was Simon's, and prayed (or asked) him to lead it a little from the land; and he sat, and taught the people out of the boat.

4 And as he ceased to speak, he said to Simon, Lead out into the depth, and slack ye your nets to take (some) fish.

5 And Simon answered, and said to him, Commander, we travailed all the night, and took nothing, but in thy word I shall lay out the net. (And Simon answered, and said to him, Master, (or Teacher), we laboured all night, and took nothing, but at thy word I shall lay out the net.)

6 And when they had done this thing, they (en)closed together a great multitude of fishes; and their net was broken.

7 And they beckoned to fellows, that were in another boat, that they should come, and help them. And they came, and filled both the boats, so that they were almost drenched (or so that they were almost drowned).

8 And when Simon Peter saw this thing, he felled down to the knees of Jesus, and said, Lord, go (away) from me, for I am a sinful man.

9 For he was on each side astonied (or

astonished), and all that were with him, in the taking of (the) fishes which they took.

10 Soothly in like manner James and John, the sons of Zebedee, that were fellows of Simon Peter. And Jesus said to Simon, Do not thou dread (or Do not fear); now from this time thou shalt take men.

11 And when the boats were led up to the land, they left all things, and they (pur)sued him (or and they followed him).

12 And it was done, when he was in one of the cities, lo! a man full of leprosy; and seeing Jesus (he) fell down on his face, and prayed him (or and beseeched him), and said, Lord, if thou wilt, thou mayest make me clean.

13 And Jesus held forth his hand, and touched him, and said, I will, be thou made clean. And anon the leprosy passed away from him (or And at once the leprosy went away from him).

14 And Jesus commanded to him, that he should say to no man; But go, show thee to a priest, and offer for thy cleansing, as Moses bade, into witnessing to them (or as a testimony to them).

15 And the word walked about the more of him (or And the story about him spread far and wide); and much people came together, to hear, and to be healed of their sicknesses.

16 And he went into (the) desert, and prayed.

17 And it was done in one of the days, he sat, and taught; and there were Pharisees sitting, and doctors of the law, that came of each castle of Galilee, and of Judea, and of Jerusalem; and the virtue of the Lord was to heal sick men. (And it was done on one of the days, he sat, and taught; and there were Pharisees, and teachers of the Law, sitting there, who had come from every village of Galilee, and from Judea, and from Jerusalem; and the power of the Lord was there to heal the sick.)

18 And lo! men bare in a bed a man that was sick in the palsy [or a man that was sick in palsy], (or And behold, men brought in a bed a man who was sick with palsy), and they sought to bear him in, and set (him) before him.

19 And they found not in what part they should bear him in, for the (crowd of) people, and (so) they went upon the roof, and by the slates they let him down with the bed, into the midst, before Jesus.

20 And when Jesus saw the faith of them, he said, Man, thy sins be forgiven to thee.

21 And the scribes and the Pharisees began to think, saying, Who is this, that speaketh blasphemies? who may forgive sins, [no] but God alone?

22 And as Jesus knew the thoughts of them, he answered, and said to them, What think ye evil things in your hearts? (or Why do ye think evil things in your hearts?)

23 What is lighter (or is easier) to say, Sins be forgiven to thee, or to say, Rise up, and walk?

24 But that ye know, that man's Son hath power in earth to forgive sins, he said to the sick man in palsy, (or But so that ye know, that man's Son hath power on the earth to forgive sins, he said to the man sick with palsy), I say to thee, rise up, take thy bed, and go into thine house.

25 And anon he rose up before them (or And at once he got up in front of them), and took the bed in which he lay, and went into his house, and magnified God.

26 And great wonder took all, and they magnified God; and they were full-filled with great dread, [or and they were filled with great dread], (or and they were filled with much fearful reverence), and said, For we have seen marvelous things today.

27 And after these things Jesus went out, and saw a publican, Levi by name, sitting at the tollbooth. And he said to him, (Pur)Sue thou me; (And after these things Jesus went out, and saw a tax-collector, named Levi, sitting at the tollbooth. And he said to him, Follow me;)

28 and when he had left all (his) things, he rose up, and (pur)sued him (or and followed

him).

29 And Levi made to him a great feast in his house; and there was a great company of publicans, and of others that were with them, sitting at the meat. (And Levi made a great feast for him in his house; and there was a great group of tax-collectors, and others who were with them, sitting at the meal.)

30 And the Pharisees and the scribes of them grudged, and said to his disciples, Why eat ye and drink with publicans, and sinful men? (And the Pharisees and their scribes grumbled, and said to his disciples, Why do ye eat and drink with tax-collectors, and sinners?)

31 And Jesus answered, and said to them, They that be whole have no need to a leech, (or Those who be whole, or be well, have no need for a physician), but (rather) they that be sick [or but they that have evil];

32 for I came not to call just men, but sinful men to penance. (for I came not to call the righteous, but sinners to repentance.)

33 And they said to him, Why (do) the disciples of John fast oft, and make prayers, also and of the Pharisees, but thine eat and drink?

34 To whom he said, Whether ye may make the sons of the spouse to fast, while the spouse is with them? (To whom he said, Can ye make the sons of the spouse to fast, while the spouse is still with them?)

35 But (the) days shall come, when the spouse shall be taken away from them, and then they shall fast in those days.

36 And he said to them also a likeness (or a parable); For no man taketh a piece from a new cloth, and putteth *it* into an old clothing, (or For no man taketh a piece from a new cloak, and putteth *it* onto an old piece of clothing); else both he breaketh the new, and the piece of the new accordeth not to the old.

37 And no man putteth new wine into old bottles; else the new wine shall break the bottles, and the wine shall be shed out, and the bottles shall perish. [And no man putteth new wine into old wine vessels; else the new wine shall break the wine vessels, and the wine shall be shed out, and the wine vessels shall perish.]

38 But new wine oweth to be put into new bottles, and both be kept. [But new wine is to be put into new wine vessels, and both be kept.] (But new wine ought to be put into new bottles, and then both shall be kept or preserved.)

39 And no man drinking the old, will anon (drink) the new (or will at once drink the new); for he saith, The old is the better [or The old is better].

CHAPTER 6

1 And it was done in the second first sabbath [or Forsooth it was done in the first second sabbath], when he passed by the corns, his disciples plucked (some) ears of corn; and they rubbing (them) with their hands, ate (them).

2 And some of the Pharisees said to them, What do ye that, that is not leaveful in the sabbaths? (or Why do ye that, which is not lawful on the Sabbath?)

3 And Jesus answered, and said to them, Have ye not read, what David did, when he hungered, and they that were with him;

4 how he entered into the house of God, and took (the) loaves of proposition, and ate (them), and gave to them that were with him; which *loaves* it was not leaveful to eat, (no) but only to priests [or no but to priests alone]. (how he entered into God's House, and took the loaves of the showbread, and ate them, and gave them to those who were with him; which *bread* it was not lawful to eat, except for the priests.)

5 And he said to them, For man's Son is Lord, yea, of the sabbath.

6 And it was done in another sabbath (or on another Sabbath), that he entered into a synagogue, and taught. And a man was there,

and his right hand was dry.

7 And the scribes and the Pharisees espied him, if he would heal him in the sabbath (or if he would heal him on the Sabbath), (so) that they should find cause, whereof they should accuse him.

8 And he knew the thoughts of them, and he said to the man that had a dry hand, Rise up, and stand in the middle (of us). And he rose, and stood (there).

9 And Jesus said to them, I ask you, if it is leaveful to do well in the sabbath [day], or evil? to make a soul safe, or to lose? (And Jesus said to them, I ask you, is it lawful to do good on the Sabbath day, or evil? to save a life, or a soul, or to destroy it?)

10 And when he had beheld all men about, he said to the man, Hold forth thine hand. And he held (it) forth, and his hand was restored to health.

11 And they were full-filled with unwisdom [or Soothly they were filled with unwisdom], and spake together, what they should do of Jesus (or what they would do about Jesus).

12 And it was done in those days, he went out into an hill to pray (or he went up onto a hill to pray); and he was all night dwelling in the prayer of God.

13 And when the day was come, he called his disciples, and chose twelve of them, which he called [or he named] also apostles;

14 Simon, whom he called Peter, and Andrew, his brother, James and John, Philip and Bartholomew,

15 Matthew and Thomas, James Alphaeus, and Simon, that is called Zelotes (or the Zealot),

16 Judas of James, and Judas Iscariot, that was (the) traitor.

17 And Jesus came down from the hill with them, and stood in a field place; and the company of his disciples, and a great multitude of people, of all Judea, and Jerusalem, and of the sea coasts, and of Tyre and Sidon, (or from all of Judea, and Jerusalem, and from the sea coasts, and from Tyre and Sidon), that came to hear him, and to be healed of their sicknesses;

18 and they that were travailed of [or with] unclean spirits, were healed. (and those who were troubled by unclean spirits, or devils and demons, were healed.)

19 And all the people sought to touch him, for virtue went out of him (or for power went out of him), and healed all.

20 And when his eyes were cast up, into his disciples, he said, (or And he turned his eyes upon his disciples, and he said), Blessed *be ye*, poor men [⁺or Blessed *be ye*, (the) poor], for the kingdom of God is yours.

21 Blessed *be ye*, that now hunger, for ye shall be full-filled. Blessed *be ye*, that now weep, for ye shall laugh. [Blessed *be ye* that hunger now, for ye shall be filled. Blessed *be ye* that weep now, for ye shall laugh.]

22 Ye shall be blessed, when men shall hate you, and separate you away, and put reproof *to you* [or and shall put shame *on you*], and cast out your name as evil, for man's Son.

23 Joy ye in that day, and be ye glad; for lo! your meed is much in heaven; for after these things the fathers of them did to (the) prophets. (Rejoice on that day, and be glad; for behold, your reward is great in heaven; for thus their fathers did to the prophets.)

24 Nevertheless woe to you, rich men, that have your comfort.

25 Woe to you that be full-filled, for ye shall hunger. Woe to you that now laugh, for ye shall mourn, and weep. [Woe to you that be filled, for ye shall hunger. Woe to you that laugh now, for ye shall mourn, and weep.]

26 Woe *to you*, when all men shall bless you; after these things the fathers of them did to [*false*] prophets (or for thus their fathers did to the *false* prophets).

27 But I say to you that hear, love ye your enemies, do ye well to them that hated you [or do ye well to them that hate you];

28 bless ye men that curse you, pray ye for

men that defame you [or that falsely challenge you].

29 And to him that smiteth thee on the one cheek, show also the other [or give also the tother]; and from him that taketh away from thee a cloth, do not thou forbid the coat, (or and as for him who taketh away a cloak from thee, give also thy coat to him).

30 And give to each that asketh thee, and if a man taketh away those things that be thine, ask thou not again (for them).

31 And as ye will that men do to you (or And as ye desire that men do to you), do ye also to them in like manner.

32 And if ye love them that love you, what thank(s), [or what grace], is to you? for sinful men love men that love them. (And if ye love those who love you, what credit is that to you? for sinners love those who love them.)

33 And if ye do well to them that do well to you, what grace, [or what thank(s)], is to you? for sinful men do this thing. (And if ye do good to those who do good to you, what credit is that to you? for sinners do this same thing.)

34 And if ye lend to them of which ye hope to take again, what thank(s), [or what grace], is to you? for sinful men lend to sinful men, to take again as much. (And if ye lend to those from whom ye hope to receive back, what credit is that to you? for sinners lend to sinners, to receive back as much.)

35 Nevertheless love ye your enemies, and do ye well, and lend ye, hoping nothing thereof, and your meed shall be much (or and your reward shall be great), and ye shall be the sons of the Highest, for he is benign, [or of good will], on unkind men and evil men.

36 Therefore be ye merciful, as your Father is merciful.

37 Do not ye deem, and ye shall not be deemed, (or Do not judge, and ye shall not be judged). Do not ye condemn, and ye shall not be condemned; forgive ye, and it shall be forgiven to you.

38 Give ye, and it shall be given to you. They shall give into your bosom a good measure, and well-filled, and shaken together, and overflowing; for by the same measure, by which ye mete, it shall be meted again to you, (or for by the same measure, by which ye measure, it shall be measured unto you).

39 And he said to them a likeness (or a parable), Whether the blind may lead the blind? nor fall they not both into the ditch? [or whether they fall not both into the ditch?]

40 A disciple is not above his master (or A student is not above his teacher); but each shall be perfect, if he be as his master.

41 And what seest thou in thy brother's eye a mote (or And why seest thou a speck in thy brother's eye), but thou beholdest not a beam, that is in thine own eye?

42 Or how mayest thou say to thy brother, Brother, suffer, (and) I shall cast out the mote of thine eye, (or Brother, allow me, and I shall take out the speck from thine eye), and thou beholdest not a beam that is in thine own eye? Hypocrite, first take out [or cast out] the beam of thine eye, and then thou shalt see to take out the mote of thy brother's eye.

43 It is not a good tree, that maketh evil fruits, neither an evil tree, that maketh good fruits;

44 for every tree is known of his fruit. And men gather not figs of thorns, neither men gather a grape of a bush of briers. (for every tree is known by its fruit. And people do not gather figs from thorns, nor do they gather grapes from a briar bush.)

45 A good man (out) of the good treasure of his heart bringeth forth good things, and an evil man (out) of the evil treasure bringeth forth evil things; for (out) of the plenty of the heart the mouth speaketh.

46 And what call ye me, Lord, Lord, (or And why do ye call me, Lord, Lord), and do not (do) those things that I say.

47 Each that cometh to me, and heareth my

words, and doeth them, I shall show to you, to whom he is like.

48 He is like to a man that buildeth an house, that digged deep, and set [or put] the foundament on a stone (or and laid its foundation on a stone). And when a great flood was made, the flood was hurled to that house, and it might not move it, for it was founded on a firm stone.

49 But he that heareth, and doeth not, is like to a man building his house on [the] earth, without (a) foundament, (or upon the ground, without a foundation); into which the flood was hurled, and anon it fell down (or and at once it fell down); and the falling down of that house was made great.

CHAPTER 7

1 And when he had fulfilled all his words into the ears of the people (or And when he had finished all his words to the people), he entered into Capernaum.

2 But a servant of a centurion, that was precious to him, was sick, and drawing to the death.

3 And when he had heard of Jesus, he sent to him the elder men of (the) Jews, and prayed him (or beseeched him), that he would come, and heal his servant.

4 And when they came to Jesus, they prayed him busily (or they earnestly beseeched him), and said to him, For he is worthy, (so) that thou grant to him this thing;

5 for he loveth our folk, and he builded to us a synagogue. (for he loveth our nation and our people, and he hath built a synagogue for us.)

6 And Jesus went with them. And when he was not far from the house, the centurion sent to him (his) friends, and said, Lord, do not thou be travailed, (or And when he was not far from the house, the centurion sent his friends to him, and said, Lord, do not be troubled), for I am not

worthy, that thou enter under my roof;

7 for which thing I deemed not myself worthy, that I come to thee; but say thou by word, and my child shall be healed. (for that reason I judged myself not worthy, that I should come to thee; but say thou the word, and my servant shall be healed.)

8 For I am a man ordained under power, and have knights under me (or and have soldiers under me); and I say to this, Go, and he goeth, and to another, Come, and he cometh, and to my servant, Do this thing, and he doeth [it].

9 And when this thing was heard, Jesus wondered; [and he turned], and said to the people (pur)suing him, Truly I say to you, neither in Israel (have) I found so great faith, [or not in Israel (have) I found so great faith], (or and he turned, and said to the people following him, I tell you the truth, I have not found such great faith in Israel).

10 And they that were sent, turned again home, and found the servant whole, that was sick. (And they who were sent, returned home, and found the servant healed, who was sick.)

11 And it was done afterward, Jesus went into a city, that is called Nain, and his disciples; and full great people went with him. [+And it was done afterward Jesus went into a city, that is called Nain, and his disciples went with him, and a full great company of people.]

12 And when he came nigh to the gate of the city (or And when he came near to the city gate), lo! the son of a woman that had no more children, was borne out dead, [or lo! an only son of his mother was borne out dead]; and this was a widow; and much people of the city [was] with her.

13 And when the Lord Jesus had seen her, he had ruth on her, [or he (was) moved by mercy on her], (or he had compassion for her), and said to her, Do not thou weep.

14 And he came nigh, and touched the bier; and they that bare *the bier* stood (there). And he

said, Young man, I say to thee, rise up.

15 And he that was dead sat up again [or And he that was dead sat up], and began to speak; and he gave him (back) to his mother.

16 And dread took all men (or And fearful reverence took hold of everyone), and they magnified God, and said, For a great prophet is risen among us, and, For God hath visited his people.

17 And this word went out of him into all Judea (or And this story about him went out into all Judea), and into all the country(side) about.

18 And John's disciples told him of all these things.

19 And John called twain of his disciples, and sent *them* to Jesus, and said, Art thou he that is to come, or abide we another? (or Art thou he who is to come, or do we wait for another?)

20 And when the men came to him, they said, John (the) Baptist sent us to thee, and said, Art thou he that is to come, or (do) we abide another?

21 And in that hour he healed many men of their sicknesses, and wounds, and [of] evil spirits (or and from evil spirits); and he gave sight to many blind men.

22 And Jesus answered, and said to them, Go ye again, and tell ye to John those things that ye have heard and seen; blind men see, crooked men go, mesels be made clean, deaf men hear, dead men rise again, poor men be taken to preaching of the gospel, (or the blind see, the lame walk, the lepers be cleansed, the deaf hear, the dead rise again, the poor be taken to the preaching of the Gospel or the Good News).

23 And he that shall not be caused to stumble in me, is blessed.

24 And when the messengers of John were gone forth, he began to say of John to the people, What went ye out into (the) desert to see? a reed wagged with the wind? [And when the messengers of John had gone away, he

began to say of John to the companies, What went ye out into (the) desert to see? a reed waved with the wind?]

25 But what went ye out to see? a man clothed with soft clothes? Lo! they that be in [a] precious cloth, (or Behold, those who wear expensive clothing), and (be) in delights, be in kings' houses.

26 But what went ye out to see? a prophet? Yea, I say to you, and more than a prophet.

27 This is he, of whom it is written, Lo! I send mine angel before thy face, which shall make ready thy way before thee.

28 Certainly I say to you, there is no man a more prophet among the children of women, than is John (the) Baptist, [or Soothly I say to you, among the children of women, no man is (a) more *prophet* (or is a greater *prophet*) than John (the) Baptist]; but he that is less in the kingdom of heavens, is more than he. (Truly I say to you, or I tell you the truth, no man is a greater prophet among the children of women, than is John the Baptist; but whoever is the least in the Kingdom of Heaven, is greater than he.)

29 And all the people hearing, and publicans (or and tax-collectors), that had been baptized with the baptism of John, justified God;

30 but the Pharisees and the wise men of the law, that were not baptized of him, despised the counsel of God against themselves. (but the Pharisees and the men wise in the Law, who were not baptized by him, rejected God's plan or purpose for themselves.)

31 And the Lord said, Therefore to whom shall I say men of this generation like, and to whom be they like?

32 They be like to children sitting in the chapping (or at the market), and speaking together, and saying, We have sung to you with pipes, and ye have not danced; we have made mourning [or lamentation] and ye have not wept.

33 For John (the) Baptist came, neither eating bread, nor drinking wine, and ye say, He hath a

fiend, (or He hath a devil, or a demon).

34 Man's Son came eating and drinking, and ye say, Lo! a man a devourer [or a glutton], and drinking wine, a friend of publicans, and of sinful men, (or and ye say, Behold, a glutton, and a wine imbiber, a friend of tax-collectors, and of sinners).

35 And wisdom is justified of [all] her sons. (And wisdom is justified by all of her sons.)

36 But one of the Pharisees prayed Jesus, that he should eat with him. And he entered into the house of the Pharisee, and sat at the meat. (But one of the Pharisees beseeched Jesus, that he would eat with him. And so he entered into the house of the Pharisee, and sat down for the meal.)

37 And lo! a sinful woman, that was in the city, as she knew, that Jesus sat at [the] meat (or sat down for a meal) in the house of the Pharisee, she brought an alabaster box of ointment;

38 and she stood behind beside his feet, and began to moist(en) his feet with (her) tears, and wiped [them] with the hairs of her head, and kissed his feet, and anointed (them) with ointment.

39 And the Pharisee seeing, that had called him, said within himself, saying, If this were a prophet, he should know, who and what manner woman it were that toucheth him, [or If this were a prophet, soothly he should know, who and what manner woman it is that toucheth him], for she is a sinful woman.

40 And Jesus answered, and said to him, Simon, I have something to say to thee. And he said, Master, say thou, (or Teacher, tell me).

41 And he answered, Two debtors were to one lender; and one owed five hundred pence, and the other fifty;

42 but when they had not whereof to yield, he forgave [freely] to both. Who [of *them*] then loveth him more?

43 Simon answered, and said, I guess, that he to whom he forgave more. And he answered to him, Thou hast deemed rightly (or Thou hast judged correctly).

44 And he turned to the woman, and said to Simon, Seest thou this woman? I entered into thine house, thou gavest no water to my feet (or thou gavest me no water for my feet); but this [*woman*] hath moist(en)ed my feet with (her) tears, and wiped (them) with her hairs.

45 Thou hast not given to me a kiss; but this [*woman*], since she entered [or since I entered], ceased not to kiss my feet.

46 Thou anointedest not mine head with oil; but this anointed my feet with ointment.

47 For which thing I say to thee, many sins be forgiven to her, for she hath loved much; and to whom is less forgiven, he loveth less.

48 And Jesus said to her, Thy sins be forgiven to thee.

49 And they that sat together at the meat (or And they who sat together at the meal), began to say within themselves, Who is this that [also], (or who even), forgiveth sins.

50 But he said to the woman, Thy faith hath made thee safe; go thou in peace, (or Thy faith hath saved thee; go in peace).

CHAPTER 8

1 And it was done afterward, and Jesus made journey by cities and castles (or by towns and villages), preaching and evangelizing the realm of God, and (the) twelve with him;

2 and some women that were healed of wicked spirits and sicknesses, Mary, that is called Magdalene, of whom seven devils went out,

3 and Joanna, the wife of Chuza, the procurator of Herod, and Susanna, and many others, that ministered to him of their riches, (or who served him out of their own resources, or with their own money).

4 And when much people was come together, and men hied [or hasted] to him, from the cities, he said by a similitude, [or by a

likeness, *or* (an) *example*], (or by a parable),

5 He that soweth, went out to sow his seed. And while he soweth, some fell beside the way, and was defouled (or and was defiled), and (the) birds of the air ate it.

6 And other fell on a stone, and it sprang up (or and it sprouted), and dried, for it had not moisture [or for it had no moisture].

7 And other fell among thorns, and the thorns sprang up together, and strangled it.

8 And other fell into good earth, and it sprang up, and made an hundredfold fruit. He said these things, and cried, He that hath ears of hearing, hear he.

9 But his disciples asked him, what this parable was.

10 And he said to them, To you it is granted to know the private [or the mystery] of the kingdom of God (or To you it is granted to know the secret of the Kingdom of God); but to other men (I speak) in parables, (so) that they seeing see not, and they hearing understand not.

11 And this is the parable. The seed is God's word;

12 and they that be beside the way, be these that hear; and afterward the fiend cometh (or and afterward the Devil cometh), and taketh away the word from their heart(s), lest they believing be made safe (or lest they believe and be saved).

13 But they that *fell* on a stone, be these that when they have heard, receive the word with joy. And these have no roots; for at a time they believe, and in time of temptation they go away (or but in the time of testing they go away).

14 But that that fell among thorns, be these that heard, and (because) of (the) busynesses (or the concerns), and (the) riches, and (the) lusts of (this) life they go forth, and be strangled, and bring forth no fruit.

15 But that that *fell* into good earth, be these that, in a good heart, and best, (or be those who, with a good and true heart), hear the word, and hold (it), and bring forth fruit in patience.

16 No man lighteth a lantern, and covereth it with a vessel, or putteth *it* under a bed, (no) but on a candlestick, (so) that men that enter (can) see light.

17 For there is no privy thing, which shall not be opened; neither hid thing, which shall not be known, and come into (the) open. (For there is nothing private, or secret, which shall not be made open; nor any hidden thing, which shall not be made known, and brought out into the open.)

18 Therefore see ye, how ye hear; for it shall be given to him that hath, and whoever hath not, also that that he weeneth, [or that he guesseth], (or that he thinketh), that he have, shall be taken away from him.

19 And his mother and brethren came to him; and they might not come to him for the people.

20 And it was told to him, Thy mother and thy brethren stand withoutforth, willing to see thee. (And he was told, Thy mother and thy brothers stand outside, desiring to see thee.)

21 And he answered, and said to them, My mother and my brethren be these, that hear the word of God, and do *it*.

22 And it was done in (or on) one of the days, he went up into a boat, and his disciples. And he said to them, Pass we over the sea (or Let us go over to the other side of the lake). And (so) they went up.

23 And while they rowed, he slept. And a tempest of wind came down into the water, and they were driven hither and thither with waves, and were in peril.

24 And they came nigh, and raised him, and said, Commander (or Master), we perish. And he rose up, and blamed the wind (or and rebuked the wind), and the tempest of the water; and it ceased, and peaceability was made.

25 And he said to them, Where is your faith?

Which dreading wondered, and said together, (or Who with fear and wonder, said to each other), Who, guessest thou, is this? for he commandeth to the winds and to the sea, and they obey to him.

26 And they rowed to the country of Gadarenes, that is against Galilee (or that is opposite Galilee).

27 And when he went out to the land, a man ran to him, that had a devil [now] (a) long time, and he was not clothed with cloth, neither dwelled in (a) house, but in sepulchres. (And when he got onto the land, a man ran over to him, who for a long time now had a demon, and he was not clothed with a cloak, nor lived in a house, but dwelt among the tombs.)

28 This (man), when he saw Jesus, fell down before him, and he crying with a great voice said, (or and he cried with a loud voice, and said), What to me and to thee, Jesus, the Son of the Highest God? I beseech thee, that thou torment me not.

29 For he (had) commanded the unclean spirit, that he should go out from the man. For he took him oft times, and he was bound with chains, and kept in stocks, and when the bonds were broken, he was led of the devil into desert (or he was led by the demon into the desert).

30 And Jesus asked him, and said, What name is to thee? And he said, A legion; for many devils were entered into him, [or for many devils had entered into him], (or for there were many demons in him).

31 And they prayed him (or And they beseeched him), that he should not command them, that they should go into hell [or that they should go into the deepness].

32 And there was a flock of many swine [or of many hogs] pasturing in an hill, and they prayed him, that he should suffer them to enter into them. And he suffered them. (And there was a herd of many pigs at pasture on a hill, and they beseeched him, that he would allow them to enter into them. And he allowed them.)

33 And so the devils went out from the man, and entered into the swine [or into the hogs]; and with a rush the flock went headlong into the pool [or into the lake of water], and was drenched. (And so the demons went out of the man, and entered into the pigs; and with a rush the herd went headlong into the lake, and were drowned.)

34 And when the herders saw this thing done, they fled, and told into the city, and into the towns.

35 And they went out to see that thing that was done. And they came to Jesus, and they found the man sitting clothed, from whom the devils went out, and in whole mind at his feet; and they dreaded (or and they had great fear).

36 And they that saw told to them, how he was made whole of the legion. (And they who saw it all, told them how he was healed from the legion of devils and demons.)

37 And all the multitude of the country of Gadarenes prayed him, that he should go (away) from them, for they were held with great dread. And he went up into a boat, and turned again (to the other side). (And all the multitude from the countryside of Gadarenes beseeched him, that he would go away from them, for they were held with great fear. And so he went up into the boat, and returned to the other side.)

38 And the man of whom the devils were gone out, [or And the man of whom the fiends went out], prayed him, that he should be with him. [Soothly] Jesus left him (or let him go), and said, (And the man from whom the demons went out, beseeched him, that he could be with him. But Jesus sent him away, and said,)

39 Go again into thine house, and tell how great things God hath done to thee. And he went through all the city, and preached, how great things Jesus had done to him. (Return to thine house, and to thy people, and tell them what great things God hath done for thee. And so he went through all the city, and preached, what great things Jesus had done for him.)

40 And it was done, when Jesus was gone (home) again [or when Jesus had gone (home) again], the people received him; for all were abiding him (or for all of them were waiting for him).

41 And lo! a man, to whom the name *was* Jairus, and he was [a] prince of a synagogue (or and he was a leader of a synagogue); and he fell down at the feet of Jesus, and prayed him (or beseeched him), that he should enter into his house,

42 for he had but one daughter [or an only daughter], almost of twelve years old, and she was dead. And it befell, the while he went, he was thronged of the people. (for he had an only daughter, almost twelve years old, and she was dying. And it befell, that while he went, he was thronged by the people.)

43 And a woman that had a flux of blood (for) twelve years, and had spended all her chattel [or all her substance] in leeches, and might not be cured of any, (And there was a woman who had a flowing, or an issue, of blood for twelve years, and had spent all of her resources on physicians, and could not be cured by any of them,)

44 and she came nigh behind, and touched the hem of his cloth, and anon the flux of her blood ceased. (and she came up close behind him, and touched the hem of his cloak, and at once the flowing, or the issue, of her blood ceased.)

45 And Jesus said, Who is it that touched me? And when all men denied (it), Peter said, and they that were with him, Commander (or Master), the people thrust [or throng] and disease thee, and thou sayest, Who touched me?

46 And Jesus said, Some man hath touched me, for [I have known] that virtue went out of me. (And Jesus said, Someone hath touched me, for I know that power hath gone out of me.)

47 And the woman seeing, that it was not hid from him, came trembling, and fell down at his feet, and for what cause she had touched him

she showed before all the people, and how anon she was healed (or and how at once she was healed).

48 And he said to her, Daughter, thy faith hath made thee safe, (or Daughter, thy faith hath saved thee, or thy faith hath healed thee); go thou in peace.

49 And yet while he spake, a man came from the (house of the) prince of the synagogue, and said to him, Thy daughter is dead, do not thou travail the Master (any further). (And while he spoke, a man came from the house of the leader of the synagogue, and said to him, Thy daughter is now dead, or Thy daughter hath died, so do not further trouble or bother the Teacher.)

50 And when this word was heard, Jesus answered to the father of the damsel, Do not thou dread, but believe thou only [or but only believe thou], and she shall be safe, (or Do not fear, but only believe, and she shall be saved, or she shall be healed).

51 And when he came to the house, he suffered no man to enter with him, [no] but Peter and John and James, and the father and the mother of the damsel. (And when he came to the house, he did not allow anyone to go in with him, except for Peter and John and James, and the father and the mother of the young girl.)

52 And all wept, and bewailed her. And he said, Do not ye weep, for the damsel is not dead, but (only) sleepeth.

53 And they scorned him, and knew that she was dead.

54 But he held her hand, and cried, and said, Damsel, rise up.

55 And her spirit turned again, and she rose anon, (or And her spirit returned, and she got up at once). And he commanded (them) to give to her (something) to eat.

56 And her father and mother wondered greatly; and he commanded them, that they should not say to any [man] (or to anyone) that

thing that was done.

CHAPTER 9

1   And when the twelve apostles were called together, Jesus gave to them virtue and power on all devils, and that they should heal sicknesses. (And when the twelve apostles were called together, Jesus gave them authority and power over all demons, and so that they could heal sicknesses.)

2   And he sent them to preach the kingdom of God, and to heal sick men.

3   And he said to them, Nothing take ye in the way (or Take nothing on or for the way), neither a staff [or a rod], nor scrip, neither bread, nor money, and neither have ye two coats.

4   And into what[ever] house ye enter, dwell ye there (remain there), and go ye not out from thence.

5   And whoever receive not you [or And whoever shall not receive you], go ye out of that city, and shake ye off the powder of your feet into witnessing on them (or and shake off the dust from your feet as a testimony against them).

6   And they went forth, and went about by castles (or and went through the villages), preaching [or evangelizing] and healing everywhere.

7   And Herod [the] tetrarch [or (the) prince of the fourth part], heard (of) all [the] things that were done of him, and he doubted, for that it was said of some men, that John was risen from death [or for (that) John had risen from (the) dead]; (And Herod, the tetrarch, or the prince of a quarter of the kingdom, heard of all of the things that were done by him, and he wondered about it, for it was said by some people, that John had risen from the dead;)

8   and of some men, that Elias had appeared; but of others, that one of the old prophets was risen. (and by some, that Elijah had appeared; but by others, that one of the prophets of old had arisen.)

9   And Herod said, I have beheaded John; and who is this, of whom I hear such things? And he sought to see him.

10   And the apostles turned again, and told to him all (the) things that they had done, (or And the apostles returned, and told him about everything that they had done). And he took them, and went beside into a desert place, that is [called] Bethsaida.

11   And when the people knew this, they followed him. And he received them, and spake to them of the kingdom of God (or and spoke to them about the Kingdom of God); and he healed them that had need of (a) cure.

12   And the day began to bow down, and the twelve came, and said to him, Leave the people, that they go, and turn into the castles and towns, that be about, that they find meat, for we be here in a desert place. (And the day began to bow down, and the Twelve came, and said to him, Let the people go, or Send them away, so that they can go, and return to the villages and towns, that be about, so that they can find some food, for we be here in this deserted place.)

13   And he said to them, Give ye to them (something) to eat. And they said, There be not to us more than five loaves and two fishes, but peradventure that we go, and buy meats to all this people, [or but peradventure we go, and buy meats for all the company], (or but perhaps we can go, and buy some food for all of these people).

14   And the men were almost five thousand. And he said to his disciples, Make ye them to sit to (the) meat by companies, a fifty together, (or And he said to his disciples, Make them to sit down for the meal in groups, fifty together).

15   And they did so, and they made all men sit to [the] meat. (And they did so, and they made everyone to sit down for the meal.)

16   And when he had taken the five loaves

and two fishes, he beheld into heaven, and blessed them, and brake (them), and dealed (them out) to his disciples, (so) that they should set [or put] (them) forth before the companies.

17 And all men ate, and were full-filled [or and were filled]; and that that (was) left to them of broken meats was taken up, twelve coffins. (And everyone ate, and were filled; and the pieces of food which were left by them were gathered up, yea, twelve baskets full.)

18 And it was done, when he was alone praying, his disciples were with him, and he asked them, and said, Whom say the people that I am?

19 And they answered, and said, John (the) Baptist, others *say* Elias, and others *say* [or but others *say*], one prophet of the former is risen (And they answered, and said, John the Baptist, others *say* Elijah, and others *say*, one of the former prophets, or one of the first prophets, is risen.)

20 And he said to them, But whom say ye that I am? Simon Peter answered, and said, The Christ of God, (or Simon Peter answered, and said, God's Messiah).

21 And he blaming them (or And he rebuking them), commanded [them] that they should say (that) to no man, [+And he blaming them commanded them that they should say to no man these things,]

22 and said these things, For it behooveth man's Son to suffer many things, and to be reproved of the elder men, and of the princes of (the) priests, and of the scribes, (or and to be rejected by the elders, and by the high priests, and by the scribes), and to be slain, and the third day to rise again.

23 And he said to all [men], If any [man] will come after me, deny he himself, and take he his cross every day, and (pur)sue he me (or and follow me).

24 For he that will make his life safe shall lose it; and he that loseth his life for me, shall make it safe.

25 And what profiteth [it to] a man, if he win all the world, and lose himself, and do impairing of himself, [or and do impairing to himself], (or and do harm to himself).

26 For whoso shameth me and my words, man's Son shall shame him, when he cometh in his majesty, and of the Father's, and of the holy angels. (For whosoever shall be ashamed of me and my words, man's Son shall be ashamed of him, when he cometh in his majesty, or in his glory, and in the glory of the Father, and of the holy angels.)

27 And I say to you, verily there be some standing here, which shall not taste death, till they see the realm of God. (Truly I say to you, or I tell you the truth, there be some standing here, who shall not taste death, until they see the Kingdom of God.)

28 And it was done after these words almost eight days, and he took Peter and James and John, and he ascended into an hill, to pray, (or and he went up onto a hill, to pray).

29 And while he prayed, the likeness of his face was changed, and his clothing was white shining.

30 And lo! two men spake with him, and Moses and Elias (And behold, two men spoke with him, yea, Moses and Elijah)

31 were seen in (their) majesty; and they said (of) his going out, which he should fulfill in Jerusalem. (were seen in their glory; and they spoke of his death, yea, of his destiny, which he would fulfill in Jerusalem.)

32 And Peter, and they that were with him, were heavy of sleep, [or were grieved, *or heavied*, with sleep], and they waking saw his majesty, and the two men that stood with him, (or but awakening they saw his glory, and the two men who stood with him).

33 And it was done, when they departed from him, Peter said to Jesus, Commander, it is good that we be here, and make we here three tabernacles, one to thee, and one to Moses, and one to Elias. And he knew not what he should

say. (And it was done, when they had left him, Peter said to Jesus, Master, it is good for us to be here, and we shall make here three tents, or three tabernacles, one for thee, and one for Moses, and one for Elijah. And he did not know what he should say.)

34 But while he spake these things, a cloud was made, and overshadowed them; and they dreaded (or and they feared), when they entered into the cloud.

35 And a voice was made out of the cloud, and said, This is my dearworthy Son, hear ye him (or listen to him).

36 And while the voice was made, Jesus was found alone. And they were still, and to no man said in those days any of those things, that they had seen, [or And they held (their) peace, and said to no man in those days aught of those things that they had seen]. (And after the voice was heard, Jesus was there alone. And they were silent, and did not tell anyone in those days, about anything that they had seen.)

37 But it was done in the day (pur)suing, when they came down of the hill, much people met them. (But it was done on the following day, when they came down from the hill, that many people met them.)

38 And lo! a man of the company cried, and said, Master, I beseech thee, behold my son, for I have no more; (And behold, a man among the people cried, and said, Teacher, I beseech thee, look at my son, for I have no other child;)

39 and lo! a spirit taketh him, and suddenly he crieth, and hurtleth [him] down, and draweth him with foam [or with froth], and scarcely he goeth away (before) drawing him all to pieces.

40 And I prayed thy disciples, that they should cast him out, and they might not. (And I beseeched thy disciples, that they should throw out the spirit, but they could not do it.)

41 And Jesus answered and said to them, A! unfaithful generation and wayward (or O unfaithful and wayward generation!), how long

shall I be with you, and suffer you? bring hither thy son.

42 And when he came nigh, the devil hurtled him down, and wrenched him. And Jesus blamed the unclean spirit, and healed the child, and yielded him (back) to his father, (or And Jesus rebuked the unclean spirit, yea, the demon, and healed the child, and gave him back to his father).

43 And all men wondered greatly in the greatness of God. And when all men wondered in all (the) things that he did, he said to his disciples, (And everyone wondered greatly at the greatness of God. And when everyone wondered at all the things that he did, he said to his disciples,)

44 Put ye these words in your hearts, for it is to come, that man's Son be betrayed into the hands of men.

45 And they knew not this word, and it was hid before them, that they feeled it not; and they dreaded to ask him of this word. (But they did not know what this meant, and it was hidden to them, so that they could not perceive or understand it; and they feared to ask him about these words.)

46 But a thought entered into them, who of them should be (the) greatest.

47 And Jesus, seeing the thoughts of the heart(s) of them, (or And Jesus, knowing the thoughts in their hearts), took a child, and setted him beside him;

48 and said to them, Whoever receiveth this child in my name, receiveth me; and whoever receiveth me, receiveth him that sent me; for he that is (the) least among you all, is the greatest.

49 And John answered and said, Commander, we saw a man casting out fiends in thy name, and we have forbidden him, for he (pur)sueth not thee with us. (And John said, Master, we saw a man throwing out devils and demons in thy name, and we have forbidden him, for he followeth not thee with us.)

50 And Jesus said to him, Do not ye forbid

(him), for he that is not against us, is for us.

51   And it was done, when the days of his taking up were fulfilled (or when it would soon be the day that he would be taken up into heaven), he set fast his face, to go to Jerusalem,

52   and sent messengers before his sight. And they went, and entered into a city of Samaritans, to make ready to him (or to prepare it for him).

53   And they received not him, for the face of him was going into Jerusalem.

54   And when James and John, his disciples, saw (that), they said, Lord, wilt thou that we say, that fire come down from heaven, and waste them, [as Elias did]? (And when James and John, his disciples, saw that, they said, Lord, desirest thou that we command, that fire come down from heaven, and destroy them, like Elijah did?)

55   And he turned, and blamed them (or and rebuked them), and said, Ye know not, whose spirits ye be;

56   for man's Son came not to lose men's souls, but to save [them]. And they went into another castle. (for man's Son came not to destroy men's souls, but to save them. And so they went to another village.)

57   And it was done, when they walked in the way, a man said to him, I shall (pur)sue thee, whither ever thou [shalt] go. (And it was done, when they walked on the way, a man said to him, I shall follow thee, wherever thou shalt go.)

58   And Jesus said to him, Foxes have dens [or ditches], and (the) birds of the air have nests, but man's Son hath not where he [shall] rest his head.

59   And he said to another, (Pur)Sue thou me. And he said, Lord, suffer me first to go, and bury my father. (And he said to another, Follow me. And he said, Lord, first allow me to go, and bury my father.)

60   And Jesus said to him, Suffer that dead men bury their dead men; but go thou, and tell (everyone about) the kingdom of God. (And Jesus said to him, Allow the dead to bury their dead; but thou go, and tell everyone about the Kingdom of God.)

61   And another said, Lord, I shall (pur)sue thee, but first suffer me to leave (in peace) all things that be at home [or but first suffer me to tell to them that be at home]. (And another said, Lord, I shall follow thee, but first allow me to say good-bye to all who be at home.)

62   And Jesus said to him, No man that putteth his hand to the plough, and beholding backward, is able to the kingdom of God. (And Jesus said to him, No man who putteth his hand to the plow, and looking backward, is fit for the Kingdom of God.)

CHAPTER 10

1   And after these things the Lord Jesus ordained also other seventy and twain (or two), and sent them by twain and twain before his face into every city and place, whither he was to come.

2   And he said to them, There is much ripe corn, and few workmen; therefore pray ye the Lord of the ripe corn, that he send workmen into his ripe corn. (And he said to them, There is a great harvest, but few workmen; and so beseech the Lord of the harvest, that he send workmen to gather in his harvest.)

3   Go ye, lo! I send you as lambs among wolves.

4   Therefore do not ye bear a satchel, neither scrip, neither shoes, and greet ye no man by the way (or and greet no one on the way).

5   Into what[ever] house that ye enter, first say ye, Peace to this house.

6   And if a son of peace be there, your peace shall rest on him; but if none, it shall turn again to you, (or but if not, it shall return to you).

7   And dwell ye in the same house, eating and drinking those things that be at them; for a workman is worthy (of) his hire. Do not ye pass

from house into house. (And live in the same house, eating and drinking those things that be there with them; for a workman is worthy of his wages. Do not go from house to house.)

8 And into whatever city ye enter, and they receive you, eat ye those things that be set [or that be put] to you (or eat those things that be put before you);

9 and heal ye the sick men (or the sick people) that be in that city. And say ye to them, The kingdom of God shall [come] nigh to you, (or The Kingdom of God hath come near to you).

10 And into what[ever] city ye enter, and they receive you not, go ye out into the streets of it, and say ye,

11 We wipe off against you the powder that cleaved to us of your city; nevertheless know ye this thing, that the realm of God shall come nigh. (We wipe off against you the dust that cleaved to us from your city; nevertheless know ye this thing, that the Kingdom of God hath come near to you.)

12 I say to you, that to Sodom it shall be easier [or it shall be less pain(ful)] than to that city in that day.

13 Woe to thee, Chorazin; woe to thee, Bethsaida; for if in Tyre and Sidon the virtues had been done, which have been done in you, sometime they would have sat in haircloth and ashes, and have done penance. (Woe to thee, Chorazin! woe to thee, Bethsaida! for if in Tyre and Sidon the works of power, or the miracles, had been done, which have been done in you, long ago they would have sat in sackcloth and ashes, and have repented.)

14 Nevertheless to Tyre and Sidon it shall be easier in the doom, than to you. (Nevertheless for Tyre and Sidon, it shall be easier at the Judgement, than for you.)

15 And thou, Capernaum, art enhanced till to heaven; thou shalt be drenched [down] till into hell. (And thou, Capernaum, art exalted unto heaven? or art raised up into the sky? thou shalt be drowned down till into hell!)

16 He that heareth you, heareth me; and he that despiseth you, despiseth me; and he that despiseth me, despiseth him that sent me.

17 And the two and seventy *disciples* turned again with joy (or And the seventy-two *disciples* returned with joy), and said, Lord, also devils be subject to us in thy name.

18 And he said to them, I saw Satan falling down from heaven, as lightning (or like lightening).

19 And lo! I have given to you power to tread on serpents, and scorpions, and on all the virtue of the enemy (or and over all the power of the enemy), and nothing shall harm you.

20 Nevertheless do not ye [have] joy in this thing, that spirits be subject to you; but joy ye, that your names be written in heavens. (Nevertheless do not rejoice over this, that the spirits, or the devils and the demons, be subject to you; rather rejoice, that your names be written in heaven.)

21 In that hour he gladded in the Holy Ghost, and said, I acknowledge to thee, Father, Lord of heaven and of earth, for thou hast hid these things from wise men and prudent, and hast showed them to small [or to little] children. Yea, Father, for so it pleased before thee [or for so it pleased to thee]. (At that time he was filled with gladness by the Holy Spirit, or At that time he rejoiced in the Holy Spirit, and said, I acknowledge to thee, Father, Lord of heaven and of earth, for thou hast hidden these things from wise and prudent men, and thou hast shown them to little children. Yes, Father, for so it pleased thee.)

22 All things be given to me of my Father (or Everything is given to me by my Father), and no man knoweth, who is the Son, but the Father; and who is the Father, but the Son, and to whom the Son will show (it).

23 And he turned to his disciples, and said, Blessed *be* the eyes, that see those things that ye see.

24 For I say to you, that many prophets and

kings would have seen those things, that ye see, and they saw not; and hear those things, that ye hear, and they heard not.

25 And lo! a wise man of the law rose up, tempting him, and saying, Master, what thing shall I do to have everlasting life? (And behold, a man wise in the Law rose up to test him, and asked, Teacher, what should I do to get eternal life?)

26 And he said to him, What is written in the law? how readest thou?

27 He answered, and said, Thou shalt love thy Lord God of all thine heart [or Thou shalt love the Lord thy God of all thine heart], and of all thy soul, and of all thy strengths, and of all thy mind; and thy neighbour as thyself. (He answered, Thou shalt love the Lord thy God with all thine heart, and with all thy soul, and with all thy strength, and with all thy mind; and thy neighbour as thyself.)

28 And Jesus said to him, Thou hast answered rightly (or Thou hast answered correctly); do this thing, and thou shalt live.

29 But he willing to justify himself, said to Jesus, And who is my neighbour? (But desiring to justify himself, he said to Jesus, And who is my neighbour?)

30 And Jesus beheld (him), and said, A man came down from Jerusalem into Jericho [or Some man came down from Jerusalem to Jericho], and fell among thieves, and they robbed him, and wounded him, and went away, and left the man half alive.

31 And it befell, that a priest came down the same way, and passed forth (or and passed by him), when he had seen him.

32 Also a deacon, when he was beside the place, and saw him, passed forth. (Also a Levite, when he was beside the place, and saw him, passed by him.)

33 But a Samaritan, going the way, came beside him; and he saw him, and had ruth on him (or and had compassion for him); [Forsooth some Samaritan, making journey, came beside the way; and he seeing him, was stirred by mercy;]

34 and came to him, and bound together his wounds, and poured in oil and wine; and laid him on his beast, and led him in to an hostelry, and did the care of him (or and took care of him).

35 And another day (or And the next day), he brought forth two pence, and gave (them) to the hosteller, and said, Have the care of him (or Take care of him); and whatever thou shalt give over, I shall yield to thee, when I come again.

36 Who of these three, seemeth to thee, was (a) neighbour to him, that fell among [the] thieves?

37 And he said (to him), He that did mercy into him, (or He who did mercy, or who was kind to him). And Jesus said to him, Go thou, and do thou in like manner.

38 And it was done, while they went, he entered into a castle (or he went into a village); and a woman, Martha by name, received him into her house.

39 And to this was a sister, Mary by name, which also sat beside the feet of the Lord, and heard his word(s).

40 But Martha busied (herself) about the oft service [or Forsooth Martha busied (herself) about much service]. And she stood, and said, Lord, takest thou no keep (or carest thou not), that my sister hath left me alone to serve? therefore say thou to her, that she help me.

41 And the Lord answered, and said to her, Martha, Martha, thou art busy, and art troubled about full many things;

42 but one thing is necessary. Mary hath chosen the best part, which shall not be taken away from her.

CHAPTER 11

1 And it was done, when he was praying in a place, as he ceased, one of his disciples said to him, Lord, teach us to pray, as John taught

his disciples.

2   And he said to them, When ye pray, say ye, Father, [or Father ours], (or Our Father), hallowed be thy name. Thy kingdom come to (or Thy kingdom come); thy will be done on earth, as it is in heaven.

3   Give to us today our each day's bread.

4   And forgive to us our sins, as we forgive to each man that oweth to us. And lead us not into temptation (or And do not bring us to the test).

5   And he said to them, Who of you shall have a friend, and shall go to him at midnight, and shall say to him, Friend, lend to me three loaves;

6   for my friend cometh to me from the way, and I have not what I shall set [or what I shall put] before him.

7   And he withinforth answer and say, Do not thou be heavy to me; the door is now shut, and my children be with me in bed; I may not rise, and give (something) to thee, (or I cannot get up, and give something to thee).

8   And if he shall dwell still knocking [or And if he shall continue knocking], I say to you, though he shall not rise, and give (anything) to him, for that that he is his friend, nevertheless for his continual asking, he shall rise, and give (something) to him, as many as he hath need to (or as much as he hath need of).

9   And I say to you, ask ye, and it shall be given to you; seek ye, and ye shall find; knock ye, and it shall be opened to you.

10   For each that asketh, taketh (or receiveth), and he that seeketh, findeth; and to a man that knocketh, it shall be opened.

11   Therefore who of you asketh his father (for) bread, whether he shall give [to] him a stone? or if he asketh (for a) fish, whether he shall give [to] him a serpent for the fish? (or shall he give him a snake instead of the fish?)

12   or if he asketh (for) an egg, whether he shall areach [to] him a scorpion?

13   Therefore if ye, when ye be evil, know how to give good gifts to your children, how

much more your Father of heaven shall give a good Spirit to men that ask him.

14   And Jesus was casting out a fiend (or And Jesus was throwing out a demon), and it was dumb. And when he had cast out the fiend, the dumb man spake; and the people wondered.

15   And some of them said, In Beelzebub, (the) prince of devils, he casteth out devils. (And some of them said, By Beelzebub, the Prince of demons, he throweth out demons.)

16   And others tempting asked of him a token from heaven. (And others testing him, asked for a sign from heaven.)

17   And as he saw the thoughts of them, he said to them, Every realm parted against itself shall be desolate(d), (or Every kingdom divided against itself shall be destroyed unto rubble), and an house shall fall on an house.

18   And if Satan be parted against himself, how shall his realm stand? For ye say, that I cast out fiends in Beelzebub. (And if Satan is divided against himself, how can his kingdom stand? For ye say, that I throw out devils and demons by Beelzebub.)

19   And if I in Beelzebub cast out fiends, in whom cast out your sons? [or in whom your sons cast out?] Therefore they shall be your doomsmen. (And if I throw out devils and demons by Beelzebub, by whom do your sons throw them out? And so they shall be your judges.)

20   But if I cast out fiends in the finger of God, then the realm of God is come among you. (But if I throw out devils and demons by the finger of God, then the Kingdom of God hath come among you, or hath come unto you.)

21   When a strong, armed man keepeth his house, all things that he wieldeth be in peace (or everything that he possesseth be at peace).

22   But if a stronger (man) than he come upon him, and overcome him, he shall take away all his armour [or all his arms] in which he trusted, (or he shall take away all his weapons in which he trusted), and shall deal abroad his robberies

[or his spoils].

23   He that is not with me, is against me; and he that gathereth not together with me, scattereth abroad.

24   When an unclean spirit goeth out of a man, he wandereth by dry places, and seeketh rest; and he finding none, saith, I shall turn again into mine house, from whence I came out, (or and he finding no place to rest, saith, I shall return to my house, where I came from).

25   And when he cometh (back), he findeth it cleansed with besoms, and fair arrayed, [or adorned], (or he findeth it swept clean, and neat and tidy).

26   Then he goeth, and taketh with him (or and getteth with him), seven other spirits worse than himself, and they enter [in], and dwell there. And the last things of that man be made worse than the former (things), (or the first things).

27   And it was done, when he had said these things, a woman of the company raised [up] her voice, and said to him, Blessed *be* the womb that bare thee, and *blessed be* the teats that thou hast sucked (or and *blessed be* the breasts that thou hast suckled).

28   And he said, But yea, blessed *be* they, [or And he said, Rather, blessed *be* they], that hear the word of God, and keep it, (or who hear the word of God, and obey it, or do it).

29   And when the people ran together, he began to say, This generation is a wayward generation; it seeketh a token (or a sign), and a token shall not be given to it, [no] but the token of Jonas the prophet (or except the sign of the prophet Jonah).

30   For as Jonas was a token to men of Nineve (or For as Jonah was a sign to the men of Nineveh), so man's Son shall be to this generation.

31   The queen of the south shall rise in (the) doom with men of this generation, and shall condemn them; for she came from the ends of the earth, to hear the wisdom of Solomon, and

lo! here is a greater (man) than Solomon. (The Queen of the South shall rise at the Judgement with men of this generation, and shall condemn them; for she came from the ends of the earth, to hear the wisdom of Solomon, and behold, here is something or someone greater than Solomon.)

32   Men of Nineve shall rise in [the] doom with this generation, and shall condemn it; for they did penance in the preaching of Jonas [or for they did penance at the preaching of Jonas], and lo! here is a greater (man) than Jonas. (Men of Nineveh shall rise at the Judgement with this generation, and shall condemn it; for they repented at the preaching of Jonah, and behold, here is something or someone greater than Jonah.)

33   No man tendeth, [or lighteneth], (or lighteth), a lantern, and putteth it in huddles (or hideth it), neither under a bushel, but (rather) on a candlestick, (so) that they that go in(side), see light.

34   The lantern of thy body is thine eye; if thine eye be simple, (or if thine eye is single, or is sound), all thy body shall be light[-full]; but if it be wayward, all thy body shall be dark-full.

35   Therefore see thou, lest the light that is in thee, be darknesses (or be darkness).

36   Therefore if all thy body be bright, and have no part of darknesses, (or And so if all thy body be bright, and have no part with darkness), it shall be all bright, and as a lantern of brightness it shall give light to thee. [Therefore if all thy body shall be light-full, not having any part of darknesses, it shall be all light-full, and as a lantern of brightness, *or shining*, it shall give light to thee.]

37   And when he spake, a Pharisee prayed him, that he should eat with him. And he entered, and sat to (the) meat [or (and) sat at the meat]. (And after he spoke, a Pharisee beseeched him, that he would eat with him. And he entered, and sat down for the meal.)

38   And the Pharisee began to say, guessing

within himself, why he was not washed before [the] meat (or why he did not wash before the meal).

39 And the Lord said to him, Now ye Pharisees cleanse that that is withoutforth of the cup and the platter; but that thing that is within of you [or but that thing of you that is within], is full of raven and wickedness.

40 Fools, whether he that made that that is withoutforth, made not also that that is within?

41 Nevertheless that that is over-plus, [or superfluous], give ye alms, and lo! all things be clean to you.

42 But woe to you, Pharisees, that tithe mint, and rue, and each herb, and leave doom and the charity of God (or and pass over the judgement and the love of God). For it behooved to do these things, and not to leave those (others).

43 Woe to you, Pharisees, that love the first chairs in synagogues, and salutations in chapping. (Woe to you, Pharisees, who love the first chairs in the synagogues, and greetings of respect at the marketplace.)

44 Woe to you, that be as sepulchres (or who be like graves), that be not seen [or which appear not], and men walking above know not.

45 But one of the wise men of the law answered, and said to him, Master, thou saying these things, also to us doest despite [or doest despite also to us]. (But one of the men wise in the Law said to him, Teacher, thou saying these things, doest disrespect to us, or insultest us.)

46 And he said, Also woe to you, wise men of [the] law, for ye charge men with burdens which they may not bear, and ye yourselves with your one finger touch not the heavinesses. (And he said, And woe to you, men wise in the Law, for ye load men with burdens which they cannot bear, but ye yourselves touch not the heavinesses with even one finger.)

47 Woe to you, that build (the) tombs [or the burials] of (the) prophets; and your fathers slew them.

48 Truly ye witness, that ye consent to the works of your fathers; for they slew them, but ye build their sepulchres. (Ye testify truthfully, that ye consent to the works of your fathers; for they killed the prophets, and ye build their tombs.)

49 Therefore the wisdom of God said, I shall send to them prophets and apostles, and of them they shall slay and pursue, (And so the wisdom of God said, I shall send them prophets and apostles, and some of them they shall persecute and kill,)

50 (so) that the blood of all [the] prophets, that was shed from the making [or from the beginning] of the world, be sought of this generation; (so that the blood of all the prophets, that was shed from the creation of the world, be sought from this generation;)

51 from the blood of just Abel to the blood of Zacharias, that was slain betwixt the altar and the House (of the Lord), [+or from the blood of Abel unto the blood of Zacharias, which perished between the altar and the house]. So I say to you, it shall be sought of this generation. (from the blood of good and righteous Abel to the blood of Zechariah, who perished between the altar and the Temple. So I tell you, it shall be sought from this generation.)

52 Woe to you, wise men of the law, for ye have taken away the key of cunning (or the key of knowing); and ye yourselves entered not [in], and ye have forbidden them that entered. (Woe to you, men wise in the Law, for ye have taken away the key of knowledge; and ye yourselves did not enter in, and ye have forbidden those who tried to enter in.)

53 And when he said these things to them, the Pharisees and the wise men of the law (or and the men wise in the Law) began grievously to against-stand [him], and (to) stop his mouth of many things,

54 ambushing him, and seeking to take something of his mouth, to accuse him. (ambushing him, and seeking to catch him with

his own words, so as to be able to accuse him.)

CHAPTER 12

1　And when much people stood about, so that they trod each on (the) other [or so that they trod (upon) each other], he began to say to his disciples, Be ye ware of the sourdough of the Pharisees, that is hypocrisy, (or Beware of the yeast, or the leaven, of the Pharisees, which is their hypocrisy).

2　For nothing is covered, that shall not be showed; neither hid, that shall not be known. (For nothing is covered, which shall not be shown, or brought out into the open; nor hidden, which shall not be made known.)

3　For why those things that ye have said in darknesses, shall be said in light; and that that ye have spoken in [the] ear in bedchambers, shall be preached in roofs. (Because everything that ye have said in the dark, shall be said in the light; and that which ye have spoken privately in the bedchambers, shall be preached from the rooftops.)

4　And I say to you, my friends, be ye not afeared of them that slay the body, and after these things have no more what they shall do.

5　But I shall show to you, whom ye shall dread; dread ye him, that after he hath slain, hath power to send into hell. And so I say to you, dread ye him. (But I shall tell you, whom ye should fear; fear him, who after he hath killed, hath power to send into hell. And so I tell you, fear him.)

6　Whether five sparrows be not sold for two halfpence [or two farthings]; and one of them is not in forgetting before God?

7　But also all the hairs of your head be numbered. Therefore do not ye dread; ye be of more price, than many sparrows, (or And so, do not fear; ye be of more value, than many sparrows).

8　Truly I say to you (or I tell you the truth), each man that acknowledgeth me before men,

man's Son shall acknowledge him before the angels of God.

9　But he that denieth me before men, shall be denied before the angels of God.

10　And each that saith a word against man's Son [or And each that saith a word against the Son of man], it shall be forgiven to him; but it shall not be forgiven to him, that blasphemeth against the Holy Ghost (or who blasphemeth against the Holy Spirit).

11　And when they lead you into synagogues, and to magistrates, and potentates, do not ye be busy (or do not be concerned), how or what ye shall answer, or what ye shall say.

12　For the Holy Ghost shall teach you in that hour (or For the Holy Spirit shall teach you at that time), what it behooveth you to say.

13　And one of the people said to him, Master, say to my brother, that he part with me the heritage, (or Teacher, tell my brother to divide the inheritance with me).

14　And he said to him, Man, who ordained me a doomsman, or a parter, on you [or over you]? (And he said to him, Man, who put me over you as a judge, or a divider?)

15　And he said to them, See ye, and beware of all covetousness; for the life of a man is not in the abundance of the things, which he wieldeth (or that he possesseth).

16　And he told to them a likeness (or a parable), and said, The field of a rich man brought forth plenteous fruits.

17　And he thought within himself, and said, What shall I do, for I have not whither I shall gather my fruits? (And he thought to himself, and said, What shall I do, for I have no place where I can store all my crops?)

18　And he saith, This thing I shall do; I shall throw down my barns, and I shall make greater (ones), and thither I shall gather all (the) things that grow to me (or and there I shall gather together all the things that grow for me), and (all) my goods.

19　And I shall say to my soul, Soul, thou hast

many goods kept into full many years; rest thou, eat, drink, and make feast.

20 And God said to him, Fool, in this night they shall take thy life from thee, [or Fool, in this night they shall ask of thee thy soul]. And (then) whose shall those things be, that thou hast arrayed?

21 So is he that treasureth to himself, and is not rich in God.

22 And he said to his disciples, Therefore I say to you, do not ye be busy to your life (or do not be concerned about your life), what ye shall eat, neither to your body, with what ye shall be clothed.

23 The life is more than meat (or Life is more than food), and the body more than clothing.

24 Behold the crows, for they sow not, neither reap, to which is neither cellar, nor barn, and God feedeth them. How much more ye be of more price than they, [or How much more be ye of more price than they], (or How much more valuable ye be than them).

25 And who of you by thinking may put [or may add] one cubit to his stature?

26 Therefore if ye may not do that that is (the) least, what be ye busy of other things? (And so if ye cannot do anything about that which is so little, why be concerned about the other things?)

27 Behold ye the lilies of the field, how they wax; they travail not, neither spin, (or Look at the lilies of the field, how they grow; they do not labour, nor spin). And I say to you, that neither Solomon in all his glory was clothed as one of these.

28 And if God clotheth thus the hay, that today is in the field, and tomorrow is cast into an oven; how much more you of little faith.

29 And do not ye seek, what ye shall eat, or what ye shall drink; and do not ye be raised (up) on high.

30 For folks of the world seek all these things; and your Father knoweth, that ye have need to all these things. (For the peoples of the world seek all these things; and your Father knoweth,

that ye have need of all these things.)

31 Nevertheless seek ye first the kingdom of God, and all these things shall be cast to you (or and all these things shall be given to thee).

32 Do not ye, little flock, dread, for it pleased to your Father to give you a kingdom. (Do not, little flock, have fear, for it pleased your Father to give you the Kingdom.)

33 Sell ye those things that ye have in possession [or that ye wield], and give ye alms. And make to you satchels that wax not old, treasure that faileth not in heavens, whither a thief nigheth not, neither moth destroyeth. (Sell those things that ye possess, and give what you receive to charity. And make for yourselves totes or bags, that do not grow old, treasure that faileth not in heaven, where a thief approacheth not, nor a moth destroyeth.)

34 For where is thy treasure, there thine heart shall be. [Forsooth where thy treasure is, there also thine heart shall be.]

35 Be your loins girded above, and lanterns burning in your hands;

36 and *be* ye like to men that abide their lord, when he shall turn again from the weddings, that when he shall come, and knock, anon they open (the door) to him. (and *be* like men who wait for their lord, when he shall return from a wedding, so that when he shall come, and knock, they open the door at once for him.)

37 Blessed *be* those servants, that when the lord shall come, he shall find (them) waking. Truly I say to you, that he shall gird himself, and make them sit to (the) meat [or sit at the meat], and he shall go, and serve them. (Blessed *be* those servants, who when their lord shall come back, he shall find them keeping watch. I tell you the truth, that he shall gird himself, and make them sit down for the meal, and he shall go, and serve them.)

38 And if he come in the second waking, and if he come in the third waking, and find so, those servants (shall) be blessed. (And if he

come in the second watch, or in the third watch, and find them so, those servants shall be blessed.)

39 And know ye this thing, for if an husbandman knew, in what hour the thief would come, soothly he should wake, and not suffer his house to be (under)mined, (or truly he would be on watch, and not allow his house to be undermined).

40 And be ye ready, for in what hour ye guess not, man's Son shall come.

41 And Peter said to him, Lord, sayest thou this parable to us, or to all?

42 And the Lord said, Who, guessest thou, is a true [or a faithful] dispenser, and prudent, whom the lord hath ordained on his household, to give them in time a measure of wheat? (And the Lord said, Who, thinkest thou, is a true, or a faithful, and prudent steward, whom the lord hath ordained on his household, to give them a measure of wheat at the proper time?)

43 Blessed *is* that servant, that the lord when he cometh, shall find so doing. [Blessed *is* that servant, whom when the lord shall come, he shall find doing so.]

44 Verily I say to you, that on all things that he wieldeth, he shall ordain him. (Truly I say to you, or I tell you the truth, that he shall ordain him over everything that he possesseth.)

45 That if that servant say in his heart (or But if that servant say in his heart), My lord tarrieth to come; and begin to smite children (or the other servants), and handmaidens, and eat, and drink, and be filled [or be full-filled] over-measure,

46 the lord of that servant shall come, in the day that he hopeth not, and in the hour that he knoweth not, and shall part him (or and shall divide him in pieces), and put his part with unfaithful men.

47 But that servant that knew the will of his lord, and made not him(self) ready, and did not after his will, shall be beaten with many *beatings.*

48 But he that knew not, and did worthy things of strokes, shall be beaten with few. For to each man to whom much is given, much shall be asked of him; and they shall ask more of him, to whom they betook much, (or and they shall ask more from him, to whom they have delivered, or entrusted, much).

49 I came to send fire into the earth, and what will I, but that it be kindled? (I came to send fire onto the earth, and how I wish, that it were already kindled!)

50 And I have to be baptized with a baptism, and how am I constrained, till that it be perfectly done?

51 Ween ye, [or Guess ye], (or Think ye), that I came to give peace into [the] earth? Nay, I say to you, but parting (or division).

52 For from this time there shall be five parted in one house; three shall be parted against twain (or two), and twain shall be parted against three;

53 the father against the son, and the son against the father; the mother against the daughter, and the daughter against the mother; the husband's mother against the son's wife, and the son's wife against her husband's mother.

54 And he said also to the people, When ye see a cloud rising from the sun going down, anon ye say (or at once ye say), Rain cometh; and so it is done.

55 And when *ye see* the south blowing, ye say, That heat shall be; and it is done.

56 Hypocrites, ye know how to prove the face of heaven and of earth, but how prove ye not this time(?). [Hypocrites, ye know how to interpret the face of heaven and of earth, but not how to interpret this present time?]

57 But what and of yourselves ye deem not that that is just? [Forsooth why and of yourselves deem ye not this thing that is just?] (But why can ye not judge for yourselves what is the right thing to do?)

58 But when thou goest with thine adversary

in the way (or on the way) to the prince [or Forsooth when thou goest with thine adversary to the prince in the way], do busyness to be delivered from him; lest peradventure he take thee to the doomsman (or lest perhaps he take thee to the judge), and the doomsman betake thee to the masterful asker, and the masterful asker send thee into prison.

59   I say to thee, thou shalt not go out from thence, till thou yield the last farthing.

CHAPTER 13

1   And some men were present in that time (or And there were some men who were present at that time), that told to him of the Galileans, whose blood Pilate (had) mingled with the sacrifices of them.

2   And he answered, and said to them, Ween ye that these men of Galilee were sinners more than all Galileans, for they suffered such things? (And he said to them, Do ye think that these men of Galilee were greater sinners than any other Galileans, because they suffered such things?)

3   I say to you, nay; all ye shall perish in like manner, [no] but ye have penance (or unless ye repent).

4   And as (for) those eighteen, on which the tower in Siloam fell down, and slew them, guess ye, that they were debtors more than all men that dwell in Jerusalem?

5   I say to you, nay; but also all ye shall perish, if ye do not penance (or if ye do not repent). [Nay, I say to you; but also ye all shall perish, if ye shall not do penance.]

6   And he said this likeness (or this parable), A man had a fig tree planted in his vineyard, and he came seeking fruit in it, and found none.

7   And he said to the tiller of the vineyard, Lo! three years be, since I come seeking fruit in this fig tree, and I find none; therefore cut it down, whereto occupieth it the earth? (or why should it take up any space in the ground?)

8   And he answering said to him, Lord, suffer it also this year, the while I delve about it, and I shall dung it [or and dung it]; (And he answering said to him, Lord, allow it to remain this year, while I dig about it, and dung it;)

9   if it shall make fruit, [(or) else] if not, in time coming thou shalt cut it down.

10   And he was teaching in their synagogue in the sabbaths (or on the Sabbath).

11   And lo! a woman, that had a spirit of sickness eighteen years, and was crooked [or and was bowed down], and neither in any manner might look upward.

12   Whom when Jesus had seen, he called [her] to him, and said to her, Woman, thou art delivered of thy sickness [or thou art left (or thou art let go) of thy sickness].

13   And he set on her his hands, and anon she stood upright, and glorified God. (And he put his hands upon her, and at once she stood upright, and praised God.)

14   And the prince of the synagogue answered, having disdain for Jesus had healed in the sabbath; and he said to the people, There be six days, in which it behooveth to work; therefore come ye in these, and be ye healed, and not in the day of sabbath. (And the leader of the synagogue spoke, indignant because Jesus had healed on the Sabbath; and he said to the people, There be six days, on which it behooveth to work; and so come here on them, and be healed, and not on the Sabbath day.)

15   But the Lord answered to him, and said, Hypocrite, whether each of you untieth not in (or on) the sabbath his ox, or ass, from the cratch (or from the feed-trough), and leadeth (it) to water? [+Forsooth the Lord answering to him said, Hypocrite, whether each of you in the sabbath untieth not his ox, or his ass, from the cratch, *or the stall,* and leadeth (it) to water?]

16   Behooved it not this daughter of Abraham, whom Satan hath bound, lo! eighteen years, to be unbound of this bond in the day of sabbath? (or on the Sabbath day?)

17 And when he said these things, all his adversaries were ashamed, and all the people joyed in all (the) things, that were gloriously done of him (or that were wonderfully done by him).

18 Therefore he said, To what thing is the kingdom of God like? and to what thing shall I guess it to be like?

19 It is like to a corn of sinapi, which a man took, and cast into his garden [or into his yard]; and it waxed, and was made into a great tree, and fowls of the air rested in the branches thereof. (It is like a kernel, or a grain, of mustard seed, which a man took, and threw into his garden; and it grew, and was made into a great tree, and the birds of the air nested in its branches.)

20 And again he said, To what thing shall I guess the kingdom of God like?

21 It is like to sourdough that a woman took, and hid *it* in three measures of meal, till all were soured. (It is like the yeast, or the leaven, which a woman took, and put *it* in three measures of meal, until all of it was leavened.)

22 And he went by cities and castles (or towns and villages), teaching and making journey into Jerusalem.

23 And a man said to him, Lord, if there be few, that be saved? And he said to them,

24 Strive ye to enter by the strait gate (or Strive to enter by the narrow gate); for I say to you, many seek to enter [in], and they shall not be able (to).

25 For when the husbandman is entered, and the door is closed, [or For when the husbandman hath entered, and closed the door], ye shall begin to stand withoutforth, and knock at the door, and say, Lord, open to us. And he shall answer, and say to you, I know you not, of whence ye be.

26 Then ye shall begin to say, We have eaten before thee and drunk [or We have eaten and drunk before thee], and in our streets thou hast taught.

27 And he shall say to you, I know you not, of whence ye be; go away from me, all ye workers of wickedness.

28 There shall be weeping and grinding of teeth, when ye shall see Abraham, and Isaac, and Jacob, and all the prophets in the kingdom of God; and you to be put out.

29 And they shall come from the east and the west, and from the north and the south, and shall sit at the meat in the realm of God. (And they shall come from the east and the west, and from the north and the south, and shall sit down for the meal in the Kingdom of God.)

30 And lo! they that were the first, be the last; and they that were the last, be the first.

31 In that day some of the Pharisees came nigh, and said to him, Go out, and go from hence, for Herod will slay thee.

32 And he said to them, Go ye, and say to that fox, Lo! I cast out fiends, and I make perfectly healings, today and tomorrow, and the third day I am ended. (And he said to them, Go, and say to that fox, Behold, today and tomorrow, I throw out devils and demons, and I make complete cures, and on the third day I have finished my work.)

33 Nevertheless it behooveth me today, and tomorrow, and the day that (pur)sueth (or the day that followeth), to walk; for it falleth not [for] a prophet to perish out of Jerusalem.

34 Jerusalem, Jerusalem, that slayest (the) prophets, and stonest them that be sent to thee, how oft would I gather together thy sons, as a bird *gathereth* his nest under (his) feathers [or under (his) wings], and thou wouldest not (let me).

35 Lo! your house shall be left to you desert(ed). And I say to you, that ye shall not see me, till it come, when ye shall say, Blessed *is* he, that cometh in the name of the Lord.

CHAPTER 14

1 And it was done, when he had entered

into the house of a prince of (the) Pharisees, in the sabbath, to eat bread, they espied him. (And it was done, when he had entered into the house of a leader of the Pharisees, on the Sabbath, to eat a meal, they watched him.)

2   And lo! a man sick in the dropsy was before him.

3   And Jesus answering spake to the wise men of [the] law, and to the Pharisees, and said, Whether it is leaveful to heal in the sabbath? (And Jesus spoke to the men wise in the Law, and to the Pharisees, and asked, Is it lawful to heal on the Sabbath?)

4   And they held (their) peace. And Jesus took (hold of him), and healed him, and let *him* go.

5   And he answered to them, and said, Whose ass or ox of you shall fall into a pit, and he shall not anon draw him out in the day of sabbath? (And he said to them, Whose ass or ox of yours shall fall into a pit, and he shall not at once pull him out on the Sabbath day?)

6   And they might not answer to him to these things.

7   He said also a parable of men bidden to a feast, and he beheld how they chose the first sitting places, and said to them, (And he also said to them a parable about men bidden to a feast, as he saw how they chose the first, or the best, places to sit, and so he said to them,)

8   When thou art bidden to bridals, sit not to (the) meat in the first place, [or When thou shalt be bidden to weddings, sit not at the meat in the first place]; lest peradventure a worthier than thou be bidden of him, (When thou art invited to a wedding, do not sit down for the meal in the first, or the best, place; lest perhaps a worthier than thou be invited by him,)

9   and lest he come that called thee and him, and say to thee, Give place to this, and then thou shalt begin with shame to hold the lowest place.

10   But when thou art bidden to a feast, go, and sit down in the last place, (so) that when he

cometh, that bade thee to the feast, he say to thee, Friend, come [up] higher. Then worship shall be to thee, before men that sit [together] at the meat, (or Then honour shall be to thee, before those who sit together at the meal).

11   For each that enhanceth himself, shall be lowed [or shall be made low]; and he that meeketh himself, shall be highed. (For everyone who exalteth himself, or who raiseth himself up, shall be made low; and he who humbleth himself, shall be put up higher.)

12   And he said to him, that had bidden him to the feast, When thou makest a meat, or a supper, do not thou call thy friends, nor thy brethren, neither thy cousins, neither neighbours, nor rich men; lest peradventure they bid thee again to the feast, and it be yielded again to thee.

13   But when thou makest a feast, call poor men, feeble [men], crooked (or the lame), and (the) blind,

14   and (then) thou shalt be blessed; for they have not whereof to yield [again] to thee, for it shall be yielded to thee in the rising again of just men (or and so it shall be requited to thee at the resurrection of the righteous).

15   And when one of them that sat together at the meat (or And when one of them who sat there at the meal), had heard these things, he said to him, Blessed *is* he, that shall eat bread in the realm of God.

16   And he said to him, A man made a great supper, and called many.

17   And he sent his servant in the hour of supper, to say to men that were bidden to the feast, that they should come, for now all things be ready.

18   And all began together to excuse them(selves). The first said [to him], I have bought a town, and I have need to go out, and see it; I pray thee, have me excused.

19   And the tother said, I have bought five yokes of oxen, and I go to prove them; I pray thee, have me excused.

20   And another said, I have wedded a wife; and therefore I may not come.

21   And the servant turned again (or And the servant returned), and told these things to his lord. Then the husbandman was wroth, and said to his servant, Go out swiftly into the great streets and the small streets of the city, and bring in hither poor men, and feeble, [and] blind *men*, and crooked (or and the lame).

22   And the servant said, Lord, it is done, as thou hast commanded, and yet there is a *void* place (or and there still be *empty* places).

23   And the lord said to the servant, Go out into (the) ways and hedges, and constrain *men* to enter, that mine house be full-filled, [or be filled], (or so that my house be filled full).

24   For I say to you, that none of those men that be called, shall taste my supper.

25   And much people went with him; and he turned, and said to them,

26   If any man cometh to me, and hateth not his father, and mother, and wife, and sons, and brethren, and sisters, or sistren, and yet his own life, he may not be my disciple (or he cannot be my disciple).

27   And he that beareth not his cross, and cometh after me, may not be my disciple (or cannot be my disciple).

28   For who of you willing to build a tower, whether he sit not first or whether he first sitteth not, and counteth the expenses that be needful, if he have (them) to perform (it)? (For who of you desiring to build a tower, will he not first sit, and count out the expenses that be needed, to see if he hath enough money to finish it or to complete it?)

29   Lest after that he hath set the foundament, and may not perform (it), all that see, begin to scorn him, (Lest after that he hath laid the foundation, and cannot finish it, all who see it, begin to scorn him,)

30   and say, For this man began to build, and might not make an end. (and say, This man began to build, but he could not finish it.)

31   Or what king that will go to do a battle against another king, whether he sitteth not first, and bethinketh, if he may with ten thousand go to meet him that cometh against him with twenty thousand?

32   Else yet while he is afar, he sendeth a messenger, and prayeth (for) those things that be of peace. (Or else while he is still far off, he sendeth a messenger, and beseecheth for those things that be of peace.)

33   So therefore each of you, that forsaketh not [or renounceth not] all (the) things that he hath, may not be my disciple (or cannot be my disciple).

34   Salt is good; but if salt vanish, in what thing shall it be savoured?

35   Neither in earth, nor in [the] dunghill it is profitable, but it shall be cast out (or but it shall be thrown away). He that hath ears of hearing, hear he.

CHAPTER 15

1   And publicans and sinful men were nighing to him, to hear him. (And tax-collectors and sinners were coming near to him, to listen to him.)

2   And the Pharisees and (the) scribes grudged, saying, For this [man] receiveth sinful men, and eateth with them. (And the Pharisees and the scribes grumbled, saying, For this *man* welcometh sinners, and eateth with them.)

3   And he spake to them this parable, and said,

4   What man of you that hath an hundred sheep, and if he hath lost one of them, whether he leaveth not ninety and nine in (the) desert, and goeth to it that perished, till he find it? (or and goeth after that which is lost, until he find it?)

5   And when he hath found it, he joyeth, and layeth [or putteth] it on his shoulders;

6   and he cometh home, and calleth together his friends and neighbours, and saith to them,

Be ye glad with me, for I have found my sheep, that had perished [or that I had lost].

7 And I say to you, so joy shall be in heaven on one sinful man doing penance, more than on ninety and nine just, that have no need to penance [or that have no need of penance]. (And I tell you, there shall be more joy in heaven over one sinner repenting, than over ninety-nine righteous men, who have no need of repentance.)

8 Or what woman having ten bezants [or ten drachmas], and if she hath lost one bezant [or one drachma], whether she tendeth not [or she lighteth not] a lantern, and turneth upside-down the house, and seeketh diligently, till she find it?

9 And when she hath found (it), she calleth together (her) friends and neighbours, and saith, Be ye glad with me, for I have found the bezant [or the drachma] that I had lost.

10 So I say to you, joy shall be before the angels of God on one sinful man doing penance. (So I tell you, there is joy among the angels of God over one sinner repenting.)

11 And he said, A man had two sons;

12 and the younger of them said to the father [or and the younger said to his father], Father, give me the portion of (the) chattel [or of the substance] that falleth to me. And he parted to them the chattel [or the substance], (or And he divided the goods between them).

13 And not after many days, when all things were gathered together, the younger son went forth in pilgrimage into a far country; and there he wasted his goods [or his substance] in living lecherously.

14 And after that he had ended all things, a strong hunger was made in that country, and he began to have need.

15 And he went, and drew him(self) to one of the citizens of that country. And he sent him into his town, to feed swine, (or to feed his pigs), [or (so) that he should feed hogs].

16 And he coveted to fill his womb of the pods that the hogs ate, and no man gave (anything) to him. (And he desired to fill his belly with the pods which the pigs ate, but no one gave him anything to eat.)

17 And he turned again to himself, and said, How many hired men in my father's house have plenty of loaves; and I perish here through hunger.

18 I shall rise up, and go to my father, and I shall say to him, Father, I have sinned (up) into heaven [or I have sinned against heaven], and before thee;

19 and now I am not worthy to be called thy son, make me as one of thine hired men.

20 And he rose up, and came to his father. And when he was yet afar, his father saw him, and was stirred by mercy. And he ran, and fell on his neck, and kissed him.

21 And the son said to him, Father, I have sinned (up) into heaven [or I have sinned against heaven], and before thee; and now I am not worthy to be called thy son.

22 And the father said to his servants, Swiftly bring ye forth the first stole, and clothe ye him, and give ye a ring in his hand (or and put a ring on his finger), and shoes on his feet;

23 and bring ye a fat calf [or and bring ye a calf made fat], and slay ye, and eat we, and make we feast.

24 For this my son was dead, and hath lived again; he perished (or he was lost), and is found. And all men began to eat [gladly].

25 But his elder son was in the field; and when he came, and nighed to the house (or and approached the house), he heard a symphony and a crowd.

26 And he called one of the servants, and asked, what these things were.

27 And he said to him, Thy brother is come (home), and thy father slew a fat calf [or and thy father hath slain a fatted calf], for he received him safe (again).

28 And he was wroth, and would not come in. Therefore his father went out, and began to

pray him (or And so his father went out to him, and began to beseech him).

29 And he answered to his father, and said, Lo! so many years I serve thee, and I never brake thy commandment(s); and thou never gave to me a kid, that I with my friends should have eaten.

30 But after that this thy son, that hath devoured his substance with whores, came, thou hast slain to him a fat calf [or a fatted calf], (or thou hast killed a fatted calf for him).

31 And he said to him, Son, thou art (for)evermore with me, (or Son, thou art always with me), and all my things be thine.

32 But it behooved to make feast, and to have joy; for this thy brother was dead, and lived again [or and liveth again]; he perished, and is found, (or for thy brother was dead, but now he liveth again; he was lost, but now he is found).

CHAPTER 16

1 He said also to his disciples, There was a rich man, that had a bailiff, [or a farmer], (or a steward, or a manager); and this was denounced to him, as he had wasted his goods.

2 And he called him, and said to him, What hear I this thing of thee? (or Why do I hear this about thee?) yield (the) reckoning (or the accounting) of thy bailiffship, for thou might not now be bailiff, [⁺or yield reason of thy farm, for now thou shalt no more hold the farm].

3 And the bailiff said within himself, What shall I do, for my lord taketh away from me the bailiffship? delve may I not, I shame to beg, (or I cannot dig, and I am ashamed to beg). [Forsooth the farmer said within himself, What shall I do, for my lord taketh away from me the farm? I may not delve, I am ashamed to beg.]

4 I know what I shall do, (so) that when I am removed from the bailiffship [or (so) that when I shall be removed from the farm], they receive me into their houses.

5 Therefore when all the debtors of his lord were called together, he said to the first, How much owest thou to my lord?

6 And he said, An hundred barrows of oil. And he said to him, Take thy caution [or Take thine obligation], and sit soon, and write fifty.

7 Afterward he said to another, And how much owest thou? Which answered, An hundred cors of wheat [or An hundred measures of wheat]. And he said to him, Take thy letters, and write fourscore.

8 And the lord praised the bailiff of wickedness [or And the lord praised the farmer of wickedness], for he had done prudently; for the sons of this world be more prudent in their generation, than the sons of light. (And the lord praised the steward for his wickedness, or his shrewdness, for he had done prudently; for the sons of this world be more prudent with their affairs, than the sons of the light be.)

9 And I say to you, make ye to you friends of the riches of wickedness, (so) that when ye shall fail, they receive you into everlasting tabernacles.

10 He that is true in the least thing, is true also in the more (thing), [or He that is faithful in the least thing, is faithful also in the more]; and he that is wicked in a little thing, is wicked also in the more (things). (He who is true in the least thing, is also true in the greater thing; and he who is wicked in a little thing, is also wicked in the greater things.)

11 Therefore if ye were not true in the wicked thing of riches [or Therefore if ye were not true in the wicked riches], who shall betake to you that that is very [or that is sooth]? (or who shall deliver unto you that which is truly valuable?)

12 And if ye were not true in other men's thing(s), who shall give to you that that is yours?

13 No servant may serve to two lords; for either he shall hate the one, and love the other; either he shall draw to the one, and despise the other. Ye may not serve to God and to riches

(or Ye cannot serve God and money, or wealth). [No manservant may serve two lords; forsooth either he shall hate one, and love the other; either he shall cleave to one, and despise the other. Ye may not serve to God and riches.]

14 But the Pharisees, that were covetous, heard all these things, and they scorned him.

15 And he said to them, Ye it be, that justify you(rselves) before men; but God hath known your hearts [or soothly God knoweth your hearts], for that that is high to men, is (an) abomination before God.

16 The law and the prophets till to John; from that time the realm of God is evangelized [or is preached], and each man doeth violence into it.

17 Forsooth it is lighter (for) heaven and earth to pass (away), than that one tittle fall from the law. (For it is easier for heaven and earth to pass away, than for one dot to fall away from the Law.)

18 Every man that forsaketh his wife, and weddeth another, doeth lechery [or doeth adultery]; and he that weddeth the *wife* forsaken of the husband, doeth adultery, (or and he who weddeth the *wife* left by her husband, doeth adultery).

19 There was a rich man, and (he) was clothed in purple, and white silk, and ate every day shiningly.

20 And there was a beggar, Lazarus by name, that lay at his gate full of boils,

21 and coveted to be fulfilled of the crumbs [⁺or coveting to be filled with the crumbs], that fell down from the rich man's board (or table), and no man gave to him; but (the) hounds came, and licked his boils.

22 And it was done, that the beggar died, and was borne of (the) angels (or was carried by the angels) into Abraham's bosom. And the rich man was dead also, and was buried in hell.

23 And he raised up his eyes, when he was in torments, and saw Abraham afar, and Lazarus in his bosom.

24 And he cried, and said, Father Abraham, have mercy on me, and send Lazarus, that he dip the end of his finger in water, and cool my tongue; for I am tormented in this flame.

25 And Abraham said to him, Son, have mind (or remember), for thou hast received good things in thy life, and Lazarus also evil things; but he is now comforted, and thou art tormented.

26 And in all these things a great dark place [or a great dark depth] is stablished betwixt us and you; that they that will from hence pass to you, may not, (or so that they who want to pass over from here to you, cannot), neither from thence (to) pass over hither.

27 And he said, Then I pray thee, father, that thou send him into the house of my father.

28 For I have five brethren, that he witness to them, (or For I have five brothers, so that he can testify to them), lest also they come into this place of torments.

29 And Abraham said to him, They have Moses and the prophets; hear they them.

30 And he said, Nay, father Abraham, but if any of dead men go to them [or but if any of (the) dead shall go to them], they shall do penance (or then they shall repent).

31 And he said to him, If they hear not Moses and the prophets, neither if any of (the) dead men rise again, they shall believe to him. (And he said to him, If they will not listen to Moses and the prophets, even if a dead man shall rise again, they shall not believe him.)

CHAPTER 17

1 And Jesus said to his disciples, It is impossible that causes of stumbling come not; but woe to that man, by whom they come.

2 It is more profitable to him, if a millstone be put about his neck, and he be cast into the sea, than that he cause to stumble one of these little (ones).

3 Take ye heed to yourselves; if thy brother hath sinned against thee, blame him; and if he

do penance, forgive him. (Keep watch over yourselves; if thy brother hath sinned against thee, rebuke him; and if he repent, forgive him.)

4 And if seven times in the day he do sin against thee, and seven times in the day he be converted to thee, and say, It forthinketh me, forgive thou him, (or and say, I repent, then forgive him).

5 And the apostles said to the Lord, Increase to us faith, [or Increase faith to us], (or Increase our faith).

6 And the Lord said, If ye have faith as (big as) the corn [or a corn] of sinapi (or If ye have faith as big as a kernel, or a grain, of mustard seed), ye shall say to this (syca)more tree, Be thou drawn up by the root, and be over-planted into the sea [or and be thou planted over into the sea], and it shall obey to you.

7 But who of you hath a servant earing, or pasturing oxen, which saith to him, when he turneth again from the field, Anon go, and sit to [the] meat; (But who of you hath a servant plowing, or pasturing oxen, who saith to him, when he returneth from the field, At once go, and sit down for your meal;)

8 and saith not to him, Make ready, (so) that I (can) sup, and gird thee, and serve me, while I eat and drink, and after this thou shalt eat and drink;

9 whether he hath grace to that servant (or shall he give thanks to that servant), for he did that that he commanded him? Nay, I guess.

10 So [also] ye, when ye have done all (the) things that be commanded to you, say ye, We be unprofitable servants, we have done that that we ought to do.

11 And it was done, the while Jesus went to Jerusalem, he passed through the midst of Samaria, and Galilee.

12 And when he entered into a castle (or And when he entered into a village), ten leprous men came to meet him, which stood afar,

13 and raised [up] their voice, and said, Jesus,

Commander (or Master), have mercy on us.

14 And as he saw them, he said, Go, show ye you(rselves) to the priests. And it was done, while they went, they were cleansed.

15 And one of them, as he saw that he was cleansed, went again, magnifying God with a great voice. (And one of them, as soon as he saw that he was healed, returned to him, praising God with a loud voice.)

16 And he fell down on the face before his feet, and did thankings, [or doing graces], (or and giving thanks); and this was a Samaritan.

17 And Jesus answered, and said, Whether ten be not cleansed (or Were ten not healed), and where be the (other) nine?

18 There is none found, that turned again, and gave glory to God, but this alien [or this stranger]. (There is no one who returned, and gave glory to God, except this foreigner.)

19 And he said to him, Rise up, go thou; for thy faith hath made thee safe, (or for thy faith hath saved thee, or thy faith hath healed thee).

20 And he was asked of the Pharisees, when the realm of God cometh, (or And he was asked by the Pharisees, when the Kingdom of God would come). And he answered to them, and said, The realm of God cometh not with espying,

21 neither they shall say, Lo! here, or lo[!] there; for lo! the realm of God is within you (or for behold, the Kingdom of God is within you).

22 And he said to his disciples, Days shall come, when ye shall desire to see one day of man's Son, and ye shall not see (it).

23 And they shall say to you, Lo! here, and lo! there. Do not ye go, neither (pur)sue (them), (or Do not go out, nor follow after them);

24 for as lightning shining from under (the) heaven(s) shineth into [or on] those things that be under (the) heaven(s), so shall man's Son be in his day.

25 But first it behooveth him to suffer many things, and to be reproved of this generation, (or and to be rebuked, or to be rejected, by this

generation).

26   And as it was done in the days of Noe (or of Noah), so it shall be in the days of man's Son.

27   They ate and drank, wedded wives, and were given to weddings, till into the day in which Noe (or Noah) entered into the ship; and the great flood came, and lost all, (or and then the great flood came, and destroyed everything).

28   Also as it was done in the days of Lot, they ate and drank, bought and sold, planted and builded;

29   but in the day that Lot went out of Sodom, the Lord rained (down) fire and brimstone from heaven, and lost all (or and destroyed everything).

30   Like this thing it shall be [or After this thing it shall be], in what day man's Son shall be showed. (It shall be like that, on the day when man's Son shall be revealed.)

31   In that hour [or In that day], he that is in the roof, (or Yea, at that time, he who is on the roof), and his vessels in the house, come he not down to take them away; and he that *shall be* in the field, also turn not again behind.

32   Be ye mindful of the wife of Lot. (Remember Lot's wife.)

33   Whoever seeketh to make his life safe, shall lose it; and whoever loseth it, shall quicken it, (or and whoever loseth it, shall save it, or shall enliven it).

34   But I say to you, in that night two shall be in one bed, one shall be taken, and the other forsaken (or and the other left);

35   two *women* shall be grinding together, the one shall be taken, and the other forsaken (or and the other left);

36   two in a field, the one shall be taken, and the other left.

37   They answer, and say to him, Where, Lord? Which said to them, Wherever the body shall be, thither shall be gathered together also the eagles. [They answering said to him,

Where, Lord? Which said to him, Wherever the body shall be, also the eagles shall be gathered together thither.]

CHAPTER 18

1   And he said to them also a parable, that it behooveth to pray (for)evermore (or that it behooveth to always pray), and not fail;

2   and said, There was a judge in a city, that dreaded not God, neither shamed of men. (and said, There was a judge in a city, who did not fear God, nor could be shamed by any man.)

3   And a widow was in that city, and she came to him, and said, (A)Venge me of mine adversary;

4   and he would not (for a) long time. But after these things he said within himself, Though I dread not God, and shame not of man, (or Though I do not fear God, and I cannot be shamed by any man),

5   nevertheless for this widow is heavy [or is dis-easeful] to me, I shall (a)venge her; lest at the last she coming condemn me [or she strangle me].

6   And the Lord said, Hear ye, what the doomsman of wickedness saith (or Listen to what the wicked judge saith);

7   and whether God shall not do [the] vengeance of his chosen, crying to him day and night, and shall have patience in them? (and so shall God not take vengeance for his chosen, those crying to him day and night, and shall also have patience with them?)

8   Soothly I say to you, for soon he shall do [the] vengeance of them. Nevertheless guessest thou, that man's Son coming shall find faith in earth? (Truly I say to you, or I tell you the truth, that soon he shall take vengeance for them. Nevertheless guessest thou, that when man's Son cometh, he shall find faith on the earth?)

9   And he said also to some men, that trusted in themselves, as *they were* rightful, [or that trusted in themselves, as rightful], (or who

believed themselves to be good and righteous), and despised others, this parable, saying,

10 Two men went up into the temple to pray; the one a Pharisee, and the other a publican (or and the other one a tax-collector).

11 And the Pharisee stood, and prayed by himself these things, and said, God, I do thankings to thee, (or God, I give thanks to thee), for I am not as other men, raveners, unjust, adulterers, as also this publican (is);

12 I fast twice in the week, I give tithes of all (the) things that I have in possession.

13 And the publican stood afar (or And the tax-collector stood far off), and would not raise [up] his eyes to heaven, but smote his breast, and said, God be merciful to me, (a) sinner.

14 Truly I say to you, this went down into his house, and was justified from the other. For each that enhanceth himself, shall be made low, and he that meeketh himself, shall be enhanced. (I tell you the truth, this man went down to his house, and was justified rather than the other man. For everyone who exalteth himself, or who raiseth himself up, shall be made low, and he who humbleth himself, shall be exalted, or shall be raised up.)

15 And they brought to him young children, that he should touch them; and when the disciples saw this thing, they blamed them. (And they brought young children to him, so that he would touch them; and when the disciples saw this, they rebuked them.)

16 But Jesus called together them, and said, Suffer ye (the) children to come to me, and do not ye forbid them, for of such is the kingdom of heavens. (But Jesus called them together, and said, Allow the children to come to me, and do not forbid them, for of such is the Kingdom of Heaven.)

17 Truly I say to you, whoever shall not take the kingdom of God as a child, he shall not enter into it. (I tell you the truth, whoever shall not receive, or shall not accept, the Kingdom of God like a child, he shall not enter into it.)

18 And a prince asked him, and said, Good master, in what thing doing shall I wield everlasting life? (And a leader of the synagogue asked him, and said, Good Teacher, what must I do to get, or to possess, eternal life?)

19 And Jesus said to him, What sayest thou me (to be) good? (or Why sayest thou that I am good?) No man *is* good, but God alone.

20 Thou knowest the commandments, Thou shalt not slay, Thou shalt not do lechery, Thou shalt not do theft, Thou shalt not say false witnessing, Worship thy father and *thy* mother. (Thou knowest the commandments, Thou shalt not kill, Thou shalt not do adultery, Thou shalt not do theft, Thou shalt not give false testimony, or Thou shalt not lie, Honour thy father and *thy* mother.)

21 Which said (or And he replied), I have kept all these things from my youth.

22 And when this thing was heard, Jesus said to him, Yet one thing faileth to thee; sell thou all (the) things that thou hast, and give to poor men, and thou shalt have treasure in heaven; and come, and (pur)sue thou me, [or and come, and (pur)sue me], (or and come, and follow me).

23 And when these things were heard, he was sorrowful, for he was full rich.

24 And Jesus seeing him made sorry [or made sorrowful] said, How hard they that have money [or riches] shall enter into the kingdom of God;

25 for it is lighter [or forsooth it is easier], (for) a camel to pass through a needle's eye, than (for) a rich man to enter into the kingdom of God.

26 And they that heard these things said, Who may be made safe? (And they who heard these things said, Then who can be saved?)

27 And he said to them, Those things that be impossible with men, be possible with God.

28 But Peter said, Lo! we have left all things, and have (pur)sued thee. (But Peter said, Behold, we have left everything, and have

followed thee.)

29   And he said to him, Truly I say to you (or I tell you the truth), there is no man that shall forsake house, or father and mother, or brethren, or wife, or children, or fields, for the realm of God (or for the Kingdom of God),

30   and shall not receive many more things in this time, and in the world to coming everlasting life, [or and in the world to come everlasting life], (or and in the world to come eternal life).

31   And Jesus took his twelve *disciples,* and said to them, Lo! we go up to Jerusalem, and (there) all things shall be ended, that be written by the prophets of man's Son (or which be written by the prophets about man's Son).

32   For he shall be betrayed to heathen men (or For he shall be handed over to the Gentiles), and he shall be scorned, and scourged, and bespat;

33   and after that they have scourged *him,* they shall slay him, and the third day he shall rise again.

34   And they understood nothing of these; and this word was hid from them (or and the meaning was hidden from them), and they understood not those things that were said.

35   But it was done, when Jesus came nigh to Jericho (or when Jesus approached Jericho), a blind man sat beside the way, and begged.

36   And when he heard the people passing (by), he asked, what this was.

37   And they said to him, that Jesus of Nazareth passed (by).

38   And he cried, and said, Jesus, the son of David, have mercy on me.

39   And they that went before, blamed him, that he should be still, (or And they who went ahead of Jesus, rebuked him, saying that he should be quiet); but he cried much the more [or soothly he cried much more], Thou son of David, have mercy on me.

40   And Jesus stood, and commanded him to be brought forth to him. And when he came

nigh, he asked him, and said,

41   What wilt thou that I shall do to thee? (or What desirest thou that I shall do for thee?) And he said, Lord, that I see.

42   And Jesus said to him, Behold; thy faith hath made thee safe, (or Behold; thy faith hath saved thee, or thy faith hath healed thee).

43   And anon he saw, and (pur)sued him, and magnified God. And all the people, as it saw, gave praising to God. (And at once he saw, and followed him, and praised God. And all the people, who saw it happen, also praised God.)

CHAPTER 19

1   And Jesus going in, walked through Jericho.

2   And lo! a man, Zacchaeus by name, and this was a prince of publicans, [or and he was (a) prince of publicans], (or and this man was a chief tax-collector), and he *was* rich.

3   And he sought to see Jesus, who he was, and he might not, for the people, for he was little in stature.

4   And he ran before (or And so he ran ahead), and ascended [up] into a sycamore tree, to see him; for he was to pass from thence.

5   And Jesus beheld up, when he came to the place, and saw him, and said to him, Zacchaeus, haste thee, and come down, for today I must dwell in thine house.

6   And he hieing [or he hasting] came down, and joying(ly) received him.

7   And when all men saw, they grudged (or they grumbled), saying, For he had turned to a sinful man.

8   But Zacchaeus stood, and said to the Lord, Lo! Lord, I (now) give the half of my goods to poor men; and if I have anything defrauded any man, I yield four so much, [or I yield fourfold], (or and if I have defrauded anyone of any amount, I shall repay them four times as much).

9   Jesus saith to him, For today health is made to this house, for that he is Abraham's

son; (Jesus said to him, Today salvation or deliverance hath come to this house, because he too is Abraham's son;)

10 for man's Son came to seek, and make safe that thing that perished. (for man's Son came to seek, and to save those who have perished.)

11 When they heard these things, he added, and said a parable, for that he was nigh to Jerusalem, and for they guessed, that anon (or at once) the kingdom of God should be showed.

12 Therefore he said, A worthy man [or Some nobleman] went into a far country, to take to him(self) a kingdom, and to turn again (or and then to return home).

13 And when his ten servants were called, he gave to them ten bezants (or he gave them ten coins); and said to them, Chaffer ye, [or Merchandize ye], (or Trade), till I come (back).

14 But his citizens hated him, and sent a messenger after him, and said, [or Forsooth his citizens hated him, and sent a message after him, saying], We will not, that he reign on us, (or We do not desire, that he reign over us, or We do not want him to rule over us).

15 And it was done, that he turned again (or that he returned), when he had taken the kingdom; and he commanded *his* servants to be called, to which he had given (the) money, to know, how much each had won by chaffering (or to learn, how much each had earned by merchandizing, or trading).

16 And the first came, and said, Lord, thy bezant hath won ten bezants, (or Lord, thy coin hath earned ten coins).

17 He said to him, Well be, thou good servant; for in little thing thou hast been true, thou shalt be having power on ten cities [or thou shalt have power upon ten cities]. (He said to him, Well done, O good servant; because in a little thing thou hast been true, thou shalt have power over ten cities.)

18 And the tother came, and said, Lord, thy bezant hath made five bezants. (And the next came, and said, Lord, thy coin hath earned five coins.)

19 And to this he said, And be thou on five cities. (And to him he said, And thou shalt be over five cities.)

20 And the third came, and said, Lord, lo! thy bezant, (or Lord, behold, thy coin), that I had, put up [or kept] in a sudarium, [*or in* (a) *sweating cloth*], (or in a napkin).

21 For I dreaded thee, for thou art an austere man; thou takest away that that thou settedest not, and thou reapest that that thou hast not sown. (For I feared thee, for thou art a stern and a hard man; thou takest away that which thou hast not brought, and thou harvestest that which thou hast not sown.)

22 He saith to him, Wicked servant, of thy mouth I deem thee. Knewest thou, that I am an austere man, taking away that thing that I setted not, and reaping that thing that I sowed not [or that I have not sown]? (He said to him, Wicked servant, with the words of thy own mouth I shall judge thee. Knewest thou, that I am a stern and hard man, taking away that which I have not brought, and harvesting that which I have not sown?)

23 and why hast thou not given my money to the board, and I coming should have asked (for) it [or should have received it] with usuries? (and why hast thou not given my money to the money-changers, and then when I came back, I would have received it with some interest?)

24 And he said to (the) men standing nigh, Take away from him the bezant, and give ye [it] to him that hath ten bezants. (And he said to the men standing near, Take away the coin from him, and give it to him who hath ten coins.)

25 And they said to him, Lord, he hath ten bezants, (or Lord, he hath ten coins!).

26 And I say to you, to each man that hath, it shall be given, and he shall increase; but from him that hath not, also that thing that he hath, shall be taken of him [or shall be taken from

him].

27 Nevertheless bring ye hither those (of) mine enemies, that would not that I reigned on them, and slay ye (them) before me. (And bring here those enemies of mine, who do not desire that I reign over them, or who do not want me to rule over them, and kill them before me.)

28 And when these things were said [or And these things said], he went before (or he went forth), and went up to Jerusalem.

29 And it was done, when Jesus came nigh to Bethphage and Bethany, at the mount, that is called of Olivet (or at the Mount of Olives), he sent his two disciples,

30 and said, Go ye into the castle that is against you (or Go into the village that is opposite you); into which as ye enter, ye shall find a colt of an ass tied, on which never (any) man sat; untie ye him, and bring ye (it) to me.

31 And if any man ask you, why ye untie (it), thus ye shall say to him, For the Lord desireth his work.

32 And they that were sent, went forth, and found as he said to them, a colt standing (there).

33 And when they untied the colt, the lords of it said to them, What untie ye the colt? [or Why untie ye the colt?]

34 And they said, For the Lord hath need to him (or For the Lord hath need of him).

35 And they led him to Jesus; and they casted their clothes on the colt, and set Jesus on him. (And they led it to Jesus; and they threw their clothes onto the colt, and then put Jesus on it.)

36 And when he went, they spreaded their clothes in the way. (And as he went, they spread their clothes on the way, or on the road.)

37 And when [now] he came nigh to the coming down of the mount of Olivet, all the people that came down began to joy, and to praise God with (a) great voice on all the virtues, that they had seen, (And when he came near to the descent of the Mount of Olives, all the people who came down began to rejoice,

and to praise God with loud voices, for all the works of power, or all the miracles, that they had seen,)

38 and said, Blessed be the king, that cometh in the name of the Lord; peace in heaven, and glory in high things.

39 And some of the Pharisees of the people said to him, Master, blame thy disciples, (or Teacher, rebuke thy disciples).

40 And he said to them, I say to you (or I tell you), for if these be still, (the) stones shall cry (out).

41 And when he nighed, he saw the city, and wept on it, (And when he approached, he saw the city, and wept over it,)

42 and said, For if thou haddest known, thou shouldest weep also; for in this [thy] day, the things be in peace to thee, but now they be hid from thine eyes. (and said, For if thou haddest only known, thou wouldest weep also; yea, in this thy day, for the things that would bring peace to thee, but now they be hidden from thine eyes.)

43 But days shall come in thee [or For days shall come to thee], and thine enemies shall environ thee with a pale, and they shall go about thee, and make thee strait on all sides (or and make thee narrow, or hemmed in, on every side),

44 and cast thee down to the earth (or and throw thee down to the ground), and thy sons [or thy children] that be in thee; and they shall not leave in thee a stone upon a stone, for thou hast not known the time of thy visitation.

45 And he entered into the temple, and began to cast out men selling therein and buying, (And he entered into the Temple, and began to throw out the men who were there buying and selling,)

46 and said to them, It is written, That mine house is an house of prayer, (or It is written, My House is a House of Prayer), but ye have made it a den of thieves.

47 And he was teaching every day in the

temple. And the princes of (the) priests, and the scribes, and the princes of the people sought to lose him; (And he was teaching every day in the Temple. And the high priests, and the scribes, and the leaders of the people sought to destroy him;)

48   and they found not, what they should do to him, for all the people was [fervently] occupied, and heard him, [or for all the people was hanged up, *or all-occupied*, hearing him]. (but they could not figure out, what they should do to him, for all the people were fervently occupied, hanging on his every word, or attentively listening to him.)

CHAPTER 20

1   And it was done in one of the days, when he taught the people in the temple, and preached the gospel [or evangelizing], the princes of (the) priests, and [the] scribes came together with the elder men; (And it was done on one of the days, when he taught the people in the Temple, and preached the Gospel or the Good News, or evangelized, the high priests, and the scribes came together with the elders;)

2   and they said to him, Say to us, in what power thou doest these things, or who is he that gave to thee this power?

3   And Jesus answered, and said to them, And I shall ask you one word; answer ye to me. (And Jesus said to them, And I shall ask you a question; you answer me.)

4   Was the baptism of John of heaven, or of men? (Was the baptism of John from heaven, or from men?)

5   And they thought within themselves, saying, For if we say, Of heaven (or From heaven), he shall say, Why then believe ye not to him?

6   and if we say, Of men (or From men), all the people shall stone us; for they be certain, that John is a prophet.

7   And they answered, that they knew not, of whence it was.

8   And Jesus said to them, Neither I say to you, in what power I do these things.

9   And he began to say to the people this parable. A man planted a vineyard, and hired it (out) to tillers; and he was gone in pilgrimage (for a) long time. (And he told the people this parable. A man planted a vineyard, and rented it to farmers, and then went on a journey for a long time.)

10   And in the time of gathering of grapes, he sent a servant to the tillers, that they should give to him of the fruit of the vineyard; which beat him, and let him go (away) void. (And at the time of gathering in the grapes, he sent a servant to the farmers, so that they could give him some of the fruit of the vineyard; but they beat him, and sent him away empty-handed.)

11   And he thought yet to send another servant; and [also] they beat this (man), and tormented him sore, and let him go (away) void (or and sent him away empty-handed).

12   And he thought yet to send the third, and him also they wounded, and casted him out (or and threw him out).

13   And the lord of the vineyard said, What shall I do? I shall send my dearworthy son; peradventure, when they see him, they shall dread (him), [or they shall be ashamed (in his presence)], (or perhaps, when they see him, they shall fear him, or surely, when they see him, they shall show reverence, or respect, for him).

14   And when the tillers saw him, they thought within themselves, and said, This is the heir, slay we him, that the heritage be ours. (But when the farmers saw him, they said to each other, He is the heir, let us kill him, and then the inheritance shall be ours.)

15   And they casted him out of the vineyard (or And they threw him out of the vineyard), and killed *him*. What shall then the lord of the vineyard do to them?

16   He shall come, and destroy these tillers,

and give the vineyard to others. And when this thing was heard, they said to him, God forbid.

17 But he beheld them, and said, What then is this that is written, The stone which men building reproved, this is made into the head of the corner?

18 Each that shall fall on that stone, shall be bruised [or shall be broken], but on whom it shall fall, it shall all-break him, [or it shall break him into small parts], (or it shall break him all to pieces).

19 And the princes of (the) priests, and (the) scribes, sought to lay on him hands in that hour, [or And the princes of the priests, and the scribes, sought to lay hands on him in that hour], and they dreaded the people; for they knew that to them he said this likeness. (And the high priests, and the scribes, wanted to lay their hands on him at that time, but they feared the people; for they knew that he had said this parable about them.)

20 And they espied, and sent spies, that feigned them[selves] (to be) just, that they should take him in word, and betake him to the power of the prince, and to the power of the justice. (And they watched him, and sent spies, who pretended to be righteous, or honest men, so that they could catch him with his own words, and then deliver him unto the power and the authority of the Governor.)

21 And they asked him, and said, Master (or Teacher), we know, that rightly thou sayest and teachest, [or Master, we know, that thou sayest and teachest rightly]; and thou takest not the person of man (or and thou favourest not any person), but thou teachest in truth the way of God.

22 Is it leaveful to us to give tribute to the emperor, [or to Caesar], or nay? (Is it lawful for us to pay taxes to Caesar, or not?)

23 And he beheld the deceit of them, and said to them, What tempt ye me? (or Why do you test me?)

24 Show ye to me a penny; whose image and superscription hath it? They answered, and said to him, The emperor's [or Caesar's].

25 And he said to them, Yield ye therefore to the emperor those things that be the emperor's, [or Yield ye therefore to Caesar those things that be Caesar's], and those things that be of God, to God.

26 And they might not reprove his word before the people; and they wondered in his answer, and held (their) peace.

27 Some of the Sadducees, that denied the again-rising from death to life [or the resurrection], came, and asked him.

28 and said, Master (or Teacher), Moses wrote to us, if the brother of any man have a wife, and he be dead [or died], and he was without heirs [or free children], that his brother take his wife, and raise (up) seed to his brother.

29 And so there were seven brethren. The first took a wife, and is dead without heirs, [or without sons, or free children];

30 and the *brother* (pur)suing took her, (or and the *brother* following took her), [or and the second took her], and he is dead without (any) son;

31 and the third took her; also and all seven, and they left not seed [or and left no seed], but be dead;

32 and the last of all the woman is dead.

33 Therefore in the rising again, whose wife of them shall she be? for seven had her to wife. (And so in the resurrection, whose wife of them shall she be? for all seven had her as their wife.)

34 And Jesus said to them, Sons of this world wed, and be given to weddings;

35 but they that shall be had worthy of that world, and of the rising again from death (or and of the resurrection from the dead), neither be wedded, nor wed wives,

36 neither they shall be able to die more; for they be even with (the) angels, and be the sons of God, since they be the sons of the rising again from death. (nor shall they be able to die any longer; for they be equal with the angels,

and be the children of God, since they be the children of the resurrection.)

37 And that dead men rise again, also Moses showed beside the bush, as he saith, (or And that the dead rise again, Moses showed beside the bush, when he said), The Lord God of Abraham, and God of Isaac, and God of Jacob.

38 And God is not (the God) of dead men, but of living men; for all men live to him. (And God is not the God of the dead, but of the living; because everyone is alive to him.)

39 And some of the scribes answering, said, Master, thou hast well said, (or Teacher, thou hast answered well).

40 And they durst no more ask him anything. (And they did not dare to ask him anything more.)

41 But he said to them, How say men, Christ to be the son of David, [Forsooth he said to them, How say men, that Christ is the son of David,] (And he said to them, How can men say, that the Messiah is the Son of David?)

42 and David himself saith in the book of Psalms, The Lord said to my Lord, Sit thou on my right half, (For David himself said in the Book of Psalms, The Lord said to my Lord, Sit at my right hand, or on my right side,)

43 till I put thine enemies a stool of thy feet? (until I make thine enemies thy footstool.)

44 Therefore David calleth him Lord, and how is he his son? (And so if David calleth him Lord, then how is he his son?)

45 And in (the) hearing of all the people, he said to his disciples,

46 Be ye ware of the scribes, that will wander in stoles, and love salutations in the chapping, and the first chairs in the synagogues, and the first sitting places in [the] feasts; (Beware of the scribes, who will walk about in stoles, and love respectful greetings at the market, and the first chairs in the synagogues, and the first sitting places at the feasts;)

47 that devour the houses of widows, and feign long praying; these shall take the more damnation. (but who rob widows of their homes, and fake piety by saying long prayers; they shall receive the greater condemnation.)

CHAPTER 21

1 And he beheld, and saw the rich men, that cast their gifts into the treasury;

2 but he saw also a little poor widow casting two farthings [or two little minutes]. (but he also saw a poor little widow throwing in two mites.)

3 And he said, Truly I say to you, that this poor widow cast (in) more than all men. (And he said, I tell you the truth, this poor widow threw in more than everyone else.)

4 For why all these of [the] thing that was plenteous [or abundant] to them cast in to the gifts of God; but this widow of that thing that failed to her, cast (in) all her livelode, [or all her lifelode], (or threw in all her livelihood), that she had.

5 And when some men said of the temple, that it was appareled [or that it was adorned] with good stones and gifts, he said,

6 These things that ye see, days shall come, in which a stone shall not be left on a stone, which shall not be destroyed.

7 And they asked him, and said, Commander (or Master), when shall these things be? and what token (or what sign) *shall be*, when they shall begin to be done?

8 And he said, See ye, that ye be not deceived; for many shall come in my name, saying, For I am, and the time shall nigh, (or for many shall come in my name, saying, I am he, and the time is near); therefore do not ye go after them.

9 And when ye shall hear (of) battles and strives [or dissensions] within, do not ye be afeared; it behooveth first these things to be done, but not yet anon *is* an end [or the end], (or but the end *will* not *come* at once).

10 Then he said to them, Folk shall rise

against folk, and realm against realm; (And he said to them, For nation shall rise against nation, and kingdom against kingdom;)

11 and great movings of the earth shall be by places, and pestilences, and hungers, and dreads from (the) heaven(s), and great tokens shall be. (and great earthquakes shall be in places, and pestilences, and famines, and there shall be fearful things and great signs in the sky.)

12 But before all these things they shall set their hands on you, and shall pursue *you*, betaking (you) into synagogues and keepings, [*either prisons*], and drawing *you* to kings and to justices, for my name; (But before all these things they shall put their hands on you, and shall persecute *you*, delivering you into synagogues and into prisons, and drawing *you* unto kings and unto governors, for my name's sake;)

13 but it shall fall to you into witnessing. (and it shall fall to you to give your testimony.)

14 Therefore put ye (it) in your hearts, not to think before, how ye shall answer;

15 for I shall give to you mouth and wisdom, to which all your adversaries shall not be able to against-stand, and gainsay. (for I shall give you the words and the wisdom, to which all your adversaries shall not be able to stand against, or to say anything against.)

16 And ye shall be taken of father [or Soothly ye shall be betrayed of father], and mother, and brethren, and cousins, and friends, and by death they shall torment [*some*] of you; (And ye shall be betrayed by father, and mother, and brothers, and cousins, and friends, and they shall torment *some* of you unto death;)

17 and ye shall be in hate to all men for my name. [and ye shall be hated of all men for my name.] (and ye shall be hated by everyone for my name's sake.)

18 And an hair of your head shall not perish; (But not a hair of your head shall perish.)

19 in your patience ye shall wield (or ye shall possess) your souls.

20 But when ye shall see Jerusalem be environed with an host [*of battle*], then know ye, that the desolation of it shall nigh. (But when ye shall see Jerusalem encompassed with an army *ready for battle*, then know ye, that its destruction is near.)

21 Then they that be in Judea, flee to the mountains; and they that *be* in the middle of it, go away; and they that *be* in the countries, enter not into it. (Then they who be in Judea, flee to the mountains; and they who *be* in its cities, go away; and they who *be* in the countryside, enter not into the cities.)

22 For these be the days of vengeance, (so) that all (the) things that be written, be fulfilled.

23 And woe to them, that be with child, and nourishing [or nursing] in those days; for a great dis-ease [or pressure] shall be on the earth (or in the land), and wrath to this people.

24 And they shall fall by the sharpness of (the) sword, and they shall be led (away as) prisoners [or led captive] into all folks; and Jerusalem shall be defouled of heathen men, till the times of (the) nations be fulfilled. (And they shall fall by the sharpness of the sword, and they shall be led away captive into all the nations; and Jerusalem shall be trodden down by the Gentiles, until the times of the nations be fulfilled.)

25 And tokens (or signs) shall be in the sun, and the moon, and in the stars; and in the earth overlaying of folks, for confusion of the sound of the sea and of floods [or of waves];

26 for men shall wax dry for dread and abiding, (or for the fear and expectation), that shall come into [or on] all the world; for (the) virtues of (the) heaven(s) shall be moved (or for the powers of the heavens shall be shaken).

27 And then they shall see man's Son coming in a cloud, with great power and majesty. (And then they shall see man's Son coming on a cloud, with great power and majesty.)

28 And when these things begin to be made

[or begin to be done], behold ye, and raise ye (up) your heads, for your redemption nigheth (or your redemption draweth near).

29 And he said to them a likeness (or a parable), See ye the fig tree, and all trees,

30 when they bring forth now of themselves fruit [or when they bring forth fruit now of them(selves)], ye know that summer is nigh (or that summer is near);

31 so [also] ye, when ye see these things to be done, know ye, that the kingdom of God is nigh (or that the Kingdom of God is near).

32 Truly I say to you, that this generation shall not pass, till all things be done. (I tell you the truth, that this generation shall not pass away, until all these things have happened.)

33 Heaven and earth shall pass (away), but my words shall not pass (away).

34 But take ye heed to yourselves (or Keep watch over yourselves), lest peradventure your hearts be grieved with gluttony, and drunkenness, and (the) busynesses of this life, and that day come suddenly on you;

35 for as a snare it shall come on all men, that sit on the face of all the earth.

36 Therefore wake ye, praying in each time, (or And so be on watch, and always pray), that ye be had worthy to flee all these things that be to come [or that ye be worthy to flee all these things that shall come], and to stand before man's Son.

37 And in days he was teaching in the temple, but in nights he went out, and dwelled in the mount, that is called of Olivet. (And during those days he was teaching in the Temple, but at night he went out, and stayed on the Mount of Olives.)

38 And all the people rose early [or And all the people came early], to come to him in the temple, for to hear him.

CHAPTER 22

1 And the holiday [or the holy day] of therf loaves, that is said pask, nighed. (And the holiday, or the holy day, of Unleavened Bread, that is called Passover, approached.)

2 And the princes of (the) priests, and the scribes sought, how they should slay Jesus, but they dreaded the people. (And the high priests, and the scribes, sought how they could kill Jesus, but they feared the people.)

3 And Satan entered into Judas, that was called Iscariot, one of the twelve.

4 And he went, and spake with the princes of (the) priests, (or And he went, and spoke with the high priests), and with the magistrates, how he should betray him to them.

5 And they joyed, and made (a) covenant to give him money. (And they rejoiced, and made a contract to give him money.)

6 And he promised, and he sought opportunity, to betray him, without the people.

7 But the days of therf loaves came, in which it was need(ful), that the sacrifice of pask were slain. (And the days of Unleavened Bread came, in which it was needed, that the Passover sacrifice was killed.)

8 And he sent Peter and John, and said, Go ye, and make ye ready to us the pask, that we eat. (And he sent off Peter and John, saying, Go, and prepare the Passover for us, so that we can eat it.)

9 And they said, Where wilt thou, that we make (it) ready? (And they said, Where do you want us to prepare it?)

10 And he said to them, Lo! when ye shall enter into the city, a man bearing a vessel of water shall meet you; (pur)sue ye him into the house (or follow him into the house), into which he entereth.

11 And ye shall say to the husbandman of the house, The master saith to thee, Where is a chamber, where I shall eat the pask with my disciples? (And ye shall say to the head of the house, The Teacher saith to thee, Where is the room, where I shall eat the Passover with my disciples?)

12   And he shall show to you a great supping place strewed, and there make ye (it) ready (or and prepare it there).

13   And (so) they went, and found (it) as he said to them, and they made ready the pask (or and they prepared the Passover).

14   And when the hour was come, he sat at the meat (or he sat down for the meal), and the twelve apostles with him.

15   And he said to them, With desire I have desired to eat with you this pask, before that I suffer; (And he said to them, With great desire I have wanted to eat this Passover with you, before that I suffer;)

16   for I say to you, that from this time I shall not eat it, till it be fulfilled in the realm of God. (for I tell you, that from this time on I shall not eat it, until it is fulfilled in the Kingdom of God.)

17   And when he had taken the cup, he did graces, [or he did thankings], and said, Take ye, and part ye among you; (And when he had taken the cup, he gave thanks, and said, Take this, and share it among you;)

18   for I say to you, that I shall not drink of the kind [or of the generation] of this vine, till the realm of God come (or until the Kingdom of God shall come).

19   And when he had taken bread, he did thankings, [or he did graces], (or he gave thanks), and brake (it), and gave (it) to them, and said, This is my body, that shall be given for you; do ye this thing in mind of me [or into my commemoration].

20   He took also the cup [or the chalice], after that he had supped, and said, This cup is the new testament in my blood, that shall be shed for you, (or This cup is the new covenant sealed with my blood, that shall be shed for you).

21   Nevertheless lo! the hand of him that betrayeth me, is with me at the table.

22   And man's Son goeth, as it is determined; nevertheless woe to that man, by whom he shall be betrayed.

23   And they began to seek among them[selves], who it was of them, that was to do this thing.

24   And strife was made among them, which of them should be seen to be (the) greatest.

25   But he said to them, Kings of heathen men be lords of them (or Kings of the Gentiles be their lords), and they that have power on them be called good doers,

26   but ye (be) not so (or but it be not so with you); but he that is [the] greatest among you, be made as a younger [or as the younger], and he that is [a] before-goer, as a servant.

27   For who is greater, he that sitteth at the meat, or he that ministereth? whether not he that sitteth at the meat? And I am in the middle [or in the midst] of you, as he that ministereth. (For who is greater, he who sitteth at the meal, or he who serveth it? whether not he who sitteth at the meal? But I am in the midst of you, like he who serveth.)

28   And ye [it] be, that have dwelled with me in my temptations; (And ye it be, who have remained with me during my tests and trials;)

29   and I assign to you, as my Father hath assigned to me, a realm (or a Kingdom). [and I dispose to you, as my Father hath disposed to me, a realm.]

30   that ye eat and drink on my board in my realm, and sit on thrones, and deem the twelve kindreds of Israel. (so that ye will eat and drink at my table in my Kingdom, and sit on thrones, and judge the twelve tribes of Israel.)

31   And the Lord said to Simon, Simon, lo! Satan hath asked (for) you, that he should riddle *you* as wheat (or so that he could sift *you* like wheat);

32   but I have prayed for thee, that thy faith fail not; and thou sometime converted [or and thou converted sometime], confirm thy brethren, (or and after thou hast returned to thy right mind, that thou strengthen thy brothers).

33   Which said to him, Lord, I am ready to go into prison and into death with thee. [+Which

said to him, Lord, I am ready to go with thee, into prison and into death.]

34 And he said, I say to thee, Peter, the cock shall not crow today, till thou thrice forsake that thou knowest me.

35 And he said to them, When I sent you without satchel, and scrip, and shoes, whether anything failed to you? And they said, Nothing.

36 Therefore he said to them, But now he that hath a satchel, take also a scrip; and he that hath none, sell his coat, and buy a sword.

37 For I say to you, that yet it behooveth that thing that is written to be fulfilled in me, And he is areckoned with wicked men; for those things that be of me have an end.

38 And they said, Lord, lo! two swords here. And he said to them, It is enough.

39 And he went out, and went after the custom into the hill of Olives [or the hill of Olivet]; and the disciples (pur)sued him. (And he went out, and as was his custom, went over to the Mount of Olives, and the disciples followed him.)

40 And when he came to the place, he said to them, Pray ye, lest ye enter into temptation, (or Pray ye, lest ye enter into, or be put to, the test).

41 And he was taken away from them, as much as is a stone's cast (or as much as a stone's throw); and he kneeled, and prayed,

42 and said, Father, if thou wilt, do away this cup from me; nevertheless not my will be done, but thine, [or nevertheless not my will, but thine be done].

43 And an angel appeared to him from heaven, and comforted him.

44 And he was made in agony [or in anguish], and prayed the longer [or (and) prayed longer]; and his sweat was made as drops of blood running down into the earth (or and his sweat was made like drops of blood running down onto the ground).

45 And when he was risen from prayer, and was come to his disciples, he found them sleeping for heaviness.

46 And he said to them, What, sleep ye? Rise ye, and pray ye, that ye enter not into temptation. (And he said to them, Why do ye sleep? Rise, and pray, so that ye do not enter into, or be put to, the test.)

47 Yet while he spake, lo! a company, and he that was called Judas, one of the twelve, went before them; and he came [nigh] to Jesus, to kiss him.

48 And Jesus said to him, Judas, betrayest thou man's Son with a kiss?

49 And they that were about him, and saw that that was to come, said to him, Lord, whether we smite (them) with (our) sword(s)? (or Lord, shall we strike them with the swords?)

50 And one of them smote the servant of the prince of (the) priests (or And one of them struck the servant of the High Priest), and cut off his right ear.

51 But Jesus answered, and said, Suffer ye till hither (or Allow this to be). And when he had touched his ear, he healed him.

52 And Jesus said to them, that came to him, the princes of (the) priests, and (the) magistrates, [or the masters], of the temple, and (the) elder men, As to a thief ye have gone out with swords and staves? (And Jesus said to those, who came to take hold of him, the high priests, and the magistrates, or the officials, of the Temple, and the elders, You have gone out with swords and bats, or clubs, like after a thief?)

53 When I was each day with you in the temple, ye stretched not out (your) hands into me; but this is your hour, and the power of darknesses.

54 And they took him, and led (him) to the house of the prince of (the) priests; and Peter (pur)sued him afar. (And they took hold of him, and then led him to the High Priest's house; and Peter followed him from afar.)

55 And when a fire was kindled in the middle of the great house, and they sat about,

Peter was in the middle of them. (And when a fire was kindled in the middle of the courtyard, they sat around it, and Peter was in their midst.)

56 Whom when a damsel, [or a handmaid, or a handmaiden], had seen sitting at the light, and had beheld him, she said, And this (man) was with him (or Yea, he was with him).

57 And he denied him (or But he denied it), and said, Woman, I know him not.

58 And after a little another man saw him, and said, And thou art (one) of them. But Peter said, A! man, I am not.

59 And when a space was made as of one hour, another affirmed, and said, Truly this was with him; for also he is of Galilee, (or Surely he was with him; for he is also from Galilee).

60 And Peter said, Man, I know not what thou sayest. And anon yet while he spake, the cock crew, (or And at once while he was still speaking, the cock crowed).

61 And the Lord turned again [or And the Lord turned], and beheld Peter; and Peter had mind of the word(s) of Jesus, as he had said, (or and Peter remembered Jesus' words, that he had said), Before that the cock crow, thrice thou shalt deny me.

62 And Peter went out, and wept bitterly.

63 And the men that held him scorned him, and smote him (or and struck him).

64 And they blindfolded him, and smote his face, and asked him, and said, Declare, thou *Christ*, to us, who is he that smote thee? [or Prophesy thou, who is it that smote thee?] (or Prophesy thou! who is it that struck thee?)

65 Also they blaspheming said against him many other things. [Also they blaspheming said many other things against him.]

66 And as the day was come, the elder men of the people, and the princes of (the) priests, and the scribes came together, (or the elders of the people, and the high priests, and the scribes came together), and led him into their council, and said,

67 If thou art Christ, say to us. And he said to them, If I say to you, ye will not believe to me; (If thou art the Messiah, tell us. And he said to them, If I tell you, ye will not believe me;)

68 and if I ask (you), ye will not answer to me, neither ye will deliver *me* [or neither ye shall (give *me*) leave]. (and if I ask you, ye will not answer me, nor will ye let *me* go.)

69 But after this time man's Son shall be sitting on the right half of the virtue of God. (But after this time man's Son shall be sitting at the right hand, or on the right side, of the power of God.)

70 Therefore all said, Then art thou the Son of God? And he said, Ye say that I am.

71 And they said, What yet desire we witnessing? for we ourselves have heard of his mouth. (And they said, Why do we need any more testimony? for we ourselves have heard it from his own mouth.)

CHAPTER 23

1 And all the multitude of them arose, and led him to Pilate.

2 And they began to accuse him, and said, We have found this (man) turning upside-down our folk, and forbidding tribute to be given to the emperor, and saying that himself is Christ a king. [Forsooth they began to accuse him, saying, We have found this man turning upside-down our folk, and forbidding tribute to be given to Caesar, and saying himself to be Christ (a) king.] (And they began to accuse him, and said, We have found this man turning our nation upside-down, subverting our people, and forbidding taxes to be paid to Caesar, and saying that he is the Messiah, a king.)

3 And Pilate asked him, and said, Art thou king of Jews? (or Art thou the King of the Jews?) And he answered, and said, Thou sayest.

4 And Pilate said to the princes of (the) priests, and to the people, I find nothing of cause (worthy of death) in this man. (And Pilate said to the high priests, and to the people, I find

no case against this man, or I see no reason to condemn this man.)

5   And they waxed stronger (or And they grew stronger and more insistent), and said, He moveth the people, teaching through all Judea, beginning from Galilee till hither.

6   And Pilate hearing Galilee asked, if he were a man of Galilee.

7   And when he knew that he was of the power of Herod, he sent him to Herod; which was at Jerusalem in those days [or and he was at Jerusalem in those days].

8   And when Herod saw Jesus, he joyed full much; for (a) long time he coveted to see him, for he heard many things of him, and hoped to see some token [or some miracle] done of him. (And when Herod saw Jesus, he greatly rejoiced; for he had desired to see him for a long time, because he had heard many things about him, and hoped to see some sign, or some miracle, done by him.)

9   And he asked him in many words; and he answered nothing to him.

10   And the princes of (the) priests (or And the high priests), and the scribes stood, steadfastly accusing him.

11   But Herod with his host despised him, and scorned him, and clothed him with a white cloth, and sent *him* again to Pilate. (But Herod and his soldiers mocked him, and scorned him, and clothed him with a white cloak, and then sent *him* back to Pilate.)

12   And Herod and Pilate were made friends from that day [or And Herod and Pilate were made friends in that day]; for before they were enemies together (or but before this day they were enemies).

13   And Pilate called together the princes of (the) priests, and the magistrates of the people, (And Pilate called together the high priests, and the magistrates of the people,)

14   and said to them, Ye have brought to me this man, as turning away the people, and lo! I asking before you find no cause (worthy of

death) in this man, of these things, in which ye accuse him; (and said to them, Ye have brought me this man, for subverting the people, and behold, I asking before you find no case against this man, or I see no reason to condemn this man, regarding those things, of which ye accuse him;)

15   neither (did) Herod, for he hath sent him again to us, and lo! nothing worthy of death is done to him. (nor did Herod, for he hath sent him back to us, and behold, nothing worthy of death hath been done by him.)

16   And therefore I shall amend him, and deliver *him*. [⁺Therefore I shall leave him amended, *or deliver him chastised*.] (And so I shall chastise him, and then let *him* go.)

17   But he must needs deliver to them one by the feast day. [Forsooth he had need to deliver to them one by the feast day.] (But he had to release one prisoner to them on the Feast Day, or at the Festival.)

18   And all the people cried together, and said, Do him away, and deliver to us Barabbas; (And all the people cried together, and shouted, Do him away, and release Barabbas to us, or and give us Barabbas;)

19   which was sent into prison for disturbing, [or some dissention, or some sedition], made in the city, and for manslaying. (who was sent into prison for sedition made in the city, and for murder.)

20   And again Pilate spake to them, and would deliver Jesus. [Forsooth again Pilate spake to them, willing to deliver Jesus.] (And again Pilate spoke to them, and wanted to release Jesus.)

21   And they cried out, and said, Crucify, crucify him.

22   And the third time he said to them, For what evil hath he done? I find no cause (worthy) of death in him; therefore I shall chastise him, and [I] shall deliver *him*, (or I find no case, or crime, worthy of death against him; and so I shall chastise him, and then I shall let

him go, or and then I shall release *him*).

23 And they continued with great voices asking [or And they continued asking with great voices], that he should be crucified; and the voices of them waxed strong. (And they continued shouting with loud voices, saying that he should be crucified; and their voices grew stronger and more insistent.)

24 And (then) Pilate deemed their asking to be done.

25 And he delivered to them him, that for manslaying (or for murder) and sedition was sent into prison, (for) whom they (had) asked; but he betook Jesus to their will (or but he delivered Jesus unto their will).

26 And when they led him (away), they took a man, Simon of Cyrene, coming from the town, and they laid on him the cross to bear after Jesus.

27 And there (pur)sued him much people (or And many people followed him), and women that bewailed, and bemourned him.

28 And Jesus turned to them, and said, Daughters of Jerusalem, do not ye weep on me, but weep ye on yourselves and on your sons, (or Daughters of Jerusalem, do not weep for me, but rather weep for yourselves and for your children).

29 For lo! days shall come, in which it shall be said, Blessed be barren women, and [the] wombs that have not born children, and the teats that have not given suck (or and the breasts that have not been suckled).

30 Then they shall begin to say to (the) mountains, Fall ye down on us, and to (the) small hills, Cover ye us.

31 For if in a green tree they do these things [or For if they do these things in a green tree], what shall be done in a dry (one)? (For if they do these things when the tree is green, what shall they do when it is dry?)

32 Also other two wicked men were led (away) with him, to be slain. (And two other wicked men were led away to be killed, or

executed, with him.)

33 And when they came into a place, that is called of Calvary, [†or And after that they came to a place, which is called Calvary], there they crucified him, and the thieves, one on the right half, and the other on the left half, (or one on his right side, and the other on his left side).

34 But Jesus said, Father, forgive them, for they know not what they do. And they parted his clothes, and cast lots (for them), (or And they divided up his clothes, and threw dice for them).

35 And the people stood abiding; and the princes scorned him with them, and said, Other men he made safe; make he himself safe, if this be Christ, the chosen of God. (And the people stood about waiting and watching; and their leaders scorned him, and said, He saved other men; let him save himself, if this be the Messiah, the chosen One of God.)

36 And the knights nighed (or And the soldiers came near), and scorned him, and proffered vinegar to him [or and offered vinegar to him],

37 and said, If thou art king of Jews, make thee safe. (and said, If thou art the King of the Jews, save thyself.)

38 And the superscription was written over him with Greek letters, and of Latin, and of Hebrew, [or And the superscription was written on, (or over, or above), him, with letters of Greek, of Latin, and of Hebrew], This is the king of Jews (or This is the King of the Jews).

39 And one of these thieves that hanged (there), [or Forsooth one of those thieves that hanged (there)], blasphemed him, and said, If thou art Christ, make thyself safe and us, (or If thou art the Messiah, save thyself and us).

40 But the other answering, blamed him, and said, Neither thou dreadest God, [thou] that art in the same condemnation [or in the same damnation]? (But the other one answering him, rebuked him, and said, Fearest thou not God, thou who art under the same condemnation, or

the same damnation?)

41   And truly we justly, for we have received worthy things to (or for) *our* works [or (for *our*) deeds]; but this did nothing of evil [or soothly this hath done no evil].

42   And he said to Jesus, Lord, have mind of me (or remember me), when thou comest into thy kingdom.

43   And Jesus said to him, Truly I say to thee (or I tell you the truth), this day thou shalt be with me in paradise.

44   And it was almost the sixth hour, and darknesses were made on all the earth, into the ninth hour [or till the ninth hour]. (And it was almost noon, and then darkness came upon all the land, until three o'clock.)

45   And the sun was made dark, and the veil of the temple was rent atwo [or was cut down the middle]. (And the sun was darkened, and the veil of the Temple was torn in two.)

46   And Jesus crying with a great voice, said, Father, into thine hands I betake my spirit, (or And Jesus crying with a loud voice, said, Father, into thine hands I deliver, or I commend, my spirit). And he saying these things, gave up the ghost, [or And he saying these things, sent out the spirit, *or died*].

47   And the centurion seeing that thing that was done, glorified God, and said, Verily, this man was just. (And the centurion, seeing all that was done, glorified God, and said, Truly, this man was good and righteous, or It is true, this man was innocent.)

48   And all the people of them that were there together at this spectacle, and saw those things that were done, smote their breasts, and turned again (or and then returned home).

49   But all his known stood afar, and (the) women that (pur)sued him from Galilee (or and the women who followed him from Galilee), seeing these things.

50   And lo! a man, Joseph by name, of Arimathaea, a city of Judea, that was a decurion, a good man and a just (man), [And lo!

a man, Joseph by name, that was a decurion, *that is, having ten men under him,* a good man and just, of Arimathaea, a city of Judea,] (And behold, a man called Joseph, of Arimathaea, a city of Judea, who was a member of the Council or the Sanhedrin, a good and righteous man,)

51   this *man* consented not to the counsel and to the deeds of them; and he abode the kingdom of God. (this *man* did not agree with, or approve of, their plan and their deeds; and he was waiting for the Kingdom of God.)

52   This *Joseph* came to Pilate, and asked (for) the body of Jesus,

53   and took it down, and wrapped it in a clean linen cloth, and laid him in a grave hewn (or and laid him in a tomb cut out of the rock), in which not yet any man had been laid [or in which not yet any man was put].

54   And the day was the even(ing) of the holiday, [or of the holy day, the making ready of pask], and the sabbath began to shine. (And that day was the evening of the day after Passover, and the Sabbath was about to begin.)

55   And the women (pur)suing (him), that came with him from Galilee, saw the grave, and how his body was laid. (And the women following him, who had come with him from Galilee, saw the tomb, and how his body was placed in it.)

56   And they turned again, and made ready sweet smelling spices, and ointments; but in the sabbath they rested, after the commandment. (And then they returned home, and prepared sweet smelling spices, and ointments; but on the Sabbath they rested, according to the commandment.)

CHAPTER 24

1   But in one day of the week full early, they came to the grave, and brought sweet smelling spices, that they had arrayed [or which they had made ready]. (But very early on the first day of

the week, they came to the tomb, and brought the sweet smelling spices, which they had prepared.)

2 And they found the stone turned away from the grave. (And they found the stone rolled away from the entrance to the tomb.)

3 And they went in, and found not the body of the Lord Jesus.

4 And it was done, the while they were astonied in thought of this thing, lo! two men stood beside them in shining cloth [or lo! two men stood beside them in shining clothing]. (And it was done, while they were astonished in their thoughts over this, behold, two men stood beside them in shining cloaks.)

5 And when they dreaded, and bowed their semblance into the earth, they said to them, What seek ye him that liveth with dead men? [or What seek ye the living with the dead?] (And they had fear, or they were afraid, and bowed their faces to the ground, but the men said to them, Why search for him who liveth among the dead?)

6 He is not here, but is risen. Have ye mind, how he spake to you, when he was yet in Galilee, (or Remember, how he spoke with you, when he was still in Galilee),

7 and said, For it behooveth man's Son to be betaken into the hands of sinful men, (or and said, For it behooveth man's Son to be delivered into the hands of sinners), and to be crucified, and the third day to rise again.

8 And they bethought on his words. (And they remembered, and thought on his words.)

9 And they went again from the grave (or And they went away from the tomb), and told all these things to the eleven, and to all [the] others.

10 And there was Mary Magdalene, and Joanna, and Mary of James, and other women that were with them, that said to the apostles these things [or that said these things to the apostles].

11 And these words were seen to them as madness, and they believed not to them (or and they did not believe them).

12 But Peter rose up, and ran to the grave (or and ran to the tomb); and he bowed down, and saw the linen clothes lying alone. And he went (away) by himself, wondering on that that was done.

13 And lo! twain of them went in that day into a castle (or And behold, two of them went that day to a village), that was from Jerusalem the space of sixty furlongs, by name Emmaus.

14 And they spake together of all these things that had befallen.

15 And it was done, the while they talked, and sought by themselves, Jesus himself nighed (or approached), and went with them.

16 But their eyes were holden, that they knew him not. (But their eyes were held, so that they did not know him.)

17 And he said to them, What be these words, that ye speak together wandering, and ye be sorrowful? (And he asked them, What be these things, that ye talk about as ye be walking, and ye be so sad?)

18 And one, whose name was Cleopas, answered, and said [to him], Thou thyself art a pilgrim in Jerusalem (or Thou thyself art a visitor, or a stranger, in Jerusalem), [or Thou alone art a pilgrim in Jerusalem (or Thou art alone and a visitor, or a stranger, in Jerusalem)], and (so) hast thou not known, what things be done in it in these days?

19 To whom he said, What things? And they said to him, Of Jesus of Nazareth, that was a man prophet, mighty in work and word before God and all the people;

20 and how the high priests and our princes betook him into condemnation [or into damnation] of death, and crucified him. (and how the high priests and our leaders delivered him unto the damnation of death, and crucified him.)

21 But we hoped, that he should have again-bought Israel, (or And we had hoped, that he

would have redeemed, or ransomed, Israel). And now on all these things the third day is today, that these things were done.

22 But also some women of ours made us afeared, which before day[light] were at the grave; (And some of our women have made us afraid, who before daylight were at the tomb;)

23 and when his body was not found, they came, and said, that they saw also a sight of angels, which said (or who said), that he liveth.

24 And some [men] of ours went to the grave, and they found so as the women said, but they found not him. (And some of our men went to the tomb, and they found it just as the women had said, but they did not find him.)

25 And he said to them, A! fools (or O fools!), and slow of heart to believe in all (the) things that the prophets have spoken.

26 Whether it behooved not Christ to suffer these things (or Did it not behoove the Messiah to suffer these things), and so to enter into his glory?

27 And he began at Moses and at all the prophets, and declared [or expounded] to them in all (the) scriptures, that were of him (or that were about him).

28 And they came nigh to the castle, whither they went, (or And they came near to the village, where they were going). And he made countenance that he would go further.

29 And they constrained him, and said, Dwell with us (or Remain with us), for it draweth to (the) night, and the day is now bowed down. And (so) he entered [in] with them.

30 And it was done, while he sat at the meat with them (or while he sat down for the meal with them), he took bread, and blessed (it), and brake (it), and (then) took (it) to them [or and (then) gave (it) to them].

31 And the eyes of them were opened, and they knew him; and he vanished from their eyes.

32 And they said together, Whether our heart was not burning in us, while he spake to us in the way, and [he] opened to us [the] scriptures? (And they said to each other, Were not our hearts burning in us, while he spoke to us on the way, and he opened the Scriptures to us?)

33 And they rose up in the same hour, and went again into Jerusalem [or (and) went again to Jerusalem], and found the eleven gathered together, and them that were with them, (And they rose up at once, and returned to Jerusalem, and found the Eleven gathered together, and those who were with them,)

34 saying, That the Lord is risen verily, and appeared to Simon. (and they were saying, Truly the Lord hath risen, or It is true that the Lord hath risen, and hath appeared to Simon.)

35 And they told what things were done in the way (or And then they told them what had happened on the way), and how they knew him in (the) breaking of (the) bread.

36 And while they spake these things, Jesus stood in the middle of them, and said to them, Peace (be) to you; I am (here), do not ye dread. (And while they spoke of these things, suddenly Jesus stood in their midst, and said to them, Peace be to you; I am here, do not fear, or do not be afraid.)

37 But they were afraid and aghast, and guessed them(selves) to see a spirit.

38 And he said to them, What be ye troubled (or Why be ye troubled), and thoughts come up into your hearts?

39 See ye my hands and my feet, for I myself am (or for I am here). Feel ye, and see ye; for a spirit hath not flesh and bones, as ye see that I have.

40 And when he had said this thing, he showed (his) hands and feet to them.

41 And yet while they believed not, and wondered for joy, he said, Have ye here anything that shall be eaten? [or Have ye anything here that shall be eaten?]

42 And they proffered to him a part of a fish roasted, and an honeycomb. [And they offered

to him a part of a fish roasted, and a comb of honey.]

43 And when he had eaten before them, he took that that (was) left, and gave (it) to them;

44 and [he] said to them, These be the words that I spake to you, when I was yet with you; for it is need(ful) that all things be fulfilled, that be written in the law of Moses, and in (the) prophets, and in (the) psalms, of me (or about me).

45 Then he opened to them wit, that they should understand [the] scriptures. (Then he opened their minds, or their thinking, so that they could understand the Scriptures.)

46 And he said to them, For thus it is written, and thus it behooved Christ to suffer (or and thus it behooved the Messiah to suffer), and rise again from death the third day [or and rise again from (the) dead the third day];

47 and penance, and remission of sins to be preached in his name to all folks, beginning at Jerusalem. (and repentance, and forgiveness of sins to be preached in his name to all the nations and all the peoples, beginning at Jerusalem.)

48 And ye be (the) witnesses of these things.

49 And I shall send the promise of my Father into you; but sit ye in the city, till ye be clothed with virtue from on high, (or but remain in the city, until ye be clothed with power from on high).

50 And he led them forth into Bethany, and when his hands were lifted up, he blessed them.

51 And it was done, the while he blessed them [or while he blessed them], he departed from them, and was borne (up) into heaven.

52 And they worshipped (him), and went again into Jerusalem with great joy,

53 and were (for)evermore in the temple (or and were always in the Temple), praising and blessing God. †

JOHN

CHAPTER 1

1 In the beginning was the word, [*that is, God's son, (or God's Son)*], and the word was at God, and God was the word.

2 This (Word) was in the beginning at (or with) God.

3 All things were made by him, and without him was made nothing [or nought], (of) that thing that was made. (Everything was made by him, and without him nothing was made, out of all that was made.)

4 In him was life, and the life was the light of men;

5 and the light shineth in darknesses, and [the] darknesses comprehended not it. (and the light shineth in the darkness, but the darkness did not understand it.)

6 A man was sent from God, to whom the name was John.

7 This man came into witnessing, that he should bear witnessing of the light, that all men should believe by him. (This man came as a witness, that he would testify about the light, so that all men could believe through him.)

8 He was not that light, but that he should bear witnessing of the light. (He was not that light, but he testified about the light.)

9 There was a very light (or There was a true light), which (en)lighteneth each man that cometh into this world.

10 He was in the world, and the world was made by him, and the world knew him not.

11 He came into his own things, and his (own) received him not.

12 But how many ever received him, he gave to them power to be made the sons of God, to them that believe in his name (or to those who believe in him);

13 the which not of bloods, neither of the will of (the) flesh, neither of the will of man, but be born of God. (who be born not of blood, nor by the desire of the flesh, nor by the desire of man, but be born of God.)

14 And the word was made man, and dwelled among us, and we have seen the glory of him, as the glory of the one begotten Son of the Father, full of grace and of truth. [And the word, *that is, God's son, (or God's Son)*, is made flesh, *or man*, and hath dwelled in us, and we have seen the glory of him, the glory as of the one begotten of the Father, *the son* full of grace and truth.]

15 John beareth witnessing of him, and crieth, and saith, (or John testified about him, and cried out, and said), This (man) is he of whom I said, He that shall come after me, is made before me, for he was before me;

16 and of the plenty of him we all have taken, and grace for grace. (and all of us have received so much from him, blessing upon blessing.)

17 For the law was given by Moses; but grace and truth is made by Jesus Christ.

18 No man saw ever God [or No man ever saw God], [no] but the one begotten Son, that is in the bosom of the Father, he hath told out (about him).

19 And this is the witnessing of John, when (the) Jews sent from Jerusalem priests and deacons to him, that they should ask him, Who art thou? (And this is the testimony of John, when the Jews sent priests and Levites from Jerusalem to him, so that they could ask him, Who art thou?)

20 He acknowledged, and denied not, and he acknowledged, For I am not Christ. (He confessed, and did not deny it, yea, he confessed, I am not the Messiah.)

21 And they asked him, What then? Art thou Elias? (or Elijah?) And he said, I am not. Art thou a prophet? [or Art thou the prophet?] (or Art thou the Prophet?) And he answered, Nay.

22 Therefore they said to him, Who art thou?

(So) That we (can) give an answer to these that sent us. What sayest thou of thyself?

23 He said, I *am* a voice of a crier in desert, Dress ye the way of the Lord, as Esaias the prophet, said. [He saith, I *am* a voice of a *man* crying in desert, Dress ye the way of the Lord, as Esaias, the prophet, said.] (He said, I *am* a voice of a *man* crying in the desert, Align or Make straight the way of the Lord, as the prophet Isaiah said.)

24 And they that were sent, were of the Pharisees.

25 And they asked him, and said to him, What then baptizest thou, if thou art not Christ, neither Elias, neither a prophet? (And they asked him, Why then do thou baptize, if thou art not the Messiah, nor Elijah, nor the Prophet?)

26 John answered to them, and said, I baptize in water, but in the middle of you hath stand [or stood] one, that ye know not; (John answered them, and said, I baptize in water, but in the midst of you hath stood one, whom ye know not;)

27 he it is, that shall come after me, that was made before me, of whom I am not worthy to loose the thong of his shoe.

28 These things were done in Bethany beyond, [or over], (the) Jordan, where John was baptizing. (These things were done in Bethany on the other side of the Jordan River, where John was baptizing.)

29 Another (or The next) day John saw Jesus coming to him, and he said, Lo! the lamb of God; lo! he that doeth away the sins of the world.

30 This is he, that I said of, After me is come a man [or After me cometh a man], which was made before me; for he was rather [or former] than I (or for he already was, before that I was).

31 And I knew him not, but that he be showed in Israel, therefore I came baptizing in water.

32 And John bare witnessing, and said, I saw the Spirit coming down as a culver from heaven, and (it) dwelled on him [or and dwelling upon him]. (And John testified, and said, I saw the Spirit coming down like a dove from heaven, and dwelling upon him.)

33 And I knew him not; but he that sent me to baptize in water, said to me, On whom thou seest the Spirit coming down, and dwelling on him, this is he, that baptizeth in the Holy Ghost, (or this is he, who baptizeth with the Holy Spirit).

34 And I saw, and bare witnessing (or and I testify), that this is the Son of God.

35 Another day John stood, and two of his disciples;

36 and he beheld Jesus walking, and saith, Lo! the lamb of God.

37 And (the) two disciples heard him speaking, and [they] followed Jesus.

38 And Jesus turned, and saw them (pur)suing him, and saith to them, What seek ye? And they said to him, Rabbi, that is to say, Master, where dwellest thou? (And Jesus turned, and saw them following him, and said to them, What do ye seek? And they said to him, Teacher, where do you live?)

39 And he saith to them, Come ye, and see. And they came, and saw where he dwelled; and dwelt with him that day. And it was as the tenth hour. (And he said to them, Come, and see. And they came, and saw where he lived; and remained with him that day. And it was about four o'clock in the afternoon.)

40 And Andrew, the brother of Simon Peter, was one of the twain, that heard of John, and had (pur)sued him. (And Andrew, the brother of Simon Peter, was one of the two, who had heard that from John, and had followed him.)

41 This found first his brother Simon, and he said to him, We have found Messias, that is to say, Christ; (And at once he found his brother Simon, and he said to him, We have found the Messiah, that is to say, the Christ;)

42 and he led him to Jesus. And Jesus beheld

him, and said, Thou art Simon, the son of Johanna (or the son of John); thou shalt be called Cephas, that is to say, Peter.

43 And on the morrow he would go out into Galilee, and he found Philip; and he saith to him, (Pur)Sue thou me, (or and Jesus said to him, Follow me).

44 Philip was of Bethsaida, the city of Andrew and of Peter.

45 Philip found Nathanael, and said to him, We have found Jesus, the son of Joseph, of Nazareth, (about) whom Moses wrote in the law and the prophets.

46 And Nathanael said to him, Of Nazareth may some good thing be? (or Can anything good come from Nazareth?) Philip said to him, Come, and see.

47 Jesus saw Nathanael coming to him, and said of him, Lo! verily a man of Israel, in whom is no guile. (Jesus saw Nathanael coming to him, and said of him, Behold, truly a man of Israel, in whom there is no deceit.)

48 Nathanael said to him, Whereof hast thou known me? Jesus answered, and said to him, Before that Philip called thee, when thou were under the fig tree, I saw thee.

49 Nathanael answered to him, and said, Rabbi (or Teacher), thou art the Son of God, thou art (the) king of Israel.

50 Jesus answered, and said to him, For I said to thee, I saw thee under the fig tree, thou believest; thou shalt see more than these things [or thou shalt see more things than these].

51 And he said to them, Truly, truly, I say to you, (or Truly, I tell you the truth), ye shall see heaven opened, and the angels of God ascending up and coming down on man's Son.

CHAPTER 2

1 And the third day weddings were made in the Cana of Galilee; and the mother of Jesus was there.

2 And Jesus was called, and his disciples, to the weddings.

3 And when wine failed, the mother of Jesus said to him, They have not wine (or They have no wine).

4 And Jesus saith to her, What to me and to thee, woman? mine hour came not yet. (And Jesus said to her, What is it to me or to thee, woman? my hour hath not come yet, or it is not yet my time.)

5 His mother saith to the ministers, Whatever thing he saith to you, do ye. (His mother said to the servants, Whatever he saith to you, do it.)

6 And there were set (there) six stone cans, after the cleansing of the Jews, holding each two or three metretes. [Forsooth there were put six stone pots, after the cleansing of (the) Jews, taking each two or three measures.] (And there were put there six stone pots, or six stone water jars, for the purification rites of the Jews, each one holding two or three measures, or twenty or thirty gallons.)

7 And Jesus saith to them, Fill ye the pots with water. And they filled them, up to the mouth [or unto the highest part].

8 And Jesus said to them, Draw ye (it) now, and bear ye to the master of the feast. And they bare (it to him).

9 And when the master of the feast had tasted the water made (into) wine, and knew not whereof it was, but the ministers knew that drew the water (or but the servants who drew the water knew), the master of the feast calleth the spouse,

10 and saith to him, Each man setteth first good wine, and when men be [full-]filled, then that that is worse; but thou hast kept the good wine into this time.

11 Jesus did this the beginning of signs (or Jesus did this, the first of his miracles), in the Cana of Galilee, and showed his glory; and his disciples believed in him.

12 After these things he came down to Capernaum, and his mother, and his brethren,

and his disciples; and they dwelled there not many days.

13 And the pask of (the) Jews was nigh (or And the Passover of the Jews was near), and Jesus went up to Jerusalem.

14 And he found in the temple men selling oxen, and sheep, and culvers, and [money-]changers sitting (there). (And he found men in the Temple selling oxen, and sheep, and doves and pigeons, and money-changers sitting there.)

15 And when he had made as it were a scourge of small cords, he drove out all of (or from) the temple, and (the) oxen, and (the) sheep; and he shedded [out] the money of (the) changers, and turned upside-down the boards, (or and he poured out the money of the money-changers, and turned upside-down their tables). [+And when he had made a scourge of small cords, he cast all out of the temple, and sheep, and oxen; and he shedded out the money of (the) changers, and turned upside-down the boards.]

16 And he said to them that sold culvers (or And he said to those who sold the doves and pigeons), Take away from hence these things, and do not ye make the house of my Father (into) an house of merchandise.

17 And his disciples had mind, for it was written, (or And his disciples remembered, that it is written), The fervent love of thine house hath eaten me. [Forsooth his disciples had mind, for it is written, The zeal of thine house hath eaten me (or My zeal for thine house hath consumed me).]

18 Therefore the Jews answered, and said to him, What token [or What sign] showest thou to us, that thou doest these things?

19 Jesus answered, and said to them, Undo ye this temple (or Destroy this temple), and in three days I shall raise it (up again).

20 Therefore the Jews said to him, In forty and six years this temple was builded, and shalt thou in three days raise it (up again)? (And so the Jews said to him, This Temple took forty-six

years to build, and shalt thou raise it up again in three days?)

21 But he said of the temple of his body.

22 Therefore when he was risen from death, his disciples had mind (or his disciples remembered), that he said these things *of his body*, [Therefore when he had risen from (the) dead, his disciples had mind, for he said this thing]; and they believed to the scripture, and to the word that Jesus said.

23 And when Jesus was at Jerusalem in pask, in the feast day, many believed in his name, seeing his signs that he did. (And when Jesus was in Jerusalem for Passover, on the Feast Day, or for the Festival, many believed in him, seeing the miracles that he did.)

24 But Jesus trusted not himself to them, for he knew all men;

25 and for it was not need(ful) to him, that any man should bear witnessing of (a) man, for he knew, what was in (each) man. (and he did not need, that anyone should testify about anyone else, for he knew, what was in each person.)

CHAPTER 3

1 And there was a man of the Pharisees, Nicodemus by name, a prince of the Jews (or a leader of the Jews).

2 And he came to Jesus by night, and said to him, Rabbi, we know, that thou art come from God a master, [or Rabbi, we know, for of God thou hast come a master]; for no man may do these signs, that thou doest, [no] but God be with him. (And he came to Jesus by night, and said to him, Teacher, we know, that thou art a teacher sent from God; for no man can do these miracles, that thou doest, unless God be with him.)

3 Jesus answered, and said to him, Truly, truly, I say to thee, [no] but a man be born again, he may not see the kingdom of God, (or Truly, I tell thee the truth, unless a man is born

again, he cannot see the Kingdom of God).

4   Nicodemus said to him, How may a man be born, when he is old? whether he may enter again into his mother's womb, and be born again?

5   Jesus answered, Truly, truly, I say to thee, [no] but a man be born again of water, and of the Holy Ghost, he may not enter into the kingdom of God. (Jesus answered, Truly, I tell thee the truth, unless a man be born again from water, and from the Holy Spirit, he cannot enter into the Kingdom of God.)

6   That that is born of the flesh, is flesh; and that that is born of the Spirit, is spirit. (That which is born from the flesh, is flesh; and that which is born from the Spirit, is spirit.)

7   Wonder thou not, for I said to thee, It behooveth you to be born again.

8   The Spirit breatheth where he will, and thou hearest his voice, but thou knowest not, from whence he cometh, nor whither he goeth; so is each man that is born of the Spirit. (The Spirit breatheth where he wanteth, and thou hearest his voice, but thou knowest not, where he cometh from, nor where he goeth; so is each man who is born from the Spirit.)

9   Nicodemus answered, and said to him, How may these things be done? (or How can these things be done?)

10   Jesus answered, and said to him, Thou art a master in Israel (or Thou art a teacher in Israel), and knowest not these things?

11   Truly, truly, I say to thee, for we speak that that we know, and we witness that that we have seen, and ye take not our witnessing. (Truly, I tell thee the truth, for we speak of that which we know, and we testify about that which we have seen, but ye do not receive or accept our testimony.)

12   If I have said to you earthly things, and ye believe not, how if I say to you heavenly things, shall ye believe?

13   And no man ascendeth [up] into heaven, [no] but he that came down from heaven, man's Son that is in heaven, [or the son of man which is in heaven], (or the Son of man who was in heaven).

14   And as Moses areared [or reared up] a serpent in (the) desert, so it behooveth man's Son to be raised [up],

15   that each man that believeth in him, perish not, but have everlasting life. (so that everyone who believeth in him, perish not, but have eternal life.)

16   For God loved so the world [or Forsooth God so loved the world], that he gave his one begotten Son, that each man that believeth in him perish not, but have everlasting life (or but have eternal life).

17   For God sent not his Son into the world, that he judge the world, but that the world be saved by him.

18   He that believeth in him, is not deemed; but he that believeth not, is now deemed, for he believeth not in the name of the one begotten Son of God. [He that believeth in to him, is not deemed, *or condemned*; forsooth he that believeth not, is now condemned, for he believeth not in the name of the only begotten son of God.]

19   And this is the doom, for light came into the world, and men loved more (the) darknesses than (the) light; for their works were evil. (And this is the judgement, yea, the light came into the world, but men loved the darkness more than the light; because their works were evil.)

20   For each man that doeth evil, hateth the light; and he cometh not to the light, (so) that his works be not reproved.

21   But he that doeth (the) truth, cometh to the light, (so) that his works be showed, that they be done in God.

22   After these things Jesus came, and his disciples, into the land of Judea, and there he dwelled with them, and baptized.

23   And John was baptizing in Aenon, beside Salim, for many waters were there; and they

came, and were baptized [or were christened].

24   And John was not yet sent into prison.

25   Therefore a question was made of John's disciples with the Jews, of the purification, (or about the purification), [or (the) cleansing].

26   And they came to John, and said to him, Master [or Rabbi], he that was with thee beyond, [or over], (the) Jordan, to whom thou hast borne witnessing, lo! he baptizeth, and all men come to him. (And they came to John, and said to him, Teacher, he who was with thee on the other side of the Jordan River, about whom thou hast witnessed, or thou hast testified, behold, he baptizeth, and all come to him.)

27   John answered, and said, A man may not take anything, [no] but it be given to him from heaven. (John answered, and said, No one can receive anything, unless it be given to him from heaven, yea, from God.)

28   Ye yourselves bear witnessing to me, that I said, I am not Christ, but that I am sent before him. (Ye yourselves can bear witness to me, or can testify about me, that I said, I am not the Messiah, but that I am sent before him.)

29   He that hath a wife, is the husband [or the spouse]; but the friend of the spouse that standeth, and heareth him, joyeth with joy, for the voice of the spouse. Therefore in this thing my joy is fulfilled.

30   It behooveth him to wax, (or It is necessary for him to grow, or to increase), but me to be made less [or to be diminished].

31   He that came from above, is above all; he that is of the earth, speaketh of the earth; he that cometh from heaven, is above all.

32   And he witnesseth that thing that he hath seen, and heard, and no man taketh (or receiveth) his witnessing. (And he testifieth about that thing that he hath seen, and heard, but no man accepteth his testimony.)

33   But he that taketh (or receiveth) his witnessing, hath confirmed that God is soothfast. (But he who accepteth his testimony, hath confirmed that God is truthful.)

34   But he whom God hath sent, speaketh the words of God; for not to measure God giveth the Spirit.

35   The Father loveth the Son, and he hath given all things into his hand.

36   He that believeth in the Son, hath everlasting life; but he that is unbelieveful to the Son, shall not see everlasting life, but the wrath of God dwelleth on him. (He who believeth in the Son, hath eternal life; but he who believeth not in the Son, shall not see eternal life, but the wrath of God shall come upon him.)

CHAPTER 4

1   Therefore as Jesus knew, that the Pharisees heard, that Jesus maketh and baptizeth more disciples than John,

2   though Jesus baptized not, but his disciples,

3   he left Judea, and went again into Galilee.

4   And it behooved him to pass by Samaria. (And it was necessary that he pass through Samaria.)

5   Therefore Jesus came into a city of Samaria, that is called Sychar, beside the place [or the field] that Jacob gave to Joseph, his son.

6   And the well of Jacob was there; and Jesus was weary of the journey, and sat thus upon the well. And the hour was, as it were the sixth. (And Jacob's well was there; and Jesus was weary from the journey, and sat down by the well. And it was about noon.)

7   And a woman came from Samaria, to draw water, (or And a woman of Samaria came to draw water). And Jesus saith to her, Give me (a) drink.

8   And his disciples were gone into the city, to buy meat (or to buy some food).

9   Therefore that woman of Samaria saith to him, How (is it that) thou, that art a Jew, askest of me (for) a drink, that am a woman of Samaria? for [the] Jews used not to deal with

[the] Samaritans.

10   Jesus answered, and said to her, If thou knewest the gift of God, and who it is, that saith to thee, Give me (a) drink, thou peradventure wouldest have asked of him, and he should have given to thee quick water (or and then he would have given thee living water).

11   The woman saith to him, Sire, thou hast not wherein to draw, and the pit is deep; whereof then hast thou quick water? (The woman said to him, Sir, thou hast nothing with which to draw up the water, and the well is deep; from where then would thou get this living water?)

12   Whether thou art greater than our father Jacob, that gave to us the pit? and he drank thereof, and his sons, and his beasts. (Art thou greater than our father Jacob, who gave us the well? and he, and his sons, and his beasts, all drank from it.)

13   Jesus answered, and said to her, Each man that drinketh of this water, shall thirst again;

14   but he that drinketh of the water that I shall give him, shall not thirst [into] without end; but the water that I shall give him, shall be made in him a well of water, springing up into everlasting life (or springing up for eternal life).

15   The woman saith to him, Sire (or Sir), give me this water, (so) that I thirst not, neither come hither to draw.

16   Jesus saith to her, Go, call thine husband, and come hither.

17   The woman answered, and said, I have none husband. Jesus saith to her, Thou saidest well, That I have none husband; [The woman answered, and said, I have not an husband. Jesus saith to her, Thou saidest well, For I have not an husband;]

18   for thou hast had five husbands, and he that thou hast [now], is not thine husband. This thing thou saidest soothly (or Thou hast spoken truthfully).

19   The woman saith to him, Lord, I see, that thou art a prophet.

20   Our fathers worshipped in this hill, and ye (Jews) say, that at Jerusalem is a place, where it behooveth (all) to worship.

21   Jesus saith to her, Woman, believe thou to me, for the hour shall come, when neither in this hill, neither in Jerusalem, ye shall worship the Father.

22   Ye worship that that ye know not; we worship that that we know; for health is of the Jews, (or for salvation is from the Jews, or salvation cometh from the Jews).

23   But the time is come, and now it is, when true worshippers shall worship the Father in spirit and truth; for also the Father seeketh such, that worship him.

24   God is a Spirit, and it behooveth them that worship him, to worship in spirit and truth.

25   The woman saith to him, I know that Messias is (to) come, that is said Christ, (or I know that the Messiah is to come, who is called Christ); therefore when he cometh, he shall tell us all things.

26   Jesus saith to her, I am he [or I am], that speaketh with thee.

27   And anon his disciples came, and wondered, that he spake with the woman; nevertheless no man said to him, What seekest thou, or, What speakest thou with her? (And at once his disciples came back, and were surprised, that he spoke with the woman; nevertheless no one said to him, Why speakest thou with her?)

28   Therefore the woman left her water pot, and went into the city, and said to the men,

29   Come ye, and see a man, that said to me all things that I have done; whether he be Christ? (or could he be the Messiah?)

30   And they went out of the city, and came to him.

31   In the meanwhile his disciples prayed him, and said, Master [or Rabbi], eat. (Meanwhile his disciples beseeched him, and said, Teacher, have something to eat.)

32   But he said to them, I have meat to eat,

that ye know not (of). (But he said to them, I have food to eat, that ye know nothing about.)

33   Therefore the disciples said together, Whether any man hath brought him meat to eat? (And so the disciples said to each other, Hath someone else brought him something to eat?)

34   Jesus saith to them, My meat is that I do the will of him that sent me, [and] that I perform the work of him. (Jesus said to them, My food is that I do the will of him who sent me, until I finish his work.)

35   Whether ye say not, that yet four months be, and ripe corn cometh? Lo! I say to you, lift up your eyes, and see ye the fields, for now they be white to reap. (Do ye not say, that there still be four months, and then the harvest shall come? Behold, I tell you, lift up your eyes, and see ye the fields, for they be ready to be harvested now!)

36   And he that reapeth taketh hire, and gathereth fruit into everlasting life, (or And he who harvesteth receiveth his wages, and gathereth crops for eternal life); (so) that both he that soweth, and he that reapeth, have joy together.

37   In this thing is the word true, For one is that soweth, and another that reapeth.

38   I sent you to reap, that that ye have not travailed, (or I sent you to harvest, that which ye have not laboured over); other men have travailed, and ye have entered into their travails.

39   And of that city many [of the] Samaritans believed in him, for the word of the woman, that bare witnessing (or who testified), That he said to me all (the) things that I have done, [or For he said to me all (the) things, whatever I did].

40   Therefore when (the) Samaritans came to him, they prayed him to dwell there (or they beseeched him to remain there); and he dwelt there two days.

41   And many more believed for his word(s),

42   and said to the woman, That now not for thy speech we believe; for we have heard, and we know, that this is verily the Saviour of the world, (or for we have heard, and we know, that he is truly the Saviour of the world).

43   And after two days he went out from thence, and went into Galilee.

44   And he bare witnessing, that a prophet in his own country hath none honour. [Soothly Jesus bare witnessing, for a prophet in his own country hath not honour, *or worship*.] (And he testified, that a prophet is not honoured in his hometown.)

45   Therefore when he came into Galilee, men of Galilee received him, when they had seen all (the) things that he had done in Jerusalem in the feast day (or for they had seen all the things that he had done in Jerusalem on the Feast Day, or at the Festival); for also they had come to the feast day.

46   Therefore he came again into the Cana of Galilee, where he made the water [into] wine. And there was a little king (or And there was a royal official), whose son was sick at Capernaum.

47   When this had heard, that Jesus should come from Judea into Galilee, he went to him, and prayed him (or beseeched him), that he should come down, and heal his son; for he began to die.

48   Therefore Jesus said to him, But ye see tokens, and great wonders, ye believe not. (And Jesus said to him, Unless ye see signs or miracles, and great wonders, ye will not believe.)

49   The little king saith to him (or The royal official said to him), Lord, come down, before that my son die.

50   Jesus saith to him, Go, thy son liveth. The man believed to the word(s), that Jesus said to him, and he went (home).

51   And now when he came down (or was close to home), the servants came to meet him, and told to him, and said, That his son lived.

52 And he asked of them the hour, in which he was amended. And they said to him, For yesterday in the seventh hour the fever left him.

53 Therefore the father knew, that that hour it was, in which Jesus said to him, Thy son liveth; and he believed, and all his house.

54 Jesus did again this second token (or Jesus did this second sign or miracle), when he came from Judea into Galilee.

CHAPTER 5

1 After these things there was a feast day of the Jews, and Jesus went up to Jerusalem.

2 And in Jerusalem is a washing place (or a pool), that in Hebrew is called Bethesda, and (it) hath five porches. [Forsooth at Jerusalem is a standing water of beasts (or a watering pool for beasts), that in Hebrew is called Bethesda, having five little gates, *or entries*.]

3 In these lay a great multitude of sick men, blind, crooked (or lame), and dry (or withered), abiding (or waiting for) the moving [or the stirring] of the water.

4 For the angel of the Lord came down (at) certain times into the [standing] water (or into the pool), and the water was moved; and he that first came down into the cistern, after the moving of the water, was made whole (or was healed) of whatever sickness he was held (by).

5 And a man was there, having eight and thirty years in his sickness.

6 And when Jesus had seen him lying (there), and had known, that he had much time (there), he saith to him, Wilt thou be made whole?

7 The sick man answered to him, Lord, I have no man, (so) that when the water is moved [or (it) is troubled], to put me into the cistern (or into the pool); for while I come, another goeth down before me.

8 Jesus saith to him, Rise up, take thy bed, and go. (Jesus said to him, Get up, pick up thy bed, and go.)

9 And anon the man was made whole, and took up his bed, and went forth. And it was sabbath in that day. (And at once the man was healed, and picked up his bed, and went forth. And that day was the Sabbath.)

10 Therefore the Jews said to him that was made whole, It is (the) sabbath, it is not leaveful to thee, to take away thy bed. (And so the Jews said to him who was healed, It is the Sabbath, and it is not lawful for thee to carry thy bed.)

11 He answered to them, He that made me whole, said to me, Take (up) thy bed, and go. (He answered to them, He who healed me, said to me, Pick up thy bed, and go.)

12 Therefore they asked him, What man is that [or Who is that man], that said to thee, Take up thy bed, and go? (or Who said to thee, Pick up thy bed, and go?)

13 But he that was made whole, wist not who it was, (or But he who was healed, did not know who it was). And Jesus (had) bowed away from the people, that was set in the place.

14 Afterward Jesus found him in the temple, and said to him, Lo! thou art made whole, (or Behold, thou art healed); now do not thou do sin [or now do not thou sin], lest any worse thing befall to thee.

15 (Then) That man went, and told to the Jews, that it was Jesus that made him whole.

16 Therefore the Jews pursued Jesus, for he did this thing in the sabbath. (And so the Jews persecuted Jesus, because he did this miracle on the Sabbath.)

17 And Jesus answered to them, My Father worketh till now, and I work.

18 Therefore the Jews sought more to slay him, for not only he brake the sabbath, but he said that God *was* his Father, and made him(self) even (or equal) to God.

19 Therefore Jesus answered, and said to them, Truly, truly, I say to you, (or Truly, I tell you the truth), the Son may not of himself do anything, [no] but that thing that he seeth the Father doing; for whatever things he doeth, the

Son doeth in like manner those things.

20 For the Father loveth the Son, and showeth to him all (the) things that he doeth; and he shall show to him greater works than these, (so) that ye wonder.

21 For as the Father raiseth dead men, and quickeneth (them), so the Son quickeneth whom he will. (For as the Father raiseth the dead, and giveth them life, so the Son giveth life to whomever he desireth.)

22 For neither the Father judgeth any man, but hath given every doom to the Son, (For the Father judgeth no one, but hath given every judgement to the Son,)

23 (so) that all men honour the Son, as they honour the Father. He that honoureth not the Son, honoureth not the Father that sent him.

24 Truly, truly, I say to you, (or Truly, I tell you the truth), that he that heareth my word, and believeth in him that sent me, hath everlasting life, and he cometh not into doom, (or hath eternal life, and he cometh not unto judgement), but passeth from death into life.

25 Truly, truly, I say to you, (or Truly, I tell you the truth), for the hour cometh, and now it is, when dead men (or when the dead) shall hear the voice of the Son of God, and they that hear (it), shall live.

26 For as the Father hath life in himself, so he gave to the Son, to have life in himself;

27 and he gave to him power to make doom, (or and he gave him the authority to pass judgement), for he is man's Son.

28 Do not ye wonder in this, for the hour cometh, in which all men that be in burials, shall hear the voice of God's Son. (Do not wonder at this, for the hour cometh, in which all those who be in graves, shall hear the voice of God's Son.)

29 And they that have done good things, shall go into again-rising of life [or shall come forth into rising again of life]; but they that have done evil things, into again-rising of doom. (And they who have done good, shall be

resurrected for life; but they who have done evil, shall be resurrected for judgement, or for condemnation.)

30 I may nothing do of myself, but as I hear, I deem, [or I may not of myself do anything, but as I hear, I judge], and my doom is just (or and my judgement is just and fair), for I seek not my will, but the will of the Father that sent me.

31 If I bear witnessing of myself, my witnessing is not true; (If I testify about myself, my testimony is not accepted as true;)

32 another is that beareth witnessing of me, and I know that his witnessing is true, that he beareth of me. (but there is another who testifieth about me, and I know that his testimony is true, what he testifieth about me.)

33 Ye sent to John, and he bare witnessing to [the] truth. (Ye sent messengers to John, and he testified about the truth, or and he testified truthfully.)

34 But I take not witnessing of (any) man; but I say these things, that ye be safe. (But I do not need the testimony of anyone; but I say these things, so that ye can be saved.)

35 He was a lantern burning and shining, [or giving light]; but ye would (be) glad, or (would have) joy, (or rejoice), at an hour in his light.

36 But I have more witnessing than John, for the works that my Father gave to me to perform them [or forsooth the works that my Father gave me that I perform them], those works that I do bear witnessing of me, that the Father sent me. (But I have a greater witness than John, or But I have better testimony than John's, for the works that my Father gave to me to complete, or to finish, those works that I do testify about me, that the Father sent me.)

37 And the Father that sent me, he bare witnessing of me, (or And the Father who sent me, he testified about me). (But) Neither ye heard ever his voice, neither ye saw his likeness, [or (his) form].

38 And ye have not his word dwelling in you; for ye believe not to him, whom he sent.

39   Seek ye the scriptures, in which ye guess to have everlasting life; and those it be, that bear witnessing of me. (Ye study the Scriptures, through which ye hope to gain eternal life; and they do indeed testify about me.)

40   And (yet) ye will not come to me, (so) that ye (can) have (eternal) life.

41   I take not clearness of men; (I do not receive my glory, or my honour, from people;)

42   but I have known you, that ye have not the love of God in you.

43   I came in the name of my Father, and ye took not me (or but ye did not receive me). If another come in his own name, ye shall receive him.

44   How may ye believe, that receive glory each of (the) other, and ye seek not the glory that is of God alone? (How can ye believe, ye who receive your glory from one another, and seek not the glory that is from God alone?)

45   Do not ye guess, that I am to accuse you with the Father; it is Moses that accuseth you, in whom ye hope.

46   For if ye believed to Moses, peradventure ye should believe also to me; for he wrote of me. (For if ye believed Moses, perhaps ye would also believe me; for he wrote about me.)

47   But if ye believe not to his letters, how shall ye believe to my words? (But if ye do not believe what he wrote, how shall ye believe what I say?)

CHAPTER 6

1   After these things Jesus went over the sea of Galilee, that is (also called the Sea of) Tiberias. (After these things Jesus went over Lake Galilee, that is also called Lake Tiberias.)

2   And a great multitude (pur)sued him; for they saw the tokens that he did on them that were sick. (And a great multitude followed him; for they saw the signs or miracles that he did for those who were sick.)

3   Therefore Jesus went into an hill (or And so Jesus went up onto a hill), and sat there with his disciples.

4   And the pask was full nigh, a feast day of the Jews. (And the Passover was very near, a Feast Day, or a Festival, for the Jews.)

5   Therefore when Jesus had lifted up his eyes, and had seen, that a great multitude came to him, he saith to Philip, Whereof shall we buy loaves, (so) that these men eat?

6   But he said this thing, tempting him (or testing him); for he knew what he was to do.

7   Philip answered to him, The loaves of two hundred pence suffice not to them, (so) that each man (can) take a little (some)what.

8   One of his disciples, Andrew, the brother of Simon Peter, saith to him,

9   A child is here, that hath five barley loaves and two fishes; but what be these among so many?

10   Therefore Jesus saith, Make them sit to the meat. And there was much hay in the place. And so men sat to the meat, as five thousand in number. [Therefore Jesus saith, Make ye men to sit at the meat. Forsooth there was much hay in the place. Therefore men sat at the meat, in number as five thousand.] (And so Jesus said, Make them to sit down for the meal. And there was much hay in that place. And so the men sat down for the meal, five thousand in number.)

11   And Jesus took [the] five loaves, and when he had done thankings, he parted (them) to the men that sat to the meat [or he parted to men sitting at the meat], and also of the fishes, as much as they would. (And Jesus took the five loaves, and when he had given thanks, he divided them to those who sat down for the meal, and also the fish, as much as they wanted.)

12   And when they were [full-]filled (or And when they were filled full), he said to his disciples, Gather ye (up) the remnants that be left, (so) that they perish not.

13   And so they gathered, and filled twelve

coffins, of the remnant(s) of the five barley loaves and two fishes, that (were) left to them that had eaten. (And so they gathered up, and filled twelve baskets, with the remnants of the five barley loaves and the two fish, that were left by those who had eaten.)

14   Therefore those men, when they had seen the sign [or the token, *or* (the) *miracle*], that he had done, said, For this is verily the prophet (or For he is truly the Prophet), that is to come into the world.

15   And when Jesus had known, that they were to come to take him, and make him king, he flew alone again into an hill (or he went by himself into the hills). [+Therefore when Jesus had known, that they were to come that they should ravish him, (or that they had come so that they could snatch him, or they could seize him), and make him king, he alone fled again into an hill.]

16   And when (the) eventide was come, his disciples went down to the sea.

17   And they went up into a boat, and they came over the sea into Capernaum. And darknesses were made then (or And it became dark then), and Jesus was not come to them [or and Jesus had not come to them].

18   And for a great wind blew, the sea rose up.

19   Therefore when they had rowed as five and twenty furlongs or thirty, they saw Jesus walking on the sea, and to be nigh the boat; and they dreaded, (or and they had fear, or and they were afraid).

20   And he said to them, I am (here); do not ye dread (or do not fear).

21   Therefore they would take him into the boat, and anon the boat was at the land (or and at once the boat was at the land), to which they went.

22   On the tother day (or On the next day), the people, that stood over the sea, saw, that there was none other boat there but that one, and that Jesus entered not with his disciples into the boat, but his disciples alone went [or but his disciples went alone].

23   But other boats came from Tiberias beside the place, where they had eaten bread, and did thankings to God (or and gave thanks to God).

24   Therefore when the people had seen, that Jesus was not there, neither his disciples, they went up into boats, and came to Capernaum, seeking Jesus.

25   And when they had found him over the sea, they said to him, Rabbi (or Teacher), how camest thou hither?

26   Jesus answered to them, and said, Truly, truly, I say to you (or Truly, I tell you the truth), ye seek me, not for ye saw the miracles, but for ye ate of the loaves, and were [ful]filled.

27   Work ye not (for) meat that perisheth, but (for) that that dwelleth into everlasting life, which *meat* man's Son shall give to you; for God the Father hath marked him. (Work not for the food that perisheth, but for that which remaineth unto eternal life, which *food* man's Son shall give to you; for God the Father hath sealed him.)

28   Therefore they said to him, What shall we do, (so) that we work the works of God?

29   Jesus answered, and said to them, This is the work of God, that ye believe to him (or so that ye believe in him), whom he sent.

30   Therefore they said to him, What token then doest thou, that we see, and believe to thee? what workest thou? (And so they said to him, Then what sign doest thou, so that we can see it, and believe in thee? what miracle workest thou?)

31   Our fathers ate manna in (the) desert, as it is written, He gave to them bread from heaven to eat.

32   Therefore Jesus saith to them, Truly, truly, I say to you, Moses gave you not bread from heaven, but my Father giveth you very bread from heaven; (And so Jesus said to them, Truly, I tell you the truth, it is not Moses that gave you the bread from heaven, but my Father, who

now giveth you the true bread from heaven;)

33   for it is very bread that cometh down from heaven (or for it is the true bread which cometh down from heaven), and giveth life to the world.

34   Therefore they said to him, Lord, (for)ever[more] give [to] us this bread.

35   And Jesus said to them, I am (the) bread of life; he that cometh to me, shall not hunger; and he that believeth in me, shall never thirst.

36   But I said to you, that ye have seen me, and ye believe(d) not.

37   All (the) thing(s) that the Father giveth to me, shall come to me; and I shall not cast him out, that cometh to me. (All whom the Father giveth to me, shall come to me; and I shall not throw him out, yea, anyone who cometh to me.)

38   For I came down from heaven, not that I do my will, but the will of him that sent me.

39   And this is the will of the Father that sent me, that all (the) thing(s) that the Father gave to me, I lose not [or nought] of it, but again-raise it in the last day. (And this is the will of the Father who sent me, that out of all those whom the Father gave to me, I shall not lose any of them, but I shall raise them all up on the Last Day.)

40   And this is the will of my Father that sent me, that each man that seeth the Son, and believeth in him, have everlasting life; and I shall again-raise him in the last day. (And this is the will of my Father who sent me, that each person who seeth the Son, and believeth in him, have eternal life; and I shall raise each one up on the Last Day.)

41   Therefore the Jews grudged of him (or And so the Jews grumbled about him), for he had said, I am (the) bread that came down from heaven.

42   And they said, Whether this is not Jesus, the son of Joseph, whose father and mother we have known. How then saith he this, That I came down from heaven?

43   Therefore Jesus answered, and said to

them, Do not ye grudge together. (And so Jesus answered, and said to them, Do not grumble to each other.)

44   No man may come to me, but if the Father that sent me, draw him, [or no but the Father that sent me, draw him]; and I shall again-raise him in the last day. (No one can come to me, unless the Father who sent me, draw him; and I shall raise each one up on the Last Day.)

45   It is written in the prophets, And all men shall be able to be taught of God (or Everyone shall be taught by God). Each man that hath heard of the Father, and hath learned, cometh to me.

46   Not for any man hath seen the Father, but this that is of God, hath seen the Father. (Not that anyone hath seen the Father, but he who is from God, hath seen the Father.)

47   Soothly, soothly, I say to you, he that believeth in me, hath everlasting life. (Truly, truly, I say to you, or Truly, I tell you the truth, he who believeth in me, hath eternal life.)

48   I am [the] bread of life.

49   Your fathers ate manna in (the) desert, and be dead.

50   This is (the) bread coming down from heaven, that if any man eat thereof, he die not, (or so that if anyone eat of it, they shall not die).

51   I am (the) living bread, that came down from heaven. If any man eat of this bread, he shall live (into) without end. And the bread that I shall give, is my flesh for the life of the world.

52   Therefore the Jews chided together, and said, How may this give to us his flesh to eat?

53   Therefore Jesus saith to them, Truly, truly, I say to you, (or Truly, I tell you the truth), [no] but ye eat the flesh of man's Son, and drink his blood, ye shall not have life in you.

54   He that eateth my flesh, and drinketh my blood, hath everlasting life, and I shall again-raise him in the last day. (He who eateth my flesh, and drinketh my blood, hath eternal life, and I shall raise him up on the Last Day.)

55   For my flesh is very meat, and my blood is

very drink. (For my flesh is the true food, and my blood is the true drink.)

56   He that eateth my flesh, and drinketh my blood, dwelleth in me, and I in him.

57   As my Father living sent me, and I live for the Father, and he that eateth me, he shall live for me. (For the living Father sent me, and I live for the Father, and he who eateth me, shall live because of me.)

58   This is (the) bread, that came down from heaven. Not as your fathers ate manna, and be dead; he that eateth this bread, shall live (into) without end.

59   He said these things in the synagogue, teaching in Capernaum.

60   Therefore many of his disciples hearing [this], said, This word is hard, who may hear it? (And many of his disciples who heard this, said, This word is hard, who can bear to hear such words? or who can listen to such words?)

61   But Jesus witting at [or within] himself, that his disciples grudged of this thing, said to them, This thing offendeth you? (And Jesus knowing within himself, that his disciples grumbled about this, said to them, This offendeth you?)

62   Therefore if ye see man's Son ascending [up], where he was before? (And so what if ye see man's Son ascending up, to the place where he was before?)

63   It is the spirit that quickeneth, the flesh profiteth nothing; the words that I have spoken to you, be spirit and life. (It is the Spirit that giveth life, the flesh profiteth nothing; the words that I have spoken to you, be of the Spirit and of life.)

64   But there be some of you that believe not. For Jesus knew from the beginning, which were believing (or who believed in him), and who was to betray him.

65   And he said, Therefore I said to you, that no man may come to me, [no] but it were given to him of my Father (or unless it was granted to him by my Father).

66   From this time many of his disciples went aback, and went not now with him.

67   Therefore Jesus said to the twelve, Whether ye will also go away?

68   And Simon Peter answered to him, Lord, to whom shall we go? Thou hast words of everlasting life (or Thou hast the words of eternal life);

69   and we believe, and have known, [or and we have believed, and know], that thou art Christ (or that thou art the Messiah), the Son of God.

70   Therefore Jesus answered to them, Whether I chose not you twelve, and one of you is a fiend? (or and yet one of you is a devil?)

71   And he said this of Judas of Simon Iscariot, for this was to betray him, when he was one of the twelve.

CHAPTER 7

1   After these things Jesus walked into Galilee, for he would not walk into Judea, for the Jews sought to slay him.

2   And there was nigh a feast day of the Jews, Scenopegia, [*that is, a feast of tabernacles, (or the Festival of Tabernacles)*].

3   And his brethren said to him, Pass from hence (or Go forth from here), and go into Judea, (so) that also thy disciples see thy works that thou doest;

4   for no man doeth anything in huddles (or in secret), and himself seeketh to be (out in the) open, [⁺or forsooth no man doeth anything in hid place, *or* (in) *privy*, (or for no one doeth anything in a hidden place, *or in private*), and he seeketh to be (out) in (the) open]. If thou doest these things, show thyself to the world.

5   For neither his brethren believed in him.

6   Therefore Jesus saith to them, My time came not yet, but your time is (for)evermore ready. (My hour hath not yet come, or It is not yet my time, but it is always your time.)

7   The world may not hate you, soothly it hateth me; for I bear witnessing thereof (or for I testify to it), that the works of it be evil.

8   Go ye up to this feast day, but I shall not go up to this feast day, for my time is not yet fulfilled, [or full-filled], (or for my time is not yet filled full, or hath not yet fully come to fruition).

9   When he had said these things, he dwelt in Galilee.

10   And after that his brethren were gone up, then he went up to the feast day, not openly, but as in private.

11   Therefore the Jews sought him in the feast day (or And so the Jews looked for him on the Feast Day, or at the Festival), and said, Where is he?

12   And much grudging was of him among the people (or And there was much grumbling about him among the people). For some said, That he is good; and others said, Nay, but he deceiveth the people;

13   nevertheless no man spake openly of him, for dread of the Jews (or for fear of the Jews).

14   But when the middle feast day came, Jesus went up into the temple (or Jesus went to the Temple), and taught.

15   And the Jews wondered, and said, How knoweth this *man* letters, since he hath not learned? (or How can this *man* know so much, since he hath not studied?)

16   Jesus answered to them, and said, My doctrine is not mine, but his that sent me.

17   If any man will do his will, he shall know of the teaching, whether it be of God, or [whether] I speak of myself.

18   He that speaketh of himself, seeketh his own glory; but he that seeketh the glory of him that sent him, is soothfast (or is truthful), and unrightwiseness is not in him.

19   Whether Moses gave not to you a law, and none of you doeth [or keepeth] the law? What seek ye to slay me? (Did not Moses give you the Law? and yet none of you obeyeth the Law. Why do ye seek to kill me?)

20   And the people answered, and said, Thou hast a devil; who seeketh to slay thee?

21   Jesus answered, and said to them, I have done one work, and all ye wonder.

22   Therefore Moses gave to you circumcision; not for it is of Moses, but of the fathers, (or not that it was from Moses, but from the fathers); and in (or on) the sabbath ye circumcise a man.

23   If a man take circumcision in the sabbath, that the law of Moses be not broken, (why) have ye indignation, [*or wrath*], to me, for I made all a man whole in the sabbath? (And if a man receive his circumcision on the Sabbath, so that the Law of Moses be not broken, then why have ye indignation, *or wrath*, against me, for I made a man all whole, or I healed him, on the Sabbath?)

24   Do not ye deem after the face, but deem ye a rightful doom. (Do not simply judge on the surface, but rather make the correct judgement.)

25   Therefore some of Jerusalem said, Whether this is not he, whom the Jews seek to slay?

26   and lo! he speaketh openly, and they say nothing to him. Whether the princes know verily that this is Christ? (or Perhaps our leaders know that he is truly the Messiah?)

27   But we know this *man*, of whence he is; but when Christ shall come, no man knoweth of whence he is. (And yet we know this *man*, where he is from; but when the Messiah shall come, no one shall know where he is from.)

28   Therefore Jesus cried in the temple (when he was) teaching, and said, Ye know me, and ye know of whence I am; and I came not of myself, but he is true that sent me, whom ye know not.

29   I know him, and if I say that I know him not, I shall be like to you, a liar; but I know him, for of him I am (or for I am from him), and he sent me.

30   Therefore they sought to take (hold of) him, and no man set on him hands, for his hour

came not yet. (And so they sought to take hold of him, but no one put his hands on him, for his hour had not yet come, or for it was not yet his time.)

31 And many of the people believed in him, and said, When Christ shall come, whether he shall do more tokens than those that this doeth? (or When the Messiah shall come, shall he do more signs, or miracles, than these which he doeth?)

32 The Pharisees heard the people musing of him, (concerning) these things; and the princes and the Pharisees sent ministers, to take him. (The Pharisees heard the people musing about him, concerning these things; and the leaders, or the high priests, and the Pharisees sent their servants, to take hold of him.)

33 Therefore Jesus said to them, Yet a little time I am with you, and (then) I go to the Father, that sent me.

34 Ye shall seek me, and ye shall not find *me*; and where I am, ye may not come (or ye cannot come).

35 Therefore the Jews said to themselves, Whither shall this go, for we shall not find him? whether he will go into the scattering of heathen men, and will teach the heathen? (And so the Jews said to themselves, Where shall he go, that we shall not be able to find him? shall he go unto the Dispersion among the Gentiles, and teach the Gentiles?)

36 What is this word, which he said, Ye shall seek me, and ye shall not find *me*; and where I am, ye may not come? (or and where I am, ye cannot come?)

37 But in the last day of the great feast, (or But on the last day of the great Feast, or the great Festival), Jesus stood, and cried (out), and said, If any man thirsteth, come he to me, and drink.

38 He that believeth in me, as the scripture saith, Rivers of quick water shall flow out of his womb. (He who believeth in me, as the Scripture saith, Rivers of living water, or Rivers

of life-giving water, shall flow out of his belly.)

39 But he said this thing of the (Holy) Spirit [or of the Holy Ghost], whom men that believed in him should take (or which those who believed in him would receive later); for the Spirit was not yet given, for Jesus was not yet glorified.

40 Therefore of that company, when they had heard these words of him, they said, This is verily a prophet (or He is truly the Prophet).

41 Others said, This is Christ. But some said, Whether Christ cometh from Galilee? (Others said, He is the Messiah. But some said, Will the Messiah come from Galilee?)

42 Whether the scripture saith not, that of the seed of David, and of the castle of Bethlehem, where David was, Christ cometh? (Saith not the Scripture, that from the seed of David, and from the village of Bethlehem, where David was, the Messiah shall come?)

43 Therefore dissension was made among the people for him.

44 And some of them would have taken (hold of) him, but no man set (his) hands on him.

45 Therefore the ministers came to the bishops, and Pharisees, and they said to them, Why brought ye not him? (And so the servants came back to the high priests, and the Pharisees, and they said to them, Why have ye not brought him back to us?)

46 The ministers answered (or The servants answered), Never (a) man spake so, as this *man* speaketh.

47 Therefore the Pharisees answered to them, Whether ye be deceived also?

48 whether any of the princes, or (we) of the Pharisees believed in him? (do any of the leaders, yea, the high priests, or we of the Pharisees believe in him?)

49 But this people, that knoweth not the law, be cursed. (Let these people, who do not know the Law, be cursed!)

50 Nicodemus saith to them, he that came to

him by night, that was one of them,

51　Whether our law deemeth a man, [no] but it have first heard of him [or no but first it have heard of him], and know what he doeth? (Certainly our Law judgeth no one, unless it first have heard from him, and know what he doeth?)

52　They answered, and said to him, Whether thou art a man of Galilee also? Seek thou (the) scriptures, and see thou, that a prophet riseth not (out) of Galilee.

53　And they turned again, each into his house. (And then each of them returned to his own house.)

CHAPTER 8

1　But Jesus went into the mount of Olivet. (And then Jesus went to the Mount of Olives.)

2　And early again (the next morning) he came into the temple; and all the people came to him; and he sat, and taught them.

3　And (the) scribes and (the) Pharisees brought a woman taken in adultery, and they setted her in the middle (or and they put her in the midst of everyone),

4　and said to him, Master, this woman is now taken in adultery. (and said to him, Teacher, this woman was caught in adultery.)

5　And in the law Moses commanded us to stone such; therefore what sayest thou?

6　And they said this thing tempting (or to test) him, (so) that they might accuse him. And Jesus bowed himself down, and wrote with his finger in the earth (or and wrote on the ground with his finger).

7　And when they abided [or continued] asking him, he raised himself (up), and said to them, He of you that is without sin, first cast a stone into her, (or He of you who is without sin, throw the first stone at her).

8　And again he bowed [down] himself, and wrote in the earth (or and wrote on the ground).

9　And they hearing these things, went away one after another, and they began from the elder men; and Jesus dwelt alone, and the woman standing in the middle.

10　And Jesus raised himself (up), and said to her, Woman, where be they that accused thee? no man hath condemned thee.

11　She said, No man, Lord. Jesus said *to her*, Neither I shall condemn thee; go thou, and now afterward do not thou (do) sin (any) more, [or and now afterward do not thou sin], (or and hereafter, do not do any more sin).

12　Therefore again Jesus spake to them, and said, I am the light of the world; he that (pur)sueth me, walketh not in (the) darknesses, (or he who followeth me, walketh not in the darkness), but shall have the light of life.

13　Therefore the Pharisees said, Thou bearest witnessing of thyself; thy witnessing is not true. (And so the Pharisees said, Thou testifiest about thyself; thy testimony is not true.)

14　Jesus answered, and said to them, And if I bear witnessing of myself, my witnessing is true, (or Jesus answered, and said to them, And if I testify about myself, then my testimony is true); for I know from whence I came, and whither I go. But ye know not from whence I came, nor whither I go.

15　For ye deem after the flesh, but I deem no man; (For ye judge after the flesh, but I judge no man;)

16　and if I deem, my doom is true, (or and if I judge, then my judgement is true), for I am not alone, but I and the Father that sent me.

17　And in your law it is written, that the witnessing of two men is true. (And in your Law it is written, that the testimony of two men who agree is true.)

18　I am, that bear witnessing of myself, and the Father that sent me, beareth witnessing of me. (I am he, who giveth testimony about myself, and the Father who sent me, also giveth testimony about me.)

19　Therefore they said to him, Where is thy Father? Jesus answered, Neither ye know me, nor ye know my Father; if ye knew me, peradventure ye should know also my Father.

20 Jesus spake these words in the treasury, teaching in the temple; and no man took (hold of) him, for his hour came not yet, (or for his hour had not yet come, or for it was not yet his time).

21 Therefore again Jesus said to them, Lo! I go, and ye shall seek me, and ye shall die in your sin; whither I go, ye may not come, (or where I go, ye cannot come).

22 Therefore the Jews said, Whether he shall slay himself, for he saith, Whither I go, ye may not come? (And so the Jews said, Shall he kill himself, for he said, Where I go, ye cannot come?)

23 And he said to them, Ye be of beneath, I am of above; ye be of this world, I am not of this world.

24 Therefore I said to you, that ye shall die in your sins; for if ye believe not that I am, ye shall die in your sins.

25 Therefore they said to him, Who art thou? Jesus said to them, The beginning, [or the first of all thing(s)], which [I] also speak to you, (or what I have told you).

26 I have many things to speak, and to deem of you, but he that sent me is soothfast; and I speak in the world these things, that I heard of him. (I have many things to say, and to judge about you, and he who sent me is truthful; and I say in the world these things, that I heard from him.)

27 And they knew not, that he called his Father God. (And they did not know or understand, that he called God his Father.)

28 Therefore Jesus said to them, When ye have araised man's Son, then ye shall know, that I am, and of myself I do nothing, (or When ye have raised up man's Son, then ye shall know, what I am, and that by myself I can do nothing); but as my Father taught me, I speak these things.

29 And he that sent me is with me, and left me not alone; for I do (for)evermore those things, that be pleasing to him, (or for I always do those things, that be pleasing to him).

30 When he spake these things, many believed in him.

31 Therefore Jesus said to the Jews, that believed in him, If ye dwell in my word, verily, ye shall be my disciples, (or If ye remain in my word, truly, ye shall be my disciples);

32 and ye shall know the truth, and the truth shall make you free.

33 Therefore the Jews answered to him, We be the seed of Abraham, and we served never to (any) man, [or and to no man we served ever], (or and we were never in servitude, or in slavery, to any man); how sayest thou, That ye shall be free?

34 Jesus answered to them, Truly, truly, I say to you, (or Truly, I tell you the truth), each man that doeth sin, is [the] servant of sin.

35 And the servant dwelleth not in the house [into] without end, but the Son dwelleth [into] without end.

36 Therefore if the Son make you free, verily, ye shall be free. (And so if the Son shall make you free, truly, or in truth, ye shall be free.)

37 I know that ye be Abraham's sons, but ye seek to slay me, for my word taketh not (hold) in you.

38 I speak those things, that I saw at my Father; and ye do those things, that ye saw at your father.

39 They answered, and said to him, Abraham is our father. Jesus saith to them, If ye be the sons of Abraham, (then) do ye the works of Abraham.

40 But now ye seek to slay me, a man that have spoken to you [the] truth, that I heard of God (or that I heard from God); Abraham did not this thing.

41 Ye do the works of your father. Therefore they said to him, We be not born of fornication; we have (but) one Father, God.

42 But Jesus saith to them, If God were your

Father, soothly ye should love me; for I passed forth of God [or forsooth I proceeded, *or came forth*, of God], and came (here); for neither I came of myself, but he sent me. (But Jesus said to them, If God were your Father, truly ye would love me, for I came forth from God, and came here; yea, I did not come here on my own accord, but he sent me.)

43   Why know ye not my speech? for ye may not hear my word. (Why do ye not understand what I say? because ye cannot hear, or ye cannot listen to, my words.)

44   Ye be of the father, the devil, and ye will do the desires of your father. He was a manslayer from the beginning, and he stood not in (the) truth; for (the) truth is not in him. When he speaketh leasing, he speaketh of his own; for he is a liar, and (the) father of it, (or When he speaketh lies, he speaketh his own language; for he is a liar, and the father of them).

45   But for I say (the) truth, ye believe not to me. (But because I speak the truth, ye do not believe me.)

46   Who of you shall reprove me of sin? if I say (the) truth, why believe ye not to me? (Who of you can prove me guilty of sin? or can convict me of sin? if I speak the truth, then why do ye not believe me?)

47   He that is of God, heareth the words of God; therefore ye hear not, (or and so ye cannot hear, or and so ye will not listen), for ye be not of God.

48   Therefore the Jews answered, and said [to him], Whether we say not well (or Do we not rightly, or correctly, say), that thou art a Samaritan, and hast a devil?

49   Jesus answered, and said, I have not a devil, but I honour my Father, and ye have unhonoured me. (Jesus answered, and said, I do not have a devil, or I am not possessed, and I honour my Father, but ye dishonour me.)

50   For I seek not my glory; there is he, that seeketh, and deemeth. (Because I do not seek my own glory; but there is He, who seeketh it,

and judgeth for me.)

51   Truly, truly, I say to you, if any man keep my word(s), he shall not taste death [into] without end. (Truly, I tell you the truth, if any man obey my words, he shall never taste death or he shall never die.)

52   Therefore the Jews said, Now we have known, that thou hast a devil. Abraham is dead, and the prophets, and thou sayest, If any man keep my word(s), (or If any man obey my words), he shall not taste death [into] without end.

53   Whether thou art greater than our father Abraham, that is dead, and the prophets be dead; whom makest thou thyself?

54   Jesus answered, If I glorify myself, my glory is nought, (or then my glory, or my boasting, is nothing); my Father is, that glorifieth me, whom ye say, that he is your God.

55   And ye have not known him, but I have known him; and if I say that I know him not, I shall be a liar like to you; but I know him, and I keep his word(s), (or and I obey his words).

56   Abraham, your father, gladded [or full out joyed] to see my day; and he saw (it), and joyed. (Your father Abraham rejoiced to see my day; yea, he saw it, and rejoiced.)

57   Then the Jews said to him, Thou hast not yet fifty years, and hast thou seen Abraham?

58   Therefore Jesus said to them, Truly, truly I say to you, (or Truly, I tell you the truth), before that Abraham should be, I am, [or before that Abraham was made, I am].

59   Therefore they took stones, to cast to him (or to throw at him); but Jesus hid him(self), and went out of the temple.

CHAPTER 9

1   And Jesus passing (by), saw a man blind from the birth.

2   And his disciples asked him, Master, who sinned, this man, or his elders, [or Rabbi, who

sinned, this man, or his father and mother], that he should be born blind? (And his disciples asked him, Teacher, who sinned, this man, or his father and mother, so that he would be born blind?)

3   Jesus answered, Neither this man sinned, neither his elders, [or Neither this man sinned, neither his father and mother]; but that the works of God be showed in him.

4   It behooveth me to work the works of him that sent me, as long as the day is [or the while the day is]; the night shall come, when no man may work (or when no one can work).

5   As long as I am in the world, I am the light of the world.

6   When he had said these things, he spat into the earth, and made clay of the spittle (or and made clay with the spittle), and anointed the clay on his eyes,

7   and said to him, Go, and be thou washed in the water, [or (in the) cistern], of Siloam, that is to say, Sent, (or Go, and be washed in the pool of Siloam, which is translated, Sent). Then he went, and washed, and came (back) seeing.

8   And so (his) neighbours, and they that had seen him before, for he was a beggar, said, Whether this is not he, that sat, and begged?

9   Other men said, That this it is, (or Some men said, Yea, it is him); and other men said, Nay, but he is like him. But he said, I am [he].

10   Therefore they said to him, How be thine eyes opened?

11   He answered, That man, that is said Jesus, made clay, and anointed mine eyes, and said to me, Go thou to the water, [or (to the) cistern], of Siloam, and wash, (or Go to the pool of Siloam, and wash); and I went, and washed, and (then I) saw.

12   And they said to him, Where is he? He said, I know not.

13   They led him that was blind to the Pharisees.

14   And it was (the) sabbath, when Jesus made clay, and opened his eyes.

15   Again the Pharisees asked him, how he had seen. And he said to them, He laid to me [or He put to me] clay on the eyes (or He put some clay on my eyes); and I washed, and (now) I see.

16   Therefore some of the Pharisees said, This man is not of God, that keepeth not the sabbath, (or And so some of the Pharisees said, This man cannot be from God, for he keepeth not the Sabbath). Other men said, How may a sinful man do these signs, [or miracles]. And strife [or division] was among them.

17   Therefore they said again to the blind man, What sayest thou of him, that opened thine eyes? And he said, That he is a prophet.

18   Therefore the Jews believed not of him, that he was blind, and had seen, till they called his father and mother, that had seen.

19   And they asked them, and said, Is this your son, which ye say was born blind? how then seeth he now?

20   His father and mother answered to them, and said, We know, that this is our son, and that he was born blind;

21   but how he seeth now, we know not, or who opened his eyes, we know not; ask ye him, he hath age, speak he of himself, (or you ask him, he is old enough, yea, let him speak for himself).

22   His father and mother said these things, for they dreaded the Jews; for then the Jews had conspired, that if any man acknowledged him (as) Christ, he should be done out of the synagogue. (His father and mother said these things, for they feared the Jews; for then the Jews had conspired together, that if anyone acknowledged him as the Messiah, they would be put out of the synagogue.)

23   Therefore his father and mother said, That he hath age, ask ye him. (And so his father and mother said, He is old enough, you ask him.)

24   Therefore again they called the man, that was blind, and said to him, Give thou glory to God; we know, that this man is a sinner.

25   Then he said, If he is a sinner, I know not; one thing I know, that when I was blind, now I see. (Then he said, If he is a sinner, I do not know; but the one thing I do know, is that before I was blind, and now I can see.)

26   Therefore they said to him, What did he (do) to thee? how opened he thine eyes?

27   He answered to them, I said to you now, and ye heard (me); what will ye again hear (it)? whether ye will be made his disciples? (He answered to them, I told you before, and ye heard me; why will ye hear it again? will ye also be made his disciples?)

28   Therefore they cursed him, and said, Be thou (made) his disciple; we be [the] disciples of Moses.

29   We know, that God spake to Moses; but we know not this (man), of whence he is.

30   That man answered, and said to them, For in this is a wonderful thing, that ye know not, of whence he is, and he hath opened mine eyes.

31   And we know, that God heareth not sinful men, but if any man be a worshipper of God, and doeth his will, he heareth him.

32   From the world it is not heard (of), that any man opened the eyes of a blind-born man (or of someone born blind);

33   [no] but this *man* were of God, he might not do anything. (unless this *man* was from God, he could not do anything.)

34   They answered, and said to him, Thou art all born in sins, and teachest thou us? [or and thou teachest us?] And they put him out.

35   Jesus heard, that they had put him out; and when he had found him, he said to him, Believest thou in the Son of God?

36   He answered, and said, Lord, who is he, (so) that I (can) believe in him?

37   And Jesus said to him, And thou hast seen him, and he it is, that speaketh with thee, (or and it is he, who speaketh with thee now).

38   And he said, Lord, I believe. And he fell down, and worshipped him.

39   Therefore Jesus said to him, I came into this world, in doom (or for judgement), (so) that they that see not, see, and they that see, be made blind.

40   And some of the Pharisees heard, that were with him (or who were with him), and they said to him, Whether we be blind?

41   Jesus said to them, If ye were blind, ye should not have sin; but now (that) ye say, That we see, your sin dwelleth still.

CHAPTER 10

1   Truly, truly, I say to you, (or Truly, I tell you the truth), he that cometh not in by the door into the fold of [the] sheep, but ascendeth [up] by another way, is a night thief and a day thief.

2   But he that entereth by the door, is the shepherd of the sheep.

3   To this the porter openeth, and the sheep hear his voice, and he calleth his own sheep by name, and leadeth them out.

4   And when he hath done out [or he hath sent out] his own sheep, he goeth before them, and the sheep (pur)sue him (or and the sheep follow him); for they know his voice.

5   But they (pur)sue not an alien, but flee from him; for they have not known the voice of aliens. (But they do not follow a stranger, but flee from him; for they do not know the voice of strangers.)

6   Jesus said to them this proverb; but they knew not what he spake to them.

7   Therefore Jesus said to them again, Truly, truly, I say to you, (or Truly, I tell you the truth), I am the door of the sheep.

8   As many as have come, were night thieves and day thieves, but the sheep heard not them (or but the sheep did not listen to them).

9   I am the door. If any man shall enter by me, he shall be saved; and he shall go in, and shall go out, and he shall find pastures.

10   A night thief cometh not, [no] but that he steal, slay, and lose, (or except to steal, kill, and

destroy); and I came, (so) that they (can) have life, and have (it) more plenteously.

11   I am a good shepherd; a good shepherd giveth his life for his sheep.

12   But an hired hind, and that is not the shepherd, (or But a hired hand, and who is not the shepherd), whose be not the sheep his own [or whose the sheep be not his own], seeth a wolf coming, and he leaveth the sheep, and fleeth; and the wolf ravisheth (or snatcheth up), and scattereth the sheep.

13   And the hired hind fleeth, for he is an hired hind, (or And the hired hand fleeth, for he is but a hired hand), and it pertaineth not to him of the sheep.

14   I am a good shepherd, and I know my sheep, and my sheep know me.

15   As the Father hath known me, I know the Father; and I put (forth or lay down) my life for my sheep.

16   I have other sheep, that be not of this fold, and it behooveth me to bring them together, and they shall hear my voice; and there shall be made one fold and one shepherd.

17   Therefore the Father loveth me, for I put (forth) my life, that again I take (it). (And so the Father loveth me, for I lay down my life, so that I can receive it back again.)

18   No man taketh it from me, but I put it of myself. I have power to put it, and I have power to take it again. This commandment I have taken of my Father. (No one taketh it from me, but I lay it down by myself. I have the power to put it forth, and I have the power to receive it back again. This commandment I have received from my Father.)

19   Again dissension was made among the Jews for these words.

20   And many of them said, He hath a devil, and maddeth, [or waxeth mad]; what hear ye him? (or why listen to him?)

21   Other men said, These words be not of *a man* that hath a devil. Whether the devil may open the eyes of blind men? [or Whether a devil may open the eyes of blind men?]

22   But the feasts of (the) hallowing of the temple (or the Feast or the Festival of Dedication) were made in Jerusalem, and it was winter.

23   And Jesus walked in the temple, in (or on) the porch of Solomon.

24   Therefore the Jews came about him, and said to him, How long takest thou away our soul? if thou art Christ (or if thou art the Messiah), say thou to us openly [or plainly].

25   Jesus answered to them, I speak to you, and ye believe not; the works that I do in the name of my Father, bear witnessing of me (or testify about me).

26   But ye believe not, for ye be not of my sheep.

27   My sheep hear my voice, and I know them, and they (pur)sue me (or and they follow me).

28   And I give to them everlasting life, and they shall not perish [into] without end, and none shall ravish them out of mine hand. (And I give them eternal life, and they shall never perish, and no one shall snatch them out of my hand.)

29   That thing that my Father gave to me, is more than all things; and no man may ravish (them), (or can snatch them), from my Father's hand.

30   I and the Father be one.

31   The Jews took up stones, to stone him.

32   Jesus answered to them, I have showed to you many good works of my Father, for which work of them stone ye me?

33   The Jews answered to him, We stone thee not of good work, but of blasphemy, (or We stone thee not for good works, but for thy blasphemy), and for thou, since thou art a man, makest thyself God.

34   Jesus answered to them, Whether it is not written in your law, That I said, Ye be gods?

35   If he said that they were gods, to whom the word of God was made, and the scripture

may not be undone (or and the Scripture cannot be destroyed),

36   that that the Father hath hallowed, and hath sent into the world, ye say, That thou blasphemest, for I said, I am God's Son?

37   If I do not the works of my Father, do not ye believe to me;

38   but if I do, though ye will not believe to me, believe ye to the works (or believe in the works); (so) that ye know and believe, that the Father is in me, and I in the Father.

39   Therefore they sought to take (hold of) him, and he went out of their hands.

40   And he went again over (the) Jordan (or And he went over again to the other side of the Jordan River), into that place where John was first baptizing, and he dwelt there.

41   And many came to him, and said, For John did no miracle [or sign]; and all things whatever John said of this (man), were sooth (or were true).

42   And many believed in him.

CHAPTER 11

1   And there was a sick man, Lazarus of Bethany, of the castle of Mary and Martha, his sisters, (or in the village of Mary and Martha, his sisters).

2   And it was Mary, which anointed the Lord with ointment, and wiped his feet with her hairs, whose brother Lazarus was sick.

3   Therefore his sisters sent to him, and said, Lord, lo! he whom thou lovest, is sick.

4   And Jesus heard, and said to them, This sickness is not to the death, but for the glory of God, (so) that man's Son be glorified by him [or (so) that God's son be glorified by it].

5   And Jesus loved Martha, and her sister Mary, and Lazarus.

6   Therefore when Jesus heard, that he was sick, then he dwelled in the same place (for) two days.

7   And after these things he said to his disciples, Go we again into Judea.

8   The disciples say to him, Master [or Rabbi], now the Jews sought to stone thee, and again goest thou thither? (The disciples said to him, Teacher, not long ago the Jews sought to stone thee there, and now thou goest there again?)

9   Jesus answered, Whether there be not twelve hours of the day? (or Be there not twelve hours in the day?) If any man wander in the day [or Whoever walketh in the day], he hurteth not (himself), for he seeth the light of this world.

10   But if he wander in the night (or But if he walk in the night), he stumbleth, for (the) light is not in (or with) him.

11   He said these things, and after these things he saith to them, Lazarus, our friend, sleepeth, but I go to raise him from sleep.

12   Therefore his disciples said, Lord, if he sleepeth, he shall be safe. (And so his disciples said, Lord, if he sleepeth, then he shall be secure or he shall be whole again.)

13   But Jesus had said of his death; but they guessed, that he said of [the] sleeping of sleep.

14   Then therefore Jesus said to them openly, Lazarus is dead;

15   and I have joy for you, that ye believe, for I was not there; but go we to him. (and I am happy for you, that your faith will increase, because I was not there; let us go to him.)

16   Therefore Thomas, that is said Didymus, said to (his) even-disciples, Go we also, that we die with him. (And Thomas, who is called the Twin, said to his fellow disciples, Let us also go, so that we can die with him.)

17   And so Jesus came, and found him having then four days in the grave.

18   And Bethany was beside Jerusalem, as it were fifteen furlongs.

19   And many of the Jews came to Mary and Martha, to comfort them of their brother (or to comfort them over their brother's death).

20   Therefore as Martha heard, that Jesus

came, she ran to him; but Mary sat at home.

21 Therefore Martha said to Jesus, Lord, if thou haddest been here, my brother had not be dead, (or Lord, if thou haddest been here, my brother would not have died).

22 But now I know, that whatever things thou shalt ask of God, God shall give to thee.

23 Jesus saith to her, Thy brother shall rise again.

24 Martha saith to him, I know, that he shall rise again in the again-rising in the last day. (Martha said to him, I know, that he shall rise again at the resurrection on the Last Day.)

25 Jesus saith to her, I am again-rising and life (or I am the resurrection and the life); he that believeth in me, yea, though he be dead, he shall live;

26 and each that liveth [or and all that liveth], and believeth in me, shall not die [into] without end. Believest thou this thing?

27 She saith to him, Yea, Lord, I have believed, that thou art Christ, the Son of the living God, that hast come into this world. (She said to him, Yes, Lord, I do believe, that thou art the Messiah, the Son of the living God, who hath come into this world.)

28 And when she had said this thing, she went, and called Mary, her sister, in silence, and said, The Master is come, and calleth thee. (And after she had said this, she went back home, and called aside her sister Mary, and said, The Teacher hath come, and calleth for thee.)

29 She, as she heard, arose anon (or got up at once), and came to him.

30 And Jesus came not yet into the castle (or And Jesus was not yet in the village), but he was yet in that place, where Martha had come to meet him.

31 Therefore the Jews that were with her in the house, and comforted her, when they saw Mary, that she rose swiftly, and went out, they (pur)sued her (or they followed her), and said, For she goeth to the grave, to weep there.

32 But when Mary was come (to) where Jesus was, she seeing him felled down to his feet, and said to him, Lord, if thou haddest been here, my brother had not be dead, (or Lord, if thou haddest been here, my brother would not have died).

33 Therefore when Jesus saw her weeping, and the Jews weeping that were with her, he made noise in (his) spirit (or he sighed loudly), and (he was) troubled himself,

34 and said, Where have ye laid him? They said to him, Lord, come, and see.

35 And Jesus wept.

36 Therefore the Jews said, Lo! how he loved him.

37 And some of them said, Whether this *man* that opened the eyes of the born-blind *man*, might not make that this (man) should not die?

38 Therefore Jesus again making noise in himself, came to the grave. And there was a den, and a stone was laid thereon. (And so Jesus again sighing loudly, came to the tomb. And it was a cave, and a stone was laid against the entrance to it.)

39 And Jesus saith, Take ye away the stone. Martha, the sister of him that was dead, saith to him, Lord, he stinketh now, for he hath lain (there) four days [or soothly he is of four days dead].

40 Jesus saith to her, Have I not said to thee, that if thou believest, thou shalt see the glory of God?

41 Therefore they took away the stone. And Jesus lifted up his eyes, and said, Father, I do thankings to thee, (or Father, I give thanks to thee), for thou hast heard me;

42 and I knew, that thou (for)evermore hearest me, (or and I know, that thou always hearest me), but for the people that standeth about, I said (this), (so) that they believe, that thou hast sent me.

43 When he had said these things, he cried with a great voice, Lazarus, come forth, [or Lazarus, come thou out].

44   And anon he that was dead, came out, bound the hands and feet with bonds, and his face bound with a sudarium, [*or* (a) *sweating cloth*], (or a napkin). And Jesus saith to them, Unbind ye him, and suffer ye him to go forth. (And at once he who was dead, came out, and his hands and his feet were bound with bonds, and his face was bound with a cloth. And Jesus said to them, Unbind him, and allow him to go forth.)

45   Therefore many of the Jews that came to Mary and Martha, and saw what things Jesus did, believed in him.

46   But some of them went to the Pharisees, and said to them, what things Jesus had done.

47   Therefore the bishops (or And so the high priests), and the Pharisees gathered a council against Jesus, and said, What do we (do)? for this man doeth many miracles [or many signs].

48   If we leave him thus, all men shall believe in him; and (then the) Romans shall come, and shall take (away) our place, and our folk. (If we leave him alone, everyone shall believe in him; and then the Romans shall come, and shall destroy our Temple, and our nation.)

49   But one of them, Caiaphas by name, when he was bishop of that year (or who was the High Priest that year), said to them, Ye know nothing,

50   nor think, that it speedeth to you, that one man die for the people, and that all the folk perish not. (nor understand, that it is more expedient for you, that one man should die for the people, so that the whole nation shall not perish.)

51   But he said not this thing of himself, but when he was bishop of that year, he prophesied, that Jesus was to die for the folk, (But he did not say this of his own accord, but as he was the High Priest that year, he had prophesied, that Jesus was to die for the nation,)

52   and not only for the folk (or and not only die for the nation), but that he should gather into one the sons of God that were scattered.

53   Therefore from that day (forth) they thought, or sought, (or made plans) for (how) to slay him.

54   Therefore Jesus walked not then openly among the Jews; but he went into a country(side) beside [the] desert (or but he went into the countryside near the desert), into a city, that is said Ephraim, and there he dwelled with his disciples.

55   And the pask of the Jews was nigh, and many of the country went up to Jerusalem before the pask, to hallow themselves. (And the Passover of the Jews was near, and many from the countryside, or and many from all over the country, went up to Jerusalem before the Passover, to sanctify or to purify themselves.)

56   Therefore they sought Jesus, and spake together, standing in the temple, What guess ye, for he cometh not to the feast day?

57   For the bishops, and the Pharisees had given a commandment, that if any man know where he is, that he show (them), that they take him. (For the high priests, and the Pharisees had given an order, that if anyone knew where he was, that they should tell them, so that they could take hold of him.)

CHAPTER 12

1   Therefore Jesus before six days of pask came to Bethany, where Lazarus had been dead, whom Jesus raised (from the dead). (And so six days before the Passover Jesus came to Bethany, where Lazarus had died, whom Jesus had raised from the dead.)

2   And they made to him a supper there, and Martha ministered to him; and Lazarus was one of the men that sat at the meat with him. (And they made a supper for him there, and Martha served him; and Lazarus was one of the men who sat at the meal with him.)

3   Therefore Mary took a pound of ointment of true nard [or spikenard] precious, and anointed the feet of Jesus, and wiped his feet

with her hairs; and the house was full-filled with the savour of the ointment.

4 Therefore Judas Iscariot, one of his disciples, that was to betray him, said,

5 Why is not this ointment sold for three hundred pence, and given to poor men? (Why is this ointment not sold for three hundred pennies, and that given to the poor?)

6 But he said this thing, not for it pertained to him of needy men, but for he was a thief, and had the purses, and bare those things that were sent (into them), (or and carried off whatever was put into them).

7 Therefore Jesus said, Suffer ye her, that into the day of my burying she keep that (which is left); (And so Jesus said, Allow her, or Let her, do this, so that on the day of my burial she can use what is left;)

8 for ye shall (for)evermore have poor men with you, but ye shall not (for)evermore have me. (for ye shall always have the poor with you, but ye shall not always have me.)

9 Therefore much people of the Jews knew, that Jesus was there; and they came, not only for Jesus, but to see Lazarus, whom he had raised from death [or whom he raised from (the) dead].

10 But the princes of (the) priests thought, or sought, to slay Lazarus, (And so the high priests also made plans to kill Lazarus,)

11 for many of the Jews went away for him, and believed in Jesus.

12 But on the morrow much people, that came together to the feast day, when they had heard, that Jesus came to Jerusalem, (But the next morning, many people who had come for the Feast Day, or the Festival, when they had heard, that Jesus had come to Jerusalem,)

13 took branches of palms, and came forth to meet him, and cried, Hosanna, blessed is the king of Israel, that cometh in the name of the Lord.

14 And Jesus found a young ass, and sat on him, as it is written,

15 The daughter of Sion, do not thou dread, (or The daughter of Zion, do not fear); lo! thy king cometh, sitting on an ass's foal [or sitting on the colt of a she ass].

16 His disciples knew not (at) first these things, but when Jesus was glorified, then they had mind, that these things were written of him, and these things they did to him. (His disciples at first did not understand the meaning of these things, but when Jesus was glorified, then they remembered, that these things were written about him, and that the people had done these things for him.)

17 Therefore the people bare witnessing, that was with him, when he called Lazarus from the grave, and raised him from death [or and raised him from (the) dead]. (And so the people, who were with him, when he called Lazarus out of the tomb, and raised him from the dead, testified about that.)

18 And therefore the people came, and met with him, for they heard that he had done this sign (or this miracle).

19 Therefore the Pharisees said to themselves, Ye see, that we profit nothing; lo! all the world hath gone after him.

20 And there were some heathen men, of them that had come up to worship in the feast day. (And there were some Gentiles, among those who had come to worship on the Feast Day, or at the Festival.)

21 And these came to Philip, that was of Bethsaida of Galilee, and prayed him, and said, Sire, we will see Jesus, [or Sire, we would (like to) see Jesus]. (And they came to Philip, who was from Bethsaida in Galilee, and beseeched him, and said, Sir, we want to see Jesus.)

22 Philip cometh, and saith to Andrew; and again Andrew and Philip said to Jesus.

23 And Jesus answered to them, and said, The hour cometh, that man's Son be clarified, (or The time hath come, for man's Son to be glorified).

24 Truly, truly, I say to you, [no] but a corn of

wheat fall into the earth, and be dead, (or Truly, I tell you the truth, unless a kernel, or a grain, of wheat fall into the earth, and it die), it dwelleth alone; but if it be dead, it bringeth [forth] much fruit.

25 He that loveth his life, shall lose it; and he that hateth his life in this world, keepeth it into everlasting life (or keepeth it safe for eternal life).

26 If any man serve me, (pur)sue he me (or follow me); and where I am, there my minister [or my servant] shall be. If any man serve me, my Father shall worship him (or my Father shall honour him).

27 Now my soul is troubled, and what shall I say? Father, save me from this hour; but therefore I came into this hour [or but for that thing I came into this hour];

28 Father, clarify thy name. And a voice came from heaven, and said, And I have clarified (it), and again I shall clarify (it). (Father, glorify thy name. And a voice came from heaven, and said, I have glorified it, and I shall glorify it again.)

29 Therefore the people that stood (there), and heard, said, that thunder was made; other men said, an angel spake to him.

30 Jesus answered, and said, This voice came not for me, but for you.

31 Now is the doom of the world, now the prince of this world shall be cast out. (Now is the Judgement of this world, now the Prince of this world shall be thrown out.)

32 And if I shall be enhanced from the earth, I shall draw all things to myself. (And if I shall be raised or lifted up from the earth, then I shall draw everyone to me.)

33 And he said this thing, signifying by what death he was to die.

34 And the people answered to him, We have heard of the law, that Christ dwelleth [into] without end; and how sayest thou, It behooveth man's Son to be areared? Who is this man's Son? (And the people said to him,

We have heard in the Law, that the Messiah remaineth forever; so how sayest thou, It behooveth the Son of man to be raised up? Who is this Son of man?)

35 And then Jesus saith to them, Yet a little light is in you; walk ye, the while ye have light, that (the) darkness(es) catch you not; he that wandereth in (the) darknesses, knoweth not whither he goeth. (And then Jesus said to them, Yet a little light is in you, or There is but a little light left to you; walk ye, the while ye have the light, so that the darkness catch you not; he who walketh, or who goeth, in the darkness, knoweth not where he goeth.)

36 While ye have (the) light, believe ye in the light, (so) that ye be the children of (the) light. Jesus spake these things, and went, and hid him(self) from them.

37 And when he had done so many miracles [or so many signs] before them, they believed not in him; (And though he had done so many miracles before them, they still did not believe in him;)

38 that the word of Esaias, the prophet, should be fulfilled, which he said, Lord, who hath believed to our hearing, and to whom is the arm of the Lord showed? (so that the word of the prophet Isaiah would be fulfilled, when he said, Lord, who hath believed our message, and to whom is the Lord's power shown or revealed?)

39 Therefore they might not believe, for again Esaias said, (And so they could not believe, for again Isaiah said,)

40 He hath blinded their eyes, and hath made hard the heart(s) of them, (so) that they see not with (their) eyes, and understand [not] with (their) heart(s); and that they be converted, and I heal them.

41 Esaias said these things, when he saw the glory of him, and spake of him. (Isaiah said these things, when he saw his glory, and spoke about him.)

42 Nevertheless of the princes, many

believed in him, but for the Pharisees they acknowledged not, that they should not be put out of the synagogue; (Nevertheless, among the leaders, many believed in him, but because of the Pharisees they did not acknowledge him publicly, so that they would not be put out of the synagogue;)

43 for they loved the glory of men, more than the glory of God.

44 And Jesus cried, and said, He that believeth in me, believeth not in me, but in him that sent me (or but in him who sent me).

45 He that seeth me, seeth him that sent me.

46 I (as a) light came into the world, that each that believeth in me, dwell not in (the) darknesses. (I came as a light into the world, so that everyone who believeth in me, remain not in darkness.)

47 And if any man heareth my words, and keepeth them not, I deem him not; for I came not, that I deem the world, but that I make the world safe. (And if anyone heareth my words, and obeyeth them not, I do not judge that person; for I came not, that I judge the world, but that I save the world.)

48 He that despiseth me, and taketh not my words, hath him that shall judge him; that word that I have spoken [or the word that I have spoken], shall deem him in the last day. (He who despiseth me, and receiveth not my words, hath that which shall judge him; yea, the words that I have spoken, will judge him on the Last Day.)

49 For I have not spoken of myself, but that Father that sent me, [he] gave to me a commandment, what I shall say, and what I shall speak.

50 And I know, that his commandment is everlasting life (or that his command bringeth eternal life); therefore those things that I speak, as the Father said to me, so I speak.

CHAPTER 13

1 But before the feast day of pask, Jesus witting, that his hour is come, [or Jesus witting, for his hour cometh], (But before the Feast Day, or the Festival, of Passover, Jesus knowing, that his hour had come), that he pass from this world to the Father, when he had loved his that were in the world, into the end he loved them.

2 And when the supper was made, when the devil had put then into the heart, that Judas of Simon Iscariot should betray him, [And the supper made, when the devil had sent now into the heart of Judas of Simon Iscariot, that he should betray him,]

3 he witting (or knowing) that the Father gave all things to him into his hands, and that he went out from God, and (now) goeth (back) to God,

4 he riseth from the supper, and doeth off his clothes; and when he had taken a linen cloth, he girded him(self).

5 And afterward he put water into a basin, and began to wash the disciples' feet, and to wipe (them) with the linen cloth, with which he was girded.

6 And so he came to Simon Peter, and Peter saith to him, Lord, washest thou my feet?

7 Jesus answered, and said to him, What I do, thou knowest not now; but thou shalt know afterward.

8 Peter saith to him, Thou shalt never wash my feet. Jesus answered to him, If I shall not wash thee, thou shalt not have (any) part with me.

9 Simon Peter saith to him, Lord, not only my feet, but both the hands and the head.

10 Jesus saith to him, He that is washed, hath no need but that he wash the feet, but he is all clean (or then he is altogether clean); and ye be clean, but not all.

11 For he knew, who it was that should betray him (or who it was that would betray him); therefore he said, Ye be not all clean.

12 And so after that he had washed their feet, he took his clothes; and when he was set to (the) meat again, again he said to them, Ye

know what I have done to you [or Know ye what I have done to you(?)]. (And so after that he had washed their feet, he took his clothes; and when he had sat down at the meal again, he said to them, Do ye understand what I have done for you?)

13 Ye call me Master and Lord, and ye say well; for I am. (Ye call me Teacher and Lord, and ye say correctly; for that is what I am.)

14 Therefore if I, Lord and Master, have washed your feet, and ye shall wash one another's feet [or ye owe to wash another the other's feet]; (And so, if I, your Lord and Teacher, have washed your feet, ye ought to wash one another's feet;)

15 for I have given to you (an) ensample, that as I have done to you, so do ye.

16 Truly, truly, I say to you, (or Truly, I tell you the truth), the servant is not greater than his lord, neither an apostle is greater than he that sent him.

17 If ye know these things, ye shall be blessed, if ye do them.

18 I say not of (or about) all (of) you, (for) I know which I have chosen; but that the scripture be fulfilled, He that eateth my bread, shall raise his heel against me.

19 Truly, I say to you before it be done, (so) that when it is done, ye believe that I am (or ye believe who I am).

20 Truly, truly, I say to you, he that taketh whomever I shall send, receiveth me, (or Truly, I tell you the truth, he who receiveth whomever I shall send, receiveth me); and he that receiveth me, receiveth him that sent me.

21 When Jesus had said these things, he was troubled in spirit, and witnessed (or testified), and said, Truly, truly, I say to you, (or Truly, I tell you the truth), that one of you shall betray me.

22 Therefore the disciples looked (around) together, doubting of whom he said.

23 And so one of his disciples was resting in the bosom of Jesus, whom Jesus loved. (And

one of his disciples, whom Jesus loved, was sitting close beside Jesus.)

24 Therefore Simon Peter beckoned to him, and said to him, Who is it, of whom he saith?

25 And so when he had rested again on the breast of Jesus, he saith to him, Lord, who is it? (And so when he was close beside Jesus again, he asked him, Lord, who is it?)

26 Jesus answered, He it is, to whom I shall areach a sop of bread. And when he had wet bread [or And when he had dipped in (some) bread], he gave (it) to Judas of Simon Iscariot.

27 And after the morsel, then Satan entered into him. And Jesus saith to him, That thing that thou doest, do thou swiftly.

28 And none of them that sat at the meat knew (or And none of those who sat at the meal knew), whereto [or what thing] he said to him.

29 For some guessed, for Judas had (the) purses, that Jesus had said to him, Buy thou those things, that be needful to us to the feast day, (or Go and buy for us those things, that we need for the Feast Day or for the Festival), or that he should give something to needy men.

30 Therefore when he had taken the morsel, he went out anon (or he left at once); and it was night.

31 Therefore when he was gone out, Jesus said, Now man's Son is clarified, and God is clarified in him. (And so when Judas had gone out, Jesus said, Now man's Son is glorified, and God is glorified in him.)

32 If God is clarified in him, and God shall clarify him in himself, and anon (or at once) he shall clarify him. (If God is glorified in him, then God shall glorify him in himself, and he shall glorify him now.)

33 Little sons, yet a little I am with you; ye shall seek me, and, as I said to the Jews, Whither I go, ye may not come, (or Where I go, ye cannot come); and to you I say (it) now.

34 I give to you a new commandment, that ye love together, as I have loved you, and that ye love together. (I give you a new

commandment, that ye love one another, as I have loved you, yea, that ye love one another.)

35 In this thing all men shall know, that ye be my disciples, if ye have love together (or if ye love one another).

36 Simon Peter saith to him, Lord, whither goest thou? Jesus answered, Whither I go, thou mayest not (pur)sue me now, but thou shalt (pur)sue me afterward. (Simon Peter said to him, Lord, where goest thou? Jesus answered, Where I go, thou cannot follow me now, but thou shalt follow me later.)

37 Peter saith to him, Why may I not (pur)sue thee now? I shall put (forth) my life for thee. (Peter said to him, Why can I not follow thee now? I shall lay down my life for thee.)

38 Jesus answered, Thou shalt put (forth) (or lay down) thy life for me? Truly, truly, I say to thee, (or Truly, I tell thee the truth), the cock shall not crow, till thou shalt deny me thrice.

39 And he saith to his disciples,

CHAPTER 14

1 Be not your heart afraid [or distroubled], nor dread it, (or Let not your heart be troubled, nor let it have fear or let it be fearful); ye believe in God, and believe ye in me.

2 In the house of my Father be many dwellings; if anything less, I had said to you, for I go to make ready to you a place (or for I go to prepare a place for you).

3 And if I go, and make ready to you a place, (or And if I go, and prepare a place for you), again I [shall] come, and I shall take you (un)to myself, (so) that where I am, ye be.

4 And whither I go, ye know, and ye know the way.

5 Thomas saith to him, Lord, we know not whither thou goest, and how may we know the way? (Thomas said to him, Lord, we do not know where thou goest, so how can we know the way?)

6 Jesus saith to him, I am (the) way, (the)

truth, and (the) life; no man cometh to the Father, but by me.

7 If ye had known me, soothly ye had known also my Father; and afterward ye shall know him, and ye have seen him.

8 Philip saith to him, Lord, show to us the Father, and it sufficeth to us.

9 Jesus saith to him, So long (a) time I am with you, and have ye not known me? Philip, he that seeth me, seeth also the Father. How sayest thou, show to us the Father?

10 Believest thou not, that I *am* in the Father, and the Father is in me? The words that I speak to you, I speak not of myself; but the Father himself that dwelleth in me, [he] doeth the works.

11 Believe ye not, that I am in the Father, and the Father is in me? Else believe ye for those works.

12 Truly, truly, I say to you, (or Truly, I tell you the truth), if a man believeth in me, also he shall do the works that I do; and he shall do greater works than these, for I go to the Father. [Truly, truly, I say to you, he that believeth in me, and he shall do the works that I do; and he shall do more works than these, for I go to the father.]

13 And whatever thing ye ask the Father in my name, I shall do this thing, (so) that the Father be glorified in the Son.

14 If ye ask anything in my name, I shall do it.

15 If ye love me, keep ye my commandments (or obey my commandments).

16 And I shall pray the Father, and he shall give to you another Comforter, the Spirit of truth, to dwell with you [into] without end (or to remain with you forever);

17 which *Spirit* the world may not take (or which *Spirit* the world cannot receive), for it seeth him not, neither knoweth him. But ye shall know him, for he shall dwell with you, and he shall be in you.

18 I shall not leave you fatherless, I shall

come to you.

19   Yet a little, and the world seeth not now me [or and the world seeth not me now]; but ye shall see me, for I live, and ye shall live.

20   In that day ye shall know, that I am in my Father, and ye in me, and I in you.

21   He that hath my commandments, and keepeth them (or obeyeth them), he it is that loveth me; and he that loveth me, shall be loved of my Father (or shall be loved by my Father), and I shall love him, and I shall show to him myself.

22   Judas saith to him, not he of Iscariot, Lord, what is done, (or Lord, why is it), that thou shalt show thyself to us, and not to the world?

23   Jesus answered, and said to him, If any man loveth me, he shall keep my word(s), (or he shall obey my words); and my Father shall love him, and we shall come to him, and we shall dwell with him.

24   He that loveth me not, keepeth not my words (or obeyeth not my words); and the word which ye have heard, is not mine, but the Father's, that sent me.

25   These things I have spoken to you, dwelling among you;

26   but that Holy Ghost, the Comforter, whom the Father shall send in my name, he shall teach you all things, and shall show, [or remember], to you all things, whatever things I shall say to you. (but the Holy Spirit, the Comforter, whom the Father shall send in my name, he shall teach you everything, and shall remind you of everything, whatever I have said to you.)

27   Peace I leave to you, my peace I give to you; not as the world giveth, I give to you; be not your heart afraid [or troubled], nor dread it, (or let not your heart be troubled, nor let it have fear or let it be fearful).

28   Ye have heard, that I said to you, I go, and (then I shall) come (back) to you. If ye loved me, forsooth ye should have joy, for I go to the Father, for the Father is greater than I.

29   And now I have said to you, before that it be done, (so) that when it is done, ye believe (it).

30   Now I shall not speak many things with you; for the prince of this world cometh, and hath not in me anything, [or and he hath not anything in me], (or and he hath no power over me).

31   But (so) that the world know, that I love the Father; and as the Father gave a commandment to me, so I do (it). Rise ye, go we hence, (or Get up, let us go now).

CHAPTER 15

1   I am a very vine, and my Father is an earth-tiller. (I am the true vine, and my Father is the farmer.)

2   Each branch in me that beareth not fruit, he shall take away it (or he shall take it away); and each that beareth fruit, he shall purge it, (so) that it bear the more fruit. [Each scion, *or branch*, not bearing fruit in me, he shall do it away; and each that beareth fruit, he shall purge it, (so) that it bear more fruit.]

3   Now ye be (made) clean, for the word that I have spoken to you. (Now ye be cleansed, or ye be purified, by the words which I have spoken to you.)

4   Dwell ye in me, and I in you; as a branch may not make fruit of itself, [no] but it dwell in the vine, so neither ye, [no] but ye dwell in me. (Remain in me, and I in you; for a branch cannot make fruit by itself, unless it remain on the vine, so neither can ye, unless ye remain in me.)

5   I am the vine, ye *be* the branches. Who that dwelleth (or remaineth) in me [or He that dwelleth in me], and I in him, this beareth much fruit, for without me ye may nothing do (or for ye can do nothing without me).

6   If any man dwelleth not in me, he shall be cast out as a branch, and shall wax dry; and they shall gather him (up), and they shall cast

him into the fire, and he shall burn. (If anyone remaineth not in me, he shall be thrown out like a branch, and shall grow dry; and they shall gather him up, and they shall throw him into the fire, and he shall be burned up.)

7 If ye dwell in me, and my words dwell in you, whatever thing ye will, ye shall ask (for it), and it shall be done to you. (If ye remain in me, and my words remain in you, whatever that ye want, ye shall ask for it, and it shall be done for you.)

8 In this thing my Father is clarified (or My Father is glorified in this), that ye bring forth full much fruit, and that ye be made my disciples.

9 As my Father loved me, I have loved you; dwell ye in my love (or remain in my love).

10 If ye keep my commandments, ye shall dwell in my love; as I have kept the commandments of my Father, and dwell in his love. (If ye obey my commandments, ye shall remain in my love; as I have obeyed my Father's commandments, and remain in his love.)

11 These things I spake to you, (so) that my joy be in you, and your joy be full-filled (or and that your joy be filled full).

12 This is my commandment, that ye love together (or that ye love one another), as I have loved you.

13 No man hath more love than this, that a man put (forth) his life for his friends.

14 Ye be my friends if ye do those things, that I command to you.

15 Now I shall not call you servants, for the servant knoweth not, what his lord shall do; but I have called you friends, for all (the) things whatever I heard of my Father, I have made known to you.

16 Ye have not chosen me, but I chose you; and I have put you, that ye go, and bring forth fruit, and your fruit dwell; that whatever thing ye ask the Father in my name, he give to you. (Ye have not chosen me, but I chose you; and I have ordained you, so that ye go, and bring forth fruit, and that your fruit remain; so that whatever ye ask the Father for in my name, he shall give it to you.)

17 These things I command to you, that ye love together (or that ye love one another).

18 If the world hate you, know ye, that it had me in hate rather than you.

19 If ye had been of the world, the world should love that thing that was his (or the world would love that which was its own); but for ye be not of the world, but I chose you from the world, therefore the world hateth you.

20 Have ye mind of my word(s), which I said to you, The servant is not greater than his lord. If they have pursued me, they shall pursue you also; if they have kept my word, they shall keep yours also. (Remember my words, which I said to you, The servant is not greater than his lord or master. If they have persecuted me, they shall also persecute you; if they have obeyed my words, they shall also obey yours.)

21 But they shall do to you all these things for my name, for they know not him that sent me.

22 If I had not come, and had not spoken to them, they should not have sin; but now they have none excusation [or not excusing] of their sin. (If I had not come, and had not spoken to them, they would not be guilty of sin; but now they have no excuse for their sin.)

23 He that hateth me, hateth also my Father.

24 If I had not done the works in them, which none other man did, they should not have sin, (or If I had not done the works among them, which no other man hath ever done, they would not be guilty of sin); but now both they have seen, and have hated me and my Father.

25 But that the word be fulfilled, that is written in their law, For they had me in hate without cause. (So that the word be fulfilled, that is written in their Law, For they hated me for no good reason.)

26 But when the Comforter shall come, which I shall send to you from the Father, the

Spirit of truth, which cometh forth [or proceedeth] of the Father, he shall bear witnessing of me; (But when the Comforter shall come, whom I shall send to you from the Father, yea the Spirit of Truth, who cometh forth from the Father, he shall testify about me;)

27 and ye shall bear witnessing (or ye shall testify), for ye be with me from the beginning.

CHAPTER 16

1 These things I have spoken to you, (so) that ye be not caused to stumble.

2 They shall make you without the synagogues, but the hour cometh, that each man that slayeth you, deem that he doeth service to God. (They shall put you out of the synagogues, and the time cometh, when each man who killeth you, shall think that he doeth a service to God.)

3 And they shall do to you these things, for they have not known the Father, neither me.

4 But these things I spake to you, that when the hour of them shall come, ye have mind, (or so that when their time shall come, ye shall remember), that I said (this) to you. I said not to you these things from the beginning, for I was with you.

5 And now I go to him that sent me, and no man of you asketh me, Whither goest thou? (And now I go to him who sent me, and none of you asketh me, Where goest thou?)

6 but for I have spoken to you these things, heaviness [or sorrow] hath full-filled your heart(s). (but because I have spoken these things to you, now sorrow hath filled your hearts full.)

7 But I say to you (the) truth, it speedeth to you, that I go, (or But I tell you the truth, it is more expedient for you, that I go away); for if I go not forth, the Comforter shall not come to you; but if I go forth, I shall send him to you. [But I say to you truth, it speedeth to you, that I go; soothly if I shall not go away, the comforter shall not come to you; forsooth if I shall go away, I shall send him to you.]

8 And when he cometh, he shall reprove the world of sin, and of rightwiseness, and of doom, (And when he cometh, he shall prove the world wrong about sin, and about righteousness, and about judgement.)

9 Of sin (or About sin), for they have not believed in me;

10 and of rightwiseness (or and about righteousness), for I go to the Father, and now ye shall not see me;

11 but of doom, for the prince of this world is now deemed. (and about judgement, for the Prince of this world is now judged.)

12 Yet I have many things to say to you, but ye may not bear them now (or but ye cannot bear them now).

13 But when the Spirit of truth cometh, he shall teach you all truth; for he shall not speak of himself, but whatever things he shall hear, he shall speak; and he shall tell to you those things that be to come.

14 He shall clarify me, for of mine he shall take, and shall tell to you. (He shall glorify me, for he shall receive it from me, and then he shall tell it to you.)

15 All things, whatever [things] the Father hath, be mine; therefore I said to you, that of mine he shall take, and (then) shall tell to you. (Everything, whatever the Father hath, is mine; and so I said to you, that he shall receive it from me, and then he shall tell it to you.)

16 A little, and then ye shall not see me; and again a little, and ye shall see me, for I go to the Father.

17 Therefore some of his disciples said together, What is this thing that he saith to us, A little, and ye shall not see me; and again a little, and ye shall see me, for I go to the Father?

18 Therefore they said, What is this that he saith to us, A little? we know not what he speaketh.

19 And Jesus knew, that they would ask him,

and he said to them, Of this thing ye seek among you(rselves), for I said, A little, and ye shall not see me; and again a little, and ye shall see me.

20 Truly, truly, I say to you, (or Truly, I tell you the truth), that ye shall mourn and weep, but the world shall have joy; and ye shall be sorrowful, but your sorrow shall turn into joy.

21 A woman when she beareth (a) child, hath heaviness [or sorrow], for her time is come; but when she hath born a son, now she thinketh not on the pain, for (or because of her) joy, for a man is born into the world.

22 And therefore ye have now sorrow, but again I shall see you, and your heart(s) shall have joy, and no man shall take from you your joy.

23 And in that day ye shall not ask (of) me anything; truly, truly, I say to you, if ye ask the Father (for) anything in my name, he shall give [it] to you. (And on that day ye shall ask nothing of me; truly, I tell you the truth, if ye ask the Father for anything in my name, he shall give it to you.)

24 Till now ye (have) asked nothing in my name; ask ye, and ye shall take, (or ask, and ye shall receive), (so) that your joy be full.

25 I have spoken to you these things in proverbs; the hour cometh, when now I shall not speak to you in proverbs, but openly of my Father I shall tell to you [or but openly of my Father I shall tell you].

26 In that day ye shall ask in my name; and I say not to you, that I shall pray (to) the Father for you;

27 for the Father himself loveth you, for ye have loved me, and have believed, that I went out from God.

28 I went out from the Father, and I came into the world; again I leave the world, and go to the Father.

29 His disciples said to him, Lo! now thou speakest openly, and thou sayest no proverb.

30 Now we know, that thou knowest all things; and it is not need(ful) to thee, [or and it is no need to thee], (or and there is no need), that any man ask thee (anything more). In this thing we believe, that thou wentest out from God.

31 Jesus answered to them, Now ye believe.

32 Lo! the hour cometh, and now it cometh, that ye be scattered, each into his own things, and that ye leave me alone; and I am not alone (or but I am not alone), for the Father is with me.

33 These things I have spoken to you, (so) that ye have peace in me; in the world ye shall have dis-ease, [or have pressing, *or over-laying*], (or in the world ye shall have pressure), but trust ye, I have overcome the world.

CHAPTER 17

1 These things Jesus spake, and when he had cast [or (had) lifted] up his eyes into heaven, he said, Father, the hour cometh, clarify thy Son, that thy Son clarify thee. (Jesus spoke these things, and when he had lifted up his eyes unto heaven, he said, Father, the time cometh, glorify thy Son, so that thy Son can glorify thee.)

2 As thou hast given to him power on each flesh, [*or man*], (so) that (of) all (the) thing(s) that thou hast given to him, he give to them everlasting life. (For thou hast given him authority over everyone, so that to all those whom thou hast given to him, he can give them eternal life.)

3 And this is everlasting life, that they know thee very God alone, and whom thou hast sent, Jesus Christ. (And this is eternal life, that they know thee, the true God alone, and whom thou hast sent, Jesus Christ.)

4 I have clarified thee on the earth, I have ended the work, that thou hast given to me to do. (I have glorified thee on the earth, I have finished the work, that thou hast given me to do.)

5 And now, Father, clarify thou me at thyself, with the clearness that I had at thee, before the world was made. (And now, Father, glorify me before thee, or in thy presence, with the glory that I had with thee, before the world was made.)

6 I have showed thy name to those men, which thou hast given to me of the world; they were thine, and thou hast given them to me, and they have kept thy word (or and they have obeyed thy command).

7 And now they have known, that all (the) things that thou hast given to me, be of thee.

8 For the words that thou hast given to me, I gave to them; and they have taken, and have known verily, that I went out from thee, (or and they have received it, and have truly known, that I went out from thee); and they believed, that thou sentest me.

9 I pray for them, *I pray* not for the world, but for them that thou hast given to me, for they be thine.

10 And all my things be thine, and thy things be mine; and I am clarified in them (or and I am glorified in them).

11 And now I am not in the world, and these be in the world, and I come to thee. Holy Father, keep them in thy name, which thou hast given to me, (so) that they be one, as we *be* (one).

12 While I was with them, I kept them in thy name; those that thou gavest to me, I kept, and none of them perished, [no] but the son of perdition, (so) that the scripture be fulfilled.

13 But now I come to thee, and I speak these things in the world, that they have my joy fulfilled in themselves. (And now I come to thee, but I say these things while I am still in the world, so that they have my joy filled full within themselves.)

14 I gave to them thy word, and the world had them in hate, (or I gave thy words to them; and the world hated them); for they be not of the world, as I am not of the world.

15 I pray not, that thou take them away from the world, but that thou keep them from evil.

16 They be not of the world, as I am not of the world.

17 Hallow thou them in (the) truth; thy word is truth.

18 As thou sentest me into the world, also I sent them into the world.

19 And I hallow myself for them, (so) that also they be hallowed in (the) truth.

20 And I pray not only for them, but also for them that shall believe into me by the word of them; (And I pray not only for them, but also for those who shall believe in me because of their words;)

21 that all [they] be one, as thou, Father, in me, and I in thee, that also they in us be one, (or that they all be one, like thou, Father, in me, and I in thee, that also they be one in us); (so) that the world believe, that thou hast sent me.

22 And I have given to them the clearness, that thou hast given to me, that they be one, as we be one; (And I have given them the glory, that thou hast given me, so that they be one, like we be one;)

23 I in them, and thou in me, that they be ended into one (or so that they perfectly or completely become one); and (so) that the world know, that thou sentest me, and hast loved them, as thou hast loved also me.

24 Father, they which thou hast given to me, I will that where I am, that they be with me, that they see my clearness, that thou hast given to me; for thou lovedest me before the making of the world. (Father, they whom thou hast given to me, I desire that where I am, that they be with me, so that they can see my glory, which thou hast given to me; for thou hast loved me before the making or the creation of the world.)

25 Father, rightfully the world knew thee not, [or Rightful Father, (or Righteous Father), the world knew not thee], but I knew thee, and these knew, that thou sentest me.

26 And I have made thy name known to them, and shall make known; that the love by which thou hast loved me, be in them, and I in them.

CHAPTER 18

1 When Jesus had said these things, he went out with his disciples over the strand of Cedron, (or he went out with his disciples across the Kidron Stream, or the Kidron Gorge, or the Kidron Valley), where (there) was a yard, *or a garden*, into which he entered, and his disciples.

2 And Judas, that betrayed him, knew the place, for oft Jesus came thither with his disciples.

3 Therefore when Judas had taken a company of knights, and ministers of the bishops, and of the Pharisees, he came thither with lanterns, and brands, and armours [or arms]. (And so when Judas had taken a company of soldiers, and servants, or officers, from the high priests, and from the Pharisees, he came there with lanterns, and torches, and weapons.)

4 And so Jesus witting all things that were to come on him, went forth, and said to them, Whom seek ye?

5 They answered to him, Jesus of Nazareth. Jesus saith to them, I am (he). And Judas that betrayed him, stood with them.

6 And when he said to them, I am (he), they went aback, and fell down on the earth. (And when he said to them, I am he, they went backward, and fell down on the ground.)

7 And again he asked them, Whom seek ye? And they said, Jesus of Nazareth.

8 He answered to them, I said to you, that I am (he); therefore if ye seek me, suffer ye these to go away, (or and so if ye came for me, allow these men to go away).

9 (So) That the word which he said should be fulfilled, For I lost not any of them, which thou hast given to me.

10 Therefore Simon Peter had a sword, and drew it out, and smote the servant of the bishop (or and struck the servant of the High Priest), and cut off his right ear. And the name of the servant was Malchus.

11 Therefore Jesus said to Peter, Put thou thy sword into thy sheath; wilt thou not, that I drink the cup, that my Father gave to me?

12 Therefore the company of knights, and the tribune, and the ministers of the Jews, took Jesus, and bound him, (And so the company of soldiers, and the tribune, and the servants, or the officers, of the Jews, took hold of Jesus, and bound him,)

13 and led him first to Annas; for he was [the] father of Caiaphas' wife, that was bishop of that year. (and first they led him to Annas; he was the father of the wife of Caiaphas, and Caiaphas was the High Priest that year.)

14 And it was Caiaphas, that gave counsel to the Jews, that it speedeth (or it was expedient), that one man (should) die for the people.

15 But Simon Peter (pur)sued Jesus, and another disciple; and that disciple was known to the bishop. And he entered with Jesus, into the hall of the bishop; (And Simon Peter, and another disciple, followed Jesus; and that disciple was known to Annas, who was a former High Priest. And he entered with Jesus, into the courtyard of the former High Priest;)

16 but Peter stood at the door withoutforth. Therefore that other disciple, that was known to the bishop, went out, and said to the woman that kept the door, and brought in Peter. (but Peter stood at the door, or at the gate, outside the courtyard. And so that other disciple, who was known to the former High Priest, went out, and spoke to the woman who kept watch at the door, or at the gate, and then brought Peter in.)

17 And the damsel, (the) keeper of the door, said to Peter, Whether thou art also of this man's disciples? He said, I am not. (And the young woman, who kept watch at the door, or

at the gate, said to Peter, Art thou also one of this man's disciples? He said, I am not.)

18   And the servants and [the] ministers stood at the coals (or And the servants and the officers stood at the coals), for it was cold, and they warmed them(selves); and Peter was with them, standing (there) and warming him(self).

19   And the bishop asked Jesus of his disciples, and of his teaching. (And the former High Priest asked Jesus about his disciples, and about his teaching.)

20   Jesus answered to him, I have spoken openly to the world; I taught evermore in the synagogue, and in the temple, whither all the Jews came together, and in huddles [or in private] I spake nothing. (Jesus answered to him, I have spoken openly to all the world; I always taught in the synagogue, and at the Temple, where all the Jews came together, and I never said anything in private.)

21   What askest thou me? (or Why askest me?) ask them that heard me, what I have spoken to them; lo! they know, what things I have said.

22   When he had said these things, one of the ministers standing nigh, gave a buffet to Jesus, and said, Answerest thou so to the bishop? (When he had said these things, one of the officers standing nearby, gave a blow to Jesus, and said, Answerest thou so to the High Priest?)

23   Jesus answered to him, If I have spoken evil, bear thou witnessing of evil; but if *I said* well, why smitest thou me? (Jesus said to him, If I have said anything wrong, testify to what that wrong was; but if *I have spoken* truthfully, why strikest me?)

24   And Annas sent him bound to Caiaphas, the bishop. (And then Annas, the former High Priest, sent Jesus while still in bonds, or still tied up, to Caiaphas, the current High Priest.)

25   And (meanwhile) Simon Peter stood, and warmed him(self); and they said to him, Whether also thou art his disciple? (or Art thou also his disciple?) He denied, and said, I am not.

26   One of the bishop's servants (or One of the former High Priest's servants), (a) cousin of him, whose ear Peter cut off, said, Saw I thee not in the yard with him? [+or Whether I saw thee not in the garden with him?]

27   And Peter again denied, and anon the cock crew. (And again Peter denied it, and at once the cock crowed.)

28   Then they led Jesus to Caiaphas, into the moot hall; and it was early, and they entered not into the moot hall, that they should not be defouled, but that they should eat pask. (And then they led Jesus **from** Caiaphas, to the Hall of Judgement, at the Governor's palace; and it was early in the morning, and they did not enter into the Hall of Judgement at the Governor's palace, so that they would not be defiled, and then they could still eat the Passover.)

29   Therefore Pilate went out withoutforth to them, and said, What accusing bring ye against this man? (And so Pilate went outside to them, and said, What accusation, or what charge, do ye make against this man?)

30   They answered, and said to him, If this were not a mis-doer, we had not betaken him to thee. (They said to him, If he were not a wrong-doer, we would not have delivered him, or we would not have brought him, to thee.)

31   Then Pilate saith to them, Take ye him, and deem ye him, after your law. And *the Jews* said to him, It is not leaveful to us, to slay any man; (Then Pilate said to them, Take him, and judge him yourselves, according to your Law. And *the Jews* said to him, It is not lawful for us, to kill any man;)

32   (so) that the word of Jesus should be fulfilled, which he said, signifying by what death he should die.

33   Therefore again Pilate entered into the moot hall, and called Jesus, and said to him, Art thou king of Jews? (And so Pilate went back into the Hall of Judgement in the Governor's palace, and called Jesus, and said to him, Art

JOHN

thou the King of the Jews?)

34 Jesus answered, and said to him, Sayest thou this thing of thyself, or others have said (it) to thee of me?

35 Pilate answered, Whether I am a Jew? Thy folk and the bishops betook thee to me (or Thy own people and the high priests have delivered thee to me); what hast thou done?

36 Jesus answered, My kingdom is not of this world; if my kingdom were of this world, my ministers would strive, that I should not be taken to the Jews; but now my kingdom is not here. (Jesus answered, My Kingdom is not of this world; if my Kingdom was of this world, my servants would fight, so that I would not be delivered, or handed over, to the Jews; but now my Kingdom is not here.)

37 And so Pilate said to him, Then art thou a king? Jesus answered, Thou sayest, that I am a king. To this thing I am born, and to this I came into the world, to bear witnessing to truth (or to testify to the truth). Each [man] that is of (the) truth, heareth my voice.

38 Pilate saith to him, What is truth? And when he had said this thing, again he went out to the Jews, and said to them, I find no cause (or crime worthy of death) in him, [or I find no cause against him], (or I find no case against him).

39 But it is a custom to you, that I deliver, [or that I leave], (or I let go), one to you in pask; therefore will ye that I deliver to you the king of Jews? (But it is a custom for you, that I release, or that I let go, one prisoner for you at Passover; and so do ye desire that I release to you the King of the Jews?)

40 All they cried again (or And they all cried again), and said, Not this (man), but Barabbas. And Barabbas was a thief.

CHAPTER 19

1 Therefore Pilate took then Jesus, and scourged him. [⁺Therefore then Pilate took

Jesus, and scourged him.]

2 And (the) knights wreathed a crown of thorns, and set (it), [or put (it)], on his head, and did about him a cloth of purple, and came to him, (And the soldiers wove, or plaited, a crown of thorns, and put it on his head, and did about him a cloak of purple, and came to him,)

3 and said, Hail, king of Jews. And they gave to him buffets. (and said, Hail, King of the Jews! And they gave him blows on his head and his body.)

4 Again Pilate went out, and said to them, Lo! I bring him out to you, that ye know, that I find no cause (or crime worthy of death) in him. (And Pilate went out again, and said to them, Behold, I bring him back out to you now, so that ye know, that I find no case against him.)

5 And so Jesus went out, bearing a crown of thorns, and a cloth of purple (or and a cloak of purple). And he saith to them, Lo! the man.

6 But when the bishops and ministers had seen him, they cried, and said, Crucify, crucify him. Pilate saith to them, Take ye him, and crucify ye [him], for I find no cause (or crime worthy of death) in him. (But when the high priests, and their servants, or their officers, had seen him, they cried, and said, Crucify him, crucify him. Pilate said to them, You take him, and you crucify him, for I find no case against him.)

7 The Jews answered to him, We have a law, and by the law he oweth to die (or and by that law he ought to die), for he made him(self) God's Son.

8 Therefore when Pilate had heard this word, he dreaded the more, [or he dreaded more], (or he was more fearful, or he was even more afraid).

9 And he went into the moot hall again, and said to Jesus, Of whence art thou? (or And he went into the Hall of Judgement again, and said to Jesus, Where do you come from?) But Jesus gave none answer to him [or Forsooth Jesus gave not (an) answer to him].

10   Pilate saith to him, Speakest thou not to me? Knowest thou not, that I have power to crucify thee, and I have power to deliver thee? (or Knowest thou not, that I have the power to crucify thee, and I have the power to release thee or to let thee go?)

11   Jesus answered, Thou shouldest not have any power against me, [no] but it were given to thee from above; therefore he that betook me to thee, hath the more sin, (or and so he who delivered me, or who handed me over to thee, hath done the greater sin).

12   From that time Pilate sought to deliver him (or From that moment on, Pilate sought to release him); but the Jews cried, and said, If thou deliverest this *man*, thou art not the emperor's friend; for each man that maketh himself king, gainsaith the emperor, [or If thou leavest this *man*, (or if thou lettest this *man* go), thou art not the friend of Caesar; for each man that maketh himself king, against-saith Caesar].

13   And Pilate, when he had heard these words, led Jesus forth, and sat for doomsman in a place, that is said Lycostratos, but in Hebrew Golgotha. (And Pilate, when he had heard these words, led Jesus forth, and sat as judge in a place, that is called Lycostratos, but in Hebrew, Gabbatha.)

14   And it was pask eve, as it were the sixth hour, [or Forsooth it was the making ready, *or even*, of pask, as the sixth hour, *or midday*]. And he saith to the Jews, Lo! your king. (And it was the eve of Passover, about noon. And he said to the Jews, Behold, here is your king!)

15   But they cried, and said, Take away, take away, [or Do away, do away]; crucify him. Pilate saith to them, Shall I crucify your king? The bishops answered, We have no king but the emperor, [or We have not a king no but Caesar], (or The high priests answered, We have no king but Caesar!).

16   And then Pilate betook him to them, that he should be crucified, (or And then Pilate delivered him, or handed him over to them, so that he could be crucified). And they took Jesus, and led *him* out.

17   And he bare to himself a cross (or And he carried his own cross), and went out into that place, that is said (or is called) Calvary, (and) in Hebrew Golgotha;

18   where they crucified him, and others twain with him, *one* on this side and *one* on that side, and Jesus in the middle.

19   And Pilate wrote a title, and set (it), [or put (it)], on the cross; and it was written, Jesus of Nazareth, king of Jews, (or the King of the Jews).

20   Therefore many of the Jews read this title, for the place where Jesus was crucified, was nigh the city, and it was written in Hebrew, Greek, and Latin.

21   Therefore the bishops of the Jews said to Pilate, Do not thou write king of Jews, but that he said, I am king of Jews. (And so the high priests of the Jews said to Pilate, Do not write The King of the Jews, but that he said, I am the King of the Jews.)

22   Pilate answered, That that I have written, I have written.

23   Therefore the knights when they had crucified him, took his clothes, and made four parts, to each knight a part, and (there was also) a coat. And the coat was without seam, and woven all about. (And so the soldiers when they had crucified him, took his clothes, and divided them into four parts, to each soldier one part, and there was also a cloak or a robe. And the cloak or the robe was without a seam, and woven in one piece.)

24   Therefore they said together, Cut we not it, but cast we lot(s), whose it is; that the scripture be fulfilled, saying, They parted my clothes to them, and on my cloth they cast lot(s). And the knights did these things. (And so they said to each other, We shall not cut it, but rather we shall throw dice, to see whose it is; so that the Scripture be fulfilled, saying, They divided my clothes among themselves, and for

my cloak or my robe they threw dice. And the soldiers did these things.)

25 But beside the cross of Jesus stood his mother, and the sister of his mother, Mary Cleophas, and Mary Magdalene.

26 Therefore when Jesus had seen his mother, and the disciple standing (there), whom he loved, he saith to his mother, Woman, lo! thy son.

27 Afterward he saith to the disciple, Lo! thy mother. And from that hour the disciple took her into (or as) his (own) *mother*.

28 Afterward Jesus witting, that now all things be ended, (so) that the scripture were fulfilled, he saith, I thirst.

29 And a vessel was set (there) full of vinegar. And they laid in hyssop about the sponge full of vinegar, and put (it) to his mouth./And a vessel was set (there) full of eisell. And they took a sponge full of eisell putting it about with hyssop, and proffered it to his mouth.

30 Therefore when Jesus had taken the vinegar, he said, It is ended. And when his head was bowed down, he gave up the ghost./And when Jesus had tasted *this* eisell, he said, It is ended. And he bowed down the head, and sent out the spirit.

31 Therefore for it was the pask eve, that the bodies should not abide [or dwell] on the cross in the sabbath, for that was a great sabbath day, the Jews prayed Pilate, that the hips of them should be broken, and they [should be] taken away. (And so because it was the eve of Passover, so that the bodies would not remain on the cross on the Sabbath, for that was a Great Sabbath day, the Jews beseeched Pilate, that their hips should be broken, and that they should be taken away.)

32 Therefore (the) knights came (or And so the soldiers came), and they brake the thighs of the first, and of the other, that was crucified with him.

33 But when they were come to Jesus [or Forsooth when they had come to Jesus], as they saw him dead then, they brake not his thighs;

34 but one of the knights opened his side with a spear, and anon blood and water went out. (but one of the soldiers opened his side with a spear, and at once blood and water went out.)

35 And he that saw (this), bare witnessing [*thereof*], and his witnessing is true; and he knoweth that he saith true things, (so) that ye (can) believe. (And he who saw this, testified *to it*, and his testimony is true; and he knoweth that he saith true things, so that ye can believe.)

36 And these things were done, (so) that the scripture should be fulfilled, Ye shall not break a bone of him.

37 And again another scripture saith, They shall see in whom they pierced through.

38 But after these things Joseph of Arimathaea prayed Pilate, that he should take away the body of Jesus, for that he was a disciple of Jesus, but privily for dread of the Jews. And Pilate suffered (him). And so he came, and took away the body of Jesus. (But after these things Joseph of Arimathaea beseeched Pilate, so that he could take away the body of Jesus, because he was a disciple of Jesus, but privately, or in secret, for fear of the Jews. And Pilate allowed him. And so he came, and took away the body of Jesus.)

39 And Nicodemus came also, that had come to him first by night, [or that had come to Jesus first in the night], (or who had first come to Jesus in the night), and brought a meddling, (or a medley, or a mixture), of myrrh and aloes, as it were an hundred pound.

40 And they took (down) the body of Jesus, and bound it in linen clothes with sweet smelling ointments [or spices], as it is (the) custom to Jews for to bury (or as is the custom of the Jews for burial).

41 And in the place where he was crucified, was a garden, and in the garden a new grave (or and in the garden was a new tomb), in which yet no man was laid [or in which not yet any

man was put].

42   Therefore there they put Jesus, for the vigil of (the) Jews' feast, for the sepulchre was nigh. (And so they put Jesus there, because it was the eve of the Jews' Feast, or Festival, and the tomb was nearby.) [Therefore there for the making ready (day) of (the) Jews, for the sepulchre was nigh, they put Jesus. (And so because it was the preparation day of the Jews, and the tomb was nearby, they put Jesus there.)]

CHAPTER 20

1   And in one day of the week, Mary Magdalene came early to the grave, when it was yet dark. And she saw the stone moved away from the grave. (And early on the first day of the week, Mary Magdalene came to the tomb, when it was still dark. And she saw the stone moved away from the tomb.)

2   Therefore she ran, and came to Simon Peter, and to another disciple, whom Jesus loved, and saith to them, They have taken (away) the Lord from the grave, (or and said to them, They have taken the Lord away from the tomb), and we know not, where they have laid him.

3   Therefore Peter went out, and that other disciple, and they came to the grave. (And so Peter went out, and that other disciple, and they came to the tomb.)

4   And they twain ran together, and that other disciple ran before Peter, and came first to the grave. (And the two men ran together, and that other disciple ran before Peter, and came to the tomb first.)

5   And when he stooped (down), he saw the sheets lying (there), nevertheless he entered not (or but he did not go in).

6   Therefore Simon Peter came (pur)suing him, and he entered into the grave, and he saw the sheets laid (there), (And so Simon Peter came following behind him, and he entered into the tomb, and he saw the sheets laid there,)

7   and the sudarium that was on his head, not laid with the sheets, but by itself wrapped into a place (or but rolled up in a place by itself).

8   Therefore then that disciple that came first to the grave, entered, and saw, and believed. (And then that disciple who first came to the tomb, entered, and saw everything, and believed.)

9   For they knew not yet the scripture, that it behooved him to rise again from death. [Forsooth they wist not yet the scripture, for it behooved him to rise again from (the) dead.]

10   Therefore the disciples went again to themselves. (And so the disciples went off by themselves.)

11   But Mary stood at the grave withoutforth weeping. And while she wept, she bowed her(self) (down), and beheld forth into the grave. (But Mary stood at the tomb outside weeping. And while she wept, she bowed herself down, and looked into the tomb.)

12   And she saw two angels sitting in white, one at the head and one at the feet, where the body of Jesus was laid.

13   And they say to her, Woman, what weepest thou? (or And they said to her, Woman, why weepest thou?) She said to them, For they have taken away my Lord, and I know not, where they have laid him.

14   When she had said these things, she turned backward [or she turned aback], and saw Jesus standing (there), and knew not that it was Jesus.

15   Jesus saith to her, Woman, what weepest thou? whom seekest thou? She guessing that he was the gardener, saith to him, Sire, if thou hast taken him up, say to me, where thou hast laid him, and I shall take him away. (Jesus said to her, Woman, why weepest thou? whom seekest thou? She thinking that he was the gardener, said to him, Sir, if thou hast taken him some place, tell me, where thou hast laid him, and I shall take him away.)

16   Jesus saith to her, Mary. She turned, and saith to him, Rabboni, that is to say, Master (or Teacher).

17   Jesus saith to her, Do not thou touch me, for I have not yet ascended to my Father; but go to my brethren, and say to them, I ascend to my Father and to your Father, to my God and to your God.

18   Mary Magdalene came, telling to the disciples, That I saw the Lord, and these things he said to me.

19   Therefore when it was even(ing) in that day, [in] one of the sabbaths, and the gates were shut, where the disciples were gathered, for dread of the Jews, Jesus came, and stood in the middle of the disciples, and he saith to them, Peace [be] to you. (And so when it was evening on that day, on one of the Sabbaths (or on the first day of the week), and the doors were shut, where the disciples were gathered, for fear of the Jews, Jesus came, and stood in the midst of the disciples, and he said to them, Peace be to you.)

20   And when he had said this, he showed to them [his] hands and side; therefore the disciples joyed (or and so the disciples rejoiced), for the Lord was seen.

21   And he saith to them again, Peace (be) to you; as the Father sent me, I send you.

22   When he had said this, he blew on them, and said, Take ye the Holy Ghost (or and said, Receive the Holy Spirit);

23   whose sins ye forgive, those be forgiven to them; and whose sins ye withhold, those be withheld.

24   But Thomas, one of the twelve, that is said Didymus (or who is called the Twin), was not with them, when Jesus came.

25   Therefore the other disciples said, We have seen the Lord. And he said to them, [No] But I see in his hands the printing of the nails, (or And he said to them, Unless I see the scarring, or the marks, from the nails in his hands), and put my finger into the place of the nails, and put mine hand into his side, I shall not believe (it).

26   And after eight days again his disciples were within, and Thomas with them. Jesus came, while the gates were shut, and stood in the middle, and said, Peace (be) to you, (or And Jesus came, while the doors were shut, and stood in their midst, and said, Peace be to you).

27   Afterward he saith to Thomas, Put in here thy finger, and see mine hands, and put hither thine hand, and put [it] into my side, and do not thou be unbelieveful, but faithful.

28   Thomas answered, and said to him, My Lord and my God.

29   Jesus saith to him, Thomas, for thou hast seen me, thou believedest; blessed be they, that saw not, and have believed.

30   And Jesus did many other signs (or miracles) in the sight of his disciples, which be not written in this book.

31   But these be written, that ye believe, that Jesus is Christ, the Son of God, and that ye believing have life in his name. (But these be written, so that ye believe, that Jesus is the Messiah, the Son of God, and that ye believing have life in his name.)

CHAPTER 21

1   Afterward Jesus again showed him(self) to his disciples, at the sea of Tiberias (or at the Sea of Galilee, that is, Lake Galilee). And he showed him(self) thus.

2   There were together Simon Peter, and Thomas, that is said Didymus (or who is called the Twin), and Nathanael, that was of the Cana of Galilee, and the sons of Zebedee, and twain other of his disciples (or and two other disciples of Jesus).

3   Simon Peter saith to them, I (shall) go to fish. They say to him, And we (shall) come with thee. And they went out, and went into a boat. And in that night they took nothing.

4   But when the morrow was come, Jesus

stood in the brink, (or But early the next morning, Jesus stood on the shore); nevertheless the disciples knew not, that it was Jesus.

5   Therefore Jesus saith to them, Children, whether ye have any supping thing? They answered to him, Nay.

6   He said to them, Put ye [or Send ye] the net into the right half of the rowing (or Throw the net onto the right side of the boat), and ye shall find (something). And they putted [or sent] the net; and then they might not draw it (in) for (the) multitude of fishes.

7   Therefore that disciple, whom Jesus loved, said to Peter, It is the Lord. Simon Peter, when he had heard that it is the Lord, girt him(self) with a coat, for he was naked, and went into the sea.

8   But the other disciples came by boat, for they were not far from the land, but as (of) a two hundred cubits [or but as it were two hundred cubits], drawing the net of fishes.

9   And as they came down into the land (or And as they came ashore), they saw coals lying (there), and fish laid on, and bread.

10   Jesus saith to them, Bring ye of the fishes, which ye have taken now.

11   Simon Peter went up, and drew the net into the land, full of great fishes, an hundred fifty and three; and when they were so many, the net was not broken. (Simon Peter went, and drew the net onto the land, full of large fish, a hundred and fifty-three of them; and although there were so many, the net was not broken.)

12   Jesus saith to them, Come ye, and eat ye. And no man of them that sat at the meat, durst ask him, Who art thou, witting that it is the Lord. (Jesus said to them, Come, and eat. And none of them who sat at the meal, dared ask him, Who art thou, knowing that it was the Lord.)

13   And Jesus came, and took bread, and gave (it) to them, and fish also.

14   Now this [is the] third time (that) Jesus was showed to his disciples, when he had risen again from death [or from (the) dead].

15   And when they had eaten, Jesus saith to Simon Peter, Simon of John (or Simon the son of John), lovest thou me more than these? He saith to him, Yea, Lord, thou knowest that I love thee. Jesus saith to him, Feed thou my lambs (or Feed my lambs).

16   Again he saith to him, Simon of John (or Simon the son of John), lovest thou me? He saith to him, Yea, Lord, thou knowest that I love thee. He saith to him, Feed thou my lambs (or Feed my male sheep).

17   He saith to him the third time, Simon of John (or Simon the son of John), lovest thou me? Peter was heavy, [or sorry], (or was grieved), for he said to him the third time, Lovest thou me, and he saith to him, Lord, thou knowest all things; thou knowest that I love thee. Jesus saith to him, Feed my sheep (or Feed my female sheep).

18   Truly, truly, I say to thee, when thou were younger, thou girdedest thee, and wanderedest where thou wouldest; but when thou shalt wax older, thou shalt hold forth thine hands, and another shall gird thee, and shall lead thee whither thou wilt not. (Truly, I tell thee the truth, when thou were younger, thou girdedest thyself, and walkedest where thou wanted to go; but when thou shalt grow older, thou shalt hold forth thine hands, and another shall gird thee, and shall lead thee where thou desirest not.)

19   He said this thing, signifying by what death he should glorify God. And when he had said these things, he saith to him, (Pur)Sue thou me (or Follow me).

20   Peter turned, and saw that disciple (pur)suing, whom Jesus loved, which also rested in the supper on his breast, and said *to him*, Lord, who is it, that shall betray thee? (Peter turned, and saw that disciple following, whom Jesus loved, who had sat close beside him at the supper, and had asked *him*, Lord,

who is it, that shall betray thee?)

21   Therefore when Peter had seen this *disciple*, he saith to Jesus, Lord, but what (about) this (man)?

22   Jesus saith to him, So I will, that he dwell till I come, what (is it) to thee? (pur)sue thou me. (Jesus said to him, If I desire, that he live until I come, what is it to thee? follow me.)

23   Therefore this word went out among the brethren, that that disciple dieth not. And Jesus said not to him, that he dieth not, but, So I will, that he dwell till I come, what (is it) to thee? (But Jesus did not say to him, that he would not die, but rather, If I desire, that he live until I come, what is it to thee?)

24   This is that disciple, that beareth witnessing of these things, and wrote them; and we know, that his witnessing is true. (This is that disciple, who testifieth about these things, and wrote them; and we know, that his testimony is true.)

25   And there be also many other things that Jesus did, which if they be written each by itself (or which if all of them be written down), I deem that the world itself shall not [be able to] take the books, that be to be written. [*Amen.*] †

DEEDS of the APOSTLES

CHAPTER 1

1 Theophilus, first I made a sermon [or a word] of all [the] things, that Jesus began to do and teach,

2 into the day of his ascension, in which he commanded by the Holy Ghost to his apostles (or on which he commanded by the Holy Spirit to his apostles), whom he had chosen; [till into the day, in which he commanding to the apostles by the Holy Ghost, whom he chose, was taken up;]

3 to whom he showed himself alive after his passion (or his suffering), by many arguments, [or provings], appearing to them (for) forty days, and speaking of the realm of God.

4 And he ate with them, and commanded [to them], that they should not depart from Jerusalem, but abide the promise of the Father (or but wait for the promise of the Father), which ye heard, he said, by my mouth;

5 for John baptized in water, but ye shall be baptized in the Holy Ghost (or but ye shall be baptized with the Holy Spirit), after these few days.

6 Therefore they that were come together, asked him, and said, Lord, whether in this time thou shalt restore the kingdom of Israel? [Therefore they that came together, asked him, saying, Lord, if in this time shalt thou restore the kingdom of Israel?]

7 And he said to them, It is not yours to know the times either moments, which the Father hath put in his power;

8 but ye shall take the virtue of the Holy Ghost coming from above into you (or but ye shall receive power when the Holy Spirit coming from above goeth into you), and ye shall be my witnesses in Jerusalem, and in all Judea, and Samaria, and to the utmost [or to the uttermost] of the earth.

9 And when he had said these things, in their sight he was lifted up, and a cloud received him from their eyes.

10 And when they beheld him going into heaven (or And after they saw him go up into the heavens), lo! two men stood beside them in white clothing,

11 and said, Men of Galilee, what stand ye beholding into heaven? This Jesus, which is taken up from you into heaven, shall come (back), as ye saw him going into heaven. (and said, Men of Galilee, why stand ye looking up into the heavens? This Jesus, who is taken up from you to heaven, shall come back, as ye saw him going to heaven.)

12 Then they turned again to Jerusalem, from the hill that is called of Olivet, which is beside Jerusalem, an holiday's journey [or having the journey of a sabbath]. (Then they returned to Jerusalem, from the Mount of Olives, which is near Jerusalem, a holy day's journey away.)

13 And when they were entered into the house, where they dwelled, they went up into the solar, [or into the higher things], (or they went up into the upper room), Peter and John, and James and Andrew, Philip and Thomas, Bartholomew and Matthew, James of Alphaeus, and Simon Zelotes (or and Simon the Zealot), and Judas of James.

14 All these were lastingly continuing [or dwelling together] with one will, in prayer, with women, and Mary, the mother of Jesus, and with his brethren.

15 In those days Peter rose up in the middle of the brethren, and said, (or In those days Peter rose up into the midst of the brothers, and said); and there was a company of men together,

almost an hundred and twenty;

16   Brethren, it behooveth that the scripture be [ful]filled, which the Holy Ghost before-said by the mouth of David (or which the Holy Spirit foretold by the mouth of David), of Judas that was (the) leader of them that took Jesus;

17   and was numbered among us, and got a part of this service [or of this ministry]. (and was numbered among us, and had a part in this ministry.)

18   And this *Judas* had a field of the hire of wickedness, and he was hanged, and burst apart the middle, and all his entrails were shed abroad. (And this *Judas* bought a field with his wicked wages, and he hanged himself, and fell to the ground, and burst open his middle, and all his bowels, or all his innards, were poured out.)

19   And it was made known to all men that dwelt in Jerusalem, so that that field was called Aceldama in the language of them, that is, the field of blood.

20   And it is written in the book of Psalms, The habitation of them be made desert [or The habitation of him be made desert], and be there none that dwell in it, and another take his bishopric.

21   Therefore it behooveth of these men, that be gathered together with us in all the time, in which the Lord Jesus entered [in], and went out among us,

22   and began from the baptism of John till into the day in which he was taken up from us, that one of these be made a witness of his resurrection with us.

23   And they ordained twain, Joseph, that was called Barsabas, that was named Justus, and Matthias.

24   And they prayed, and said, Thou, Lord, that knowest the hearts of all men, show whom thou hast chosen of these twain,

25   that one take the place of this service [or of this ministry] and apostlehood, of which Judas trespassed, that he should go into his place (or so that he can take his place).

26   And they gave lots to them, and the lot felled on Matthias; and he was numbered with the eleven apostles.

CHAPTER 2

1   And when the days of Pentecost were [ful]filled, all the disciples were together in the same place.

2   And suddenly there was made a sound from heaven (or from the heavens), as of a great wind coming, and it filled all the house where they sat.

3   And diverse tongues as (flames of) fire appeared to them [or And tongues diversely parted as (flames of) fire appeared to them], and it sat on each of them.

4   And all were filled with the Holy Ghost, and they began to speak in diverse languages [or with diverse tongues], as the Holy Ghost gave to them to speak. (And all were filled with the Holy Spirit, and they began to speak in different languages, which the Holy Spirit made them able to speak.)

5   And there were in Jerusalem dwelling Jews (or And there were Jews living in Jerusalem), religious men, of each nation that is under heaven.

6   And when this voice was made, the multitude came together, and were astonied, (or were astonished), [or was confounded], in thought, (or And when this sound was made, the multitude came together, and were bewildered in their understanding), for each man heard them speaking in his own language [⁺or in his own tongue].

7   And all were astonied (or astonished), and wondered, and said together, Whether not all these that speak be men of Galilee [or Whether not all these that speak be Galileans],

8   and how heard we [or have we heard] each man our (own) language (or and how have each of us heard our own language) in which

we be born?

9 Parthians, and Medes, and Elamites, and they that dwell at [or in] Mesopotamia, Judea, and Cappadocia, Pontus, and Asia,

10 Phrygia, and Pamphylia, Egypt, and the parts of Libya, that is about Cyrene, and comelings (or and newcomers), Romans, and Jews, and proselytes,

11 men of Crete, and of Arabia, we have heard them speaking in our (own) languages [or in our (own) tongues] the great things of God.

12 And all were astonied, and wondered, saying together, What will this thing be? (And all were astonished, and wondered, and they said to each other, What meaneth this thing?)

13 And others scorned, and said, For these men be full of must. (But others scorned them, and said, These men be full of wine.)

14 But Peter stood with the eleven, and raised up his voice, and spake to them, Ye Jews, and all that dwell at Jerusalem (or and all who live in Jerusalem), be this known to you, and with ears perceive ye my words.

15 For not as ye ween [or not as ye guess], these be drunken, when it is the third hour of the day; (For it is not as ye think, that these be drunk, when it is but nine o'clock in the morning;)

16 but this it is, that was said by the prophet Joel,

17 And it shall be in the last days, the Lord saith, I shall pour out my Spirit on each flesh [or I shall pour out my Spirit on all flesh]; and your sons and your daughters shall prophesy, and your young men shall see visions, and your elders shall dream swevens (or your old men shall dream dreams).

18 And on my servants and on mine handmaidens in those days I shall pour out (a portion) of my Spirit, and they shall prophesy.

19 And I shall give great wonders in (the) heaven(s) above, and signs in (or on the) earth beneath, blood, and fire, and heat [or vapour] of smoke.

20 The sun shall be turned into darkness, and the moon into blood, before that the great and the open day of the Lord [shall] come.

21 And it shall be, each man whichever shall call to help the name of the Lord [or each man whoever shall in-call the name of the Lord], shall be safe (or shall be saved).

22 Ye men of Israel, hear ye these words. Jesus of Nazareth, a man proved of God before you by virtues, and wonders, and tokens, which God did by him in the middle of you, as ye know, (Israelites, listen to these words. Jesus of Nazareth, a man of God proved before you by works of power, or miracles, and wonders, and signs, which God did by him in the midst of you, as ye know,)

23 ye tormented, and killed him by the hands of wicked men, by counsel determined and betaken by the fore-knowing [or by the prescience] of God. (ye tormented, and killed him by the hands of wicked men, delivered up by the predetermined plan and in the foreknowledge of God.)

24 Whom God raised, when [the] sorrows of hell were unbound, by that that it was impossible that he were holden of it (or because it was impossible that he would be held by it).

25 For David saith of him, I saw afar the Lord before me (for)evermore, for he is on my right half, that I be not moved. (For David said of him, I saw the Lord always before me, for he is on my right side, or at my right hand, so that I shall not be moved.)

26 For this thing mine heart joyed, and my tongue made full out joy [or gladded], and moreover my flesh shall rest in hope.

27 For thou shalt not leave my soul in hell, neither thou shalt give thine Holy (One) to see corruption.

28 Thou hast made known to me the ways of life, thou shalt [full-]fill me with mirth with thy face (or thou shalt fill me full of joy by thy presence).

29   Brethren, be it leaveful boldly to say to you of the patriarch David, for he is dead and buried, and his sepulchre is among us into this day. (Brothers, may it be lawful for me to boldly say this to you about the patriarch David, that he is dead and buried, and his tomb is here among us unto this day.)

30   Therefore when he was a prophet, and knew, that with a great oath God had sworn to him, that of the fruit of his loins should one sit on his seat (or that a man from the fruit of his loins should sit on his throne),

31   he seeing afar spake of the resurrection of Christ (or he seeing far ahead spoke of the resurrection of the Messiah), for neither he was left in hell, neither his flesh saw corruption.

32   God raised this Jesus, to whom we all be witnesses.

33   Therefore he was enhanced by the right hand of God, and through the promise of the Holy Ghost that he took of the Father, he shedded out this *Spirit,* that ye see and hear. (And so he was exalted, or raised up, by the right hand of God, and through the promise of the Holy Spirit that he received from the Father, he poured out this *Spirit,* that ye now see and hear.)

34   For David ascended not into heaven; but he saith, The Lord said to my Lord, Sit thou on my right half, (or Sit on my right side, or at my right hand),

35   till I put thine enemies the stool of thy feet. (until I make thine enemies thy footstool.)

36   Therefore most certainly know all the house of Israel, that God made him both Lord and Christ, this Jesus, whom ye crucified. (And so let all the house of Israel most certainly know, that God made this Jesus, whom ye crucified, both Lord and Messiah.)

37   When they heard these things, they were compuncted in heart; and they said to Peter and [to] (the) other apostles, Brethren (or Brothers), what shall we do?

38   And Peter said to them, Do ye penance, and each of you be baptized in the name of Jesus Christ, into remission of your sins; and ye shall take the gift of the Holy Ghost. (And Peter said to them, Repent, and each of you be baptized in the name of Jesus Christ, for the forgiveness of your sins; and then ye shall receive the gift of the Holy Spirit.)

39   For the promise is to you, and to your sons, and to all that be far (off), whichever our Lord God hath called. [Forsooth repromission is to you, and to your sons, and to all that be far, whomever the Lord our God hath called to (him).]

40   Also with other words full many he witnessed to them, and admonished them, and said, Be ye saved from this shrewd [or from this wicked] generation. (And with a great many other words he testified to them, and admonished them, and said, Save yourselves from this depraved generation.)

41   Then they that received his word were baptized, and in (or on) that day souls were increased, about three thousand;

42   and [they] were lasting stably in the teaching of the apostles, and in (the) communing of the breaking of bread, and in prayers.

43   And dread was made to each man. And many wonders and signs were done by the apostles in Jerusalem, and great dread was in all. (And there was fearful reverence in each man. And many wonders and miracles were done by the apostles in Jerusalem, and great and fearful reverence was in all.)

44   And all that believed were together, and had all things (in) common.

45   They sold (their) possessions and chattel, [or substances, *or goods*], and parted those things to all men, as it was need(ful) to each. (They sold their possessions and goods, and divided those things to everyone, as it was needed by each person.)

46   And each day they dwelled stably with one will in the temple, and brake bread about

houses (or and broke bread in their houses), and took meat (or meals) with full out joy [or gladness] and simpleness of heart,

47 and praised together God, and had grace to (or favour with) all the folk [or all the people]. And the Lord increased them that were made safe, each day into the same thing (or And the Lord added to those who were saved, each and every day).

CHAPTER 3

1 And Peter and John went up into the temple, at the ninth hour of praying, [or at the ninth hour of prayer], (or at three o'clock in the afternoon).

2 And a man, that was lame from the womb of his mother, was borne (there), and was laid [or was put] each day at the gate of the temple, that is said 'Fair' (or that is called 'Beautiful'), to ask (for) alms of men that entered into the temple.

3 This (man), when he saw Peter and John beginning to enter into the temple, prayed, that he should take alms. (And when he saw Peter and John entering the Temple, he beseeched, or asked for, some money.)

4 And Peter with John beheld on him, and said, [or Forsooth Peter with John beholding him, said], Behold thou into us. (And Peter and John looked at him, and Peter said, Look at us.)

5 And he beheld into them, and hoped, that he should take somewhat [or something] of them. (And he looked at them, and hoped that he would receive something from them.)

6 But Peter said, I have neither silver nor gold; but that that I have, I give to thee. In the name of Jesus Christ of Nazareth, rise up, and go.

7 And he took him by the right hand, and lifted him up; and anon (or at once) his legs and his feet were strengthened together;

8 and he leaped, and stood, and wandered (or and walked about). And he entered with them into the temple, and wandered, and leaped, and praised God.

9 And all the people saw him walking, and praising God.

10 And they knew him, that he it was that sat at alms at the fair gate of the temple, (or And they knew him, that it was he who sat at the Beautiful Gate of the Temple begging for money). And they were filled with wondering, and astonishing, in that thing that befelled to him.

11 But when they saw Peter and John, all the people ran to them at the porch that was called of Solomon (or that was named for Solomon), and wondered greatly.

12 And Peter saw, and answered to the people, Men of Israel, what wonder ye in this thing? either what behold ye us, as (if) by our (own) virtue, either power, we made this man for to walk? [+or as (if) by our virtue, either piety, we make this *man* to walk?] (And Peter saw them, and said to the people, Israelites, why wonder ye at this thing? or why look at us, as if by our own power, we made this man to walk?)

13 God of Abraham, and God of Isaac, and God of Jacob, [and] God of our fathers, hath glorified his Son Jesus, whom ye betrayed, and denied before the face of Pilate, when he deemed him to be delivered, [or left], (or to be let go), (or when he judged him, and would have released him).

14 But ye denied the holy and the rightful (*man*), [or Ye forsooth denied the holy and just *man*], and asked (for) a manslayer to be given to you. (But ye rejected this holy and just *man*, and asked for a murderer to be given to you.)

15 And ye slew the maker of life, whom God raised from death [or whom God raised from (the) dead], of whom we be witnesses.

16 And in the faith of his name he hath confirmed this *man*, whom ye see and know; the name of him, and the faith that is by him, gave to this man full healing [or full health] in

the sight of all (of) you.

17   And now, brethren, I wot that by unwitting ye did, as also your princes (did). (And now, brothers, I know, that ye did this by unknowing, or ignorance, as also your leaders did.)

18   But God that before-told by the mouth of all (the) prophets, that his Christ should suffer (or that his Messiah should suffer), hath fulfilled so.

19   Therefore be ye repentant, and be ye converted, (so) that your sins be done away, (so) that when the times of refreshing shall come from the sight of the Lord,

20   and (then) he shall send that Jesus Christ, that is now preached to you.

21   Whom it behooveth heaven to receive, into the times of restitution of all things, which the Lord spake by the mouth of his holy prophets from the (beginning of the) world (or of which the Lord spoke by the mouth of his holy prophets from long ago, or from the creation of the world).

22   For Moses said, For the Lord your God shall raise to you a prophet, of your brethren; as me, ye shall hear him by all things [or ye shall hear him upon all things], whatever he shall speak to you (or whatever he shall say to you).

23   And it shall be, that every man [or every soul] that shall not hear that prophet (or who shall not listen to that prophet), shall be destroyed, [or exiled], from the people.

24   And all (the) prophets from Samuel and afterward, that spake, told (of) these days.

25   But ye be the sons of (the) prophets, and of the testament that God ordained to our fathers (or and of the covenant that God ordained to our fathers), and said to Abraham, In thy seed all the families of earth shall be blessed.

26   God raised his Son first to you, and sent him blessing you, that each man convert him(self) from his wickedness (or so that each man be turned from his own wickedness).

CHAPTER 4

1   And while they spake to the people, the priests and the magistrates of the temple, and the Sadducees came upon them,

2   and sorrowed, that they taught the people, and told in Jesus the again-rising from death [or and told by Jesus (the) again-rising from (the) dead]. (and were vexed, that they taught the people, and told them about the resurrection from the dead through Jesus.)

3   And they laid (their) hands on them, and putted them into (the) ward [or into (the) keeping] into the morrow (or and put them in the prison until the morning); for it was then eventide [or evening].

4   But many of them that had heard the word, believed; and the number of men was made five thousands [or and the number of them is made five thousand].

5   And amorrow it was done [or Forsooth in the morrow it was done], that the princes of them, and elder men and scribes were gathered in Jerusalem; (And the next morning it was done, that their high priests, and elders, and scribes were gathered together in Jerusalem;)

6   and Annas, (the) prince of priests, (or and Annas, the former High Priest), and Caiaphas, and John, and Alexander, and how many ever were of the kind [or of the kindred] of priests.

7   And they set them in the middle, and asked, In what virtue, either in what name, have ye done this thing? (And they set them in their midst, and asked, By what power, or in what name, have ye done this thing?)

8   Then Peter filled with the Holy Ghost, said to them, Ye princes of the people, and ye elder men, hear ye. (Then Peter filled with the Holy Spirit, said to them, Ye high priests of the people, and ye elders, listen.)

9   If we today be deemed in the good deed of a sick man, in whom [or in which] this man is made safe, (If today we be judged for this

good deed for a sick man, by which this man is saved,)

10   be it known to you all, and to all the people of Israel, that in the name of Jesus Christ of Nazareth, whom ye crucified, whom God raised from death [or whom God raised from (the) dead], in this (man) [or in him], this man standeth whole before you.

11   This is the stone, which was reproved of (or rejected by) you (when) building, which is made into the head of the corner;

12   and health is not in any other. For neither (any) other name under heaven is given to men, in which it behooveth us to be made safe. (and salvation, or deliverance, is not by any other. For no other name under heaven is given to men, by which it behooveth us to be saved.)

13   And they saw the steadfastness of Peter and of John, and *when* it was found that they were men unlettered [or without letters], and lay men, they wondered, and they knew them that they were with Jesus.

14   And they saw the man that was healed, standing with them, and they might nothing gainsay (them), (or and they could not say anything against them).

15   But they commanded them to go forth without the council (or And they ordered them to go outside the Council chamber). And they spake together,

16   and said, What shall we do to these men? for the sign (or this miracle) is made known by them to all men, that dwell at Jerusalem; it is open, and we be not able to deny (it), [or and we may not deny (it)].

17   But that it be no more published into the people, menace we to them (or let us threaten them), (so) that they speak no more in this name to any man.

18   And they called them, and announced (or commanded) to them, that on no manner they should speak, neither teach, in the name of Jesus.

19   But Peter and John answered, and said to them, If it be rightful in the sight of God to hear you rather than God, deem ye (or ye judge).

20   For we must needs speak those things, that we have seen and heard. [Forsooth we may not not speak (about) the things that we have seen and heard.]

21   And they menaced them, and left them, and found not how they should punish them, for the people; for all men clarified (God, for) that thing that was done in that that was befallen. (And they threatened them, and then let them go, for they could not find any way to punish them, because of the people; for all the people glorified God, for what was done in all that befell.)

22   For the man was more than forty years *old*, in whom this sign of healing [or this sign of health] was made. (For the man was more than forty years *old*, in whom this miracle of a cure was done.)

23   And when they were delivered, [or were left], (or were let go), they came to their *fellows*, and told to them, how great things [or how many things] the princes of (the) priests and the elder men had said to them. (And when they were delivered, or released, they came back to their *fellows*, and told them everything that the high priests and the elders had said to them.)

24   And when they heard, with one heart they raised (up their) voice to the Lord, and said, Lord, thou that madest heaven and earth, (the) sea, and all things that be in them,

25   which saidest by the Holy Ghost, by the mouth of our father David, thy child, Why heathen men gnashed with (their) teeth together [or wrathed], and the peoples thought vain things? (who said by the Holy Spirit, by the mouth of our father David, thy servant, Why did the Gentiles gnash with their teeth together, or be enraged, and the peoples thought empty and futile things?)

26   (The) Kings of the earth stood nigh, and (the) princes came together into one, against the Lord, and against his Christ (or and against his

Messiah).

27   For verily, Herod and Pontius Pilate, with heathen men, and peoples of Israel, came together in this city against thine holy child Jesus, whom thou anointedest, (For truly, Herod and Pontius Pilate, with the Gentiles, and the people of Israel, came together in this city against thine holy servant Jesus, whom thou anointedest,)

28   to do the things, that thine hand and thy counsel (or thy plan or thy purpose) deemed to be done.

29   And now, Lord, behold into the threatenings of them, and grant to thy servants to speak thy word with all trust,

30   in that thing that thou hold forth thine hand, that healings and signs (or miracles) and wonders be made by (or through) the name of thine holy Son Jesus.

31   And when they had prayed, the place was moved, in which they were gathered; and all were filled with the Holy Ghost (or and everyone was filled with the Holy Spirit), and spake the word of God with trust.

32   And of the multitude of men believing was (of) one heart and one will; neither any man said (that) anything of those things that he wielded (or he possessed) to be his own, but all things were (held in) common to them.

33   And with great virtue, the apostles yielded witnessing of the again-rising of Jesus Christ our Lord, and great grace was in all (of) them [or and great grace was in them all]. (And with great power, the apostles testified about the resurrection of Jesus Christ our Lord, and everyone was richly blessed.)

34   For neither any needy man was among them, for how many ever were possessors of fields, either of houses, they sold (them), and brought the prices of those things that they sold (or and brought the payments for those things that they sold),

35   and laid (them) before the feet of the apostles. And it was parted to each, as it was need(ful) to each, (or And it was divided unto each, as it was needed by each).

36   Forsooth Joseph, that was named Barnabas of [the] apostles (or who was called Barnabas by the apostles), that is to say (or which is translated), the son of comfort, of the lineage (or of the tribe) of Levi, [or a Levite by kin], a man of Cyprus,

37   when he had a field, sold it, and brought the price (or and brought the payment for it), and laid it before the feet of the apostles.

CHAPTER 5

1   But a man, Ananias by name, with Sapphira, his wife, sold a field,

2   and defrauded of the price of the field (or and lied about the payment for the field); and his wife was witting. And he brought (only) a part, and laid [it] before the feet of the apostles.

3   And Peter said to him, Ananias, why hath Satan tempted thine heart, that thou lie to the Holy Ghost, and to defraud (God) of the price of the field? (And Peter said to him, Ananias, why hath thou let Satan test thine heart, so that thou lie to the Holy Spirit, and defraud God of the payment for the field?)

4   Whether it unsold was not thine; and when it was sold, it was in thy power? Why hast thou put this thing in thine heart? Thou hast not lied to men, but to God.

5   Ananias heard these words, and felled down, and was dead [or and died]. And great dread was made on all that heard (about this), (or And great and fearful reverence came upon all who heard about this).

6   And young men rose (up), and moved him away, and bare him out, and buried (him).

7   And there was made a space of three hours, and his wife knew not that thing that was done, and entered.

8   And Peter answered to her, Woman, say to me, whether ye sold the field for so much? And she said, Yea, for so much.

9 And Peter said to her, What befelled to you [or What soothly came together to you, *or accorded*], to tempt the Spirit of the Lord? (or What befell to you, to test the Spirit of the Lord?) Lo! the feet of them that have buried thine husband *be* at the door, and they shall bear thee out.

10 Anon she felled down at his feet, and died. And the young men entered, and found her dead, and they bare her out, and buried [her] to (or beside) her husband. (At once she fell down at his feet, and died. And the young men returned, and found her dead, and they carried her out, and buried her beside her husband.)

11 And great dread was made in all the church, and into all that heard (of) these things. (And great and fearful reverence came upon all the church, and upon all who heard about these things.)

12 And by the hands of the apostles signs (or miracles) and many wonders were made in the people. And all were of one accord in the porch of Solomon.

13 But no man of others durst (or dared to) join himself with them, but the people magnified them.

14 And the multitude of men and of women believing in the Lord was more increased,

15 so that they brought out sick men into (the) streets, and laid (them) in (or on) little beds and couches, (so) that when Peter came, namely the shadow of him should shadow each of them, and they should be delivered from their sicknesses (or and they would be released from their sicknesses). [so that into (the) streets they brought out sick men, and put (them) in little beds and couches, (so) that when Peter came, namely the shadow of him should shadow each of them, and they were delivered from all sicknesses.]

16 And the multitude(s) of cities nigh to Jerusalem ran, bringing sick men, and (they) that were travailed of unclean spirits (or and

those who were troubled by unclean spirits, or demons), which all were healed.

17 But the prince of priests rose up (or But the High Priest rose up), and all that were with him, that is the heresy of (the) Sadducees, and (they) were filled with envy;

18 and they laid hands on the apostles, and put them in the common ward [or in the common keeping]. (and they laid their hands on the apostles, and put them in the prison.)

19 But the angel of the Lord opened by night the gates of the prison, and led them out, and said, [Forsooth the angel of the Lord by night opened the gates of the prison, and leading them out, said,]

20 Go ye, and stand ye, and speak in the temple to the people all the words of this life.

21 Whom when they had heard, they entered early into the temple, and taught. And the prince of priests came (or And the High Priest came), and they that were with him, and called together the council (or the Sanhedrin), and all the elder men of the children of Israel; and sent (men) to the prison, (so) that they should be brought forth.

22 And when the ministers came, and found them not, and for the prison was opened, [or Soothly when the ministers came, and, the prison opened, found them not], they turned again and told (them), (But when the servants, or the officers, came, and opened the prison, and did not find them, they returned, and told them,)

23 and said, We found the prison shut with all diligence, and the keepers standing at the gates (or and the guards standing at the gates); but we opened (it), and found no man therein.

24 And as the magistrates of the temple, and the princes of (the) priests heard these words, they doubted of them, what was done. (And when the Temple magistrate, and the high priests, heard these words, they wondered, what had become of them.)

25 But a man came, and told to them, For lo!

those men which ye have put into prison, be in the temple, and stand (there), and teach the people.

26 Then the magistrate went with the ministers, and brought them without violence; for they dreaded the people, lest they should be stoned. (Then the magistrate went with the servants. or the officers, and brought them in without force; because they feared the people, lest they should be stoned.)

27 And when they had brought them, they set them in the council; and the prince of priests asked them, (And when they had brought them in, they put them before the Council; and the High Priest spoke to them,)

28 and said, In commandment we commanded you, that ye should not teach in this name, and lo! ye have filled Jerusalem with your teaching, and ye will bring on us the blood of this man.

29 And Peter answered, and the apostles, and said, It behooveth (us) to obey to God, more than to men.

30 [The] God of our fathers raised Jesus, whom ye slew, hanging in a tree. (The God of our fathers raised Jesus, whom ye killed, by hanging him on a tree, or on the cross.)

31 God enhanced with his right hand this prince and Saviour, that penance were given to Israel [or for to give penance to Israel], and remission of sins. (With his right hand God exalted, or raised up, this Leader and Saviour, to give repentance to Israel, and forgiveness for their sins.)

32 And we be witnesses of these words, and the Holy Ghost (or as is the Holy Spirit), whom God gave to all obeying to him.

33 When they heard these things, they were tormented, and thought to slay them.

34 But a man rose in the council, a Pharisee, Gamaliel by name, a doctor of the law, a worshipful man to all the people, and (he) commanded the men to be put withoutforth for a while. (But a man stood up in the Council, a

Pharisee, named Gamaliel, a teacher of the Law, a man honoured by all the people, and he commanded the men to be put outside for a while.)

35 And he said to them, Ye men of Israel (or Israelites), take attention to yourselves on these men, what ye shall do.

36 For before these days (there was) Theudas, that said himself to be some man, to whom a number of men consented, about four hundred; which was slain, and all that believed to him, were scattered, and brought to nought.

37 After this, Judas of Galilee was in the days of profession, and turned away the people after him; and all how many ever consented to him, were scattered, and he perished. (After this, there was Judas of Galilee during the days of professing, or during the census, and he turned away the people after him; but all whomever consented to him, were scattered, after that he perished.)

38 And now therefore I say to you, depart ye from these men, and suffer ye them; for if this counsel either work is of men, it shall be undone; (And so now I say to you, go away from these men, and let them be; for if this plan, or this work, is from men, it shall be destroyed, or it shall be ended;)

39 but if it is of God, ye may not undo them, lest peradventure ye be found to repugn *against* God. (but if it is from God, ye cannot stop, or destroy, them, lest perhaps ye be found to fight *against* God.) [forsooth if it is of God, ye may not undo them. But suffer ye them, lest peradventure ye be found for to repugn God. (but if it is from God, ye cannot stop them. So let them be, lest perhaps ye be found to be fighting with God.)]

40 And they consented to him; and they called together the apostles, and announced (or commanded) to them, (after) that (they) were beaten, that they should no more speak in the name of Jesus, and (then) they let them go.

41 And they went joying from the sight of the

council, that they were had worthy to suffer despising for the name of Jesus.

42 But each day they ceased not in the temple, and about houses, to teach and preach Jesus Christ. (But each day they did not cease in the Temple, and in their houses, to teach and to preach about Jesus Christ.)

CHAPTER 6

1 But in those days, when the number of disciples increased, the Greeks grudged against the Hebrews, for that their widows were despised in every day's ministering. (But in those days, when the number of disciples increased, the Greeks grumbled against the Hebrews, because their widows did not receive their portion of each day's sharing, or of the daily distribution.)

2 And the twelve called together the multitude of (the) disciples, and said, It is not rightful, that we leave the word of God, and minister to boards, (or It is not right, that we leave the word of God, to serve tables).

3 Therefore, brethren, behold ye men of you of good fame [or of good witnessing], [seven], full of the Holy Ghost, and of wisdom, whom we shall ordain on this work; (And so, brothers, look for, or find, men among you of good reputation, seven who be full of the Holy Spirit, and of wisdom, whom we shall ordain upon this work;)

4 for we shall be busy to prayer, and to preach, [or and (the) ministry, *or preaching*, of] the word of God. (for we shall be busy with prayer, and with the preaching, or the ministering, of the word of God.)

5 And the word pleased before all the multitude [or And the word pleased to all the multitude]; and they chose Stephen, a man full of faith and of the Holy Ghost (or a man full of faith and of the Holy Spirit), and Philip, and Prochorus, and Nicanor, and Timon, and Parmenas, and Nicolas, a comeling, [or a

guest], (or a newcomer), a man of Antioch.

6 They ordained these before the sight of the apostles, and they prayed, and laid (their) hands on them.

7 And the word of the Lord waxed, and the number of the disciples in Jerusalem was much multiplied; also a much company of priests obeyed to the faith. (And the word of the Lord grew, or spread, and the number of the disciples in Jerusalem greatly increased; and also a great number of priests obeyed the faith.)

8 And Stephen, full of grace and of strength, made wonders and great signs in the people. (And Stephen, full of grace and strength, made great wonders and miracles among the people.)

9 But some rose of the synagogue, that was called of Libertines, and Cyrenians, and of men of Alexandria, and of them that were of Cilicia and of Asia, and disputed with Stephen.

10 And they might not withstand the wisdom and the spirit, that (he) spake.

11 Then they privily sent men, that should say, that they [have] heard him saying words of blasphemy against Moses and God.

12 And so they moved together the people, and the elder men (or the elders), and the scribes; and they came together, and took (hold of) him, and brought (him) into the council.

13 And they ordained false witnesses, that said, This man ceaseth not to speak words against the holy place, and the law.

14 For we heard him saying, That this Jesus of Nazareth shall destroy this place, and shall change the traditions, which Moses betook (or delivered) to us.

15 And all men that sat in the council beheld him, and saw his face as the face of an angel.

CHAPTER 7

1 And the prince of priests said to Stephen, Whether these things have them so? (And the High Priest said to Stephen, Be these things true?)

2   Which said, Brethren and fathers, hear ye, (or And he said, Brothers and fathers, listen). [The] God of glory appeared to our father Abraham, when he was in Mesopotamia, before that he dwelt in Charran,

3   and said to him, Go out of thy land, and of thy kindred, (or Go out of thy land, and away from thy kinfolk), and come into the land, which I shall show to thee.

4   Then he went out of the land of (the) Chaldeans, and dwelt in Charran. And from thence after that his father was dead, he translated him into this land (or he led him to this land), in which ye dwell now.

5   And he gave not to him heritage in it (or But he did not give him any inheritance in it), neither a pace of a foot, but he promised to give him it into possession, and to his seed after him, when he had not a son.

6   And God spake to him, That his seed shall be [a] comeling [or a guest] in an alien land, and they shall make them subject to servage, and shall evil treat them, (for) four hundred years and thirty [or (for) four hundred years]; (And God said to him, That his descendants shall be newcomers in a foreign or a strange land, and they shall make them subject to servitude, or to slavery, and shall treat them wickedly, for four hundred years;)

7   and I shall judge the folk to whom they shall serve, (or and I shall judge the nation for whom they shall be slaves), saith the Lord. And after these things they shall go out, and they shall serve to me in this place.

8   And he gave to him the testament of circumcision; and so he engendered Isaac, and circumcised him in the eighth day. And Isaac engendered Jacob, and Jacob *engendered* the twelve patriarchs. (And he gave to him the covenant of circumcision; and so he begat Isaac, and circumcised him on the eighth day. And Isaac begat Jacob, and Jacob *begat* the twelve patriarchs.)

9   And the patriarchs had envy to Joseph, and sold him into Egypt. And God was with him,

10   and delivered him (out) of all his tribulations, and gave him grace and wisdom in the sight of Pharaoh, king of Egypt. And he ordained him sovereign on Egypt, and on all his house.

11   And hunger came into all Egypt, and Canaan, and great tribulation; and our fathers found not meat (or and our fathers could not find any food).

12   But when Jacob had heard, that wheat was in Egypt, he sent our fathers (on their) first (visit).

13   And in the second time Joseph was known of his brethren (or And on the second visit Joseph made himself known to his brothers), and his kin was made known to Pharaoh.

14   And Joseph sent, and called (for) Jacob, his father, and all his kindred, seventy and five men [or souls].

15   And Jacob came down into Egypt, and was dead, he and our fathers;

16   and they were translated into Sychem, and were laid in the sepulchre, that Abraham bought by price of silver of the sons of Emmor, the son of Sychem. (and they were taken to Shechem, and were laid in the tomb, that Abraham bought with silver from the sons of Hamor, the father of Shechem.)

17   And when the time of (the) promise came nigh, which God had acknowledged to Abraham, the people waxed (or grew), and multiplied in Egypt,

18   till another king (a)rose in Egypt, which knew not Joseph.

19   This (man) beguiled our kin, and tormented our fathers, that they should put away [or they should put out] their young children, for they should not live.

20   In the same time Moses was born, and he was loved of God [or he was accepted of God], (or At that time Moses was born, and he was loved by God); and he was nourished (or was

nursed) three months in the house of his father.

21 And when he was put out *in the river*, the daughter of Pharaoh took him up, and nourished him into her son (or and raised him as her own son).

22 And Moses was learned in all the wisdom of (the) Egyptians, and he was mighty in his words and works.

23 But when the time of forty years was [full-]filled to him, it rose up into his heart, that he should visit his brethren, the sons of Israel.

24 And when he saw a man suffering wrong, he (a)venged him, and did vengeance for him that suffered the wrong, and killed the Egyptian.

25 For he guessed that his brethren should understand, that God should give to them health (or deliverance) by the hand of him; but they understood not.

26 For in the day (pur)suing he appeared to them (who were) chiding (or For on the following day he appeared to two men who were fighting), and he accorded them [or he reconciled them] in peace, and said, Men, ye be brethren; why annoy (or harm) ye each other?

27 But he that did the wrong to his neighbour, putted him away, and said, Who ordained thee prince and doomsman on us? (But he who did the wrong to his neighbour, pushed him away, and said, Who made thee lord and judge over us?)

28 Whether thou wilt slay me, as yesterday thou killedest the Egyptian?

29 And in this word Moses flew, and was made a comeling in the land of Madian (or and was made a newcomer in the land of Midian), where he begat two sons.

30 And when he had [ful]filled forty years, an angel appeared to him in (the) fire of (the) flame of a bush, in desert of the mount of Sina (or in the desert of Mount Sinai).

31 And Moses saw, and wondered on the sight. And when he nighed to behold, the voice of the Lord was made to him, (And Moses saw, and wondered at the sight. And when he approached to look at it, the voice of the Lord was made to him,)

32 and said, I am (the) God of your fathers, (the) God of Abraham, God of Isaac, [and] God of Jacob. Moses was made trembling, and durst (or dared) not behold.

33 But God said to him, Do off the shoes of thy feet, for the place in which thou standest is holy earth (or for the place where thou standest is holy ground).

34 I seeing saw the tormenting [or the affliction] of my people that is in Egypt, and I heard the mourning of them, and came down to deliver them. And now come thou, and I shall send thee into Egypt.

35 This Moses whom they denied, saying, Who ordained thee prince and doomsman on us? God sent this prince and again-buyer, with the hand of the angel, that appeared to him in the bush. (This Moses whom they denied, saying, Who ordained thee lord and judge over us? God sent this leader and this redeemer, by the hand of the angel, who appeared to him in the bush.)

36 This *Moses* led them out, and did wonders and signs (or miracles) in the land of Egypt, and in the Red Sea (or and in the Sea of Reeds), and in (the) desert (for) forty years.

37 This is Moses, that said to the sons of Israel, God shall raise to you a prophet of your brethren, [and] as me ye shall hear him.

38 This it is, that was in the church in wilderness, with the angel that spake to him in the mount of Sina, and with our fathers; which took words of life to give to us. (This is he, who was with the congregation in the wilderness, with the angel who spoke to him on Mount Sinai, and with our fathers; who received the Words of Life to give to us.)

39 To whom our fathers would not obey, but putted him away, and were turned away in their hearts into Egypt (or and their hearts were turned back to Egypt),

40   saying to Aaron, Make thou to us gods, that shall go before us; for to this Moses that led us out of the land of Egypt, we know not what is done to him.

41   And they made a calf in those days, and offered a sacrifice to the maumet, [or to the simulacrum], (or and offered a sacrifice to the idol); and they were glad in the works of their hands.

42   And God turned, and betook them to serve to the knighthood (or to the host) of heaven, (or And God turned away from them, and delivered them over to serve, or to worship, the stars of the heavens), as it is written in the book of [the] prophets, Whether ye, house of Israel, offered to me slain sacrifices, either sacrifices, (for) forty years in (the) desert?

43   And ye have taken the tabernacle of Moloch, and the star of your god Remphan, figures that ye have made to worship them; and I shall translate you into Babylon (or and so I shall lead you to Babylon).

44   The tabernacle of witnessing was with our fathers in desert, (or The Tabernacle, or the Tent, of the Testimony was with our fathers in the desert), as God assigned to them, and spake to Moses, that he should make it after the form that he saw.

45   Which also our fathers took with Jesus, (or he) *that was* (called) *Joshua*, and brought into the possession of (the) heathen men, which God putted away from the face of our fathers, till into the days of David,

46   that found grace with God, and asked that he should find a tabernacle to (the) God of Jacob. (who found grace with God, and asked if he could make a Tabernacle for the God of Jacob.)

47   But Solomon builded the house to him. [Solomon forsooth built an house to him.] (But it was Solomon who built a House, or the Temple, for him.)

48   But the high *God* dwelleth not in things made by hand, as he saith by the prophet,

49   Heaven is a seat to me (or Heaven is my throne), and the earth *is* the stool of my feet; what house shall ye build to me, saith the Lord, either what place is of my resting? [or which *is* the place of my resting?]

50   Whether mine hand made not all these things?

51   With hard noll, and uncircumcised hearts and ears, ye withstand (for)evermore the Holy Ghost; and as your fathers, so ye. (With a stiff neck, and uncircumcised hearts and ears, ye always stand against the Holy Spirit; and so ye be just like your fathers.)

52   Whom of the prophets have not your fathers pursued (or Whom of the prophets have your fathers not persecuted), and have slain them that before-told of the coming of the rightful man [or of the just man], whose traitors and manslayers ye were now?

53   Which took the law in ordinance of angels, and have not kept *it*. (Who received the Law through the facility of angels, but have not obeyed *it*.)

54   And they heard these things, and were diversely tormented in their hearts, and they grinded, *or gnashed*, with (their) teeth on (or at) him.

55   But when Stephen was full of the Holy Ghost, he beheld into heaven, and saw the glory of God, and Jesus standing on the right half of the virtue of God. (But when Stephen was full of the Holy Spirit, he beheld into heaven, and saw the glory of God, and Jesus standing on the right side, or at the right hand, of the power of God.)

56   And he said, Lo! I see heavens opened, and man's Son [or the Son of man] standing on the right half of the virtue of God. (And he said, Behold, I see the heavens opened, and the Son of man standing on the right side, or at the right hand, of the power of God.)

57   And they cried with a great voice, and stopped their ears, and made with one will an

assault into him.

58   And they brought him out of the city, and stoned [him]. And the witnesses did off their clothes, beside the feet of a young man, that was called Saul.

59   And they stoned Stephen, that called *God* to help (or who called *to God* for help), saying, Lord Jesus, receive my spirit.

60   And he kneeled, and cried with a great voice, and said, Lord, set not to them this sin, (or Lord, do not hold this sin against them). And when he had said this thing, he died [or he slept in the Lord].

CHAPTER 8

1   But Saul was consenting to his death. And great persecution was made that day in the church, that was in Jerusalem. And all men were scattered by the countries (or into the provinces) of Judea and Samaria, except the apostles.

2   But good [or dread-full] men buried Stephen, and made great mourning on him. (And some good or devout men buried Stephen, and greatly mourned over him.)

3   But Saul greatly destroyed the church, and entered by houses, and drew out men and women, and betook them into prison [or into keeping], (or and delivered them to prison).

4   And they that were scattered, passed forth, preaching the word of God.

5   And Philip came down into a city of Samaria, and preached to them Christ. (And Philip came down to a city in Samaria, and preached to them about the Messiah.)

6   And the people gave attention to these things that were said of (or by) Philip, with one will hearing and seeing the signs that he did.

7   For many of them that had unclean spirits, cried with (a) great voice, and (they) went out. And many sick in the palsy, and crooked (or and lame), were healed.

8   Therefore great joy was made in that city.

9   But there was a man in that city, whose name was Simon, a witch, that had deceived the folk of Samaria (or who had deceived the Samaritan people), saying, that himself was some great man.

10   [To] Whom all harkened, from the least to the most, and said, This is the virtue (or the power) of God, which is called great.

11   And they believed him, for (a) long time he had madded them (or he had astonished them) with his witchcrafts. [Forsooth they beheld him, for this thing, that much time he had made them mad with his witchings.]

12   But when they had believed to Philip, preaching of the kingdom of God, men and women were baptized in the name of Jesus Christ. [Soothly when they had believed to Philip, evangelizing of the kingdom of God, in the name of Jesus Christ, men and women were baptized.]

13   And then also Simon himself believed; and when he was baptized, he drew (himself) (un)to Philip; and he saw also that signs and great virtues were done, he was astonied, and wondered, (or and when he saw that miracles and great works of power were done, he was astonished, and wondered).

14   But when the apostles that were at Jerusalem, had heard that Samaria had received the word of God, they sent to them Peter and John.

15   And when they came (there), they prayed for them, that they should receive the Holy Ghost (or so that they would receive the Holy Spirit);

16   for he came not yet into any of them [or forsooth not yet he came into any of them], but they were baptized only in the name of the Lord Jesus.

17   Then they laid (their) hands on them, and they received the Holy Ghost (or and they received the Holy Spirit).

18   And when Simon had seen, that the Holy Ghost was given by (the) laying on of [the]

hands of the apostles, and he proffered [or he offered] to them money, (And when Simon had seen, that the Holy Spirit was given by the laying on of the hands of the apostles, then he offered them money,)

19 and said, Give ye also to me this power, that whomever I shall lay on mine hands [or that on whomever I shall put on hands], that he receive the Holy Ghost. (and said, Give also to me this power, so that whomever I shall lay my hands on, he shall receive the Holy Spirit.)

20 But Peter said to him, Thy money be with thee into perdition, for thou guessedest that the gift of God should be had for money [or for thou guessedest the gift of God to be had (or gotten), or wielded, (or possessed), by money].

21 There is no part, nor lot to thee, in this word, for thine heart is not rightful before God.

22 Therefore do thou penance for this wickedness of thee (or And so repent for this wickedness of thine), and pray God, if peradventure this thought of thine heart be forgiven to thee.

23 For I see that thou art in the gall of bitterness and in the bond of wickedness.

24 And Simon answered, and said, Pray ye for me to the Lord, (so) that nothing of these things that ye have said, come on me.

25 And they witnessed, and spake the word of the Lord, and went again to Jerusalem, and preached [or evangelized] to many countries of Samaritans. (And they testified, and spoke the word of the Lord, and then returned to Jerusalem, preaching in many villages of the Samaritans as they went forth.)

26 And an angel of the Lord spake to Philip, and said, Rise thou, and go to meet the south, to the way that goeth down from Jerusalem into Gaza; this is (the) desert.

27 And he rose (up), and went forth. And lo! a man of Ethiopia, a mighty manservant, a gelding of Candace, the queen of (the) Ethiopians, which was on all her riches, came to worship in Jerusalem. (And he got up, and

went forth. And behold, an Ethiopian man, a powerful manservant, a eunuch of Candace, the Ethiopian queen, who was over, or was in charge of, all of her wealth, came to worship in Jerusalem.)

28 And he turned again, sitting on his chariot, and reading Esaias, the prophet. (And he was returning home, sitting in his chariot, and reading the prophet Isaiah.)

29 And the Spirit said to Philip, Nigh thou, and join thee to this chariot. (And the Spirit said to Philip, Approach him, and join thyself to this chariot.)

30 And Philip ran to, and heard him reading Esaias, the prophet, (or And Philip ran over, and heard him reading the prophet Isaiah). And he said, Guessest thou, whether thou understandest, what things thou readest?

31 And he said, How may I, if no man show to me? And he prayed Philip (or And he beseeched Philip), that he should come up, and sit with him.

32 And the place of the scripture that he read, was this, As a sheep he was led to slaying, and as a lamb before a man that sheareth him is dumb without voice, so he opened not his mouth.

33 In meekness his doom was taken up; who shall tell out the generation(s) of him? For his life shall be taken away from the earth. (He was humbled, or He was humiliated, and was denied justice; now who can tell out about his descendants? For his life was taken away from the earth.)

34 And the gelding answered to Philip, and said (or And the eunuch said to Philip), I beseech thee, of what prophet saith he this thing? of himself, or of any other?

35 And Philip opened his mouth, and began at this scripture, and preached [or evangelized] to him (about) Jesus.

36 And while they went by the way, they came to a water [or they came to some water]. And the gelding said, Lo! water; who forbiddeth

me to be baptized?

37   And Philip said, If thou believest of all thine heart, it is leaveful, (or And Philip said, If thou believest with all thine heart, it is lawful). And he answered, and said, I believe that Jesus Christ is the Son of God.

38   And he commanded the chariot to stand still. And they went down both into the water, Philip and the gelding, and *Philip* baptized him, (or And they both went down into the water, Philip and the eunuch, and *Philip* baptized him).

39   And when they were come up (out) of the water, the Spirit of the Lord ravished (or snatched up) Philip, and the gelding saw him no more; and he went in his way joying (or and he went on his way rejoicing).

40   And Philip was found in Azotus; and he passed forth, and preached [or evangelized] to all (the) cities, till he came to Caesarea.

CHAPTER 9

1   But Saul, yet a blower [or a breather] of menaces, and of beatings, [or slaying(s)], against the disciples of the Lord, came to the prince of (the) priests, (But Saul, still a breather of threats, and killings, against the disciples of the Lord, came to the High Priest,)

2   and asked of (or from) him letters into Damascus, to the synagogues; that if he found any men or women of this life, he should lead *them* bound (back) to Jerusalem.

3   And when he made his journey, it befelled, that he came nigh to Damascus. And suddenly a light from heaven shone about him;

4   and he fell to the earth, and heard a voice saying to him, Saul, Saul, what pursuest thou me? (or Saul, Saul, why persecutest thou me?)

5   And he said, Who art thou, Lord? And he *said*, I am Jesus of Nazareth, whom thou pursuest. It is hard to thee, to kick against the prick. (And he said, Who art thou, Lord? And he *said*, I am Jesus of Nazareth, whom thou persecutest. It is hard for thee, to kick against

the prod.)

6   And he trembled, and wondered, and said, Lord, what wilt thou that I do? And the Lord *said* to him, Rise up, and enter into the city, and it shall be said to thee, what it behooveth thee to do.

7   And those men that went with him, stood astonied, (or astonished), [or were made afeared, *or out of mind*]; for they heard a voice, but they saw no man.

8   And Saul rose from the earth; and when his eyes were opened, he saw nothing. And they drew him by the hands, and led *him* into Damascus.

9   And he was three days not seeing; and he ate not, neither drank.

10   And a disciple, Ananias by name, was at Damascus. And the Lord said to him in a vision, Ananias. And he said, Lo! I, Lord.

11   And the Lord *said* to him, Rise thou, and go into a street that is called Rectus; and seek, in the house of Judas, Saul by name, of Tarsus. For lo! he prayeth;

12   and he saw a man, Ananias by name, entering and laying on him hands, that he receive sight (or so that he can see again).

13   And Ananias answered, Lord, I have heard of many of this man, how great evil he did to thy saints in Jerusalem; (And Ananias answered, Lord, I have heard about this man from many people, what great evil he did to God's people in Jerusalem;)

14   and this hath power of the princes of (the) priests, to bind all men that call thy name to help. (and he hath received authority from the high priests, to bind up, or to take captive, all who call on thy name for help.)

15   And the Lord said to him, Go thou, for this is to me a vessel of choosing, that he bear my name before heathen men, and kings, and before the sons of Israel. (And the Lord said to him, Go, for he is a vessel that I have chosen, to bring my name before the Gentiles, and kings, and before the Israelites.)

16   For I shall show to him, how great things it behooveth him to suffer for my name.

17   And Ananias went, and entered into the house; and laid on him his hands, and said, Saul brother, the Lord Jesus sent me, that appeared to thee in the way, in which thou camest, that thou see, and be full-filled with the Holy Ghost, (or Brother Saul, the Lord Jesus sent me, who appeared to thee on the way, in which thou camest, so that thou may see again, and be filled with the Holy Spirit).

18   And anon as the scales felled from his eyes (or And at once as the scales fell from his eyes), he received (his) sight (again). And he (a)rose, and was baptized.

19   And when he had taken meat, he was comforted, (or And when he had eaten some food, he was strengthened). And he was by some days with the disciples, that were at (or in) Damascus.

20   And anon, he entered into the synagogues, (or And at once, he went to the synagogues), and preached (about) the Lord Jesus, for this is the Son of God.

21   And all men that heard him, wondered, and said, Whether this is not he that impugned in Jerusalem them that called to help this name? and hither he came for this thing [or and hither for this thing he came], that he should lead them bound (back) to the princes of (the) priests? (And everyone who heard him, wondered, and said, Is this not he who attacked those in Jerusalem who called on this name for help? and did he not come here for this purpose, that he would lead such believers bound and captive back to the high priests?)

22   But Saul much the more waxed strong [or Forsooth Saul much more waxed strong], and confounded the Jews that dwelled at Damascus, and affirmed that this is Christ. (But Saul grew stronger, and confused the Jews who lived in Damascus, and affirmed that Jesus is the Messiah.)

23   And when many days were [ful]filled, (the) Jews made a counsel, that they should slay him. (And after many days had passed, the Jews made a plan, that they would kill him.)

24   And the ambushes of them were made known to Saul. And they kept (watch on) the gates day and night, that they should slay him (or so that they could kill him).

25   But his disciples took him by night, and delivered him, and let him down in a basket by the wall.

26   And when he came into Jerusalem, he assayed [or he attempted] to join him(self) to the disciples; and all dreaded him (or but everyone feared him), and believed not that he was a disciple.

27   But Barnabas took, and led him to the apostles, and told to them, how in (or on) the way, (that) he had seen the Lord, and that he spake to him, and how in Damascus he did trustily in the name of Jesus.

28   And he was with them, and entered (in), and went out in Jerusalem, and did trustily in the name of Jesus.

29   And he spake with heathen men, and disputed with Greeks (or And he spoke and disputed with the Greek-speaking Jews). And they sought to slay him.

30   Which thing when the brethren had known, they led him by night to Caesarea, and let him go to Tarsus.

31   And the church by all Judea, and Galilee, and Samaria, had peace, and was edified, and walked in the dread of the Lord, and was [full-]filled with (the) comfort of the Holy Ghost. (And the church in all of Judea, and Galilee, and Samaria, had peace, and was edified, and walked in fearful reverence of the Lord, and was filled with the strength of the Holy Spirit.)

32   And it befelled, that Peter, the while he passed about all, came to the holy men that dwelled at Lydda.

33   And he found [there] a man, Aeneas by name, that from eight years (old) he had lain bed-ridden; and he was sick in the palsy.

34 And Peter said to him, Aeneas, the Lord Jesus Christ heal thee; rise thou, and array, *either make ready*, thee. And anon he rose (or And at once he rose up).

35 And all (the) men that dwelt at Lydda, and at Saron, saw him, which were converted to the Lord. (And everyone who dwelt at Lydda, and at Saron, who saw him, were converted to the Lord.)

36 And in Joppa was a discipless, whose name was Tabitha, that is to say, Dorcas. This was full of good works and almsdeeds, that she did.

37 And it befelled in those days, that she was sick, and died. And when they had washed her, they laid her in a solar (or they laid her in an upper room).

38 And for Lydda was nigh Joppa, the disciples heard that Peter was therein, and sent two men to him, and prayed (or beseeched), That thou tarry not to come to us.

39 And Peter rose up, and came with them. And when he was come, they led him into the solar (or into the upper room). And all the widows stood about him, weeping, and showing coats and clothes, which Dorcas made to them (or which Dorcas had made for them).

40 And when all men were put withoutforth (or And after everyone was sent out of the room), Peter kneeled, and prayed. And he turned to the body, and said, Tabitha, arise thou. And she opened her eyes, and when she saw Peter, she sat up.

41 And he took her by the hand, and raised her (up). And when he had called the holy men and widows, he assigned her alive.

42 And it was made known by all Joppa; and many believed in the Lord.

43 And it was made, that many days he dwelled in Joppa, at (or with) one Simon, a currier [or a tanner].

CHAPTER 10

1 A man was in Caesarea, Cornelius by name, a centurion of the company of knights, that is said of Italy; (There was a man in Caesarea, named Cornelius, who was a centurion, or the leader, of a group of soldiers, called the Italian Company;)

2 a religious man, and dreading the Lord, with all his household; doing many alms to the people, and praying (to) the Lord (for)evermore. (a religious man, who had fearful reverence for the Lord, with all his family; giving many gifts to the Jewish people, and always praying to the Lord.)

3 This saw in a vision openly, as in the ninth hour of the day, [*or* (at) *noon*], an angel of God entering in to him, and saying to him, Cornelius.

4 And he beheld him, and was adread (or and was afraid), and said, Who art thou, Lord? And he said to him, Thy prayers and thine almsdeeds have ascended up into mind, in(to) the sight of the Lord.

5 And now send thou men into Joppa, and call one Simon, that is named Peter.

6 This is harboured at a man, Simon, (a) currier [or a tanner], whose house is beside the sea. This shall say to thee, what it behooveth thee to do.

7 And when the angel that spake to him, was gone away [or had gone away], he called two men of his house, and a knight that dreaded the Lord (or and a soldier who had fearful reverence for the Lord), which were at his bidding [or that obeyed to him].

8 And when he had told to them all these things, he sent them into Joppa.

9 And on the day (pur)suing, while they made journey, and nighed to the city, Peter went up into the highest place of the house to pray, about the sixth hour. (And on the following day, while they journeyed, and approached the city, Peter went up to the highest place of the house to pray, at about noon.)

10 And when he was hungered, he would

have eaten. But while they made ready, a ravishing of the spirit, [or an excess of soul], felled on him;

11   and he saw heaven opened, and a vessel coming down, as a great sheet with four corners [or with four cords], to be let down from heaven into earth (or to be let down from heaven onto the earth),

12   in which were all (the) four-footed beasts, and (the) creeping [things] of the earth, and (the) volatiles of (the) heaven(s), [either of the air], (or and the birds of the air).

13   And a voice was made to him, Rise thou, Peter, and slay, and eat.

14   And Peter said, Lord, forbid [it], for I never eat any common thing, and unclean (or unclean).

15   And again the second time the voice was made to him, That thing that God hath cleansed, say thou not unclean.

16   And this thing was done by thrice; and anon the vessel was received again into heaven (or and then at once the vessel was taken up again into heaven).

17   And while that Peter doubted within himself, what the vision was that he saw, lo! the men, that were sent from Cornelius, sought the house of Simon, and stood at the gate.

18   And when they had called, they asked if Simon, that is named Peter, had there harbour. (And they called out, and asked if Simon, who was called Peter, was harboured there.)

19   And while Peter thought on the vision, the Spirit said to him, Lo! three men seek thee.

20   Therefore rise thou, and go down, and go with them, and doubt thou nothing, for I sent them.

21   And Peter came down to the men, and said, Lo! I am (he), whom ye seek; what is the cause, for which ye be come? [or for which ye have come?]

22   And they said, Cornelius, the centurion, a just man, and dreading God, and having good witnessing of all the folk of Jews, took answer

of an holy angel, to call thee into his house, and to hear words of thee. (And they said, Cornelius, the centurion, a righteous man, and revering God, and receiving good testimony from all the Jewish people, received a word from a holy angel, to call thee to his house, and to hear some words from thee.)

23   Therefore he led them in, and received (them) in harbour; and that night they dwelled with him. And in the day (pur)suing he rose (or And on the following day he rose up), and went forth with them; and some of the brethren followed him from Joppa [or and some of (the) brethren from Joppa followed him], (so) *that they be witnesses to Peter.*

24   And the tother day (or And the next day), he entered into Caesarea. And Cornelius abode them, with his cousins, and necessary friends, that were called together.

25   And it was done, when Peter was come in [or when Peter had entered], Cornelius came meeting him, and fell down at his feet, and worshipped (or and honoured) *him.*

26   But Peter raised him (up), and said, Arise thou, also I myself am a man, as thou.

27   And he spake with him, and went in, and found many that were come together.

28   And he said to them, Ye know, how abominable it is to a Jew, to be joined either to come to an alien (or to a foreigner); but God showed to me, that no man say a man common, either unclean (or unclean).

29   For which thing I came, when I was called, without doubting. Therefore I ask you, for what cause have ye called me?

30   And Cornelius said, Today, four days into this hour [or From the fourth day passed till to this hour], I was praying and fasting in the ninth hour in mine house. And lo! a man stood before me in a white cloth (or a man stood before me in a white cloak),

31   and said, Cornelius, thy prayer is heard, and thine almsdeeds be in mind in the sight of God (or and thy acts of charity be remembered

before God).

32 Therefore send thou into Joppa, and call Simon, that is named Peter; this (man) is harboured in the house of Simon (the) currier, beside the sea. This (man), when he shall come, shall speak to thee.

33 Therefore anon I sent to thee (or And so at once I sent for thee), and thou didest well in coming to us. Now therefore we all be present in thy sight, to hear the words, whatever be commanded to thee of the Lord.

34 And Peter opened his mouth, and said, In truth I have found, that God is no acceptor of persons, (or In truth I have found, that God hath no favourites among people);

35 but in each folk he that dreadeth God, and worketh rightwiseness, is accept(able) to him. (but among all people and every nation, he who hath fearful reverence for God, and worketh righteousness, is acceptable to him.)

36 God sent a word to the children of Israel, showing peace by Jesus Christ; this is (the) Lord of all things, [or this is the Lord of all men], (or he is the Lord of everyone).

37 Ye know the word that is made (or the tidings that be told) through(out) all Judea, and (that) began at Galilee, after the baptism that John preached, (about) Jesus of Nazareth;

38 how God anointed him with the Holy Ghost, and virtue; which passed forth in doing well [or which passed forth in well-doing], and healing all men oppressed of the devil, for God was with him. (how God anointed him with the Holy Spirit, and with power; and he went forth doing good, and healing everyone oppressed by the Devil, for God was with him.)

39 And we be witnesses of all things, which he did in the country of (the) Jews, and of Jerusalem; whom they slew, hanging on a tree.

40 And God raised this (man) in (or on) the third day, and gave him to be made known,

41 not to all the people, but to witnesses before-ordained of God; to us that ate and drank with him, after that he rose again from death [or after that he rose again from (the) dead].

42 And he commanded to us to preach to the people, and to witness, that he it is, that is ordained of God doomsman of the quick and of the dead. (And he commanded us to preach to the people, and to testify, that it is he, who is ordained by God to be the Judge of the living and of the dead.)

43 To this all (the) prophets bear witnessing [or To this all prophets bear witness], that all men that believe in him, shall receive remission of sins by his name. (And all the prophets testify about him, that all who believe in him, shall receive forgiveness for their sins through his name.)

44 And yet while that Peter spake these words, the Holy Ghost felled on all that heard the word. (And while Peter spoke these words, the Holy Spirit fell upon all who heard the word.)

45 And the faithful men of (the) circumcision, that came with Peter, wondered, that also into nations the grace of the Holy Ghost is shed out. (And the faithful men of the circumcision, who came with Peter, wondered and were amazed, that the gift of the Holy Spirit was also poured out on heathen men, that is, upon the Gentiles.)

46 For they heard them speaking in languages [or speaking with tongues], and magnifying God. Then Peter answered (or Then Peter asked),

47 Whether any man may forbid water, that these be not baptized, that have also received the Holy Ghost as we? (Would anyone forbid the water, with which these people can be baptized, yea, they who have also received the Holy Spirit like we have?)

48 And he commanded them to be baptized in the name of the Lord Jesus Christ. Then they prayed him, that he should dwell with them some days.

CHAPTER 11

1 And the apostles, and the brethren that were in Judea, heard that also heathen men received the word of God, and they glorified God. (And the apostles, and the brothers who were in Judea, heard that the Gentiles had also accepted the word of God, and they glorified God.)

2 But when Peter came to Jerusalem, they that were of (the) circumcision, disputed against him,

3 and said, Why enteredest thou to men that have prepuce, and hast eaten with them? (and said, Why hast thou gone to those who have foreskin, or who be uncircumcised, and hast eaten with them?)

4 And Peter began, and expouned to them by order, and said,

5 I was in the city of Joppa, and prayed, and I saw in (the) ravishing of my mind, [or in (the) excess of my soul], a vision, that a vessel came down, as a great sheet with four cords [or with four corners], and was sent down from heaven; and it came to me.

6 Into which I looking beheld, and saw (the) four-footed beasts of the earth, and (other) beasts, and (the) creeping beasts, and (the) volatiles of (the) heaven(s), [or of the air], (or and the birds of the air).

7 And I heard also a voice that said to me, Peter, rise thou, and slay, and eat.

8 But I said, Nay, Lord; for common thing either unclean entered never into my mouth. (But I said, No, Lord; for a common or an unclean thing hath never entered into my mouth.)

9 And the voice answered the second time from heaven, That thing that God hath cleansed, say thou not unclean.

10 And this was done by thrice, and (then) all (the) things were received again into heaven.

11 And lo! three men anon stood in the house, in which I was, (or And behold, three men at once arrived at the house, where I was); and they were sent from Caesarea to me.

12 And the Spirit said to me, that I should go with them, and doubt nothing. Yea, and these six brethren came with me, and we entered into the house of the man.

13 And he told to us, how he saw an angel in his house, standing and saying to him, Send thou into Joppa, and call Simon, that is named Peter,

14 which shall speak to thee words, in which thou shalt be safe, and all thine house. (who shall speak to thee the words, by which thou shalt be saved, and all of thine house.)

15 And when I had begun to speak, the Holy Ghost fell on them, as into us in the beginning. (And when I had begun to speak, the Holy Spirit fell upon them, as upon us at the beginning.)

16 And I bethought on the word of the Lord, as he said, For John baptized in water, but ye shall be baptized in the Holy Ghost (or For John baptized with water, but ye shall be baptized with the Holy Spirit).

17 Therefore if God gave to them the same grace, as to us that believed in the Lord Jesus Christ, who was I, that might forbid the Lord, that he give not the Holy Ghost [or that he should not give the Holy Ghost] to them that believed in the name of Jesus Christ? (And so if God gave them the same gift, as to us who believed in the Lord Jesus Christ, who was I, who would forbid the Lord, yea, that he should not give the Holy Spirit to those who believed in the name of Jesus Christ?)

18 When these things were heard, they held peace, and glorified God, and said, Therefore also to heathen men God hath given penance to life. (When they heard these things, they held their peace, and glorified God, and said, And so God hath given life-giving repentance also to the Gentiles.)

19 And they that were scattered of the

tribulation that was made under Stephen (or Now those who were scattered after the persecution that was made after Stephen's death), walked forth to Phenice, and to Cyprus, and to Antioch, and spake the word to no man, but to (the) Jews alone.

20 But some of them were men of Cyprus, and of Cyrene; which when they had entered into Antioch, they spake to the Greeks, and preached the Lord Jesus.

21 And the hand of the Lord was with them, and much number of men believing was converted to the Lord.

22 And the word came to the ears of the church, that was at Jerusalem, on these things; and they sent Barnabas to Antioch.

23 And when he was come, and saw the grace of the Lord, he joyed, and admonished all men to dwell in the Lord in purpose of heart; (And when he had come, and saw the blessing of the Lord, he rejoiced, and admonished everyone to remain in the Lord with a resolute heart;)

24 for he was a good man, and full of the Holy Ghost (or and full of the Holy Spirit), and of faith. And much people was increased to the Lord.

25 And he went forth to Tarsus, to seek Saul;

26 and when he had found him, he led (him) to Antioch. And all a year they lived there in the church, and taught much people, so that the disciples were named first at Antioch christian men (or were first called Christians at Antioch).

27 And in these days prophets came over from Jerusalem to Antioch.

28 And one of them rose up, Agabus by name, and signified by the Spirit a great hunger to coming [or a great hunger to come] in all the world, which *hunger* was made under Claudius (or and this *famine* occurred during the reign of Claudius).

29 And all the disciples purposed, after that (that) each had, for to send (or to contribute) into (the) ministry to (the) brethren that dwelled

in Judea.

30 Which thing also they did, and sent *it* to the elder men, by the hands of Barnabas and Saul.

CHAPTER 12

1 And in the same time Herod the king sent power, [or hands], (or his men), to torment some men of the church.

2 And he slew by (the) sword James, the brother of John.

3 And he saw that it pleased to the Jews, and cast to take also Peter; and the days of therf loaves were. (And he saw that it pleased the Jews, and sent forth men to take hold of Peter; and it was during the Days, or the Feast, of Unleavened Bread.)

4 And when he had caught Peter, he sent him into prison; and betook *him* to four quaternions of knights, to keep him, and would after pask bring him forth to the people. (And when he had caught Peter, he put him into prison; and gave *him* over to four squads of four soldiers each, to guard him, and intended after Passover to bring him before the people.)

5 And Peter was kept in prison; but prayer was made of the church without ceasing to God for him (or but prayer without ceasing was made by the church to God for him).

6 But when Herod should bring him forth, in that night Peter was sleeping betwixt two knights, and was bound with two chains; and the keepers before the door kept the prison. (But on the night before Herod would bring him before the people, Peter was sleeping between two soldiers, and was bound with two chains; and the guards outside at the door, or at the gate, kept watch over the prison.)

7 And lo! an angel of the Lord stood nigh, and light shone in the prison house. And when he had smitten the side of Peter, he raised, [or *waked*], him, and said, Rise thou swiftly. And

anon the chains felled down from his hands (or And at once the chains fell off his hands).

8 And the angel said to him, Gird thee, and do on thine hoses. And he did so. And he said to him, Do about thee thy clothes, and (pur)sue me (or and follow me).

9 And he went out, and (pur)sued him; and he wist not that it was sooth, that (it) was done by the angel, (or And he went out, and followed him; and he knew not that it was true, that it was done by the angel); for he guessed himself to have seen a vision.

10 And they passed the first and the second ward, and came to the iron gate that leadeth to the city, which anon (or at once) was opened to them, [or the which willfully, (or on its own accord), is opened to them]. And they went out, and came [forth] into one street, and anon (or at once) the angel passed away from him.

11 And Peter turned again to himself, and said, Now I know verily (or Now I truly know), that the Lord sent his angel, and delivered me from the hand of Herod, and from all the abiding of the people of (the) Jews.

12 And he beheld, and came to the house of Mary, the mother of John, that is named Mark, where many were gathered together, and praying.

13 And when he knocked at the door of the gate, a damsel [or a wench], Rhoda by name, came forth to see (who it was).

14 And when she knew the voice of Peter, for joy she opened not the gate, but ran in, and told (them), that Peter stood at the gate.

15 And they said to her, Thou maddest [or Thou art mad]. But she affirmed, that it was so. And they said, It is his angel.

16 But Peter abode still, and knocked. And when they had opened the door, they saw him, and wondered.

17 And he beckoned to them with his hand to be still, and told how the Lord had led him out of the prison. And he said, Tell ye to James and to the brethren these things. And he went

out, and went into another place (or and went to another place).

18 And when the day was come, there was not little troubling among the knights, what was done of Peter. (And when the daylight had come, there was a great deal of concern among the soldiers, about what had become of Peter.)

19 And when Herod had sought him, and found (him) not, after that he had made inquiring of the keepers, he commanded them to be brought to him, (or And when Herod had them search for him, and he was not found, after that he had questioned the guards, he commanded that they be put to death). And he came down from Judea into Caesarea, and dwelled there.

20 And he was wroth to (the) men of Tyre and of Sidon. And they of one accord came to him, when they had counselled with Blastus, that was the king's chamberlain, (and) they asked (for) peace, for as much as their countries (or their provinces) were victualed of him [or were nourished by him].

21 And in a day that was ordained, Herod was clothed with king's clothing, and sat for doomsman, and spake to them, (or and sat as judge, and spoke to them).

22 And the people cried, The voice of God, and not of man.

23 And anon an angel of the Lord smote him, for he had not given honour to God; and he was wasted of worms, and died. (And at once an angel of the Lord struck him, for he had not given honour to God; and he was wasted by worms, and died.)

24 And the word of the Lord waxed, (or grew, or spread), and was multiplied.

25 And Barnabas and Saul turned again from Jerusalem, when the ministry was [ful]filled, and (they) took John, that was named Mark. (And Barnabas and Saul returned from Jerusalem, when their service, or work, was completed, and they took John, who was called Mark, with them.)

DEEDS of the APOSTLES

CHAPTER 13

1   And prophets and doctors (or teachers of the Law) were in the church that was at Antioch, in which Barnabas, and Simon, that was called Black, and Lucius Cyreneus, and Manaen, that was the suckling-frère of Herod tetrarch (or who was the foster-brother of Herod the tetrarch), *that is, (a) prince of the fourth part*, and Saul *were.*

2   And when they ministered to the Lord, and fasted, the Holy Ghost said to them, Separate ye to me Saul and Barnabas, into the work to which I have taken them. (And when they served the Lord, and fasted, the Holy Spirit said to them, Set apart Saul and Barnabas, for the work to which I have called them.)

3   Then they fasted, and prayed, and laid hands on them, and let them go.

4   But they were sent of the Holy Ghost (or And they were sent by the Holy Spirit), and went forth to Seleucia, and from thence they went by boat to Cyprus.

5   And when they came to Salamis, they preached the word of God in the synagogues of (the) Jews; and they had also John in ministry [or in service].

6   And when they had walked by all the isle to Paphos, they found a man, a witch, [or they found some man witch], a false prophet, a Jew, to whom the name was Barjesus, (who was also called Elymas),

7   that was with the proconsul Sergius Paulus, a prudent man. This (man) called Barnabas and Paul, and desired to hear the word of God.

8   But (this) Elymas the witch withstood them; for his name is expounded so [or (it) is interpreted so]; and he sought to turn away the proconsul from belief.

9   But Saul, which *is said* also Paul, was filled with the Holy Ghost, and beheld into him, (But Saul, who *is* also *called* Paul, was

filled with the Holy Spirit, and looked at him,)

10   and said, A! thou full of all guile, and all falseness, thou son of the devil, thou enemy of all rightwiseness, thou leavest not (off) to turn upside-down, [or to subvert, *or to destroy*], the rightful ways of the Lord.

11   And now lo! the hand of the Lord *is* on thee, and thou shalt be blind, and not seeing the sun into a time. And anon, (or at once), [a] mist and darkness felled down on him; and he went about, and sought him that should give [the] hand to him.

12   Then the proconsul, when he had seen the deed, believed, wondering on the teaching of the Lord.

13   And when from Paphos Paul had gone by boat, and they that were with him, they came to Perga of Pamphylia; but John departed from them, and turned again to Jerusalem (or and returned to Jerusalem).

14   And they went from Perga, and came to Antioch of Pisidia; and they entered into the synagogue in the day of sabbaths, and sat, (or and they entered into the synagogue on the Sabbath day, and sat down).

15   And after the reading of the law and of the prophets, the princes of the synagogue sent to them (or the leaders of the synagogue sent word to them), and said, Brethren, if any word of exhortation to the people is in you, say ye.

16   And Paul rose, and with hand bade silence, and said, Men of Israel, and ye that dread God, hear ye. (And Paul rose up, and with his hand ordered silence, and said, Israelites, and ye who have fearful reverence for God, listen to me.)

17   God of the people of Israel chose our fathers, and enhanced the people, when they were comelings in the land of Egypt, and in an high arm he led them out of it; (God of the people of Israel chose our fathers, and raised up the people, when they were foreigners in the land of Egypt, and with an outstretched arm he led them out of it;)

18 and by the time of forty years he suffered their manners (or their ways) in (the) desert.

19 And he destroyed seven folks in the land of Canaan, and by sort parted to them their land, (And he destroyed seven nations in the land of Canaan, and by lot, or for an inheritance, divided up their land to them,)

20 as after four hundred and fifty years. And after these things he gave doomsmen (or judges), [till] to Samuel, the prophet.

21 And from that time they asked (for) a king, and God gave to them Saul, the son of Cis, a man of the lineage of Benjamin, by forty years. (And at that time they asked for a king, and God gave them Saul, the son of Cis, a man of the tribe of Benjamin, for forty years.)

22 And when he was done away, he raised to them David the king, to whom he bare witnessing (or of whom he testified), and said, I have found David, the son of Jesse, a man after mine (own) heart, which (or who) shall do all my will.

23 Of whose seed by the promise God hath led out to Israel a Saviour Jesus,

24 when John preached before the face of his coming the baptism of penance (or the baptism of repentance) to all the people of Israel.

25 But when John [ful]filled his course, he said, I am not he, whom ye deem me to be (or whom ye judge me to be); but lo! he (that) cometh after me, and I am not worthy to do off [or to unbind] the shoes of his feet.

26 Brethren, and sons of the kind of Abraham, and which that in you dread God, to you the word of this health is sent. (Brothers, and sons of the kindred of Abraham, and those of you who have fearful reverence for God, to you the message of this salvation is sent.)

27 For they that dwell at Jerusalem, and (the) princes of it, (or For they who live in Jerusalem, and their leaders), that knew not this Jesus, and the voices of (the) prophets, that by every sabbath be read, deemed, and fulfilled;

28 and they found in him no cause (worthy)

of death, and (yet) asked of Pilate, that they should slay him. (and they found in him no crime worthy of death, but yet they asked of Pilate, that he should be killed, or executed.)

29 And when they had ended all things that were written of him, they took him down off the tree, and laid him in a grave (or and laid him in a tomb).

30 And God raised him from death in the third day; [Forsooth God raised him from (the) dead the third day;]

31 which was seen by many days to them that went up together with him from Galilee into Jerusalem, which be till now his witnesses to the people. (who was seen for many days by those who went up together with him from Galilee to Jerusalem, who up to the present be his witnesses to the people.)

32 And we show to you the promise that was made to our fathers;

33 for God hath fulfilled this to their sons, and again-raised Jesus (or and raised up Jesus); as in the second psalm it is written, Thou art my Son, today I begat thee.

34 And he that again-raised him from death [or Forsooth that he again-raised him from (the) dead], that he should not turn again into corruption, said thus, For I shall give to you the holy true things of David. (And he who raised him from the dead, so that he would never return to corruption, or to death and destruction, said thus, I shall give you the holy and true blessings which I promised to David.)

35 Therefore and in another stead he saith, Thou shalt not give thine holy (One) to see corruption. (And so in another place he saith, Thou shalt not allow thine Holy One to experience death and destruction, that is, to rot in the grave.)

36 But David in his generation, when he had ministered to the will of God (or when he had served the will of God), died [or slept], and was laid with his fathers, and saw corruption;

37 but he whom God raised from death [or

soothly he whom God raised from (the) dead],
saw not corruption (or did not suffer corruption,
or rot in the grave).

38 Therefore, brethren, be it known to you,
that by him remission of sins is told to you, (And
so brothers, let it be known to you, that through
him forgiveness of sins is now told to you.)

39 from all sins, of which ye might not be
justified in the law of Moses (or under the Law
of Moses). In this each man that believeth, is
justified.

40 Therefore see ye, that it come not to you,
that is before-said in the prophets,

41 Ye despisers, see ye, and wonder ye, [+or
See ye, despisers, and wonder ye], and be ye
scattered abroad; for I work a work in your
days, a work that ye shall not believe, if any
man shall tell *it* [out] to you.

42 And when they went out, they prayed,
that in the sabbath (pur)suing (or that on the
following Sabbath), they should speak to them
these words.

43 And when the synagogue was left, many
of the Jews and comelings worshipping God
(pur)sued Paul and Barnabas; that spake, and
counselled them, that they should dwell in the
grace of God. (And when the synagogue was let
go, many of the Jews and newcomers
worshipping God followed after Paul and
Barnabas; who spoke, and counselled them,
that they should remain in the grace of God.)

44 And in the sabbath (pur)suing (or And on
the following Sabbath), almost all the city came
together, to hear the word of God.

45 And (the) Jews saw the people, and (they)
were filled with envy, and gainsaid these things
that were said of Paul (or and spoke against
those things that were said by Paul), and
blasphemed.

46 Then Paul and Barnabas steadfastly said,
To you it behooved (us) first to speak the word
of God; but for ye put it away, and have
deemed you(rselves) unworthy to everlasting
life [+or and have deemed you(rselves)

unworthy of everlasting life], lo! we turn to (the)
heathen men. (Then Paul and Barnabas
resolutely said, It behooved us first to speak the
word of God to you; but because ye have
pushed it away, and have deemed yourselves
unworthy of eternal life, behold, we shall turn
to the Gentiles.)

47 For so the Lord commanded us, I have set
thee into (a) light of (the) heathen men, that
thou be into health to the utmost [or to the
uttermost] of the earth. (For so the Lord
commanded us, I have ordained thee to be a
light for the Gentiles, so that thou be a means
of salvation unto the uttermost terms, or limits,
of the earth.)

48 And (the) heathen men heard, and joyed,
and glorified the word of the Lord; and
believed, as many as were before-ordained to
everlasting life. (And the Gentiles heard, and
rejoiced, and glorified the word of the Lord;
and believed, as many as were foreordained, or
predestined, for eternal life.)

49 And the word of the Lord was [far] sown
in all that country (or region).

50 But the Jews stirred religious women, and
honest, and the worthiest [or the first] men of the
city, and stirred persecution against Paul and
Barnabas, and drove them out of their countries.
(But the Jews excited some honest and religious
women, and the worthiest men of the city, and
stirred up persecution against Paul and
Barnabas, and drove them out of their region.)

51 And they shook away into them the dust
of their feet [or And they shook away the powder
of (their) feet into them], and came to Iconium.

52 And the disciples were filled with joy and
the Holy Ghost. (And so the disciples were
filled with joy and the Holy Spirit.)

CHAPTER 14

1 And it befelled at Iconium, that they
entered together into the synagogue of (the)
Jews, and spake, so that [a] full great multitude

of Jews and Greeks believed.

2 But the Jews that were unbelieveful, raised persecution, and stirred to wrath the souls of (the) heathen men against the brethren; but the Lord gave soon peace (or but the Lord soon gave peace).

3 Therefore they dwelled much time, and did trustily in the Lord, bearing witnessing to the word of his grace (or testifying to the message of his grace), giving signs (or miracles) and wonders to be made by the hands of them.

4 But the multitude of the city was parted (or But the multitude in that city was divided), and some were with the Jews, and some with the apostles.

5 But when there was made an assault of the heathen men and the Jews, with their princes (or with their leaders), to torment (them), and to stone them,

6 they understood, and fled together to the cities of Lycaonia, and Lystra, and Derbe, and into all the country(side) about.

7 And they preached there the gospel, and all the multitude was moved together in the teaching of them. (And so) Paul and Barnabas dwelt at Lystra. (And they preached the Gospel or the Good News there, and everyone was greatly moved by their teaching. And so Paul and Barnabas remained at Lystra.)

8 And a man at Lystra was sick in the feet, and had sat crooked from his mother's womb, which never had gone. (And a man at Lystra was sick in the feet, and had been lame from his mother's womb, and had never walked.)

9 This (man) heard Paul speaking; and Paul beheld him and saw that he had faith, that he should be made safe, (He listened as Paul spoke; and Paul looked at him, and saw that he had firm faith, so that he could be saved,)

10 and said with a great voice, Rise thou upright on thy feet. And he leaped (up), and walked.

11 And the people, when they had seen that that Paul did, reared their voice in Lycaonian tongue, and said, Gods made like to men be come down to us.

12 And they called Barnabas, Jupiter, and Paul, Mercury, for he was (the) leader of the word.

13 And the priest of Jupiter that was before the city (or And the priest of Jupiter, whose temple was just outside the city), brought bulls and crowns (or garlands) before the gates, with (the) peoples, and would have made (a) sacrifice (there).

14 And when the apostles Barnabas and Paul heard this, they rent their coats (or they tore their coats); and they skipped out among the people, and cried,

15 and said, Men, what do ye this thing? and we be deadly men like you, and show (these tidings) to you, that ye be converted from these vain things to the living God, that made heaven, and earth, and the sea, and all things that be in them; (and said, Men, why do ye this? for we be mortal men just like you, and we tell these tidings to you, so that ye be converted from these futile and useless things to the living God, who made heaven, and earth, and the sea, and all the things that be in them;)

16 which in generations passed suffered all folks to go into their own ways. (who in generations passed allowed all the peoples to go their own ways.)

17 And yet he left not himself without witnessing in well-doing, for he gave rains from heaven, and times of bearing fruit, and full-filled your hearts with meat, and gladness. (And yet he did not leave himself without testimony or evidence of his good deeds, for he gave rain from the heavens, and times of bearing fruit, and filled you full with food, and your hearts with gladness.)

18 And they saying these things, scarcely assuaged the people, (so) that they offered not to them.

19 But some Jews came over from Antioch and Iconium, and counselled [or stirred (up)]

the people, and [they] stoned Paul, and drew *him* out of the city, and guessed that he was dead.

20 But when [the] disciples were come about him, he (a)rose, and went into the city; and in the day (pur)suing, [or and in the (pur)suing day], (or and on the following day), he went forth with Barnabas into Derbe.

21 And when they had preached [or had evangelized] to that city, and taught many, they turned again to Lystra (or they returned to Lystra), and Iconium, and to Antioch;

22 confirming the souls of the disciples, and admonishing, that they should dwell in the faith, (or that they should remain in the faith, or that they should live in the faith), and said, That by many tribulations it behooveth us to enter into the kingdom of heavens.

23 And when they had ordained priests to them by all cities, and had prayed with fastings, they betook them to the Lord (or they delivered them unto the Lord), in whom they believed.

24 And they passed (through) Pisidia, and came to Pamphylia;

25 and they spake the word of the Lord in Perga, and came down into Italy.

26 And from thence they went by boat to Antioch, from whence they were taken to the grace of God (or from where they had been committed, or delivered, unto God's grace), into the work that they (had now) [ful]filled.

27 And when they were come, and had gathered the church, they told how great things (that) God did with them [or they told how many things (that) God did with them], and that he had opened to heathen men the door of faith (or and that he had opened the door of faith to the Gentiles).

28 And they dwelled not a little time with the disciples.

CHAPTER 15

1 And some men came down from Judea,

and taught (the) brethren, That but ye be circumcised after the law of Moses, ye may not be made safe, [or ye may not be saved], (or ye cannot be saved).

2 Therefore when there was made not a little dissension to Paul and Barnabas against them, they ordained, that Paul and Barnabas, and some others of them, should go up to the apostles and (the) priests in Jerusalem, on this question.

3 And so they were led forth of the church, and passed by Phenice and Samaria; and they told the conversation [or the living] of heathen men, and they made great joy to all the brethren. (And so they were led forth from the church, and went through Phoenicia and Samaria; and they told them the news of the conversion of the Gentiles, and they gave great joy to all the brothers.)

4 And when they came to Jerusalem, they were received of the church, and of the apostles, and of the elder men, (or they were received by the church, and by the apostles, and by the elders), and told, how great things (that) God did with them [or how many things (that) God did with them].

5 But some of the heresy of the Pharisees, that believed, rose up, and said, That it behooveth them to be circumcised, and to command to keep also the law of Moses.

6 And the apostles and elder men came together, to see of this word.

7 And when there was made a great seeking thereof, Peter rose, and said to them, Brethren, ye know, that of old days in you, God chose by my mouth heathen men, to hear the word of the gospel, and to believe, (or Brothers, ye know, that in the old days, or in the early days, God chose that the Gentiles would hear the word of the Gospel or the Good News, from my mouth, and believe it);

8 and God, that knew the hearts, bare witnessing, and gave to them the Holy Ghost, as also to us; (and God, who knew their hearts,

testified, and gave them the Holy Spirit, as he also gave to us;)

9   and nothing diversed betwixt us and them, cleansing the hearts of them by faith.

10   Now then what tempt ye God (or Then why now do ye test God), to put a yoke on the neck of the disciples, which neither we, neither our fathers might bear?

11   But by the grace of our Lord Jesus Christ we believe to be saved, as also they. (For we believe it is by the grace of our Lord Jesus Christ that we be saved, as they also be.)

12   And all the multitude held (their) peace, and heard Barnabas and Paul, telling how great signs and wonders, [or how many signs and wonders], (that) God did by them in (the) heathen men. (And all the multitude held their peace, and listened to Barnabas and Paul, telling how many miracles and wonders that God did by them among the Gentiles.)

13   And after that they held (their) peace, James answered, and said, Brethren, hear ye me.

14   Simon told, how God visited, first to take (out) of heathen men, a people to his name. [Simon told, how first God visited, to take (out) of (or from among) (the) heathen men a people to his name.] (Simon told, how God first visited, to take, or to choose, from among the Gentiles, a people to his name.)

15   And the words of (the) prophets accord to him, as it is written,

16   After this I shall turn again (or After this I shall return), and build the tabernacle of David, that fell down; and I shall build again the cast-down things of it, and I shall raise it (up);

17   that other men seek the Lord, and all folks, on whom my name is called to help, [or in-called], (or so that other men seek the Lord, yea, all the peoples and nations, who call on my name for help); the Lord doing this thing, saith.

18   From the (beginning of the) world, the work of the Lord is known to the Lord. (From

long ago, or from the creation of the world, the Lord's work was made known.)

19   For which thing I deem them that of (the) heathen men be converted to God, to be not dis-eased [or unquieted],

20   but to write to them, that they abstain them from (the) defoulings of maumets [or of simulacra], and from fornication, and strangled things, and blood. (but to write to them, that they abstain themselves from the defilements of idols, that is, from food offered to idols, and from fornication, and from strangled things, and from blood.)

21   For Moses of (or from the) old times hath in all (the) cities them that preach him in (the) synagogues, whereby each sabbath he is read.

22   Then it pleased to the apostles, and to the elder men (or to the elders), with all the church, to choose (some) men of them, and send (them) to Antioch, with Paul and Barnabas, (that is), Judas, that was named Barsabas, and Silas, the first men among (the) brethren;

23   and wrote by the hands of them, Apostles and elder brethren to them that be at Antioch, and Syria, and Cilicia, brethren of heathen men (or to the Gentile brothers), greeting(s).

24   For we heard that some went out from us, and troubled you with words, and turned upside-down your souls, to which men we commanded not,

25   it pleased to us gathered into one, to choose men, and send (them) to you, with our most dearworthy Barnabas and Paul,

26   men that gave their lives for the name of our Lord Jesus Christ.

27   Therefore we sent Judas and Silas, and they shall tell the same things to you by words.

28   For it is seen to the Holy Ghost, and to us, to put to you nothing more of charge, than these needful things, (For it is seen by the Holy Spirit, and by us, to put no other burden upon you, other than these necessary things,)

29   that ye abstain you from the offered things of maumets [or of simulacra], and blood

strangled, and fornication, (or that ye abstain yourselves from the food offered to idols, and from blood, and from strangled things, and from fornication). From which ye keeping you(rselves), shall do well. Fare ye well.

30   Therefore they were let go [or dismissed], and came down to Antioch; and when the multitude was gathered, they (be)took the epistle (or they delivered the letter);

31   which when they had read (it), they joyed on the comfort. (and when they had read it, they rejoiced over the encouragement that it gave to them.)

32   And Judas and Silas and they, for they were prophets, comforted (or strengthened) (the) brothers, and confirmed [them] with full many words.

33   But after that they had been there a little while, they were let go of (the) brethren with peace, (or they were sent forth by the brothers with peace), [or they were dismissed with peace of (or from) (the) brethren], (back) to them that had sent them.

34   But it was seen to Silas, to dwell there; and Judas went alone to Jerusalem.

35   And Paul and Barnabas dwelt at Antioch, teaching and preaching the word of the Lord, with others many [or with many others].

36   But after some days, Paul said to Barnabas, Turn we again, and visit we [our] brethren by all (the) cities, in which we have preached the word of the Lord, how they have them. (But after some days, Paul said to Barnabas, Let us return, and visit our brothers in all the cities, in which we have preached the word of the Lord, to learn how they be doing.)

37   And Barnabas would take with him John, that was named Mark (or who was called Mark).

38   But Paul prayed him, that he that departed from them from Pamphylia, and went not with them into the work, should not be received. (But Paul beseeched him, saying that he who had left them at Pamphylia, and did not go with

them in the work, should not be taken with them now.)

39   And dissension was made, so that they departed atwain. And Barnabas took Mark, and came by boat to Cyprus.

40   And Paul chose Silas, and went forth from the brethren, and was betaken to the grace of God (or and was delivered unto God's grace).

41   And he went by Syria and Cilicia, and confirmed the church, commanding to keep the behests [or the precepts] of the apostles and (the) elder men.

CHAPTER 16

1   And he came into Derbe and Lystra. And lo! a disciple was there, by (the) name (of) Timothy, the son of a Jewess christian, and of the father heathen (or and of a Gentile father).

2   And [the] brethren that were in Lystra and Iconium, yielded good witnessing to him. (And the brothers who were in Lystra and Iconium, testified good things about him, or spoke approvingly about him.)

3   And Paul would, that this man should go forth with him, and he took, and circumcised him, for (the) Jews that were in those places. For all knew, that his father was heathen. (And Paul wanted, that this man would go forth with him, and he took, and circumcised him, for the Jews who were in those places. For everyone knew, that his father was a Gentile.)

4   When they passed by (the) cities, they betook to them to keep the teachings, that were deemed of (the) apostles and elder men, that were at Jerusalem.

5   And the churches were confirmed in faith, and increased in number each day.

6   And they passed (through) Phrygia, and the country of Galatia, and were forbidden of the Holy Ghost to speak the word of God in Asia (or but they were forbidden by the Holy Spirit to speak the word of God in Asia).

7   And when they came to Mysia, they

assayed [or they attempted] to go into Bithynia, and the Spirit of Jesus suffered not them, [or and the Spirit of Jesus suffered them not], (or but the Spirit of Jesus did not allow them).

8 But when they had passed by Mysia, they came down to Troas;

9 and a vision by night, [or in (the) night], was showed to Paul. But a man of Macedonia [or Some man of Macedonia] that stood, prayed him (or beseeched him), and said, Go thou into Macedonia, and help us.

10 And as he had seen the vision, anon we sought to go forth into Macedonia (or at once we took action to go forth to Macedonia), and were made certain, that God had called us to preach [or to evangelize] to them.

11 And we went by ship from Troas, and came to Samothracia with straight course, [or Soothly we going by boat, *or sailing*, from Troas, with straight course came to Samothracia]; and the day (pur)suing to Neapolis (or and the following day to Neapolis);

12 and from thence to Philippi, that is the first part of Macedonia, the city colony. And we were in this city some days, and spake together.

13 And in the day of sabbaths we went forth without the gate beside the river, where prayer seemed to be [or where prayer was seen to be]; and we sat, and spake to women that came together.

14 And a woman, Lydia by name, a purpless of the city of Thyatira, worshipping God, heard; whose heart the Lord opened to give attention to these things, that were said of Paul.

15 And when she was baptized and her house, she prayed (or she beseeched us), and said, If ye have deemed that I am faithful to the Lord, enter ye into mine house, and dwell (there). And she constrained us.

16 And it was done, when we went to prayer, that a damsel [or a wench] that had a spirit of divination, met us, which gave great winning to her lords in divining, (or who brought much profit to her masters by her divining, or through her fortune-telling).

17 This **(woman)** (pur)sued Paul and us, and cried, and said, These men be servants of the high God, that tell to you the way of health. (She followed Paul and the rest of us, and cried, and said, These men be servants of the Most High God, who can tell you the way of salvation.)

18 And this she did in many days (or And she did this for many days). And Paul sorrowed, and turned, and said to the spirit, I command thee in the name of Jesus Christ, that thou go out of her. And he went out in the same hour.

19 And the lords of her saw, that the hope of their winning went away, and they took (hold of) Paul and Silas, and led [*them*] into the chapping, *either doom place*, to the princes. (And her masters saw, that their hope for more profit went away, and they took hold of Paul and Silas, and led *them* to the market, *or to the seat of judgement*, that is, the city square, to the city leaders.)

20 And they brought them to the magistrates, and said, These men disturb [or distrouble] our city, for they be Jews,

21 and show a custom, which [it] is not leaveful to us to receive (or which it is not lawful for us to accept), neither do, since we be Romans.

22 And the people and magistrates ran against them, and when they had rent to pieces the coats of them (or and when they had torn their coats to pieces), they commanded them to be beaten with rods.

23 And when they had given to them many wounds, they sent them into prison, and commanded to the keeper, that he should keep them diligently. (And after they had given them many wounds, they threw them into prison, and commanded the warden, that he should guard them carefully.)

24 And when he had taken such a precept, he put them into the inner prison, and

restrained the feet of them in a tree (or and restrained their feet in the stocks).

25 And at midnight Paul and Silas worshipped, and praised God; and they that were in [the] keeping (or and those who were in the prison), heard them.

26 And suddenly a great earth-moving was made, so that the foundaments of the prison were moved. And anon all the doors were opened, and the bonds of all were loosed. (And suddenly there was a great earthquake, so strong that the foundations of the prison were shaken. And at once all the doors were opened, and everyone's bonds were loosened.)

27 And the keeper of the prison was awaked (or And the warden was awakened), and saw the gates of the prison opened, and with a sword drawn out he would have slain himself, and guessed that the men that were bound had fled.

28 But Paul cried with a great voice, and said, Do thou none harm to thyself [or Do thou nothing of evil to thyself], for all we be here. (But Paul cried with a loud voice, and said, Do not harm thyself, for all of us still be here.)

29 And he asked (for) light, and entered [in], and trembled, and fell down to Paul and to Silas at *their* feet.

30 And he brought them withoutforth, and said, Lords, what behooveth me to do, that I be made safe? (And he brought them outside, and said, Lords, what must I do, so that I can be saved?)

31 And they said, Believe thou in the Lord Jesus, and thou shalt be safe, and thine house. (And they said, Believe in the Lord Jesus, and thou, and thy family, shall be saved.)

32 And they spake to him the word of the Lord, with all that were in his house.

33 And he took them in the same hour of the night, and washed their wounds. And he was baptized, and all his house anon, (or And he, and his whole family, or and all his household, were baptized at once).

34 And when he had brought them into his house, he set to them a board. And he was glad with all his house, and believed to God. (And when he had brought them into his house, he set a table for them, or he gave them a meal. And he had joy with all his household, and believed in God.)

35 And when (the) day was come, the magistrates sent constables, and said, Deliver thou those men [or Dismiss ye those men].

36 And the keeper of the prison told these words to Paul, That the magistrates have sent, that ye be delivered; now therefore go ye out, and go ye in peace. (And the warden of the prison said to Paul, The magistrates have sent word, that ye should be released; and so now go out, and go thy way in peace.)

37 And Paul said to them, They sent us men of Rome into prison, that were beaten openly and uncondemned, and now privily they bring us out; not so (fast), but come they themselves, and deliver us out, (or no! let them come here themselves, and release us).

38 And the constables told these words to the magistrates; and they dreaded, for they heard that they were Romans, (or and they had great fear, when they learned that they were Romans).

39 And they came, and besought them, and they brought them out, and prayed, that they should go out of the city. (And so they came, and found them, and they brought them out, and beseeched them, that they would go away from their city.)

40 And they went out of the prison, and entered [in]to (the house of) Lydia. And when they saw (the) brethren, they comforted them, and went forth. (And they left the prison, and went to Lydia's house. And when they saw the brothers, they strengthened or encouraged them, and then they went forth.)

CHAPTER 17

1 And when they had passed by Amphipolis

and Apollonia, they came to Thessalonica, where was a synagogue of (the) Jews.

2　And by custom Paul entered to them, and by three sabbaths he declared to them of the scriptures, (And as was his custom, Paul went to them, and on three Sabbaths he declared the Scriptures to them,)

3　and opened, and showed that it behooved Christ to suffer, and rise again from death, [or to suffer, and rise again from (the) dead], and that this is Jesus Christ, whom I tell to you. (and expounded upon them, and showed that it behooved the Messiah to suffer, and to rise again from the dead, and that this is Jesus Christ, about whom I tell you.)

4　And some of them believed, and were joined to Paul and to Silas; and a great multitude of heathen men worshipped God, and noble women not a few.

5　But the Jews had envy, and took of (or from) the common people some evil men, and when they had made a company, they moved the city. And they came to Jason's house, and sought to bring *them* forth among the people (or out to the people).

6　And when they found them not, they drew Jason and some brethren to the princes of the city, and cried, That these it be, that moved the world, and hither they came, (And when they found them not, they dragged Jason and some of the brothers to the leaders of the city, and cried, These it be, who stirred up the world, and now they have come here,)

7　whom Jason received. And these all do against the commandments of the emperor [or against the commandments of Caesar], and say, that Jesus is another king.

8　And they moved the people, and the princes of the city, hearing these things. (And they stirred up the people, and the leaders of the city, when they heard these things.)

9　And when satisfaction was taken of Jason, and of others, they let Paul and Silas go.

10　And anon by night, (the) brethren let [Paul and] Silas go into Berea, [or (the) brethren sent Paul and Silas into Berea], (or And at once in the night, the brothers sent Paul and Silas to Berea). And when they came thither, they entered into the synagogue of the Jews.

11　But these were the worthier [or the nobler] of them that be at Thessalonica, which received the word with all desire, each day seeking [the] scriptures, if these things had them so.

12　And many of them believed, and of heathen women honest and men not a few (or and more than a few honourable heathen men and women). [And soothly many of them believed, and of honest heathen women and men not (a) few.]

13　But when the Jews in Thessalonica had known, that also at Berea the word of God was preached of Paul (or that also at Berea the word of God was preached by Paul), they came thither, moving and disturbing [or distroubling] the multitude.

14　And then anon (the) brethren delivered [or dismissed] Paul, that he should go to the sea; but Silas and Timothy dwelt there. (And then at once the brothers sent off Paul, so that he could go down to the seacoast; but Silas and Timothy remained there.)

15　And they that led forth Paul, led him to Athens. And when they had taken a commandment of him to Silas and Timothy (or And when they had received an order from him for Silas and Timothy), that full hieingly they should come to him, they went forth.

16　And while Paul abode them at Athens (or And while Paul waited for them in Athens), his spirit was moved in him, for he saw the city given to idolatry.

17　Therefore he disputed in the synagogue with the Jews, and with men that worshipped God, and in the doom place, [or in the chapping], by all days to them that heard. (And so he disputed in the synagogue with the Jews, and with the men who worshipped God, and also in the city square, or at the market, every day with all those who would listen.)

18   And some Epicureans, and Stoics, and philosophers disputed with him. And some said, What will this sower of words say? And others said, He seemeth to be a teller of new fiends; for he told to them (of) Jesus, and (of) the again-rising, (or for he told them about Jesus, and about the resurrection).

19   And they took, and led him to Areopagus, [*that is*, *a common school*], and said, May we know, what is this new doctrine, that is said of thee?

20   For thou bringest in some new things to our ears; therefore we will know, what these things will be.

21   For all men of Athens and comelings (or newcomers) harboured (there), gave attention to none other thing, but either to say, either to hear, some new thing.

22   And Paul stood in the middle of Areopagus, and said, Men of Athens, by all things I see you as vain (or as futile) worshippers.

23   For I passed (by), and saw your maumets, [or your simulacra], (or and I saw your idols), and found an altar, in which was written, To the unknown God. Therefore which thing ye unknowing (or not knowing) worship, (or which ye worship in ignorance), this thing I (shall) show to you.

24   God that made the world and all things that be in it, this (God), for he is (the) Lord of heaven and earth, dwelleth not in temples made with hand [or made by hand],

25   neither is worshipped by man's hands, neither hath need of anything, for he giveth life to all men, and breathing, and all things;

26   and made of one all the kind of men to inhabit on all the face of the earth, determining times ordained, and (the) terms of the dwelling [or of the habitation] of them,

27   to seek God, if peradventure they feel him, either find (him), though he be not far from each of you.

28   For in him we live, and move, and be. As also some of your poets said, And we be also the kind [or the kin] of him.

29   Therefore since we be the kind [or the kin] of God, we shall not deem [or guess] that (a) godly thing is like gold, and silver, either stone, either to (the) (en)graving of craft and thought of man.

30   For God despiseth the times of this uncunning, and now showeth to men, that all everywhere do penance; (For God despiseth the times of this unknowing, or this ignorance, and now showeth to all, so that everyone everywhere shall repent;)

31   for that he hath ordained a day, in which he shall deem the world in equity (or on which he shall judge the world with fairness), in a man in which he ordained, and gave faith to all men, and raised him from death [or raising him from (the) dead].

32   And when they had heard (of) the again-rising of dead men, [or Soothly when they had heard (of) the again-rising of (the) dead], (or And when they had heard of the resurrection of the dead), some scorned, and some said, We shall hear thee again of this thing.

33   So Paul went out of the middle of them. (And then Paul went away from their midst.)

34   But some men drew [or cleaved] to him, and believed. Among which Dionysius Areopagite *was*, and a woman, by name Damaris, and other men with them.

CHAPTER 18

1   After these things Paul went out of Athens, and came to Corinth.

2   And he found a man, a Jew, Aquila by name, of Pontus by kind, that (of) late came from Italy, and Priscilla, his wife, for that Claudius commanded all Jews to depart from Rome; and he came to them.

3   And for that he was of the same craft, he dwelled with them, and wrought; and they

were of rope-makers craft [or soothly they were of tent-makers craft, *that is, to make coverings to* (or for) *travelling men*].

4 And he disputed in the synagogue by each sabbath, putting among (them) the name of the Lord Jesus; and he counselled (the) Jews and Greeks.

5 And when Silas and Timothy came from Macedonia, Paul gave busyness to the word, and witnessed to the Jews, that Jesus is Christ, (or and testified to the Jews, that Jesus is the Messiah).

6 But when they gainsaid and blasphemed, he shook away his clothes, [or he shook off his clothes], (or he shook out his clothes), and said to them, Your blood *be* on your head; I shall be clean from henceforth, and I shall go to (the) heathen men (or to the Gentiles).

7 And he passed from thence, and entered into the house of a just man, Titus by name, that worshipped God, whose house was joined to the synagogue.

8 And Crispus, (the) prince of the synagogue, believed to the Lord, with all his house. And many of the Corinthians heard, and believed, and were christened. (And Crispus, the leader of the synagogue, believed in the Lord, with all his house. And many of the Corinthians heard, and believed, and were baptized.)

9 And the Lord said by night to Paul by a vision, Do not thou dread, but speak, and be not still; (And the Lord said to Paul one night in a vision, Do not fear, or Fear not, but continue to speak, and do not be silent;)

10 for I am with thee, and no man shall be put to thee to harm thee, for much people is to me in this city (or for many people be with me in this city).

11 And he dwelled there a year and six months, teaching among them the word of God.

12 But when Gallio was proconsul of Achaia, [the] Jews rose up with one will against Paul, and led him to the doom (place), (or and led him to the seat of judgement or the court),

13 and said, Against the law this (man) counseleth men to worship God.

14 And when Paul began to open his mouth, Gallio said to the Jews, If there were any wicked thing, either evil trespass [or worst trespass], ye Jews, rightly I should suffer you, (or certainly I would allow you to present your case);

15 but if questions be of the word, and of (the) names of your law, busy yourselves [or ye yourselves see]; I will not be doomsman of these things (or I will not be the judge of these matters).

16 And he drove them from the doom place.

17 And all took Sosthenes, (the) prince of the synagogue, and smote him before the doom place; and nothing of these was to care to Gallio. (And all the people took hold of Sosthenes, the leader of the synagogue, and beat him there in front of the seat of judgement or the court; but none of this was of any concern to Gallio.)

18 And when Paul had abided many days, he said farewell to (the) brethren, and by boat came to Syria. And Priscilla and Aquila came with him, which had clipped his head in Cenchrea; for he had a vow.

19 And he came to Ephesus, and there he left them (or and he departed from them there); and he went into the synagogue, and disputed with (the) Jews.

20 And when they prayed (him), that he should dwell more time (there), he consented not, (And when they beseeched him, that he would spend more time there, he would not agree to it,)

21 but he made farewell to (the) brethren, and said, [It behooveth me to make the solemn day coming at Jerusalem, and (then)] again I shall turn again to you, (or and then I shall return to you), if God will [or God willing]; and he went forth from Ephesus.

22 And he came down to Caesarea, and he

went up, and greeted the church, and came down to Antioch.

23 And when he had dwelled there somewhat of time, he went forth, walking by row [or walking by order] through the country of Galatia, and (then) Phrygia, and confirmed all the disciples.

24 But a Jew, Apollos by name, a man of Alexandria of kind, a man eloquent (or an eloquent man), came to Ephesus; *and he was* mighty in (the) scriptures.

25 This man was taught the way of the Lord, and was fervent in spirit, and spake, and taught diligently those things that were of Jesus, and knew only the baptism of John (or but he only knew of the baptism by John).

26 And this man began to do trustily in the synagogue. Whom when Priscilla and Aquila heard, they took him, and more diligently expounded to him the way of the Lord.

27 And when he would go to Achaia, (the) brethren (were) excited [or (the) brethren admonished, *or counselled*], and wrote to the disciples, that they should receive him; which when he came, gave much to them that believed.

28 For he greatly overcame (the) Jews, and showed openly by (the) scriptures, that Jesus is Christ (or that Jesus is the Messiah).

CHAPTER 19

1 And it befell, when Apollos was at Corinth, that Paul when he had gone (to) the higher coasts, he came to Ephesus, and found some of the disciples (there).

2 And he said to them, Whether ye that believe have received the Holy Ghost? And they said to him, But neither have we heard [or But neither we have heard], if the Holy Ghost is. (And he said to them, Have ye who believe received the Holy Spirit? And they said to him, None of us have heard that there is a Holy Spirit?)

3 And he said, Therefore in what thing be ye baptized? And they said, In the baptism of John.

4 And Paul said, John baptized the people in the baptism of penance (or John baptized the people with a baptism of repentance), and taught, that they should believe in him that was to coming after him, [or and taught, that they should believe into him that was to come after him], that is, in Jesus.

5 When they heard these things, they were baptized in the name of the Lord Jesus.

6 And when Paul had laid on them his hands, the Holy Ghost came into them [or the Holy Ghost came (up)on them], and they spake with languages, and prophesied. (And when Paul had laid his hands on them, the Holy Spirit came upon them, and they spoke in strange and ecstatic tongues, and prophesied.)

7 And all were almost twelve men.

8 And he went into the synagogue, and spake with trust (for) three months, disputing and treating, [or softly moving], of the kingdom of God (or arguing about and quietly discussing the Kingdom of God).

9 But when some were harded [or were made hard], and believed not, and cursed the way of the Lord before the multitude, he went away from them, and separated (or set apart) the disciples, and disputed in the school of a mighty man each day.

10 This was done by two years, so that all that dwelled in Asia heard the word of the Lord, Jews and heathen men. (This was done for two years, so that all who lived in Asia heard the word of the Lord, yea, both Jews and Gentiles.)

11 And God did virtues not small [or little] by the hand of Paul, (And God did works of power or miracles, that were not small or insignificant, by Paul's hand,)

12 so that on sick men the sudaria, [or *sweating clothes*], (or napkins), were borne from his body, and sicknesses departed from them, and wicked spirits went out.

13   But also some of the Jewish exorcists went about, and assayed [or attempted] to [in-]call the name of the Lord Jesus Christ on them that had evil spirits, and said, I conjure you by Jesus, whom Paul preacheth.

14   And there were [some] seven sons of a Jew, Sceva, a prince of (the) priests (or a high priest), that did this thing.

15   But the evil spirit answered, and said to them, I know Jesus, and I know Paul; but who be ye?

16   And the man in which was the worst devil, leaped on them, and had victory [or lordship] on both (or over all of them), and was (so) strong against them, that they naked and wounded fled away from that house.

17   And this thing was made known to all the Jews and heathen men, that dwelled at Ephesus; and dread fell down on them all, and they magnified the name of the Lord Jesus. (And this was made known to all the Jews and Gentiles, who lived in Ephesus; and fearful reverence fell upon them, and they magnified the name of the Lord Jesus.)

18   And many men believed, and came, acknowledging and telling their deeds.

19   And many of them that (pur)sued curious things, brought together (their) books, and burned them before all (the) men; and when the prices of those were accounted, they found money of fifty thousand pence; (And many of them who followed curious things, brought together all their books, and burned them before everyone; and when the value of those books was reckoned, they found that they were worth about fifty thousand pence;)

20   so strongly the word of God waxed, (or grew, or spread), and was confirmed.

21   And when these things were [ful]filled, Paul purposed in spirit, after that Macedonia was passed (through) and Achaia (also), to go to Jerusalem, and said, For after that I shall be there, it behooveth me also to see Rome [or it behooveth me to see also Rome].

22   And he sent into Macedonia two *men*, that ministered to him (or who served him), Timothy, and Erastus, and he dwelled for a time in Asia.

23   And a great troubling was made in that day, of the way of the Lord [or in the way of the Lord].

24   For a man, Demetrius by name, a worker in silver, made silver houses to Diana, [*that is, a false goddess*], and gave to craftsmen much winning (or great profit);

25   which he called together them that were such manner workmen, and said, Men, ye know that of this craft winning is to us, (or Men, ye know that from this craft there is great profit for us);

26   and ye see and hear, that this Paul counseleth and turneth away much people, not only of Ephesus, but almost of all Asia, and said, that they be not gods, that be made with hands.

27   And not only this part shall be in peril to us, to come into reproof, but also the temple of the great Diana shall be accounted into nought (or but even the temple of the great Diana shall be reckoned as worthless); yea, and the majesty of her shall begin to be destroyed [or but and the majesty of her shall be destroyed], whom all Asia and the world worshippeth.

28   When these things were heard, they were [full-]filled with ire, and cried, and said, Great *is* the Diana of the Ephesians.

29   And the city was filled with confusion, and they made an assault with one will into the theatre, and took Gaius and Aristarchus, men of Macedonia, (and) fellows of Paul.

30   And when Paul would have entered into the people, the disciples suffered not. (And when Paul wanted to go out to the people, the disciples would not allow him to go.)

31   And also some of the princes of Asia, that were his friends, sent to him, and prayed (him), that he should not give himself into the theatre. (And also some of the leaders of Asia, who

were his friends, sent word to him, and beseeched him, so that he himself would not go to the theatre.)

32 And other men cried other thing(s); for the church was confused, and many knew not for what cause they were come together.

33 But of the people they drew away one Alexander, while (the) Jews putted him forth. And Alexander asked with his hand silence, and would yield reason to the people.

34 And as they knew that he was a Jew, one voice of all (the) men was made, crying as by twain (or by two) hours, Great *is* Diana of (the) Ephesians.

35 And when the scribe, *that is, a town clerk*, had ceased the people, he said, Men of Ephesus, what man is he, that knoweth not, that the city of Ephesians is the worshipper of the great Diana, and of the child of Jupiter?

36 Therefore when it may not be gainsaid to these things, it behooveth you to be ceased [or to be assuaged], and to do nothing follily; (And so since these things cannot be denied, or argued against, it behooveth you to cease your uproar, and to do nothing foolish;)

37 for ye have brought these men, neither sacrilegers, neither blaspheming your goddess.

38 That if Demetrius, and the workmen that be with him, have cause against any man, there be courts, and dooms, and judges; accuse they each other (there).

39 If ye seek aught of any other thing, it may be absolved in the lawful church, (or it can be resolved, or settled, in a lawful assembly).

40 For why we be in peril to be reproved of this day's dissension [or sedition], since no man is guilty, of whom we may yield (a) reason of this running together.

41 And when he had said this thing, he let the people go.

CHAPTER 20

1 And after [that] the noise (had) ceased, Paul called the disciples, and admonished them, and said farewell; and he went forth, to go into Macedonia.

2 And when he had walked by those coasts [or those parts], and had admonished them by many words, he came to Greece.

3 Where when he had been (there) three months, the Jews laid ambush for him, that was to sail into Syria; and he had counsel to turn again by Macedonia. (And when he had been there for three months, the Jews laid ambush for him, as he was about to sail to Syria; and so he made plans to return by way of Macedonia.)

4 And Sopater of Pyrri Berea (pur)sued him (or And Sopater the son of Pyrrhus, from Berea, followed him); of (the) Thessalonians, Aristarchus, and Secundus, and Gaius Derbeus, and Timothy; and (the) Asians, Tychicus and Trophimus.

5 These (men) for they went before, abode us at Troas. (And because these men went ahead of us, they waited for us at Troas.)

6 For we shipped after the days of therf loaves from Philippi (or For we set sail from Philippi after the Feast of Unleavened Bread), and came to them at Troas in five days, where we dwelt seven days.

7 And in the first day of the week (or And on the first day of the week), when we came to break bread, Paul disputed with them, and should go forth in the morrow; and he drew along the sermon till into midnight.

8 And many lamps were in the solar (or And there were many lamps in the upper room), where we were gathered together.

9 And a young man, Eutychus by name, sat on the window, (and) when he was fallen into an heavy sleep, while Paul disputed long, all sleeping he fell down from the third stage; and he was taken up, and was brought (in) dead.

10 To whom when Paul came down, he lay on him, and embraced (him), and said, Do not ye be troubled; for his soul is in him.

11 And he went up, and brake bread, and

ate, and spake enough unto the day [or till into the light]; and so he went forth.

12 And they brought the child alive, and they were comforted greatly. (And they brought the young man home alive, and they were greatly comforted.)

13 And we went up into a ship, and shipped into Assos, to take Paul from thence; for so he had assigned [or he had disposed] to make (the) journey by land.

14 And when he found us in Assos, we took him, and came to Mitylene.

15 And from thence we shipped in the day (pur)suing, and we came against Chios, and another day we havened at Samos, and in the day (pur)suing, we came to Miletus. (And we sailed from there on the following day, and we came opposite Chios, and the next day we havened at Samos, and on the following day, we came to Miletus.)

16 And Paul purposed to ship over to Ephesus, lest any tarrying were made to him in Asia; for he hied, if it were possible to him, that he should be in the day of Pentecost at Jerusalem, (or for he made haste, so that if it was possible for him, he would be in Jerusalem on the Day of Pentecost).

17 From Miletus he sent to Ephesus, and called the greatest men of birth [or the more through birth, *either the elder men*], of the church.

18 And when they came to him, and were together, he said to them, Ye know from the first day, in which I came into Asia, how with you by each time I was,

19 serving to the Lord with all meekness, and mildness, and tears, and temptations, that felled to me of (the) ambushings of (the) Jews; (serving the Lord with all humility, amid the tears, and tests, that came to me from the ambushing of the Jews;)

20 how I withdrew not [or nought] of profitable things to you, that I told not to you, and taught you openly, and by houses; (how I

kept nothing profitable from you, yea, that I did not tell you, but rather, I taught you openly, or in public, and also in your homes;)

21 and I witnessed to Jews and to heathen men penance into God, and faith into our Lord Jesus Christ. (and I testified to Jews and to Gentiles alike, the need for repentance unto God, and faith in our Lord Jesus Christ.)

22 And now lo! I am bound in spirit, and go into Jerusalem; and I know not what things shall come to me in it,

23 [no] but that the Holy Ghost by all cities witnesseth to me, and saith, that bonds and tribulations at Jerusalem abide me. (except that the Holy Spirit in every city testifieth to me, that bondage, or imprisonment, and troubles await me in Jerusalem.)

24 But I dread nothing of these, neither I make my life preciouser than myself, so that I end, [*or fulfill*], my course, and the ministry of the word, which I received of the Lord Jesus, to witness the gospel of the grace of God. (But I fear none of that, nor do I make my life of any great value, I only desire that I fulfill my course, and the ministry of the word, which I received from the Lord Jesus, yea, to testify to the Gospel, or the Good News, of the grace of God.)

25 And now lo! I know, that ye shall no more see my face, all ye by which I passed (or all ye of whom I have been among), preaching the kingdom of God.

26 Wherefore I witness to you this day (or And so I testify to you this day), that I am clean of the blood of all men.

27 For I fled not away [or For I flew not away], that I told not to you all the counsel of God. (For I did not fly away, or hold anything back, so that I did not tell you all of God's plans.)

28 Take ye attention to you(rselves), and to all (of) the flock, in which the Holy Ghost hath set you, [or hath put you], (as) bishops (or among whom the Holy Spirit hath made you

overseers), to rule the church of God, which he purchased with his blood.

29   I know, that after my departing, ravening (or snatching) wolves shall enter into you, not sparing the flock;

30   and men speaking shrewd [or wayward] things shall rise (up out) of yourselves (or and men speaking depraved things shall rise up from among you), (so) that they lead away (the) disciples after them.

31   For which thing wake ye, holding in mind, (or For which thing be on watch, keeping in mind), that by three years night and day I ceased not, (along) with (my) tears, admonishing each of you.

32   And now I betake you to God and to the word of his grace, that is mighty to edify and give heritage in all that be made holy. (And now I deliver you unto God and unto the word of his grace, that is mighty to edify and to give an inheritance to all who be made holy.)

33   And of no man I coveted silver, and gold, either cloth (or cloak),

34   as [ye] yourselves know; for to those things that were needful to me, and to these that be with me, these hands ministered. (as you yourselves know; for my own hands served, or worked, to acquire those things that were needed by me, and by those who were with me.)

35   All these things I showed to you, for so it behooveth men travailing to receive sick men, and to have mind of the word of the Lord Jesus; for he said, It is more blissful to give, than to receive, [or It is more blessed to give, more than to receive]. (I showed all of these things to you, because it behooveth all of us who labour, to accept, or to help, the frail or the weak, and to remember the words of the Lord Jesus; for he said, It is more blessed to give, than to receive.)

36   And when he had said these things, he kneeled, and prayed with all (of) them.

37   And great weeping of all men was made; and they felled on the neck of Paul, and kissed him,

38   and sorrowed most(ly) in the word that he said, for they shall no more see his face. And (then) they led him to the ship.

CHAPTER 21

1   And when it was done, that we should sail, and were passed away from them, with straight course we came to Coos, and the day (pur)suing to Rhodes, and from thence to Patara, and from thence to Myra. (And it was done, that we should set sail, and when we were gone away from them, with straight course we came to Cos, and the following day to Rhodes, and from there to Patara, and from there to Myra.)

2   And when we found a ship passing over to Phenicia (or Phoenicia), we went up into it, and sailed forth.

3   And when we appeared to Cyprus, we left it at the left half, and sailed into Syria, and came to Tyre. For there the ship should be uncharged. (And when Cyprus appeared to us, we left it on the left side, or the port side, and sailed unto Syria, and came to Tyre. For the ship was to be unloaded there.)

4   And when we found (some) disciples, we dwelled there seven days; which said by (the Holy) Spirit to Paul, that he should not go up to Jerusalem.

5   And when the days were [ful]filled, we went forth, and all men with wives and children led forth us without the city; and we kneeled in the sea brink, and we prayed. (And when the days were fulfilled, we went forth, and all the men with their wives and children led us outside the city; and we kneeled on the seashore, and we prayed.)

6   And when we had made farewell together, we went up into the ship; and they turned again into their own places (or and they returned to their own homes).

7   And when the ship sailing was filled from

Tyre, we came down to Ptolemais, and when we had greeted well the brethren, we dwelled one day at them, (or and after we had warmly greeted the brothers, we stayed there one day with them).

8 And another day we went forth, and came to Caesarea. And we entered into the house of Philip (the) evangelist, that was one of the seven, and dwelled at him. (And the next day we went forth, and came to Caesarea. And we entered into the house of Philip the evangelist, who was one of the Seven, and stayed with him.)

9 And to him were four daughters, virgins, that prophesied.

10 And when we dwelled there some days, a prophet, Agabus by name, came over from Judea.

11 This (man) when he came to us, took (hold of) the girdle of Paul, and bound together his feet and hands, and said, The Holy Ghost saith these things, Thus [the] Jews shall bind in Jerusalem the man, whose is this girdle; and they shall betake *him* into heathen men's hands. (And when he came to us, he took hold of Paul's belt, and then bound up his own hands and feet with it, and said, The Holy Spirit saith these things, Thus shall the Jews in Jerusalem bind the man, whose belt this is; and they shall deliver *him* into the hands of the Gentiles.)

12 Which thing when we heard, we prayed, and they that were of that place, that he should not go up to Jerusalem (or that he would not go up to Jerusalem).

13 Then Paul answered, and said, What do ye, weeping and tormenting mine heart? (or Why be ye weeping, and tormenting my heart so?) For I am ready, not only to be bound, but also to die in Jerusalem for the name of the Lord Jesus.

14 And when we might not counsel him, we were still, and said, The will of the Lord be done.

15 And after these days we were made ready, and went up to Jerusalem. [Soothly after these days we made ready, ascended (or went up) to Jerusalem.]

16 And some of the disciples came with us from Caesarea, and led with them a man, Jason of Cyprus, an old disciple, at whom we should be harboured.

17 And when we came to Jerusalem, brethren received us willfully. (And when we arrived at Jerusalem, the brothers willingly, or gladly, received us.)

18 And in the day (pur)suing, Paul entered with us to James, and all the elder men were gathered (there). (And on the following day, Paul came with us to James, and all the elders were gathered there.)

19 Which when he had greeted (them), he told by all things, what [things] God had done in heathen men, by the ministry of him. (And when he had greeted them, he told them everything that God had done among the Gentiles, through his ministry.)

20 And when they heard, they magnified God, and said to him, Brother, thou seest how many thousands be in (the) Jews, that have believed to God, and all be lovers [or (pur)suers] of the law (or and all of them be ardent followers of the Law).

21 And they heard of thee, that thou teachest departing from Moses of those Jews that be by heathen men, that say, that they owe not to circumcise their sons, neither owe to enter by [or after] custom. (But they have heard about thee, that thou teachest going away from Moses for those Jews who live among the Gentiles, and say, that they ought not to circumcise their sons, nor ought to go after, or to follow, our customs.)

22 Therefore what is [this]? (or And so what is it?) It behooveth that the multitude come together; for they shall hear, that thou art come (here).

23 Therefore do thou this thing, that we say

to thee. There be to us four men, that have a vow on them.

24   Take thou these men, and hallow thee with them; hang on them, that they shave their heads; and that all men know, that those things that they heard of thee be false, but that thou walkest, and thyself keepest the law. (Take these men, and purify thyself, along with them; yea, hang on them, so that they shave their heads; and so that all men know, that those things that they have heard about thee be false, and that thou walkest in, and thou obeyest, the Law.)

25   But of these that believed of heathen men (or But to those who believe among the Gentiles), we have written, deeming that they abstain them(selves) from thing(s) offered to idols, and from blood, and also from strangled thing(s), and from fornication.

26   Then Paul took the men, and in the day (pur)suing (or and on the following day), he was purified with them, and entered into the temple, and showed the [ful]filling of (the) days of purifying, till the offering was offered for each of them.

27   And when seven days were ended, the Jews that were of Asia, when they saw him in the temple, stirred all the people, and laid hands on him,

28   and cried, Men of Israel, help ye us. This is the man, that against the people and the law and this place teacheth everywhere all men, moreover and (he) hath led heathen men into the temple, and hath defouled this holy place. (and cried, Israelites, help us! This is the man, who teacheth everyone everywhere against our people and the Law and this place, and moreover he hath even led Gentiles into the Temple, and hath defiled this holy place.)

29   For they saw Trophimus of Ephesus in the city with him, whom they guessed that Paul had brought into the temple.

30   And all the city was moved, and a running together of the people was made. And they took Paul, and drew (or dragged) him out of the temple; and anon the gates were closed (or and at once the Temple gates were closed).

31   And when they sought to slay him, it was told to the tribune of the company of knights, that all Jerusalem is confounded. (And when they tried to kill him, it was told to the commander of the company of the soldiers stationed there, that all of Jerusalem was in an uproar.)

32   Which anon took knights, and centurions, and ran to them. And when they had seen the tribune, and the knights, they ceased to smite Paul. (Who at once took some soldiers, and centurions, and ran to them. And when they had seen the commander, and the soldiers, they ceased to strike Paul.)

33   Then the tribune came, and caught (hold of) him, and commanded, that he were bound with two chains; and asked, who he was, and what he had done.

34   But others cried other thing(s) among the people. And when he might know no certain thing for the noise/And when he might not know (any) certain thing for the noise, he commanded him to be led into the castles (or he commanded that he be brought into the fortress).

35   And when Paul came to the grees, it befell that he was borne of (the) knights, for (the) strength of the people. (And when Paul came to the steps, it befell that he had to be carried by the soldiers, because of the pressing of the people.)

36   For the multitude of the people (pur)sued him (or For the crowd followed him), and cried, Take him away.

37   And when Paul began to be led into the castles, he said to the tribune, Whether it is leaveful to me, to speak anything to thee? And he said, Knowest thou Greek? (And as Paul was brought into the fortress, he said to the commander, Is it lawful for me, to say anything to thee? And he asked, Knowest thou how to

speak Greek?)

38   Whether thou art not the Egyptian, which before these days movedest a noise, and leddest out into (the) desert four thousand of men, menslayers? (Art thou not that Egyptian, who before these days caused a commotion, and led out into the desert four thousand men, all murderers?)

39   And Paul said to him, For I am a Jew, of Tarsus of Cilicia, a citizen, which city is not unknown. And I pray thee, suffer me to speak to the people, (or And I beseech thee, allow me to speak to the people).

40   And when he suffered (him), Paul stood in the grees, and beckoned with the hand to the people, (or And when he allowed him to speak, Paul stood on the steps, and beckoned with his hand to the people). And when a great silence was made, he spake in Hebrew tongue, and said,

CHAPTER 22

1   Brethren and fathers, hear ye what reason I yield now to you.

2   And when some heard that in (the) Hebrew tongue he spake to them, they gave the more silence [or they gave more silence]. And he said,

3   I am a man a Jew, born at Tarsus of Cilicia, nourished and in this city beside the feet of Gamaliel [or nourished forsooth in this city beside the feet of Gamaliel], taught by the truth of (our) fathers' law, a lover [or a (pur)suer] of the law, (or an ardent follower of the Law), as also ye all be today.

4   And I pursued this way till to the death, binding [together] and betaking into holds men and women, (And I persecuted the followers of this way unto the death, taking them captive, and delivering them to prison, yea, both men and women,)

5   as the prince of priests yieldeth witnessing to me, and all the greatest of birth [or and all

the more in birth]. Of whom also I took epistles to (the) brethren, and went to Damascus, to bring from thence men bound into Jerusalem, that they should be pained. (as the High Priest, and all the greatest of birth, or the elders, have testified about me. And from whom I took letters to the brothers, and went to Damascus, to bring back to Jerusalem from there men in bondage, so that they could be punished.)

6   And it was done, while I went, and nighed to Damascus (or and approached to Damascus), at midday suddenly from heaven a great plenty of light [or a copious light] shone about me.

7   And I felled down to the earth, and heard a voice from heaven, saying to me, Saul, Saul, what pursuest thou me? It is hard to thee, to kick against the prick, [⁺or It is hard for thee, to kick against the prick]. (And I fell down to the ground, and heard a voice from heaven, saying to me, Saul, Saul, why persecutest thou me? It is hard for thee, to kick against the prod.)

8   And I answered, Who art thou Lord? And he said to me, I am Jesus of Nazareth, whom thou pursuest, (or I am Jesus of Nazareth, whom thou persecutest).

9   And they that were with me saw but the light, but they heard not the voice of him, that spake with me, (or but they did not hear the voice of him, who spoke with me).

10   And I said, Lord, what shall I do? And the Lord said to me, Rise thou, and go to Damascus; and there it shall be said to thee, of all (the) things which it behooveth thee to do.

11   And when I saw not, for the clarity of that light, I was led by the hand of fellows, and I came to Damascus. (And when I saw not, because of the brightness of that light, I was led by the hands of my fellows, and I came to Damascus.)

12   And a man, Ananias, that by the law had (the) witnessing of all (the) Jews dwelling in Damascus, (And a man, Ananias, who lived by the Law, and received good testimony from all

the Jews living in Damascus,)

13   came to me, and stood nigh, and said to me, Saul, brother, behold. And I in the same hour beheld into him (or And at that very moment I saw him).

14   And he said, (The) God of our fathers hath before-ordained thee, that thou shouldest know the will of him, and shouldest see the rightful man, [that is, (the) just *Christ*], and hear the voice of his mouth.

15   For thou shalt be his witness to all men, of those things that thou hast seen and heard.

16   And now, what dwellest thou? (or And now, why waitest thou?) Rise up, and be baptized, and wash away thy sins, by the name of him called to help, [or Rise up, and be baptized, and wash away thy sins, (and) in-call the name of him].

17   And it was done to me, as I turned again into Jerusalem (or after I returned to Jerusalem), and prayed in the temple, that I was made in (a) ravishing of (the) soul,

18   and I saw him saying to me, Hie thou, and go out fast of Jerusalem, for they shall not receive thy witnessing of me. (and I saw him saying to me, Haste thou, and quickly go out of Jerusalem, for they shall not accept thy testimony about me.)

19   And I said, Lord, they know, that I was (en)closing together in prison, and beating by synagogues them that believed into thee [or and beating by synagogues them that believed in thee]. (And I said, Lord, they know, that I was enclosing in prison, and beating in the synagogues, those who believed in thee.)

20   And when the blood of Stephen, thy witness, was shed out, I stood nigh, and consented, and kept the clothes of (the) men that slew him.

21   And he said to me, Go thou, for I shall send thee far (away) to (the) nations.

22   And they heard him till [to] this word; and they raised their voice, and said, Take away from the earth such a manner man; for it is not

leaveful that he live. (And they listened to him until this word; and then they raised up their voices, and said, Take away such a manner man from the earth; for it is not lawful that he live.)

23   And when they cried, and cast away their clothes, and threw dust in the air,

24   the tribune commanded him to be led into the castles, and to be beaten with scourges, and to be tormented, that he knew [or that he should know], for what cause they cried so to him. (the commander ordered him to be brought into the fortress, and then to be beaten with scourges, and to be tormented, so that he could know, for what reason they shouted so about him.)

25   And when they had bound him with cords [or And when they had restrained him with ropes], Paul said to a centurion standing nigh to him, Whether it is leaveful to you (or Is it lawful for you), to scourge a Roman, and (someone) uncondemned?

26   And when this thing was heard, the centurion went to the tribune, and told to him, and said, What art thou to doing? for this man is a citizen of Rome.

27   And the tribune came nigh, and said to him, Say thou to me, whether thou art a Roman? And he said, Yea.

28   And the tribune answered, I with much sum got this freedom. And Paul said, And I was born *a citizen of Rome.*

29   Therefore anon, they that should have tormented him, departed away from him. And the tribune dreaded, after that he knew, that he was a citizen of Rome, and for he had bound him [or and that he had bound him]. (And so at once, those who would have tormented him, went away from him. And the commander feared, after that he knew, that he was a citizen of Rome, and because he had bound him.)

30   But in the day (pur)suing he would know more diligently, for what cause he were accused of the Jews, and unbound him, and

commanded (the) priests and all the council to come together. And he brought forth Paul, and set him among them. (But on the following day, because he wanted to know, for what reason Paul was accused by the Jews, he unbound him, and commanded the priests and all the Council to come to him. And then he brought forth Paul, and set him among them.)

CHAPTER 23

1 And Paul beheld into the council (or And Paul looked at the Council), and said, Brethren, I with all good conscience have lived before God, till into this day.

2 And Ananias, (the) prince of priests, commanded to men that stood nigh to him, that they should smite his mouth. (And Ananias, the High Priest, commanded to the men who stood near to him, that they should strike him on his mouth.)

3 Then Paul said to him, Thou whited wall [or Thou wall made white], God [shall] smite thee; thou sittest, and deemest me by the law, and against the law thou commandest me to be smitten. (Then Paul said to him, Thou whitewashed wall, God shall strike thee; thou sittest, and judgest me by the Law, and then against the Law thou commandest me to be struck?)

4 And they that stood nigh, said, Cursest thou the highest priest of God? [or Cursest thou the high priest of God?] (And they who stood nearby, said, Cursest thou the High Priest of God?)

5 And Paul said, Brethren, I knew not, that he is [the] prince of priests; for it is written, Thou shalt not curse the prince of thy people. (And Paul said, Brothers, I did not know, that he is the High Priest; for it is written, Thou shalt not curse the leader of thy people.)

6 But Paul knew, that one part was of (the) Sadducees, and the other (was) of (the) Pharisees; and he cried in the council, Brethren,

I am a Pharisee, the son of Pharisees; I am deemed of the hope and of the again-rising of dead *men*, [or of the hope and (the) again-rising of (the) dead I am deemed], (or I am on trial over the hope for the resurrection of the dead).

7 And when he had said this thing, dissension was made betwixt the Pharisees and the Sadducees, and the multitude was parted (or and so the gathering was divided).

8 For (the) Sadducees say, that no rising again of dead men is, (or For the Sadducees say, that there is no resurrection of the dead), neither angel, neither spirit; but (the) Pharisees acknowledge ever either. [+Forsooth Sadducees say, that no rising again is of (the) dead, neither angel, neither spirit; forsooth Pharisees acknowledge both.]

9 And a great cry was made. And some of the Pharisees rose up, and fought, saying, We find nothing of evil in this man; what if a spirit, either an angel, spake to him?

10 And when great dissension was made, the tribune dreaded, lest Paul should be drawn to pieces of them; and he commanded knights to go down, and to take [or to ravish] him (away) from the middle of them, and to lead him into the castles. (And when great dissension was made, the commander feared, lest Paul should be drawn to pieces by them; and he commanded some soldiers to go down, and to snatch him from their midst, and to bring him into the fortress.)

11 And in the night (pur)suing the Lord stood nigh to him, and said, Be thou steadfast; for as thou hast witnessed of me in Jerusalem, so it behooveth thee to witness also at Rome. (And on the following night the Lord stood near to him, and said, Be thou resolute; for as thou hast testified about me in Jerusalem, it behooveth thee to also testify about me in Rome.)

12 And when the day was come, some of the Jews gathered them(selves), and made a vow, and said, that they should neither eat, nor drink, till they slew Paul.

13 And there were more than forty men, that made this swearing together [or this conjuration]. (And there were more than forty men, who formed this conspiracy.)

14 And they went to the princes of (the) priests, and elder men, (or And they went to the high priests, and the elders), and said, With devotion we have avowed [us], that we shall not taste anything, till we have slain Paul.

15 Now therefore make ye known to the tribune (or And so make it known to the commander), with the council, that he bring him forth to you, as if ye should know something more certainly of him; and we (shall) be ready to slay him, before that he come [nigh].

16 And when the son of Paul's sister had heard (of) the ambush [or the treason], he came, and entered into the castles (or into the fortress), and told to Paul.

17 And Paul called to him(self) one of the centurions, and said, Lead this young man to the tribune, for he hath something to show to him, (or Lead this young man to the commander, for he hath something to tell him).

18 And he took him, and led to the tribune, and said, Paul, that is bound, prayed me to lead to thee this young man, that hath something to speak to thee. (And he took him, and brought him to the commander, and said, Paul, who is bound, beseeched me to bring this young man to thee, for he hath something to say to thee.)

19 And the tribune took his hand, and went with him asides half, and asked him, What thing is it, that thou hast to show to me? (And the commander took his hand, and drew him aside, and asked him, What is it, that thou hast to tell me?)

20 And he said, The Jews be accorded to pray thee (or The Jews be in agreement to beseech thee), that tomorrow thou bring forth Paul into the council, as if they should inquire something more certainly of him.

21 But believe thou not to them; for more than forty men of them ambush him, which have avowed, that they shall neither eat nor drink, till they slay him; and now they be ready, abiding thy promise.

22 Therefore the tribune left the young man (or And so the commander let the young man go, or dismissed him), and commanded, that he should speak to no man, that he had made these things known to him.

23 And he called together two centurions, and he said to them, Make ye ready two hundred knights, that they go to Caesarea, and horsemen seventy, and spearmen two hundred, from the third hour of the night. (And he called together two centurions, and he said to them, Make ready two hundred soldiers, so that they can go to Caesarea, and seventy horsemen, and two hundred spearmen, at nine o'clock this evening.)

24 And make ye ready an horse, for Paul to ride on, to lead him safe to Felix, the president. For the tribune dreaded, lest the Jews would take him by the way, and slay him, and afterward he might be challenged, as (if) he had taken money. (And prepare a horse, for Paul to ride on, and lead him safely to Governor Felix. Because the commander feared, that the Jews might take hold of him on the way, and kill him, and afterward he might be challenged, that he had received some money.)

25 [And] He wrote to him an epistle, containing these things.

26 Claudius Lysias to the best Felix, president, health. (Claudius Lysias to the most excellent Governor Felix, greetings and best wishes.)

27 This man that was taken (hold) of (by) the Jews, and began to be slain, I came upon them with mine host (or I came upon them with my army), and delivered him from them, when I knew that he was a Roman.

28 And I would know the cause, which they putted against him; and I led him [in] to the council of them (or and I brought him in to

their Council).

29   And I found, that he was accused of questions of their law, but he had no crime worthy (of) the death, either (of) bonds (or of bondage, or imprisonment).

30   And when it was told me of the ambush, that they (had) arrayed for him, [or And when it was told to me of the treasons, that they (had) made ready to him], I sent him to thee, and I warned also the accusers, that they say at thee, (or and I have told his accusers, that they must tell their charges to thee). Farewell.

31   And so the knights (or the soldiers) as they were commanded, took Paul, and led him by night into Antipatris.

32   And in the day (pur)suing, when the horsemen were left, that should go with him, they turned again to the castles. (And on the following day, the soldiers returned to the fortress, leaving the horsemen, who would go with him.)

33   And when they came to Caesarea, they took the epistle to the president, and they set also Paul before him. (And when they arrived at Caesarea, they delivered the letter to the Governor, and they also put Paul before him.)

34   And when he had read, and asked, of what province he was, and knew that he was of Cilicia,

35   I shall hear thee, he said, when thine accusers come. And he commanded him to be kept in the moot hall of Herod (or And he commanded that Paul be kept in Herod's Judgement Hall, in his palace).

CHAPTER 24

1   And after five days, Ananias, prince of priests, came down with some elder men, and Tertullus, a fair speaker, [or an orator, or an advocate], which went to the president against Paul. (And five days later, Ananias, the High Priest, came down with some elders, and Tertullus, an advocate, and they went before the Governor against Paul.)

2   And when Paul was summoned, Tertullus began to accuse him, and said, When in much peace we do by thee, and many things be amended by thy wisdom,

3   (for)evermore and everywhere, thou best Felix, we have received with all doing of thankings. (always and in every place, O most excellent Felix, we be most grateful for this opportunity.)

4   But lest I tarry thee longer, I pray thee, shortly hear us for thy meekness.

5   We have found this wicked man stirring dissension, to all (the) Jews in all the world, and (the) author of dissension of the sect of Nazarenes; [We have found this man bearing venom, or pestilence, and stirring sedition, or dissention, to all the Jews in all the world, and (the) author of sedition of the sect of Nazarenes;]

6   and he also enforced to defoul the temple; whom also we took (hold of), and would deem after our law. (and he also endeavored to defile the Temple; whom we then took hold of, and would judge according to our Law.)

7   But Lysias, the tribune, came above with great strength, and delivered him from [or out of] our hands; (But Lysias, the commander, came upon us with great strength, and delivered him out of our hands;)

8   and commanded his accusers to come to thee, of whom thou deeming (or of whom thou judging), mayest know of all these things, of which we accuse him.

9   And (the) Jews put to (or And the Jews agreed), and said, that these things had them so.

10   And Paul answered, when the president granted him to say, Of many years I know thee, that thou art doomsman to this folk, and I shall do enough for me with good reason. (And Paul answered, when the Governor allowed him to speak, For many years I know thee, that thou art the judge of these people, and I shall defend myself with sound reasoning.)

11   For thou mayest know, for to me be not

more than twelve days [or for to me be no more than twelve days], since I came up to worship in Jerusalem;

12 and neither in the temple they found me disputing with any man, neither making concourse of the people, neither in the synagogues, neither in (the) city;

13 neither they may prove to thee, of the which things they now accuse me. (nor can they prove to thee, the things of which they now accuse me.)

14 But I acknowledge to thee this thing, that after the sect which they say (to be) heresy, so I serve to God the Father, believing to all things that be written in the law and (the) prophets;

15 and I have hope in God, which also they themselves abide, the again-rising to coming of just men and wicked [or the again-rising to come of just men and wicked]. (and I have this hope in God, which they also wait for, yea, the resurrection to come of both the good or the righteous, and the wicked.)

16 In this thing I study without hurting, to have conscience to God, and to men (for)evermore. (In this thing I work diligently, to always have a clear conscience before God, and before men.)

17 But after many years, I came to do almsdeeds to my folk (or I came to give gifts of charity to my people), and offerings, and avows [or and vows];

18 in which they found me purified in the temple, not with company, neither with noise. And they caught (hold of) me, and they cried, and said, Take away our enemy. And some Jews of Asia,

19 which it behooved to be now present at thee, [or whom it behooved to be now present at thee], (or here before thee), and accuse (me), if they had anything against me,

20 either these themselves say, if they (have) found in me anything of wickedness, since I stand in the council,

21 but only of this [one] voice, by which I

cried standing among them, For of the again-rising of dead men [or For of the again-rising of (the) dead] I am deemed this day of you. (but only because of this one thing, which I cried out while standing among them, yea, Because of the resurrection of the dead I am judged, or I am on trial, this day before you.)

22 Soothly Felix delayed [or deferred] them, and knew most certainly of the way, and said, When Lysias, the tribune (or the commander), shall come down, I shall hear you.

23 And he commanded to a centurion to keep him, and that he had rest [or and to have (some) rest], neither to forbid any man to minister of his own things to him.

24 And after some days Felix came, with Drusilla his wife, that was a Jewess, and called Paul, and heard of him the faith that is in Christ Jesus (or and heard from him about faith in the Messiah Jesus).

25 And while he disputed of rightwiseness, and chastity, and of doom to coming [or and of doom to come], Felix was made trembling, and answered, That pertaineth now, go; but in time covenable, I shall call thee. (And while he disputed about righteousness, and love, and the judgement to come, Felix began to tremble, and answered, That pertaineth for now, now go; but at a suitable time, I shall call for thee again.)

26 Also he hoped, that money should be given to him of Paul (or And he hoped, that Paul would give him some money); for which thing again [or oft] he called him, and spake with him.

27 And when two years were [ful]filled, Felix took a successor, Porcius Festus; and Felix would give grace to the Jews, and left Paul bound, [or forsooth Felix willing to give grace to (the) Jews, left Paul bound].

CHAPTER 25

1 Therefore when Festus came into the

province, after the third day he went up to Jerusalem from Caesarea.

2   And the princes of (the) priests, and the worthiest [or the first] of the Jews went to him against Paul, and prayed him, (And the high priests, and the leaders of the Jews went before him against Paul, and beseeched him,)

3   and asked grace against him, that he should command him to be led to Jerusalem; and they set ambush to slay him in the way (or and they prepared to kill him on the way).

4   But Festus answered, that Paul should be kept in Caesarea; soothly that he himself should proceed more advisedly [or more hastily].

5   Therefore he said, They that in you (who) be mighty, come down together; and if any crime is in the man (or and if the man hath done any crime), accuse they him.

6   And he dwelled among them no more than eight either ten days, and came down to Caesarea; and the tother day he sat for doomsman (or and the next day he sat as judge), and commanded Paul to be brought (to him).

7   And when he was brought forth, (the) Jews stood about him, which came down from Jerusalem, putting against him many and grievous causes, which they might not prove. (And when he was brought forth, the Jews who had come down from Jerusalem, stood about him, making many serious charges against him, that they could not prove.)

8   For Paul yielded reason in all things, (saying), That neither against the law of (the) Jews, neither against the temple, neither against the emperor [or neither against Caesar], I sinned anything.

9   But Festus would do grace to the Jews [or Forsooth Festus (was) willing to give grace to the Jews], and answered to Paul, and said, Wilt thou go up to Jerusalem, and there be deemed of these things before me? (or and be judged about these things before me there?)

10   And Paul said, At the doom place of the emperor I stand [or At the doom place of Caesar I stand], where it behooveth me to be deemed, (or And Paul said, I stand now at the Emperor's seat of judgement or the court, where it behooveth me to be judged). I have not annoyed (or harmed) the Jews, as thou knowest well.

11   For if I have annoyed (or harmed), either done anything worthy (of) death, I forsake not to die; but if nothing of those is, that they accuse me (of), no man may give me to them. I appeal to the emperor [or I appeal to Caesar].

12   Then Festus spake with the council, and answered, (or Then Festus spoke with the Council, and said), To the emperor thou hast appealed, to the emperor thou shalt go, [or To Caesar thou hast appealed, to Caesar thou shalt go].

13   And when some days were passed, Agrippa king (or King Agrippa), and Bernice came down to Caesarea, to welcome [or to greet] Festus.

14   And when they dwelled there many days, Festus showed to the king of Paul, and said, A man is left bound of Felix, (And after they had been there for many days, Festus told the king about Paul, and said, There is a man left here in bondage by Felix,)

15   of which, when I was at Jerusalem, (the) princes of (the) priests, and the elder men of the Jews came to me, and asked damnation against him. (of whom, when I was at Jerusalem, the high priests, and the elders of the Jews came to me, and asked for condemnation against him.)

16   To whom I answered, That it is not custom to Romans, to damn any man, (or It is not the Roman custom, to condemn any man), before that he that is accused have his accusers present, and take (the) place of defending, to put away the crimes, that be put against *him*.

17   Therefore when they came together hither, without any delay, in the day (pur)suing I sat for doomsman (or on the following day I sat as judge), and commanded the man to be

brought.

18   And when his accusers stood [nigh], they said no cause of which things I had suspicion of evil. (And when his accusers stood here before me, they made no case in which I found any suspicion of wrong-doing.)

19   But they had against him some questions of their vain worshipping, [or (their futile) *religion*], and of one Jesus (who was) dead, whom Paul affirmed to live.

20   And I doubted of such manner questions, and said, Whether he would go to Jerusalem, and there be deemed of these things? (And I was uncertain about such matters, and asked, Would he go to Jerusalem, and be judged on these matters there?)

21   But for Paul appealed, that he should be kept to the knowing of the emperor (or of Caesar), I commanded him to be kept, till I send him to the emperor [or till I shall send him to Caesar]. (But because Paul appealed, that he should be sent to the Emperor for judgement, or for a decision, or for sentencing, I commanded him to be kept under guard, until I could send him to the Emperor.)

22   And Agrippa said to Festus, I myself would (like to) hear the man. And he said, Tomorrow thou shalt hear him.

23   And on the tother day (or And on the next day), when Agrippa and Bernice came with great desire, [or (with much) *pride of state*], and entered into the auditorium, with tribunes and the principal men of the city, when Festus bade, Paul was brought (in).

24   And Festus said, King Agrippa, and all men that be with us, ye see this man, of which all the multitude of Jews prayed me at Jerusalem, and asked, and cried, that he should live no longer. (And Festus said, King Agrippa, and all those who be with us, ye see this man, about whom all the multitude of the Jews at Jerusalem beseeched me, and asked, and cried, that he should no longer live.)

25   But I found, that he had done nothing

worthy of death; and I deemed to send *him* to the emperor (or and I decided to send *him* to Caesar), for he appealed this thing, [or soothly him appealing this thing to the emperor, I deemed to send (him to him)].

26   Of which man I have (it) not certain, what thing I shall write to the lord. For which thing I (have) brought him to you, and most(ly) to thee, thou king Agrippa [or O king Agrippa], that when asking is made (or so that after he is questioned), I have what I shall write.

27   For it is seen to me without reason, to send a bound man, and not to signify the cause of him, (or and not to specify his case, or the charges, against him).

CHAPTER 26

1   And Agrippa said to Paul, It is suffered to thee (or It is allowed for thee), to speak for thyself. Then Paul held forth the hand, and began to yield reason.

2   Of all (the) things, in which I am accused of the Jews, thou king Agrippa, I guess me blessed at thee, when I shall defend me this day; (Because of all the things, that I am accused of by the Jews, O King Agrippa, I believe that I am most fortunate to be before thee, when I shall defend myself today;)

3   most(ly) for thou knowest all things that be among (the) Jews, (their) customs and questions. For which thing, I beseech (thee), hear me patiently.

4   For all (the) Jews that before knew me from the beginning, know my life from youth;

5   that from the beginning was in my folk in Jerusalem, if they will bear witnessing [or if they will bear witness], that by the most certain sect of our religion, I lived a Pharisee. (who from the beginning was among my people in Jerusalem, and they can testify, that by the most strictest sect of our religion, I lived as a Pharisee.)

6   And now for the hope of repromission, that is made to our fathers of God, I stand

subject in (the) doom (place); (And now for the hope of the promise, that was made to our fathers by God, I stand before the court;)

7   in which *hope* our twelve lineages, serving night and day hope to come; of which hope, sir king, [or of which hope, thou king], I am accused of the Jews. (of which *hope* our twelve tribes, serving night and day hope to come; because of which hope, O King, I am now accused by these Jews.)

8   What unbelieveful thing is deemed at you, if God raiseth dead men? (Why is it so unbelievable in your judgement, that God raiseth the dead?)

9   And soothly I guessed, that I ought to do many contrary things against the name of Jesus of Nazareth.

10   Which thing(s) also I did in Jerusalem, and I enclosed many of the saints in prison, when I had taken power of the princes of (the) priests. And when they were slain, I brought the sentence [or I gave the sentence]. (Which things I did in Jerusalem, and I imprisoned many of God's people, when I had been given the authority by the high priests. And when it was deemed that they should be executed, I voted for that punishment, or for that sentence.)

11   And by all synagogues oft I punished them, and constrained (them) to blaspheme; and more I waxed mad against them, and pursued (them) [till] into alien cities. (And in all the synagogues I often punished them, and compelled them to blaspheme; and I grew more mad against them, and I persecuted them even in foreign cities.)

12   In which, [the] while I went to Damascus, with power and suffering of the princes of (the) priests, (In which, while I was on my way to Damascus, with power and authority from the high priests,)

13   at midday, in the way I saw, sir king, [or thou king], (or in the middle of the day, on the way I saw, O King), that from heaven a light shined about me, (sur)passing the shining of the sun, and about them that were together with me.

14   And when we all had fallen down into the earth, I heard a voice saying to me in (the) Hebrew tongue, Saul, Saul, what pursuest thou me? it is hard to thee, to kick against the prick, [or it is hard for thee, to kick against the prick]. (And after we all had fallen down to the ground, I heard a voice saying to me in the Hebrew language, Saul, Saul, why persecutest thou me? it is hard for thee, to kick against the prod.)

15   And I said, Who art thou, Lord? And the Lord said, I am Jesus, whom thou pursuest, (or I am Jesus, whom thou persecutest).

16   But rise up, and stand on thy feet. For why to this thing I appeared to thee, that I ordain thee minister and witness of those things that thou hast seen, and of those things in which I shall show to thee [or and of those things in which I shall appear to thee]. (But rise up, and stand on thy feet. Because I have appeared to thee for this reason, so that I can ordain thee to be my servant and witness of those things that thou hast seen, and of those things which I shall yet show to thee, or in which I shall yet appear to thee.)

17   And I shall deliver thee from (the) peoples and folks, to which now I send thee, (And I shall rescue thee from the peoples and nations, to whom I now send thee,)

18   to open the eyes of them, that they be converted [or turned] from darkness to light, and from (the) power of Satan to God, that they take remission of sins, and (their) part among (the) saints, by faith that is in me. (to open their eyes, so that they be turned from the darkness to the light, and from the power of Satan to God, so that they receive forgiveness for their sins, and their place among God's people, by their faith that is in me.)

19   Wherefore, sir king Agrippa [or thou king Agrippa], I was not unbelieveful to the heavenly vision; (And so, O King Agrippa, I did not

disobey the heavenly vision;)

20   but I told [or I showed] to them, that be at Damascus first, and at Jerusalem, and by all the country of Judea, and to (the) heathen men, that they should do penance, and be converted to God, and do worthy works of penance. (but I told first to those who be at Damascus, and then to those at Jerusalem, and then to those throughout all the country of Judea, and then to the Gentiles, that they should repent, and be converted to God, and do worthy works of repentance.)

21   For this cause, (the) Jews took (hold of) me, when I was in the temple, to slay me [or and would slay me]. (And because of this, or for this reason, the Jews took hold of me, when I was in the Temple, to kill me.)

22   But I was helped by the help of God [till] into this day, and stand, witnessing to less and to more (or testifying to the least and to the greatest). And I say nothing else than which things the prophets and Moses spake that shall come,

23   if Christ *is* to suffer, if he is the first of the again-rising of dead men [or if (he is) the first of the again-rising of (the) dead], that shall show light to the people and to heathen men. (that the Messiah *is* to suffer, and that he is the first of the resurrection of the dead, who shall show light to the (Jewish) people and to the Gentiles.)

24   When he spake these things, and yielded reason, Festus said with (a) great voice, Paul, thou maddest, [or Paul, thou waxest (or thou growest) mad]; many letters turn thee to madness. (And when he had said these things, and made his defence, Festus said with a loud voice, Paul, thou art mad; too much study hath driven thee mad.)

25   And Paul said, I mad not, thou best Festus, (or But Paul said, I am not mad, O most excellent Festus), but I speak out the words of truth and of soberness.

26   For also the king, to whom I speak steadfastly, knoweth of these things; for I deem,

that nothing of these is hid from him (or that none of this is hidden from him); for neither in a corner was aught (or anything) of these things done.

27   Believest thou, king Agrippa, to prophets? I know that thou believest.

28   And Agrippa said to Paul, In little thing thou counselest me [for] to be made a christian man(?).

29   And Paul *said*, I desire with God, both in little and in great (or both for the least and the greatest), (yea), not only (for) thee, but (for) all these (people) that hear (me) today, to be made such as I am, except (for) these bonds.

30   And the king rose up, and the president, and Bernice, and they that sat nigh to them.

31   And when they went away, they spake together, and said, That this man hath not done anything worthy (of) death, neither (of) bonds [or (of) bonds]. (And when they went away, they spoke together, and said, This man hath not done anything worthy of death, or of bondage, or imprisonment.)

32   And Agrippa said to Festus, This man might be delivered, if he had not appealed to the emperor. [Forsooth Agrippa said to Festus, This man might be dismissed, if he had not appealed to Caesar.]

CHAPTER 27

1   But as it was deemed (for) him to ship into Italy, they betook Paul with other keepers [or with other men kept] to a centurion, by (the) name (of) Julius, of the company of knights of the emperor. (And when it was decided that he should sail to Italy, they delivered Paul with other prisoners to a centurion, named Julius, from the Emperor's cohort or regiment of soldiers.)

2   And we went up into the ship of Adramyttium, and began to sail, and were borne about the places of Asia, while Aristarchus of Macedonia, Thessalonica,

dwelled still with us.

3   And in the day (pur)suing, we came to Sidon; and Julius treated courteously Paul, and suffered [him] to go to friends, and to do his needs [or and to do the care of him]. (And on the following day, we came to Sidon; and Julius treated Paul courteously, and allowed him to go to his friends, and to get his needs filled, or and for them to take care of him.)

4   And when we removed from thence [or And when we were taken up from thence], we under-sailed to Cyprus, for that (the) winds were contrary.

5   And we sailed in the sea of Cilicia and Pamphylia, and came to Lystra, that is Lycia.

6   And there the centurion found a ship of Alexandria, sailing into Italy, and putted us over into it.

7   And when in many days we sailed slowly, and scarcely came against Cnidus, for the wind hindered us, we sailed to Crete, beside Salmone.

8   And scarcely we sailed beside, and came into a place, that is called of good haven, to whom the city Lasea was nigh.

9   And when much time was passed, and when sailing then was not secure, for that (the time of) fasting was passed, Paul comforted them (or Paul strengthened them),

10   and said to them, Men, I see that (the) sailing beginneth to be with wrong and much harm, not only of the charge, and of the ship, but also of our lives, (or not only for the cargo, and for the ship, but also even for our own lives).

11   But the centurion believed more to the governor, and to the lord of the ship, than to these things that were said of Paul. (But the centurion trusted more in what the captain and the owner of the ship said, than what was said by Paul.)

12   And when the haven was not able [for] to dwell in (over) winter, full many ordained counsel to sail from thence, if on any manner

[or if in any manner] they might come to Phenice, (for) to dwell in winter at the haven of Crete, which beholdeth to Africa, *that is*, (to the) *southwest*, and to Corum, *that is*, (to the) *northwest*.

13   And when the south blew, they guessed them(selves) to hold purpose; and when they had removed [or had taken up] from Assos, they sailed to Crete.

14   And not after much [time], the wind Tifonyk, that is called (the) northeast, [*or* (the) *wind of tempest*], was against it.

15   And when the ship was ravished, and might not enforce against the wind [or into the wind], when the ship was given (over) to the blowings of the wind, we were borne (And when the ship was snatched, or was seized, and could not endeavour against the wind, when the ship was given over to the blowing of the wind, we were borne)

16   with course into an isle, that is called Cauda; and scarcely we might get a little boat (under control in these circumstances). (with course by an island called Cauda; and we were barely able to control the ship's little boat under such circumstances.)

17   And when this (little boat) was taken up, they used helps, girding together the ship; and dreaded (or and feared), lest they should fall into sandy places. And when the vessel was under-set, so they were borne.

18   And for we were thrown with (a) strong tempest, in the day (pur)suing they made casting out. (And because we were tossed about by a strong tempest, on the following day they began to throw out the cargo.)

19   And the third day with their hands they cast away the instruments of the ship.

20   And when [neither] the sun neither the stars were seen by many days, and tempest not a little nighed, now all the hope of our health was done away. (And when neither the sun nor the stars were seen for many days, and a great tempest approached, now all the hope for our

deliverance was gone.)

21   And when much fasting had been, then Paul stood in the middle of them, and said, A! men [or O! men], it behooved, when ye heard me, not to have taken away *the ship* from Crete, and get this wrong and (this) casting out.

22   And now I counsel you to be of good comfort [or of good heart], for loss of no person of you shall be [or soothly there shall be loss of no soul of you], (no), except of the ship.

23   For an angel of God, whose I am, and to whom I serve, stood nigh to me in this night,

24   and said, Paul, dread thou not (or fear not); it behooveth thee to stand before the emperor [or it behooveth thee to stand nigh to Caesar]. And lo! God hath given to thee all that be in the ship with thee.

25   For which thing, ye men, be of good comfort [or be of good heart]; for I believe to my God (or for I believe my God), that so it shall be, as it is said to me.

26   And it behooveth us to come into some isle.

27   But afterward that in the fourteen day the night came on us sailing in the stony sea (or But then on the fourteenth day when the night came upon us sailing on the stormy sea), about midnight the shipmen supposed some country to appear to them.

28   And they cast down a plummet [or Which sent down a plummet], and found twenty fathoms *of deepness*. And after a little they were departed from thence, and found fifteen fathoms.

29   And they dreaded (or feared), lest we should have fallen into sharp places; and from the last part of the ship they sent (out) four anchors, and desired that the day had become. [Soothly they dreaded, lest we should fall into sharp places; and from the last part of the ship they sent (out) four anchors, and desired that the day were made.]

30   And when the shipmen sought to flee from the ship, when they had sent a little boat into the sea (or when they had sent the little boat into the sea), under colour as they should begin to stretch forth the anchors from the former part of the ship,

31   Paul said to the centurion and to the knights, But these dwell in the ship, ye may not be made safe. (Paul said to the centurion and to the soldiers, Unless these men stay on the ship, ye shall not be saved.)

32   Then [the] knights cutted away the cords of the little boat, and suffered it to fall away. (So the soldiers cut away the cords of the little boat, and allowed it to fall away.)

33   And when the day was come, Paul prayed all (the) men to take meat (or Paul beseeched all the men to have some food), and said, The fourteenth day this day ye abide, and dwell fasting, and take nothing.

34   Wherefore I pray you to take meat, for your health, (or And so I beseech you to have some food, for your own well-being); for of none of you the hair of the head shall perish.

35   And when he had said these things, *Paul* took bread, and did thankings to God in the sight of all (the) men (or and gave thanks to God before all the men); and when he had broken (it), he began to eat (it).

36   And all were made of better comfort, [or (were) made more patient, *or hardy*], and they took meat. (And all were strengthened, after they had eaten some food.)

37   And we were all (the) men in the ship, two hundred seventy and six.

38   And they were [full-]filled with meat, and discharged the ship, and cast (the) wheat into the sea. (And they were filled full with the food, and discharged the ship, and threw the wheat into the sea.)

39   And when the day was come, they knew no land; and they beheld an haven that had a water-bank, into which they thought, if they might (or if they could), to bring up the ship.

40   And when they had taken up the anchors, they betook them [in]to the sea (or they

dropped them in the sea), and slacked together the jointures of (the) rudders. And with a little sail lifted up, by (the) blowing of the wind they went (forth) to the bank.

41 And when we felled into a place of gravel gone all about with the sea, they hurtled the ship. And when the former part was fixed, it dwelled unmoveable, and the last part (of it) was broken of [or by] the strength of the sea.

42 And [the] counsel of the knights' was, to slay (the) men that were in (the) ward [or in the keeping], lest any should escape, when he had swimmed out. (And the soldiers' plan, or their thinking, was to kill the men who were in the hold, lest anyone would escape, after he had swam away.)

43 But the centurion would keep Paul (alive), and forbade it to be done. And he commanded them that might swim, to go [first] into the sea, and escape, and go out to the land.

44 And they bare some others on boards, (and) some on those things that were of the ship. And so it was done, that all [the] men escaped to the land.

CHAPTER 28

1 And when we had escaped, then we knew that the isle was called Melita.

2 And the heathen men did to us not (just a) little courtesy, [or Soothly (the) barbarians gave to us not (just a) little humanity], (or And the Gentiles there did not just a little courtesy to us). And when a fire was kindled, they refreshed us all, for the rain that came, and the cold.

3 But when Paul had gathered a quantity of cuttings of vines, and laid (them) on the fire, an adder came forth from the heat (or a snake came out because of the heat), and took him by the hand.

4 And when the heathen men of the isle saw the beast hanging in his hand, they said together, For this man is a manslayer; and when

he escaped from the sea, God's vengeance suffereth him not to live in (the) earth. (And when the Gentiles of that island saw the beast hanging on his hand, they said to each other, This man is a murderer; and although he escaped from the sea, God's vengeance shall not allow him to live upon the earth.)

5 But he shook away the beast into the fire, and had none harm, [or and suffered nothing of evil], (or and was not harmed).

6 And they guessed that he should be turned into swelling, and fall down suddenly, and die. But when they abided long, and saw that nothing of evil was done in him, they turned (to) them(selves) together, and said, that he was God (or a god).

7 And in those places were manors [or fields] of the prince of the isle, Publius by name, which received us by three days benignly [or with good will], and 'found' us.

8 And it befell, that the father of Publius lay travailed with fevers and bloody flux (or dysentery). To whom Paul entered, and when he had prayed, and laid his hands on him, he healed him.

9 And when this thing was done, all that in the isle had sicknesses came (or all those on the island who had sicknesses came), and were healed [or were cured].

10 Which also honoured us with many worships (or And they honoured us with many gifts), and putted (on board) what things were necessary to (or for) us, when we shipped.

11 And after three months we shipped (out) in (or on) a ship of Alexandria, that had wintered in (or at) the isle, to which was an excellent sign of Castor.

12 And when we came to Syracuse, we dwelled there three days.

13 From thence we sailed about, and came to Rhegium; and after one day, while the south blew, in the second day we came to Puteoli.

14 Where when we found (some) brethren, we were prayed to dwell there with them seven

days (or we were beseeched to stay there with them for seven days). And so we (finally) came to Rome.

15 And from thence, when brethren had heard, they came to us to the chapping of Appii, and to the Three Taverns. And when Paul had seen them, he did thankings to God, and took trust. (And from there, when the brothers had heard, they came to meet us at the market, or at the city square, of Appii, and to the Three Taverns. And when Paul had seen them, he gave thanks to God, and took trust.)

16 And when we came to Rome, it was suffered to Paul to dwell by himself, with a knight keeping him. (And when we came to Rome, Paul was allowed to live by himself, with a soldier guarding him.)

17 And after the third day, he called together the worthiest of the Jews. And when they came, he said to them, Brethren, I did nothing against the people either custom(s) of (our) fathers, and I was bound at Jerusalem, and was betaken into the hands of (the) Romans. (And after three days, he called together the leaders of the Jews. And when they came, he said to them, Brothers, I did nothing against our people, or against our fathers' customs, but I was taken captive in Jerusalem, and was delivered into the hands of the Romans.)

18 And when they had asked of me, (they) would have delivered me, for that no cause (worthy) of death was in me. (And after they had questioned me, they would have released me, because no case, or crime, worthy of death was found against me.)

19 But for the Jews gainsaid (me), I was constrained to appeal to the emperor [or to Caesar], (or But because the Jews spoke against me, I was compelled to appeal to the Emperor); not as having anything to accuse my people (of).

20 Therefore for this cause I prayed to see you, and speak to you, (or And so for this reason I asked to see you, and to speak to you);

for for the hope of Israel I am gird about with this chain.

21 And they said to him, Neither we have received letters of thee from Judea, neither any of (the) brethren coming showed, either spake, any evil thing of thee. (And they said to him, We have not received any letters about thee from Judea, nor have any of the brothers coming here shown, or spoken, anything bad about thee.)

22 But we pray to hear of thee, what things thou feelest; for of this sect it is known to us, that everywhere men gainsaith it. (But we would like to listen to thee, whatever thou would like to say; for this sect is known to us, and everywhere people speak against it.)

23 And when they had ordained a day to him, many men came to him into the inn. To which he expounded, witnessing the kingdom of God, and counselled them of Jesus, of the law of Moses, and [of] (the) prophets, from the morrow till to [the] eventide. (And so when they had ordained a day for him, many came to him at the inn. To whom he expounded, testifying about the Kingdom of God, and counselled them about Jesus, and the Law of Moses, and the prophets, from the morning until the evening.)

24 And some believed to these things that were said of Paul, some believed not. (And some believed these things that were said by Paul, and some did not believe them.)

25 And when they were not consenting together, they departed. And Paul said one word, For the Holy Ghost spake well by Esaias, the prophet, to our fathers, (or And so Paul said this last thing to them, For the Holy Spirit spoke rightly by the prophet Isaiah, to our fathers),

26 and said, Go thou to this people, and say to them, With ear ye shall hear, and ye shall not understand; and ye seeing shall see, and ye shall not behold.

27 For the heart of this people is greatly fatted, and with ears they heard heavily, and

they closed together their eyes, lest peradventure they see with (their) eyes, and with (their) ears hear, and by (their) heart understand, and be converted, and I heal them.

28 Therefore be it known to you, that this health of God, is sent to (the) heathen men, and they shall hear. (And so let it be known to you, that this salvation of God is now sent to the Gentiles, and they shall listen.)

29 And when he had said these things, (the) Jews went out from him, and had much question, *or musing*, [or seeking], among themselves.

30 And he dwelled (a) full two years in his hired place; and he received all that entered to him,

31 and preached the kingdom of God, and taught those things that be of the Lord Jesus Christ, with all trust, without forbidding. Amen. †

ROMANS

CHAPTER 1

1   Paul, the servant of Jesus Christ, called an apostle, separated into the gospel of God, (or set apart for the Gospel, or the Good News, of God);

2   which he had promised before by his prophets in (the) holy scriptures

3   of his Son, which is made to him of the seed of David by the flesh, [of his Son, the which is made of the seed of David after the flesh,] (of his Son, who was made for him from the seed of David by the flesh,)

4   and he was before-ordained, [or predestined *by grace*], the Son of God in virtue, by the Spirit of hallowing of the again-rising of dead men, of Jesus Christ our Lord, (and he was predestined *by grace* the Son of God in power, by the Spirit, by the consecrating of the resurrection from the dead, yea, Jesus Christ our Lord,)

5   by whom we have received grace and the office of apostle [or apostlehood] to obey to the faith in all folks, for his name, (or to lead to the faith in his name those in all nations and peoples),

6   among which ye be also called of Jesus Christ,

7   to all that be at Rome, darlings [or the (be)loved] of God, and called holy, grace [*be*] to you, and (the) peace of God our Father, and of the Lord Jesus Christ.

8   First I do thankings to my God (or First I give thanks to my God), by Jesus Christ, for all (of) you, for your faith is showed in all the world.

9   For God is a witness to me, to whom I serve in my spirit, in the gospel of his Son, that without ceasing I make mind of you (for)ever[more] in my prayers, (For God is my

witness, to whom I serve in my spirit, in the Gospel, or the Good News, of his Son, so that without ceasing I always remember you in my prayers,)

10   and beseech [or praying], if in any manner sometime I have a speedy way in the will of God to come to you.

11   For I desire to see you, to (im)part somewhat *to you* of spiritual grace [or that I give to you something of spiritual grace], (so) that ye be confirmed,

12   that is, to be comforted together in you (or to be strengthened by you), by [that] faith that is both yours and mine together.

13   And, brethren, I will not, that ye not know, that oft I purposed to come to you, and I am hindered till this time, that I have some fruit in you, as in other folks. (And brothers, I do not desire, that ye do not know, that I often planned to come to you, but I am hindered until this time, so that I can have some fruit in you, as I have in other nations and peoples.)

14   To Greeks and to barbarians, to wise men and to unwise men, I am (a) debtor,

15   so that that is in me is ready to preach the gospel [or to evangelize] also to you that be at Rome.

16   For I shame not the gospel, for it is the virtue of God into health, to each man that believeth, to the Jew first, and to the Greek. (For I am not ashamed of the Gospel or the Good News, for it is the power of God unto salvation, to everyone who believeth, to the Jew first, and to the Greek.)

17   For the rightwiseness (or the righteousness) of God is showed in it, of faith into faith, as it is written, For a just man liveth of faith.

18   For the wrath of God is showed from heaven on all unpiety and wickedness [or unrightwiseness] of those men, that withhold [or that hold aback] the truth of God in unrightwiseness.

19   For that thing of God that is known, is showed [or is made open] to them, for God

hath showed (it) to them.

20 For the invisible things of him, that be understood, be beheld of the creature of the world (or be seen from the creation of the world), by those things that be made, yea, and the everlasting virtue of him (or and his eternal power), and the Godhead, so that they may not be excused [or they be unexcusable].

21 For when they had known God, they glorified *him* not as God, neither did thankings (or nor gave thanks); but they vanished in their thoughts, and the unwise heart of them was darked [or made dark].

22 For they saying that themselves were wise, they were made fools.

23 And they (ex)changed the glory of (the) uncorruptible God into the likeness of an image of a deadly [or a corruptible] man, and of birds, and of four-footed beasts, and of serpents. (And they exchanged the glory of the incorruptible or the immortal God, for the likeness of an image of a mortal man, and those of birds, and of four-footed beasts, and of serpents.)

24 For which thing God betook them into the desires of their heart (or For which thing God delivered them unto the desires of their hearts), into uncleanness, (so) that they punish with wrongs their bodies in themselves.

25 The which [*men*] changed the truth of God into leasing (or into lying), and praised and served a creature rather than the Creator, that is blessed into worlds of worlds [or into without end]. Amen. (And these *men* changed the truth of God into lies, and praised and served creatures, or the Creation, rather than the Creator, who is blessed forever and ever. Amen.)

26 Therefore God betook them into (the) passions of shame [or of evil fame]. For the women of them changed the natural use into that use that is against kind. (And so God delivered them unto their shameless passions. And their women changed from the natural use, or the natural way, to that way that is against

nature.)

27 Also the men forsook the kindly use of women, and burned in their desires together, and men into men wrought filthhood, and received into themselves the meed that behooved (them) of their error. (And the men gave up the natural use of women, and burned in their desires for one another, and men with men wrought filthhood, and received unto themselves the reward that they deserved for their error.)

28 And as they proved that they had not God in knowing, God betook them into a reprovable wit, that they do those things that be not covenable; (And as they proved that they did not have true knowledge of God, God delivered them unto their corrupted minds, or their corrupted way of thinking, so that they do those things that be not suitable;)

29 that they be full-filled with all wickedness (or so that they be filled full with all wickedness), malice, fornication, covetousness, waywardness, full of envy, manslayings, strife, guile, evil will,

30 privy backbiters, detractors, hateful to God, debaters [or despisers], proud, and high over-measure, finders of evil things, not obedient to father and mother,

31 unwise, unmannerly, without love [or without affection], without (a) bond of peace, without mercy.

32 The which when they had known the rightwiseness (or the righteousness) of God, understood not, that they that do such things be worthy (of) the death, not only they that do those things (or not only they who do such things), but also they that consent to the doers.

CHAPTER 2

1 Therefore thou art unexcusable, each man that deemest (or each one who judgest), for in what thing thou deemest another, thou condemnest thyself; for thou doest the same

things which thou deemest.

2   And we know, that the doom of God is after (the) truth against them, that do such things. (And we know, that the judgement of God is according to the truth against those, who do such things.)

3   But guessest thou, man, that deemest them that do such things, and thou doest those things, that thou shalt escape the doom of God? (or that thou shalt escape God's judgement?)

4   Whether thou despisest the riches of his goodness, and the patience, and the long abiding? Knowest thou not, that the benignity, [or (the) *good will*], of God leadeth thee to forthinking, (or to repenting), [or to penance]?

5   But after thine hardness and unrepentant heart, thou treasurest to thee wrath in[to] the day of wrath, and of (the) showing of the rightful doom of God (or and of the showing of God's righteous judgement),

6   that shall yield to each man after his works;

7   soothly to them that be by patience of good work, glory, and honour, and uncorruption, to them that seek everlasting life; (truly to those who patiently do good works, and seek glory, and honour, and incorruption, he shall give eternal life;)

8   but to them that be of strife (or but to those who argue and fight), and that assent not to (the) truth, but believe to wickedness, wrath and indignation,

9   tribulation and anguish, into each soul of man that worketh evil, to the Jew first, and to the Greek; (he shall give troubles and anguish, yea, unto each person who worketh evil, to the Jew first, and to the Greek;)

10   but glory, and honour, and peace, to each man that worketh good thing(s), (or to each person who doeth good things), to the Jew first, and to the Greek.

11   For acception of persons, [*that is, to put one before another without desert*, (or without deserving it)], is not with God. (For favouring people is not God's way.)

12   For whoever have sinned without the law, shall perish without the law; and whoever have sinned in the law, they shall be deemed by the law. (For whoever have sinned without the Law, shall perish without the Law; and whoever have sinned in the Law, they shall be judged by the Law.)

13   For the hearers of the law be not just with God, but the doers of the law shall be made just.

14   For when heathen men that have not (the) law, do kindly those things that be of the law, (or For when the Gentiles who do not have the Law, do by kind, or naturally, those things that be in the Law), they not having such manner [of] law, be (a) law (un)to themselves,

15   that show the work of the law written in their hearts (or who show the work of the Law written on their hearts). For the conscience of them yieldeth to them a witnessing (or a testimony) betwixt themselves of thoughts that be accusing or defending,

16   in the day when God shall deem the privy things of men after my gospel, by Jesus Christ. (on the day when God shall judge the private, or the secret, things of men, according to my Gospel or Good News, through Jesus Christ.)

17   But if thou art named a Jew, and restest in the law, and hast glory (or pride) in God, (But if thou art called a Jew, and leanest on the Law, and hast boasted about God,)

18   and hast known his will, and thou learned by the law (ap)provest [or hast proved] the more profitable things,

19   and trustest thyself to be a leader of blind men, the light of them that be in darknesses (or the light for those who be in darkness),

20   a teacher of unwise men, a master of young children (or a teacher of young children), that hast the form of cunning, (or of knowing), [or of science], (or of knowledge), and of (the) truth in the law;

21   what then teachest thou another, and

teachest not thyself? (or why then teachest thou someone else, but teachest not thyself?) Thou that preachest that me/that men shall not steal, stealest? [or Thou that preachest to not steal, stealest?]

22 Thou that teachest that me/that men shall not do lechery, doest lechery? [or Thou that sayest to not do lechery, doest lechery?] Thou that loathest maumets [or idols], doest sacrilege? (Thou who teachest that me or that men shall not do adultery, doest adultery? Thou who loathest idols, doest sacrilege?)

23 Thou that hast glory in the law, unworshippest God by breaking of the law? (Thou who hast boasted about the Law, dishonourest God by breaking the Law?)

24 For the name of God is blasphemed by you among (the) heathen men, as [it] is written.

25 For circumcision profiteth, if thou keep the law; but if thou be a trespasser against the law, thy circumcision is made prepuce. (For circumcision profiteth, if thou keep the Law; but if thou be a trespasser against the Law, thy circumcision is made uncircumcision.)

26 Therefore if (the) prepuce (or the heathen men) keep the rightwiseness of the law, whether his prepuce shall not be areckoned into circumcision? (And so if the uncircumcised, or the Gentiles, keep the righteousness of the Law, shall not his uncircumcision be reckoned as circumcision?)

27 And the prepuce of kind that fulfilleth the law, shall deem thee, that by (the) letter and circumcision art a trespasser against the law. (And the uncircumcised, or the Gentiles, who by kind, or naturally, fulfill the Law, shall judge thee, who by the letter and thy circumcision art a trespasser against the Law.)

28 For he that is in (the) open (or only by appearance) is not a Jew, neither it is [the] circumcision that is openly in the flesh;

29 but he that is a Jew in hid, and the circumcision of (the) heart, in spirit, not by the letter [or not in (the) letter], whose praising is not of men, but of God. (but he who is a Jew inside, or internally, and whose heart is circumcised by the work of the Spirit, not simply by following the written Law, and whose praising is not from men, but from God.)

CHAPTER 3

1 What then is more to a Jew, or what (is the) profit of circumcision?

2 Much by all wise [or by all manner]; first, for the speakings of God were betaken to them, (or first, for the speakings of God, or God's messages, were delivered to them, or were given to them).

3 And what if some of them believed not? Whether the unbelief of them hath voided the faith of God? (or Hath their lack of faith made God's faithfulness null and void?)

4 God forbid. For God is soothfast, [or true], (or truthful), but each man (is) a liar; as it is written, That thou be justified in thy words, and overcome, when thou art deemed (or when thou art judged).

5 But if our wickedness commend the rightwiseness of God, what shall we say? Whether God is wicked, that bringeth in wrath? After man I say.

6 God forbid. Else how shall God deem this world? (God forbid. Or how else would God judge this world?)

7 For if the truth of God hath abounded in my leasing (or in my lying), into the glory of him, what yet am I deemed as a sinner? (For if God's truth hath abounded in my lies, unto his glory, why am I still judged like a sinner?)

8 And not as we be blasphemed, and as some say that we say, Do we evil things, (so) that good things come. Whose damnation is just.

9 What then? (Sur)pass we them? Nay; for we have showed by skill, that all both Jews and Greeks be under sin, [What therefore? Pass we them? Nay; soothly we have showed by skill,

the Jews and Greeks all to be under sin,]

10   as it is written, For there is no man (that is) just; (as it is written, For there is no one who is righteous;)

11   there is no man understanding, neither seeking God.

12   All bowed away, together they be made unprofitable; there is none that doeth (any) good thing, there is none till to one.

13   The throat of them is an open sepulchre; with their tongues they did guilefully, [or treacherously]; the venom of snakes is under their lips.

14   The mouth of whom is full of cursing and bitterness;

15   the feet of them be swift to shed blood.

16   Sorrow and cursedness be in the ways of them, [⁺Contrition, or defouling together, and infelicity/unhappiness be in the ways of them,]

17   and they knew not the way of peace;

18   the dread of God is not before their eyes. (the fear of God, or fearful reverence for God, is not in their thoughts.)

19   And we know, that whatever things the law speaketh, it speaketh to them that be in the law, (so) that each mouth be stopped, and each world be made subject to God.

20   For of the works of the law each flesh shall not be justified before him; for by the law there is knowing of sin.

21   But now without the law the rightwiseness of God is showed, that is witnessed of the law and the prophets. (But now without the Law God's righteousness is shown, which is testified to by the Law and the prophets.)

22   And the rightwiseness of God is by the faith of Jesus Christ into all men and on all men that believe in him; for there is no parting [or distinction].

23   For all men sinned, and have need to the glory of God; (For all have sinned, and have need of God's glory;)

24   and be justified freely by his grace, by the again-buying [or by the redemption] that is in

Christ (or that is in the Messiah).

25   Whom God ordained (the) forgiver [or purposed (as) an helper], by faith in his blood, to the showing of his rightwiseness, for [the] remission of before-going sins, in the bearing up of God,

26   to the showing of his rightwiseness in this time, that he be just, and justifying him that is of the faith of Jesus Christ.

27   Where then is thy glorying? (or Then where is thy boasting?) It is excluded. By what law? Of deeds doing? Nay, but by the law of faith.

28   For we deem a man to be justified by faith, without works of the law.

29   Whether of the Jews is God only? Whether he is not also of (the) heathen men? Yes, and of (the) heathen men. (Is God only for the Jews, or only of the Jews? Is he not also for or of the Gentiles? Yes, he is also for, or of, the Gentiles.)

30   For there is one God, that justifieth (the) circumcision by faith, and (the) prepuce (or the heathen men) by faith. (For there is one God, who justifieth the circumcised by faith, and the uncircumcised, or the Gentiles, by faith.)

31   Destroy we therefore the law by faith? God forbid; but we stablish the law.

CHAPTER 4

1   What then shall we say, that Abraham, our father after the flesh, found?

2   For if Abraham is justified of works of the law, he hath glory, but not with God. (For if Abraham is justified by works of the Law, he can boast, but not of God or not before God.)

3   For what saith the scripture? Abraham believed to God (or Abraham believed God), and it was areckoned to him to rightwiseness.

4   And to him that worketh, meed is not areckoned by grace, but by debt. (And to him who worketh, his wages, or his reward, is not reckoned as a gift, but as a debt that is owed to

him.)

5 Soothly to him that worketh not, but believeth into him that justifieth a wicked [or an unpious] man, his faith is areckoned to rightwiseness, after the purpose of God's grace.

6 As David saith the blessedness of a man, whom God accepteth, he giveth to him rightwiseness without works *of the law*,

7 Blessed *be* they, whose wickednesses be forgiven, and whose sins be hid, [or be covered], (or and whose sins be hidden, or covered over).

8 Blessed *is* that man, to whom God areckoned not sin.

9 Then whether dwelleth this blessedness only in (the) circumcision, or also in (the) prepuce? (or also among the uncircumcised, or among the Gentiles?) For we say, that the faith was areckoned to Abraham to rightwiseness.

10 How then was it areckoned? in circumcision, or in prepuce? Not in circumcision, but in prepuce. (But when was it reckoned? when he was circumcised, or when he was uncircumcised? Not when he was circumcised, but when he was uncircumcised.)

11 And he took a sign of circumcision, a token [or a marking] of (the) rightwiseness of the faith which is in (the) prepuce, that he be (the) father of all men believing by prepuce, that it be areckoned also to them to rightwiseness; (And he later received the sign of circumcision, a marking of the righteousness of his faith, when he was still uncircumcised, and so he is the father of all believing men who be uncircumcised, so that righteousness is also reckoned to them;)

12 and that he be (the) father of (the) circumcision, not only to them that be of (the) circumcision, but also to them that (pur)sue the steps of the faith, which *faith* is in (the) prepuce of our father Abraham. [and that he be (the) father of (the) circumcision, not only to them that be of circumcision, but and to them that (pur)sue the steps of the faith of our father Abraham, that is in (the) prepuce (or who was uncircumcised).] (and so he is the father of the circumcised, not only to those who be of the circumcision, but also to those who follow the steps of the faith, which *faith* Abraham had while he was still uncircumcised.)

13 For not by the law is [the] promise to Abraham, or to his seed, that he should be [the] heir of the world, but by the rightwiseness of faith.

14 For if they that be of the law, be heirs, faith is destroyed, (the) promise is done away.

15 For the law worketh wrath; for where (there) is no law, there is no trespass, neither is (there) trespassing [or prevarication].

16 Therefore *rightwiseness is* of (the) faith, (so) that by grace (the) promise be stable [or be steadfast] to each seed, not to that seed only that is of the law, but to that that is of the faith of Abraham, which (or who) is (the) father of us all.

17 As it is written, For I have set thee father of many folks (or For I have made thee the father of many nations and peoples), before God to whom thou hast believed. The which *God* quickeneth dead men, [or The which quickeneth the dead], (or The which *God* giveth life to the dead), and calleth those things that be not, as those that be.

18 [The] Which *Abraham* against hope believed into hope, that he should be made father of many folks (or that he would be made the father of many nations and peoples), as it was said to him [or after that it is said to him], Thus shall thy seed be, as the stars of (the) heaven(s), and as the gravel [or the sand] that is in the brink of the sea (or and like the sand that is on the seashore).

19 And he was not made unsteadfast in the belief, neither he beheld his body then nigh dead, when he was almost of an hundred years (old), nor the womb of Sarah nigh dead.

20 Also in the promise of God he doubted not with untrust; but he was comforted in (his)

belief, giving glory to God,

21 witting most fully (or fully knowing) that whatever things (that) God hath promised, he is mighty also to do (them).

22 Therefore it was areckoned to him to rightwiseness.

23 And it is not written only for him, that it was areckoned to him to rightwiseness,

24 but also for us, to whom it shall be areckoned, that believe in him that raised our Lord Jesus Christ from death. [but and for us, to which it shall be reckoned, believing into him that raised our Lord Jesus Christ from (the) dead.]

25 Which was betaken for our sins (or Who was delivered, or given over, for our sins), and rose again for our justifying.

CHAPTER 5

1 Therefore we, justified of faith, have we peace at God by our Lord Jesus Christ. (And so we, justified by faith, let us have peace with God through our Lord Jesus Christ.)

2 By whom we have nigh going to (or access), by faith into this grace, in which we stand, and have glory in the hope of the glory of God's children.

3 And not this only, but also we glory in tribulations, witting that tribulation worketh patience, (And not only this, but also we can boast, or we can rejoice, in trials and troubles, knowing that trouble worketh patience,)

4 and patience proving, and proving hope.

5 And hope confoundeth not, for the charity of God is spread abroad in our hearts by the Holy Ghost, that is given to us. (And hope shameth not us, for the love of God is spread abroad in our hearts by the Holy Spirit, who is given to us.)

6 And while that we were sick after the time, what died Christ for wicked men? (And while that we were frail or weak at the time, why did the Messiah die for wicked men?)

7 For scarcely dieth any man for the just man [or Soothly scarcely dieth any man for the just]; and yet for a good man peradventure some man (might) dare die.

8 But God commendeth his charity in us; for if when we were yet sinners, after the time Christ was dead for us, (But God showeth his love for us; for if when we were still sinners, at that time the Messiah died for us,)

9 then much more now we justified in his blood, shall be safe from wrath by him. (then much more now we having been justified by his blood, shall be saved from God's wrath, or from his righteous anger, through him.)

10 For if when we were enemies, we be reconciled to God by the death of his Son, much more we reconciled shall be safe in the life of him. (For if when we were enemies, we were reconciled to God by the death of his Son, then much more now we who be reconciled shall be saved by his life.)

11 And not only this, but also we glory in God, (or but also we can boast, or we can rejoice, in God), by our Lord Jesus Christ, by whom we have received now reconciling.

12 Therefore as by one man sin entered into this world, and by sin death, and so death passed forth into all men, in which *man* all men sinned.

13 For unto the law sin was in the world; but sin was not reckoned, when [the] law was not.

14 But death reigned from Adam unto Moses, also into them that sinned not in (the) likeness of the trespassing of Adam, the which is (the) likeness of *Christ* to coming, [or the which is (the) form, *or* (the) *likeness*, of (the) *one* to come], (or who was the likeness of *the Messiah* to come).

15 But not as [the] guilt [or as the trespass], so the gift; for if through the guilt [or through the trespass] of one many be dead, much more the grace of God and the gift in the grace of one man Jesus Christ hath abounded into many men.

16 And not as by one sin, so by the gift; for the doom, (or the judgement, or the sentence), of one into condemnation, but the (gift of) grace of (or over) many guilts [or many trespassings] into justification.

17 For if in the guilt of one death reigned through one, much more men that take plenty of grace (or those who receive an abundance of grace), and of giving, and of rightwiseness, shall reign in life by one Jesus Christ.

18 Therefore as by the guilt of one into all men into condemnation, so by the rightwiseness of one into all men into (the) justifying of life.

19 For as by (the) unobedience of one man many be made sinners, so by the obedience of one many shall be [ordained] just.

20 And the law entered, (so) that guilt should be plenteous; but where guilt was plenteous, grace was more plenteous [or abounded].

21 That as sin reigned into death, so grace reign by rightwiseness into everlasting life (or so grace reign by righteousness unto eternal life), by Jesus Christ our Lord.

CHAPTER 6

1 Therefore what shall we say? Shall we dwell in sin, (so) that grace be plenteous?

2 God forbid. For how shall we that be dead to sin, live yet therein?

3 Whether, brethren, ye know not, that whichever we be baptized in Christ Jesus, we be baptized in his death? (Brothers, do ye not know, that whoever is baptized into union with the Messiah Jesus, is baptized into his death?)

4 For we be together buried with him by baptism into death; that as Christ arose from death by the glory of the Father, [or that as Christ rose from (the) dead by (the) glory of the father], (or that as the Messiah rose from the dead by the glory of the Father), so walk we in a newness of life.

5 For if we planted together be made to the likeness of his death, also we shall be of the likeness of his rising again (or we shall also be made to the likeness of his resurrection);

6 witting this thing (or knowing this), that our old man is crucified together (with him), (so) that the body of sin be destroyed, (so) that we serve no more to sin.

7 For he that is dead [to sin], is justified from sin.

8 And if we be dead with Christ (or And if we have died with the Messiah), we believe that also we shall live together with him;

9 witting that Christ, rising again from death [or rising again from (the) dead], now dieth not, death shall no more have lordship on him. (knowing that the Messiah, rising again from the dead, now dieth not, death shall no more have lordship over him.)

10 For that he was dead to sin, he was dead once; but that he liveth, he liveth to God.

11 So ye deem yourselves to be dead to sin, but living to God in Jesus Christ our Lord.

12 Therefore reign not sin in your deadly body, that ye obey to his covetings. (And so do not let sin reign in your mortal body, so that ye obey its desires.)

13 Neither give ye your members (as) armours, (or as arms, or as instruments), of wickedness to sin, but give ye yourselves to God, as they that live of dead men, and your members (as) armours, (or as arms, or as instruments), of rightwiseness to God.

14 For sin shall not have lordship over you; for ye be not under the law, but under grace.

15 What therefore? Shall we do sin, for we be not under the law, but under grace? God forbid.

16 Know ye not, that to whom ye give your*selves* (as) servants to obey to, ye be (the) servants of that thing, to which ye have obeyed, either of sin to death, either of obedience to rightwiseness?

17 But I thank God, that (once) ye were servants of sin; but ye have obeyed of heart into

that form of teaching, in which ye be betaken. (But I thank God, that before ye were servants of sin; but now ye have obeyed with your heart that form of teaching, which was delivered unto you, or unto which ye be delivered.)

18 And ye delivered from sin, be made (the) servants of rightwiseness.

19 I say that thing that is of man, for the unsteadfastness, [or the infirmity, *or unstableness*], of your flesh, (or for the frailty, or the weakness, of your flesh). But as ye have given your members to serve to uncleanness, and to wickedness into wickedness, so now give ye your members to serve to rightwiseness into holiness.

20 For when ye were servants of sin, ye were free of rightwiseness. (For when ye were the servants of sin, ye were free from the control of righteousness.)

21 Therefore what fruit had ye then in those things, in which ye shame now? For the end of them is death. (And so what fruit had ye then in those things, of which ye now be ashamed? For their end is death.)

22 But now ye delivered from sin, and made servants to God, have your fruit into holiness, and the end everlasting life (or and the end is eternal life).

23 For the wages of sin *is* death; the grace of God *is* everlasting life in Christ Jesus our Lord. (For the wages of sin *be* death; but the gift of God *is* eternal life in the Messiah Jesus.)

CHAPTER 7

1 Brethren, whether ye know not; for I speak to men that know the law; for the law hath lordship in a man (or for the Law hath lordship over a man), as long (a) time as he liveth?

2 For that woman that is under an husband, is bound to the law, while the husband liveth; but if her husband is dead, she is delivered [or she is unbound] from the law of the husband.

3 Therefore she shall be called (an) adulteress, if she be with another man, while the husband liveth; but if her husband is dead, she is delivered from the law of the husband, (or but if her husband dieth, she is released from the marriage law), (so) that she be not (an) adulteress, if she be with another man.

4 And so, my brethren, ye be made dead to the law by the body of Christ, (so) that ye be of another, that rose again from death (or who rose again from the dead), (so) that ye bear fruit to God. [Truly, brethren, and ye be made dead to the law through the body of Christ, that ye be another's, that rose again from (the) dead, (so) that we bear fruit to God.]

5 For when we were in (the) flesh, (the) passions of sins, that were by the law (or which were stirred up by the Law), wrought in our members, to bear fruit to death.

6 But now we be unbound from the law of death, in which we were held, so that we serve in (a) newness of spirit, and not in (the) oldness of (the) letter.

7 What therefore shall we say? The law is sin? God forbid. But I knew not sin, [no] but by [the] law, (or But I did not know sin, except for the Law); for I knew not that coveting was sin, [no] but for the law said, Thou shalt not covet.

8 And through occasion taken, sin by the commandment hath wrought in me all covetousness; for without the law, sin was dead.

9 And I lived without the law sometime; but when the commandment was come [or but when the commandment had come], sin lived again. But I was dead,

10 and this commandment that was to life, was found to me, to be to death.

11 For sin, through occasion taken by the commandment, deceived me, and by that it slew *me*.

12 Therefore the law *is* holy, and the commandment *is* holy, and just, and good.

13 Is then that thing that is good, made death

to me? God forbid. But sin, that it seem sin, through good thing wrought death to me, (so) that me sin over-manner/(so) that men sin over-manner through the commandment. [Therefore that that is good, is made death to me? Far be it. But that sin appear, *or be known,* (as) sin, through good thing wrought death to me, (so) that there be made sin sinning over-manner or over-measure, by (the) commandment.]

14 And we know, that the law is spiritual; but I am fleshly, sold under sin.

15 For I understand not that that I work; for I do not the good thing that I will, (or for I do not do the good thing that I desire to do), but I do that evil thing that I hate.

16 And if I do that thing that I will not, (then) I consent to the law, that it is good. (And if I do that which I do not desire to do, then I agree with the Law, that it is good, or that it is right.)

17 But now I work not it now, but the sin that dwelleth in me. [Now soothly I work not it now/Now soothly I work not that thing now, but that sin that dwelleth in me.]

18 But I know, that in me, that is, in my flesh, dwelleth no good; for will lieth to me, (or for the will, or the desire, to do good, lieth before me), but I find not (how) to perform (any) good thing.

19 For I do not that good thing that I will, but I do that evil thing that I will not. (For I do not do that good thing that I desire to do, but I do that evil thing that I do not desire to do.)

20 And if I do that *evil* thing that I will not (or And if I do that *evil* thing that I do not desire to do), (then) I work not it, but the sin that dwelleth in me.

21 Therefore I find the law to me willing to do good thing [or Therefore I find a law to me willing (or desiring) to do (the) good thing], for evil thing lieth to me. (And so I find this law in me; I desire to do the good thing, but only the evil thing lieth *before* me.)

22 For I delight (al)together to the law of God, after the inner man. (For I greatly delight in the Law of God, in my inner man.)

23 But I see another law in my members, fighting against the law of my soul, and making me captive in the law of sin, that is in my members.

24 I am an unhappy [or a woeful] man; who shall deliver me from the body of this sin?

25 The grace of God, by Jesus Christ our Lord. Therefore I myself by the soul serve to the law of God; but by the flesh to the law of sin.

CHAPTER 8

1 Therefore now nothing of condemnation is to them that be in Christ Jesus, which wander not after the flesh. (And so now there is no condemnation for those who be in the Messiah Jesus, who do not walk, or do not go, after the flesh.)

2 For the law of the Spirit of life in Christ Jesus hath delivered me from the law of sin, and of death [or and death]. (For the law of the Spirit of life in the Messiah Jesus hath delivered me from the law of sin, and of death.)

3 For that that was impossible to the law, in what thing it was sick by (the) flesh, (or For that which was impossible for the Law, because the flesh was frail or weak), God sent his Son into the likeness of (the) flesh of sin, and of sin condemned sin in (the) flesh;

4 (so) that the justifying of the law were fulfilled in us, (so) that [we] go not after the flesh, but after the Spirit.

5 For they that be after the flesh, understand [or savour] those things that be of the flesh; but they that be after the Spirit, feel (or experience) those things that be of the Spirit.

6 For the prudence (or the wisdom) of (the) flesh is death; but the prudence (or the wisdom) of (the) Spirit *is* life and peace.

7 For the wisdom of the flesh is enemy to God; for it is not subject to the law of God, for neither it may [*be subject to the law*], (or nor

could it *be subject to the law*).

8   And they that be in (the) flesh, may not please to God. (And those who be in the flesh, cannot please God.)

9   But ye be not in (the) flesh, but in (the) Spirit; if nevertheless the Spirit of God dwelleth in you. But if any man hath not the Spirit of Christ, this is not his.

10   For if Christ is in you, the body is dead for sin [or the body is dead from sin], but the Spirit liveth for justifying. (For if the Messiah is in you, then though the body shall die because of sin, the Spirit shall give life to you, because you have been justified.)

11   And if the Spirit of him that raised Jesus Christ from death dwelleth in you, (then) he that raised Jesus Christ from death, shall quicken also your deadly bodies, for the Spirit of him that dwelleth in you. [⁺For if the Spirit of him that raised Jesus Christ from (the) dead dwelleth in you, (then) he that raised Jesus Christ from (the) dead, shall quicken also your deadly bodies, for the Spirit of him is dwelling in you.] (And if the Spirit of him who raised Jesus Christ from the dead liveth in you, then he who raised Jesus Christ from the dead, shall also enliven, or shall give life, to your mortal bodies, through the Spirit of him who liveth in you.)

12   Therefore, brethren, we be debtors, not to the flesh, (so) that we live after (or according to) the flesh.

13   For if ye live after (or according to) the flesh, ye shall die; but if ye by the Spirit slay the deeds of the flesh, ye shall live.

14   For whoever be led by the Spirit of God, these be the sons of God.

15   For ye have not taken again the spirit of servage in dread, but ye have taken the Spirit of adoption of sons, *that is, sons of God by grace,* in which we cry, Abba, Father. (For ye have not received the spirit of servitude, or of slavery, in fear, but ye have received the Spirit of the adoption of sons, *that is, sons of God by grace,*

in which we cry, Abba, or Father.)

16   And that Spirit yieldeth witnessing (or testifieth) to our spirit, that we be the sons of God;

17   if sons, and heirs, heirs forsooth of God, and heirs together with Christ, [or soothly heirs of God, truly even-heirs of Christ], (or truly heirs of God, and fellow heirs with the Messiah); if nevertheless we suffer together, (so) that also we be glorified together.

18   And I deem, that the passions of this time be not even worthy, to the glory to coming [or to the glory to come], that shall be showed in us. (And I judge, that the sufferings of this time be not worthy of any comparison, to the glory that is to come, that shall be showed to us, or which shall be given to us.)

19   For the abiding of creature (or of all Creation) abideth the showing of the sons of God.

20   But the creature is subject to vanity, not willing(ly), but for him that made it subject in hope; (But all Creation is subject to emptiness and futility, not out of free will, or of its own choice, but because of him who made it so, but also with hope;)

21   for that creature shall be delivered from servage of corruption into the liberty of the glory of the sons of God. (for that Creation shall be set free from the servitude, or the slavery, of corruption into the freedom of the glory of the sons of God.)

22   And we know, that each creature (or that all Creation) sorroweth, and travaileth with pain till yet.

23   And not only it, but also we us-selves, that have the first fruits of the Spirit, and we us-selves sorrow within us for the adoption of God's sons, abiding the again-buying of our body (or awaiting the redemption of our body).

24   But by hope we be made safe (or But through hope we be saved). For hope that is seen, is not hope; for who hopeth (for) that thing, that he seeth?

25   And if we hope (for) that thing that we see not, we abide by patience.

26   And also the Spirit helpeth our infirmity; for what we shall pray, as it behooveth, we know not, but that Spirit asketh for us with sorrowings, that may not be told out. (And the Spirit also helpeth our frailty or weakness; because we do not know what we ought to pray for, or because we do not know how we should pray, but that Spirit asketh for us with groanings, that cannot be told out.)

27   For he that seeketh the hearts, knoweth what the Spirit desireth, for by God, [*that is, after God's will*], he asketh for (the) holy men.

28   And we know, that to men that love God, all things work together into good, to them that after (the) purpose be called saints (or for them who according to his purpose be called God's people).

29   For those that he knew before, he before-ordained by grace to be made like to the image of his Son, (so) that he be the first begotten among many brethren.

30   And those that he before-ordained to bless, them he called; and whom he called, them he justified; and whom he justified, them he glorified.

31   What then shall we say to these things? If God *be* for us, who *is* against us?

32   Which also spared not his own Son, but betook him for us all (or but delivered him for us all), how also gave he not to us all things with him?

33   Who shall accuse against the chosen men of God? It is God that justifieth,

34   who is it that condemneth? It is Jesus Christ that was dead, yea, the which rose again, the which is on the right half of God, and the which prayeth for us. (who is it who condemneth? It is Jesus Christ, who died, yea, who rose again, who is on the right side, or at the right hand, of God, and who prayeth for us.)

35   Who then shall part us from the charity of Christ? (or What then shall separate us from the love of the Messiah?) tribulation, or anguish, or hunger, or nakedness, or persecution, or peril, or (the) sword?

36   As it is written, For we be slain all day for thee; we be guessed as (the) sheep of slaughter, [or we be guessed as sheep to slaughter], (or we have been thought of, or we have been treated like, sheep for the slaughter).

37   But in all these things we overcome, for him that loved us (or through him who loved us).

38   But I am certain, that neither death, neither life, neither angels, neither principats (or principalities), neither virtues (or powers), neither present things, neither things to coming [or neither things to come], neither strength,

39   neither height, neither deepness, neither any other creature, may part us from the charity of God, that is in Christ Jesus our Lord. (neither height, nor depth, nor anything else in all Creation, can separate us from the love of God, that is in the Messiah Jesus our Lord.)

CHAPTER 9

1   I say (the) truth in Christ Jesus, I lie not, for my conscience beareth witnessing to me in the Holy Ghost, (I tell the truth in the Messiah Jesus, I do not lie, for my conscience testifieth to me by the Holy Spirit,)

2   for great heaviness is to me, and continual sorrow to my heart.

3   For I myself desired to be parted (or to be cursed) from Christ for (the sake of) my brethren, that be my cousins after the flesh, (For I myself desired to be separated from the Messiah, that is, to be accursed for the sake of my brothers, who be my cousins after the flesh,)

4   that be men of Israel [or that be Israelites]; whose is (the) adoption of sons, and glory, and testament (or and the covenant), and (the) giving of the law, and service, and promises;

5   whose be the fathers, and of which *is* Christ after the flesh, that is God above all

things, blessed into worlds. Amen. (whose be the fathers, and whom *is* the Messiah according to the flesh, who is above everything, and blessed by God forever. Amen.)

6   But not that the word of God hath fallen down, [*or failed unfulfilled*]. For not all that be of Israel, these be Israelites.

7   Neither they that be [the] seed of Abraham, all be sons; but in Isaac the seed shall be called to thee;

8   that is to say, not they that be (the) sons of the flesh, *be* (the) sons of God, but they that be (the) sons of [the] promise be deemed (or be judged to be) in the seed.

9   For why this is the word of promise, After this time I shall come, and a son shall be (given) to Sarah.

10   And not only she, but also Rebecca had two sons of one lying-by, [*or of one knowing of man*], of Isaac, our father.

11   And when they were not yet born, neither had done anything of good either evil, (so) that the purpose of God should dwell by election, not of works, but of God calling,

12   it was said to him [or it is said to her], That the more should serve the less,

13   as it is written, I loved Jacob, but I hated Esau.

14   What therefore shall we say? Whether wickedness be with God? God forbid.

15   For he saith to Moses, I shall have mercy on whom I shall have mercy; and I shall give mercy on whom I shall have mercy.

16   Therefore it is not neither of [a] man willing (or desiring), neither running, but of God having mercy.

17   And the scripture saith to Pharaoh, For to this thing I have stirred thee, that I show in thee my virtue (or so that I show my power through dealing with thee), and that my name be told in all [the] earth.

18   Therefore of whom God will, he hath mercy; and whom he will, he endureth. (And so for whom God desireth, he hath mercy; and for whom he desireth, he maketh hard or he maketh stubborn.)

19   Then sayest thou to me, What is sought yet? [or What thing is yet sought?] for who withstandeth his will?

20   O! man, who art thou, that answerest to God? Whether a made thing saith to him that made it, What hast thou made me so? (or Why hast thou made me so?)

21   Whether a potter of clay hath not power to make of the same gobbet one vessel into honour, another into despite, [*or low office*]? (Hath not a potter of clay the power, or the right, to make out of the same piece one vessel to be honoured, and another to be despised?)

22   And if God willing to show his wrath, and to make his power known, hath suffered in great patience vessels of wrath able into death, [or into perdition, *or damnation*],

23   to show the riches of his glory into vessels of mercy, which he made ready into glory.

24   Which also he called [us], not only of the Jews, but also of (the) heathen men, (And so he hath called us, not only from among the Jews, but also from among the Gentiles,)

25   as he saith in Osee (or in Hosea), I shall call not my people my people, and not my (be)loved my (be)loved, and not getting mercy getting mercy [or and not having mercy having mercy];

26   and it shall be in the place, where it is said to them, Not ye my people, there they shall be called the sons of (the) living God.

27   But Esaias crieth for Israel, If the number of children of Israel shall be as [the] gravel of the sea, the remnants shall be made safe. (But Isaiah crieth for Israel, Even if the number of the children of Israel shall be like the sand of the sea, only a remnant shall be saved.)

28   Forsooth a word making an end, and abridging in equity, for the Lord shall make a word abridged, [*or made short*], on all the earth.

29   And as Esaias before-said, [No] But (the)

God of hosts had left to us seed, we had been made as Sodom, and we had been like as Gomorrha. (And as Isaiah said before, If the God of hosts had not left us some seed or a few descendants, we would have become like Sodom, and we would have been like Gomorrah.)

30 Therefore what shall we say? That heathen men that (pur)sued not rightwiseness, have gotten [or have caught] rightwiseness, yea, the rightwiseness that is of faith. (And so then what shall we say? That the Gentiles, who did not follow righteousness, have gotten righteousness, yea, the righteousness that is from faith.)

31 But Israel (pur)suing the law of rightwiseness, came not perfectly to the law of rightwiseness. (But Israel following the law of righteousness, did not perfectly come to, or attain, the law of righteousness.)

32 Why? For not of faith, but as of works. And they spurned against the stone of offence, [or (against the stone of) spurning], (Why? Because their efforts were not based on faith, but rather on works. And so they stumbled against the stone of stumbling,)

33 as it is written, Lo! I put a stone of offence (or a stone of spurning) in Sion, and a stone of stumbling; and each that shall believe in it, shall not be confounded, [or shamed]. (as it is written, Behold, I put a stone of offense in Zion, yea, a stone of stumbling; and everyone who shall believe in it, shall not be put to shame.)

CHAPTER 10

1 Brethren, the will of mine heart and my beseeching is made to God for them into health. (Brothers, my heart's desire and my beseeching be made to God for their salvation.)

2 But I bear witnessing to them, that they have the love of God, but not after cunning (or knowing). (For I can testify about them, that they have the love of God, but it is not based on true knowledge.)

3 For they unknowing (or not knowing) God's rightwiseness, and seeking to make steadfast their own rightwiseness, be not subject to the rightwiseness of God.

4 For the end of the law is Christ, to rightwiseness to each man that believeth. (For the end of the law is the Messiah, unto righteousness for each man who believeth.)

5 For Moses wrote, For the man that shall do rightwiseness that is of the law, shall live in it.

6 But the rightwiseness that is of belief, saith thus, Say thou not in thine heart, Who shall ascend into heaven? that is to say, to lead down Christ, (or that is to say, to bring down the Messiah);

7 or who shall go down into hell? that is, to again-call Christ from death, (or that is, to bring the Messiah up from the dead). [+or who shall go down into (the) deepness, or into (the) depth(s)? that is, to again-call Christ from the dead.]

8 But what saith the scripture? The word is nigh in thy mouth, and in thine heart; this is the word of belief (or this is the word of faith), which we preach.

9 That if thou acknowledge in thy mouth the Lord Jesus Christ, and believest in thine heart, that God raised him from death [or that God raised him from (the) dead], thou shalt be safe. (If thou acknowledge with thy mouth that Jesus Christ is the Lord, and believest in thine heart, that God raised him from the dead, then thou shalt be saved.)

10 For by heart me believeth to rightwiseness [or Forsooth by heart men believeth to rightwiseness], but by mouth acknowledging is made to health (or unto salvation).

11 For why the scripture saith, Each that believeth in him, shall not be confounded. (Because the Scripture saith, Everyone who believeth in him, shall not be shamed.)

12 And there is no distinction of Jew and of Greek (or And there is no difference between

Jew and Greek); for the same Lord of all *is* rich into all, that inwardly call him [or that in-call him].

13 For each man, whoever shall inwardly call the name of the Lord [or whoever shall in-call the name of the Lord], shall be safe (or shall be saved).

14 How then shall they inwardly call him [or How therefore shall they in-call him], into whom they have not believed? or how shall they believe to him, whom they have not heard? (or how shall they believe in him, whom they have not heard?) How shall they hear, without a preacher?

15 and how shall they preach, but (that) they be sent? As it is written, How fair *be* the feet of them that preach [or that evangelize] peace, of them that preach good things.

16 But not all men obey to the gospel. For Esaias saith, Lord, who believed to our hearing? (But not everyone obeyeth the Gospel or the Good News. For Isaiah saith, Lord, who believed our message?)

17 Therefore faith *is* of hearing [or Therefore faith by hearing], but hearing by the word of Christ (or through the word of the Messiah).

18 But I say, Whether they heard not? Yes, soothly, the sound of them went out into all the earth, (Yes, truly, their voices went out unto all the earth), and their words into the ends of the world.

19 But I say, Whether Israel knew not? First Moses saith, I shall lead you to envy, that ye be no folk (or so that ye be not a nation), [or First Moses saith, I shall lead you to envy, to not a folk]; (for) that ye be an unwise folk, I shall send you into wrath.

20 And Esaias is bold, and saith, I am found of men that seek me not; openly I appeared to them, that asked not (about) me. (And Isaiah is bold, and saith, I am found by men who did not seek me; openly I appeared to them, who did not ask for me.)

21 But to Israel he saith, All day I stretched out mine hands to a people that believed not [to me], but gainsaid me. (But to Israel he says, All day I have stretched out my hands to a people that did not believe me, but rather, spoke against me.)

CHAPTER 11

1 Therefore I say, Whether God hath put away his people? God forbid. For I am an Israelite, of the seed of Abraham, of the lineage of Benjamin. (And so I say, Hath God discarded his people? God forbid. For I am an Israelite, of the seed of Abraham, of the tribe of Benjamin.)

2 God hath not put away his people, which he before-knew. Whether ye know not, what the scripture saith in Elias? (or Do ye not know, what the Scripture saith in the story about Elijah?) How he prayeth God against Israel,

3 Lord, they have slain thy prophets, they have under-delved thine altars, and I am left alone, and they seek my life.

4 But what saith God's answer to him? I have left to me seven thousands of men, that have not bowed their knees before Baal.

5 So therefore also in this time, the remnants be made safe, (or And so also in this time, a remnant hath been saved), by the choosing of the grace of God.

6 And if *it be* by the grace of God, *it is* not now of works; else grace is not now grace.

7 What then? Israel hath not gotten this that he sought, but (the) election hath gotten (it); and the others be blinded.

8 As it is written, God gave to them a spirit of compunction, eyes that they see not, and ears, that they hear not, into this day.

9 And David saith, Be the board of them made into a snare before them (or Let their table, or their feasts, be made into a snare for them), and into catching, and into (a) cause of stumbling, and into yielding [again] to them.

10 Be the eyes of them made dark, (so) that they see not; and bow thou down always the

back of them.

11   Therefore I say, Whether they offended so, that they should fall down? God forbid. But by the guilt of them health is made to heathen men, that they, (the Israelites), (pur)sue them, (or But because of their guilt, salvation hath come to the Gentiles, so that they, the Israelites, follow them).

12   (So) That if the guilt of them be (the) riches of the world, and the making less [or the diminishing] of them be (the) riches of heathen men (or of the Gentiles), how much more the plenty of them?

13   But I say to you, heathen men, for as long as I am (an) apostle of heathen men, I shall honour my ministry [or my service], (But I say to you, Gentiles, that as long as I am an apostle to the Gentiles, I shall give honour to my ministry,)

14   if in any manner I stir my flesh for to follow, and that I make some of them safe (or and that I save some of them).

15   For if the loss of them is the reconciling of the world, what is the taking up [of them], but (the giving of) life of dead men? [+or no but (the giving of) life to (the) dead?] (or nothing less than the giving of life to the dead! or the giving of life from the dead!)

16   For if a little part of that that is tasted be holy, the whole gobbet is holy; and if the root is holy, also the branches.

17   What if any of the branches be broken, when thou were a wild olive tree, art grafted [or art set in] among them, and art made (a) fellow of the root, and of the fatness of the olive tree,

18   do not thou have glory (or boast) against the branches. For if thou gloriest (or For if thou boastest), thou bearest not the root, but the root thee.

19   Therefore thou sayest, The branches be broken, (so) that I be grafted in [or so that I be inset].

20   Well, for unbelief the branches be broken; but thou standest by faith. Do not thou understand [or savour] high things, but dread

thou (them), (or fear them),

21   for if God spared not the kindly branches (or for if God did not spare the natural branches), [see thou] lest peradventure he spare not thee.

22   Therefore see the goodness, and the fierceness of God; yea, the fierceness into them that fell down, but the goodness of God into thee, if thou dwellest in goodness, else also thou shalt be cut down.

23   Yea, and they shall be set in [or they shall be inset], if they dwell not in unbelief. For God is mighty, to set them in again.

24   For if thou art cut down of the kindly wild olive tree, and against kind art set into a good olive tree, how much more they that be by kind, shall be set in their olive tree? (For if thou art cut down from the naturally wild olive tree, and against nature art grafted into a good or a cultivated olive tree, how much more then they who be of that very nature, shall be able to be grafted into their olive tree?)

25   But, brethren, I will not, that ye not know this mystery, that ye be not wise to yourselves; for blindness hath fallen a part in Israel, till that the plenty of heathen men entered, (But, brothers, I do not desire, that ye do not know this mystery, so that ye do not think yourselves to be wise; for blindness hath fallen in part upon Israel, until the multitude of the Gentiles have entered,)

26   and so all Israel should be made safe. As it is written, He shall come of Sion, that shall deliver, and turn away the wickedness [or the unpiety] of Jacob. (and so all Israel shall be saved. As it is written, He shall come from Zion, who shall deliver them, and shall take away wickedness or impiety from Jacob.)

27   And this testament to them of me (or And this is my covenant with them), when I shall do away their sins.

28   After the gospel they be enemies for you, but they be most dearworthy by the election [or after the election] for the fathers.

29 And the gifts and the calling of God be without forthinking, (or repenting), [*or revoking*].

30 And as sometime also ye believed not to God, but now ye have gotten mercy for the unbelief of them;

31 so and these now believed not into your mercy, (so) that also they get mercy.

32 For God closed all things together in unbelief [or Forsooth God closed together all things in unbelief], (so) that he have mercy on all.

33 O! the highness of the riches of the wisdom and of the cunning, (or the knowing, or the knowledge), of God [⁺or O! the depth of the riches of wisdom and cunning of God]; how incomprehensible be his dooms (or how incomprehensible be his judgements), and his ways *be* unsearchable.

34 For why who knew the wit of the Lord (or For who knew the mind, or the thinking, of the Lord), or who was his counsellor?

35 or who former gave to him (or who first gave to him), and (after) it shall be requited [again] to him?

36 For of him, and by him, and in him be all things. To him *be* glory into worlds [of worlds], (or To him *be* glory forever and ever). Amen.

CHAPTER 12

1 Therefore, brethren, I beseech you by the mercy of God, that ye give your bodies (as) a living sacrifice, holy, pleasing to God, and your service reasonable (or which is your reasonable service).

2 And do not ye be conformed to this world, but be ye reformed in (the) newness of your wit, that ye prove which is the will of God, (or but be ye reformed in the renewing of your mind, or in your thinking, so that ye prove what is the will of God), good, and well pleasing, and perfect.

3 For I say, by the grace that is given to me, to all that be among you, that ye understand not more than it behooveth to understand, but for to understand to soberness, [or to not savour, *or know,* more than it behooveth to know, but to know to soberness]; and to each man, as God hath parted the measure of faith.

4 For as in one body we have many members, but all the members have not the same deed [or the same act];

5 so we many be one body in Christ, and each *be* members one of another. (so we many bodies be but one body in the Messiah, and each of us *be* members of one another.)

6 Therefore we that have gifts diversing [or Therefore having gifts diversing], after the grace that is given to us, either prophecy, after the reason of faith;

7 either service [or ministry], in ministering; either he that teacheth, in teaching;

8 he that stirreth softly, in admonishing [or in exhortation]; he that giveth, in simpleness (or with sincerity); he that is sovereign, [or is (a) prelate, or is before], in busyness (or with zeal and concern); he that hath mercy, in gladness.

9 Love without feigning, hating evil, drawing [or *fast*(ly) cleaving] to (the) good;

10 loving together the charity of brotherhood. Each come before to worship (the) other [or Coming before together in honour];

11 not slow in busyness, fervent in spirit, serving to the Lord,

12 joying in hope, patient in tribulation, busy in prayer,

13 giving good to the needs of (the) saints, keeping hospitality. (giving what is needed to God's people, being hospitable.)

14 Bless ye men that pursue you; bless ye, and do not ye curse (them); (Bless those who persecute you; yea, bless them, and do not curse them;)

15 for to joy with men that joy, for to weep with men that weep.

16 Feel ye the same thing together; not understanding high things, [or not savouring, *or cunning*, (or knowing), high things], but

consenting to meek (or to humble) things, [*following meek* (or humble) *fathers*]. Do not ye be prudent with yourselves (or Do not think yourselves to be overly wise);

17   to no man yielding evil for evil, but purvey ye good things, not only before God, but also before all men.

18   If it may be done, that that is of you, have ye peace with all men.

19   Ye most dear brethren, not defending, [*or venging*], yourselves, but give ye place to wrath [or ire]; for it is written, The Lord saith, To me vengeance, and I shall yield (it).

20   But if thine enemy hungereth, feed thou him; if he thirsteth, give thou drink to him; for thou doing this thing shalt gather together coals on his head [or forsooth doing these things thou shalt gather together coals on his head].

21   Do not thou be overcome of evil, but overcome thou evil by good. (Do not be overcome by evil, but overcome evil with good.)

CHAPTER 13

1   Every soul be subject to higher powers. For there is no power but of God (or For there is no authority except from God), and those things that be of God, be ordained.

2   Therefore he that against-standeth power, against-standeth the ordinance of God; and they that against-stand (that), get to themselves damnation.

3   For princes be not to the dread of good work(s), but of evil (works), (or For rulers or leaders should not be feared by those who do good works, but by those who do evil works). But wilt thou, that thou dread not power? Do thou (a) good thing, and thou shalt have (the) praising of it; [For why princes be not to the dread of good work(s), but of evil. Soothly wilt thou not dread power? Do good, and thou shalt have (the) praising of it;]

4   for he is the minister of God to thee into good. But if thou doest evil, dread thou; for not

without cause he beareth the sword, for he is the minister of God, venger into wrath to him that doeth evil. (for he is God's servant for your own good. But if thou doest evil, fear thou; for not without cause he beareth the sword, for he is God's servant, the avenger unto wrath of those who do evil.)

5   And therefore by need be ye subject, not only for wrath, but also for conscience.

6   For therefore ye give tributes, they be the ministers of God, and serve for this same thing. (And so for this ye pay taxes, for they be God's servants, and serve by these duties.)

7   Therefore yield ye to all men (your) debts, to whom tribute, tribute, to whom toll, [*or* (a) *custom* (duty) *for things borne about*], toll, [*or such* (a) *custom* (duty)], to whom dread, dread, to whom honour, honour. (And so yield to all men your debts, to whom taxes, taxes, to whom a custom duty or a toll, a custom duty or a toll, to whom fear, fear, to whom honour, honour.)

8   To no man owe ye anything, [no] but that ye love together (or except that ye love one another). For he that loveth his neighbour, hath fulfilled the law.

9   For, Thou shalt do no lechery (or Thou shalt not do adultery), Thou shalt not slay, Thou shalt not steal, Thou shalt not say false witnessing (or Thou shalt not give false testimony), Thou shalt not covet the thing of thy neighbour, and if there be any other commandment, it is enstored, *or included*, [*or enclosed*], in this word, Thou shalt love thy neighbour as thyself.

10   The love of thy neighbour worketh not evil; therefore love is the fulfilling of the law.

11   And we know (at) this time, that the hour is now, that we rise from sleep; for now is our health near(er), [or soothly now our health is nearer], (or for now our salvation, or our deliverance, is nearer), than when we (first) believed.

12   The night went before, but the day hath nighed. Therefore cast we away the works of

darknesses, and be we clothed in the armours of light [or and be we clothed with the armours of light]. (The night went before, but now the day hath approached. And so let us throw off the works of darkness, and be we clothed in the armour of light.)

13   As in [the] day wander, (or walk, or go), we honestly (or decently), not in superfluous feasts [or in oft eatings], and drunkennesses, not in beds (or bedchambers) and unchastities, not in strife and in envy;

14   but be ye clothed in the Lord Jesus Christ, and do ye not the busyness [or the cares] of (the) flesh in desires.

CHAPTER 14

1   But take ye a sick man in belief, not in deemings of thoughts, [or not in deceptions, *or disputations*, of thoughts]. (Accept a man frail or weak in the faith, without judging or arguing about his thoughts and beliefs.)

2   For another man believeth, that he may eat all things; but he that is sick, [*or unsteadfast*], eat worts. (For one man believeth, that he can eat anything and everything; but he who is frail or weak, eateth only vegetables and herbs.)

3   He that eateth, despise not him that eateth not; and he that eateth not, deem not him that eateth (or judge not him who eateth). For God hath taken him (un)to him(self), [or For why God hath taken him], (or Because God hath accepted him).

4   Who art thou, that deemest another's servant? (or Who art thou, who judgest another's servant?) To his lord he standeth, or falleth *from him*, [or To his lord he standeth, or falleth down]. But he shall stand; for the Lord is mighty to make him perfect, [or to ordain him, *or make* (him) *steadfast*].

5   For why one deemeth a day betwixt a day, another deemeth each day. Each man increase in his wit (or Each man increase in his understanding, or in his thinking).

6   He that understandeth the day, understandeth to the Lord, [or He that savoureth the day, savoureth to the Lord]. And he that eateth, eateth to the Lord, for he doeth thankings to God (or for he giveth thanks to God). And he that eateth not, eateth not to the Lord, and doeth thankings to God.

7   For no man of us liveth (un)to himself, and no man dieth (un)to himself.

8   For whether we live, we live to the Lord; and whether we die, we die to the Lord. Therefore whether we live or die, we be of the Lord [or we be (the) Lord's].

9   For why for this thing Christ was dead, and rose again, that he be (the) Lord both of quick and of dead men [or of quick and of dead]. (Because the Messiah died, and rose again for this, so that he be the Lord both of the living and of the dead.)

10   But what deemest thou thy brother? or why despisest thou thy brother? for all we shall stand before the throne of Christ. (But why judgest thy brother? or why despisest thy brother? for all of us shall stand before the throne of the Messiah.)

11   For it is written, I live, saith the Lord, for to me each knee shall be bowed, and each tongue shall acknowledge to God.

12   Therefore each of us shall yield reason to God for himself. (And so each of us shall have to answer to God for himself, or give an account of himself.)

13   Therefore no more deem we (or judge) each other; but more deem ye this thing, that ye put not hurting, or (any) cause of stumbling, to a brother.

14   I know and trust in the Lord Jesus, that nothing is (made) unclean by him, no but to him that deemeth anything to be unclean, to him it is unclean.

15   And if thy brother be made sorry, [*or heavy*], in (his) conscience for meat, now thou walkest not after charity. Do not thou through thy meat lose him, for whom Christ died. (And

if thy brother be grieved in his conscience over food, now thou walkest not with love. Do not because of thy food, or by thy eating, destroy him for whom the Messiah died.)

16 Therefore be not your good thing blasphemed [or despised].

17 For why the realm of God is not meat and drink, but rightwiseness and peace and joy in the Holy Ghost. (Because the Kingdom of God is not food and drink, but righteousness and joy in the Holy Spirit.)

18 And he that in this thing serveth Christ, pleaseth God, and is proved to men. (And he who doeth this serveth the Messiah, pleaseth God, and is approved by men.)

19 Therefore (pur)sue we those things that be of peace, and keep we together those things that be of edification. (And so follow those things that be about peace, and hold we together those things that be for our edification.)

20 Do not thou for meat lose the work of God. For all things be clean, but it is evil to the man that eateth by offending. (Do not because of food, or by thy eating, destroy the work of God. For all things be clean, but it becometh evil to the man who, by his eating, causeth someone else to stumble.)

21 It is good to not eat flesh, and to not drink wine, neither in what thing thy brother offendeth, or is caused to stumble, or is made sick, [or unsteadfast], (or is made frail, or weak).

22 Thou hast faith with thyself, have thou (it) before God. Blessed is he that deemeth not himself in that thing that he (ap)proveth [or Blessed is he that deemeth not, or condemneth not, himself in that thing that he proveth].

23 For he that deemeth, is condemned [or is damned], if he eateth; for it, [his eating], is not of faith (or is not based on faith). And all thing that is not of faith, is sin.

CHAPTER 15

1 But we firmer men owe to sustain [or to bear up] the feeblenesses of sick men, [or (those) unfirm in (the) faith], and not [to] please to ourselves. (But we stronger men ought to bear up the weakness of frail or weak men, or those unstable in the faith, and not to please ourselves.)

2 Each of us please to his neighbour in[to] good, to edification.

3 For Christ pleased not to himself (or For the Messiah did not please himself), [but], as it is written, The reproofs of men despising thee, felled on me, [or The reproofs, or shames, of men despising thee, fell on me].

4 For whatever things be written, those be written to our teaching, (so) that by (the) patience and (the) comfort of (the) scriptures we have hope.

5 But (the) God of patience and of solace give to you to understand the same thing, each into (the) other, after (the example of) Jesus Christ, (And may the God of patience and of solace help you to agree on matters, with one another, after the example of Jesus Christ,)

6 (so) that ye of one will with one mouth worship God and the Father of our Lord Jesus Christ.

7 For which thing take ye together, as also Christ took you into the honour of God. (For which thing accept one another, as also the Messiah hath accepted you, for the honour or the glory of God.)

8 For I say, that Jesus Christ was a minister (or a servant) of (the) circumcision for the truth of God, to confirm the promises of (the) fathers.

9 And (the) heathen men owe to honour God for mercy (or And the Gentiles ought to honour God for his mercy); as it is written, Therefore, Lord, I shall acknowledge to thee among (the) heathen men, and I shall sing to thy name.

10 And again he saith, Ye heathen men, be ye glad [or (make) joy] with his people. (And again it saith, Ye Gentiles, rejoice with his people!)

11   And again, All heathen men, praise ye the Lord; and all peoples, magnify ye him. (And again, All the Gentiles, praise the Lord; yea, all the peoples, praise him.)

12   And again Esaias saith, There shall be a root of Jesse, that shall rise up to govern heathen men, and heathen men shall (have) hope in him. (And again, Isaiah saith, There shall be a root of Jesse, that shall rise up to govern the Gentiles, and the Gentiles shall have hope in him.)

13   And God of hope full-fill you in all joy and peace in believing, that ye increase [or ye abound] in hope and virtue of the Holy Ghost. (And may the God of hope fill you full with all joy and peace by your believing, or by your faith in him, so that ye increase or abound in the hope and the power of the Holy Spirit.)

14   And, brethren, I myself am certain of you, that also ye be full of love, and ye be [full-]filled with all cunning, (or with all knowing), [or with all science], so that ye may admonish each other. (And, brothers, I myself am certain about you, that ye also be full of love, and that ye be filled full with all knowledge, so that ye can admonish one another.)

15   And, brethren, more boldly I wrote to you a part, as bringing you into mind, for the grace that is given to me of God, (And, brothers, more boldly I wrote to you in part, as bringing you into remembrance, of the gift that is given to me by God,)

16   that I be the minister of Christ Jesus among heathen men. And I hallow the gospel of God, that the offering of heathen men be accepted [or be made acceptable], and hallowed in the Holy Ghost. (that I be the servant of the Messiah Jesus among the Gentiles. And I consecrate the Gospel, or the Good News, of God, so that the offering of the Gentiles be made acceptable, and consecrated by the Holy Spirit.)

17   Therefore I have glory in Christ Jesus to God. (And so I have glory in the Messiah Jesus to God.)

18   For I dare not speak anything of those things, which Christ doeth not by me, into obedience of (the) heathen men, in word and deeds, (For I dare not say anything about those things, which the Messiah doeth not by me, to bring the Gentiles into obedience to God, by word and deed,)

19   in virtue of tokens and great wonders, in virtue of the Holy Ghost, so that from Jerusalem by compass to the Illyricum sea [or till unto Illyricum], I have [full-]filled the gospel of Christ. (by the power of miracles, *or signs*, and great wonders, by the power of the Holy Spirit, so that from Jerusalem all around unto Illyricum, I have fully preached the Gospel, or the Good News, of the Messiah.)

20   And so I have preached this gospel, not where Christ was named, (or not where the Messiah hath already been spoken of, or not where the Messiah hath already been heard of), lest I build upon another's ground,

21   but as it is written, For to whom it is not told of him, they shall see, and they that heard not, shall understand.

22   For which thing I was hindered full much to come to you, and I am hindered till [to] this time.

23   And now I have not further place, [*or cause of longer dwelling* (there)], in these countries (or in these regions), but I have (a) desire to come to you, of many years that [now] be passed.

24   When I begin to pass into Spain (or When I go forth to Spain), I hope that in my going I shall see you, and of you I shall be led thither, if I [shall] use you first in part.

25   Therefore now I shall pass forth to Jerusalem, to minister to (the) saints. (But now I shall go forth to Jerusalem, to serve God's people.)

26   For Macedonia and Achaia have assayed to make some gift, [or some collection, *or* (a) *gathering of money*], to (the) poor men of (the)

saints, that be in Jerusalem. (For the churches in Macedonia and in Achaia have decided to make a gift of some money, for those of God's people in Jerusalem who be poor.)

27 For it pleased to them, and they be debtors of them; for if heathen men be made partners of their ghostly things, they owe also in fleshly things to minister to them. (For it pleased them to do this, and they be their debtors; for if the Gentiles be made the partners of their spiritual things, then they, the Gentiles, ought also to serve them with fleshly things.)

28 Therefore when I have ended this thing, and have assigned to them this fruit, I shall pass by you into Spain (or I shall pass by you as I go to Spain).

29 And I know, that I coming to you, shall come in the abundance, [or (in the) plenty], of the blessing of Christ. (And I know, that when I come, I shall come with a full measure of the Messiah's blessing.)

30 Therefore, brethren, I beseech you by our Lord Jesus Christ, and by the charity of the Holy Ghost, that ye help me in your prayers [for me] to the Lord, (And so, brothers, I beseech you by our Lord Jesus Christ, and by the love of the Holy Spirit, that ye help me by your prayers for me to the Lord,)

31 that I be delivered from the unfaithful men, that be in Judea, and that the offering of my service be accepted in Jerusalem to (the) saints; (so that I be delivered from the unfaithful men, who be in Judea, and that the offering of my service be accepted by, or acceptable to, God's people in Jerusalem;)

32 (so) that I come to you in joy, by the will of God, and that I be refreshed with you.

33 And (may the) God of peace be with you all. Amen.

CHAPTER 16

1 And I commend to you Phebe, our sister, which is in the service of the church that is at Cenchrea, (And I commend to you our sister Phoebe, who is in the service of the church that is at Cenchrea,)

2 that ye receive her in the Lord worthily to (the) saints, and that ye help her in whatever cause she shall need of you (or and that ye help her with whatever she shall need from you). For she hath helped many men, and myself.

3 Greet Priscilla and Aquila, mine helpers in Christ Jesus, (Greetings to Priscilla and Aquila, my helpers in the Messiah Jesus,)

4 which under-putted their necks for my life; to whom not I alone do thankings, but also all the churches of (the) heathen men. (who risked their necks for me; for whom not I alone give thanks, but also all the churches of the Gentiles.)

5 And greet ye well their household church [or their home-church]. Greet well Epaenetus, (be)loved to me, that is the first of Asia in Christ, Jesus (or Hearty greetings to Epaenetus, beloved to me, who is the first Asian convert in the Messiah Jesus).

6 Greet well Mary, the which hath travailed much in us. (Hearty greetings to Mary, who hath laboured much with us, or for us.)

7 Greet well Andronicus and Junia, my cousins, and mine even-prisoners, which be noble among the apostles, and which were before me in Christ. (Hearty greetings to Andronicus and Junia, my cousins, and my fellow prisoners, who be of note among the apostles, and who were in the Messiah before me.)

8 Greet well Amplias (or Hearty greetings to Amplias), most dearworthy to me in the Lord.

9 Greet well Urbane, our helper in Christ Jesus, and Stachys, my darling [or my (be)loved]. (Hearty greetings to Urbane, our helper in the Messiah Jesus, and Stachys, my beloved.)

10 Greet well Apelles, the noble in Christ [or noble in Christ]. Greet well them that be of Aristobulus' house.

11 Greet well Herodion, my cousin. Greet well them that be of Narcissus' house, that be in the Lord.

12 Greet well Tryphena and Tryphosa, which *women* travail in the Lord. Greet well Persis, most dearworthy *woman*, that hath travailed much in the Lord.

13 Greet well Rufus, chosen in the Lord, and his mother, and mine.

14 Greet well Asyncritus, Phlegon, Hermes, Patrobas, Hermas, and brethren that be with them (or and the brothers who be with them).

15 Greet well Philologus, and Julia, and Nereus, and his sister, and Olympas, and all the saints that be with them (or and all of God's people who be with them).

16 Greet ye well together in holy kiss. All the churches of Christ greet you well. (Give hearty greetings to one another with a holy kiss. All the churches of the Messiah send you hearty greetings.)

17 But, brethren, I pray you, that ye espy them that make dissensions and hurtings [or offences], besides the doctrine that ye have learned, and bow away from them.

18 For such men serve not to the Lord Christ, but to their womb, (or For such men do not serve the Lord Messiah, but their own bellies), and by sweet words and blessings deceive the hearts of innocent men.

19 But your obedience is published into every place, therefore I have joy in you. But I will (or I desire), that ye be wise in good thing(s), and simple in evil (things).

20 And (may the) God of peace tread Satan under your feet swiftly. The grace of our Lord Jesus Christ be with you.

21 Timothy, mine helper, greeteth you well (or sendeth hearty greetings), and also Lucius, and Jason, and Sosipater, my cousins.

22 I Tertius greet you well, that wrote this epistle, in the Lord. (I Tertius, who wrote this letter, send you hearty greetings, in the Lord.)

23 Gaius, mine host, greeteth you well, and all the church. Erastus, (the) treasurer, [or (the) *keeper*], of the city, greeteth you well, and Quartus [the] brother. (My host Gaius, sendeth you hearty greetings, and all the church. Erastus, the treasurer of the city, sendeth you hearty greetings, and also our brother Quartus.)

24 The grace of our Lord Jesus Christ *be* with you all. Amen.

25 And honour and glory be to him, that is mighty to confirm you by my gospel, and (the) preaching of Jesus Christ, by the revelation of (the) mystery held still, in times everlasting; [Forsooth to him, that is mighty to confirm you by my gospel, and (the) preaching of Jesus Christ, after the revelation of (the) mystery holden still, *that is, not showed*, in times everlasting;]

26 which *mystery* is now made open by (the) scriptures of (the) prophets, by the commandment of God without beginning and ending, to the obedience of faith in all heathen men (or to bring all the Gentiles to faith and obedience),

27 *the mystery* known by Jesus Christ to God alone wise [or *the mystery* known to God alone wise by Jesus Christ], to whom *be* honour and glory into worlds of worlds. Amen. (to God who alone is wise, through Jesus Christ, to whom *be* honour and glory forever and ever. Amen.) †

1ST CORINTHIANS

CHAPTER 1

1 Paul, called (an) apostle of Jesus Christ, by the will of God, and Sosthenes, (a) brother,

2 to the church of God that is at Corinth, to them that be hallowed in Christ Jesus, and called saints, (or to those who be consecrated in the Messiah Jesus, and be called God's people), with all that inwardly call the name of our Lord Jesus Christ [or with all that in-call the name of our Lord Jesus Christ], in each place of them and of ours (or in every place of theirs and of ours),

3 grace (be) to you and (the) peace of God, our Father, and of the Lord Jesus Christ.

4 I do thankings to my God (for)evermore for you, in the grace of God that is given to you in Christ Jesus. (I give thanks always to my God for you, for the grace of God which is given to you in the Messiah Jesus.)

5 For in all things ye be made rich in him, in each word, and in each cunning, (or knowing), [or science], (or in all knowledge),

6 as the witnessing of Christ is confirmed in you; (as the testimony of the Messiah is confirmed in you;)

7 so that nothing fail to you in any grace (or of any blessing), that abide the showing [or the revelation] of our Lord Jesus Christ;

8 which also shall confirm you into the end without crime, [or great sin], in the day of the coming of our Lord Jesus Christ.

9 A true God [or Forsooth God is true], by whom ye be called into the fellowship of his Son Jesus Christ our Lord.

10 But, brethren, I beseech you, by the name of our Lord Jesus Christ, that ye all say the same thing, and that dissensions, [or schisms, or divisions, or discords], be not among you; but

be ye perfect in the same wit, (or in the same thinking, or of the same mind), and in the same cunning, (or the same knowing, or with the same knowledge).

11 For, my brethren, it is told to me of them that be at Chloe's, that strives (or arguments) be among you.

12 And I say that, that each of you saith, For I am of Paul, and I *am* of Apollos, and I *am* of Cephas, [*that is*, Peter], but I *am* of Christ.

13 Whether Christ is parted? (or Is the Messiah divided?) whether Paul was crucified for you, either ye be baptized in the name of Paul?

14 I do thankings to my God (or I give thanks to my God), that I baptized none of you, but Crispus and Gaius;

15 lest any man say, that ye be baptized in my name.

16 And I baptized also the house of Stephanas, but I know not, that I baptized any other.

17 For Christ sent me not to baptize, but to preach the gospel [or to evangelize]; not in (the) wisdom of word(s), that the cross of Christ be not voided away (or so that the cross of the Messiah be made of no consequence).

18 For the word of the cross is folly to them that perish; but to them that be made safe, that is to say, to us, it is the virtue of God. (For the word of the cross is foolishness to those who perish; but for those who be saved, that is to say, for us, it is the power of God.)

19 For it is written, I shall destroy the wisdom of wise men, and I shall reprove the prudence of prudent men.

20 Where is the wise man? where is the wise lawyer? [or where is the writer, or the man of (the) law?] where is the purchaser of this world? Whether God hath not made the wisdom of this world fond [or foolish]?

21 For the world, in (the) wisdom of God, knew not God by wisdom, [or For why for in the wisdom of God, the world knew not God

by wisdom], it pleased to God, by [the] folly of preaching, to make them safe that believed, (or it pleased God, by the foolishness of preaching, to save those who believed).

22   For Jews seek signs, and Greeks seek wisdom;

23   but we preach Christ crucified, to the Jews (a) cause of stumbling, and to heathen men folly; (but we preach the crucified Messiah, to the Jews a stumbling block, and to the Gentiles foolishness;)

24   but to those Jews and Greeks that be called, *we preach* Christ the virtue of God, and the wisdom of God. (but to those Jews and Greeks who be called, *we preach* the Messiah to be the power of God, and the wisdom of God.)

25   For that that is (a) folly thing of God, is wiser than men; and that that is the feeble, [*or* (the) *frail*], thing of God, is stronger than men. (For that which is a foolish thing of God, is wiser than men; and that which is the frail or the weak thing of God, is stronger than men.)

26   But, brethren, see ye your calling, (or But, brothers, see to your calling); for not many (of you be) wise men after the flesh, not many mighty, not many noble.

27   But God chose those things that be fond [or that be foolish] of the world, to confound wise men; and God chose the feeble, [*or* (the) *frail*], things of the world, to confound the strong things; (But God chose those things that be foolish in the world, to shame the wise; and God chose the frail or the weak things of the world, to shame the strong;)

28   and God chose the unnoble things and (the) despisable things of the world, and those things that be not, to destroy those things that be;

29   that each man have not glory in his sight. (so that no one can boast in the presence of God or before God.)

30   But of him ye be in Christ Jesus, which is made of God to us wisdom, and rightwiseness, and holiness, and again-buying; (For ye be in the Messiah Jesus, whom God made to be for us our wisdom, and righteousness, and holiness, and redemption;)

31   that, as it is written, He that glorieth, have glory in the Lord. (so that, as it is written, He who boasteth, boast of the Lord.)

CHAPTER 2

1   And I, brethren, when I came to you, came not in the highness of word(s), either of wisdom, telling, [*or showing*], to you the witnessing of Christ (or telling the testimony of the Messiah).

2   For I deemed not me to know anything among you, but Christ Jesus, and him crucified. (For I judged, or I determined, that when I was among you, I did not know anything, except the Messiah Jesus, and his crucifixion.)

3   And I in sickness, and dread, and in much trembling, was among you [or was with you]; (And I in frailty or weakness, and in fear, and in much trembling, was with you;)

4   and my word(s) and my preaching was not in (or with) subtly stirring [or persuadable] words of man's wisdom, but in (the) showing of (the) Spirit and of virtue (or and of the power);

5   (so) that your faith be not in the wisdom of men, but in the virtue of God (or but in the power of God).

6   For we speak wisdom among perfect men, but not (the) wisdom of this world, neither of (the) princes of this world, that be destroyed, (or nor of the rulers of this world, who be destroyed);

7   but we speak the wisdom of God in mystery, which wisdom is hid; which *wisdom* God before-ordained before (the) worlds into our glory, (but we speak God's secret wisdom, which wisdom is hidden; which *wisdom* God before-ordained before the making or the creation of the world for our glory,)

8   which none of the princes of this world

knew; for if they had known (it), they should never have crucified the Lord of glory. (which none of the rulers of this world knew; for if they had known it, they would never have crucified the Lord of glory.)

9   But as it is written, That eye saw not, nor ear heard, neither it ascended into the heart of man, what things God arrayed [or made ready before] to them that love him (or what things God hath prepared for those who love him);

10   but God showed to us by his Spirit. For why the Spirit searcheth all things, yea, the deep things of God.

11   And who of men knoweth, what things be of man, but the spirit of man that is in him? So what things be of God, no man knoweth, but the Spirit of God.

12   And we have not received the spirit of this world, but the Spirit that is of God, that we know what things be given to us of God. (And we have not received the spirit of this world, but the Spirit that is from God, so that we know what things be given to us from God.)

13   Which things we speak also, not in wise [or in taught] words of man's wisdom, but in the doctrine of the Spirit, and make a likeness [or a comparison] of spiritual things to ghostly men (or and make a comparison of spiritual things for spiritual men).

14   For a beastly man perceiveth not those things that be of the Spirit of God; for it is folly to him, and he may not understand, for it is examined, [or assayed], ghostly. (For a fleshly man perceiveth not those things that be of God's Spirit; for it is foolishness to him, and he cannot understand, for it is examined spiritually.)

15   But a spiritual man deemeth (or judgeth) all things, and he is deemed of no man.

16   As it is written, And who knew the wit of the Lord, or who taught him? And we have the wit of Christ. (As it is written, And who knew the mind, or the thoughts, of the Lord, or who taught him? And we have the mind of the

Messiah.)

CHAPTER 3

1   And I, brethren, might not speak to you as to spiritual men, but as to fleshly *men*; as to little children in Christ,

2   I gave to you milk to drink, not meat (or solid food); for ye might not yet *understand*, neither ye may now (or nor can ye now),

3   for yet ye be fleshly. For while envy and strife is among you, whether ye be not fleshly, and ye go after man?

4   For when some saith, I am of Paul, and another, But I am of Apollos, whether ye be not [*fleshly*] men?

5   What therefore is Apollos, and what Paul? They be ministers (or servants) of him, to whom ye have believed; and to each man as God hath given.

6   I planted, Apollos moisted (or Apollos watered), but God gave increasing.

7   Therefore neither he that planteth is anything, neither he that moisteth (or nor he who watereth), but God that giveth increasing.

8   And he that planteth, and he that moisteth, be one; and each shall take his own meed, after his travail. (And he who planteth, and he who watereth, be one; and each shall receive his own reward, according to his labour.)

9   For we be the helpers of God; ye be the earth-tilling of God, ye be the building of God.

10   After the grace of God that is given to me, as a wise master carpenter I setted the foundament, (or By the grace of God that is given to me, like a wise master carpenter I set the foundation); and another buildeth above. But each man see, how he buildeth above, [or Soothly each man see, how and what things he buildeth upon].

11   For no man may set another foundament, except [or besides] that that is set, which is Christ Jesus. (And no other foundation can be

laid by any man, besides that which was laid, which is the Messiah Jesus.)

12   For if any man buildeth over [or upon] this foundament, (with) gold, silver, precious stones, sticks, hay, or stubble,

13   every man's work shall be open; for the day of the Lord shall declare (it), for it shall be showed in fire; the fire shall prove the work of each man, what manner work it is.

14   If the work of any man dwell still, which he builded above [or upon], he shall receive meed (or he shall receive a reward).

15   If any man's work burn, he shall suffer harm, *either impairing*; but he shall be safe, so nevertheless as by fire, (or but he shall be saved, as if from a fire).

16   Know ye not, that ye be the temple of God, (or Do ye not know, that ye be God's temple), and the Spirit of God dwelleth in you?

17   And if any [man] defouleth the temple of God, God shall lose him; for the temple of God is holy, which ye be. (And if any man defileth God's temple, God shall destroy him; for God's temple is holy, which ye be.)

18   No man deceive himself. If any man among you is seen to be wise in this world, be he made a fool, (so) that he (can truly) be wise.

19   For the wisdom of this world is folly with God (or For this world's wisdom is foolishness to God); for it is written, I shall catch wise men in their fell wisdom, [*or subtle guile*];

20   and again, The Lord knoweth the thoughts of wise men, for those be vain (or for they be empty and useless).

21   Therefore no man have glory in men (or And so let no man boast about men). For all things be yours,

22   either Paul, either Apollos, either Cephas (or Peter), either the world, either life, either death, either things present, either things to coming [or either things to come]; for all things be yours,

23   and ye *be* of Christ, and Christ *is* of God. (and ye *be* of the Messiah, and the Messiah *is* of God.)

CHAPTER 4

1   So a man guess, [*or deem*], us as ministers of Christ, (or So think of us as servants of the Messiah), and (as) dispensers of the mysteries of God.

2   Now it is sought here among the dispensers, that a man be found true.

3   And to me it is for the least thing, that I be deemed of you (or if I be judged by you), or of man's day; but neither I deem (or I judge) myself.

4   For I am nothing over-trusting, [*or guilty*], to myself, but not in this thing I am justified; for he that deemeth me, is the Lord.

5   Therefore do not ye deem before the time, till that the Lord come, which shall lighten the hid things of (the) darknesses, and shall show the counsels of (the) hearts; and then praising shall be to each man of God. (And so do not judge before the time, until that the Lord come, who shall lighten things hidden in the darkness, and shall reveal the plans in the hearts; and then praises shall be to each person in God.)

6   And, brethren, I have transfigured these things into me and into Apollos, for you; that in us ye learn (or so that ye can learn from us), lest over that it is written [or lest over that that is written], one against another be blown with pride for another [*man*].

7   Who deemeth thee? (or Who judgeth thee?) And what hast thou, that thou hast not received? And if thou hast received (it), what gloriest thou (or why boastest thou), as (if) thou haddest not received (it)?

8   Now ye be [full-]filled, now ye be made rich; ye reign without us; and I would that ye reign, (so) that also we (could) reign with you.

9   And I guess, that God showed us the last apostles, (or For I think, that God hath made us apostles the last, or the lowest), (yea), as those that be sent to the death; for we be made a

spectacle to the world, and to angels, and to men.

10 We fools for Christ, but ye prudent in Christ; we sick, but ye strong; ye noble, but we unnoble. (We be fools for the Messiah, but ye be wise in the Messiah; we be frail or weak, but ye be strong; ye be noble, but we be ignoble.)

11 Till into this hour we hunger, and thirst, and be naked, and be smitten with buffets, and we be unstable, [moving from place to place],

12 and we travail working with our hands; we be cursed, and we bless; we suffer persecution, and we abide long;

13 we be blasphemed, and we beseech; as cleansings of this world we be made the out-casting(s) of all things till yet.

14 I write not these things, (so) that I confound you, but (that) I warn you as my most dearworthy sons.

15 For why if ye have ten thousand of under-masters in Christ, but not many fathers; for in Christ Jesus I have (en)gendered you by the gospel. (For ye may have ten thousand tutors in the Messiah, but only one father; for in the Messiah Jesus I have begat you, by preaching the Gospel or the Good News.)

16 Therefore, brethren, I pray you, be ye followers of me, as I of Christ. (And so brothers, I beseech you, be followers of me, like I am of the Messiah.)

17 Therefore I sent to you Timothy, which is my most dearworthy son, and faithful in the Lord, which shall teach you [or shall admonish you (in)] my ways, that be in Christ Jesus, (or who shall teach you my way of life, that is in the Messiah Jesus); as I teach everywhere in each church.

18 As though I should not come to you, so some be blown with pride;

19 but I shall come to you soon, if God will (or God willing); and I shall know not the word(s) of them that be blown with pride, but the virtue (or but the power).

20 For the realm of God is not in word(s), but in virtue. (For the Kingdom of God is not of words, but of power.)

21 What will ye? Shall I come to you in a rod, or in charity, and in a spirit of mildness? (What desire ye? Shall I come to you with a rod, or with love, and in a spirit of meekness and humility?)

CHAPTER 5

1 Yet all manner of fornication is heard among you, and such fornication, which is not among heathen men (or which is not even seen among the Gentiles), so that some man have the wife of his father.

2 And ye be swollen [or blown] with pride, and not more had wailing, that he that did this work, be taken away from the middle of you.

3 And I absent in body, but present in spirit, now have deemed (or now have judged), as (if I were) present, him that hath thus wrought,

4 when ye be gathered together in the name of our Lord Jesus Christ, and my spirit, with the virtue of the Lord Jesus (or with the power of the Lord Jesus),

5 to betake such a man to Satan, into the perishing of flesh, that the spirit be safe in the day of our Lord Jesus Christ. (to deliver such a man unto Satan, into the perishing of the flesh, so that his spirit be saved on the Day of our Lord Jesus Christ.)

6 Your glorying is not good. Know ye not, that a little sourdough impaireth [or corrupteth] all the gobbet? (Your boasting, or your pride, is not good. Know ye not, that a little yeast corrupteth all the piece?)

7 Cleanse ye out the old sourdough, (so) that ye be (a) new sprinkling together, as ye be therf, [or without souring], (or unleavened). For Christ offered is our pask, [or Forsooth Christ is offered our pask], (or For the sacrificed Messiah is our Passover).

8 Therefore eat we, not in old sourdough, neither in sourdough of malice and

waywardness, but in therf things of clearness, and of truth. (And so, let us not eat the old yeast, yea, the yeast of malice and wickedness, but the unleavened things of sincerity, and of truth.)

9 I wrote to you in an epistle, that ye be not meddled, [or mingled, *or commune not*], with lechers,

10 not with (the) lechers of this world, nor *with* covetous men, nor raveners, nor with men serving to maumets [or to idols], else ye should have gone out of this world (or else ye would have had to have gone out of this world).

11 But now I have written to you, that ye be not meddled, [or mingled, *or commune not with such*]. If he that is named a brother among you, and is a lecher, or covetous, or serving to idols, or a curser, or full of drunkenness, or a ravener, to take no meat with such, (or to have no meals, or to eat no food, with such people).

12 For what *is* it to me to deem of them that be withoutforth? Whether ye deem not of things [or of them] that be withinforth? (For why *should* I judge those who be outside of us? Ye should judge those who be inside with us.)

13 For God shall deem them that be withoutforth (or And God shall judge those who be outside of us). Do ye away evil from yourselves.

CHAPTER 6

1 Dare any of you that hath a cause against another, be deemed at wicked men, and not at holy men [or saints]? (Dare any of you who hath a case against another, be judged by wicked men, and not by God's people?)

2 Whether ye know not, that (the) saints shall deem this world? And if the world shall be deemed by you, be ye unworthy to deem the least things? (Do ye not know, that God's people shall judge this world? And so if the world shall be judged by you, be ye unworthy to judge these least things?)

3 Know ye not, that we shall deem angels? (or Do ye not know, that we shall judge the angels?) (and so then) how much more (the) worldly things?

4 Therefore if ye have worldly dooms (or And so if ye have worldly judgements to make), ordain ye those contemptible men, [*or of little reputation*], that be in the church, to deem (them).

5 I say (this) to make you ashamed [or I say (this) to your shame]. So there is not any wise man, that may deem betwixt a brother and his brother, (or So is there not any wise man, who can judge between a brother and his brother);

6 but brother with brother striveth in doom, and that among unfaithful men. (but a brother must fight, or argue, with another brother in court, and in front of men who be out of the faith?)

7 And (so) now trespass is always among you, for ye have dooms among you (or because ye have legal wranglings among you). Why rather take ye not (the) wrong? why rather suffer ye not (the) deceit [or (the) fraud]?

8 But also ye do wrong, and do fraud [or and defraud], and that to brethren.

9 Whether ye know not, that wicked men shall not wield the kingdom of God? Do not ye err; neither lechers, neither men that serve maumets, neither adulterers, neither lechers against kind, neither they that do lechery with men, (Do ye not know, that the wicked shall not possess the Kingdom of God? Do not err; neither lechers, nor men who serve idols, nor adulterers, nor lechers against nature, nor those who do lechery with men,)

10 neither thieves, neither avaricious [or covetous] men, neither *men* full of drunkenness, neither cursers, neither raveners, shall wield the kingdom of God (or shall possess the Kingdom of God).

11 And ye were sometime these things; but ye be washed, but ye be hallowed (or but ye be consecrated), but ye be justified in the name of

our Lord Jesus Christ, and in the Spirit of our God.

12   All things be leaveful to me, but not all things be speedful. All things be leaveful to me, but I shall not be brought down under any man's power. (All things be lawful for me, but not all things be expedient. All things be lawful for me, but I shall not be brought down under the power of any man.)

13   Meat to the womb, and the womb to meats; and God shall destroy both this and that. And the body not to fornication, but to the Lord, and the Lord to the body. (Food for the belly, and the belly for food; and God shall destroy both this and that. And the body is not for fornication, but for the Lord, and the Lord is for the body.)

14   For God raised the Lord, and shall raise us by his virtue. (For God raised the Lord, and he shall also raise us by his power.)

15   Know ye not, that your bodies be members of Christ? Shall I then take the members of Christ, and shall I make *them* the members of a whore? God forbid. (Do ye not know, that your bodies be parts of the Messiah? Shall I then take the parts of the Messiah, and make *them*, or join *them*, to the parts of a whore? God forbid.)

16   Whether ye know not, that he that cleaveth to a whore, is made one body? For he saith, There shall be twain in one flesh.

17   And he that cleaveth to the Lord, is one Spirit.

18   Flee ye fornication; all sin whatever sin a man doeth, is without the body (or is outside the body); but he that doeth fornication, sinneth against his body.

19   Whether ye know not, that your members be the temple of the Holy Ghost, that is in you, whom ye have of God, and ye be not your own? (Do ye not know, that your bodies be the temple of the Holy Spirit, who is in you, whom ye have received from God, and ye be not your own?)

20   For ye be bought with (a) great price. Glorify ye, and bear ye God in your body, (or Glorify, and carry or bear about God in your body).

CHAPTER 7

1   But of those things that ye have written to me, it is good to a man to touch not a woman (or it is good for a man not to touch a woman).

2   But for fornication each man have his own wife, and each woman have her own husband.

3   The husband yield debt to the wife, and also the wife to the husband.

4   The woman hath not power of her body, but the husband; and the husband hath not power of his body, but the woman [or but the wife]. (The woman hath not power over her body, but the husband; and the husband hath not power over his body, but the wife.)

5   Do not ye defraud each to (the) other (or Do not deny yourselves to one another), [no] but peradventure of consent for a time, (so) that ye give attention to prayer; and again turn again to the same thing (or and then return to being together), lest Satan tempt you for your uncontinence.

6   But I say this thing as giving leave [or by indulgence], not by commandment.

7   For I will (or I desire), that all men be as myself. But each man hath his proper gift of God (or But each man hath his own gift from God); one thus, and another thus.

8   But I say to them, that be not wedded, and to widows, it is good to them, if they dwell so as I. (But I say to them, who be not wedded, and to widows, it is good for them, if they remain like I am.)

9   And if they contain not themselves, [*or be not chaste*], be they wedded; for it is better to be wedded, than to be burnt. (And if they cannot contain themselves, *or remain chaste*, then let them be married; for it is better to be married, than to burn alone.)

10 But to them that be joined in matrimony, I command, not I, but the Lord, that the wife depart not from the husband;

11 and that if she departeth, that she dwell unwedded, or be reconciled to her husband; and the husband forsake not the wife (or and the husband must not desert the wife).

12 But to others I say, not the Lord. If any brother hath an unfaithful, [or heathen], wife, (or If any brother hath a Gentile wife), and she consenteth to dwell with him, leave he her not.

13 And if any woman hath an unfaithful (or heathen) husband (or And if any woman hath a Gentile husband), and this consenteth to dwell with her, leave she not the husband.

14 For the unfaithful husband is hallowed by the faithful woman, and the unfaithful woman is hallowed by the faithful husband. Else your children were unclean, but now they be holy.

15 That if the unfaithful departeth, depart he. For why the brother or sister is not subject to servage in such; for God hath called us in peace. (But if the unfaithful departeth, then let him depart. Because the brother or the sister is not subject to servitude or to slavery in such; for God hath called us to live in peace.)

16 And whereof knowest thou, woman, if thou shalt make the man safe; or whereof knowest thou, man, if thou shalt make the woman safe? (And whereof knowest thou, woman, if thou shalt save the man; or whereof knowest thou, man, if thou shalt save the woman?)

17 [No] But as the Lord hath parted to each, and as God hath called each man, so go he, as I teach in all (the) churches.

18 A man circumcised is called, bring he (himself) not (back) to (being) prepuce (or bring he himself not back to being uncircumcised). A man is called in prepuce, be he not circumcised.

19 Circumcision is nought, and prepuce is nought, but the keeping of the commandments of God (is everything). (Being circumcised is nothing, and being uncircumcised is nothing, but keeping, or obeying, the commandments of God is everything.)

20 Each man in what calling he is called, in that dwell he.

21 Thou [a] servant art called, be it no charge to thee (or do not let that be a burden to you); but if thou mayest be made free, use it rather.

22 He that is a servant, and is called in the Lord, is a free man of the Lord. Also he that is a free man, and is called, is the servant of Christ (or is a servant of the Messiah).

23 With (a) price ye be bought; do not ye be made (the) servants of men.

24 Therefore each man in what thing (that) he is called a brother, dwell he in this with God (or remain he in this with God).

25 But of virgins I have no commandment of God; but I give counsel, as he that hath gotten mercy of the Lord (or as he who hath received mercy from the Lord), (so) that I be true.

26 Therefore I guess, that this thing is good for the present need; for it is good to a man to be so [or for it is good for a man to be so].

27 Thou art bound to a wife, do not thou seek unbinding; thou art unbound from a wife, do not thou seek a wife.

28 But if thou hast taken a wife, thou hast not sinned; and if a maiden is wedded, she sinned not; nevertheless such shall have tribulation of flesh. But I spare you.

29 Therefore, brethren, I say this thing, The time is short. Another is this, that they that have wives, be as though they had none;

30 and they that weep, as they wept not; and they that joy, as they joyed not; and they that buy, as they had not;

31 and they that use this world, as they that use [it] not. For why the figure, [or (the) fairness], of this world passeth (or Because the beauty of this world passeth away).

32 But I will, that ye be without busyness (or But I desire, that ye be without cares or concerns), for he that is without (a) wife, is busy

(with) what things (that) be of the Lord, how he shall please God.

33 But he that is with a wife, is busy (with) what things (that) be of the world, how he shall please the wife [or how he shall please his wife], and he is parted (or and he is divided).

34 And a woman unwedded and [a] maiden thinketh what things be of the Lord, (so) that she be holy in body and spirit. But she that is wedded, thinketh what things be of the world, how she shall please the husband [or how she shall please her husband].

35 And I say these things to your profit, not that I cast to you a snare, but to that that is seemly, and that giveth easiness [or facility], without hindering to make prayers [or to beseech] to the Lord.

36 And if any man guesseth himself to be seen foul on his virgin, that she is full waxen [or that she is well old], and so it behooveth to be done, do she that that she will [⁺or do she what he will]; she sinneth not, if she be wedded, [⁺or s/he sinneth not, if s/he be wedded].

37 For he that ordained stably, [or steadfast(ly)], in his heart, not having need, but having power of his will, and hath deemed in his heart this thing, to keep his virgin(ity), doeth well. (For he who resolutely ordained in his heart, not having need, but having power over his will, and hath determined in his heart, to keep his virginity, doeth well.)

38 Therefore he that joineth his virgin (or his betrothed) in matrimony, doeth well, (or And so he who alloweth his daughter to be joined in matrimony, doeth well); and he that joineth not, doeth better.

39 The woman is bound to the law, as long (a) time as her husband liveth; and if her husband is dead, she is delivered from the law of the husband, be she wedded to whom she will, only in the Lord.

40 But she shall be more blessed, if she dwelleth thus, after my counsel; and I ween (or I guess), that I have the Spirit of God.

CHAPTER 8

1 But of these things that be sacrificed to idols, we know, for all we have cunning, (or knowing, or knowledge). But cunning, (or knowing), [or science], bloweth [with pride], charity edifieth, (or But such knowledge swelleth a man with pride, while love edifieth).

2 But if any man guesseth, [or deem(eth)], that he knoweth anything, he hath not yet known how it behooveth him to know.

3 And if any man loveth God, this is known of him (or this is known by him).

4 But of meats (or of foods) that be offered to idols, we know, that an idol is nothing in the world, and that there is no God but one.

5 For though there be some that be said gods, either in heaven, either in earth, as there be many gods, and many lords;

6 nevertheless to us (there) is one God, the Father, of whom be all things, and we in him; and one Lord Jesus Christ, by whom be all things, and we by him.

7 But not in all men is cunning (or knowing). For some men with (the) conscience of idol(s), that is, they guess that the idol is some divine thing, till now eat (such food) as (a) thing offered to idols; and (so) their conscience is defouled, for it is sick. (But not all men have this knowledge. For some men with the consciousness, or the experience, of idols, that is, they think that the idol is some divine thing, till now eat such food that was offered to idols; and so their conscience is defiled, for it is frail or weak.)

8 Meat commendeth us not to God (or Food commendeth us not to God); for neither we shall fail, if we eat not, neither if we eat, we shall have plenty [or we shall abound].

9 But see ye, lest peradventure this your leave be made (a) hurting to sick men (or to frail and weak men). [⁺See ye forsooth, lest peradventure this your license, or leave, be

made (a) hurting to sick men, *or* (to the) *frail*.]

10 For if any man shall see him, that hath cunning, (or knowing), (or who hath knowledge of God), eating in a place where idols be worshipped, whether his conscience, since it is sick, (or it is frail or weak), shall not be edified to eat things offered to idols?

11 And the sick, [*or unsteadfast*], brother, for whom Christ died, shall perish in thy cunning (or in thy knowing). (And the frail or weak brother, for whom the Messiah died, shall now perish because of thy so-called knowledge.)

12 For thus ye sinning against (the) brethren, and smiting their sick conscience, sin against Christ. (For thus ye sinning against the brothers, and striking or wounding their frail or weak conscience, sin against the Messiah.)

13 Wherefore if meat causeth my brother to stumble (or And so if any food causeth my brother to stumble), I shall never eat flesh, lest I cause my brother to stumble.

CHAPTER 9

1 Whether I am not free? Am I not (an) apostle? Whether I saw not Jesus Christ, our Lord? Whether ye be not my work in the Lord?

2 And though to others I am not (an) apostle, but nevertheless to you I am; for ye be the little sign of mine apostlehood in the Lord.

3 My defence to them that ask me, that is. [My defence to them that ask me, is this.]

4 Whether we have not (the) power to eat and drink?

5 Whether we have not (the) power to lead about a woman, a sister, as also other apostles, and (the) brethren of the Lord, and Cephas? (or and Peter?)

6 Or I alone and Barnabas have not (the) power to work these things?

7 Who travaileth any time with his own wages? (or Who laboureth any time at his own expense?) Who planteth a vineyard, and eateth not of his fruit? Who keepeth a flock, and eateth not of the milk of the flock? [⁺Who fighteth, *or holdeth knighthood*, anytime with his own soldiers? Who planteth a vineyard, and eateth not of the fruits? Who feedeth a flock, and eateth not of the milk of the flock?]

8 Whether after man I say these things? whether also the law saith not these things?

9 For it is written in the law of Moses, Thou shalt not bind [up] the mouth of the ox that thresheth. Whether of oxen is (a) charge to God? (or Whether oxen be of any concern to God?)

10 Whether for us he saith these things? For why those be written for us; for he that eareth, oweth to ear in hope, and he that thresheth, in hope to take (some) fruits. (Whether he saith these things for us? Yea, they be written for us; for he that ploweth, ought to plow in hope, and he that reapeth, in hope to take some fruits.)

11 If we sow spiritual things to you, is it great, if we reap your fleshly things? (If we sow spiritual things for you, is it too much to ask, that we be able to harvest your fleshly things?)

12 If others be partners of your power, why not rather we? But we use not this power, but we suffer all things, that we give no hindering to the evangel of Christ. (If ye give others this right, why not also to us? But we do not need this right, rather we endure everything, so that we do not hinder the Gospel, or the Good News, of the Messiah.)

13 Know ye not, that they that work in the temple, eat those things that be of the temple, and they that serve to the altar, be partners of the altar?

14 So the Lord ordained to them that tell the gospel, to live of the gospel. (So the Lord hath ordained for those who tell the Gospel or the Good News, to live from the Gospel or the Good News.)

15 But I used none of these things; and I wrote not these things, that they be done so in me (or so that they be done for me); for it is good rather for me to die, than that any man

should make my rejoicing [or my glory] void.

16   For if I preach the gospel, glory is not to me, (or there is no boasting, or any glory, for me), for need-like I must do it; for woe to me, if I preach not the gospel.

17   But if I do this thing willfully [or willing(ly)], I have meed, (or But if I do this of my own free will, I have a reward); but if against my will, dispensing [or (a) dispensation] is betaken to me.

18   What then is my meed? (or Then what is my reward?) That I preaching the gospel, put the gospel without others' cost, [or expense, *either taking of sustenance therefore*], that I use not my power in the gospel, [or that I mis-use not my power in the gospel], (or so that I do not mis-use my power in the Gospel or the Good News).

19   For why when I was free of all men, I made me (a) servant of all men (or I made myself a servant to all men), to win the more men [or (so) that I should win more men].

20   And (so) to (the) Jews I am made as a Jew, to win the Jews; to them that be under the law, as (if) I were under the law, when I was not under the law, to win them that were under the law;

21   to them that were without (the) law, as (if) I were without (the) law, when I was not without [the] law of God, but I was in the law of Christ, to win them that were without [the] law, (or but I was in the law of the Messiah, to win those who were without the Law, or outside the Law).

22   I am made sick to sick men, to win sick men; to all men I am made all things, to make all men safe. (I am made frail or weak to frail or weak men, to win frail or weak men; to all men I am made all things, to save all men.)

23   But I do all things for the gospel, (so) that I be made (a) partner of it.

24   Know ye not, that they that run in a furlong, all run, but one taketh the prize? So run ye, that ye catch (it), (or So run, so that ye win it).

25   Each man that striveth in (a) fight, abstaineth him(self) from all things; and they, that they take a corruptible crown, (or and they, so that they receive or they win a corruptible crown), but we an uncorrupt(ed) (one).

26   Therefore I run so, not as to an uncertain thing; thus I fight, not as beating the air;

27   but I chastise my body, and bring *it* into servage, [or into servitude], (or into slavery); lest peradventure when I preach to others, I myself be made reprovable.

CHAPTER 10

1   Brethren, I will not, that ye unknow (or that ye not know), that all our fathers were under [a] cloud, and all passed (through) the (Red) sea; (Brothers, I do not desire, that ye do not know, that all our fathers were under the protection of a cloud, and all passed through the Sea of Reeds;)

2   and all were baptized in Moses, in the cloud and in the sea;

3   and all ate the same spiritual meat, (and everyone ate the same spiritual food,)

4   and all drank the same spiritual drink; and they drank of the spiritual stone following them; and the stone was Christ (or and that stone was the Messiah).

5   But not in full many of them it was well pleasant to God; for why they were cast down in [the] desert. (But not very many of them pleased God; and because of that they were thrown down in the desert.)

6   But these things were done in figure of us (or But these things were done as an example for us), (so) that we be not coveters of evil things, as they coveted.

7   Neither be ye made idolaters, as some of them; as it is written, The people sat to eat and drink, and they rose up to play.

8   Neither do we fornication, as some of them did fornication, and three and twenty

thousand were dead in one day.

9 Neither tempt we Christ, as some of them tempted, and perished of serpents. (Nor let us test the Lord, as some of them tested him, and perished from the bites of snakes.)

10 Neither grudge ye, as some of them grudged, and they perished of a destroyer [or of the waster]. (And do not grumble, like some of them grumbled, and they perished by the Destroyer.)

11 And all these things fell to them in figure; but they be written to our amending, into whom the ends of the worlds be come, [or soothly they be written to our correction, into whom the ends of the world have come]. (And all these things were examples for them; but they were written for our correction, unto whom the ends of the world have come.)

12 Therefore he that guesseth him(self), that he standeth, see he, that he fall not.

13 Temptation take not you, but man's *temptation*; for God is true, which shall not suffer you to be tempted above that that ye may; but he shall make with temptation also purveyance, that ye may suffer [or sustain] (it). (Do not let yourselves be overtaken or defeated by any test, for it is but each man's *testing*; and God is true, and he shall not allow you to be tested beyond what ye can endure; and he shall also make provision with any test, so that ye can endure it, or so that ye can sustain it.)

14 Wherefore, ye most dearworthy to me, flee ye from the worshipping of maumets [or flee from worshipping of idols].

15 As to prudent men I speak, deem ye (or judge) yourselves that thing that I say [or ye yourselves deem that thing that I say].

16 Whether the cup of blessing which we bless, is not the communing of Christ's blood? and whether the bread which we break, is not the *part*-taking of the body of the Lord? (The cup of blessing which we bless, is it not the sharing of the Messiah's blood? and the bread which we break, is it not the partaking of the

Lord's body?)

17 For we many be one bread and one body, all we that take part of one bread and of one cup.

18 See ye Israel after the flesh, whether they that eat sacrifices, be not partners of the altar?

19 What therefore say I, that a thing that is offered to idols is anything, or that the idol is anything?

20 But those things that heathen men offer, they offer to devils, and not to God. But I will not, that ye be made fellows of fiends; (But those things which the Gentiles offer, they offer to demons, and not to God. But I do not desire, that ye be made the partners of devils and demons;)

21 for ye may not drink the cup of the Lord, and the cup of fiends; ye may not be partners of the board of the Lord, and of the board of fiends. (for ye cannot drink the cup of the Lord, and the cup of devils and demons; ye cannot be partners of the table of the Lord, and partners of the table of devils and demons.)

22 Whether we have envy to the Lord? whether we be stronger than he? (Could the Lord ever envy us? be we stronger than him?)

23 All things be leaveful to me, but not all things be speedful. All things be leaveful to me, but not all things edify. (All things be lawful for me, but not all things be expedient. All things be lawful for me, but not all things edify.)

24 No man seek (to protect or to esteem) that thing that is his own, but that thing that is of another (man).

25 All thing that is sold in the butchery, eat ye, asking nothing for conscience.

26 The earth and the plenty of it, is the Lord's.

27 If any of heathen [or of unfaithful] men call you to supper (or If any of the Gentiles invite you to dinner), and ye will go, all thing that is set to you, eat ye, asking nothing for conscience.

28   But if any man saith, This thing is offered to idols, do not ye eat (it), for him that showed [*this thing*], and for conscience;

29   and I say not, thy conscience, but of another [*man's*] (conscience). But whereto is my freedom [or my liberty] deemed of (or judged by) another man's conscience?

30   Therefore if I take part with grace, what am I blasphemed, for that that I do thankings [or I do graces]? (And so if I take part after saying grace, why am I blasphemed or criticized for that over which I have said grace, or for which I have given thanks?)

31   Therefore whether ye eat, or drink, or do any other thing, do ye all things to the glory of God.

32   Be ye without offence to Jews, and to heathen men, and to the church of God; (Give no offence to Jews, or to Gentiles, or to the church of God;)

33   as I by all things please to all men, not seeking that that is profitable to me [or not seeking what is profitable to me], but that that *is profitable* to many men, that they be made safe (or so that they can be saved).

CHAPTER 11

1   Be ye my followers, as I *am* of Christ. (Be followers of me, like I *am* of the Messiah.)

2   And, brethren, I praise you, that by all things ye be mindful of me; and as I betook to you my commandments, ye hold (onto them), [or ye keep (them)]. (And, brothers, I praise you, because ye always remember me; and as I delivered to you my teachings, ye follow and obey them.)

3   But I will that ye know, that Christ is [the] head of each man; but the head of the woman is the man; and the head of Christ *is* God. (But I desire that ye know, that the Messiah is the head of every man; and the head of the woman is the man; and the head of the Messiah *is* God.)

4   Each man praying, or prophesying, when his head is covered, defouleth his head (or defileth his head).

5   But each woman praying, or prophesying, when her head is not covered, defouleth her head (or defileth her head); for it is one (or for it is such), as if she were polled, [or if she were made bald, *or clipped*].

6   And if a woman be not covered [or veiled], be she polled; and if it is (a) foul thing to a woman to be polled, or to be made bald, (or and if it is a foul thing for a woman to be clipped, or to be cropped, or to be made bald), cover she her head.

7   But a man shall not cover his head, for he is the image and (the) glory of God; but a woman is the glory of man.

8   For a man is not of the woman, but the woman of the man.

9   And the man is not made for the woman, but the woman for the man.

10   Therefore the woman shall have a covering on her head, (and) also (out of regard) for (the) angels. (And so the woman shall have a covering upon her head, out of respect for the angels.)

11   Nevertheless neither the man *is* without the woman, neither the woman *is* without [the] man, in the Lord.

12   For why as the woman *is* of the man, so the man *is* by the woman; but all things *be* of God.

13   Deem ye yourselves (or You yourselves judge); beseemeth it [or becometh it] (for) a woman not covered on the head to pray to God?

14   Neither the kind itself teacheth us [*that*] (or Neither nature itself teacheth us *that*), for if a man nourish long hair, it is (a) shame to him;

15   but if a woman nourish long hair, it is (a) glory to her, for hairs be given to her for covering.

16   But if any man is seen to be full of strife (or And if anyone is seen to be always arguing),

we have none such custom, neither (hath) the church of God.

17 But this thing I command, not praising, that ye come together not into the better, but into the worse.

18 First for when ye come together into the church, I hear that dissensions, *either partings*, be, and in part I believe (it).

19 For it behooveth heresies to be, (so) that they that be (ap)proved, be openly known in you.

20 Therefore when ye come together into one, now it is not to eat the Lord's supper;

21 for why each man before taketh his supper to eat, and one is (still) hungry, and another is (now) drunken.

22 Whether ye have not houses to eat and (to) drink (in), or ye (so) despise the church of God, and confound, [*or shame*], them that have none [or them that have not]? What shall I say to you? I praise you, but herein I praise *you* not, [or I praise you; in this thing I praise *you* not].

23 For I have taken of the Lord that thing, which I have betaken to you, (or For I have received from the Lord, that which I have delivered to you). For the Lord Jesus, in what night he was betrayed, took bread,

24 and did thankings [or graces], and brake (it), and said, Take ye, and eat ye; this is my body, which shall be betrayed for you; do ye this thing into my mind (or do this in remembrance of me).

25 Also [*he took*] the cup, after that he had supped, and said, This cup is the new testament in my blood; do ye this thing, as oft as ye shall drink [*it*], into my mind. (And *he took* the cup, after that he had supped, and said, This cup is the New Covenant sealed by my blood; do this, as often as ye shall drink *it*, in remembrance of me.)

26 For as oft as ye shall eat this bread, and drink this cup, ye shall tell the death of the Lord, till that he come, [or ye shall show the death of the Lord, till he come].

27 Therefore whoever eateth the bread, or drinketh the cup of the Lord unworthily, he shall be guilty of the body and of the blood of the Lord.

28 But prove a man himself, and so eat he of that bread, and drink he of the cup.

29 For he that eateth and drinketh unworthily, eateth and drinketh doom, [*or damnation*], (or judgement), (un)to him[self], not wisely deeming the body of the Lord.

30 Therefore among you many *be* sick and feeble [or unstrong], and many sleep, [*or die*]. (And so among you there be many who be frail and weak, and many who have died.)

31 And if we deemed wisely us-selves, we should not be deemed; (And if we wisely judged ourselves, then we would not be judged or come under God's judgement;)

32 but while we be deemed of the Lord (or but when we be judged by the Lord), we be chastised, (so) that we be not condemned with this world.

33 Therefore, my brethren, when ye come together to eat, abide ye together. (And so, my brothers, when ye come together to eat, wait for one another.)

34 If any man hungereth, eat he at home, that ye come not together into doom (or so that ye do not come together under judgement). And I shall dispose other things, when I come.

CHAPTER 12

1 But of spiritual things, brethren, I will not that ye unknow. (But regarding spiritual matters, brothers, I do not desire that ye do not know or be ignorant about such things.)

2 For ye know, that when ye were heathen men, how ye were led going to dumb maumets [or to dumb simulacra]. (For ye know, how that when ye were Gentiles, ye were led like sheep unto mute and lifeless idols.)

3 Therefore I make known to you, that no

man speaking in the Spirit of God, saith departing from Jesus; and no man may say the Lord Jesus [is], [no] but in the Holy Ghost, (or and no one can say that Jesus *is* the Lord, unless he is guided by the Holy Spirit).

4   And diverse graces there be, (or And there be many different gifts or blessings), but *it is* all one Spirit;

5   and diverse services *there be*, but *it is* all one Lord;

6   and diverse workings there be, but *it is* all one God, that worketh all things in all things. (and there be many different kinds of works, but *it is* all one God, who worketh everything in everything.)

7   And to each man the showing of (the) Spirit is given to (his) profit (or for his benefit).

8   And the word of wisdom is given to one by (the) Spirit; to another the word of cunning, (or of knowing), (or to another the word of knowledge), by the same Spirit;

9   faith to another, in the same Spirit; to another, grace(s) of healings [or of healths], in one Spirit; (faith to another, by the same Spirit; to another, gifts of healing, by the one Spirit;)

10   to another, the working of virtues, (or works of power, or miracles); to another, prophecy; to another, very knowing, [or discretion], (or true discerning), of spirits; to another, kinds of (strange and ecstatic) languages [or tongues]; to another, (the) expounding [or (the) interpreting] of words.

11   And one and the same Spirit worketh all these things, parting to each by themselves as he will, (or dividing, or imparting, to each as he so desireth).

12   For as there is one body, and (it) hath many members, and all the members of the body when those be many [or when they be many], be one body, so also Christ (or so also the Messiah).

13   For in one Spirit all we be baptized into one body, either Jews, either heathen, either servants, either free; and all we be filled with drink in one Spirit [or and all we have drunk in one Spirit]. (For by one Spirit or in one Spirit, we all were baptized into one body, whether Jews, or Gentiles, servants, or free men; and we all have drunk from the one Spirit, or of one Spirit.)

14   For the body is not one member, but many.

15   If the foot shall say, For I am not the hand, I am not of the body; not therefore it is not of the body.

16   And if the ear saith, For I am not the eye, I am not of the body; not therefore it is not of the body.

17   If all the body is the eye, where is [the] hearing? and if all the body is hearing, where is [the] smelling?

18   But now God hath set members [or Now forsooth God hath put members], and each of them in the body, as he would (or as he wanted them to be).

19   And if all were one member, where *were* the body? (or where would the body *be*?)

20   But now there be many members, but one body.

21   And (so) the eye may not say to the hand, I have no need to thy works (or I have no need of thy works); or again the head to the feet, Ye be not necessary to me.

22   But much more those that be seen to be the lower members of the body, [or the more sick], (or the more frail, or weaker, members of the body), be more needful;

23   and those that we guess to be the unworthier [or the unnobler] members of the body, to them we give more honour; and those members that be unhonest, have more honesty, (or and those members that be unseemly, have more seemliness).

24   For our honest members have need of none; but God tempered the body, giving more worship to it, to whom it failed, (For our seemly members have need of no one else; but God tempered the body, giving more honour to

those parts, that seemed lacking,)

25   (so) that debate be not in the body, but that the members be busy into the same thing each for (the) other (or for one another).

26   And if one member suffereth anything, all members suffer therewith; either if one member joyeth [or glorieth], all members joy together.

27   And ye be the body of Christ (or And ye be the body of the Messiah), and members of member.

28   But God set some men in the church, first apostles, the second time prophets [or the second prophets], the third teachers, afterward virtues, (or works of power, or miracles), afterward graces of healings (or gifts of healing), helpings, governings, kinds of (strange and ecstatic) languages (or tongues), interpretations of words.

29   Whether all [be] apostles? whether all [be] prophets? whether all (be) teachers? whether all (be) virtues? (or whether all be works of power or miracles?)

30   whether all have (the) grace of healings? whether all speak with (strange and ecstatic) languages? whether all expound [or interpret]? (whether all have the gift of healing? whether all speak with tongues? whether all interpret?)

31   But (pur)sue ye the better ghostly gifts (or But follow, or go after, the better spiritual gifts). And yet I (shall) show to you a more excellent, [or worthy], way.

CHAPTER 13

1   If I speak with tongues of men and of angels, and I have not charity, I am made as brass sounding, or a cymbal tinkling. (If I speak with the tongues of men and of angels, but I have no love, I am made like a sounding brass, or like a tinkling cymbal.)

2   And if I have prophecy, and know all mysteries, and all cunning, (or all knowing), [or science], and if I have all faith, so that I (can) move hills from their place(s), [or from one place to another], and I have not charity, I am nought. (And if I have prophecy, and know all mysteries, and all knowledge, and if I have all faith, so that I can move mountains from one place to another, but I have no love, I am nothing.)

3   And if I part all my goods into the meats of poor men, and if I betake my body, so that I burn, and if I have not charity, it profiteth to me nothing. (And if I part with, or divide up, all my goods, to provide food for the poor, and if I deliver, or give up, my body, to be burned, but I have no love, it profiteth nothing to me.)

4   Charity is patient, it is benign; charity envieth not, it doeth not wickedly, it is not blown [with pride], (Love is patient, it is kind; love envieth not, it doeth not wickedly, it is not swollen with pride,)

5   it is not covetous, [or it is not ambitious, or covetous of worships, (or honours)], it seeketh not those things that be his own [or her own], it is not stirred to wrath, it thinketh not evil,

6   it joyeth not on wickedness, but it joyeth together to (the) truth; [it joyeth not in wickedness, forsooth it joyeth together with (the) truth;]

7   it suffereth all things, it believeth all things, it hopeth all things, it sustaineth all things.

8   Charity falleth never down, whether prophecies shall be voided, either languages shall cease, either science shall be destroyed. (Love never falleth down, whether prophecies shall be made null and void, or strange and ecstatic languages shall cease, or knowledge shall be destroyed.)

9   For a part we know, and a part we prophesy;

10   but when that shall come that is perfect, that thing that is of part shall be voided. (but when that shall come which is complete, or which is finished, that which is but partial, or is unfinished, shall be done away.)

11 When I was a little child, I spake as a little child, I understood as a little child, I thought as a little child; but when I was made a man, I avoided those things/I voided those things that were of a little child. (When I was a little child, I spoke like a little child, I understood like a little child, I thought like a little child; but when I became a man, I put away those things that were a little child's.)

12 And we see now by a mirror in darkness, but then face to face; now I know of part, but then I shall know, as I am known. (And we see now by a mirror in the dark, but then face to face; now I know a part, but then I shall know, like I am known by God.)

13 And now dwelleth faith, hope, charity, these three; but the most of these is charity. (And now remaineth faith, hope, love, these three; but the greatest of these is love.)

CHAPTER 14

1 (Pur)Sue ye charity, (or Follow or Go after love), (and) love ye spiritual things, but more that ye prophesy.

2 And he that speaketh in tongue(s), speaketh not to men, but to God; for no man heareth (it), (or And he who speaketh in a strange and ecstatic language, speaketh not to men, but to God; for no one can understand it). But the Spirit speaketh mysteries.

3 For he that prophesieth, speaketh to men to edification (or speaketh to men for edification), and admonishing, and comforting.

4 He that speaketh in tongue(s), *that is, in* (a) *strange language*, edifieth himself, (or He who speaketh in a strange and ecstatic language, edifieth himself); but he that prophesieth, edifieth the church of God.

5 And I will, that all ye speak in tongues, but more that ye prophesy. For he that prophesieth, is more than he that speaketh in (strange and ecstatic) languages, [or in tongues]; but peradventure he expound, [or interpret, *or*

declare], that the church take edification. (And I do desire, that ye all speak in strange and ecstatic languages, or in tongues, but more importantly, that ye all prophesy. For he who prophesieth, is more helpful to others than he who speaketh in a strange and ecstatic language; unless of course, the speaker in tongues can also expound or interpret, so that the entire church can receive edification.)

6 But now, brethren, if I come to you, and speak in tongues, what shall I profit to you [or what shall it profit to you], [no] but if I speak to you either in revelation, either in science, either in prophecy, either in teaching? (But now, brothers, if I come to you, and speak in a strange and ecstatic language, what shall it profit you, unless I also speak to you either in revelation, or in knowledge, or in prophecy, or in teaching?)

7 For those things that be without soul, [*or life*], and giveth voices (or maketh sounds), (yea), either pipe, either harp, but those give (a) distinction of soundings [or no but if they shall give (a) distinction of soundings], how shall it be known that that is sung, either that that is trumped [or is harped].

8 For if a trumpet give an uncertain sound, who shall make himself ready to battle? (or who shall prepare himself for battle?)

9 So but ye give an open word by tongue(s), how shall that that is said be known? (or And so, unless ye open, or ye interpret, the words spoken in a strange and ecstatic language, how shall what is said be understood?) For ye shall be speaking in vain [or in the air].

10 There be many kinds of languages [or tongues] in this world, and nothing is without voice (or and none of them is without sound or meaning).

11 But if I know not the virtue of a voice (or But if I do not know the meaning of a sound), I shall be to him, to whom I shall speak, (like) a barbaric; and he that speaketh to me, *shall be* (like) a barbaric.

12   So ye, for ye be lovers of spirits, [*that is, of ghostly*, (or spiritual) *gifts*], seek ye that ye be plenteous to (the) edification of the church.

13   And therefore he that speaketh in (a strange and ecstatic) language [or in tongue(s)], pray, that he expound (it), [or pray, that he interpret (it)]. (And so he who speaketh in a strange and ecstatic language, beseech him to interpret it.)

14   For if I pray in tongue(s), my spirit prayeth; mine understanding, [or my mind, *or reason*ing], is without fruit. (For if I pray in a strange and ecstatic language, my spirit prayeth; but my thinking, *or my reasoning*, is without fruit.)

15   What then? I shall pray in (my) spirit, I shall pray in (my) mind; I shall say psalm in (my) spirit, I shall say psalm also in (my) mind.

16   For if thou blessest in (thy) spirit, who filleth the place of an idiot, (or For if thou blessest from thy spirit, if an unlearned man be there), how shall he say Amen on thy blessing, for he knoweth not, what thou sayest?

17   For thou doest well (thy) thankings [or (thy) graces], but another man is not edified.

18   I thank my God, for I speak in the language of all (of) you; [I do graces to my God, for I speak in the tongue of all (of) you;]

19   but in the church I will (rather) speak five words in my wit, (or but in the church I would rather speak five words from my mind, or out of my thoughts), (so) that also I teach other men, than ten thousand words in (a) tongue [*not understood*].

20   Brethren, do not ye be made children in wits, (or Brothers, do not be made like children in your minds, or in your thoughts), but in malice be ye children; but in wits be ye perfect.

21   For in the law it is written, That in other tongues and other lips I shall speak to this people, and neither so they shall hear me, saith the Lord.

22   Therefore (strange and ecstatic) languages be into (a) token, not to faithful men, but to men out of the faith; but prophecies be not to men out of the faith, but to faithful men. (And so tongues be a sign, not for men in the faith, but for men out of the faith; and prophecies be a sign, not for men out of the faith, but for men in the faith.)

23   Therefore if all the church come together into one, and all men speak in tongues, if idiots, either men out of the faith enter, whether they shall not say, What, be ye mad? (And so if all the church come together as one, and everyone speak in a strange and ecstatic language, if the unlearned, or those not in the faith enter, shall they not say, What is this? ye be crazy!)

24   But if all men prophesy, if any unfaithful man or idiot enter, he is convicted of all, he is wisely deemed of all (these words). (But if everyone prophesy, if anyone not in the faith, or someone unlearned, enter, he is convicted by all of these words, he is wisely judged by all of them.)

25   For the hid things of his heart be known, and so he shall fall down on the face, and shall worship God, and show verily that God is in you. (For the hidden things of his heart be known, and so he shall fall down on his face, and shall worship God, and truly show that God is there with you.)

26   What then, brethren? When ye come together, each of you hath a psalm, he hath teaching, he hath apocalypse, [*or revelation*], he hath tongue(s), (or he hath a strange and ecstatic language), he hath expounding [or interpreting]; all (these) things be they done to edification.

27   Whether a man speaketh in tongue(s), (or And if someone speaketh in a strange and ecstatic language), [*be this done*] by two men, either three at the most, and by parts, (so) that (some)one (can) interpret.

28   But if there be not an interpreter, be he still [or speak he not] in the church, and speak he (only) to himself and to God.

29 Prophets twain or three say, and others wisely deem. (Let two or three prophets speak, and others wisely judge what they say.)

30 But if anything be showed to a sitter [or (to) one (who is) sitting], the former be still (or the first speaker stop speaking).

31 For ye may all prophesy, each by himself, that all men learn (or so that everyone can learn), and all admonish.

32 And the spirits of (the) prophets be subject to (other) prophets;

33 for why God is not of dissension, but of peace; as I teach in all churches of holy men. (for God is not *the God* of conflict or discord, but *the God* of peace; as I teach in all the churches of the saints or of God's people.)

34 Women in churches be still; for it is not suffered to them to speak, but to be subject, as the law saith. (Women should be silent in church; for it is not allowed for them to speak, but they should be subordinate, or in submission, like the Law saith.)

35 But if they will anything learn, ask they their husbands at home; for it is foul thing to a woman to speak in the church. (And if they desire to learn anything, let them ask their husbands at home; for it is a foul thing for a woman to speak in the church.)

36 Whether the word of God came forth of you, or to you alone it came? (Did the word of God come forth from you, or did it come to you alone?)

37 If any man is seen to be a prophet, or spiritual, know he those things that I write to you, for those be the commandments of the Lord [or for they be the commandments of the Lord].

38 And if any man unknoweth (or not knoweth), he shall be unknowing. (And if anyone is ignorant, let him be ignorant.)

39 Therefore, brethren, love ye to prophesy, and do not ye forbid to speak in tongues. (And so brothers, love prophesy, and do not forbid any to speak in strange and ecstatic languages.)

40 But be all things done honestly, and by due order in you. (But let all things be done with seemliness, and by due order among you.)

CHAPTER 15

1 Soothly, brethren, I make the gospel known to you, which I have preached to you, which also ye have taken, in which ye stand, (Truly, brothers, I make the Gospel, or the Good News, known to you, which I have preached to you, and which ye have received, and in which ye stand,)

2 by which also ye shall be saved; by which reason I have preached to you, if ye hold, if ye have not believed idly. (and by which ye shall be saved; for which reason I have preached to you, if ye will hold onto it, and if ye have not idly believed it.)

3 For I betook to you at the beginning [or in the first] that thing which also I have received; that Christ was dead for our sins, by the scriptures; (For I delivered or I gave to you, from the beginning, that which also I have received; that the Messiah died for our sins, according to the Scriptures;)

4 and that he was buried, and that he rose again in the third day, after [the] scriptures; (and that he was buried, and that he rose again on the third day, according to the Scriptures;)

5 and that he was seen to Cephas, and after these things to (the) eleven; (and that he was seen by Peter, and afterward by the Eleven;)

6 afterward he was seen to more than five hundred brethren together, of which many live yet, but some be dead; (afterward he was seen by more than five hundred brothers together, of whom many still live, but some of whom have died;)

7 afterward he was seen to James, and afterward to all the apostles. (afterward he was seen by James, and afterward by all the apostles.)

8 And last of all he was seen also to me, as

to a dead-born child. (And last of all he was also seen by me, as if to a dead-born child.)

9 For I am the least of the apostles, that am not worthy to be called (an) apostle, for I pursued the church of God (or for I persecuted God's church).

10 But by the grace of God I am that thing that I am; and his grace was not void in me. For I travailed more plenteously than all they; but not I, but the grace of God with me. (But by the grace of God I am what I am; and his grace was not given to me in vain. For I worked harder than all of them; but not me really, but the grace of God working through me.)

11 But whether I, or they, so we have preached, and so ye have believed.

12 And if Christ is preached, that he rose again from death [or that he rose again from (the) dead], how say some men among you, that the again-rising of dead men is not? (And if it be preached, that the Messiah rose again from the dead, then how can some men among you say, that there is no resurrection of the dead?)

13 And if the again-rising of dead men is not, neither Christ rose again from death. (And if there is no resurrection of the dead, then the Messiah did not rise again from the dead.)

14 And if Christ rose not, our preaching is vain, our faith is vain. (And if the Messiah did not rise again, then our preaching is in vain, and our faith is in vain.)

15 And we be found false witnesses of God, for we have said witnessing against God, that he raised Christ, whom he raised not, if dead men rise not again. (And we be found to be false witnesses about God, for we have said false testimony about God, that he raised the Messiah, whom he did not raise, if the dead do not rise again.)

16 For why if dead men rise not again, neither Christ rose again; (Because if the dead do not rise again, then neither did the Messiah rise again;)

17 and if Christ rose not again, our faith is vain; and yet ye be in your sins. (and if the Messiah did not rise again, then our faith is in vain; and ye still be in your sins.)

18 And then they that have died [or that (have) slept] in Christ, have perished. (And then those who have died in the Messiah, have truly perished.)

19 If in this life only we be hoping in Christ, we be more wretches than all men. (If it is only for this life that we have hope in the Messiah, then we be greater wretches than anyone.)

20 But now Christ hath risen again from death [or Now forsooth Christ rose again *from dead men*], the first fruit(s) of dead men; (But the Messiah hath risen again from the dead, yea, he is the first fruits of the dead;)

21 for death *was* by a man, and by a man *is* again-rising (or the resurrection) from death. [+for soothly by a man (came) death, and by a man (the) again-rising of (the) dead.]

22 And as in Adam all men die, so in Christ all men shall be quickened. (And so as in Adam all men die, so in the Messiah all men shall be enlivened or shall be given life.)

23 But each man in his order; the first fruit(s), Christ, [or (the) first fruits, Christ], afterward they that be of Christ, that believed in the coming of Christ; (But each one in the proper order; the first fruits, the Messiah, afterward they who be of the Messiah, yea, those who believe at the coming of the Messiah;)

24 afterward an end, when he shall betake the kingdom to God and to the Father, when he shall void all princehood, and power, and virtue. (and then the end, when he shall deliver the Kingdom to God the Father, when he shall make void, or shall do away, all princehood, and power, and authority.)

25 But it behooveth him to reign, till he put all his enemies under his feet.

26 And at the last, death the enemy shall be destroyed;

27 for he hath made subject all things under his feet. And when he saith, all things be

subject to him, without doubt except him that subjected all things to him.

28 And when all things be subjected to him, then the Son himself shall be subject to him, that made all things subject to him, (so) that God be all things in all things.

29 Else what shall they do, that be baptized for dead men, if in no wise dead men rise again? whereto be they baptized for them? (Or else what shall they do, who be baptized for the dead, if in no way the dead rise again? why then be they baptized for them?)

30 And whereto be we in peril every hour? (And why be we in danger every hour?)

31 Each day I die for your glory, brethren, which *glory* I have in Christ Jesus our Lord. (Every day I die for your glory, brothers, which *glory* I have in the Messiah Jesus our Lord.)

32 If after man I have fought to beasts, [*or against beasts*], at Ephesus, what profiteth it to me, if dead men rise not again? (or what is the benefit to me, if the dead do not rise again?) Eat we, and drink we, for we shall die tomorrow.

33 Do not ye be deceived; for evil speeches destroy good conduct. [+Do not ye be deceived *by false teaching*; forsooth evil speeches, *or false doctrine*, corrupt good virtues.]

34 Awake ye, just men, and do not ye do sin [*or and do not ye sin*]; for some men have ignorance of God, but to reverence, *that is, to your shame*, I speak to you (or I speak about you).

35 But some man saith, How shall dead men rise again (or How can the dead rise again), or in what manner body shall they come?

36 [O!] Unwise man, that thing that thou sowest, is not quickened, [no] but it die first; (O unwise man! that which thou sowest, is not brought back to life, unless it first die;)

37 and that thing that thou sowest, thou sowest not the body that is to come, but a naked corn, (or a kernel, or a grain), as of wheat, or of some other *seeds*;

38 and God giveth to it a body, as he will, and to each of (the) seeds a proper body. (and God giveth it a body, as he so desireth, yea, to each seed its own body.)

39 Not each flesh *is* the same flesh (or All flesh *is* not the same flesh), but one *is* of men, another *is* of beasts, another *is* of birds, another *is* of fishes.

40 And *there be* heavenly bodies, and *there be* earthly bodies; but one glory *is* of heavenly bodies, and another *is* of earthly [*bodies*]. (And *there be* heavenly bodies, and *there be* earthly bodies; but one beauty or splendour *is* for heavenly bodies, and another beauty or splendour *is* for earthly *bodies*.)

41 Another clearness *is* of the sun, another clearness *is* of the moon, and another clearness *is* of the stars; and a star diverseth from a star in clearness. (And there *is* one beauty or splendour for the sun, another beauty or splendour *is* for the moon, and another beauty or splendour *is* for the stars; and a star diverseth from a star in its beauty or splendour.)

42 And so the again-rising of dead men (or And so the resurrection of the dead). It is sown in corruption, it shall rise in uncorruption;

43 it is sown in unnobleness, it shall rise in glory; it is sown in infirmity, it shall rise in virtue, (or it is sown in frailty and weakness, it shall rise in strength and power);

44 it is sown a beastly body, it shall rise a spiritual body, (or it is sown as a fleshly body, it shall rise as a spiritual body). If there is a beastly body, (then) there is also a spiritual body;

45 as it is written, The first man Adam was made into a soul living, the last Adam into a spirit quickening. (as it is written, The first Adam was made into a living soul, the last Adam into the enlivening, or the life-giving, Spirit.)

46 But the first *is* not that [*body*] that is spiritual, but that that is beast-like (or that is fleshly), afterward that that is spiritual.

47　The first man of earth *is* earthly; the second man of heaven *is* heavenly. (The first man from earth *is* earthly; the second Man from heaven *is* heavenly.)

48　Such as the earthly man *is*, such *be* the earthly men; and such as the heavenly man *is*, such *be* also the heavenly men.

49　Therefore as we have borne the image of the earthly man, bear we also the image of the heavenly *man*. (And so as we have worn the image of the earthly man, let us also wear the image of the heavenly *Man*.)

50　Brethren, I say this thing, that flesh and blood may not wield the kingdom of God, neither corruption shall wield uncorruption [or incorruption]. (Brothers, I say this, that flesh and blood cannot possess the Kingdom of God, nor shall that which is corrupted or is mortal, possess incorruption or immortality.)

51　Lo! I say to you (a) private [or a mystery] of holy things, (or Behold, I shall tell you a secret about the holy things). And all we shall rise again, but not all we shall be changed *to the state of glory*;

52　in a moment, in the twinkling of an eye, in the last trump; for the trump shall sound, and dead men shall rise again, without corruption [or incorrupt], and we shall be changed. (in a moment, in the twinkling of an eye, at the last trumpet call; for the trumpet shall sound, and the dead shall rise again, without corruption, or incorrupt, or immortal, and so we shall be changed.)

53　For it behooveth this corruptible thing to clothe uncorruption [or incorruption], and this deadly thing to put away [or to clothe] undeadliness. (For it behooveth that this corruptible thing be clothed with incorruption, yea, that this mortal thing put on, or be clothed with, immortality.)

54　But when this deadly thing shall clothe undeadliness, then shall the word be done [or be fulfilled], that is written, Death is sopped up in victory. (But when this mortal thing shall be clothed with immortality, then shall the word be fulfilled that is written, Death is swallowed up in victory!)

55　Death, where is thy victory? Death, where is thy prick? (Death, where is thy victory? Death, where is thy prod?)

56　But the prick of death is sin; and the virtue of sin is the law. (And the prod of death is sin; and the power of sin cometh from the Law.)

57　But do we thankings to God, that gave to us victory by our Lord Jesus Christ. (But we give thanks to God, who gave us victory by our Lord Jesus Christ.)

58　Therefore, my dearworthy brethren, be ye steadfast, and unmoveable, being plenteous in (the) work of the Lord, (for)evermore witting that your travail is not idle in the Lord (or always knowing that your labour is never in vain, or futile, in, or done for, the Lord).

CHAPTER 16

1　But of the gatherings [or of the collects] *of money* that be made into (the) saints (or Regarding the collection of money that be made for the saints or God's people), as I *have* ordained in the churches of Galatia, so also do ye

2　one day of the week (or the first day of the week). Each of you keep, [*or lay up*], at himself, keeping that that pleaseth to him(self), (so) that when I come, the gatherings be not made.

3　And when I shall be present, which men ye (ap)prove, I shall send them by epistles to bear your grace into Jerusalem. (And then when I shall be there, whichever men ye shall approve, I shall send them with letters to take your gift to Jerusalem.)

4　That if it be worthy that also I go, they shall go with me. (And if it be worthwhile that I also go, they shall go with me.)

5　But I shall come to you, when I shall pass by Macedonia; for why I shall pass by

Macedonia. (But I shall come to you, when I shall pass through Macedonia; for I shall go through Macedonia.)

6   But peradventure I shall dwell at you (or But perhaps I shall remain with you), or also dwell the winter, (so) that ye (can) lead me whither ever I shall go.

7   And I will not now see you in my passing (through), [or Soothly I will not now see you in (or while) passing (through)], for I hope to dwell with you a while, if the Lord shall suffer, (or for I hope to remain with you for a while, if the Lord will allow it).

8   But I shall dwell at Ephesus, unto Whitsuntide.

9   For a great door and an open [or (an) evident] (one) is opened to me (or For a great door is opened to me for effective work), and (there be) many adversaries.

10   And if Timothy come, see ye that he be without dread with you (or see that he be without anything to fear from you), for he worketh the work of the Lord, as I (do).

11   Therefore no man despise him; but lead him forth in peace, (so) that he come to me; for I abide him with (the) brethren (or for I wait for him with the brothers).

12   But, brethren, I make known to you of Apollos, that I prayed (or beseeched) him much, that he should come to you, with (some) brethren. But it was not his will to come now (or But it was not his desire to come now); but he shall come, when he shall have leisure [or when it shall be able to him].

13   Walk ye, and stand ye in the faith; do ye manly, and be ye comforted in the Lord, (or be brave, and be strong in the Lord),

14   and be all your things done in charity. (and let everything ye do be done in love, or with love.)

15   And, brethren, I beseech you, ye know the house(hold) of Stephanas, and of Fortunatus, and Achaicus, for they be the first fruits of Achaia, and into (the) ministry of (the) saints they have ordained themselves (or and they have committed themselves unto the service of God's people);

16   that also ye be subjects to such, and to each working together and travailing.

17   For I have joy in the presence of Stephanas, and Fortunatus, and Achaicus; for they [full-]filled that thing that failed to you (or for they did fully what you were unable to do, because of your absence);

18   for they have refreshed both my spirit and yours. Therefore know ye them, that be such manner *men* (or And so know and respect those who be such kind of *men*).

19   All the churches of Asia greet you well (or All the Asian churches send you hearty greetings). Aquila and Priscilla, with their home-church, greet you much in the Lord, at the which also I am harboured.

20   All (the) brethren greet you well. Greet ye well together in holy kiss. (All the brothers send you hearty greetings. Give hearty greetings to one another with a holy kiss.)

21   My greeting by Paul's hand.

22   If any man loveth not our Lord Jesus Christ, be he cursed, Maranatha, *that is, in the coming of the Lord, or in the day of doom.* (If anyone loveth not our Lord Jesus Christ, let him be cursed on the Day of Judgement.)

23   The grace of our Lord Jesus Christ be with you.

24   My charity be with you all in Christ Jesus our Lord. Amen. (My love be with you all in the Messiah Jesus our Lord. Amen.) †

2ND CORINTHIANS

CHAPTER 1

1 Paul, (an) apostle of Jesus Christ, by the will of God, and Timothy, (a) brother, to the church of God that is at Corinth, with all (the) saints that be in all Achaia (or with all of God's people who be in all of Achaia),

2 grace (be) to you, and (the) peace of God our Father and of the Lord Jesus Christ.

3 Blessed *be* God and the Father of our Lord Jesus Christ, (the) Father of mercies, and (the) God of all comfort,

4 which comforteth us in all our tribulation, that also we may comfort them, that be in all dis-ease [or in all pressure] by the admonishing by which also we be admonished of God. (who comforteth us in all our trials, so that we can also comfort those, who be under great pressure, by the admonishing by which we also be admonished by God.)

5 For as the passions of Christ be plenteous in us, so also by Christ our comfort is plenteous. (For as the sufferings of the Messiah be plentiful in us, so also through the Messiah our comfort is plentiful.)

6 And whether we be in tribulation, [or be troubled, *or be pursued*], (or be persecuted), for your tribulation and health (or salvation), either we be comforted, for your comfort, either we be admonished, for your admonishing and health (or salvation). Which worketh in you the suffering of the same passions (or the same sufferings), which also we suffer,

7 that our hope be firm for you; witting for as ye be fellows of passions, so ye shall be also of comfort. (so that our hope for you be firm; knowing that as ye be my fellows in sufferings, so ye shall also be my fellows in comfort.)

8 For, brethren, we will, that ye know of our tribulation, that was done in Asia; for over-measure we were grieved over-might [or above virtue], so that it distressed us, yea, to live. (For brothers, we desire, that ye know of our trouble, that we had in Asia; for over-measure we were grieved more than our strength could endure, so that it distressed us, yea, to live.)

9 But we in us-selves had (the) answer, [*or* (the) *certainty*], of death, (so) that we trust not in us, but in God that raiseth dead men (or but in God who raiseth the dead).

10 Which delivered us, and delivereth from so great perils, into whom we hope, also yet he shall deliver,

11 while also ye help in prayer for us; (so) that of the persons of many faces of that giving that is in us, thankings [or graces] be done for us by many men to God.

12 For our glory is this, the witnessing of our conscience (or the testimony of our conscience), that in (the) simpleness and cleanness of God (or with godly sincerity), and not in fleshly wisdom, but in the grace of God, we lived in this world, but more plenteously to you.

13 And we write not other things to you, than those that ye have read and know, and I hope that into the end ye shall know,

14 as also ye have known us a part; for we be your glory, as also ye be ours in the day of our Lord Jesus Christ.

15 And in this trusting I would first come to you, that ye should have the second grace (or so that ye would have a second blessing),

16 and pass by you into Macedonia, (or and pass by you, or visit you, on the way to Macedonia), and again from Macedonia come to you, and of you be led into Judea.

17 But when I would (do) this thing, whether I used unsteadfastness, either those things that I think, I think after the flesh, (so) that at me be, it is and it is not? [⁺Forsooth when I would (do) this thing, whether I used lightness, *either unsteadfastness*, or those things that I think, I

think after the flesh, (so) that there be at me, is and is not, *or yea and nay*?]

18   But God is true, for our word that was at you, is and is not, is not therein, but is is in it. [⁺Forsooth God is true, for our word that was at you, there is not in it yea and nay/there is not in it is and nay, but is, *that is* (the) *truth*, is in it.]

19   For why Jesus Christ, the Son of God, which is preached among you by us (or who was preached among you by us), by me, and Silvanus, and Timothy, there was not in him, is and is not, but is was in him. [⁺Soothly Jesus Christ, the son of God, that is preached in you by us, by me, and by Silvanus, and Timothy, there was not in him yea and nay, but is, *or yea*, was in him/but in him was is.]

20   For why how many ever be (the) promises of God, in that is, *be fulfilled*, [or Forsooth how many ever be (the) promises of God, in him is, *that is, they be fulfilled in him*]. And therefore by him we say Amen to God, to our glory.

21   Soothly it is God that confirmeth us with you in Christ, and which anointed us, (Truly it is God who confirmeth us with you in the Messiah, and who anointed us,)

22   and which marked us, and gave (the) earnest [or a wed] of the Spirit in our hearts. (and who sealed us, and put the pledge of the Spirit in our hearts.)

23   For I call God to witness against my soul (or For I call upon God to testify about my soul), that I sparing you came not over to Corinth;

24   not that we be lords of your faith, but (that) we be helpers of your joy; for through belief ye stand (or for ye stand by faith).

CHAPTER 2

1   And I ordained this [same] thing at me, that I should not come again in heaviness [or in sorrow] to you.

2   For if I make you sorry, [*or heavy*], who is he that gladdeth me, but he that is sorrowful of me? (For if I make you sorrowful, who is he who maketh me glad, but he whom I have made sorrowful?)

3   And this same thing I wrote to you, (so) that when I come, I have not sorrow on sorrow, of the which it behooved me to have joy. And I trust in you all, that my joy is of all you [or that my joy is of you all].

4   For of much tribulation and anguish of heart I wrote to you by many tears, not that ye be sorry, but that ye know what charity I have more plenteously in you. (For I wrote to you out of much trouble and anguish in my heart, and through many tears, not that ye be made sorrowful, but so that ye know of the love which I have most plentifully for you.)

5   For if any man hath made me sorrowful, he hath not made me sorrowful but a part [or but in part], that I charge not you all (or so that I do not be a burden to all of you).

6   This blaming that is made of many, sufficeth to him, that is such one [or that is such a manner *man*];

7   so that on the contrary ye rather forgive and comfort (or strengthen), lest peradventure he that is such a manner *man*, be swallowed up, [or be sopped up, *or despair*], by more great heaviness.

8   For which thing I beseech you, that ye confirm charity into him (or that ye confirm your love for him).

9   For why therefore I wrote this, that I know your proof, whether in all things ye be obedient.

10   For to whom ye have forgiven anything, also I have forgiven. For I, that that I forgave, if I forgave anything, *have forgiven* for you in the person of Christ (or *have forgiven* it for you in the presence of the Messiah),

11   that we be not deceived of Satan (or so that we be not deceived by Satan); for we know his thoughts.

12   But when I was come to Troas for the gospel of Christ, and a door was opened to me

298

in the Lord, (But when I had come to Troas with the Gospel, or the Good News, of the Messiah, and a door was opened to me by the Lord,)

13 I had not rest to my spirit (or I had no rest for my spirit), for I found not my brother Titus, but I said to them farewell, and I passed (forth) into Macedonia.

14 And I do thankings to God, that (for)evermore maketh us to have victory in Christ Jesus, and showeth by us the odour, [or (the) *savour, or* (the) *sweetness*], of his knowing in each place; (And I give thanks to God, who always maketh us to have victory in the Messiah Jesus, and showeth by us the aroma, *or the fragrance, or the sweetness*, of his knowledge in every place;)

15 for we be the good odour, [*or savour*], of Christ to God, among these that be made safe, and among these that perish. (for we be the good aroma, *or the sweet fragrance*, of the Messiah to God, among those who be saved, and among those who perish.)

16 To other soothly, (or Truly to the one), [*we be*] (the) odour of death into death, but to the other *we be* (the) odour of life into life. And to these things who *is* so able?

17 For we be not as [full] many, that do adultery by the word of God [or adulterating the word of God], but we speak of cleanness as of God, before God in Christ. (For we do not do like a great many, adulterating the word of God, but we speak with godly sincerity, before God in the Messiah.)

CHAPTER 3

1 Begin we therefore again to praise (or to commend) us-selves? or whether we need, as some men, epistles [or letters] of praising to you, or of you? (or from you?)

2 Ye be our epistle, written in our hearts, which is known and read of all men (or which is known and read by all men),

3 and [*ye be*] made open, for ye be the epistle of Christ ministered of us, and written, not with ink, but by the Spirit of the living God; not in stone tables, but in fleshly tables of heart. (and *ye be* made open, for ye be the letter of the Messiah served by us, and written, not with ink, but by the Spirit of the living God; not on stone tablets, but on the fleshly tablets of the heart.)

4 For we have such trust by Christ to God;

5 not that we be sufficient to think anything of us[-selves], as of us, but our sufficience is of God (or but our sufficiency is from God).

6 Which also made us able ministers of the new testament, not by (the) letter, but by (the) Spirit; for the letter slayeth, but the Spirit quickeneth. (Who also made us able servants of the new covenant, not by the letter, but by the Spirit; for the letter killeth, but the Spirit enliveneth or giveth life.)

7 And if the (ad)ministration of death written by letter(s) in stones was in glory, so that the children of Israel might not behold into the face of Moses, for the glory of his face, which [*glory*] is voided (or is done away),

8 how shall not the (ad)ministration of the Spirit be more in glory?

9 For if the (ad)ministration of condemnation was in glory, much more the (ad)ministration of rightwiseness is plenteous in glory.

10 For neither that that was clear (or that that was glorious) was glorified in this part for the excellent glory;

11 and if that that is voided (or that that was done away) was by glory, much more that that dwelleth still is in glory.

12 Therefore we that have such hope, use much trust;

13 and not as Moses laid [or put] a veil on his face, that the children of Israel should not behold into his face, which *veil* is voided. (and not as Moses put a veil on his face, so that the children of Israel could not behold his face, which *veil* is now done away.)

14   But the wits of them be astonied; for into this day the same veil in [the] reading of the old testament, dwelleth not showed, for it is voided in Christ, (But their minds be astonished; for unto this day the same veil remaineth when they read from the Old Covenant, though it is not shown, but it is done away in the Messiah,)

15   but into this day, when Moses is read, the veil is put on their hearts.

16   But when Israel shall be converted to God, the veil shall be done away.

17   And the Spirit is the Lord; and where the Spirit of the Lord is, there *is* freedom. [Forsooth the Lord is a Spirit; forsooth where is the Spirit of God, there *is* liberty.]

18   And all we that with open face see the glory of the Lord, be transformed into the same image, from clearness into clearness (or from glory unto glory), as of the Spirit of the Lord.

CHAPTER 4

1   Therefore we that have this administration, [*or office*], after this that we have gotten mercy, fail we not,

2   but do we away the privy, (or the private, or the secret), things of shame, not walking in subtle guile, neither doing adultery by the word of God [or neither adulterating the word of God], but in (the) showing of the truth commending us-selves to each conscience of men before God.

3   For if also our gospel is covered, *or is hid*, in these that perish it is covered; (And if our Gospel or Good News is covered, *or it is hidden*, it is only hidden for those who perish, or who go to destruction;)

4   in which [the] god of this world, *that is, the devil*, hath blinded the souls of unfaithful men, (so) that the (en)lightening [or the lighting] of the gospel of the glory of Christ, which is the image of God, shine not. (in which the god of this world, *that is, the Devil*, hath blinded the souls of the unfaithful or the unbelievers, so

that the light of the Gospel, or the Good News, of the glory of the Messiah, who is the image of God, cannot shine for them.)

5   But we preach not us-selves, but our Lord Jesus Christ [or but Jesus Christ our Lord]; and us (as) your servants by Jesus.

6   For God, that said [the] light to shine of darknesses, he hath given light in our hearts, to the lightening [or the illumining] of the science of the clearness of God, in the face of Jesus Christ. (For God, who commanded the light to shine in the darkness, he hath given, or he hath put, the light in our hearts, to give the light of the knowledge of the glory of God, in the face of Jesus Christ.)

7   And we have this treasure in brittle vessels, that the worthiness [or the highness] be of God's virtue (or so that the worthiness be of God's power), and not of us.

8   In all things we suffer tribulation, but we be not anguished, *or annoyed*, (or harmed); we be made poor, but we lack nothing [or we be not destitute];

9   we suffer persecution, but we be not forsaken; we be made low, but we be not confounded; we be cast down, but we perish not, (or we be thrown down, but we do not perish).

10   And (for)evermore we bear about the slaying [or the mortifying] of Jesus in our body (or And we always carry about the death of Jesus in our body), (so) that also the life of Jesus be showed in our bodies.

11   For evermore we that live, be taken into death, for Jesus, that the life of Jesus be showed in our deadly flesh. (For we who live, always be taken unto death, for the sake of Jesus, so that the life of Jesus be shown in our mortal flesh.)

12   Therefore death worketh in us, but life in you.

13   And we have the same spirit of faith, as it is written, I have believed, wherefore I have spoken; and we believe, wherefore also we speak;

14   witting that he that raised Jesus (or knowing that he who raised up Jesus), shall raise up also us with Jesus, and shall ordain [us] with you.

15   And all things [be done] for you, (so) that a plenteous grace by many thankings be plenteous into the glory of God. [Soothly all things be done for you, (so) that grace being plenteous by many in doing of thanks be plenteous into (the) glory of God.]

16   For which thing we fail not, for though our outer man be corrupted; nevertheless the inner man is renewed from day to day.

17   But that light, [or easy], thing of our tribulation that lasteth now, but as it were by a moment, worketh in us over-measure an everlasting burden [or an everlasting weight] into the highness of glory;

18   while that we behold not those things that be seen, but those [things] that be not seen. For those things that be seen, be but during for a short time [or temporal]; but those things that be not seen, be everlasting [or eternal].

CHAPTER 5

1   And we know, that if our earthly house of this dwelling be dissolved, that we have a building of God, an house not made with hands, everlasting in (the) heavens (or eternal in heaven).

2   For why in this thing we mourn, coveting to be clothed above with our dwelling, which is of heaven (or which is from heaven);

3   if nevertheless we be found clothed, and not naked.

4   For why we that be in this tabernacle, sorrow within, and be heavied [or be grieved], for that we will not be (de)spoiled, but be clothed above; that that thing that is deadly, be sopped up of life, (or that that is mortal, shall be swallowed up by life or into eternal life).

5   But who is it that maketh us into this same thing? God, that gave to us the earnest, either

(the) wed, of the Spirit, (or God, who gave us the pledge, or the guarantee, of it, by the Spirit). [Forsooth he that maketh us into this same thing, is God, that gave to us the earnest, or a wed, of (the) Spirit.]

6   Therefore we be hardy always (or And so we shall always be bold), and know that the while we be in this body, we go in pilgrimage from the Lord;

7   for we walk by faith, and not by clear sight.

8   But we be hardy, and have good will, more to be in pilgrimage from the body, and to be present to God. (But we be bold, and be willing, rather to be in pilgrimage from the body, and to be present with God.)

9   And therefore we strive, whether absent, whether present, to please him.

10   For it behooveth us all to be showed before the throne of Christ, that every man tell [or receive] the proper things of the body, as he hath done, either good, either evil. (For it behooveth us all to be shown before the throne of the Messiah, so that every man receive his due, or that which he deserveth, because of what he hath done in the body, either good, or evil.)

11   Therefore we witting the dread of the Lord, (or And so we knowing the fear of the Lord, or And so we having reverence for the Lord), counsel men, for to God we be open; and I hope, that we be open also in your consciences.

12   We commend not us-selves again to you, but we give to you occasion to have glory for us, (so) that ye have [understanding] to them (or of them) that glory in the face, and not in the heart.

13   For either we by mind [or by reason] pass (forth), (or go away from sanity, or from soberness), [it is] to God, either we be sober, [it is] to you.

14   For the charity of Christ driveth us (or For the love of the Messiah compelleth us); guessing

[or deeming] this thing, that if one died for all, then all were dead.

15 And Christ died for all (or And the Messiah died for all), (so) that they that live, live not now to themselves, but to him that died for them, and rose again.

16 Therefore we from this time know no man after the flesh; though we (have) known Christ after the flesh, but now we know not.

17 Therefore if any new creature is in Christ, the old things be passed. Lo! all things be made new, (And so if anyone is in the Messiah, he is a new creature, or a new creation, and the old things be passed away. Behold, all things be made new,)

18 and all things be of God, which reconciled us to him by Christ (or who reconciled us to him through the Messiah), and gave to us the service [or the ministry] of reconciling.

19 And [for] God was in Christ (or And because God was in the Messiah), reconciling to him the world, not reckoning to them their guilts (or their trespasses), and putted in us the word of reconciling.

20 Therefore we use (this) message for Christ, as if God admonisheth by us; we beseech you for Christ, be ye reconciled to God. (And so we give this message for the Messiah, or from the Messiah, as if God admonisheth by us; we beseech you for the Messiah, be ye reconciled to God.)

21 God the Father made him sin for us, which knew not sin, (so) that we should be made [the] rightwiseness of God in him.

CHAPTER 6

1 But we helping [*you in work and word*] admonish [you], that ye receive not the grace of God in vain (or so that ye did not receive God's grace in vain).

2 For he saith, In time well pleasing I have heard thee, and in the day of health, I have helped thee. Lo! now a time acceptable, lo! now a day of health. (For he saith, In my time of favour I heard thee, and on the Day of Deliverance, or on the Day of Salvation, I helped thee. Behold, now is a time of favour, behold, now is the Day of Deliverance, or the Day of Salvation.)

3 Give we to no man any offence, (so) that our service be not reproved; [To no man giving any offence, *or hurting*, (so) that our ministry, *or service*, be not reproved;]

4 but in all things give we us-selves as the ministers (or the servants) of God, in much patience, in tribulations, in needs, in anguishes,

5 in beatings, [*or scourgings*], in prisons, in dissensions within, in travails, in wakings, in fastings,

6 in chastity, in cunning, (or in knowing), [or in science], in long abiding, in sweetness, in the Holy Ghost, in charity not feigned, (in chastity or in purity, in knowledge, in patience, in sweetness, in the Holy Spirit, in sincere love,)

7 in the word of truth, in the virtue of God; by armours of rightwiseness on the right half and on the left half; (in the word of truth, in the power of God; by the arms, or the weapons, of righteousness on the right side, or at the right hand, and on the left side, or at the left hand;)

8 by glory and unnobleness; by evil fame and good fame; as deceivers, and true men;

9 as they that be unknown and known; as men dying, and lo! we live; as chastised, and not made dead;

10 as sorrowful, and (for)evermore joying, [or as sorrowful, but evermore joying]; as having need, but making many men rich; as nothing having, and wielding all things. (as sorrowful, and yet always joyful; as having need, yet making many men rich; as having nothing, and yet possessing everything.)

11 A! ye Corinthians, our mouth is open to you, our heart is alarged; (O ye Corinthians! we have spoken openly or frankly to you, and our

heart was enlarged, or was open wide to you;)

12 ye be not anguished in us, but ye be anguished in your inwardnesses. [+ye be not made strait in us, but ye be made strait, *or be ye anguished*, in your entrails.]

13 And I say as to sons, ye that have the same reward, be ye alarged (or be ye enlarged, or open wide your hearts to us).

14 Do not ye bear the yoke with unfaithful men. For what parting, [*or communing*], of rightwiseness with wickedness? or what fellowship of light to darknesses? (Do not carry the yoke with the unfaithful or with unbelievers. For what sharing is there of righteousness with wickedness? or what fellowship of light with darkness?)

15 and what according of Christ to Belial? or what part of a faithful [*man*] with the unfaithful, [*or* (the) *heathen*]? (and what agreement is there between the Messiah and Belial or the Devil? or what sharing or communing is there between a believer and an unbeliever or a Gentile?)

16 and what consent to the temple of God with maumets? (or and what consent between God's temple and idols?) And ye be the temple of the living God, as the Lord saith, For I shall dwell in them, and I shall walk among them; and I shall be [the] God of them, and they shall be a people to me.

17 For which thing go ye out of the middle of them, and be ye separated (or be set apart), saith the Lord, and touch not (any) unclean thing; and I shall receive you,

18 and I shall be to you into a Father, and ye shall be to me into sons and daughters, saith the Lord almighty.

CHAPTER 7

1 Therefore, most dearworthy *brethren*, we that have these promises, cleanse we us from all (the) filth of the flesh and of the spirit, doing holiness in the dread of God, (or being holy in the fear of God, or with reverence for God).

2 Take ye us; we have hurt no man, we have impaired no man [or we have corrupted no man], we have beguiled no man.

3 I say not to your condemning; for I said before, that ye be in our hearts, to die together and to live together.

4 Much trust is to me with you, much glorying is to me for you. I am [full-]filled with comfort, I am plenteous in joy [or I abound in joy] in all our tribulation.

5 For when we were come to Macedonia, our flesh had no rest, but we suffered all tribulation; withoutforth fightings, and dreads within (or and fears within).

6 But God that comforteth meek men, comforted us in the coming of Titus.

7 And not only in the coming of him, but also in the comfort by which he was comforted in you, telling to us your desire, your weeping, your love for me, so that I joyed (all the) more.

8 For though I made you sorry, in an epistle, it rueth me not; though it rued, [I] seeing that though that epistle made you sorry at an hour, (For though I made you sorrowful, by my letter, I do not regret it now; and though I did regret it, I seeing that though that letter made you sorrowful for a time,)

9 now I have joy; not for ye were made sorrowful, but for ye were made sorrowful to penance. For why ye be made sorry after God, that in nothing ye suffer impairment of us. (now I have joy; not for ye were made sorrowful, but for ye were made sorrowful unto repentance. For ye were made sorrowful by God, and ye did not suffer any impairment or any harm from us.)

10 For the sorrow that is after God, worketh penance into steadfast health; but sorrow of the world worketh death. (For the sorrow that is from God, worketh repentance unto certain salvation; but the sorrow of the world worketh death.)

11 For lo! this same thing, that ye be sorrowful after God, how much busyness it

worketh in you; but defending, but indignation, but dread (or but fear), but desire, but love, but vengeance. In all things ye have given yourselves to be undefouled in the cause.

12 Therefore though I wrote to you, *I wrote* not for him that did the injury, neither for him that suffered, but to show our busyness (or our zeal), which we have for you before God.

13 Therefore we be comforted, but in your comfort more plenteously [or but in our comfort more plenteously] we joyed more on the joy of Titus, for his spirit is fulfilled of all you. (And so we were comforted by your comfort, or And so we were encouraged, yea our own encouragement was great, but we rejoiced even more abundantly over Titus' joy, for his spirit was filled full by all of you.)

14 And if I gloried anything with him of you, I am not confounded, [or shamed]; but as we have spoken to you all things [in truth], so also our glory that was at Titus, is made truth. (And if I have boasted of anything about you to him, I am not ashamed; for as we have spoken to you everything in truth, so also our boasting about you to Titus, is shown to be true.)

15 And the inwardness of him be more plenteously in you, which hath in mind the obedience of you all, how with dread and trembling ye received him. (And his inward affection for you hath grown more plentiful, when he hath remembered all of your obedience, and how with fear and trembling ye received him.)

16 I have joy, that in all things I trust in you (or I trust you).

CHAPTER 8

1 But, brethren, we make known to you the grace of God, that is given in the churches of Macedonia,

2 that in much assaying of tribulation, the plenty [or the abundance] of the joy of them was, and the highest poverty of them was

plenteous into the riches of the simpleness of them (or their sincerity).

3 For I bear witnessing to them, after might, [or after power], and above might they were willful, (For I testify about them, yea, about their power, and even over their power, or beyond their limit, they were willing,)

4 with much admonishing beseeching us (for) the grace and the communing of (the) ministering [or of the ministry] that is made to holy men.

5 And not as we hoped, but they gave themselves first to the Lord, afterward to us by the will of God.

6 So that we prayed Titus, that as he began, so also he perform in you this grace.

7 But as ye abound in all things, in faith, and word, and cunning, (or and knowing), [or and science], and all busyness, moreover and in your charity into us, that also in this grace ye abound. (But as ye abound in all things, in faith, and word, and knowledge, and all zeal, and moreover in your love for us, so that also in this gift ye abound.)

8 I say not as commanding, but by the busyness of other men proving also the good wit of your charity. (I say not as commanding, but by *telling you of* the concern of other men, I am proving, or testing, the good thoughts or the sincerity of your love.)

9 And ye know the grace of our Lord Jesus Christ, for he was made needy for you, when he was rich, (so) that ye should be made rich by his neediness.

10 And I give counsel in this thing; for this is profitable to you, that not only have begun to do, but also ye began to have will (or to have desire) from the former year.

11 But now perform ye in deed, that as the discretion of will is ready [*to desire good*], so be it also of performing of that that ye have.

12 For if the will be ready, it is accepted after that that it hath, not after that that it hath not.

13 And not that it be (a) remission, [*or*

idleness, or sloth], to other *men*, and to you tribulation;

14 but of evenness in the present time your abundance fulfill the need of them, (so) that also the abundance of them be a fulfilling of your need, (so) that evenness be made;

15 as it is written, He that gathered much, was not increased, and he that *gathered* little, had not less.

16 And I do thankings to God, that gave the same busyness for you in the heart of Titus, (And I give thanks to God, who put the same concern for you in Titus' heart,)

17 for he received exhortation; but when he was busier, by his will he went forth to you.

18 And we sent with him a brother, whose praising is in the gospel by all (the) churches. (And we sent a brother with him, who is praised by all the churches for his service to, or his preaching of, the Gospel or the Good News.)

19 And not only praised, but also he is ordained of churches (as) the fellow of our pilgrimage into this grace, that is (ad)ministered of us, to the glory of the Lord, and to our ordained will; (And not only praised, but he is also ordained by the churches as the partner of our pilgrimage in this grace, that is administered by us, for the glory of the Lord, and unto our ordained will;)

20 eschewing this thing, that no man blame us in this plenty, that is (ad)ministered of us, to the glory of the Lord. (shunning this, so that no one can reproach us regarding this plenty, that is administered by us, for the glory of the Lord.)

21 For we purvey good things, not only before God, but also before all men.

22 For we sent with them also our brother, whom we have proved in many things oft, that he was busy, but now much busier, for much trust in you,

23 either for Titus, that is my fellow and helper in you, either for our brethren, (the) apostles of the churches of the glory of Christ.

(either for Titus, who is my fellow and helper with you, or for our brothers, the apostles of the churches to the glory of the Messiah.)

24 Therefore show ye to them in the face of (the) churches, that showing that is of your charity (or that showing of your love), and of our glory for you.

CHAPTER 9

1 For of the ministry that is made to holy men, it is to me of plenty to write to you. (And as for the service, or the aid, that is sent to the saints, or to God's people, it is unnecessary for me to write to you.)

2 For I know your [ready] will, for the which I have glory of you with (the) Macedonians, for also Achaia is ready from a year passed, and your love hath stirred full many.

3 And we have sent brethren, that this thing that we glory of you, be not voided in this part, that as I said, ye be ready. (And we have sent these brothers, so that our boasting about you in this matter, be not empty words, but as I said, so that ye be prepared.)

4 Lest when (the) Macedonians come with me, and find you unready, we be shamed, that we say you not or that we saw you not, in this substance.

5 Therefore I guessed (it) necessary to pray (the) brethren, that they come before to you, and make ready this promised blessing to be ready, so as blessing, and not as avarice, (or as a blessing, or as a gift, and not as an example of greed).

6 For I say this thing, he that soweth scarcely, shall also reap scarcely; and he that soweth in blessings, shall reap also of blessings.

7 Each man as he casted in his heart, not of heaviness, or of need; for God loveth a glad(ful) giver.

8 And God is mighty to make all grace abound in you, that ye in all things (for)evermore have all sufficience, and abound

into all good work; (And God is powerful enough to give all necessary gifts in abundance to you, so that ye always have all sufficiency in everything, and can abound in all good works;)

9   as it is written, He dealed abroad, he gave to poor men, his rightwiseness dwelleth [into] without end (or his righteousness remaineth forever and ever).

10   And he that ministereth seed to the sower (or And he who serveth up seed to the sower), shall give also bread to eat, and he shall multiply your seed, and make much the increasings of (the) fruits of your rightwiseness;

11   that in all things ye made rich wax plenteous [or abound] into all simpleness, which worketh by us (the) doing of thankings to God. (so that in all things ye made rich grow plenteous, or abound, in all sincerity, which worketh in us the giving of thanks to God.)

12   For the ministry (or the service) of this office not only filleth those things that fail to holy men, but also multiplieth many thankings to God,

13   by the proving of this ministry, which glorify God in the obedience of your acknowledging in the gospel of Christ (or in the Gospel, or the Good News, of the Messiah), and in (the) simpleness (or the sincerity) of (the) communication into them and into all [others],

14   and in the beseeching of them for you, that desire you for the excellent grace of God in you.

15   I do thankings to God of the gift of him, that may not be told (out). [I give thankings to God upon the unnarrable, (or unnarrative-able, or untellable), or that may not be told (out), gift of him.] (I give thanks to God, for his gift, thanks that can never be sufficiently told out or described.)

CHAPTER 10

1   And I myself, Paul, beseech you, by the mildness (or by the meekness) and (the)

softness, [or (the) patience], of Christ, (or And I, Paul, beseech you, by the meekness, and the gentleness of the Messiah), which in the face am meek among you, and I absent trust in you.

2   For I pray you, that lest I present be not bold [or be not hardy] by the trust, in which I am guessed to be bold [or to be hardy] into some, that deem us, as if we wander after the flesh. (For I pray you, lest that when I am present I be not bold with the confidence, in which I am thought to be bold by some, who judge us, as if we walk or if we go after the flesh.)

3   For we walking in the flesh, fight not after the flesh.

4   For the armours of our knighthood be not fleshly, but mighty by God to the destruction of strengths [or of wardings]. (For the arms or the weapons of our combat be not fleshly, but be made mighty by God for the destruction of strongholds.)

5   And we destroy counsels, and all highness that higheth [or raised] itself against the science of God, and drive into captivity all understanding into the service of Christ. (And we destroy plots and plans, and all the highness that raiseth itself against the knowledge of God, and drive into captivity all understanding in the service of, or obedience to, the Messiah.)

6   And we have ready to (a)venge all unobedience (or And we be ready to punish all disobedience or rebellion), when your obedience shall be [ful]filled.

7   See ye the things that be after the face. If any man trusteth to himself, that he is of Christ, think he this thing again with himself, for as he is Christ's, so also we (be). (Look at what is before you. If any man trusteth himself, that he is the Messiah's, then think he this within himself, that as he is the Messiah's, so we also be the Messiah's.)

8   For if I shall glory (or For if I shall boast), (in) anything more of our power, which the Lord gave to us into edifying, and not into your

destruction, I shall not be shamed.

9 But that I be not guessed as to fear you by epistles, (So that I do not be thought to frighten you by my letters,)

10 for they say, That epistles be grievous [or be heavy] and strong, but the presence of the body is feeble, and the word (is) worthy to be despised [or it is contemptible]. (for they say, His letters be weighty and strong, but in person he is frail or weak, and his speech contemptible.)

11 He that is such one, think this, for such as we absent be in word by epistles (or letters), such we be present in deed.

12 For we dare not put us among, or comparison us to some men, that commend themselves; but we measure us in us-selves, and comparison us-selves to us.

13 For we shall not have glory over-measure, but by the measure of the rule which God measured to us, the measure that stretcheth [till] to you.

14 For we overstretch not forth us, as not stretching to you. For to you we came in the gospel of Christ (or For we came to you to preach the Gospel, or the Good News, of the Messiah),

15 not glorying over-measure in other men's travails. For we have hope of your faith that waxeth in you (or For we have hope that by the faith that groweth in you), to be magnified by our rule in abundance,

16 also to preach into those things that be beyond you, not to have glory in (an)other man's rule (or not to boast about, or over, another man's field of work), in these things that be made ready.

17 He that glorieth, have glory in the Lord. (He who boasteth, boast of the Lord.)

18 For not he that commendeth himself is (ap)proved, but whom God commendeth.

CHAPTER 11

1 I would that ye would suffer a little thing of mine unwisdom (or I wish that ye would allow me a little foolishness), but also support ye me [or bear me up].

2 For I love you by the love of God; for I have espoused you to one husband, to yield a chaste virgin to Christ, [or to give you, a chaste virgin, to one man, Christ], (or to give you as a pure virgin to the Messiah).

3 But I dread, lest as the serpent deceived Eve with his subtle fraud, so your wits be corrupted, and fallen down from the simpleness that is in Christ. (But I fear, that just as the serpent deceived Eve with his subtle fraud, so your minds now be corrupted, and have fallen away from your sincere devotion to the Messiah.)

4 For if he that cometh, preacheth another Christ, (or For if he who cometh, preacheth another Messiah), whom we preached not, or if ye take another spirit, whom ye took not [or whom ye received not], or another gospel, which ye received not, rightly ye should suffer.

5 For I ween (or I think) that I have done nothing less than the great apostles.

6 For though I be unlearned in word, but not in cunning (or in knowing), [or For why though I be unlearned in sermon, but not in science], (or For although I am not learned in giving sermons or in public speaking, I have some knowledge). For in all things I am open to you [or I am showed, or made known, to you].

7 Or whether I have done sin, meeking, [or making low], myself, that ye be enhanced (or so that ye be raised up), for freely I preached to you the gospel (or the Good News) of God?

8 I made naked, [or I spoiled, or I took gifts of], other churches, and I took wages to your service. (Yes, I robbed other churches, or I received gifts from other churches, and so I received my wages for my service or my ministry to you.)

9 And when I was among you, and had need, I was chargeous to no man; for brethren that came from Macedonia, fulfilled [or

supplied] that that failed to me. And in all things I have kept [me], and shall keep me without charge to you. (And when I was among you, and had need, I was not a burden to anyone; for the brothers who came from Macedonia, supplied what I needed. And so in everything I have looked after myself, and shall not be a burden to you.)

10 The truth of Christ is in me (or The truth of the Messiah is in me); for this glory shall not be broken in me in the countries [or in the regions] of Achaia.

11 Why? for I love not you? God knoweth.

12 For that that I do, and that I shall do, *is* that I cut away the occasion of them that will (an) occasion, that in the thing, in which they glory, they be found [such] as we. (For what I do, and what I shall do, *is* that I cut away the occasion of those who desire an occasion, so that in that, in which they boast, they be found such as we.)

13 For such false apostles be treacherous, [*or guileful*], workmen, and transfigure them(selves) into apostles of Christ. (For such false apostles be workers of deceit, who transform themselves into apostles of the Messiah.)

14 And no wonder, for Satan himself transfigureth him(self) into an angel of light. (And no wonder, for Satan himself transformeth himself into an angel of light.)

15 Therefore it is not great, if his ministers be transfigured as the ministers of rightwiseness, whose end shall be after their works. (And so it is no great thing, if his servants be transformed into the servants of righteousness, whose end shall be after their works.)

16 Again I say, lest any man guess me, [or deem me], (or think me), to be unwise; else take ye me as unwise, that also I have glory a little (some)what (or so that I can also boast a little).

17 That that I speak, I speak not after God, but as in unwisdom, in this substance of glory (or in this matter of boasting).

18 For many men glory after the flesh, and I shall glory. (For many men boast about fleshly matters, and so I shall boast.)

19 For ye suffer gladly unwise men, when ye yourselves be wise.

20 For ye suffer, if any man driveth you into servage, if any man devoureth (you), if any man taketh (you), if any man is enhanced [*by pride*], if any man smiteth you on the face. (For ye allow it, if any man driveth you into servitude or into slavery, if any man devoureth you, if any man catcheth you, if any man is raised up over you *by pride*, if any man striketh you on the face.)

21 By unnobleness I say, as if we were sick in this part (or as if we were frail or weak in this matter). In what thing any man dare, in unwisdom I say, and I dare.

22 They be Hebrews, and I; they be Israelites, and I; they be the seed of Abraham, and I;

23 they be the ministers of Christ, and I, (or they be the servants of the Messiah, like I am). As less wise I say, I more; in full many travails (or in many great labours), in prisons more plenteously, in wounds above-manner, [*or over-measure*], in deaths oft times.

24 I received of the Jews five times forty *strokes* one less; (I received from the Jews five times forty *strikes* less one;)

25 thrice I was beaten with rods, once I was stoned, thrice I was at ship-break (or three times I was shipwrecked), a night and a day I was in the deepness of the sea;

26 in ways oft, in perils of floods (or in danger from rivers), in perils of thieves, in perils of kin, in perils of heathen men (or in danger from the Gentiles), in perils in [the] city, in perils in (the) desert, in perils in the sea, in perils among false brethren,

27 in travail and neediness, in many wakings, in hunger, in thirst, in many fastings, in cold and nakedness.

28 Without those things that be withoutforth, mine each day's travailing [or mine each day's

studying] *is* the busyness of all (the) churches.

29   Who is sick, and I am not sick? (or Who is frail or weak, and I am not frail or weak?) who is caused to stumble (or to fall), and I am not burnt?

30   If it behooveth to glory, I shall glory *in those things* that be of mine infirmity, [*or frailty*]. (If it behooveth to boast, then I shall boast *about those things* that tell of, or show, my weakness, *or frailty*.)

31   God and the Father of our Lord Jesus Christ, that is blessed into worlds, (or who is blessed forever, or forever be he blessed), knoweth that I lie not.

32   The provost of Damascus, of the king of the folk of Aretas, [or of the king of the folk, Aretas], kept the city of Damascenes to take me; (The governor of Damascus, under King Aretas, kept watch in the city of the Damascenes to take me captive;)

33   and by a window in a basket I was let down by the wall, and so I escaped his hands.

CHAPTER 12

1   If it behooveth to have glory, it speedeth not (or It is not expedient to boast); but I shall come to the visions and the revelations of the Lord.

2   I know a man in Christ that before fourteen years; whether in body, whether out of body, I know not, God knoweth; that such a man was ravished unto the third heaven. (I know a man in the Messiah who fourteen years ago; whether in the body, or out of the body, I do not know, but God knoweth; that man was snatched up into the third heaven.)

3   And I know such a man; whether in body, or out of body, I know not, God knoweth; (And I know that man, whether in the body, or out of the body, I do not know, but God knoweth;)

4   that he was ravished into paradise, and heard privy words, which it is not leaveful to a man to speak. (that he was snatched up into paradise, and heard private or secret words, which it is not lawful for a man to speak or tell out.)

5   For such manner things I shall glory (in); but (as) for me nothing, but in mine infirmities. (About such a man as this, I shall boast; but about myself nothing, except my frailties and weaknesses.)

6   For if I shall desire to glory (or For if I wish to boast), I shall not be unwise, for I shall say (the) truth; but I spare (thee), lest any man guess me over that thing that he seeth in me, or heareth anything of me.

7   And lest the greatness of (these) revelations enhance me, (or exalt me, or raise me up), *in pride*, the prick of my flesh, an angel of Satan, is given to me, (so) that he buffet me.

8   For which thing thrice I prayed the Lord, that it should go away from me.

9   And he said to me, My grace sufficeth to thee; for virtue is perfectly made in infirmity. Therefore gladly I shall glory in mine infirmities, that the virtue of Christ dwell in me. (And he said to me, My grace sufficeth for thee; for power is made perfect in frailty or weakness. And so I shall gladly boast of my frailties and weaknesses, so that the power of the Messiah can live in me.)

10   For which thing I am pleased in mine infirmities, in despisings, [*or reprovings*], in needs, in persecutions, in anguishes, for Christ; for when I am sick, then I am mighty. (And so I am content in my frailties and weaknesses, in despisings, *or reproaches*, in needs, in persecutions, in anguishes, for the Messiah; for when I am frail or weak, then I am mighty.)

11   I am made unwitty (or witless), ye constrained me. For I ought to be commended of you; for I did nothing less than they that be apostles over-measure. Though I am nought, (But I am being foolish, and ye compelled me. For I ought to be commended by you; for I did nothing less than those who be apostles over-measure or who be the greatest apostles.

Although I am nothing,)

12 nevertheless the signs of mine apostlehood be made on you, in all patience, and signs (or miracles), and great wonders, and virtues (or works of power).

13 And what is it, that ye had less than (the) other churches, [no] but that I myself grieved you not, [*betaking* (nothing) *of you*]? (*or taking* nothing *from you*?) Forgive ye to me this wrong.

14 Lo! this third time I am ready to come to you, and I shall not be grievous to you; for I seek not those things that be yours, but you. For neither sons owe to [*make*] treasure to father and mother (or For sons ought not to give treasure to their father and mother), but the father and mother to the sons.

15 For I shall give most willfully (or For I shall give most willingly or out of my free will), and I myself shall be given over for your souls; though I more love you, and be less loved.

16 But (so) be it; I grieved not you, but when I was subtle [or wily], I took you with guile.

17 Whether I deceived you by any of them, which I sent to you?

18 I prayed Titus, and I sent with him a brother. Whether Titus beguiled you? whether we went not in the same spirit? whether not in the same steps?

19 Sometime ye ween (or ye guess), that we shall excuse us with you. Before God in Christ we speak (or In the presence of or before God, we speak in the Messiah); and, most dear brethren, all things for your edifying.

20 But I dread, lest when I come, I shall not find you such as I will, and I shall be found of you such as ye will not, (or But I fear, that when I come there, I shall not find you such as I want, or as I desire, and that I shall be found by you such as ye do not want, or as ye do not desire); lest peradventure strivings, envies, indignations, dissensions and detractions, privy speeches of discord, swellings *by pride*, debates be among you;

21 *and* lest again when I come, God make me low [or make me humble] with you, and I bewail many of them, that before sinned, and did not penance on the uncleanness (or and who did not repent for the uncleanness), and fornication, and unchastity, that they have done.

CHAPTER 13

1 Lo! this third time I come to you, and in the mouth of two or of three witnesses every word shall stand.

2 I said before, and say before, as present twice, and now absent, to them that before have sinned, and to all others; for if I come again, I shall not spare (you).

3 Whether ye seek the proof [or (the) assaying] of that Christ, that speaketh in me, which is not feeble in you, [but is mighty in you]? (Do ye seek the proof of that Messiah, who speaketh through me, who is not frail or weak in you, but is mighty and powerful?)

4 For though he was crucified of infirmity, but he liveth of the virtue of God. For also we be sick in him, but we shall live with him of the virtue of God in us. (For though he was crucified in weakness, now he liveth by the power of God. For we also be frail or weak in him, but we shall live with him by the power of God in us.)

5 Assay yourselves, if ye be in the faith; ye yourselves prove (it). Whether ye know not yourselves, for Christ Jesus is in you? [no] but in hap ye be reprovable. (Test yourselves, if ye be in the faith; ye yourselves prove it. Do ye not know, that the Messiah Jesus is in you? unless perhaps ye be reproachable.)

6 But I hope, that ye know, that we be not reprovable. (But I hope, that ye know, that we be not reproachable.)

7 And we pray the Lord, that ye do nothing of evil; not that we seem proved (or not that we be seen as to have been proven correct), but

that ye do that that is good, and that we be as reprovable.

8   For we may do nothing against (the) truth, but, (rather), for the truth.

9   For we joy, when we be sick, but ye be mighty; and we pray (for) this thing, (yea), your perfection. (For we rejoice, when we be frail or weak, but ye be strong or powerful; and we pray for this thing, yea, for your completion.)

10   Therefore I absent write these things, that (when) I (am) present do not harder, (or so that when I come there, I do not have to be harsher), by the power, which the Lord gave to me into edification, and not into *your* destruction.

11   Brethren (or Brothers), henceforward joy ye, be ye perfect, excite ye [or and teach ye]; understand ye the same thing; have ye peace, and (the) God of peace and of love shall be with you.

12   Greet ye well together in holy kiss. (Give hearty greetings to one another with a holy kiss.)

13   All holy men greet you well. (All the saints, or All of God's people, send you hearty greetings.)

14   The grace of our Lord Jesus Christ, and the charity of God, and the communing of the Holy Ghost, be with you all. Amen. (The grace of our Lord Jesus Christ, and the love of God, and the communing of the Holy Spirit, be with you all. Amen.) †

GALATIANS

CHAPTER 1

1   Paul the apostle, not of men, nor by man, but by Jesus Christ, and God the Father, that raised him from death [or that raised him from (the) dead],

2   and all the brethren that be with me, to the churches of Galatia, (and all the brothers who be with me, to the churches in Galatia,)

3   grace (be) to you and (the) peace of God the Father, and of the Lord Jesus Christ,

4   that gave himself for our sins, to deliver us from the present wicked world, by the will of God and our Father,

5   to whom is honour and glory into worlds of worlds. Amen. (to whom be honour and glory forever and ever. Amen.)

6   I wonder, that so soon ye be thus moved from him that called you into the grace of Christ, into another evangel [or into another gospel]; (I am amazed, that so quickly ye be moved away from him who called you into the grace of the Messiah, to another gospel;)

7   which is not another, but that there be some that trouble you, and will mis-turn the evangel of Christ. (which is not truly another gospel, but that there be some who trouble you, and will pervert the Gospel, or the Good News, of the Messiah.)

8   But though we, or an angel of heaven, preached to you, besides that that we have preached to you, be he accursed. [But though we, or an angel of heaven, evangelized to you, besides that that we have evangelized to you, cursed be he.]

9   As I have said before, and now again I say, if any *man* preach to you besides that that ye have received, be he accursed [or cursed be he].

10   For now whether counsel I men, or God? or whether I seek to please men? If I pleased yet men, I were not Christ's servant, (or If I still sought to please men, I would not be the Messiah's servant).

11   For, brethren, I make known to you the evangel [or the gospel], that was preached of me (or by me), for it is not by man;

12   nor I took it of man (or nor I received it from any man), nor learned (it from any man), but by [the] revelation of Jesus Christ.

13   For ye have heard my conversation sometime in the Jewry, that I pursued (sur)passingly, [or over-manner, *or* (over-) *measure*], the church of God, and fought against it. (For ye have heard about my life before among the Jewry, how I persecuted God's church beyond measure, and fought so very hard against it.)

14   And I profited in the Jewry above many of mine even-elders in my kindred, and was more abundantly a follower [or a lover] of my fathers' traditions.

15   But when it pleased him, that parted me (or who separated me) from my mother's womb, and called (me) by his grace,

16   to show his Son in me, that I should preach him among the heathen, anon I drew me not to flesh and blood; (to show his Son to me, so that I would preach him among the Gentiles, at once I drew me not to flesh and blood;)

17   nor I came to Jerusalem to the apostles, that were before me, but I went into Arabia, and again I turned again into Damascus. (nor did I come to Jerusalem to those who were apostles before me, but I went to Arabia, and then I returned to Damascus.)

18   And since three years after I came to Jerusalem [or Afterward after three years I came to Jerusalem], to see Peter, and I dwelled with him fifteen days;

19   but I saw none other of the apostles, but James, *our* Lord's brother.

20   And these things which I write to you, lo! before God I lie not.

21   Afterward I came into the coasts of Syria

and Cilicia.

22   But I was unknown by face to the churches of Judea, that were in Christ (or who were in the Messiah);

23   and they had only an hearing, that he that pursued us sometime (ago), preacheth now the faith, against which he fought sometime (ago); (and they had only heard it said, that he who had persecuted us before, now preacheth the faith, which before he fought so very hard against;)

24   and in me they glorified God. (and they praised God for me.)

CHAPTER 2

1   And since fourteen years after [or Afterward after fourteen years], again I went up to Jerusalem with Barnabas, and took with me Titus.

2   I went up by revelation, and spake with them the evangel [or the gospel], which I preach among the heathen, (or I went up by revelation, and spoke, or shared, the Gospel, or the Good News, with them, which I preach among the Gentiles); and by themselves to these that seemed to be somewhat, lest I run [or lest peradventure I should run], or had run in vain.

3   And neither Titus, that had been with me, while he was heathen, was compelled to be circumcised; (And Titus, who had been with me, while he was a Gentile, was not compelled to be circumcised;)

4   but for false brethren that were brought in, which had [privily] entered to espy our freedom [or our liberty], which we have in Jesus Christ, to bring us [or to drive us] into servage (or to drive us into servitude, or into slavery).

5   But we gave no place to subjection, that the truth of the gospel should dwell with you. (But we did not submit to their domination, so that the truth of the Gospel or the Good News would remain with you.)

6   But of these that seemed to be somewhat (or to be esteemed); which they were sometime, it pertaineth not to me, for God taketh not the person of (a) man (or for God favoureth not any person); for they that seemed to be somewhat (or to be esteemed), gave me nothing.

7   But on the contrary, when they had seen, that the evangel of (the) prepuce (or for the uncircumcision) was given to me [or that the gospel of heathen men is betaken to me], as the evangel of (the) circumcision *was given* to Peter; (But on the contrary, when they had seen, that the Gospel, or the Good News, for the uncircumcised, or the heathen, or the Gentiles, was given to me, like the Gospel, or the Good News, for the circumcised, or the Jews, *was given* to Peter;)

8   for he that wrought to Peter in apostlehood of (the) circumcision, wrought also to me among the heathen; (for he who made Peter the apostle to the circumcised, also made me the apostle to the Gentiles;)

9   and when they had known the grace *of God*, that was given to me, James, and Peter [or Cephas], and John, which were seen to be the pillars, they gave the right hand of fellowship to me and to Barnabas, that we [*preach*] among the heathen (or that we *preach* among the Gentiles), and they into the circumcision;

10   only that we had mind of, [or that we should be mindful of], (the) poor men, the which thing I was full busy to do. (only that we should remember the poor, which I already was always doing.)

11   But when Peter was come to Antioch, I against-stood him in the face, (or I stood up against him, or I opposed him, to his face), for he was worthy to be reproved.

12   For before that there came some men from James [or Forsooth before that some came from James], he ate with heathen men; but when they were come, he withdrew, and departed him(self), dreading them that were of (the) circumcision. (For before that some men came from James, he ate with the Gentiles; but

when they had come, he withdrew, and separated himself, fearing those who were of the circumcision.)

13   And the other *Jews* assented [or consented] to his feigning, so that Barnabas was drawn of them into that feigning.

14   But when I saw, that they walked not rightly to the truth of the gospel, I said to Peter [or to Cephas] before all men, If thou, that art a Jew, livest heathen-like, and not Jew-like, how constrainest thou heathen men to become Jews? (or how can thou compel Gentiles to become Jews?)

15   We Jews of kind, and not sinful men of the heathen, (We Jews by kind, or naturally, and not of the sinners of the Gentiles, as they be called,)

16   know that a man is not justified of the works of the law, but by the faith of Jesus Christ; and we believe in Jesus Christ, that we be justified of [or by] the faith of Christ, and not of the works of the law. Wherefore of the works of the law each flesh shall not be justified. (know that a man is not justified by the works of the Law, but by faith in Jesus Christ; and we believe in Jesus Christ, that we be justified by faith in the Messiah, and not by doing the works of the Law. And so by doing the works of the Law each flesh shall not be justified.)

17   And if we seek to be justified in Christ, we ourselves be found sinful men [or to be sinners], whether Christ be (a) minister of sin? God forbid. (And if we seek to be justified in the Messiah, and we ourselves be found to be sinners, then is the Messiah a servant of sin? God forbid.)

18   And if I build again things that I have destroyed, I make myself a trespasser.

19   For by the law I am dead to the law, [For by the law I am dead to the law, that I live to God;]

20   and I am fixed to the cross, that I live to God with Christ. And now live not I, but Christ liveth in me, (or and I am fixed to the cross, so that I live to God with the Messiah. But now I do not live, but the Messiah who liveth in me).

But that I live now in (the) flesh, I live in the faith of God's Son, that loved me, and gave himself for me. [with Christ I am fixed to the cross. Forsooth I live now, not I, but Christ liveth in me. Forsooth that I live now in (the) flesh, I live in the faith of God's son, the which loved me, and betook (or delivered) himself for me.]

21   I cast not away the grace of God; for if rightwiseness be through (the) law [or for if rightwiseness is by the law], then Christ died without cause. (I do not throw away God's grace; because if righteousness can be gained through the Law, then the Messiah died without any reason or for no purpose.)

CHAPTER 3

1   O! unwitty Galatians, before whose eyes Jesus Christ is exiled, [or O! ye witless men of Galatia, before whose eyes Jesus Christ is damned or condemned], and is crucified in you, who hath deceived you, that ye obey not to truth? (O foolish Galatians! before whom Jesus was shown to be condemned, and crucified, who hath deceived you, so that ye do not obey the truth?)

2   This only I desire to learn of you, whether ye have received the Spirit of the works of the law, or of hearing of belief? (I only desire to learn this from you, did ye receive the Spirit by doing the works of the Law, or by hearing and believing?)

3   So ye be fools, that when ye have begun in Spirit (or because what ye have begun in the Spirit), [now] ye be ended in (the) flesh.

4   So great things [or So many things] ye have suffered without cause, (or without any reason, or for any purpose), if it be without cause.

5   He that giveth to you [the] Spirit, and worketh virtues in you, whether of works of the law, or of hearing of belief? [Therefore he that giveth to you the spirit, and worketh virtues in you, whether of the works of the law, or of hearing of faith?] (Giveth he the Spirit to you,

and worketh works of power among you, because of ye doing the works of the Law, or because of ye hearing and believing?)

6　　As it is written, Abraham believed to God, and it was reckoned to him to rightwiseness.

7　　And therefore know ye, that these that be of belief, be the sons of Abraham. [+Therefore know ye, that they that be of faith, they be the sons of Abraham.]

8　　And the scripture seeing afar, that God justifieth the heathen of belief, [or Forsooth the scripture purveying, for God justifieth of faith heathen men], told before to Abraham, That in thee all the heathen [or all (the) folks] shall be blessed. (And the Scripture seeing afar off, that God justifieth the Gentiles by faith, said ahead of time to Abraham, Through thee all the nations and all the peoples shall be blessed.)

9　　And therefore these that be of belief, [or Therefore they that be of faith], (or And so they who be of the faith or who have faith), shall be blessed with faithful Abraham.

10　　For all that be of the works of the law, be under (a) curse; for it is written, Each man *is* cursed, that abideth not [or that dwelleth not] in all (the) things that be written in the book of the law (or in the Book of the Law), to do those things.

11　　And that no man is justified in the law before God, it is open, for a rightful man liveth of belief. [Forsooth for no man is justified in the law with God, it is known, for a rightful man liveth by faith.]

12　　But the law is not of belief (or But the Law is not a matter of faith), but he that doeth those things *of the law*, shall live in them.

13　　But Christ again-bought us [or delivered us] from the curse of the law (or But the Messiah redeemed us from the curse of the Law), and was made accursed for us; for it is written, Each man *is* cursed that hangeth in (or on) the tree;

14　　that among the heathen the blessing of Abraham were made in Jesus Christ, that we

receive the promise of (the) Spirit through belief. [that the blessing of Abraham in heathen men should be made in Christ Jesus, that we take the promise of (the) Spirit by faith.] (so that among the Gentiles the blessing of Abraham came through, or by, Jesus Christ, and so we receive the promise of the Spirit through faith.)

15　　Brethren, I say after man, no man despiseth the testament (or the covenant) of a man that is confirmed, or ordaineth above, (or can add, or subtract), (any) [*other thing*].

16　　The promises were said to Abraham and to his seed; he saith not, In [the] seeds, as in many, but as in one, And to thy seed, that is, Christ (or the Messiah).

17　　But I say, this testament *is* confirmed of God, (or But I say, this covenant *is* confirmed by God); the law that was made after four hundred and thirty years, maketh not the testament (in) vain to void away the promise [or maketh (it) not void for to do away the promise].

18　　For if [the] heritage *were* of the law, *it were* not now of (the) promise, (or For if the inheritance *is* by the Law, *it is* not by the Promise).　But God granted [or gave] to Abraham through (the) promise.

19　　What then the law? that is, Whereto is the law profitable? [or What therefore *profiteth* the law?] It was set for trespassing, till the seed came, to whom he had made the promise. *Which law was* ordained by angels, in the hand of a mediator.

20　　But a mediator is not of one. But God is one.

21　　*Is* then the law against the promises of God? God forbid.　For if the law were given, that might quicken, verily were rightfulness of (the) law, [or verily rightwiseness were of (the) law], (or For if a law had been given, that could enliven, or that could give life, then truly righteousness would have come from keeping or obeying the Law).

22　　But the scripture hath concluded all things under sin, (so) that the promise of the faith of

Jesus Christ were given to them that believe.

23 And before that belief came, they were kept under the law, enclosed into that belief that was to be showed. [Forsooth before that the faith came, we were kept under the law, shut together into that faith that was to be showed.]

24 And so the law was our under-master in Christ, that we be justified of belief. [+Therefore the law was our little master (or our teacher) in Christ, that we be justified of faith.] (And so the Law was our tutor in the Messiah, so that we would be justified through faith.)

25 But after that belief came, we be not now under the under-master. [But after that the faith came, now we be not under the little master (or under the teacher).] (But now that faith hath come, we be not under the tutor any longer.)

26 For all ye be the children of God through the belief of Jesus Christ. [For all ye be the sons of God by faith in Christ Jesus.] (For all of ye be God's children through faith in the Messiah Jesus.)

27 For all ye that be baptized, be clothed with Christ. (For all of ye who be baptized, be clothed with the Messiah.)

28 There is no Jew, nor Greek, no bondman, nor free man, no male, nor female; for all ye be one in Christ Jesus (or for all of ye be one in the Messiah Jesus).

29 And if ye *be one* in Jesus Christ, then ye be the seed of Abraham, *and* heirs by (the) promise.

CHAPTER 4

1 But I say, as long (a) time as the heir is a little child, he diverseth nothing from a servant, when he is (the) lord of all things, [or when he is lord of all], (or even though he is the lord of all);

2 but he is under keepers and tutors, into the time determined of the father (or until the time determined by his father).

3 So we, when we were little children, we

served under the elements of the world.

4 But after that the fulfilling of time came, God sent his Son, made of a woman, made under the law,

5 that he should again-buy them that were under the law, that we should receive the adoption of sons. (so that he would redeem those who were under the Law, so that we could receive adoption as sons.)

6 And for ye be God's sons, God sent his Spirit into your hearts, crying, Abba, Father. [Forsooth for ye be the sons of God, God sent the Spirit of his Son into your hearts, crying, Abba, *that is*, father.]

7 And so there is not now a servant, but a son; and if *he is* a son, *he is* an heir by God.

8 But then ye unknowing God, served to them that in kind were not gods. (But when ye did not know God, ye served those who by their very nature were not gods.)

9 But now when ye have known God, and be known of God, how be ye turned again to the feeble [or to the sick] and needy elements, to the which ye will again serve? (But now when ye have known God, and ye be known by God, how can ye return to those elements which be frail or weak, and lacking, yet which ye will serve again?)

10 Ye take keep to days, [or Ye keep, *or wait* (upon), days], (or Ye care about special days), and months, and times, and years.

11 But I dread you, lest without cause, I have travailed among you, [or lest peradventure I have travailed in you without cause]. (But you make me fear, that I have laboured among you for no good reason, or for no good purpose, or without any good result.)

12 Be ye as I, for I *am* as ye. Brethren, I beseech you, ye have hurt me nothing, [or Brethren, I beseech you, ye have nothing hurt me].

13 But ye know, that by, (or with), (an) infirmity of (the) flesh I have preached to you [or I have evangelized to you] now before;

14   and ye despised not, neither forsook your temptation in my flesh, but ye received me as an angel of God, as Christ Jesus (or like the Messiah Jesus himself).

15   Where then is your blessing? [or Where is therefore your blessedness, *that ye had before time*?] For I bear you witness (or For I testify about you), that if it might have been done, ye would have put out your eyes, and have given them to me.

16   Am I then made an enemy to you, saying to you the sooth? (Am I then made your enemy, by telling you the truth?)

17   They love not you well [or They love you not well], but they will exclude you, that ye (pur)sue them (or so that ye follow them).

18   But (pur)sue ye the good (for)evermore in good, (or But instead, always follow, or go after, the good, simply because it is good), and not only when I am present with you.

19   My small children, which I bear again, till that Christ be formed in you, [My little sons, whom I child, *or I bring forth by travail*, again, till Christ be formed in you,] (My young children, whom I bring forth through travail, or with great labour, until the Messiah is formed within you,)

20   and I would now be at you, and change my voice, for I am confounded among you. (I wish that I could be with you, and change my tone, for I am confused about you.)

21   Say to me, ye that will be under the law, have ye not read the law?

22   For it is written, that Abraham had two sons, one of a servant [or of a handmaiden], and one of a free woman [or of a wife].

23   But he that *was* of the servant [or of the handmaiden] was born after the flesh; but he that *was* of the free woman [or of the wife] by a promise.

24   The which things be said by another understanding. For these be two testaments (or For they be two covenants); one in the hill of Sinai, (en)gendering into servage, (or begetting

into servitude, or into slavery), which is Agar. [+Which things be said by allegory. For why these things be two testaments; soothly the one in the mount Sinai, (en)gendering into servage, that is Agar.]

25   For Sinai is an hill *that is* in Arabia, which *hill* is joined to it that is now Jerusalem, and serveth with her children.

26   But that Jerusalem that is above, is free, which is our mother.

27   For it is written, Be glad, thou barren, that bearest not; break out and cry, [thou] that bringest forth no children; for many sons *be* of her that is left of her husband, more than of her that hath an husband, (or for there *shall be* more sons of her who was deserted by her husband, than of her who hath a husband).

28   For, brethren, we be [the] sons of (the) promise after Isaac;

29   but now as this that was born after the flesh pursued him that *was* after the Spirit, so now. (but just as he who was born after the flesh persecuted him who *was* born according to the Spirit, so it is also today.)

30   But what saith the scripture? Cast out the servant [or the handmaiden] and her son, for the son of the servant shall not be heir with the son of the free *wife*.

31   And so, brethren, we be not sons of the servant [or of the handmaiden], but of the free *wife*, by which freedom [or liberty] Christ hath made us free. (And so brothers, we be not the sons of the handmaid, but the sons of the free *wife*, by which freedom the Messiah hath made us free.)

CHAPTER 5

1   Stand ye therefore, and do not ye again be held in the yoke of servage. (And so stand firm, and do not be held again in the yoke of servitude or slavery.)

2   Lo! I, Paul, say to you, that if ye be circumcised, Christ shall nothing profit to you.

(Behold, I, Paul, say to you, that if ye be circumcised, the Messiah shall be of no profit to you.)

3   And I witness again to each man that circumciseth himself (or And I testify again to each man who circumciseth himself), that he is a debtor of all the law to be done.

4   And ye be voided away from Christ, and ye that be justified in the law, ye have fallen away from grace. (And ye be devoid of the Messiah, yea, ye who be justified by the Law, ye have fallen away from grace.)

5   For we through the Spirit of belief abide the hope of rightwiseness. [For we by (the) Spirit of faith abide the hope of rightwiseness.]

6   For in Jesus Christ neither circumcision is anything worth, neither prepuce, but the belief that worketh by charity [or but (the) faith that worketh by charity]. (For in Jesus Christ circumcision is not worth anything, nor is uncircumcision, but only faith that worketh through love.)

7   Ye ran well; who hindered you that ye obeyed not to the truth?

8   Consent ye to no man; for this counsel is not of him that hath called you.

9   A little sourdough impaireth [or maketh sour] all the gobbet. (A little leaven maketh the whole piece sour.)

10   I trust on you in our Lord, that ye should understand none other thing. And who that disturbeth you [or Forsooth he that distroubleth you], shall bear doom (or shall receive God's judgement), whoever he be.

11   And, brethren, if I preach yet circumcision, what suffer I yet persecution? then the stumbling of the cross is avoided/is voided. (And, brothers, if I still preach circumcision, why do I still suffer persecution? for then the stumbling of the cross is made null and void.)

12   I would that they were cut away, that disturb you. [I would that they that distrouble you, be also cut off.] (I wish that those who

disturb or trouble you, wanting you to be circumcised just like they be, would cut it all off!)

13   For, brethren, ye be called into freedom [or into liberty]; only give ye not freedom [or liberty] into (an) occasion of (the) flesh, but by charity of [the] Spirit serve ye together (or but in the love of the Spirit serve one another).

14   For every law [or all the law] is fulfilled in one word (or For all the Law is fulfilled in a single sentence), Thou shalt love thy neighbour as thyself.

15   And if ye bite, and eat each other, see ye, lest ye be wasted each from (the) other (or lest ye destroy one another).

16   And I say *to you in Christ* (or And I say *to you in the Messiah*), walk ye in (the) Spirit, and ye shall not perform the desires of the flesh.

17   For the flesh coveteth against the Spirit, and the Spirit against the flesh; for these be adversaries together, that ye do not all things that ye will, (or for they be adversaries with each other, so that ye do not do the things that ye desire to do).

18   That if ye be led by [the] Spirit, ye be not under the law. (But if ye be led by the Spirit, ye shall not be under the Law.)

19   And the works of the flesh be open, which be fornication, uncleanness, unchastity, lechery,

20   service of false gods [or serving of idols], witchcrafts, enmities, strivings [or strives], indignations, wraths, chidings, dissensions, sects [or heresies],

21   envies, manslayings, drunkennesses, unmeasurable eatings [or gluttonies], and things like to these, which I say to you before, as I have told to you before, for they that do such things, shall not have the kingdom of God, (or for they who do such things, shall not possess the Kingdom of God).

22   But the fruit of the Spirit is charity (or love), joy, peace, patience, long abiding (or endurance), benignity, [*or good will*], goodness, mildness (or meekness and humility), faith,

23   temperance, continence, chastity; against such things (there) is no law.

24   And they that be of Christ, have crucified their flesh with vices and covetings [or concupiscences]. (And they who belong to the Messiah, have crucified their flesh with its vices and its coveting.)

25   If we live by (the) Spirit, walk we by (the) Spirit;

26   be we not made covetous of vain glory, stirring each other to wrath, *or* having envy each to (the) other. (be we not made covetous of empty boasting, stirring each other to anger, *or* having envy with one another.)

CHAPTER 6

1   Brethren, if a man be occupied in any guilt [or overcome in any trespass], ye that be spiritual, inform ye [or teach] such one in (the) spirit of softness, [*or meekness*], beholding thyself, lest that thou be tempted, [*falling in the same wise*], (or lest thou be tested, *failing in the same way, or in like manner*).

2   Each bear (the) other's charges, and so ye shall fulfill the law of Christ. (Bear each other's burdens, and so ye shall fulfill the law of the Messiah.)

3   For who that troweth [or guesseth] that he be aught, when he is nought, he beguileth himself. (For he who thinketh that he is something, when he is really nothing, fooleth himself.)

4   But each man prove his own work, and so he shall have glory [only] in himself, and not in another.

5   For each man shall bear his own charge. (For each man shall bear his own burden.)

6   He that is taught in word, commune he with him that teacheth him, in all goods [or in all good things].

7   Do not ye err, God is not scorned; for those things that a man soweth, those things he shall reap, [or for why what things a man soweth, also these things he shall reap].

8   For he that soweth in his flesh, of the flesh he shall reap corruption; but he that soweth in the Spirit, of the Spirit he shall reap everlasting life.

9   And doing good fail we not; for in his time we shall reap, not failing.

10   Therefore while we have time, work we good to all men; but most(ly) to them that be home-like [or that be the household members] of the faith. (And so while we have the time, do we good to all; but most of all to those who be members of the household, or the family, of faith.)

11   See ye, what manner letters I have written to you with mine own hand.

12   For whoever will please in the flesh, these constrain you to be circumcised, only that they suffer not the persecution of Christ's cross (or so that they themselves shall not suffer persecution for the cross of the Messiah).

13   For neither they that be circumcised keep the law; but they will (or they desire) that ye be circumcised, (so) that they have glory in your flesh.

14   But far be it from me to have glory, [no] but in the cross of our Lord Jesus Christ, by whom the world is crucified to me, and I to the world.

15   For in Jesus Christ neither circumcision is anything (of) worth, nor prepuce, but a new creature. (For in Jesus Christ being circumcised is not worth anything, nor being uncircumcised, but only being a new creation.)

16   And whoever [shall] (pur)sue this rule (or And whoever shall follow this rule), peace (be) on them, and mercy, and on (the) Israel of God.

17   And hereafter [or From henceforth], no man be heavy to me; for I bear in my body the tokens, [*or the wounds*], of our Lord Jesus Christ (or for I bear on my body the signs, or the marks, of our Lord Jesus Christ).

18   The grace of our Lord Jesus Christ *be* with your spirit, brethren. Amen. †

EPHESIANS

CHAPTER 1

1 Paul, the apostle of Jesus Christ, by the will of God, to all the saints that be at Ephesus (or to all of God's people who be at Ephesus), and to the faithful men in Jesus Christ,

2 grace *be* to you and (the) peace of God, our Father, and of our Lord Jesus Christ.

3 Blessed *be* God and the Father of our Lord Jesus Christ, that hath blessed us in all spiritual blessing in heavenly things in Christ,

4 as he hath chosen us in himself before the making of the world, that we were holy [or that we should be holy], and without wem in his sight, in charity. (as he hath chosen us for himself before the creation of the world, so that we were holy, and without spot or blemish before him, in love.)

5 Which hath before-ordained us into [the] adoption of sons by Jesus Christ into him, by the purpose of his will,

6 into the praising of the glory of his grace; in which he hath glorified us in his dearworthy Son. [into the praising of the glory of his grace; in which he made us able to his grace in his dearworthy Son.]

7 In whom we have redemption by his blood, [and] forgiveness of sins, after the riches of his grace,

8 that abounded greatly in us in all wisdom and prudence,

9 to make known to us the sacrament (or the mystery) of his will, by the good pleasance of him; (to make known to us his secret plan, by his good pleasure;)

10 the which *sacrament* he purposed in him in the dispensation of (the) plenty of times, to store up all things in Christ (or to include everything in the Messiah), which be in heavens, and which *be* in earth, in him.

11 In whom [also] we be called by lot, before-ordained by the purpose of him that worketh all things by the counsel of his will;

12 that we be into the praising of his glory, we that have hoped before in Christ [or we that before hoped in Christ]. (so that we can praise his glory, we who first hoped in the Messiah, or we who were the first to hope in the Messiah.)

13 In whom also ye *were called*, when ye heard the word of truth, the gospel of your health, in whom ye believing be marked with the Holy Ghost of promise, (In whom also ye *were called*, when ye heard the Word of Truth, the Gospel, or the Good News, of your salvation, in whom ye believing be sealed with the Holy Spirit, as was promised,)

14 which is the earnest [or a wed] of our heritage (or which is the pledge of our inheritance), into the redemption of purchasing, into [the] praising of his glory.

15 Therefore and I hearing (of) your faith, that is in Christ Jesus, and the love into all (the) saints, (And so I hearing of your faith, that is in the Messiah Jesus, and your love for all of God's people,)

16 cease not to do thankings for you, making mind of you in my prayers; (never cease to give thanks for you, remembering you in my prayers;)

17 (so) that (the) God of our Lord Jesus Christ, the Father of glory, give to you the spirit of wisdom and of revelation, into the knowing of him;

18 and the eyes of your heart lightened, that ye know, which is the hope of his calling, and which be the riches of the glory of his heritage in saints; (and that the eyes of your hearts be enlightened, so that ye know, what is the hope of his calling, and what be the riches and the glory of his inheritance for God's people;)

19 and which is the excellent greatness of his virtue, into us that have believed, by the working of the might of his virtue, (and what is the excellent greatness of his power, for those

of us who have believed, by the working of the might of his power,)

20 which he wrought in Christ, raising him from death [or raising him from (the) dead], and setting *him* on his right half in heavenly things, (which he worked in the Messiah, raising him from the dead, and setting *him* at his right hand, or on his right side, in heavenly things,)

21 above each principat, and potentate, and virtue, and domination, (or above each principality, and authority, and power, and dominion), and *above* each name that is named, not only in this world, but also in the world to coming [or but also in the world to come];

22 and made all things subject under his feet, and gave him to be (the) head over all the church,

23 that is the body of him, and the plenty of him, which is all things in all things fulfilled.

CHAPTER 2

1 And when ye were dead in your guilts and sins,

2 in which ye wandered sometime, (or in which ye walked, or ye went some time ago), after the course of this world, after the prince of the power of this air, of the spirit that worketh now into the sons of unbelief;

3 in which also we all lived sometime in the desires of our flesh, doing the wills of the flesh and of the thoughts (or doing the desires of the flesh and of the thoughts, or of the mind), and we were by kind (or by nature) the sons of wrath, as other men;

4 but God, that is rich in mercy, for his full much charity in which he loved us, (but God, who is rich in mercy, for his very great love with which he loved us,)

5 yea, when we were dead in (our) sins, quickened us together in Christ (or made us alive together with the Messiah), by whose grace ye be saved,

6 and again-raised together, and made together to sit in heavenly things in Christ Jesus; (and ye be raised up, and allowed to sit in heavenly things with the Messiah Jesus;)

7 that he should show in the worlds above coming the plenteous riches of his grace in goodness on us in Christ Jesus. (so that he could show in the world to come the plentiful riches of his grace in goodness for us in the Messiah Jesus.)

8 For by grace ye be saved by faith, and this not of you (or and this is not by your own doing); for it is the gift of God,

9 not of works, that no man have glory. (and not by works, so that no one can boast.)

10 For we be the making of him, made of nought in Christ Jesus, in good works, (or made out of nothing in the Messiah Jesus, for good works), which God hath ordained, that we go in those *works*.

11 For which thing be ye mindful that sometime ye were heathen in (the) flesh, which were said prepuce (or who were called the uncircumcision), from that that is said (the) circumcision made by hand in (the) flesh; (For which thing remember that sometime ago ye were Gentiles in the flesh, ye who were called the uncircumcised, by those who be called the circumcised, which is made in the flesh by our hands;)

12 and ye were in that time without Christ, aliened [or strangers] from the living (community) of Israel, and guests of the testaments, not having (any) hope of (the) promise, and without God in this world. (and at that time ye were without the Messiah, alienated from, or strangers to, the living community of Israel, and outside of the covenants, not having any hope of the Promise, and without God in this world.)

13 But now in Christ Jesus ye that were sometime far, be made nigh in the blood of Christ. (But now in the Messiah Jesus ye who were sometime far off, be made near by the

blood of the Messiah.)

14 For he is our peace, that made both one, and unbinding the middle wall of a wall without mortar,

15 enmities in his flesh; and voided the law of commandments by dooms (or and voided the Law with its commandments and ordinances), (so) that he make two in himself into a new man, making peace,

16 to reconcile both in one body to God by the cross, slaying the enmities in himself.

17 And he coming preached peace to you that were far, and peace to them that were nigh; (And he coming preached peace to you who were far off, and peace to those who were near;)

18 for by him we both have nigh coming in one Spirit to the Father.

19 Therefore now ye be not guests and strangers, but ye be citizens of saints, and [the] household members of God; (And so now ye be not guests and strangers, but ye be citizens along with God's people, and members of God's household, or of God's family.)

20 above builded on the foundament of (the) apostles and of (the) prophets, upon that highest cornerstone, Christ Jesus; (built upon the foundation of the apostles and of the prophets, and the highest cornerstone is the Messiah Jesus;)

21 in whom each building made waxeth into an holy temple in the Lord.

22 In whom also ye be builded together into the habitation of God, in the Holy Ghost (or in the Holy Spirit).

CHAPTER 3

1 For the grace of this thing I, Paul, the bound of Christ Jesus, for you heathen men, (For the grace of this thing I, Paul, the prisoner of the Messiah Jesus, for you Gentiles,)

2 if nevertheless ye have heard the dispensation of God's grace, that is given to me

in you.

3 For by revelation the sacrament is made known to me, as I above wrote in short thing,

4 as ye may read, and understand my prudence in the mystery of Christ. (so ye can read, and understand my comprehension of the secret of the Messiah.)

5 Which was not known to other generations to the sons of men, as it is now showed to his holy apostles and prophets in the Spirit,

6 that heathen men be even-heirs, and of one body, and partners together of his promise in Christ Jesus by the evangel; (that the Gentiles be equal heirs, and of one body, and partners together of his promise in the Messiah Jesus by the Gospel or the Good News;)

7 whose minister I am made, by the gift of God's grace, which is given to me by the working of his virtue (or which is given to me by the working of his power).

8 To me, least of all (the) saints, this grace is given to preach [or to evangelize] among heathen men the unsearchable riches of Christ, (To me, least of all of God's people, this grace is given to preach among the Gentiles the immeasurable riches of the Messiah,)

9 and to (en)lighten all men, which is the dispensation of [the] sacrament hid from worlds in God, that made all things of nought; (and to enlighten all men, which is the dispensation of the mystery, or the secret, hidden from the beginning, or from the Creation, in God, who made everything out of nothing;)

10 (so) that the much-fold wisdom of God be known to princes and potentates in heavenly things by the church,

11 by the before-ordinance of worlds [or after the setting of worlds], which he made in Christ Jesus our Lord. (according to his eternal purpose, which he made in the Messiah Jesus our Lord.)

12 In whom we have trust and nigh coming [to], in trusting by the faith of him.

13   For which thing I ask, that ye fail not in my tribulations for you, which is your glory.

14   For grace of this thing I bow my knees to the Father of our Lord Jesus Christ,

15   of whom each fatherhood (or every family) in heavens and in earth is named, [of whom each fatherhood in heaven and in earth is named,]

16   (so) that he give to you, after the riches of his glory, (the) virtue (or the power) to be strengthened by his Spirit in the inner man,

17   that Christ dwell by faith in your hearts; that ye rooted and grounded in charity, (so that the Messiah live by faith in your hearts; so that ye rooted and grounded in love,)

18   may (be able to) comprehend with all (the) saints, which is the breadth, and the length, and the highness, and the deepness; (can grasp along with all of God's people, what is the breadth, and the length, and the highness, and the depth;)

19   also to know the charity of Christ more excellent(ly) than science, that ye be [full-]filled in all the plenty of God. (and also to know the love of the Messiah more completely than knowledge itself, so that ye be filled full with all the abundance of God.)

20   And to him that is mighty to do all things more plenteously than we ask or understand, by the virtue that worketh in us (or by the power that worketh in us),

21   to him be glory in the church, and in Christ Jesus, into all the generations of the world(s) of worlds. Amen. (to him be glory in the church, and in Messiah Jesus, from generation unto generation forever and ever. Amen.)

CHAPTER 4

1   Therefore I bound for the Lord beseech you, that ye walk worthily in the calling, in which ye be called,

2   with all meekness and mildness, with patience supporting each other in charity, (in all humbleness and humility, with forbearance supporting each other in love,)

3   busy to keep (the) unity of (the) Spirit in the bond of peace.

4   One body and one Spirit, as ye be called in one hope of your calling;

5   one Lord, one faith, one baptism,

6   one God and Father of all, which is above all men, and by all things, and in us all.

7   But to each of us grace is given by [or after] the measure of the giving of Christ; (But each of us is given grace according to the measure of the giving of the Messiah;)

8   for which thing he saith, He ascending on high, led captivity captive, he gave gifts to men.

9   But what is it, that he ascended up, no but that also he came down first into the lower parts of the earth?

10   He it is that came down, and that ascended [up]on (or above) all (the) heavens, (so) that he should fill all things.

11   And he gave some apostles (or And he made some *of us* apostles), some prophets, others evangelists, others shepherds and teachers,

12   to the full ending of (the) saints, into the work of (the) ministry, into [the] edification of Christ's body, (for the perfection or the completion of God's people, for the work of the ministry, for the instruction of the Messiah's body,)

13   till we run all, into (the) unity of (our) faith and of (our) knowing of God's Son, [or till we run all, in unity of faith and of knowing of God's Son], into a perfect man, after the measure of the age of the plenty of Christ (or according to the measure of the stature of the fullness of the Messiah);

14   (so) that we be not now little children, moving as (the) waves, and be not borne about with each wind of teaching, in the waywardness of men, in subtle wit, to the deceiving of error.

15   But do we (the) truth in charity, and wax in him by all things, that is Christ our head; (But speak we the truth in love, and grow in him in every way, who is the Messiah our head;)

16   of whom all the body set together, and bound together by each jointure of under-serving, by (the) working into the measure of each member, maketh increasing of the body, into [the] edification of itself in charity (or in love).

17   Therefore I say and witness (to) this thing in the Lord, that ye walk not now, as heathen men walk, in the vanity of their wit; (And so I say and testify to this in the Lord, that ye walk not now, like the Gentiles walk, in the emptiness and uselessness of their reasoning or of their thinking;)

18   that have understanding darkened with darknesses (or who have their understanding darkened with darkness), and be aliened, (or alienated), [or made far], from the life of God, by (the) ignorance that is in them, for the blindness of their heart(s).

19   Which despairing betook (or delivered) themselves to unchastity, into the working of all uncleanness in covetousness.

20   But ye have not so learned Christ, (But ye have not so learned the Messiah,)

21   if nevertheless ye heard him, and be taught in him, as is (the) truth in Jesus.

22   Do ye away by the old living, [or after the first living], the old man, that is corrupt by the desires of error;

23   and be ye renewed [or made new again] in the spirit of your soul;

24   and clothe ye the new man, which is made after God in rightwiseness and (in the) holiness of truth. [and clothe ye the new man, which after God is made of nought (or out of nothing) in rightwiseness and holiness of truth.]

25   For which thing put ye away leasing (or lying), and speak ye (the) truth each man with his neighbour, for we be members each to (the) other, [or together], (or for we be members with one another of one body).

26   Be ye wroth, and do not do sin [or and do not ye sin]; the sun fall not down on your wrath.

27   Do not ye give stead (or a place) to the devil.

28   He that stole, now steal he not; but more *rather* travail he in working with his hands that that is good, (so) that he have whereof he shall give to the needy.

29   Each evil word go not out of your mouth; but if any (word) is good to the edification of (the) faith, (so) that it give grace to men that hear (it).

30   And do not ye make the Holy Ghost of God sorry, [*or heavy*], in which ye be marked in the day of redemption. (And do not make the Holy Spirit of God sorrowful, in whom, and by whom, ye be sealed unto the Day of Redemption.)

31   All bitterness, and wrath, and indignation, and cry, and blasphemy be taken away from you, with all malice;

32   and be ye together benign, [*or of good will*], merciful, forgiving together, as also God forgave to you in Christ. (and be benign, *or have good will*, with one another, merciful, and forgiving each other, as also God forgave you in the Messiah.)

CHAPTER 5

1   Therefore be ye followers of God, as most dearworthy sons;

2   and walk ye in love, as Christ loved us (or as the Messiah loved us), and gave himself for us (as) an offering and a sacrifice to God, into the odour of sweetness.

3   And fornication, and all uncleanness, or avarice (or greed), be not named among you, as it becometh holy men;

4   either filth, or folly speech, or buffoonery [or harlotry], that pertaineth not to profit, but more *rather* doing of thankings. (or filth, or

foolish speaking, or buffoonery, all that pertaineth not to profit, but more *rather* the giving of thanks or thanksgiving.)

5   For know ye this, and understand, that each lecher [or each fornicator], or unclean man, or covetous [man], that serveth to maumets [or to idols], hath not heritage in the kingdom of Christ and of God (or hath not an inheritance in the Kingdom of the Messiah and of God).

6   No man deceive you by vain words (or Let no one deceive you with empty and useless words); for why for these things the wrath of God came upon the sons of unbelief.

7   Therefore do not ye be made partners of them.

8   For ye were sometime darknesses, (or For before ye were in darkness, or For before ye were darkness), but now *ye be* light in the Lord. Walk ye as the sons of light.

9   For the fruit of light is in all goodness, and rightwiseness, and truth.

10   And prove ye what thing is well pleasing to God.

11   And do not ye commune to unfruiteous works of darknesses; but more *rather* reprove ye [*them*]. (And do not share, or take part in, unfruitful works of darkness, but rather, rebuke *them*.)

12   For what things be done of them in privy, it is foul, yea, to speak.

13   And all things that be reproved of the light, be openly showed [or be made open]; for all thing that is showed, is light. (And everything that is reproved is first brought into the light, so that it can be openly shown, or made open; for everything that is shown, is light.)

14   For which thing he saith, Rise thou that sleepest, and rise up from death, and Christ shall lighten thee. [For which thing he saith, Rise thou that sleepest, and rise up from (the) dead, and Christ shall illumine thee.] (For which thing he saith, Rise thou who sleepest,

yea, rise up from the dead, and the Messiah shall shine upon thee.)

15   Therefore, brethren (or brothers), see ye, how warily ye shall go; not as unwise men, but as wise men, (And so, people, see how prudently you should go; not as unwise people, but as wise people,)

16   again-buying the time (or redeeming the time), for the days be evil.

17   Therefore do not ye be made unwise, but understanding which is the will of God [or of the Lord]. (And so do not be made unwise, but rather seek understanding of what is God's will.)

18   And do not ye be drunk of wine, in which is lechery [or in which is luxury], but be ye filled with the Holy Ghost; (And do not be drunk with wine, which leadeth to lechery, and to self-indulgence, but be filled with the Holy Spirit;)

19   and speak ye to yourselves in psalms, and hymns, and spiritual songs, singing and saying psalm(s) in your hearts to the Lord;

20   (for)evermore doing thankings for all things (or always giving thanks for everything), in the name of our Lord Jesus Christ to God and to the Father.

21   *Be ye* subject together in the dread of Christ. (*Be* subject to one another out of reverence for the Messiah.)

22   Women, be they subject to their husbands, as to the Lord,

23   for the man is (the) head of the woman, as Christ is head of the church (or as the Messiah is the head of the church); he *is* (the) Saviour of his body.

24   But as the church is subject to Christ (or And just as the church is subject to the Messiah), so (let) women (be subject) to their husbands in all things.

25   Men, love ye your wives, as Christ loved the church (or as the Messiah loved the church), and gave himself for it,

26   to make it holy; and cleansed it with the washing of water, in the word of life,

27   to give the church glorious to himself, that it had no wem, [or spot], nor rivelling [or wrinkle], or any such thing, but that it be holy and undefouled. (to give the church glorious to himself, so that it had no blemish, *or spot*, or wrinkle, or any such thing, but that it be holy and undefiled.)

28   So and men shall love their wives, as their own bodies. He that loveth his wife, loveth himself;

29   for no man hated ever his own flesh, but nourisheth and fostereth it, as Christ *doeth* the church (or as the Messiah nourisheth and fostereth the church).

30   And we be (the) members of his body, of his flesh, and of his bones.

31   For this thing a man shall forsake his father and mother (or a man shall leave his father and his mother), and he shall draw [or he shall cleave] to his wife; and they shall be twain in one flesh.

32   This sacrament is great; yea, I say in Christ, and in the church. (In this is a great mystery or a great secret; yes, I speak here about the Messiah, and about the church.)

33   Nevertheless ye all, each man love his wife as himself; and the wife dread her husband (or and the wife revere her husband).

CHAPTER 6

1   Sons, obey ye to your father and mother, in the Lord; for this thing is rightful, [or (it) is just], (or for this is the right thing to do).

2   Honour thou thy father and mother, that is the first commandment in [the] promise;

3   (so) that it be well to thee, and that thou be long living on the earth.

4   And, fathers, do not ye provoke your sons to wrath; but nourish ye them in the teaching and (the) chastising of the Lord [or but nourish ye them in the discipline and (the) correction of the Lord].

5   Servants, obey ye to fleshly lords with dread and trembling, in simpleness of your heart, as to Christ; (Servants, obey your human lords with fearful reverence and trembling, and with sincerity in your hearts, as unto the Messiah;)

6   not serving at the eye, as pleasing to men, but as servants of Christ (or but as the Messiah's servants); doing the will of God by discretion,

7   with good will serving as to the Lord, and not as to men;

8   witting (or knowing) that each man, whatever good thing he shall do, he shall receive this of the Lord, whether servant, whether free man.

9   And, ye lords, do the same things to them, forgiving menacings; witting that both their Lord and yours is in heavens, and the taking of persons is not with God. (And, ye lords, do the same thing for them, forgiving threats; knowing that both their Lord and yours is in heaven, and that the favouring of persons is not done by God.)

10   Here afterward, brethren, be ye comforted in the Lord, and in the might of his virtue. (Here afterward or Henceforth, brothers, be strengthened in the Lord, and in the power of his might.)

11   Clothe you(rselves) with the armour of God, that ye may stand against the ambushings, [or (the) *assailings*], of the devil. (Clothe yourselves with the armour of God, so that ye can stand against the Devil's assaults.)

12   For why striving [or battle] is not to us against flesh and blood, but against [the] princes and (the) potentates, against (the) governors of the world of these darknesses, (or against the rulers of the darkness in this world, or the rulers of this dark world), against spiritual things of wickedness, in heavenly things.

13   Therefore take ye the armour of God, that ye may against-stand in the evil day, (or And so take or put on God's armour, so that ye can withstand, or stand against, *the Devil*, on the Day of Evil); and in all things stand perfect.

14   Therefore stand ye, and be girded about your loins in soothfastness, and clothed with the habergeon of rightwiseness, (And so stand, with your loins girded in truthfulness, or with truth, and clothed with the breastplate of righteousness,)

15   and your feet shod in (the) making ready of the gospel of peace. (and your feet shod in the preparation of the Gospel, or the Good News, of peace.)

16   In all things take ye the shield of faith, in which ye may quench all the fiery darts of *him that is* (the) most wicked or (of *him who is*) the worst.

17   And take ye the helmet of health, and the sword of the Ghost, that is, the word of God. (And take or put on the helmet of salvation, and the sword of the Holy Spirit, that is, the word of God.)

18   By all prayer and beseeching pray ye all time in (the) Spirit, and in him waking in all busyness, and beseeching for all holy men [or for all (the) saints]. (By all prayer and beseeching pray all the time in the Spirit, and in him keeping watch with all diligence, and beseeching for all of God's people.)

19   and for me; that word be given to me in (the) opening of my mouth, with trust to make known the mystery of the gospel,

20   for which I am set in message in a chain (or for which I am an ambassador in a chain); so that in it I be hardy (or I be bold) to speak, as it behooveth me [*to speak out*].

21   And (so that) ye know, what things be about me, (and) what I do, Tychicus, my most dear brother, and true minister in the Lord (or and a true servant in the Lord), shall make all things known to you;

22   whom I sent to you for this same thing, (so) that ye know what things be about us, and that he comfort your hearts (or and so that he strengthen your hearts).

23   Peace to brethren, and charity, (or Peace be to the brothers, and love), with (the) faith of God our Father, and of the Lord Jesus Christ.

24   Grace (be) with all men that love our Lord Jesus Christ in uncorruption. Amen, *that is, So be it.* †

PHILIPPIANS

CHAPTER 1

1 Paul and Timothy, servants of Jesus Christ, to all the holy men in Christ Jesus, (or to all the saints, or to all of God's people, in the Messiah Jesus), that be at Philippi, with (the) bishops and (the) deacons,

2 grace and peace to you of God our Father, and of the Lord Jesus Christ. (grace and peace be to you from God our Father, and from the Lord Jesus Christ.)

3 I do thankings to my God in all mind of you (I give thanks to my God in every remembrance of you)

4 (for)evermore in all my prayers for all (of) you with joy, and make beseeching (always in all my prayers for all of you, and make beseeching)

5 on your communing in the gospel of Christ, from the first day till now; (regarding your sharing in the Gospel, or the Good News, of the Messiah, from the first day until now;)

6 trusting this same thing, that he that began in you a good work, shall perform *it* till into the day of Jesus Christ.

7 As it is just to me to feel this thing for all (of) you (or And it is right for me to feel this for all of you), for that I have you in (my) heart, and in my bonds, and in (the) defending and (in the) confirming of the gospel, (so) that all (of) ye be fellows of my joy.

8 For God is a witness to me (or For God is my witness), how I covet all (of) you in the bowels of Jesus Christ.

9 And this thing I pray, that your charity be plenteous more and more in cunning, (or in knowing), [or in science], and in all wit; (And this I pray, that your love be more and more plentiful in knowledge, and in understanding all things;)

10 that ye prove the better things, that ye be clean and without offence in the day of Christ; (that ye approve the better things, so that ye be clean and without blemish on the Day of the Messiah;)

11 [full-]filled with the fruit of rightwiseness by Jesus Christ, into the glory and praising of God. (filled full with the fruit of righteousness by Jesus Christ, unto the glory and the praising of God.)

12 For, brethren, I will that ye know, that the things that be about me have come more to the profit of the gospel, (Because, brothers, I want you to know, that what happened to me hath truly helped to advance the work of the Gospel or the Good News,)

13 so that my bonds were made known in Christ, in each moot hall, and in all other places; (for my bondage or my imprisonment for the sake of the Messiah hath been made known, throughout the Hall of Judgement here, and in many other places as well;)

14 that more of [the] brethren trusting in the Lord more plenteously for my bonds, durst without dread speak the word of God. [that more of the brethren in the Lord trusting in my bonds, more plenteously durst without dread speak the word of God.] (and because of my imprisonment, more of the brothers trusting more in the Lord, dare to speak the word of God without any fear.)

15 But some for envy and strife, some for good will, preach Christ; (But some out of envy and strife, and some out of good will, preach the Messiah;)

16 and some of charity, witting that I am put in the defence of the gospel. (and some out of love, knowing that I am put in the defence of the Gospel or the Good News.)

17 But some (out) of strife [or (out) of contention] show Christ not cleanly, guessing them(selves) to raise tribulation to my bonds. (But some to be contentious, do not reveal the Messiah purely, or do not sincerely proclaim

the Messiah, thinking to make trouble for me here in prison.)

18   But what? while on all manner, either by occasion, either by truth, Christ is showed (or the Messiah is shown); and in this thing I have joy, but also I shall have joy.

19   And I know, that this thing shall come to me into health, by your prayer(s), and the under-ministering of the Spirit of Jesus Christ, (And I know, that this shall be my salvation, or my deliverance, by your prayers, and by the ministering of the Spirit of Jesus Christ,)

20   by mine abiding and hope. For in nothing I shall be ashamed, but in all trust as (for)evermore and now, Christ shall be magnified in my body, either by life, either by death. (by my abiding and hope. For I shall be ashamed of nothing, but in complete trust now and always, the Messiah shall be magnified in my body, either in life, or in death.)

21   For [to] me to live is Christ, and to die is winning. (For to me to live is the Messiah, and to die is gain, or it is better for me.)

22   That if to live in (the) flesh, [this] is (the) fruit of work to me, lo! what I shall choose, I know not. (But if to live in the flesh, this is the fruit of my work, behold, what I shall choose, I do not know.)

23   But I am constrained of two things, I have desire to be departed [*from the body*], and to be with Christ, *it is* much more better; (For I am constrained by two things, I have a desire to be departed *from this body*, and to be with the Messiah, *it is* so much better than living;)

24   but to dwell in (the) flesh, is needful for you. (but to remain in the flesh, is necessary for your benefit.)

25   And I trusting this thing, know that I shall dwell, and perfectly dwell to all you, to your profit and joy of faith, (And I trusting in this thing, know that I shall remain, yea, I shall remain with all of you, for your profit and your joy in the faith,)

26   that your thanking abound in Christ Jesus in me, by my coming again to you. (so that your thanksgiving abound in the Messiah Jesus for me, by my coming again to you.)

27   Only live ye worthily to the gospel of Christ, that whether when I come and see you, either absent I hear of you, that ye stand in one spirit of one will, travailing together to the faith of the gospel. (Only be sure to live worthily unto the Gospel, or the Good News, of the Messiah, so that whether when I come and see you, or if absent I hear about you, that ye stand in one spirit of one will, working together in the faith for the Gospel or the Good News.)

28   And in nothing be ye afeared of adversaries, which is to them (a) cause (or a sign) of perdition, but to you *a cause* of health (or but for you a sign of your salvation). And this thing *is* of God.

29   For it is given to you for Christ (or For it is given to you for the Messiah), that not only ye believe in him, but also that ye suffer for him;

30   having the same strife, which ye saw in me, and now ye have heard of me.

CHAPTER 2

1   Therefore if any comfort *is* in Christ, if any solace of charity, (or And so if there *is* any comfort in the Messiah, if any consolation of love), if any fellowship of (the) Spirit, if any inwardness of mercy doing,

2   [ful]fill ye my joy, that ye understand the same thing, and have the same charity, of one will, and feel the same thing; (fulfill my joy, in that ye understand the same thing, have the same love, be of one will, and of one purpose;)

3   nothing [*doing*] by strife, neither by vain glory, but in meekness, deeming each other to be higher [*in virtue*] than himself; (doing *nothing* by contention, nor by conceit, but in humility, judging others to be *of* greater *virtue* than thyself;)

4   not beholding each by himself what things be his own, but those things that be of other

men.

5   And feel ye this thing in you, which *was* also in Christ Jesus; (Have the same attitude in you, which *was* also in the Messiah Jesus;)

6   which when he was in the form of God, deemed (it) not raven, that himself were even to God, [or deemed (it) not raven, himself to be even to God], (who when he was in the form of God, reckoned it not robbery, that although he was equal to God,)

7   but he lowed [or he meeked] himself (or but he humbled himself), taking the form of a servant, and was made into the likeness of men,

8   and in habit was found as a man. He meeked himself, and was made obedient to the death, yea, to the death of the cross. (and in appearance was found as a man. He humbled himself, and was obedient unto death, yea, unto his death on the cross.)

9   For which thing God enhanced him (or For which thing God exalted him), and gave to him a name that is above all name(s);

10   that in the name of Jesus each knee be bowed (or so that at the name of Jesus every knee shall be bowed), of heavenly things, [and] of earthly things, and of hell's;

11   and each tongue (shall) acknowledge, that the Lord Jesus Christ is in the glory of God the Father.

12   Therefore, my most dearworthy *brethren*, as (for)evermore ye have obeyed, not in my presence only, but much more now in mine absence, work ye with dread and trembling your health. (And so, my most dearworthy *brothers*, as ye have always obeyed, not only in my presence, but much more now in my absence, work out your own salvation with fearful reverence and trembling.)

13   For it is God that worketh in you, both to will, and to perform, for good will. (For it is God who worketh in you, both to desire, and to perform, for his own good purpose.)

14   And do ye all things without grudgings (or grumblings), and doubtings;

15   that ye be without (com)plaint, and simple as the sons of God, without reproof, in the middle of a shrewd nation and a wayward (one); among which ye shine as (the) givers of light in the world. (so that ye be without fault, and sincere as the sons of God, yea, without reproach, in the midst of a depraved and a wicked nation; among whom ye shine as the givers of light in the world.)

16   And hold ye together the word of life to my glory in the day of Christ; for I have not run in vain, neither I have travailed in vain. (And hold on firmly to the Word of Life unto my glory, or to be my boasting, on the Day of the Messiah; and thus show that I have not run in vain, nor have I laboured in vain.)

17   But though I be offered or slain on the sacrifice and service of your faith, I have joy, and I thank you all (or and I thank all of you).

18   And for the same thing have ye joy, and [together] thank ye me.

19   And I hope in the Lord Jesus, that I shall send Timothy soon to you, (so) that I (may) be of good comfort, when those things be known that be about you.

20   For I have no man so of one will, that is (so) busy for you with clean affection.

21   For all men seek those things that be their own, not those that be of Christ Jesus (or not those things that be of the Messiah Jesus).

22   But know ye the assay of him, for as a son to the father he hath served with me in the gospel.

23   Therefore I hope that I shall send him to you, anon as I see what things be about me. (And so I hope that I shall send him to you, as soon as I see what things be about me here.)

24   And I trust in the Lord, that also myself shall come to you soon.

25   And I guessed it needful to send to you Epaphroditus, my brother and even-worker, and mine even-knight, (or my brother and fellow worker, and my fellow soldier), but your apostle, and the minister of my need(s).

26   For he desired you all, and he was sorrowful, therefore that ye heard that he was sick.

27   For he was sick to the death, but God had mercy on him; and not only on him, but also on me, lest I had heaviness on heaviness.

28   Therefore more hastily I sent him, (so) that when ye have seen him, ye have joy again, and I be without heaviness.

29   Therefore receive ye him with all joy in the Lord, and have ye such with *all* honour.

30   For the work of Christ he went to (the) death, giving his life, that he should fulfill that that failed of you with my service. (For the work of the Messiah he went unto death, giving his life, so that he could do for me, or so that he could fulfill for me, that service which you could not do.)

CHAPTER 3

1   Henceforward, my brethren, have ye joy in the Lord. To write to you the same things, to me *it is* not slow, and to you *it is* necessary.

2   See ye hounds, see ye evil workmen, see ye division [or concision].

3   For we be (the) circumcision, which by (the) Spirit serve to God, and glory in Christ Jesus, (or who by the Spirit serve God, and glory in, or boast about, the Messiah Jesus), and have not trust in the flesh,

4   though I have trust, yea, in the flesh. If any other man is seen to trust in the flesh, I more,

5   that *was* circumcised in the eighth day, of the kin [or of the kindred] of Israel, of the lineage of Benjamin, an Hebrew of Hebrews, by the law a Pharisee, (who was circumcised on the eighth day, of the kindred of Israel, of the tribe of Benjamin, a Hebrew of Hebrews, a Pharisee by the Law,)

6   by love pursuing the church of God, by rightwiseness that is in the law living without (com)plaint. (zealously persecuting God's

church, by the righteousness that is in the Law living without any fault.)

7   But which things were to me winnings, I have deemed these impairings for Christ. (And those things which were to me winnings, now I have judged to be losses because of the Messiah.)

8   Nevertheless I guess all things to be impairment for the clear science (or for the glorious knowledge) of Jesus Christ my Lord. For whom I made all things impairment, and I deem as drit [or as turds], that I win Christ (or so that I may win the Messiah),

9   and that I be found in him, not having my rightwiseness that is of the law, but that that is of the faith of Christ Jesus, that is of God the rightwiseness in faith, (and that I be found in him, not having my righteousness that is from the Law, but the righteousness that is from faith in the Messiah Jesus, which is the righteousness from God through faith,)

10   to know him, and the virtue of his rising again, and the fellowship of his passion, and to be made like [or (to be) configured] to his death, (to know him, and the power of his resurrection, and the sharing of his suffering, and to be made like him in his death,)

11   if on any manner (or in any manner) I come to the resurrection that is from death. [⁺if on any manner I shall come to the resurrection that is of (the) dead.]

12   Not that now I have taken (hold of it), or now I am perfect; but I (pur)sue, if in any manner I comprehend [or I take (hold of)] in which thing also I am comprehended of Jesus Christ. (Not that now I have caught it, or that now I am perfect, or am completed; but I continue to pursue it, if by any means I can catch hold of that for which also I am caught by Jesus Christ.)

13   Brethren, I deem me not that I have comprehended, (or Brothers, I do not reckon that I have taken hold of it, or that I have caught it); but one thing, I forget those things that be

behind, and stretching forth myself to those things that be before,

14 and pursue to the ordained meed [or to the prize] of the high calling of God in Christ Jesus. (and pursue toward the ordained prize of the high calling of God in the Messiah Jesus.)

15 Therefore whoever we be perfect, feel we this thing. And if ye understand in other manner anything, this thing God shall show to you.

16 Nevertheless to what thing we have come, (so) that we understand the same thing, and that we perfectly dwell in the same rule.

17 Brethren, be ye my followers, and wait ye (on) them that walk so, as ye have our form. (Brothers, follow me, and watch those who walk so, so that ye have our form.)

18 For many walk, which I have said oft to you, but now I weeping say, [them], the enemies of Christ's cross (or the enemies of the Messiah's cross),

19 whose end *is* death, whose god is the womb, and the glory in [the] confusion of them, that savour [or that understand] earthly things.

20 But our living is in (the) heavens [or Forsooth our living is in heaven]; from whence also we abide (or we wait for) the Saviour our Lord Jesus Christ,

21 which shall reform the body of our meekness, *that is* made like [or (that is) configured] to the body of his clearness (or of his glory), by the working by which he may also make all things subject to him.

CHAPTER 4

1 Therefore, my brethren most dearworthy and most desired, my joy and my crown, so stand ye in the Lord, most dear *brethren*.

2 I pray Euodias, and beseech Syntyche, to understand the same thing in the Lord.

3 Also I pray and thee, germane fellow, help thou those *women* that travailed with me in the gospel, (or help those *women* who laboured

with me in the Gospel or the Good News), with Clement and other mine helpers, whose names be in the book of life.

4 Joy ye in the Lord (for)evermore; again I say, joy ye. (Always have joy in the Lord; again I say, have joy!)

5 Be your patience [or your temperance] known to all men; the Lord is nigh (or the Lord is near).

6 Be ye nothing busy, but in all prayer and beseeching, with doing of thankings, (or with the giving of thanks, or with thanksgiving), be your askings known at God.

7 And the peace of God, that passeth all wit, keep your hearts and understandings in Christ Jesus. (And the peace of God, which passeth all reasoning or all understanding, keep your hearts and understandings in the Messiah Jesus.)

8 From henceforth, brethren, whatever things be sooth (or whatever things be true), whatever things chaste (or pure), whatever things just, whatever things holy, whatever things able to be loved, [or amiable, or lovable], whatever things of good fame, if any virtue, if any praising of discipline, think ye (on) these things,

9 that also ye have learned, and taken, and heard, and seen in me. Do ye these things, and (the) God of peace shall be with you.

10 But I joyed greatly in the Lord, that sometime afterward ye flowered again to feel for me, as also ye feeled (before). But ye were occupied,

11 I say not as for need, for I have learned to be sufficient in which things I am.

12 And I know also how to be lowed, [or how to be bowed, *or meeked*], I know also how to have plenty [or how to abound], (And I know how to be humbled, and I know how to abound). Everywhere and in all things I am taught to be [full-]filled, and to hunger, and to abound, and to suffer need.

13 I may all things in him that comforteth me.

(I can do all things through him who strengtheneth me.)

14 Nevertheless ye have done well, communing to my tribulation.

15 For ye, Philippians, know also, that in the beginning of the gospel, when I went forth from Macedonia, no church communed with me in reason, of thing given and taken, (or no other church shared things given and received with me), but ye alone.

16 Which sent to Thessalonica once and twice also into use to me. (Ye who sent sustenance to Thessalonica not once but twice for my use.)

17 Not for I seek (a) gift, but I require, [*or* (I) *seek again*], fruit abounding in your reason.

18 For I have all things, and abound; I am [full-]filled [or replete] with those things taken of Epaphroditus (or with those things received from Epaphroditus), which ye sent into the odour of sweetness, a covenable (or a suitable) sacrifice, pleasing to God.

19 And my God [ful]fill all your desire(s), by his riches in glory in Christ Jesus. (And my God shall fulfill all your desires, or shall fill all of your desires full, with his riches in glory through the Messiah Jesus.)

20 But to God and our Father be glory into worlds of worlds. Amen. (But to God and our Father be glory forever and ever. Amen.)

21 Greet ye well every holy *man* in Christ Jesus. Those brethren that be with me, greet you well. (Give hearty greetings to every saint, or to all of God's people, in the Messiah Jesus. Those brothers who be with me, send you hearty greetings.)

22 All holy men greet you well, most soothly they that be of the emperor's [or of Caesar's] house. (All the saints, or all of God's people, send hearty greetings to you, most particularly those who be in the household of the Emperor.)

23 The grace of our Lord Jesus Christ be with your spirit. Amen. †

COLOSSIANS

CHAPTER 1

1   Paul, (an) apostle of Jesus Christ, by the will of God, and Timothy, (a) brother,

2   to them that be at Colosse, holy and faithful brethren in Christ Jesus, grace and peace to you of God our Father and of the Lord Jesus Christ. (to those who be at Colosse, holy and faithful brothers in the Messiah Jesus, grace and peace be to you from God our Father, and from the Lord Jesus Christ.)

3   We do thankings to God, and to the Father of our Lord Jesus Christ, (for)evermore praying for you, (We give thanks to God, and to the Father of our Lord Jesus Christ, always praying for you,)

4   hearing (of) your faith in Christ Jesus, and the love that ye have to all holy men, (hearing of your faith in the Messiah Jesus, and of the love that ye have for all the saints, or for all of God's people,)

5   for the hope that is kept to you in heavens. Which ye heard in the word of truth of the gospel, (for the hope which is kept for you in heaven. Which ye heard in the Word of Truth, yea, the Gospel or the Good News,)

6   that came to you, as also it is in all the world, and maketh fruit, and waxeth (or and groweth), as [it is] in you, from that day in which ye heard and knew the grace of God in truth.

7   As ye learned of Epaphras, our fellow [or our even-servant], most dearworthy, which is a true minister of Jesus Christ for you; (As ye learned from Epaphras, our fellow servant, and most dearworthy, who is a true servant of Jesus Christ for you;)

8   which also showed to us your loving in (the) Spirit.

9   And therefore we from the day in which we heard, cease not to pray for you, and to ask, that ye be filled with the knowing of his will in all wisdom and ghostly (or spiritual) understanding;

10   (so) that ye walk worthily to God pleasing by all things, and make fruit in all good work, and wax in the science of God (or and grow in the knowledge of God),

11   and be comforted in all virtue, by the might of his clearness, in all patience and long abiding with joy, (and be strengthened in all power, by his glorious might, in all endurance and in long abiding with joy,)

12   that ye do thankings to God and to the Father, which made you worthy into the part of heritage of holy men in light. [⁺doing thankings to God the Father, the which made us worthy into the part of heritage of holy men in light.] (so that ye give thanks to God the Father, who made you worthy to share in the inheritance of the saints, or of God's people, in the light.)

13   Which delivered us from the power of darknesses, and translated [us] into the kingdom of the Son of his loving,

14   in whom we have again-buying, and remission of sins. (in whom we have redemption, and the forgiveness of sins.)

15   Which is the image of God invisible, the first begotten of each creature. (Who is the image of the invisible God, the first-born before every created thing, or he who holdeth primacy over all Creation.)

16   For in him all things be made, in heavens and in earth, visible and invisible, either thrones, either dominations, either princehoods, either powers, all things be made of nought by him, and in him, (For in him all things be made, in heaven and on earth, visible and invisible, yea, thrones, and dominions, and principalities, and powers, all things be made out of nothing, by him, and in him,)

17   and he is before all, and all things be in him.

18   And he is (the) head of the body of the church; which is the beginning, and the first

begotten of dead *men*, (or who is the Source, and the first-born to be raised from the dead), (so) that he hold the first dignity, in all things. [⁺And he is (the) head of the body of the church; the which is the beginning, *or the first of all*, and the first begotten of (the) dead, that he be holding primacy, *or the first dignity*, in (or over) all things.]

19 For in him it pleased all plenty to inhabit,

20 and by him all things to be reconciled into him, and made peace by the blood of his cross, those things that be in earths, either that be in heavens. (and by him all things were reconciled to God, and he made peace by the blood of his cross, yea, for those things that be on earth, and those things that be in heaven.)

21 And when ye were sometime aliened [or made strangers], and enemies by wit, in evil works, (or and enemies in thought, and by evil works), now he hath reconciled *you*

22 in the body of his flesh by death, to have you holy, and unwemmed (or without spot), and without reproof before him.

23 If nevertheless ye dwell in the faith, founded, and stable, and unmoveable from the hope of the gospel that ye have heard, which is preached in all creature that is under heaven (or which is preached in all Creation that is under heaven). Of which I, Paul, am made a minister,

24 and now I have joy in passion(s) for you, and I [ful]fill those things that fail of the passions of Christ in my flesh, for his body, that is the church. (and now I have joy in my sufferings for you, and through them I fulfill that which fail of the sufferings of the Messiah in my flesh, for his body, that is the church.)

25 Of which I Paul am made (a) minister [or a servant] by the dispensation of God, that is given to me in you, that I [ful]fill the word of God,

26 the private [or the mystery] that was hid from worlds and generations. But now it is showed to his saints, (the secret that was hidden for countless generations. But now it is shown, or revealed, to God's people,)

27 to whom God would make known the riches of the glory of this sacrament in heathen men, which is Christ in you, the hope of glory. (to whom God would make known the riches of the glory of this secret among the Gentiles, which is the Messiah in you, the hope of glory.)

28 Whom we show, reproving each man, and teaching each man in all wisdom, that we offer each man perfect in Christ Jesus (or so that we offer each person complete in the Messiah Jesus).

29 In which thing also I travail, in striving by the working of him, that he worketh in me in virtue (or that he worketh in me in power).

CHAPTER 2

1 But I will (or But I desire) that ye know, what busyness I have for you, and for them that be at Laodicea, and whichever saw not my face in (the) flesh,

2 that their hearts be comforted, and they *be* taught in charity, (or so that their hearts be strengthened, and they *be* taught in love), into all the riches of the plenty of understanding, into the knowing of [the] mystery of God, the Father of Jesus Christ,

3 in whom all the treasures of wisdom and of science, [or of cunning], (or of knowing), be hid. (in whom all the treasures of wisdom and of knowledge be hidden.)

4 For this thing I say, that no man deceive you in height of words. (And I say this to you, so that no one shall deceive you with high-sounding arguments.)

5 For though I be absent in body, [but] by spirit I am with you, joying and seeing your order and the firmness of your belief that is in Christ (or rejoicing and seeing your order and the firmness of your belief that is in the Messiah).

6 Therefore as ye have taken Jesus Christ our Lord, walk ye in him, (And so as ye have received Jesus Christ our Lord, now walk in him, or now live in him,)

7   and be ye rooted and builded above in him, (that is, in Christ, or the Messiah), and confirmed in the belief, as ye have learned, abounding in him in (the) doing of thankings, (or and abounding in thanksgiving, or in the giving of thanks, to him).

8   See ye that no man deceive you by philosophy and vain, (or empty and futile), fallacy, after the tradition(s) of men, after the elements of the world, and not after Christ.

9   For in him dwelleth body-like all the fullness of the Godhead.

10   And ye be [ful]filled in him, that is (the) head of all principat and power.

11   In whom also ye be circumcised in (a) circumcision not made with hand(s), in (the) despoiling [or in (the) nakedness] of the body of flesh, but in (the) circumcision of, (or made by), Christ;

12   and ye be buried together with him in baptism, in whom also ye have risen again by (the) faith of the working of God, that raised him from death [or that raised him from (the) dead].

13   And when ye were dead in your guilts, and in the prepuce of your flesh, he quickened together *you* with him; forgiving to you all guilts [or all (your) trespasses], (And when ye were dead in your trespasses, and in the uncircumcision of your flesh, or with your flesh uncircumcised, he enlivened *you* with the Messiah; forgiving all of your trespasses,)

14   doing away that writing of (the) decree that was against us, that was contrary to us; and he took away that from the middle, pitching it (or fixing it) on the cross;

15   and he spoiled principats and powers, and led out trustily, openly overcoming them in himself.

16   Therefore no man judge you in meat, or in drink, or in part of feast day, or of new moon, or of sabbaths, (And so let no man judge you about food, or drink, or taking part in Feast Days, or about new moons, or about the Sabbath,)

17   which be (but a) shadow of things to coming [or which be (but a) shadow of things to come]; for the body *is* of Christ.

18   (Let) No man deceive you, willing *to teach* in meekness (or with humility), and [the] religion of angels, those things which he hath not seen, walking vainly, swollen [or in-blown] with (the) wit of his flesh (or with a worldly mind),

19   and not holding the head, of which all the body, by bands and joinings together under-ministered and made, waxeth into [the] increasing of God.

20   For if ye be dead with Christ from the elements of the world, what yet as men living to the world deem ye? (For if ye be with the Messiah, and so dead to the elements of the world, then why do ye judge like men still living in the world?)

21   That ye touch not, neither taste, neither treat with hands those things,

22   which all be into death by that use, after the commandments and teachings of men;

23   which have a reason of wisdom in vain religion [or in superstition] and meekness, and not to spare the body, not in any honour to the fulfilling of the flesh.

CHAPTER 3

1   Therefore if ye have risen together with Christ, seek ye those things that be above, where Christ is sitting on the right half of God, (or at the right hand, or on the right side, of God).

2   Savour ye [or Understand ye] those things that be above, not those (things) that *be* on the earth.

3   For ye be dead, and your life is hid with Christ in God.

4   For when Christ shall appear, (who is) your life, then also ye shall appear with him in glory.

5   Therefore slay ye your members, which be on the earth, fornication, uncleanness, lechery, evil covetousness, and avarice (or greed), which is (the) service of maumets, [or of simulacra], (or which is being in service to idols);

6   for which things the wrath of God came on the sons of unbelief;

7   in which also ye walked sometime, when ye lived in them (or when ye lived among them).

8   But now put ye away all things, wrath, indignation, malice, blasphemy and foul words of your mouth.

9   Do not ye lie, [or gab], together; despoil ye you(rselves) from the old man with his deeds,

10   and clothe ye the new man, that is made new again into the knowing of God, after the image of him that made him;

11   where is not male and female, heathen man and Jew, circumcision and prepuce, barbarous and Scythian, bondman and free, but all things and in all things Christ. (where there is not male and female, Gentile and Jew, circumcised and uncircumcised, barbarian and Scythian, slave and free man, but the Messiah is all and in all.)

12   Therefore ye, as the chosen of God, holy and loved, clothe [ye] you with the entrails of mercy, benignity, and meekness (or humility), temperance, patience;

13   and support ye each one (the) other [or bearing up together], and forgive to yourselves, if any man against any (other) hath a quarrel; as the Lord [Christ] forgave to you, so also ye. (and support one another, and forgive each other, if anyone hath a quarrel against another; like the Lord Messiah forgave you, so ye also should forgive.)

14   And upon all these things have ye charity (or love), that is the bond of perfectness [or the bond of perfection].

15   And the peace of Christ enjoy in your hearts, in which ye be called in one body, and be ye kind.

16   The word of Christ dwell in you plenteously, in all wisdom; and teach and admonish yourselves in psalms, and hymns, and spiritual songs, in grace singing in your hearts to the Lord. (Let the Messiah's words remain plentifully in you, providing all wisdom; and teach and admonish each other with psalms, and hymns, and spiritual songs, singing with thanksgiving in your hearts to the Lord.)

17   All thing(s), whatever thing ye do, in word or in deed, all things in the name of our Lord Jesus Christ, doing thankings to God and to the Father by him, [or doing thankings to God the Father by him], (or giving thanks to God the Father through him).

18   Women, be ye subject to your husbands, as it behooveth in the Lord.

19   Men, love ye your wives, and do not ye be bitter to them.

20   Sons, obey ye to your father and mother by all things [or in all things]; for this is well pleasing in the Lord. (Sons, obey your father and mother in everything, for this is greatly pleasing to the Lord.)

21   Fathers, do not ye provoke your sons to indignation, (so) that they be not made feeble-hearted.

22   Servants, obey ye by all things to fleshly lords, not serving at the eye, as pleasing to men, but in simpleness of heart, dreading the Lord [God], (or but with an honest, or a sincere, heart, having fearful reverence for the Lord).

23   Whatever ye do, work ye of will as to the Lord and not to men; (Whatever ye do, do it or work it with the thought that it is done for the Lord and not for men;)

24   witting that of the Lord ye shall take yielding of heritage. Serve ye to the Lord Christ. (knowing that from the Lord ye shall receive your inheritance as a reward. Serve the Lord Messiah.)

25   For he that doeth injury [or wrong] shall receive that that he did evil; and (the) acception [or (the) taking] of persons is not with God, (or

and the favouring of persons is not done by God).

CHAPTER 4

1   Lords, give ye to (your) servants that that is just and even (or what is just and fair), witting (or knowing) that also ye have a Lord in heaven.

2   Be ye busy in prayer, and wake in it, in doing of thankings; (Be diligent in prayer, and be watchful in it, and in thanksgiving, or in the giving of thanks;)

3   and pray each for (the) other, and for us, that God open to us the door of word, to speak the mystery of Christ; for which also I am bound, (and pray for one another, and for us, that God would open for us the door, or the occasion, to preach, yea, to speak about the secret of the Messiah; for which I am now in prison,)

4   that I show it, so as it behooveth me to speak.

5   Walk ye in wisdom to them that be withoutforth, again-buying (the) time. (Walk with wisdom, or Show wisdom, to those who be outside, redeeming the time.)

6   Your word be savoured with salt (for)evermore in grace; that ye know, how it behooveth you to answer to each man. (Let your words always be gracious, and savoured with salt; so that ye know, how it behooveth you to answer to everyone.)

7   Tychicus, most dear brother, and faithful minister, and my fellow [or my even-servant] in the Lord, (or Tychicus, most dear brother, and faithful servant, and my fellow servant in the Lord), shall make all things known to you, that be about me.

8   Whom I sent to you to this same thing, (so) that he know what things be about you, and comfort your hearts,

9   with Onesimus, most dear and faithful brother, which is of you (or who is one of you); which shall make all things that be done here,

known to you.

10   Aristarchus, (a) prisoner with me [or mine even-captive], greeteth you well (or sendeth you hearty greetings), and Marcus, the cousin of Barnabas, of whom ye have taken commandments; if he come to you, receive ye him;

11   and Jesus, that is said Justus; which be of (the) circumcision; they alone be mine helpers in the kingdom of God, that were to me in solace. (and Jesus, who is also called Justus; all of whom be of the circumcision; they alone be my helpers in the Kingdom of God, and were a great solace to me.)

12   Epaphras, that is of you, the servant of Jesus Christ, greeteth you well (or sendeth you hearty greetings); ever busy for you in prayers, (so) that ye stand perfect and full in all the will of God.

13   And I bear witnessing to him, that he hath much travail for you, and for them that be at Laodicea, and that be at Hierapolis. (And I testify about him, that he hath laboured much for you, and for those who be at Laodicea, and who be at Hierapolis.)

14   Luke, the leech, most dear, and Demas, greet you well. (Luke, the most dear physician, and Demas, send you hearty greetings.)

15   Greet ye well the brethren that be at Laodicea (or Give hearty greetings to the brothers who be at Laodicea), and *the woman* Nymphas, and the church that is in her house, [or and Nymphas, and the church that is in his house].

16   And when this epistle is read among you, do ye, that it be read in the church of (the) Laodiceans; and read ye that *epistle* that is of (the) Laodiceans.

17   And say ye to Archippus, See the ministry, that thou hast taken in the Lord (or that thou hast received from the Lord), that thou [ful]fill it.

18   My salutation, by the hand of Paul. Be ye mindful of my bonds. The grace of our Lord Jesus Christ be with you. Amen. †

1ST THESSALONIANS

CHAPTER 1

1   Paul, and Silvanus, and Timothy, to the church of (the) Thessalonians, in God the Father, and in the Lord Jesus Christ, grace and peace (be) to you.

2   We do thankings to God (for)evermore for all (of) you, and we make mind of you in our prayers without ceasing; (We always give thanks to God for all of you, and we remember you in our prayers without ceasing;)

3   having mind of the work of your faith [⁺or mindful of the work of your faith], and travail, and charity, and abiding of the hope of our Lord Jesus Christ, before God and our Father. (remembering the work of your faith, and your labour, and your love, and the endurance of your hope in our Lord Jesus Christ, before God and our Father.)

4   Ye beloved brethren of God, we witting your choosing, (You beloved brothers in God, we knowing of your choosing, or of your election,)

5   for our gospel was not at you in word only, but also in virtue, and in the Holy Ghost, and in much plenty; as ye know, which we were among you for you; (and so we brought you the Gospel or the Good News, not in words alone, but also in power, and in the Holy Spirit, or but also in the power of the Holy Spirit, and with great certitude; and ye know, what manner of men we were when we were among you for your own sakes;)

6   and ye be made followers of us, and of the Lord, receiving the word in much tribulation, with joy of the Holy Ghost, (or with joy in the Holy Spirit or from the Holy Spirit);

7   so that ye be made (an) ensample to all men that believe, in Macedonia and in Achaia.

8   For of you the word of the Lord is published [or is much told (out)], not only in Macedonia and Achaia, but your faith that is to God, in each place is gone forth, [or but in each place your faith that is to God, is gone forth]; so that it is not need(ful) to us to speak anything (or so that it is not needed or necessary for us to say anything more).

9   For they show of you, what manner entry we had to you, and how ye be converted to God from maumets [or from simulacra], to serve to the living God and very; (For they tell about you, and how we visited you, and thereafter how ye be turned from idols, to serve the living and true God;)

10   and to abide his Son from heavens (or and to wait for his Son to come from heaven), whom he raised from death, the Lord Jesus, that delivered us from (the) wrath to coming. [and for to abide his son from heavens, whom he raised from (the) dead, Jesus, that delivered us from (the) wrath to come.]

CHAPTER 2

1   For, brethren, ye know our entry to you, for it was not (in) vain;

2   but first we suffered, and were punished with wrongs, as ye know in Philippi, and had trust in our Lord, to speak to you the gospel of God in much busyness (or to tell you about the Gospel, or the Good News, of God with much diligence).

3   And our exhortation [or our teaching] is not of error, neither of uncleanness, neither in guile,

4   but as we be (ap)proved of God, that the gospel of God should be taken to us, so we speak, (or but as we be approved by God, that the Gospel, or the Good News, of God should be given to us, and so we speak); not as pleasing to men, but to God that proveth our hearts.

5   For neither we were anytime in word(s) of glossing [or of flattering], as ye know, neither in

occasion of avarice (or nor as an occasion for greed); God is (our) witness;

6 neither seeking glory of men, neither of you, neither of others, when we, as Christ's apostles, might have been in charge to you. (neither seeking praise from people, nor from you, nor from others, when we, as Christ's apostles, might have been in charge of you or might have been a burden to you.) might have been in charge of you, or might have been a burden to you). [neither seeking glory of men, neither of you, neither of others, when we might have been chargeous (or burdensome) to you, as Christ's apostles.]

7 But we were made little in the middle of you, as if a nurse foster her sons;

8 so we desiring you with great love, would have betaken to you not only the gospel of God (or would have delivered to you not only the Gospel, or the Good News, of God), but also our lives, for ye be made most dearworthy to us.

9 For, brethren, ye be mindful of our travail and weariness; we worked night and day, that we should not grieve any of you, and preached to you the gospel of God. (Because, brothers, ye remember our labour and our weariness; yea, we worked night and day, so that we would not grieve any of you, and preached to you the Gospel, or the Good News, of God.)

10 God and ye be witnesses, how holily (or how devoutly), and justly, and without (com)plaint [or quarrel], we were to you that believed.

11 As ye know, how we prayed you (or how we beseeched you), and comforted each of you, as the father his sons,

12 and we have witnessed (or and we have testified), that ye should go worthily to God, that called you into his kingdom and glory.

13 Therefore we do thankings to God without ceasing. For when ye had taken of us the word of the hearing of God, ye took it not as the word of men, but as it is verily, the word of God, that worketh in you that have believed.

(And so we give thanks to God without ceasing. Because when ye had received from us the word of God, which ye heard, ye took it not as the word of men, but as it truly is, the word of God, which worketh in you who have believed.)

14 For, brethren, ye be made followers of the churches of God, that be in Judea, in Christ Jesus, for ye have suffered the same things of your even-lineages, as they of the Jews, (or and ye have suffered the same things from your fellow countrymen, as they have from the Jews).

15 Which slew both the Lord Jesus and the prophets, and pursued us (or and persecuted us), and they please not to God, and they be adversaries to all men;

16 forbidding us to speak to heathen men, that they be made safe, that they [full-]fill their sins (for)evermore; for the wrath of God came on them into the end. (forbidding us to speak to the Gentiles, so that they can be saved, so that they fill their sins full forevermore; but God's wrath hath come upon them in the end.)

17 And, brethren, we desolate from you for a time, by mouth and in beholding, [as in presence], but not in heart, have hied more plenteously to see your face with great desire.

18 For we would come to you, yea, I, Paul, once and again, but Satan hindered us.

19 For why what is our hope, or joy, or crown of glory? Whether ye be not before our Lord Jesus Christ in his coming? (or Shall it not be you, when we stand before our Lord Jesus Christ at his coming?)

20 For ye be our glory and joy. (Yea, ye be our glory and our joy.)

CHAPTER 3

1 For which thing we suffered (it) no longer, and it pleased to us to dwell alone at Athens; (For which thing we could no longer bear it, and it pleased us to remain alone at Athens;)

2 and we sent Timothy, our brother, and minister of God in the evangel of Christ, (or and

so we sent Timothy, our brother, and the servant of God in the Gospel, or the Good News, of the Messiah), to you to be confirmed, and to be taught, [or admonished], for your faith,

3   that no man be moved in these tribulations (or so that no one be moved, or be shaken, by these troubles). For [ye] yourselves know, that in this thing we be set.

4   For when we were at you, we before-said to you, that we should suffer tribulations; as it is (now) done, and ye know (it). (For when we were with you, we said ahead of time to you, or we warned you, that we would suffer troubles; as it is now done, and ye know it.)

5   Therefore I, *Paul*, no longer abiding, sent to know your faith, lest peradventure he that tempteth [shall] tempt you, and your travail be made (in) vain [or and our travail be made (in) vain]. (And so I, *Paul*, no longer waiting, sent to know your faith, lest perhaps he who testeth shall test you, and my labour be made in vain.)

6   But now, when Timothy shall come to us from you, and (shall) tell to us your faith and charity, and that ye have good mind of us, (for)ever[more] desiring to see us, as we also you; [Now forsooth Timothy coming to us from you, and telling to us your faith and charity, and for ye have evermore good mind of us, desiring for to see us, as we also you;] (But now, Timothy hath come back to us from you, and hath told us about your faith and love, and that ye have a fond remembrance of us, always desiring to see us, as we also you;)

7   therefore, brethren, we be comforted in you, in all our need and tribulation, by your faith. (and so, brothers, we be strengthened by you, in all our need and troubles, by your faith.)

8   For now we live, if ye stand in the Lord.

9   For what doing of thankings may we yield to God for you (or For what doing of thanks can we give to God for you), in all joy, in which we joy for you before our Lord?

10   night and day more plenteously praying, that we see your face, and fulfill those things

that fail to your faith [or and fulfill those things that fail of your faith].

11   But God himself and our Father, and the Lord Jesus Christ, (ad)dress our way to you. (But God himself and our Father, and the Lord Jesus Christ, direct our way to you.)

12   And the Lord multiply you, and make your charity to be plenteous of each to (the) other [or and make your charity for to abound together], and into all men, as also we in you; (And may the Lord make your love for one another be plentiful, or to abound more and more, and for all men, as also we for you, or and also our love for you;)

13   that your hearts be confirmed without (com)plaint in holiness, before God and our Father, in the coming of our Lord Jesus Christ with all his saints. Amen. (so that your hearts be confirmed in holiness without fault or blemish, before God and our Father, in the coming of our Lord Jesus Christ with all his people. Amen.)

CHAPTER 4

1   Therefore, brethren, from henceforward we pray you, and beseech in the Lord Jesus, that as ye have received of us (or that as ye have received from us), how it behooveth you to go and to please God, so walk ye, (so) that ye abound more.

2   For ye know what commandments I have given to you by the Lord Jesus.

3   For this is the will of God, (yea), your holiness, that ye abstain you(rselves) from fornication.

4   That each of you know how to wield his vessel in holiness, and honour; (So that each of you know how to control his body with holiness, and with honour;)

5   not in (the) passion(s) of lust, as (the) heathen men that know not God. (not in lustful passions, like the Gentiles who do not know God.)

6   And that no man over-go, neither deceive

his brother, in chaffering. For the Lord is (the) (a)venger of all these things, as we before-said to you, and have witnessed. (And that no one overreach, or take advantage of, or deceive his brother, in merchandising or in trading. For the Lord is the avenger of all these things, as we said to you before, or as we warned you, and have so testified.)

7   For God called not us into uncleanness, but into holiness.

8   Therefore he that despiseth these things, despiseth not man, but God, that also gave his Holy Spirit in us (or who also gave us his Holy Spirit).

9   But of the charity of brotherhood, we had no need to write to you; ye yourselves have learned of God, that ye love together; (But about the love for the brotherhood, we had no need to write to you; ye yourselves have learned from God, that ye should love one another;)

10   for ye do that into all (the) brethren in all (of) Macedonia. And, brethren, we pray you, that ye abound more; (and in fact ye do love all the brothers in all of Macedonia. And, brothers, we beseech you, that ye abound all the more;)

11   and take keep, that ye be quiet, [or and give work, *or busyness*, that ye be quiet], (or and take care, that ye be calm, or that ye live quietly); and that ye do your need, and that ye work with your [own] hands, as we have commanded to you;

12   and that ye wander honestly to them that be withoutforth, and that of no man ye desire anything. (and that ye walk honestly, or properly, with those who be outside of us, and that ye desire nothing from anyone.)

13   For, brethren, we will not, that ye unknow of men that die, that ye be not sorrowful, as others that have not hope. (And, brothers, we do not desire, that ye do not know about men who die, so that ye do not sorrow, like others who have no hope.)

14   For if we believe, that Jesus was dead, and rose again, so God shall lead with him them

that be dead by Jesus. (For we believe, that Jesus died, and rose again, and so God shall bring back with him those who have died as believers.)

15   And we say this thing to you in the word of the Lord, that we that live, that be left in the coming of the Lord, shall not come before them that be dead. (And we say this to you by the word of the Lord, that we who live, who be left alive until the coming, or the return, of the Lord, shall not go before those who have died.)

16   For the Lord himself shall come down from heaven, in the commandment [or in the commanding], and in the voice of an archangel, and in the trump of God; and the dead men that be in Christ, shall rise again first. (For the Lord himself shall come down from heaven, at the command, and at the sounding of God's trumpet; and the dead who believe in the Messiah, shall rise again first.)

17   Afterward we that live, that be left, shall be ravished together with them in (the) clouds, meeting Christ in the air; and so (for)evermore we shall be with the Lord. (Afterward we who live, who be left alive, shall be snatched up together with those in the clouds, meeting the Messiah in the air; and then forevermore, we shall be with the Lord.)

18   Therefore be ye comforted together in these words. (And so comfort ye or strengthen one another with these words.)

CHAPTER 5

1   But, brethren, of times and moments ye need not that I write to you.

2   For ye yourselves know diligently, that the day of the Lord shall come, as a thief in the night. (For ye yourselves assuredly know, that the Day of the Lord shall come, like a thief in the night.)

3   For when they shall say peace *is*, and secureness, then sudden death shall come on them [⁺or then suddenly perishing shall come

on them], as sorrow to a woman that is with child, and they shall not escape.

4 But, brethren, ye be not in darknesses, that that day as a thief catch you. (But, brothers, ye do not be in darkness, so that that day shall catch you like a thief.)

5 For all ye be the sons of light, and sons of [the] day; we be not of night, neither of darknesses. (For all of ye be the children of the light, and the children of the day; we do not be of the night, nor of the darkness.)

6 Therefore sleep we not as others; but wake we, and be we sober. (And so let us not sleep like others; but watch, and be resolute.)

7 For they that sleep, sleep in the night, and they that be drunken, be drunken in the night.

8 But we that be of the day, be sober, clothed in the habergeon of faith and of charity, and in the helmet of hope of health. (But we who be of the day, be resolute, clothed in the breastplate of faith and of love, and in the helmet of the hope of salvation.)

9 For God putted not us into wrath, but into the purchasing of health (or but unto the getting of salvation), by our Lord Jesus Christ,

10 that was dead for us (or who died for us); (so) that whether we wake, whether we sleep, we live together with him.

11 For which thing comfort ye together (or For which thing strengthen ye one another), and edify ye each other, as ye do.

12 And, brethren, we pray you, that ye know them that travail among you, and be sovereigns to you [or be before to you] in the Lord, and (who) teach you, (And, brothers, we beseech you, that ye acknowledge and honour those who labour among you, and be your leaders in the Lord, and who teach you,)

13 that ye have them more abundantly in charity (or and that ye have more love for them); and for the work of them, have ye peace with them.

14 And, brethren, we pray you, reprove unpeaceable men, [or reprove ye, *or chastise,*

unquiet men]. Comfort ye men of little heart, receive ye sick men, be ye patient to all men. (And, brothers, we beseech you, rebuke the unpeaceable, or chastise the troublesome. Strengthen men of faint heart, receive the frail, or support the weak, and be patient with all men.)

15 See ye, that no man yield evil for evil to any man; but (for)evermore (pur)sue ye that that is good, each to (the) other, and to all *men.* (Ensure, that no one give back evil for evil to anyone; but always pursue that which is good, for one another, and for all *people.*)

16 (For)Evermore joy ye; (Always have joy;)

17 without ceasing pray ye;

18 in all things do ye thankings. For this is the will of God in Christ Jesus, in all you. (in all things give thanks. For this is the will of God in the Messiah Jesus, for all of you.)

19 Do not ye quench the Spirit,

20 do not ye despise prophecies.

21 But prove ye all things, and hold ye (fast, or firm), (to) that thing that is good.

22 Abstain [ye] you(rselves) from all evil species, [*or* (all evil) *likeness*]. (Absent yourselves from anything that hath even the appearance of evil.)

23 And God himself of peace make you holy by all things, that your spirit be kept whole, and soul, and body, without (com)plaint, in the coming of our Lord Jesus Christ. (And God himself, the God of peace, make you holy in everything, so that your spirit, and your soul, and your body, be kept whole, yea, without fault, into the coming of our Lord Jesus Christ.)

24 God is true, that called you, which also shall do [(a) *work of grace in you*].

25 Brethren, pray ye for us.

26 Greet ye well all (the) brethren in (a) holy kiss. (Give hearty greetings to all the brothers with a holy kiss.)

27 I charge you by the Lord, that this epistle be read to all (of the) holy brethren.

28 The grace of our Lord Jesus Christ *be* with you. Amen. †

2ND THESSALONIANS

CHAPTER 1

1 Paul, and Silvanus, and Timothy, to the church of (the) Thessalonians, in God our Father, and in the Lord Jesus Christ,

2 grace (be) to you and (the) peace of God, our Father, and of the Lord Jesus Christ.

3 We owe to do thankings (for)evermore to God for you, brethren, so as it is worthy, for your faith over-waxeth [or ever-waxeth], and the charity of each of you to (the) other aboundeth. (We ought to always give thanks to God for you, brothers, for it is worthy to do so, for your faith ever-increaseth, and the love each of you have for the other aboundeth, or and the love you have for one another aboundeth.)

4 So that we us-selves glory in you in the churches of God, for your patience and faith in all your persecutions and tribulations. Which ye sustain

5 into the ensample of the just doom of God, that ye be had worthy in the kingdom of God, for which ye suffer. (as an example of the righteous judgement of God, so that ye become worthy of the Kingdom of God, for which ye suffer.)

6 If nevertheless it is just before God to requite tribulation to them that trouble you,

7 and to you that be troubled, rest with us in the showing of the Lord Jesus from heaven, with (the) angels of his virtue (or with the angels of his power),

8 in the flame of fire, that shall give vengeance to them that know not God, and that obey not to the gospel of our Lord Jesus Christ. (in the flames of fire, who shall give vengeance to those who do not know God, and who do not obey the Gospel, or the Good News, of our Lord Jesus Christ.)

9 Which shall suffer everlasting pains, in perishing from the face of the Lord, and from the glory of his virtue (or and from the glory of his power),

10 when he shall come to be glorified in his saints, and to be made wonderful in all men that believed, for our witnessing is believed on you, in that day. (when he shall come to be glorified among his people, and to be held wonderful among all those who believe, for ye have believed our testimony, on that Day.)

11 In which thing also we pray (for)evermore for you, that our God make you worthy to his calling, and [ful]fill all the will of his goodness, and the work of faith in virtue; (In which thing also we always pray for you, that our God make you worthy of his calling, and fulfill all the purpose, or all the intention, of his goodness, and the work of faith in power;)

12 that the name of our Lord Jesus Christ be clarified in you (or so that the name of our Lord Jesus Christ be glorified in you), and ye in him, by the grace of our Lord Jesus Christ.

CHAPTER 2

1 But, brethren, we pray you by the coming of our Lord Jesus Christ, and of our congregation into the same coming [or and our congregation into the same thing],

2 that ye be not moved soon from your wit, neither be afeared, (or that ye be not soon moved away from your reason, nor be made afraid), neither by spirit, neither by word, neither by epistle as sent by us, as if the day of the Lord be nigh.

3 (Let) No man deceive you in any manner. For but dissension [or departing away] come first, and the man of sin be showed, the son of perdition,

4 that is (the) adversary, and is enhanced over all thing that is said God, or that is worshipped, so that he sit in the temple of God, and show himself as if he were God. (that is the

344

Adversary, and he is exalted over all that is called a god, or that is worshipped, so that he even sit in God's Temple, and show himself as if he were God.)

5 Whether ye hold not, that yet when I was at you, I said these things to you? (Do ye not remember, that while I was still with you, I said these things to you?)

6 And now what withholdeth, [or letteth], (or hindereth), [him], ye know, (so) that he be showed in his time.

7 For the private, [or the mystery], (or the secret), of wickedness worketh now; (so) only that he that holdeth (onto it) now, hold (firm), till he be done away.

8 And then that wicked man shall be showed, whom the Lord Jesus shall slay with the spirit of his mouth, and shall destroy with (the) lightening, [or the Illumining, or (the) shining], of his coming;

9 him, whose coming is by the working of Satan, in all virtue (or in all power), and signs (or miracles), and great wonders, false, [or leasing, (or lying)],

10 and in all deceit of wickedness, to them that perish. For that they received not the charity of (the) truth, that they should be made safe, (or Because they have not received the love of the truth, so that they could be saved).

11 And therefore God shall send to them a working of error, that they believe to leasing (or so that they believe the lie),

12 that all be deemed, [or be damned], (or condemned), which believed not to truth, (or so that all be judged, who did not believe the truth), but consented to wickedness.

13 But, brethren (be)loved of God, we owe to do thankings (for)evermore to God for you, that God chose us the first fruits into health, in (the) hallowing of (the) Spirit and in (the) faith of (the) truth; (But, brothers beloved by God, we ought to always give thanks to God for you, because God chose all of us as the first fruits unto salvation, by the sanctifying of the Spirit

and by faith in the truth;)

14 in which also he called you by our gospel, (or in which he also called you by the Gospel, or the Good News, which we brought), into the getting of the glory of our Lord Jesus Christ.

15 Therefore, brethren, stand ye, (or And so, brothers, stand), and hold ye the traditions, that ye have learned, either by word, either by our epistle.

16 And our Lord Jesus Christ himself, and God our Father, which loved us (or who loved us), and gave everlasting comfort and good hope in grace,

17 stir [or admonish] your hearts, and confirm [you] in all good work and word.

CHAPTER 3

1 Brethren, from henceforward pray ye for us, that the word of God run, and be clarified (or and be glorified), as it is with you;

2 and that we be delivered from noxious (or harmful) and evil men; for faith is not of (or in) all men.

3 But the Lord is true, that shall confirm you, and shall keep [us] from evil.

4 And, brethren, we trust of you in the Lord, for whatever things we command to you, both ye do and shall do.

5 And the Lord (ad)dress your hearts, in the charity of God, and in the patience of Christ. (And the Lord direct your hearts, in the love of God, and in the endurance of the Messiah.)

6 But, brethren, we announce to you in the name of our Lord Jesus Christ, that ye withdraw you(rselves) from each brother that wandereth out of order, [or against good order], and not after the teaching, that they received of us. (But, brothers, we command you in the name of our Lord Jesus Christ, that ye withdraw yourselves from each brother who walketh, or who goeth, out of order, or against good order, and not after the teaching, that they received from us.)

7 For ye yourselves know, how it behooveth

to (pur)sue us (or how it behooveth to follow us). For we were not unpeaceable [or unquiet] among you,

8   neither without our own travail, we ate bread of any man, but in travail and weariness wrought night and day, that we grieved none of you. (nor without our own work, did we eat anyone's bread, but with labour and in weariness worked night and day, so that we grieved none of you.)

9   Not as we had not power, but that we should give us-selves ensample to you to (pur)sue us. (Not as though we did not have the power, but so that we could give ourselves as an example for you to follow.)

10   For also when we were among you, we announced (or we commanded) this thing to you, that if any man will not work, neither eat he.

11   For we have heard that some among you go unrestfully, [or unquietly, *or unpeaceably*],

and nothing work, but do curiously.

12   But we announce (or command) to them that be such men, and beseech in the Lord Jesus Christ, that they work with silence, and eat their own bread.

13   But do not ye, brethren, fail well-doing.

14   (So) That if any man obey not to our word [*sent*] by (this) epistle, mark ye him, and commune ye not with him, (so) that he be ashamed;

15   and do not ye guess him as an enemy, but reprove ye him as a brother. (but do not think of him like an enemy, but rebuke him like a brother.)

16   And God himself of peace give to you everlasting peace in all place(s). The Lord be with you all.

17   My salutation by the hand of Paul; which sign in each epistle I write thus.

18   The grace of our Lord Jesus Christ be with you all. Amen. †

1ˢᵗ TIMOTHY

CHAPTER 1

1 Paul, [the] apostle of Jesus Christ, by the commandment of God our Saviour, and of Jesus Christ our hope,

2 to Timothy, beloved son in the faith, grace and mercy and (the) peace, of God the Father, and of Jesus Christ, our Lord.

3 As I prayed thee, that thou shouldest dwell at Ephesus, when I went into Macedonia, that thou shouldest command to some men, that they should not teach (any) other way,

4 neither give attention to fables and genealogies that be uncertain [or without end], which give questions, more than edification of God, that is in the faith.

5 For the end of the commandment is (the) charity of (a) clean heart, and good conscience, and of faith not feigned. (For the goal of this command is the love of a pure heart, and a good conscience, and true and sincere faith.)

6 From which things some men have erred, and be turned into vain speech;

7 and will to be teachers of the law (or and desire to be teachers of the Law), and understand not what things they speak, neither of what things they affirm.

8 And we know that the law is good, if any man use it lawfully;

9 and witting this thing, that the law is not set [or is not put] to a just man, but to unjust men and not subject, to wicked men and to sinners, to cursed men and defouled, to slayers of father, and slayers of mother, to manslayers (and knowing this, that the Law is not made, or it is not ordained, for a good man, but for evil men and those disobedient, for wicked men and for sinners, for cursed men and defiled men, for killers of father, and killers of mother, for manslayers)

10 and lechers, to them that do lechery with men, leasing-mongers and forsworn, and if any other thing is contrary to the wholesome teaching, [⁺and fornicators, to them that trespass with males *against kind*, sellers, *or stealers*, of men, to leasing-mongers and to forsworn men, and if any other thing is contrary to wholesome teaching,] (and lechers, for those who do lechery with men, for liars and perjurers, and if any other thing is contrary to the wholesome teaching,)

11 that is after the gospel of the glory of blessed God, which is betaken to me. (that is found in the Gospel or the Good News of the glory of the blessed God, or of the glorious and the blessed God, which was delivered to me.)

12 I do thankings to him, that comforted me in Christ Jesus our Lord, for he guessed me faithful, and put me in ministry, (I give thanks to him, who strengthened me, yea, the Messiah Jesus our Lord, for he believed me to be faithful, and set me in service,)

13 that first was a blasphemer, and a pursuer, and full of wrongs. But I have gotten the mercy of God, for I unknowing(ly) did in unbelief. (who before was a blasphemer, and a persecutor, and full of wrongs. But I have received God's mercy, for I unknowingly acted in unbelief, or out of ignorance.)

14 But the grace of our Lord over-abounded, with faith and love that is in Christ Jesus. (But the grace of our Lord was most plentiful, with the faith and love which is ours in the Messiah Jesus.)

15 A true word and worthy (of) all receiving, for Christ Jesus came into this world to make sinful men safe, of which I am the first. (Here is a true word and worthy of all acceptance, that the Messiah Jesus came into this world to save sinful men, of whom I am the first or of whom I am the worst.)

16 But therefore I have gotten mercy, that Christ Jesus should show in me first all patience, to the informing of them that shall

believe to him into everlasting life. (And so I have received mercy, so that the Messiah Jesus could first show in me all his patience, for the informing of those who shall believe in him unto eternal life.)

17 And to the king of worlds, undeadly, and invisible God alone, be honour and glory into worlds of worlds. Amen. (And to the King of all the worlds, or the eternal King, immortal, and invisible God alone, be honour and glory forever and ever. Amen.)

18 I betake this commandment to thee, thou son Timothy, after the prophecies that have been heretofore in thee, that thou travail [or fight] in them a good travail,

19 having faith and good conscience, which some men cast away, and perished about the faith. (having faith and a good conscience, which some men threw away, and perished amid their faith.)

20 Of which is Hymenaeus and Alexander, whom I betook to Satan (or whom I delivered unto Satan), (so) that they learn not to blaspheme.

CHAPTER 2

1 Therefore I beseech first of all things, that beseechings, prayers, askings, (and) doing of thankings, (or and thanksgiving, or the giving of thanks), be made for all men,

2 for kings and all that be set in highness, (so) that we (can) lead a quiet and a peaceable life, in all piety and chastity.

3 For this thing is good and accepted before God, our Saviour, (For this is something good and acceptable before God, our Saviour,)

4 that will that all men be made safe (or who desireth that all men be saved), and that they come to the knowing of (the) truth.

5 For one God and one mediator is of God and of men, a man Christ Jesus, (For there is one God, and one mediator between God and men, a man, the Messiah Jesus,)

6 that gave himself (as a) redemption for all men. Whose witnessing is confirmed in his times; (who gave himself for the redemption of all men. Whose testimony was confirmed in his time or at his time;)

7 in which I am set a preacher and an apostle. For I say (the) truth [in Christ Jesus], and I lie not, that am a teacher of heathen men in faith and in truth. (in whom I am put or am made a preacher and an apostle. For I tell the truth in the Messiah Jesus, and I do not lie, I who am a teacher of the Gentiles about faith and about truth, or I who am a teacher of the Gentiles in the true faith.)

8 Therefore I will (or And so I desire), that men pray in all place(s), lifting up clean hands without wrath and strife [or disputing].

9 Also women in suitable habit, with shamefastness and soberness arraying themselves, not in wreathed hairs, either in gold, or pearls, or precious cloth (or expensive clothing);

10 but that that becometh women, promising piety by good works.

11 A woman learn [she] in silence, with all subjection.

12 But I suffer not a woman to teach, neither to have lordship on the husband [or on the man], but to be in silence. (But I do not allow a woman to teach, or to have lordship over a man, but rather, to be silent or to be quiet.)

13 For Adam was first formed, afterward Eve;

14 and Adam was not deceived, but the woman was deceived, in (the) breaking of the law [or in prevarication].

15 But she shall be saved by (the) generation of children, if she dwell perfectly in faith, and love, and holiness, with soberness.

CHAPTER 3

1 A faithful word [I shall say]. If any man desireth a bishopric, he desireth a good work.

2 Therefore it behooveth a bishop to be

without reproof, the husband of one wife, sober, prudent, chaste, virtuous, holding hospitality, a teacher;

3   not given much to wine, not a smiter, but temperate [or patient], not full of chiding [or full of strife], not covetous,

4   well-ruling his house, and have sons subject with all chastity;

5   for if any man know not how to govern his house, how shall he have (the) diligence [or the keeping] of the church of God?

6   not new(ly) converted to the faith, lest he be borne up into pride, and fall into [the] doom of the devil. (not newly converted to the faith, lest he be raised up into pride, and then fall into the judgement of the Devil, or and then fall down under the same condemnation as the Devil.)

7   For it behooveth him to have also good witnessing of them that be withoutforth (or And it behooveth him to have good testimony from those who be outside the church), (so) that he fall not into reproof, and into the snare of the devil.

8   Also *it behooveth* deacons to be chaste, not double-tongued, not given much to wine [or not given to much wine], not following foul winning;

9   that have the mystery of faith in clean conscience. (who hold to the mystery of the faith with a clear conscience.)

10   But be they proved first, and minister they so, having no crime, [*or great sin*].

11   Also *it behooveth* women to be chaste, not backbiting, sober, faithful in all things.

12   Deacons be husbands of one wife; which govern well their sons and their houses.

13   For they that minister well, shall get a good degree to themselves, and much trust in the faith, that is in Christ Jesus (or that is in the Messiah Jesus).

14   Son Timothy, I write to thee these things, hoping that I shall come soon to thee;

15   but if I tarry, that thou knowest, how it behooveth thee to live in the house of God, that is the church of (the) living God, (as) a pillar and (a) firmness of (the) truth.

16   And openly it is a great sacrament of piety, that thing that was showed in (the) flesh, it is justified in (the) Spirit, it appeared to angels, it is preached to heathen men, it is believed in the world, it is taken up into glory.

CHAPTER 4

1   But the Spirit saith openly, that in the last times some men shall depart from the faith, giving attention to spirits of error, and to (the) teachings of devils (or and to the doctrines of demons);

2   that speak leasing in hypocrisy (or who speak lies and hypocrisy), and have their conscience corrupted,

3   forbidding to be wedded, and to abstain from meats, which God made to take with (the) doing of thankings, to faithful men, and them that have known the truth. (forbidding to be wedded, and to abstain from foods, which God made to be received with thanksgiving, or with the giving of thanks, by faithful men, and by those who have known the truth.)

4   For each creature of God is good, and nothing is to be cast away, which is taken with (the) doing of thankings; (For each creation of God is good, and nothing is to be thrown away, which is received with thanksgiving, or with the giving of thanks;)

5   for it is hallowed by the word of God, and by prayer.

6   Thou putting forth these things to brethren, shalt be a good minister of Christ Jesus; nourished with words of faith and of good doctrine, which thou hast gotten [in (pur)suing]. (Thou putting forth these things to the brothers, shalt be a good servant of the Messiah Jesus; nourished with words of faith and of good doctrine, which thou hast followed.)

7 But eschew thou [or shun thou] uncovenable fables (or But shun unsuitable fables), and old women's *fables*; haunt thyself to piety.

8 For bodily exercitation is profitable to little thing; but piety is profitable to all things, that hath a promise of life that now is, and that is to come.

9 A true word, and worthy (of) all acceptation [or (of) all acception]. (This word is true, and worthy of all acceptance.)

10 And in this thing we travail, and be cursed, for we hope in (the) living God, that is (the) Saviour of all men, most(ly) of faithful men (or and most of all the faithful).

11 Command thou this thing, and teach (it).

12 No man despise thy youth, but be thou ensample of faithful men (or but be an example to those in the faith), in word, in living, in charity (or in love), in faith, in chastity.

13 Till I come, take attention to reading, to exhortation and teaching.

14 Do not thou little care (for), [or despise], the grace which is in thee, that is given to thee by prophecy, with (the) putting on of the hands of [the] priesthood.

15 Think thou (on) these things, in these be thou, (so) that thy profiting be showed to all men.

16 Take attention to thyself and to doctrine; be busy in them. For thou doing these things, shalt make both thyself safe, and them that hear thee (or For thou doing these things, shalt save thyself, and those who listen to thee).

CHAPTER 5

1 Blame thou not an elder man (or Do not admonish, or rebuke, an older man), but beseech [him] as a father, young men as brethren;

2 old women as mothers, young women as sisters, in all chastity.

3 Honour thou [the] widows, that be very widows. (Honour the widows, who be true widows, or who be all alone.)

4 But if any widow hath children of sons, learn she first to govern her house, and requite to (her) father and mother; for this thing is accepted before God, (or for this is acceptable before God, or for God approveth of this).

5 And she that is a widow verily, and desolate, hope [she] into God, (or And she who is truly a widow, and desolate, let her put her hope in God), and be busy in beseechings and prayers night and day.

6 For she that is living in delights, is dead [*in* (her) *soul*].

7 And command thou this thing, (so) that they be without reproof.

8 For if any man hath not care of his own, and most(ly) of his household members (or of his own family), he hath denied the faith, and is worse than an unfaithful, [*or* (a) *heathen*], man.

9 A widow be chosen [*into the temple*] not less than sixty years (old), that was (the) wife of one husband,

10 and hath witnessing in good works (or and hath testimony of good works), (yea), if she nourished children, if she received poor men to harbour, if she hath washed the feet of holy men, if she ministered to men that suffered tribulation, if she followed all good work(s).

11 But eschew thou younger widows; for when they have done lechery, they will be wedded in Christ, [or forsooth when they have done lechery in Christ, they will be wedded], (But shun younger widows; for when, while yet in the Messiah, they shall feel passion, or shall do lechery, and they will be wedded,)

12 having damnation (or and so shall receive condemnation), for they have made void the(ir) first faith.

13 Also they (being) idle learn to go about houses, not only idle, but [*they be*] full of words and curious [*or and curiosity*], speaking things that it behooveth not.

14 Therefore I will (or And so I desire), that

younger *widows* be wedded, and bring forth children, and be housewives, to give none occasion to the adversary, because of (any) cursed thing.

15 For now some be turned aback after Satan.

16 If any faithful man hath widows, minister he to them, that the church be not charged, that it suffice to them that be very widows. (If anyone in the faith hath a widow in their family, let them minister unto her, so that the church be not burdened, and so that it can provide sufficiently for those who be true widows, or who be all alone.)

17 The priests that be well governors, [*that is*, (that) *truly keep well* (the) *priesthood*], be they had worthy to double honour; most(ly) they that travail in word and teaching (or and most of all those who labour in speaking and teaching).

18 For the scripture saith, Thou shalt not bridle the mouth of the ox threshing, and, A workman is worthy (of) his hire (or A worker is worthy of their wages).

19 Do not thou receive accusing against a priest, [no] but under twain or three witnesses.

20 But reprove thou men that sin before all men, that also others have dread. (And rebuke those who sin before everyone, so that others also have fearful reverence.)

21 I pray thee [or I adjure thee] before God, and Jesus Christ, (or I beseech thee before God, and Jesus Christ), and his chosen angels, that thou keep these things without prejudice, and do nothing in bowing to the other side.

22 Put thou hands to no man, neither anon commune thou with other men's sins. Keep thyself chaste. [Put thou hands to no man soon, neither commune thou with other men's sins. Keep thyself chaste.] (Do not at once, or too hastily, lay hands upon any man for ordination, nor share thou in other men's sinning. Keep thyself pure.)

23 Do not thou yet drink water, but use a little wine, for thy stomach, and for thine oft falling infirmities.

24 Some men's sins be open, before going to doom (or before going unto Judgement); but of some men they come after [or they follow].

25 And also good deeds be open, and those that have them in other manner, may not be hid. (And some good deeds be done in the open, but those which be not, cannot be kept hidden forever.)

CHAPTER 6

1 Whatever servants be under yoke, deem they their lords worthy (of) all honour, lest the name of the Lord and the doctrine be blasphemed [⁺or lest the name of their Lord *God* and his doctrine be blasphemed].

2 And they that have faithful, [*or christian*], lords, despise *them* not, for they be brethren; but more serve they [*them*], for they be faithful and loved, which be partners of beneficence, [*or* (of) *good-doing*]. Teach thou these things, and admonish thou these things.

3 If any man teach otherwise, and accordeth not to the wholesome words of our Lord Jesus Christ, and to that teaching that is by piety,

4 he is proud, and knoweth nothing, but languisheth about questions and strivings [or fightings] of words, of the which be brought forth envies, strives, blasphemies, evil suspicions,

5 fightings of men, that be corrupt in soul [or in reason], and that be deprived from (the) truth, that deem winning to be piety, (or who believe their gain to be proof of their piety, or who believe their increase to be a reward for their piety).

6 But a great winning is piety, with sufficience. (But piety, in and of itself, is a great gain or a great reward, yea, with abundance.)

7 For we brought in nothing into this world, and no doubt, that we may not bear anything away. [⁺Forsooth we brought nothing into this world, (and) no doubt, that we may not bear

away anything.] (For we brought nothing into this world, and there is no doubt, that we cannot take anything out of it or away from it.)

8 But we having foods, and with what things we shall be covered [or and with what things we shall be clothed], be we satisfied with these things.

9 For they that will be made rich, fall into temptation, and into the snare of the devil, and into many unprofitable desires and noxious, which drench men (down) into death and perdition. (For those who will be made rich, fall into testing, and into the Devil's snare, and into many unprofitable and harmful desires, which drown men down into death and destruction.)

10 For the root of all evils is covetousness, which some men coveting erred from the faith, and besetted them(selves) with many sorrows.

11 But, thou, man of God, flee these things; but follow thou rightwiseness, piety, faith, charity (or love), patience, (and) mildness (or and meekness and humility).

12 Strive thou a good strife of faith, catch everlasting life, into which thou art called, and hast acknowledged a good acknowledging before many witnesses.

13 I command to thee before God, that quickeneth all things, and *before* Christ Jesus, that yielded a witnessing under Pilate of Pontii, a good confession, (I command thee before God, who enliveneth all things, or who giveth life to everything, and *before* the Messiah Jesus, who gave his testimony to Pontius Pilate, yea, a worthy testimony,)

14 that thou keep the commandment without wem, without reproof, into the coming of our Lord Jesus Christ; (that thou obey, or follow thy orders, without spot or blemish, and without reproof, unto the coming of our Lord Jesus Christ;)

15 whom the blessed and alone almighty King of kings and Lord of lords shall show in his times.

16 Which alone hath undeadliness [or immortality], and dwelleth in light, to which *light* no man may come; whom no man saw, neither may see (or nor can see); to whom glory, and honour, and empire *be* without end, [or to whom (be) glory, and honour, and empire into without end]. Amen.

17 Command thou to the rich men of this world, that they understand not highly [or proudly], neither that they hope in (the) uncertainty of riches, but in the living God, that giveth to us all things plenteously to use;

18 to do well, to be made rich in good works, lightly to give (or easy, or quickly, to give), to commune,

19 to treasure to themselves a good foundament, into (the) time to coming [or into (the) time to come], that they catch everlasting life. (to treasure unto themselves a good foundation, into the time to come, so that they can grasp eternal life.)

20 Thou Timothy, keep the thing [or the deposit] betaken to thee, eschewing cursed novelties of voices, and opinions of (the) false name of cunning (or of knowing); (O Timothy, guard the deposit delivered unto thee, shunning the cursed novelties, or chattering, of voices, and opinions in the name of false knowledge;)

21 which some men promising, about the faith fell down [or the which some men promising, fell down about the faith]. The grace of God *be* with thee. Amen. †

2ND TIMOTHY

CHAPTER 1

1 Paul, [the] apostle of Jesus Christ, by the will of God, by the promise of life that is in Christ Jesus, (Paul, the apostle of Jesus Christ, by the desire of God, by the promise of life that is in the Messiah Jesus,)

2 to Timothy, his most dearworthy son, grace, mercy, and (the) peace of God the Father, and of Jesus Christ, our Lord.

3 I do thankings to my God, to whom I serve from my progenitors [or from my ancestors], in clean conscience, that without ceasing I have mind of thee in my prayers, night and day, (I give thanks to my God, whom I serve, like my ancestors, with a clean conscience, so that without ceasing I remember thee in my prayers, night and day,)

4 desiring to see thee; having mind of thy tears, [or mindful of thy tears], (or remembering thy tears), (so) that I be [ful]filled with joy.

5 And I bethink of that faith, that is in thee not feigned, which also dwelled first in thine aunt Lois, and in thy mother Eunice. And I am certain, that (is) also in thee.

6 For which cause I admonish thee, that thou raise again the grace of God, that is in thee by the setting on of mine hands [or by the on-putting of mine hands].

7 For why God gave not to us the spirit of dread, but of virtue, and of love, and of soberness. (Because God did not give us the spirit of fear, but of power, and of love, and of resoluteness.)

8 Therefore do not thou shame the witnessing of our Lord Jesus Christ, neither (of) me, his prisoner; but travail thou together (with others) in the gospel by the virtue of God; (And so do not be ashamed of the testimony of our Lord Jesus Christ, nor of me, his prisoner or a

prisoner for his sake; but labour together with others for the Gospel or the Good News, by the power of God;)

9 that delivered us, and called (us) with his holy calling, not after our works, but by his purpose and grace, that is given [to us] in Christ Jesus before worldly times; (who delivered us, and called us with his holy calling, not according to our works, but by his purpose and grace, that is given to us in the Messiah Jesus before the creation of the world or before time began;)

10 but now it is open by the lightening of our Saviour Jesus Christ, which destroyed death, and lightened life and uncorruption by the gospel. (but now it is made open by the appearance of our Saviour Jesus Christ, who destroyed death, and lightened life and uncorruption by the Gospel or the Good News.)

11 In which I am set a preacher and apostle, and master of heathen men. (In which I am ordained a preacher and an apostle, and a teacher of the Gentiles.)

12 For which cause also I suffer these things; but I am not confounded. For I know to whom I have believed, and I am certain that he is mighty to keep that (which) is taken to my keeping (or that which is delivered unto my keeping), into that day.

13 Have thou the form of wholesome words, which thou heardest of me in (the) faith and love in Christ Jesus. (Have thou the form of wholesome words, which thou hast heard from me in the faith and love in the Messiah Jesus.)

14 Keep thou the good [deposit, or (the good) thing], taken to thy keeping by the Holy Ghost, that dwelleth in us. (Keep thou, or Guard, the good deposit delivered unto thy keeping by the Holy Spirit, who dwelleth in us.)

15 Thou knowest this, that all that be in Asia be turned away from me, of which is Phygellus and Hermogenes.

16 The Lord give mercy to the house of Onesiphorus, for oft he refreshed me, and

shamed not my chain. (May the Lord show kindness to the family of Onesiphorus, for he often refreshed me, and he was not ashamed of my bonds, or my imprisonment.)

17 But when he came to Rome, he sought me (out) busily, and found [*me*].

18 The Lord give to him to find (the) mercy of God in that day. And how great things he ministered to me at Ephesus, thou knowest better.

CHAPTER 2

1 Therefore thou, my son, be comforted in (the) grace that is in Christ Jesus. (And so, my son, be thou strengthened by the grace that is ours in the Messiah Jesus.)

2 And what things thou hast heard of me by many witnesses, betake thou these to faithful men, which shall be able also to teach other men. (And those things that thou hast heard from me, in the presence of many witnesses, deliver them to the faithful, or share them with the faithful, who then shall be able to also teach others.)

3 Travail thou as a good knight of Christ Jesus. (Labour thou, or Endure thou, like a good soldier of the Messiah Jesus.)

4 No man holding knighthood to God, [en]wrappeth himself with worldly needs, (so) that he please to him, to whom he hath proved himself.

5 For he that fighteth in a battle, shall not be crowned, [no] but he fight lawfully.

6 It behooveth an earth-tiller to receive (the) first of the fruits.

7 Understand thou what things I say. For the Lord shall give to thee understanding in all things.

8 Be thou mindful that the Lord Jesus Christ of the seed of David hath risen again from death, after my gospel, [⁺Be thou mindful that the Lord Jesus Christ of the seed of David hath risen again from (the) dead, after my gospel,]

(Remember, that the Lord Jesus Christ of the seed of David hath risen again from the dead, according to my Gospel or my Good News,)

9 in which I travail unto bonds, as (if) working evil, but the word of God is not bound.

10 Therefore I suffer [*or I sustain*] all things for the chosen (ones), that also they get the health that is in Christ Jesus, with heavenly glory. (And so I endure everything for the chosen ones, so that they also get the salvation that is in the Messiah Jesus, along with heavenly glory.)

11 A true word [*is this that I say*], that if we be dead together [*to the world*], also we shall live together [*in bliss*];

12 if we suffer [*or if we sustain*], we shall reign together [*with Christ*], (or if we endure, we shall reign together with the Messiah); if we deny [*him*], he shall deny us;

13 if we believe not, he dwelleth faithful, he may not deny himself. (if we do not believe, he remaineth faithful, for he cannot deny himself.)

14 Teach thou these things, witnessing before God. Do not thou strive in words; for to nothing it is profitable, [no] but to the subverting of men that hear (it). (Teach these things, testifying before God. And do not argue; because it is profitable for nothing, but to the undermining of those who hear it.)

15 Busily keep [*or Take care*] to give thyself (as) a proved, praiseable workman to God, without shame, rightly treating the word of truth. (Work hard to make thyself an approved, praiseworthy workman for God, without shame, correctly proclaiming the Word of Truth.)

16 But eschew thou [*or shun thou*] unholy and vain (or empty and useless) speeches, for why those profit much to unfaithfulness,

17 and the word of them creepeth as a canker. Of whom Philetus is, and Hymenaeus,

18 which felled down from the truth, saying that the rising-again is now done (or saying that the resurrection hath happened already), and

they subverted [or they turned upside-down] the faith of some men.

19 But the firm foundament of God standeth, having this mark, The Lord knoweth which be his, and, Each man that nameth the name of the Lord, departeth from wickedness. (But the firm foundation of God standeth, having this sign or this inscription, The Lord knoweth whom be his, and, Each man who nameth the name of the Lord, goeth away from wickedness.)

20 But in a great house be not only vessels of gold and of silver, but also of tree, and of earth, (or but also of wood, and of clay); and so some be into honour, and some into despite.

21 Therefore, if any man cleanseth himself from these, he shall be a vessel hallowed into honour, and profitable to the Lord, ready to (do) all good work.

22 And flee thou [the] desires of youth, but follow thou rightwiseness, faith, charity (or love), (and) peace, with them that inwardly call the Lord of a clean heart, [or with them that in-call the Lord of a clean heart], (or with those who call upon the Lord from a pure heart).

23 And eschew thou [or shun] foolish questions, and without knowing, [or without discipline], (or without knowledge), witting (or knowing) that those (en)gender chidings.

24 But it behooveth the servant of the Lord to chide not; but to be mild to all men (or but to be meek and humble with everyone), able to teach, patient,

25 with temperance reproving them that against-stand the truth, that sometime God give to them forthinking, (or repenting), [or penance], (so) that they know the truth,

26 and that they rise again from the snares of the devil, of whom they be held prisoners at his will (or by whom they be held prisoners by his desire).

CHAPTER 3

1 But know thou this thing, that in the last days perilous times shall nigh, (But know this, that in the Last Days perilous times shall approach,)

2 and men shall be loving themselves, covetous, high of bearing, proud, blasphemers, not obedient to (their) father and mother, unkind, cursed,

3 without affection, [or good will], without peace, false blamers [or false challengers], uncontinent, [or unchaste], unmild, without benignity,

4 traitors, over-thwart [or froward], swollen [or blown] with proud thoughts, blind, lovers of lusts more than of God,

5 having the likeness of piety, but denying the virtue of it (or but denying its power). And eschew thou (or shun) these men.

6 Of these they be that pierce houses, and lead women captives [or and lead little women captive], charged (or burdened) with sins, which be led with diverse desires,

7 (for)evermore learning, and never perfectly coming to the science, [or to the cunning], (or to the knowing), of truth. (always learning, and never perfectly coming to the knowledge of the truth.)

8 And as Jannes and Jambres against-stood Moses, so these against-stand the truth, men corrupt in understanding [or in soul], reproved about the faith.

9 But further they shall not profit, for the unwisdom of them shall be known to all men, as theirs was.

10 But thou hast gotten my teaching [or my doctrine], (or But thou hast received my teaching), ordinance, purposing [or purpose], faith, long abiding, love, patience,

11 persecutions, passions, which were made to me at Antioch, at Iconium, at Lystra, what manner persecutions I suffered, and the Lord hath delivered me of all (or but the Lord hath delivered me from all of them).

12 And all men that will live faithfully [or piously] in Christ Jesus, shall suffer persecution.

(And all who will live faithfully, or piously, in the Messiah Jesus, shall suffer persecution.)

13 But evil men and deceivers shall increase into worse, erring [themselves], and sending [others] into error.

14 But dwell thou in these things that thou hast learned, and that be betaken to thee, witting of whom thou hast learned (them); (But remain thou in these things that thou hast learned, and that be delivered to thee, knowing from whom thou hast learned them;)

15 for thou hast known holy letters from thy youth, which may learn thee [or which may inform thee] to health, by (the) faith that is in Christ Jesus. (for thou hast known the holy Scriptures from thy youth, which can lead thee to salvation, through faith that is in the Messiah Jesus.)

16 For all scripture inspired of (or by) God is profitable to teach, to reprove, to chastise, [for] to learn in rightwiseness,

17 (so) that the man of God be perfect, learned to (do) all good work(s).

CHAPTER 4

1 I witness before God and Christ Jesus, that shall deem the quick and the dead, by the coming of him, and the kingdom of him, (I testify before God and the Messiah Jesus, who shall judge the living and the dead, by his coming, and his reign,)

2 preach the word, be thou busy covenably without rest, (or be thou suitably busy, or be thou busy at every opportunity, without any rest, or without ceasing), reprove thou, beseech thou, blame thou in all patience and doctrine.

3 For (the) time shall be, when men shall not suffer [or shall not sustain] wholesome teaching (or when men shall not allow or permit wholesome teaching), but at their desires they shall gather together to themselves masters (or teachers) itching [or pleasing] to the ears.

4 And truly they shall turn away the(ir) hearing from (the) truth, but to fables they shall turn (or and instead they shall turn their attention to fables).

5 But wake thou (or Watch), in all things travail thou, do [thou] the work of an evangelist, fulfill thy service, [or (thine) office], be thou sober (or be resolute).

6 For I am sacrificed now, and the time of my departing is nigh (or and the time of my departure is near).

7 I have striven a good strife (or I have fought a good fight), I have ended the course, I have kept the faith.

8 In the tother time a crown of rightwiseness is kept to me, which the Lord, a just doomsman, shall yield to me in that day; and not only to me, but also to these that love his coming. (In the time to come a crown of righteousness is kept for me, which the Lord, a righteous Judge, shall give to me on that Day; and not only to me, but also to those who await his coming with love.)

9 Hie thou to come to me soon.

10 For Demas, loving this world, hath forsaken me, and went to Thessalonica, Crescens into Galatia, Titus into Dalmatia;

11 Luke alone is with me. Take thou Mark, and bring (him) with thee; for he is profitable to me into service.

12 Forsooth I sent Tychicus to Ephesus.

13 The cloth which I left at Troas at Carpas (or The cloak which I left with Carpas in Troas), when thou comest, bring with thee, and the books, but most(ly) the parchments.

14 Alexander, the treasurer, showed to me much evil; the Lord shall yield to him after his works.

15 Whom also thou eschew; for he against-stood full greatly our words. (Whom also thou should shun; for he very strongly stood against our words.)

16 In my first defence no man helped me, but all forsook me; be it not areckoned to them.

17 But the Lord helped me [or Forsooth the Lord stood nigh to me], and comforted me, that the preaching be [full-]filled by me, and that all folks hear, (and) that I am delivered from the mouth of the lion. (But the Lord stood near to me, or by me, and strengthened me, so that the preaching was fully proclaimed by me, and all the nations heard it, and I was delivered from the lion's mouth.)

18 And the Lord delivered me from all evil work, and shall make me safe into his heavenly kingdom, to whom *be* glory into worlds of worlds. Amen. (And the Lord shall deliver me from all evil works, and shall bring me safely into his heavenly kingdom, to whom *be* glory forever and ever. Amen.)

19 Greet well Prisca, and Aquila, and the house of Onesiphorus. (Give hearty greetings to Prisca, and Aquila, and Onesiphorus' household or family.)

20 Erastus (was) left [or dwelt] at Corinth, and I left Trophimus sick at Miletum.

21 Hie thou to come before winter. Eubulus, and Pudens, and Linus, and Claudia, and all brethren, greet thee well, (or and all the brothers, send hearty greetings).

22 Our Lord Jesus Christ *be* with thy spirit. The grace of God *be* with you. Amen. †

TITUS

CHAPTER 1

1   Paul, the servant of God, and (an) apostle of Jesus Christ, by the faith of the chosen of God, and by the knowing of the truth, which is after piety,

2   into the hope of everlasting life, which *life* God that lieth not, promised before (the) times of the world; (in the hope of eternal life, which *life* God who lieth not, promised before the creation of the world;)

3   but he hath showed in his times his word in preaching, that is betaken to me (or that is delivered to me), by the commandment of God, our Saviour,

4   to Titus, most dearworthy son [or beloved son], by the common faith, grace and (the) peace of God the Father, and of Christ Jesus, our Saviour, (or and of the Messiah Jesus, our Saviour).

5   For cause of this thing I left thee at Crete, (so) that thou amend those things that fail, and ordain priests by cities, as also I assigned to thee [or I disposed to thee].

6   If any man is without crime, [*or great sin*], an husband of one wife, and hath faithful sons, not in accusation of lechery, or not subject.

7   For it behooveth a bishop to be without crime, [as] a dispenser of God, not proud, not wrathful, not given to drunkenness, not [a] smiter, not covetous of foul winning(s);

8   but holding hospitality, benign, prudent, sober, just, holy, continent,

9   taking [or embracing] that true word, that is after doctrine; that he be mighty to admonish in wholesome teaching [or doctrine], and to reprove them that gainsay (or and to rebuke those who speak against it).

10   For there be many unobedient, and vain speakers, and deceivers, most(ly) they that be of (the) circumcision, (or mostly those who be of the circumcision, or who be circumcised),

11   which it behooveth to be reproved (or who it behooveth to be rebuked); which subvert all houses, teaching which things it behooveth not, for [the] love of foul winning.

12   And one of them, their proper prophet said (or their own prophet said), Men of Crete *be* (for)evermore liars, evil beasts, of slow womb.

13   This witnessing is true. For which cause blame them sore, that they be (made) whole in (the) faith, (This testimony is true. For which reason sharply rebuke them, so that they can be made whole in the faith,)

14   not giving attention to (the) fables of (the) Jews, and to (the) commandments of men, that turn away them from (the) truth [or (that) turn them away from (the) truth].

15   And all things be clean to clean men; but to unclean men and to unfaithful (men), nothing is clean, for the soul and (the) conscience of them be made unclean.

16   They acknowledge that they know God, but by (their) deeds they deny [*him*]; when they be abominable, and unbelieveful, and reprovable to all good work(s), (or and unfit for any good work).

CHAPTER 2

1   But speak thou those things that beseem [or that become] wholesome teaching;

2   that old men be sober, chaste, prudent, whole in faith, in love, and patience;

3   also old women in holy habit, not slanderers [or backbiters], not serving much to wine, well-teaching, (so) that they teach prudence.

4   *Admonish thou* young women, that they love their husbands, that they love their children;

5   and that they be prudent, chaste, sober, having care of the house, benign, subject to

their husbands, (so) that the word of God be not blasphemed.

6 Also admonish young men, that they be sober (or that they be temperate).

7 In all things give thyself ensample of good works, in teaching, in wholeness [or in holiness of living], *that is, in cleanness of soul and body,* in firmness [*of virtues*].

8 An wholesome word, and unreprovable (or unreproachable); that he that is of the contrary side, be ashamed, having none evil thing to say of you.

9 *Admonish thou* servants to be subject to their lords; in all things pleasing, not gainsaying, (or not speaking back to them, or not speaking against them),

10 not defrauding, but in all things showing good faith, (so) that they honour in all things the doctrine of God, our Saviour.

11 For the grace of God, our Saviour, hath appeared to all men,

12 and taught us, that we (should) forsake wickedness [or unpiety], and worldly desires, and live soberly, and justly, and piously in this world,

13 abiding the blessed hope and the coming of the glory of the great God, and our Saviour Jesus Christ;

14 that gave himself for us, to again-buy us from all wickedness, and make clean to himself a people acceptable, and (pur)suer of good works. (who gave himself for us, to redeem us from all wickedness, and to make clean an acceptable people unto himself, who be pursuers of good works.)

15 Speak thou these things, and admonish thou, and reprove thou with all commandment; no man despise thee. (Speak these things, and admonish, and rebuke them with all authority; let no man despise thee.)

CHAPTER 3

1 Admonish them to be subjects to princes [or Admonish them to be subject to princes], and to powers; to obey to that that is said, and to be ready to (do) all good work(s);

2 to blaspheme no man, to be not full of chiding, but temperate [or patient], showing all mildness to all men (or showing meekness and humility to everyone).

3 For we were sometime unwise, unbelieveful, erring, and serving to desires, and to diverse lusts, doing in malice and envy, worthy to be hated, hating each other.

4 But when the benignity and the manhood [or the humanity] of our Saviour God appeared,

5 not of works of rightwiseness that we did, but by his mercy he made us safe, by [the] washing, [or (the) *baptism*], of (the) again-begetting, and (the) again-newing of the Holy Ghost, (not because of works of righteousness that we did, but by his mercy he saved us, by the washing, *or the baptism*, of rebirth, and the renewing power of the Holy Spirit,)

6 whom he shedded [out] into us plenteously by Jesus Christ, our Saviour,

7 that we justified by his grace, be heirs by hope of everlasting life. (so that we who be justified by his grace, be heirs through the hope of eternal life.)

8 A true word is [*this*], and of these things I will that thou confirm others, that they that believe in God, be busy to be above others [or to be before others] in good works. These things be good, and profitable to men. (*This* is a true word, and I desire that thou confirm these things to others, so that they who believe in God, be busy to be before others, or ahead of others, in doing good works. These things be good, and profitable for everyone.)

9 And eschew thou foolish questions, and genealogies, and strivings [or and strives], and fightings of the law; for those be unprofitable and vain. (And shun foolish questions, and genealogies, and fights, and arguments over the Law; for they be empty and useless.)

10 Eschew thou [or Shun thou] a man heretic,

after one and the second correction;

11 witting that he that is such a manner *man* is subverted, and trespasseth, and is condemned by his own doom (or by his own judgement).

12 When I send to thee Artemas, or Tychicus, hie thou [or (make) haste] to come to me to Nicopolis; for I have purposed to dwell in winter there. (When I send Artemas, or Tychicus, to thee, hasten to come to me at Nicopolis; for I have decided to remain there for the winter.)

13 Busily before send Zenas [or Busily send before Zenas], a wise man of (the) law, and Apollos, (so) that nothing fail to them. (With whatever assistance you can provide, send forth Zenas, a man wise in the Law, and Apollos, so that nothing is lacking for to them.)

14 They that be of ours, learn to be governors [or to be before] in good works, (or Those who be of us, learn to be leaders in good works, or the first to do good works), to necessary uses, (and) that they be not without fruit.

15 All men that be with me greet thee well. Greet thou well them, that love us in [the] faith. The grace of God *be* with you all. Amen. (All who are with me send hearty greetings to thee. Give hearty greetings to those in the faith who love us. The grace of God *be* with you all. Amen.) †

PHILEMON

1   Paul, the bound of Christ Jesus, and Timothy, (a) brother, to Philemon, beloved, and our helper, (Paul, a prisoner of the Messiah Jesus, or a prisoner for the sake of the Messiah Jesus, and Timothy, a brother, to Philemon, beloved, and our helper,)

2   and to Apphia, most dear sister, and to Archippus, our even-knight (or our fellow soldier), and to the church that is in thine house,

3   grace *be* to you, and (the) peace of God our Father, and of the Lord Jesus Christ.

4   I do thankings to my God, (for)evermore making mind of thee, in my prayers, (I give thanks to my God, always remembering thee, in my prayers,)

5   hearing (of) thy charity, and faith, that thou hast in the Lord Jesus, and to all holy men, (hearing of thy love, and the faith, which thou hast in the Lord Jesus, and for all the saints, or all of God's people,)

6   that the communing of thy faith be made open, in (the) knowing of all good thing(s) in Christ Jesus. (so that the sharing of thy faith be made open, in the knowledge of all the good things in the Messiah Jesus.)

7   And I had great joy and comfort in thy charity, for the entrails of holy men rested [or were refreshed] by thee, brother. (And I had great joy and strength in thy love, for the hearts of the saints, or of God's people, were refreshed by thee, brother.)

8   For which thing I having much trust in Christ Jesus (or For which thing I having much trust in the Messiah Jesus), to command to thee that that pertaineth to profit;

9   but I beseech more for charity, since thou art such as the old Paul, and now the bound of Jesus Christ. (but I beseech thee more out of love, since thou art like old Paul, now the prisoner of Jesus Christ, or now a prisoner for the sake of Jesus Christ.)

10   I beseech thee for my son Onesimus, whom I in bonds begat,

11   which sometime was unprofitable to thee, but now profitable, both to thee and to me;

12   whom I sent again to thee. And receive thou him as mine entrails (or And receive him as thou would receive me);

13   whom I would withhold with me, that he should serve for thee to me in (the) bonds of the gospel; (whom I would keep here with me, so that he could serve me for thee here where I am in prison for the sake of the Gospel or the Good News;)

14   but without thy counsel I would not do anything, that thy good should not be as of need, but willful. (but without thy counsel, or without thy consent, I would not do anything, so that thy good doing would not be done as out of necessity, but out of thy own free will or willingly.)

15   For peradventure therefore he departed from thee for a time, (so) that thou shouldest receive him [into] without end;

16   now not as a servant, but for a servant a most dear brother [or but more than a servant, (yea), (a) most dear brother], most(ly) to me; and how much more to thee, both in [the] flesh and in the Lord?

17   Therefore if thou hast me a fellow, receive him as me;

18   for if he hath anything annoyed (or harmed) thee, either oweth (thee), areckon thou this thing to me.

19   I, Paul, wrote with mine (own) hand, (and) I shall yield (it); (and) that I say not to thee, that also thou owest to me thyself.

20   So, brother, I shall use thee in the Lord; [full-]fill thou mine entrails in Christ (or fill thou my heart full with the Messiah).

21   I trusting of thine obedience wrote to thee, witting that thou shalt do over that that I say (or

knowing that thou shalt do even more than what I ask you to do).

22   Also make thou ready to me an house to dwell in; for I hope that by your prayers I shall be given to you.

23   Epaphras, (a) prisoner with me in Christ Jesus, greeteth thee well, (Epaphras, a prisoner like me of the Messiah Jesus, or a prisoner like me for the sake of the Messiah Jesus, heartily greeteth thee,)

24   and Marcus, Aristarchus, Demas, Lucas, mine helpers.

25   The grace of our Lord Jesus Christ *be* with your spirit. Amen. †

HEBREWS

CHAPTER 1

1 God, that spake sometime by prophets in many manners to our fathers,

2 at the last in these days he hath spoken to us by the Son; whom he hath ordained (the) heir of all things, and by whom he made the worlds.

3 Which when also he is the brightness of glory, and [the] figure of his substance, and beareth all things by (the) word of his virtue, he maketh purgation of sins, and sitteth on the right half of the majesty in heavens; (Who when he is also the brightness of glory, and the example, or the image, of his substance, and beareth all things by the word of his power, he maketh purgation of sins, and sitteth at the right hand, or on the right side, of the Majesty in heaven;)

4 and so much is made better than angels, by how much he hath inherited a more diverse name before them. (and is made so much better than the angels, for he hath inherited a more excellent name than they have.)

5 For to which of the angels said God any time, Thou art my Son, I have (en)gendered thee today? And again, I shall be to him into a Father, and he shall be to me into a Son? (For to which of the angels did God say at any time, Thou art my Son, I have begotten thee today? And again, I shall be like a Father to him, and he shall be like a Son to me?)

6 And when again he bringeth in the first begotten Son into the world, he saith, And all the angels of God worship him.

7 But he saith to (the) angels, He that maketh his angels spirits (or wind), and his ministers (a) flame of fire.

8 But to the Son *he saith*, God, thy throne *is* into the world of world(s), (or thy kingdom, or

thy rule, *is* forever and ever); a rod of equity *is* the rod of thy realm;

9 thou hast loved rightwiseness, and hatedest wickedness; therefore the God [or therefore God], thy God, anointed thee with (the) oil of joy, more than thy fellows.

10 And, Thou, Lord, in the beginning foundedest the earth, and (the) heavens be (the) works of thine hands;

11 they shall perish, but thou shalt perfectly dwell; and all shall wax old as a cloth (or and all things shall grow old like a cloak),

12 and thou shalt change them as a cloth (or and thou shalt change them like a cloak), and they shall be changed. But thou art the same thyself, and thy years shall not fail.

13 But to which of the angels said God at any time, Sit thou on my right half, till I put thine enemies a stool of thy feet? (But to which of the angels did God say at any time, Sit thou at my right hand, or on my right side, until I make thine enemies thy footstool?)

14 Whether they all be not serving spirits, sent to serve for them that take the heritage of health? (Be they not all spirits that serve, yea, sent to serve those who receive the inheritance of salvation?)

CHAPTER 2

1 Therefore more plenteously it behooveth us to keep those things, that we have heard, lest peradventure we float away.

2 For if that word that was said by (the) angels, was made firm, and each breaking of the law [or each trespassing], and unobedience took just retribution of meed, (For if that word that was said by the angels, was made firm, and each trespass, and disobedience, received just retribution as a reward,)

3 how shall we escape, if we despise so great an health? (or then how shall we escape, if we despise so great a salvation, or so great a deliverance?) Which, when it had taken

beginning to be told out by the Lord, of them that heard (him), (it) is confirmed into us.

4 For God witnessed together by miracles [or by signs], and wonders, and great marvels, and diverse virtues, and partings [or distributions] of the Holy Ghost, by his will. (Because God testified by miracles or signs, and wonders, and great marvels, and various works of power, and distributions of the Holy Spirit, according to his will.)

5 But not to (the) angels God subjected the world that is to coming, of which we speak. [Forsooth not to angels God subjected the roundness of the earth to come, of which we speak.]

6 But some man witnessed in a place, and said, What thing is man, that thou art mindful of him, or man's son, for thou visitest him? (But someone testified, in some place, and said, What is a man, that thou rememberest him, or a man's son, that thou visitest him?)

7 Thou hast made him a little less than (the) angels; thou hast crowned him with glory and honour; and thou hast ordained him on (or over) the works of thine hands.

8 Thou hast made all things subject under his feet. And in that that he subjected all things to him, he left nothing unsubject to him. But now we see not yet all things subject to him;

9 but we see him that was made a little less than (the) angels, Jesus, for the passion of death (or through the suffering of death), crowned with glory and honour, (so) that he through [the] grace of God should taste death for all men.

10 For it beseemed him, for whom all things, and by whom all things *were made*, which had brought many sons into glory, *and was* [the] author [or the maker] of the health of them, that he had an end by passion. (For it seemed appropriate for him, for whom all things, and by whom all things *were made*, who had brought many sons unto glory, *and was* the Maker of their salvation, that he met his end in

suffering.)

11 For he that halloweth, and they that be hallowed, *be* all of one; for which cause he is not ashamed to call them brethren,

12 saying, I shall tell thy name to my brethren; in the middle of the church I shall praise thee.

13 And again, I shall be trusting into him; and again, Lo! I and my children, which God gave to me.

14 Therefore for children communed to flesh and blood, and he also took part of the same, that by death he should destroy him that had lordship of death (or so that by death he would destroy him who had authority over death), that is to say, the devil,

15 and that he should deliver them that by dread of death, by all life were bound to servage. (and that he would deliver those who by fear of death, for all their lives were bound in servitude or in slavery.)

16 And he took never (the) angels, but he took the seed of Abraham.

17 Wherefore he ought to be likened to brethren by all things, that he should be made merciful and a faithful bishop to God, that he should be merciful to the trespasses of the people. (And so he ought to be likened to *his* brothers in all things, so that he would be made a merciful and faithful High Priest to God, and so that he would be merciful to the people's trespasses.)

18 For in that thing in which he suffered, and was tempted, he is mighty to help also them that be tempted.

CHAPTER 3

1 Therefore, holy brethren (or holy brothers), and partners of heavenly calling, behold ye the apostle and the bishop (or the High Priest) of our confession, Jesus,

2 which is true to him that made him, as also Moses in all the house(hold) of him.

3   But this *bishop* (or this *High Priest*) is had worthy of more glory than Moses, by as much as he hath more honour of the house(hold), that made the house.

4   For each house is made of some man; [forsooth] he that made all things (out) of nought is God. (For every house is made by someone; but he who made everything out of nothing is God.)

5   And Moses was true in all his house, as a servant, into witnessing of those things that were to be said; (And in all his household, Moses was a true or a faithful servant, testifying about those things that would be said later, or in the future;)

6   but Christ (is) as a son in his house. Which house we be, if we hold firm (our) trust and (the) glory of hope into the end. (but the Messiah is like a son in his household, or in his family. Which household or family we be, if we hold firm to our trust and the glory of hope unto the end.)

7   Wherefore as the Holy Ghost saith (or And so as the Holy Spirit said), Today, if ye have heard his voice,

8   do not ye harden your hearts, as in (the) wrathing, like the day of temptation in (the) desert; (do not harden your hearts, like in the rebellion, like on the day of testing in the desert;)

9   where your fathers tempted me, and proved (me), (or where your fathers tested me, and proved me), and saw my works (for) forty years.

10   Wherefore I was wroth to this generation, and I said, (For) Evermore they err in heart, for they knew not my ways; (And so I was angry with that generation, and I said, They always go astray in their hearts, because they do not know my ways;)

11   to which I swore in my wrath (or to whom I swore in my anger), they shall not enter into my rest.

12   Brethren (or Brothers), see ye, lest peradventure in any of you be an evil heart of unbelief, to depart from the living God.

13   But admonish yourselves by all days, the while today is named, that none of you be hardened by (the) fallacy [or by (the) falseness] of sin.

14   For we be made partners of Christ (or For we become the Messiah's partners), if nevertheless we hold the beginning of his substance firm into the end.

15   While it is said, today, if ye have heard the voice of him, do not ye harden your hearts, as in that wrathing, (or do not harden your hearts, like in that rebellion).

16   For some men hearing wrathed (or rebelled), but not all they that went out of Egypt by Moses.

17   But to whom was he wrathed forty years? Whether not to them that sinned, whose carrions were cast down in (the) desert? (But by whom was he angered for forty years? Whether not by those who sinned, whose carcasses were thrown down in the desert?)

18   And to whom swore he, that they should not enter into the rest of him, no but to them that were unbelieveful? [⁺To whom he swore soothly, for to not enter into his rest, no but to them that were unbelieveful?]

19   And (so) we see, that they might not enter into the rest of him for unbelief.

CHAPTER 4

1   Therefore dread we, lest peradventure while the promise of entering into his rest is left (open), that any of us be guessed to be away, [or (that) any of us be guessed, *or deemed*, for to fail]. (And so let us be fearful, lest perhaps while the promise of entering into his rest is left open, that any of us be thought to miss our opportunity.)

2   For it is told also to us, as to them. And the word that was heard profited not to them, not mingled to (the) faith of those things that

they heard.

3   For we that have believed, shall enter into (his) rest, as he said, As I swore in my wrath, they shall not enter into my rest, (or As I swore in my anger, They shall not enter into my rest), [or As I swore in my wrath, if they shall enter into my rest]. And when the works were made perfect at the ordinance of the world,

4   he said thus in a place [or in some place] of the seventh day, And God rested in the seventh day from all his works.

5   And in this *place* again, They shall not enter into my rest. [And in this *place* again, If they shall enter into my rest.]

6   Therefore for it (pur)sueth (or And so it followeth), that some men shall enter into it, and they to which it was told to before [or and they first to whom it is told], entered not for their unbelief.

7   Again, he determineth some day, and saith in David, Today, after so much time of time, as it is before-said, Today if ye have heard his voice, do not ye harden your hearts.

8   For if Jesus, *that is, Joshua*, had given rest to them, he should never speak of (an)other (rest) after this day.

9   Therefore the sabbath [or (a) rest] is left to the people of God.

10   For he that is entered into his rest, rested of his works, as also God of his. (For he who is entered into his rest, rested from his own works, like God rested from his.)

11   Therefore haste we to enter into that rest, (so) that no man fall into the same ensample of unbelief.

12   For the word of God is quick (or alive), and speedy in working, and more able to pierce than any twain-edged sword, and stretcheth forth [till] to the parting of the soul and of the spirit, and of the jointures and (the) marrows, and [*it is* the] deemer (or the judge) of thoughts, and of (the) intents of hearts.

13   And no creature is invisible in the sight of God. For all things be naked and open to his eyes, to whom a word to us.

14   Therefore we that have a great bishop, that pierced heavens, Jesus, the Son of God, hold we the acknowledging [or the confession] of our hope. (And so we who have a great High Priest, who pierced the heavens, Jesus, the Son of God, let us hold onto the confession of our hope.)

15   For we have not a bishop, that may not have compassion on our infirmities, (or For we do not have a High Priest, who cannot have compassion on our frailties or our weaknesses), but (One who) was tempted by all things by likeness, without sin.

16   Therefore go we with trust to the throne of his grace, (so) that we get mercy, and find grace in covenable, (or in opportune, or in timely), help.

CHAPTER 5

1   For each bishop taken of men (or For every high priest taken from among men), is ordained for men in these things that be to God, (so) that he offer gifts and sacrifices for sins.

2   Which may together sorrow with them (or Who can feel compassion for those), that be uncunning, (or unknowing, or ignorant), and err; for also he is environed with infirmity.

3   And therefore he oweth (or And so he ought), as for the people, so also for himself, to offer for sins.

4   Neither any man taketh to him honour, but he that is called of God, as Aaron *was*.

5   So Christ clarified not himself, that he were bishop, but he that spake to him, Thou art my Son, today I (en)gendered thee. (So the Messiah did not glorify himself, so that he became High Priest, but he who spoke to him, and said, Thou art my Son, today I begat thee.)

6   As in another place he saith, Thou art a priest [into] without end, after the order of Melchisedec, (or Thou art a priest forever, after

the order of Melchizedek).

7 Which in the days of his flesh offered, with great cry and tears, prayers and beseechings to him that might make him safe from death (or prayers and beseechings to him who could save him from death), and was heard for his reverence.

8 And when he was God's Son, he learned obedience of these things that he suffered;

9 and he brought to the end [or he led to perfection] is made (the) cause of everlasting health to all that obey him, (and he brought to perfection is made the Source of eternal salvation for all who obey him,)

10 *and is* called of God a bishop, by the order of Melchisedec. (*and is* named the High Priest by God, in the order of Melchizedek.)

11 Of whom *there is* to us a great word for to say, and able to be expounded, for ye be made feeble to hear.

12 For when ye ought to be masters for a time (or For although ye ought to be teachers by this time), again ye need that ye be taught, which be the letters [or the elements] of the beginning of God's words. And ye be made those, to whom is need of milk, and not [of] firm meat (or of solid food).

13 For each that is (a) partner of milk, is without (a) part (or a portion) of the word of rightwiseness, for he is (but) a little child.

14 But of perfect men is firm meat, of them that for custom have [their] wits exercised to (the) discretion of good and of evil. (But for grown men there is solid food, yea, for those who by custom have their minds, or their thoughts, exercised by the discretion of good and of evil.)

CHAPTER 6

1 Therefore we bringing in a word of the beginning of Christ, be we born to the perfection *of him*, not again laying the foundament of penance from dead works, and

of the faith to God, (And so, having brought to you the beginning of the words, or the first lessons, about the Messiah, now let us be born unto *his* perfection, not again laying the foundation of repentance from dead works, and of faith in God,)

2 and of teaching of baptisms, and of laying on of hands, and of (the) rising again of dead men, and of everlasting doom. (and of the teaching of baptisms, and of the laying on of hands, and of the resurrection of the dead, and of eternal judgement.)

3 And this thing we shall do, if God shall suffer. (And we shall do this, if God shall allow it.)

4 But it is impossible, that they that be once (en)lightened [or illumined], and have tasted also an heavenly gift, and be made partners of the Holy Ghost (or and be made partners of the Holy Spirit),

5 and nevertheless have tasted the good word of God, and the virtues of the world to coming, [or and the virtues of the world to come], (or and the powers of the world to come),

6 and be slid far away, that they be renewed again to penance. *Which* again crucify to themselves the Son of God, and have him to scorn.

7 For the earth that drinketh rain oft coming on it, and bringeth forth covenable (or suitable) herb(s), to them of which it is tilled, taketh blessing of God.

8 But that that is bringing forth thorns and briars, is reprovable, (or is reproachable, or is worthy to be rebuked), and next to curse, whose ending shall be into burning.

9 But, ye most dearworthy, we trust of you better things, and near(er) to health (or and nearer to salvation), though we speak so.

10 For God is not unjust, that he forget your work and love, which ye have showed in his name; for ye have ministered to (the) saints, and (do) minister, (or for ye have served God's

people, and continue to serve them).

11 And we covet that each of you show the same busyness to the [full-]filling of hope into the end;

12 that ye be not made slow, but also (pur)suers of them, which by faith and patience shall inherit the promises. (so that ye be not made slow, but also followers of those, who by faith and patience, or endurance, shall inherit the promises.)

13 For God promising to Abraham, for he had none greater, by whom he should swear, swore by himself,

14 and said, I blessing shall bless thee, and I multiplying shall multiply thee;

15 and so he long abiding had the promise. [and so he long suffering got repromission.]

16 For men swear by a greater than themselves, and the end of all their plea, [or all their controversy, *or debate*], is an oath to confirmation.

17 In which thing God willing to show plenteouslier (or In which God desiring to show more plentifully), to the heirs of his promise the firmness [or the unmoveableness] of his counsel, put betwixt an oath,

18 (so) that by two things unmoveable, by which it is impossible that God lie, we have (the) strongest solace, [*or comfort*], we that flee together to hold the hope that is put forth to us.

19 Which *hope* as an anchor we have secure to the soul, and firm, and going into the inner things of hiding;

20 where the before-goer, Jesus, that is made bishop [into] without end by the order of Melchisedec, entered for us. (where the foregoer, Jesus, who is made High Priest forever in the order of Melchizedek, entered for us.)

CHAPTER 7

1 And this Melchisedec, king of Salem, and [the] priest of the highest God, which met Abraham, as he turned again from the slaying of the kings, and blessed him; (And this Melchizedek, the king of Salem, and the priest of the Most High God, who met Abraham, as he returned from the killing of the kings, and blessed him;)

2 to whom also Abraham parted tithes of all things (or to whom Abraham gave tithes of all that he had taken); first he is said (the) king of rightwiseness, and afterward (the) king of Salem, that is to say, (the) king of peace,

3 without father, without mother, without genealogy, neither having beginning of days, neither end of life; and he *is* likened to the Son of God, and dwelleth (a) priest [into] without end (or and remaineth a priest forever).

4 But behold ye how great is this [*man*], to whom Abraham the patriarch gave tithes of the best things.

5 For men of the sons of Levi taking priesthood have commandment to take tithes of the people, by the law, that is to say, of their brethren, though also they went out of the loins of Abraham. (For the men of the descendants of Levi who become priests have a command to receive tithes from the people, according to the Law, that is to say, from their brothers, even though they also came from the loins of Abraham.)

6 But he whose generation is not numbered in them, took tithes of Abraham; and he blessed this *Abraham*, which had repromissions (or who received the promises).

7 Without any gainsaying, that that is less, is blessed of the better. (For without a doubt or without any contradiction, that that is less, is blessed by the better.)

8 And here deadly men take tithes; but there he beareth witnessing, that he liveth. (And here mortal men, or those who die, receive tithes; but there, as the Scripture testifieth, he who yet liveth.)

9 And that it be said so, by Abraham also Levi, that took tithes (or who received tithes), was tithed;

10   and yet he was in his father's loins, when Melchisedec met him.

11   Therefore if perfection was by the priesthood of Levi, for under him the people took the law, what yet was it needful, (for) another priest to rise, by the order of Melchisedec, and not to be said by the order of Aaron? (And so if perfection had truly come by means of the priesthood of the sons of Levi, for under him the people received the Law, why then was it still necessary for another priest to arise, by the order of Melchizedek, and not to be called by, or to come from, the order of Aaron?)

12   For why when the priesthood is translated, it is need[ful] that also [the] translation of the law be made. (Because when there is a change in the priesthood, it is also necessary that there be a change in the Law.)

13   But he in whom these things be said, is of another lineage (or of another tribe), of which no man was priest to the altar.

14   For it is open [or it is openly known], that our Lord is born of Judah, in which lineage Moses spake nothing of priests. (For it is openly known, that our Lord was born from Judah, from which tribe Moses said nothing about priests.)

15   And more yet it is known, if by the order of Melchisedec another priest is risen up; (And more yet it is known, if by the order of Melchizedek another priest hath arisen;)

16   which is not made by the law(s) of fleshly commandment(s), but by [the] virtue of (a) life that may not be undone [or is indissoluble]. (who is made a priest not by a system of human laws, but by the power of a life that cannot be destroyed, or be dissolved.)

17   For he witnesseth, That thou art a priest [into] without end, by the order of Melchisedec; (For the Scripture testifieth, Thou art a priest forever, in the order of Melchizedek;)

18   (so) that reproving of the commandment before-going is made, for the unfirmness and unprofit of it.

19   For why the law brought nothing to perfection, but there is a bringing in of a better hope, by which we nigh to God. (Because the Law brought nothing to perfection, but there is the bringing in of a better hope, by which we can come near to God, or by which we can approach God.)

20   And how great it is, not without swearing, [that Christ is made priest after the order of Melchisedec], (or that the Messiah is made a priest in the order of Melchizedek);

21   but the others be made priests without an oath; but this priest with an oath, by him that said to him, The Lord swore, and it shall not rue him, Thou art a priest [into] without end, by the order of Melchisedec; (but the others be made priests without an oath; but this priest with an oath, by him who said to him, or as the Scripture said about him, The Lord swore, and he shall not regret it, Thou art a priest forever, in the order of Melchizedek;)

22   in so much Jesus is made (a) [better] promiser of the better testament (or of a better covenant).

23   And [soothly] the others were made many priests, therefore for they were forbidden by death to dwell still; (And truly there were many priests of those others, because they were forbidden by death to remain alive forever;)

24   but this man, for he dwelleth [into] without end, hath an everlasting priesthood. (but this man, because he liveth forever, hath an eternal priesthood.)

25   Wherefore also he may save [into] without end, coming nigh by himself to God, and (for)evermore liveth to pray for us. (And so he can also save forever, those who come near to God through him, and he always liveth to pray for us.)

26   For it beseemed that such a man were a bishop to us, holy, innocent, undefouled, clean, separated from sinful men, and made higher than (the) heavens; (For it is indeed appropriate

that such a man became the High Priest for us, holy, innocent, undefiled, clean, separated from sinners, and made higher than the heavens;)

27   which hath not need each day, as priests, first for his own guilts (or his own trespasses) to offer sacrifices, and afterward for the people; for he did this thing in offering himself once.

28   And the law ordained men priests having sickness, [or frailty]; but the word of swearing, which is after the law, *ordained* the Son perfect [into] without end. (And the Law ordained men to be high priests who were weak, *or frail*; but the words of the oath, which came after the Law, *ordained* the Son to be perfect forever.)

CHAPTER 8

1   But a capital, *that is, a short comprehending of many things*, on those things that be said. We have such a bishop, that sat on the right half of the seat of greatness in heavens, (But a recapitulation of those things that have already been said. We have such a High Priest, who sat on the right side, or at the right hand, of the throne of the Greatness in heaven,)

2   the minister of (the) saints, and of the very tabernacle, that God made [or set], and not man. (the minister of God's people, and of the true Tabernacle, or the true Tent, that God made, *or pitched*, and not man.)

3   For each bishop is ordained to offer gifts and sacrifices; wherefore it is need(ful), that also this *bishop* have something that he shall offer. (For every high priest is ordained to offer gifts and sacrifices; and so it is necessary, that also this *High Priest* have something that he shall offer.)

4   Therefore if he were on (the) earth, he were no priest, when there were (priests) that should offer gifts by the law,

5   which serve to the exemplar, [or (the) figure], and (the) shadow of heavenly things. As it was answered to Moses, when he should

end [or when he should make] the tabernacle, See [thou], he said, make thou all things by the exemplar, that is showed to thee in the mount, (or make all things by the example, or the pattern, that was shown to thee on Mount Sinai).

6   But now he hath gotten a better ministry, by so much as he is a mediator of a better testament (or because he is a mediator of a better covenant), which is confirmed with better promises.

7   For if that first had lacked blame, the place of the second should not have been sought.

8   For he reproving them saith, Lo! days come, saith the Lord, and I shall make perfect a new testament on the house of Israel, and on the house of Judah; (For he rebuking them said, Behold, the days shall come, saith the Lord, and I shall complete a new covenant with the house of Israel, and with the house of Judah;)

9   not like the testament that I made to their fathers, in the day in which I caught their hand, that I should lead them out of the land of Egypt; for they dwelled not perfectly in my testament, and I have despised them, saith the Lord. (not like the covenant which I made with their fathers, on the day in which I took their hands, so that I could lead them out of the land of Egypt; for they did not remain perfectly, or faithfully, in my covenant, and so I have despised them, saith the Lord.)

10   But this is the testament which I shall assign [or I shall dispose] to the house of Israel after those days, saith the Lord, in giving my laws into the souls of them, and into the hearts of them I shall above write them; and I shall be to them into a God [or and I shall be to them into God], and they shall be to me into a people. (But this is the covenant which I shall allot to the house of Israel after those days, saith the Lord, in putting my laws into their minds, and I shall write them upon their hearts; and I shall be their God, and they shall be my people.)

11   And each man shall not teach his

neighbour, and each man his brother, saying, Know thou the Lord; for all men shall know me, from the least to the more of them, (or for all shall know me, from the least unto the greatest of them).

12 For I shall be merciful to the wickedness of them, and now I shall not bethink on the sins of them (or and now I shall not remember their sins).

13 But in saying a new (testament) the former (testament) waxed old; and that that is of many days, and waxeth old, is nigh the death. (But in proclaiming a new covenant, the former covenant hath grown old; and that which is of many days, and groweth old, is nearly dead, or shall soon die.)

CHAPTER 9

1 And the former *testament* had justifyings of worship (or And the former *covenant* had rules for worship), and holy thing(s) (en)during for a time.

2 For the tabernacle was made first, in which were candlesticks, and [a] board (or a table), and (the) setting forth [or (the) putting forth] of loaves, which is said holy.

3 And after the veil, the second tabernacle, that is said sanctum sanctorum, *that is*, (the) *holy of holy things* (or the Holy of Holies);

4 having a golden censer, and the ark of the testament (or the Covenant Box), covered about on each side with gold, in which *was* a pot of gold having manna, and the rod of Aaron that flowered, and the tables of the testament (or and the Tablets of the Covenant);

5 on which things were cherubims of glory, overshadowing the propitiatory, [*or* (the) *mercyable place*], (or over which things were the cherubims of God's glory, or the heavenly cherubim, overshadowing the mercyseat); of which things it is not now to say by all.

6 But when these were made thus together, priests entered (for)evermore in(to) the former tabernacle, (or the priests always went into the first tabernacle or tent), doing the offices of (the) sacrifices;

7 but in the second *tabernacle*, the bishop, (or the high priest), [alone] *entered* once in the year, not without blood, which he offered for his ignorance and (for) the people's.

8 For the Holy Ghost signified this thing, that not yet the way of (the) saints was opened, while the former tabernacle had state. (For the Holy Spirit signified this, that the way for God's people was not yet opened, or was not yet revealed, while the first tabernacle still stood.)

9 Which parable is of this present time, by which also gifts and sacrifices be offered, which may not make a man serving perfect by conscience, (Which parable is for this present time, in which gifts and sacrifices also be offered, which cannot make the man who serveth there, or who worshippeth there, inwardly perfect,)

10 only in meats (or they only be food), and drinks, and diverse washings, and rightwisenesses of (the) flesh, that were set [till] to the time of correction.

11 But Christ being a bishop of goods to coming, *entered* by a larger and perfecter tabernacle, not made by hand, that is to say, not of this making, (But the Messiah being the High Priest of the good things to come, *entered* into a larger and more perfect Tabernacle, or Tent, not made by hands, that is to say, not of this making,)

12 neither by (the) blood of goat bucks, or of calves, but by his own blood, entered once into the holy things, that were found by an everlasting redemption. (nor with the blood of goat bucks, or of calves, but with his own blood, he entered once into the Holy of Holies, and obtained eternal deliverance for us.)

13 For if the blood of goat bucks, and of bulls, and the ashes of a cow calf sprinkled, halloweth unclean men (un)to the cleansing of (the) flesh,

14 how much more the blood of Christ, which by the Holy Ghost offered himself unwemmed to God, shall cleanse our conscience from dead works, to serve (the) God that liveth? [or for to serve to (the) living God?] (then how much more the blood of the Messiah, who by the Holy Spirit offered himself without fault, or without blemish, to God, shall cleanse our conscience from dead works, to serve the living God?)

15 And therefore he is a mediator of the new testament, that by death falling betwixt, into redemption of the trespassings that were under the former testament, they that be called take the behest of everlasting heritage. (And so he is the mediator of the new covenant, which by death falling between, for the redemption of the trespasses that were under the former covenant, they who be called receive the promise of the eternal inheritance.)

16 For where a testament is, it is need(ful), (or For where there is a testament, it is needed), that the death of the testament-maker come betwixt.

17 For a testament is confirmed in dead *men*; (or) else it is not (of) worth, [(or) else it is (of) no worth], while he liveth, that made the testament (or who made the testament).

18 Wherefore neither the first testament was hallowed without blood.

19 For when each commandment of the law was read of Moses to all the people (or Because when Moses read each commandment of the Law to the people), he took the blood of calves, and of bucks of goats, with water, and red wool, and hyssop, and besprinkled both that book and all the people,

20 and said, This is the blood of the testament that God commanded to you. (and said, This is the blood that sealeth the covenant which God hath commanded that you obey.)

21 Also he sprinkled with blood the tabernacle, and all the vessels of the service in like manner.

22 And almost all things be cleansed in blood by the law; and without shedding of blood remission of sins is not made (or and without the shedding of blood there is no forgiveness of sins).

23 Therefore it is need(ful), (or And so it is needed), that the exemplars of heavenly things be cleansed with these things; but those heavenly things with better sacrifices than these (sacrifices).

24 For Jesus entered not into (the) holy things made by hands, *that be* [the] exemplars of very things, but into heaven itself, that he appear now to the face of God for us; (Because Jesus did not enter into the Holy Place made with hands, *which is* the example, or the figure, or the shadow, of the true place, but into heaven itself, so that now he appear before God or in the presence of God, for us;)

25 neither that he offer himself oft, as the bishop entered into (the) holy things by all years in alien blood, (nor that he offer himself often, like the high priest who entered into the Holy of Holies each year with blood not his own,)

26 (or) else it behooved him to suffer oft from the beginning of the world; but now once in the ending of the worlds, to the destruction of sin by his sacrifice he appeared.

27 And as it is ordained to men, once to die, but after this *is* the doom (or but after this *is* the Judgement),

28 so Christ was offered once, to void, [*or* (to) *do away*], the sins of many men; the second *time* he shall appear without sin to men that abide him into health. (so the Messiah was offered once, to do away the sins of many men; the second *time* he shall appear without sin to those who wait for him unto salvation, or for deliverance.)

CHAPTER 10

1 For the law having, (or containing, or

being but) a shadow of (the) good things to come, not that image of things, may never make men nighing [or coming nigh] perfect by those same sacrifices, (or can never make those who approach become perfect by those same sacrifices), which they offer without ceasing by all years;

2   (or) else they should have ceased to be offered, for as much as the worshippers cleansed once, had not furthermore conscience of sin.

3   But in them [*by oft offering*], (the) mind of sins is made by all years (or a remembrance of sins is made year after year).

4   For it is impossible that sins be done away by (the) blood of bulls, and of (the) bucks of goats.

5   Therefore he entering into the world, saith, Thou wouldest not sacrifice and offering; but thou hast shaped a body to me; (And so he entering into the world, saith, Thou desirest not sacrifice and offering; but thou hast shaped, or thou hast prepared, a body for me;)

6   [and] burnt sacrifices also for sin pleased not to thee.

7   Then I said, Lo! I come; in the beginning of the book it is written of me (or from the beginning of the Book it is written about me), that I do thy will, [thou] God.

8   He saying before, That thou wouldest not sacrifices, and offerings, and burnt sacrifices for sin, nor those things be pleasant to thee, which be offered by the law, (He saying first, Thou desirest not sacrifices, and offerings, and burnt sacrifices for sin, nor those things be pleasing to thee, which be offered by the Law,)

9   then I said, Lo! I come, that I do thy will, God. He doeth away the first, that he make steadfast the second.

10   In which will we be hallowed by the offering of the body of Christ Jesus once. (By whose will we be consecrated, or we be sanctified, by the offering of the body of the Messiah Jesus once.)

11   And each priest is ready ministering each day, and oft times offering the same sacrifices, which may never do away sins (or which can never do away sins).

12   But this *man* offering one sacrifice for sins, forevermore sitteth in the right half of God the Father [or forevermore sitteth on the right half of God the Father]; (But this *man* offering one sacrifice for sins, forevermore sitteth at the right hand, or on the right side, of God the Father;)

13   from thenceforth abiding, till his enemies be put a stool of [or under] his feet. (where he waiteth henceforth, until his enemies be made a footstool under his feet.)

14   For by one offering he made perfect forever[more] hallowed men.

15   And the Holy Ghost witnesseth to us (or And the Holy Spirit testifieth to us); for after that he said,

16   This is the testament, which I shall witness to them after those days, the Lord saith, in giving my laws in(to) the hearts of them, and in the souls of them I shall above write them; (This is the covenant, about which I shall testify to them after those days, saith the Lord, in putting my laws in their hearts, and I shall write them upon their minds;)

17   and now I shall no more think on the sins and the wickedness(es) of them.

18   And where remission of these is, now *is* there none offering for sin. [+Forsooth where (there) is remission of these, now *is* none offering for sin.] (And where there is forgiveness for sins, now *there is* no more any need of offerings for sins.)

19   Therefore, brethren, having trust into the entering of (the) holy things, in the blood of Christ, (And so brothers, having trust to enter into the Holy of Holies, by the blood of the Messiah,)

20   which [he] hallowed to us a new way (or the new way which he hath consecrated for us), and living by the covering [or by a veil], that is to say, his flesh,

21 and *we having* the great priest on the house of God, (and *we having* the Great Priest over the household of God,)

22 nigh we with very heart (or let us approach with a true heart), in the plenty of faith; and be our hearts sprinkled from an evil conscience, and our bodies washed with clean water,

23 and hold we the confession of our hope, bowing to no side, [or unbowing, *or unpliable*]; for he is true that hath made the promise.

24 And behold we together in the stirring of charity (or of love), and of good works;

25 not forsaking our gathering together, as it is the custom to some men, but comforting [*them*], and by so much the more, by how much ye see the day nighing.

26 For why now a sacrifice for sins is not left to us, that sin willfully, after that we have taken the knowing of truth. (Because now there is no longer any sacrifice for sins for us, we who sin willingly, or with our free will, after that we have received the knowledge of the truth.)

27 For why some abiding of doom is dreadful, and the (pur)suing of fire, which shall waste (his) adversaries. (But instead, only waiting for fearful Judgement, and the fire following, which shall waste all his adversaries.)

28 Who that breaketh Moses' law, dieth without any mercy, by two or three witnesses (or on the evidence given by two or three witnesses);

29 how much more guess ye, that he deserveth worse torments, which defouleth the Son of God, and holdeth the blood of the testament polluted, in which he is hallowed, and doeth despite [or wrong] to the Spirit of grace? (then how much more do ye think, that he deserveth worse torments, who defileth the Son of God, and holdeth the blood of the covenant polluted, by which he was consecrated, or he was sanctified, and despiseth or doeth wrong to the Spirit of grace?)

30 For we know him that said, To me vengeance, and I shall yield (it). And again, For the Lord shall deem his people. (For we know him who said, Vengeance is mine, and I shall yield it. And again, The Lord shall judge his people.)

31 It is fearedful to fall into the hands of God living. [⁺It is fearful to fall into the hands of (the) living God.]

32 And have ye mind on the former days, in which ye were (en)lightened, and suffered great strife of passions. (And remember the early days, when ye were first enlightened, and struggled through great sufferings.)

33 And in the tother ye were made a spectacle by shames, and tribulations, (or by reproofs, and troubles); in another ye were made fellows of men living so.

34 For also to bound men ye had compassion, and ye received with joy the robbing of your goods, knowing that ye have a better and a dwelling substance.

35 Therefore do not ye lose your trust, which hath great rewarding.

36 For patience is needful to you, that ye do the will of God, and bring again the promise. (Because it is necessary that ye be patient, or that ye endure, so that ye do God's will, and win the promise, or and receive the promise.)

37 For yet a little, and he that is to come shall come, and he shall not tarry.

38 For my just man liveth of faith (or For my righteous man liveth by faith); (so) that if he withdraweth himself, he shall not please to my soul.

39 But we be not the sons of withdrawing away into perdition, but of faith into [the] getting of (the) soul (or but of faithfulness unto the getting of life, or unto the saving of our souls).

CHAPTER 11

1 But faith is the substance of things that be

to be hoped [or Forsooth faith is the substance of things to be hoped], and an argument, [or (a) certainty], of things not appearing.

2　And in this *faith* old men have gotten witnessing. (And by this *faith* men of old have received a good witness or a good testimony.)

3　By faith we understand that the worlds were made [or were shaped] by God's word, that visible things were made (out) of invisible things.

4　By faith Abel offered a much more sacrifice than Cain to God [or By faith Abel offered full much more host, *or sacrifice*, to God than Cain], by which he got witnessing to be just, for God bare witnessing to his gifts; and by that *faith* he dead speaketh yet. (By faith Abel offered a much better sacrifice than Cain to God, by which he received testimony that he was righteous, for God gave testimony regarding his gifts; and through that *faith* though he is dead still speaketh.)

5　By faith Enoch was translated, that he should not see death; and he was not found, for the Lord translated him. For before [the] translation he had witnessing that he pleased God. (By faith Enoch was transferred, or was carried away, so that he did not see death; and he was not found, because the Lord carried him away. For before he was carried away, it is the testimony of Scripture that he had pleased God.)

6　And it is impossible to please God without faith. For it behooveth that a man coming to God, believe that he is, and that he is [a] rewarder of men that seek him.

7　By faith Noe dreaded, through (an) answer taken of these things that yet were not seen, and shaped a ship [or an ark] into the health of his house, (or By faith Noah feared, through an answer received regarding those things that were not yet seen, and made an ark for the salvation, or the deliverance, of his family); by which he condemned the world, and is ordained (an) heir of rightwiseness, which is by faith.

8　By faith he that is called Abraham, obeyed to go out into a place, which he should take into heritage (or which he would receive for an inheritance); and he went out, not witting whither (or knowing where) he should go.

9　By faith he dwelt in the land of promise, as in an alien *land*, (or like in a strange, or a foreign, *land*), dwelling in little houses with Isaac and Jacob, even-heirs of the same promise.

10　For he abode a city having foundaments (or For he was waiting for a city with firm foundations), whose craftsman and maker is God.

11　By faith also that Sara barren, took virtue in conceiving of seed, (or Also by faith Sarah who was barren, received strength to conceive by seed), yea, against the time of age; for she believed him true, that had promised (it).

12　For which thing of one, and yet nigh dead, there were born as (the) stars of (the) heaven(s) in multitude, and as (the) gravel, that is at the seaside out of number. [For which thing, and of one, and him nigh dead, *men* be born as stars of heaven in multitude, and as gravel, *or* (the) *sand*, that is at the seaside unnumerable.]

13　By faith all these be dead, when the behests were not taken, (or when the promises were not yet received, or were not yet fulfilled), but they beheld them afar, and greeting them well, and acknowledged that they were pilgrims, and harboured men on the earth.

14　And they that say these things, signify that they seek a country.

15　If they had had mind of that, of which they went out, they had time of turning again; (And if they had remembered, or had thought upon, the place from which they had gone out, they would have found the way, or a time, to return;)

16　but now they desire a better, that is to say, (a) heavenly (country). Therefore God is not confounded, [or ashamed], to be called the God of them; for he made ready to them a city (or for he prepared a city for them).

17 By faith Abraham offered Isaac, when he was tempted; and he offered the one begotten [son], which had taken the behests; (By faith Abraham offered Isaac, when he was tested; yea, he offered his only begotten son, he who had received the promises;)

18 to whom it was said, For in Isaac the seed shall be called to thee.

19 For he deemed (or For he judged), that God is mighty to raise him, yea, from death [or from (the) dead]; wherefore he took him also into a parable.

20 By faith also of things to coming [or By faith and of things to come], Isaac blessed Jacob and Esau.

21 By faith Jacob dying blessed all the sons of Joseph, and honoured the highness of his staff [or the highness of his rod].

22 By faith Joseph dying had mind of the passing forth of the children of Israel, and commanded of his bones. (By faith when Joseph was dying, he spoke of the going forth of the children of Israel from Egypt, and commanded about his bones.)

23 By faith Moses born, was hid three months of his father and mother, for that they saw the young child fair, [or seemly]; and they dreaded not the commandment of the king. (By faith after Moses was born, he was hidden for three months by his father and mother, for they saw that the young child was beautiful; and they did not fear, or they were not afraid of, the king's command.)

24 By faith Moses was made great, and denied that he was the son of Pharaoh's daughter,

25 and chose more [or rather] to be tormented with the people of God, than to have (the) mirth of temporal sin;

26 deeming the reproof of Christ (to be) more riches, than the treasures of [the] Egyptians, (or judging the rebuke of the Messiah to be greater riches, than the treasures of the Egyptians); for he beheld into the rewarding.

27 By faith he forsook Egypt, and dreaded not the hardness of the king, (or By faith he left Egypt, and did not fear the king's wrath); for he abode, as seeing him that was invisible.

28 By faith he hallowed pask, (or By faith he consecrated, or he sanctified, the Passover), and the shedding out of (the) blood, (so) that he that destroyed the first things of [the] Egyptians, should not touch them.

29 By faith they passed (through) the Red Sea, as by dry land, (or By faith they crossed over the Sea of Reeds, like on dry land), which (same) thing (the) Egyptians assaying were devoured [in the waters].

30 By faith the walls of Jericho felled down, by (the) (en)compassing of seven days.

31 By faith Rahab the whore received the spies with peace, and perished not with (the) unbelieveful men.

32 And what yet shall I say? For time shall fail to me telling of Gedeon (or Gideon), Barak, Samson, Jephthae (or Jephthah), David, and Samuel, and of (the) other prophets;

33 which by faith overcame realms, wrought rightwiseness, got repromissions; they stopped the mouths of lions, (who by faith overcame kingdoms, worked righteousness, received the promises; they stopped the mouths of lions,)

34 they quenched the fierceness of fire, they drove away the edge of (the) sword, they recovered of sickness, they were made strong in battle, they turned (back) the hosts of aliens (or they turned back the armies of the foreigners).

35 Women received their dead children from death to life; but others were held forth, [or died], not taking redemption, that they should find a better again-rising. (Women received their dead raised from death back to life; but others died, not accepting release or deliverance, so that they would receive, or could get, a better resurrection.)

36   And others assayed scornings and beatings, moreover and bonds and prisons.

37   They were stoned, they were sawed, they were tempted, they were dead in (or by) slaying of (the) sword. They went about in badger skins, and in skins of goats, needy, anguished, tormented;

38   to which the world was not worthy. They wandered in (the) wildernesses (or They went about in the wilderness), and in (the) mountains and dens, and [in] (the) caves of the earth.

39   And all these, proved by (the) witnessing of faith, took not repromission; (And all these, approved by the testimony of their faith, did not receive the promise;)

40   for God provided some better thing for us, that they should not be made perfect without us (or so that they would not be made perfect without us).

CHAPTER 12

1   Therefore we that have so great a cloud of witnesses put (forth) to [us], do we away all charge, and sin standing about us, and by patience run we to the battle, [or to the strife, *or* (the) *fight*], purposed to us, (And so we who have such a great crowd of witnesses put before us, let us do away every burden, and every sin standing about us, and then girded with endurance let us run to the battle, or to the strife, *or the fight*, purposed for us,)

2   beholding into the maker of faith, and the perfect ender, Jesus; which when joy was purposed to him, he suffered the cross, and despised confusion, and sitteth on the right half of the seat of God. (beholding the maker and the perfect finisher of faith, Jesus; who when joy was purposed to him, he suffered the cross, and despised its shame, and now sitteth at the right hand, or on the right side, of God's throne.)

3   And bethink ye on him that suffered such gainsaying of sinful men against himself, that ye be not made weary, failing in your souls. (And so think upon him who suffered such opposition, or such railing, against himself from sinners, so that ye be not made weary, and lose heart.)

4   For ye against-stood not yet unto (the) blood, fighting against sin.

5   And ye have forgotten the comfort that speaketh to you as to sons, and saith, My son, do not thou despise the teaching [or the discipline] of the Lord, neither be thou made weary, the while thou art chastised of him.

6   For the Lord chastiseth him that he loveth; he beateth [or he scourgeth] every son that he receiveth.

7   Abide ye still in chastising; God proffereth him(self) to you as to sons [⁺or Last ye therefore in discipline; God offereth him(self) to you as to sons]. For what son is it, whom the father chastiseth not?

8   That if ye be out of chastising, whose partners be ye all made [⁺or That if ye be out of discipline, of which all ye be made partners], then ye be adulterers (or ye be bastards), and not sons.

9   And afterward we had fathers of our flesh, (yea), teachers, and we with reverence dreaded them (or and we had fearful reverence for them). Whether not much more we shall obey to the Father of spirits, and (then) we shall live?

10   And they in time of few days taught us by their will; but this Father teacheth to that thing that is profitable, in(to) receiving (of) the hallowing of him. (And they taught us for only a few days, or they disciplined us for only a short time, out of their own desires; but this Father teacheth or disciplineth that which is profitable, unto the receiving or the sharing of his holiness.)

11   And each chastising in [this] present *time* seemeth to be not of joy, but of sorrow; but afterward it shall yield (the) fruit of rightwiseness most peaceable to men exercised

by it.

12 For which thing raise ye [up] slow hands, and knees unbound,

13 and make ye rightful steps to your feet; (so) that no man halting err, but (that) more be healed.

14 (Pur)Sue ye peace with all men (or Seek peace with everyone), and holiness, without which no man shall see God.

15 Behold ye, that no man fail to the grace of God, (so) that no root of bitterness burrowing upward hinder [us], and many be defouled by it (or and by which many be defiled);

16 that no man be (a) lecher, either unholy, as Esau (was), which for one [*meal's*] meat sold his first things, [*or* (his) *heritage*], (or who for the food of one meal sold his birthright, *or his inheritance*).

17 For know ye, that afterward he coveting to inherit (a) blessing, was reproved. For he found not (a) place of penance, though he sought it with tears. (For know ye, that afterward he coveting to inherit a blessing, was rebuked. For he could not find a way to repentance, though he sought it with tears.)

18 But ye have not come to the fire able to be touched, and able to come to, and to the whirlwind [or the great wind], and (the) mist, and (the) tempest,

19 and sound of trump, and voice of words, (or and the sound of the trumpet, and the sound of words); which they that heard, excused them(selves), (so) that the word should not be made to them.

20 For they bare not that that was said, And if a beast touched the hill, it was stoned [or it shall be stoned].

21 And so dreadful it was that was seen (or And what was seen was so fearful), that Moses said, I am afeared, and full of trembling.

22 But ye have come nigh to the hill [of] Sion, and to the city of God living, [or and to the city of living God], (or But ye have come near to Mount Zion, and to the city of the living

God), the heavenly Jerusalem, and to the multitude of many thousand angels,

23 and to the church of the first men, which be written in (the) heavens, and to God, doomsman of all, and to the spirit(s) of just (and) perfect men, (and to the congregation or to the assembly of the first-born, whose names be written in heaven, and to God, the Judge of all, and to the spirits of righteous or good people made perfect,)

24 and to Jesus, mediator of the new testament, (or and to Jesus, the mediator of the new covenant), and to the sprinkling of blood, speaking better than Abel [or better speaking than Abel's *blood*].

25 See ye, that ye forsake not [or that ye refuse (not)] the speaker; for if they that forsaked [or refusing] him that spake on the earth, escaped not, much more we that turn away from him that speaketh to us from (the) heavens. (See, that ye do not refuse to listen to the speaker; for if those who refused to listen to him, who spoke on the earth, did not escape, then how much more we who turn away from him, who now speaketh to us from heaven.)

26 Whose voice then moved the earth, but now he again promiseth, and saith, Yet once and I shall move not only the earth, but also heaven. (Whose voice then shook the earth, and now he again promiseth, and saith, Yet once more I shall shake not only the earth, but also heaven.)

27 And that he saith, Yet once (more), he declareth the translation of moveable things, as of made things, that those things dwell, that be unmoveable. (And that he saith, Yet once more, he declareth the shaking of moveable things, that is, of made or created things, so that those other things remain, which be unmoveable.)

28 Therefore we receiving the kingdom unmoveable, have we grace, by which serve we pleasing to God with dread and reverence. (And so having received an unshakeable

kingdom, let us be grateful, and let our service please God, yea, with fearful reverence.)

29 For our God is (a) fire that wasteth.

CHAPTER 13

1 The charity of (the) brotherhood dwell in you, (Keep the love for the brotherhood dwelling in you,)

2 and do not ye forget hospitality; for by this some men pleased to angels, that were received to harbour.

3 Think ye on bound men, as (if) ye were together bound (with them), and of travailing men, as yourselves dwelling in the body. (Remember those in prison, as if ye were in prison together with them, and those who be struggling, like ye yourselves who remain in the body.)

4 Wedding *is* in all things honourable, and (the) bed unwemmed, [or undefouled, or undefiled]; for God shall deem fornicators and adulterers (or for God shall judge fornicators and adulterers).

5 Be *your* manners without covetousness, satisfied with present things; for he said, I shall not leave thee, neither forsake (thee),

6 so that we say trustily, The Lord is an helper to me; I shall not dread what a man shall do to me (or I shall not fear what anyone shall do to me).

7 Have ye mind of your sovereigns [or your provosts], that have spoken to you the word of God; of whom behold ye the going out of living, and (pur)sue ye the faith of them, (Remember your leaders, who have spoken the word of God unto you; think about their living and their dying, and follow the example of their faith,)

8 Jesus Christ, yesterday, and today, he *is* also into worlds. (Jesus Christ, he *is* yesterday, and today, and forevermore.)

9 Do not ye be led away with diverse and strange teachings. For it is best to stable the heart with grace, not with meats (or not with food), which profited not to men wandering [or going] in them.

10 We have an altar, of which they that serve to the tabernacle, have not (the) power [or (the) leave] to eat. (We have an altar, from which those who serve in the Tabernacle, or the Tent, do not have the right to eat off of.)

11 For of which beasts the blood is borne in for sin into (the) holy things by the bishop, the bodies of them be burnt without the castles. (For of which beasts the blood for sin is carried into the Holy of Holies by the high priest, and their bodies be burned up outside the camp.)

12 For which thing Jesus, that he should hallow the people by his blood, suffered without the gate. (For which thing Jesus, so that he could consecrate, or he could sanctify, the people with his own blood, suffered outside the gate.)

13 Therefore go we out to him without the castles, bearing his reproof. (And so let us go out to him outside the camp, carrying the same rebuke or sharing the same reproach.)

14 For we have not here a city dwelling, but we seek a city to coming. [⁺Soothly we have not here a dwelling city, but we seek a city to come.]

15 Therefore by him offer we a sacrifice of praising (for)evermore to God, that is to say, the fruit of (our) lips acknowledging to his name.

16 And do not ye forget well-doing, and communing; for by such sacrifices God is well-served, (or is pleased, or is well-satisfied).

17 Obey ye to your sovereigns, [or to your provosts, *or prelates*], and be ye subject to them; for they perfectly wake (or for they diligently watch), as to yielding reason for your souls, (so) that they do this thing with joy, and not sorrowing; for this thing speedeth not to you (or for that would not be expedient for you).

18 Pray ye for us, and we trust that we have good conscience in all things, willing to live

well (or desiring always to do the right thing).

19   Moreover I beseech you to do [*this thing*], (so) that I be restored the sooner to you.

20   And God of peace, that led out from death the great shepherd of (the) sheep, in the blood of [the] everlasting testament (or by the blood of the eternal covenant), our Lord Jesus Christ,

21   shape you in all good thing(s), [⁺or make you able in each good work], (so) that ye do the will of him; and he do in you that thing that shall please before him, by Jesus Christ, to whom be glory into worlds of worlds (or to whom be glory forever and ever). Amen.

22   And, brethren, I pray you, that ye suffer a word of solace; for by full few things I have written to you.

23   Know ye our brother Timothy, that is sent forth, with whom if he shall come more hastily, I shall see you. (Know that our brother Timothy hath been set free, or is now at liberty, and if he shall come in time, he shall be with me when I shall see you.)

24   Greet ye well all your sovereigns, and all (the) holy men, [or Greet well all your provosts, and all (the) saints]. The brethren of Italy greet you well. (Give a hearty greeting to all of your leaders, and to all of the saints, or to all of God's people. The brothers in Italy send you hearty greetings.)

25   The grace of God *be* with you all. Amen. †

JAMES

CHAPTER 1

1   James, the servant of God, and of our Lord Jesus Christ, to the twelve kindreds, that be in (the) scattering abroad, health. (James, the servant of God, and of our Lord Jesus Christ, to the twelve tribes, who be in the scattering abroad, or in the dispersion, or the Diaspora, greetings.)

2   My brethren, deem ye (it) all joy, when ye fall into diverse temptations, (My brothers, judge it to be most joyful, when ye undergo different tests,)

3   witting that the proving of your faith worketh patience; (knowing that the proving of your faith produceth patience, or increaseth endurance;)

4   and patience hath a perfect work, that ye be perfect and whole, and fail in nothing.

5   And if any of you needeth wisdom, ask he of God, which giveth to all men largely (or who giveth generously to everyone), and upbraideth not; and it shall be given to him.

6   But ask he in faith, and doubt nothing; for he that doubteth, is like to a wave of the sea, which is moved and borne about of the wind. (But ask he with faith, and do not doubt; for he who doubteth, is like a wave of the sea, which is moved and carried about by the wind.)

7   Therefore guess not that man, that he shall take anything of the Lord. (And so do not let that man think, that he shall receive anything from the Lord.)

8   A man double in soul is unstable in all his ways.

9   And a meek brother have glory in his enhancing, (And a humble man have glory in his exalting,)

10   and a rich man in his lowness; for as the flower of grass he shall pass (away).

11   The sun rose up with heat, and dried the grass [or the hay], and the flower of it felled down, and the fairness of his cheer perished (or and the beauty of his face perished); and so a rich man withereth in his ways.

12   Blessed *is* the man, that suffereth temptation, (or Happy *is* the man, who undergoeth testing); for when he shall be proved, he shall receive the crown of life, which God promised to men that love him.

13   No man when he is tempted, say, that he is tempted of God; for why God is not a tempter of evil things, for he tempteth no man. (Let no man say, when he is tempted or tested, that he was tempted or tested by God; for God cannot be tempted by evil, and he tempteth no one.)

14   But each man is tempted, drawn (away) and stirred, of his own coveting. [Soothly each man is tempted of (or by) his own coveting, drawn (away) *from reason*, and snared, *or deceived*.] (But each person is tempted or tested, drawn away and stirred, by his own lusts and envies.)

15   Afterward coveting [or Then coveting], when it hath conceived, bringeth forth sin; but sin, when it is [ful]filled, (en)gendereth death.

16   Therefore, my most dearworthy brethren, do not ye err.

17   Each good gift, and each perfect gift is from above, and cometh down from the Father of lights, with whom is none other changing, nor overshadowing of reward. [⁺Each best thing given, and all perfect gift is from above, coming down from the Father of lights, with whom is not any changing, neither shadowing of whileness, *or* (of) *time*.]

18   For willfully he begat us by the word of truth, that we be a beginning of his creature(s). (For willingly, or by free will, he begat us by the Word of Truth, so that we hold the first rank among all his creatures.)

19   Know ye, my brethren most (be)loved, be each man swift to hear, but slow to speak, and

slow to wrath;

20 for the wrath of man worketh not the rightwiseness of God.

21 For which thing cast ye away all uncleanness, and plenty of malice, and in mildness (or and in meekness and humility), receive ye the word that is planted, that may save your souls (or that can save your souls).

22 But be ye doers of the word, and not hearers only, deceiving yourselves.

23 For if any man is an hearer of the word, and not a doer, this shall be likened to a man that beholdeth the cheer of his birth in a mirror (or he shall be like a man who seeth his face in a mirror);

24 for he beheld himself, and went away, and anon he forgot which [or what] he was (or and at once he forgot what he was).

25 But he that beholdeth into the law of perfect freedom, and dwelleth in it, and is not made a forgetful hearer, but a doer of work(s), this shall be blessed in his deed(s).

26 And if any man guesseth himself to be religious, and refraineth not his tongue, but deceiveth his heart, the religion of him is vain (or his religion is empty and useless).

27 A clean religion, and unwemmed with God and the Father, is this, to visit fatherless and motherless children, and widows in their tribulation, and to keep himself undefouled from this world. (A clean religion, and unspotted, or without blemish, with God the Father, is this, to visit fatherless and motherless children, and widows in their distress, and to keep himself undefiled from this world.)

CHAPTER 2

1 My brethren, do not ye have the faith of our Lord Jesus Christ of glory, in (the) acception of persons. [My brothers, do not in acception, *or taking*, of persons, have the faith of our Lord Jesus Christ of glory.] (My brothers, ye who have faith in our Lord Jesus Christ in glory, do

not favour, or have respect for, certain people over others.)

2 For if a man that hath a golden ring, and in a fair clothing, (or For if a man who hath a gold ring, and beautiful clothes), cometh in your company, and a poor man entereth in a foul clothing,

3 and if ye behold into him that is clothed with clear clothing, and if ye say to him, Sit thou here well, (or and if ye see him who is clothed with beautiful clothes, and ye say to him, Sit thou here in this favoured place); but to the poor man ye say, Stand thou there, either sit under the stool of my feet;

4 whether ye deem not with yourselves, and be made doomsmen of wicked thoughts? (do not ye judge, and make yourselves judges, with your wicked thoughts?)

5 Hear ye, my most dearworthy brethren, whether God chose not poor men in this world, rich in faith, and heirs of the kingdom, that God promised to men that love him?

6 But ye have despised the poor man. Whether rich men oppress not you by power, and they draw you to dooms? (or and do they not drag you to the courts?)

7 Whether they blaspheme not the good name, that is called to help on you? [Whether they blaspheme not the good name, that is in-called of you?] (Do they not blaspheme the good name, that you call upon for help?)

8 Nevertheless if ye perform the King's law, by (the) scriptures, Thou shalt love thy neighbour as thyself, ye do well.

9 But if ye take persons, ye work sin, and be reproved of the law, as trespassers [or as transgressors]. (But if ye favour, or have respect for, certain people over others, ye work sin, and be rebuked by the Law, as trespassers or as transgressors.)

10 And whoever keepeth all the law, but offendeth in one, he is made guilty of all (of it).

11 For he that said, Thou shalt do no lechery [or Thou shalt not do lechery], said also, Thou

shalt not slay; (so) that if thou doest no lechery, but thou slayest, thou art made [a] trespasser of the law.

12   Thus speak ye, and thus do ye, as beginning to be deemed (or to be judged) by the law of freedom.

13   For why doom without mercy *is* to him, that doeth no mercy; but mercy above raiseth doom. (For judgement without mercy *is* for him, who doeth no mercy; but mercy riseth above or triumpheth over judgement.)

14   My brethren, what shall it profit, if any man say that he hath faith, but he hath not works? whether faith shall be able to save him?

15   And if a brother or sister be naked, and have need of each day's livelode [or of each day's lifelode], (And if a brother or sister be naked, and have need of each day's livelihood,)

16   and if any of you say to them, Go ye in peace, be ye made hot, and be ye [full-]filled; but if ye give not to them those things that be necessary to the body, what shall it profit?

17   So also faith, if it hath not works, is dead in itself.

18   But some man shall say, Thou hast faith, and I have works; show thou to me thy faith without works, and I shall show to thee my faith of works, (or show to me thy faith without works, and I shall show to thee my faith by my works).

19   Thou believest, that one God is; thou doest well; and (the) devils believe, and [together] tremble.

20   But wilt thou know, thou vain man (or O empty and useless man), that faith without works is idle?

21   Whether Abraham, our father, was not justified of works, (or Was not our father Abraham justified by works), offering Isaac, his son, on the altar?

22   Therefore thou seest, that faith wrought with his works, and his faith was [ful]filled of works. (And so thou seest, that faith was at work in his works, and his faith was fulfilled, or

was brought to fruition, by his works.)

23   And the scripture was [ful]filled, saying, Abraham believed to God, and it was areckoned to him to rightwiseness, and he was called the friend of God.

24   Ye see that a man is justified of works, and not of faith only. (And so ye see that a man is justified by works, and not by faith alone.)

25   In like manner, whether also Rahab, the whore, was not justified of works, (or In like manner, was not Rahab, the whore, justified by works), and received the messengers, and sent them out by another way?

26   For as the body without (the) spirit is dead, so also faith without works is dead.

CHAPTER 3

1   My brethren, do not ye be made (into) many masters, witting that ye take the more doom. (My brothers, do not let many of you become teachers, knowing that if ye do, ye shall receive a sterner judgement, or a greater condemnation.)

2   For all we offend in many things. If any man offendeth not in word, this is a perfect man, (or If some man offendeth not by speaking unkindly, or harshly, then he is a perfect man); for also he may lead about all the body with a bridle.

3   For if we put bridles into horses' mouths, for to consent to us, and (so) we lead about all the body of them.

4   And lo! ships, when they be great, and be driven of strong winds, yet they be borne about of a little rudder, where the moving of the governor will. (And behold, ships, although they be great, and be driven by strong winds, yet they can be turned about by a little rudder, wherever the captain desireth.)

5   So also the tongue is but a little member, and raiseth great things. Lo! how little fire burneth [or kindleth] a full great wood, (or Behold, how a little fire burneth a very large

forest).

6 And our tongue is (a) fire, the university of wickedness. The tongue is ordained in our members, which defouleth all the body; and it is enflamed, [or set afire], of hell (or and it is set on fire from hell), and enflameth the wheel of our birth.

7 And all the kind(s) of beasts, and of fowls, and of serpents, and of others is chastised, and those be made tame of man's kind (or and they all can be tamed by mankind); [Soothly all kind(s) of beasts, and fowls, and serpents, and of others, be overcome, or under-yoked, and be made tame, of mankind, (or and can be made tame by mankind);]

8 but no man may chastise the tongue (or but no one can discipline the tongue), for it is an unpeaceable evil, and full of deadly venom.

9 In it we bless God, the Father, and in it we curse men, that be made to the likeness of God. (With it we bless God the Father, and with it we curse men, who be made in the likeness of God.)

10 (Out) Of the same mouth passeth forth [or cometh forth] blessing and cursing. My brethren (or My brothers), it behooveth not that these things be done so.

11 Whether a well of the same hole bringeth forth sweet (water), and salt water?

12 My brethren (or My brothers), whether a fig tree may make grapes, either a vine figs? So neither salt water may make sweet water.

13 Who is wise, and taught among you? show he of good living his working [or show he of good living his work], in mildness of his wisdom. (Who is wise, and learned among you? show he by good living his work, along with the humility and the meekness of his wisdom.)

14 (So) That if ye have bitter envy, and strivings [or strives] be in your hearts, do not ye have glory (or do not boast), and be liars against the truth.

15 For this wisdom is not from above coming down, but earthly, and beastly, and fiendly (or and devilish).

16 For where (there) is envy and strife, there is unsteadfastness and all shrewd work (or and every depraved work).

17 But wisdom that is from above, first it is chaste, afterward peaceable, mild (or meek and humble), able to be counselled [or persuadable], consenting to good things, full of mercy and of good fruits, deeming without feigning (or judging with sincerity).

18 And the fruit of rightwiseness is sown in peace, to men that make peace. (And the fruit of righteousness is sown in peace, by men who make peace.)

CHAPTER 4

1 Whereof be battles and chidings among you? Whether not (out) of your covetings, that fight in your members? (Where do battles and arguments among you come from? Whether not from your lusts and your envies, that fight among your members?)

2 Ye covet, and ye have not; ye slay, and ye have envy, and ye may not get (or and ye cannot get). Ye chide, and make battle; and ye have not, for that ye ask not.

3 Ye ask, and ye receive not; for that ye ask (with) evil (intent), as ye show openly in your covetings.

4 Adulterers, know not ye, that the friendship of this world is enemy to God? [+or that the friendship of this world is enmity to God?] (or that friendship with this world, or love of or for this world, is enmity to God?) Therefore whoever will be the friend of this world, is made the enemy of God.

5 Whether ye guess, that the scripture saith vainly, (or Do ye think, that the Scripture saith emptily, or for no purpose), The spirit that dwelleth in you, coveteth to envy?

6 But he giveth the more grace; for which thing he saith, God withstandeth proud men,

but to meek men he giveth grace, (or God opposeth the proud, but he giveth grace to the humble).

7   Therefore be ye subject to God; but withstand ye the devil, and he shall flee from you.

8   Nigh ye to God, and he shall nigh to you. Ye sinners, cleanse ye the hands, and ye double in soul [or and ye double of will], purge ye the hearts. (Come near to God, and he shall come near to you. Ye sinners, cleanse your hands, and ye of two minds, purge your hearts.)

9   Be ye wretches, and wail ye [or and weep ye]; your laughing be turned into weeping, and [your] joy into (the) sorrow of heart.

10   Be ye meeked in the sight of the Lord, and he shall enhance you. (Be ye humble before the Lord, and he shall raise you up.)

11   My brethren, do not ye backbite each other. He that backbiteth his brother, either that deemeth his brother, backbiteth the law, and deemeth the law. And if thou deemest the law, thou art not a doer of the law, but a doomsman. (My brothers, do not slander each other. He who slandereth his brother, or who judgeth his brother, slandereth the Law, and judgeth the Law. And if thou judgest the Law, thou art not a doer of the Law, but a judge.)

12   But one is maker of the law, and judge, that may lose and deliver. And who art thou, that deemest thy neighbour? (But there is One who is the Maker of the Law, and the Judge, who can destroy and save. And so who art thou, who judgest thy neighbour?)

13   Lo! now ye, that say, Today either tomorrow we shall go into that city, and there we shall dwell a year, and we shall make merchandise, and we shall make winning(s), (or and we shall have great success, and make great profits);

14   which know not, what is to you in the morrow. For what is your life? A smoke [or A vapour] appearing at a little time, and afterward it shall be wasted.

15   Therefore that ye say, If the Lord will, and if we live, we shall do this thing, either that thing. (And so ye should say, If the Lord desireth it, and if we live, we shall do this, or that.)

16   And now ye make full out joy in your prides; every such joying is wicked.

17   Therefore it is sin to him, that knoweth to do good, and doeth not.

CHAPTER 5

1   Do now, ye rich men, weep ye, yelling in your wretchednesses that shall come to you.

2   Your riches be rotten, and your clothes be eaten of moths. (Your riches have rotted, and your clothes have been eaten by moths.)

3   Your gold and silver hath rusted, and the rust of them shall be to you into witnessing, and shall eat your fleshes, as fire. Ye have treasured to you wrath in the last days. (Your gold and silver have rusted, and their rust shall be the testimony against you, and shall eat your flesh, like fire. Ye have piled up wealth for yourselves in the Last Days.)

4   Lo! the hire of your workmen, that reaped your fields, which is defrauded of you, crieth; and the cry of them hath entered into the ears of the Lord of hosts. (Behold, the wages of your workers, who harvested your fields, and who were defrauded by you, crieth out; and their cry hath entered into the ears of the Lord of hosts.)

5   Ye have eaten on the earth, and in your lecheries ye have nourished your hearts. In the day of slaying

6   ye brought, and slew the just Man, and he against-stood not you. [ye led to, and slew the just man, and he withstood you not (or and he did not withstand you).] (ye condemned, and killed the Just Man, and he did not oppose you, or and he did not stand against you.)

7   Therefore, brethren, be ye patient, till to the coming of the Lord. Lo! an earth-tiller abideth [the] precious fruit of the earth,

patiently suffering, till he receive timeful and lateful *fruit*. (And so brothers, endure, until the coming of the Lord. Behold, a farmer waiteth for the precious fruit from the earth, yea, patiently waiting, until he receive the *fruit* in its time, and then even a later harvest.)

8 And be ye patient, and confirm ye your hearts, for the coming of the Lord shall nigh. (And so be patient, and make your hearts firm, for the coming of the Lord shall approach, or it is near.)

9 Brethren, do not ye be sorrowful [or do not ye be scornful] each to (the) other, that ye be not deemed (or so that ye be not judged). Lo! the judge standeth nigh before the gate.

10 Brethren, take ye (an) ensample of evil going out, and of long abiding, and travail, [or and of (the) long abiding of travail], and of patience, the prophets, that spake to you in the name of the Lord, (or the prophets, who spoke to you in the name of the Lord).

11 Lo! we bless them that suffered. Ye have heard (of) the patience of Job, and ye saw the end of the Lord (or and ye saw his end with the Lord), for the Lord is merciful, and doing mercy.

12 Before all things, my brethren, do not ye swear, neither by heaven, neither by earth, neither by whatever other oath. But be your word Yea, yea, Nay, nay, that ye fall not under doom (or so that ye do not fall under judgement).

13 And if any of you is sorrowful, [*or* (is) *heavy*], pray he with (a) patient soul, and say he a psalm.

14 If any of you is sick, lead he in (some) priests of the church (or send he for some priests from the church), and pray they for him, and anoint him with oil in the name of the Lord;

15 and the prayer of faith shall save the sick *man* [or and the prayer of faith shall save the sick], and the Lord shall make him light (or and the Lord shall put him at ease); and if he be in sins, they shall be forgiven to him.

16 Therefore acknowledge ye each to (the) other your sins, and pray ye each for (the) other, (so) that ye be saved. For the continual prayer of a just man is (of) much worth.

17 Elias was a deadly man like us (or Elijah was a mortal man like us), and in prayer he prayed, that it should not rain on the earth, and it rained not (for) three years and six months.

18 And again he prayed, and heaven gave rain, and the earth gave his fruit (or and the land brought forth its fruit).

19 And, brethren, if any of you erreth from (the) truth, and any converteth him,

20 he oweth to know, that he that maketh a sinner to be turned from the error of his way(s), shall save the soul of him from death, and covereth the multitude of sins. [Amen.] (he ought to know, that he who maketh a sinner to turn from the error of his ways, shall save his soul from death, and covereth a multitude of sins. Amen.) †

1ST PETER

CHAPTER 1

1 Peter, (an) apostle of Jesus Christ, to the chosen men, to the comelings of (the) scattering abroad, [or to the chosen guests, *or (the) comelings*, of (the) dispersion, *or the scattering abroad*], (or who be the newcomers, or the strangers, in the scattering abroad, or in the dispersion, or the Diaspora), of Pontus, of Galatia, of Cappadocia, of Asia, and of Bithynia,

2 by the before-knowing [or the prescience] of God, the Father, in (the) hallowing of (the) Spirit, (or by the consecrating, or the sanctifying, of the Spirit), by (the) obedience, and (the) sprinkling of the blood of Jesus Christ, grace and peace be multiplied to you.

3 Blessed *be* God, and the Father of our Lord Jesus Christ, which by his great mercy begat us again into (a) living hope, by the again-rising of Jesus Christ from death, [or by the again-rising of Jesus Christ from (the) dead], (or by the resurrection of Jesus Christ from the dead),

4 into (a) heritage uncorruptible, and undefouled, and that shall not fade, that is kept in heavens for you, (to an incorruptible and undefiled inheritance, that shall not fade, and that is kept for you in heaven,)

5 that in the virtue of God be kept by the faith into health, and is ready to be showed in the last time. (who by the power of God be kept by the faith unto salvation, and is ready to be shown on the Last Day or at the Time of the End.)

6 In which ye shall make joy, though it behooveth now a little to be sorry in diverse temptations; (On which Day ye shall have joy, though it behooveth now to be sorrowful for a while, enduring different tests;)

7 (so) that the proving of your faith be much more precious than gold, that is proved by fire; and be found into praising, and glory, and honour, in the revelation of Jesus Christ.

8 Whom when ye have not seen, ye love; into whom also now ye not seeing, believe; but ye that believe shall have joy, and gladness that may not be told out, (or but ye who believe shall have joy, yea, joy that cannot be told out), and ye shall be glorified,

9 and have [or bring again] the end of your faith, the health of your souls. (and receive the completion of your faith, yea, the salvation of your souls.)

10 Of which health prophets sought [out], (or Of which salvation the prophets sought out), and searched into, that prophesied of the grace to coming in you, [Of which health prophets sought out, and ensearched, that prophesied of the grace to come into you,]

11 and sought which either what manner time the Spirit of Christ signified in them, and before-told those passions that be in Christ, and the latter glories. (and sought at what time and in what manner the Spirit of the Messiah signified to them, and foretold the sufferings that be for the Messiah, and the latter glories.)

12 To which it was showed, for not to themselves, but to you they ministered those things, that now be told to you by them that preached to you by the Holy Ghost (or which now be told to you by those who preached to you through the Holy Spirit), sent from heaven, into whom angels desire to behold.

13 For which thing be ye gird the loins of your soul, sober (or resolute), perfect, *and* hope ye into that grace that is proffered to you by the showing of Jesus Christ [or and hope ye into that grace that is offered to you by the revelation of Jesus Christ],

14 as sons of obedience, not made like to the former desires of your uncunningness, (or your unknowingness), [or of your ignorance],

15 but like him that hath called you holy; (so)

that also yourselves be holy in all living;

16   for it is written, Ye shall be holy, for I am holy.

17   And if ye inwardly call him Father, which deemeth without acception of persons by the work of each man, live ye in dread in the time of your pilgrimage [*in*, (or on), (the) *earth*]; (And if ye inwardly call him Father, who judgeth without respect for persons, or without favouritism, but rather, according to the works of each man, live ye in fearful reverence during the time of your pilgrimage *on the earth*;)

18   witting that not by corruptible gold, either silver, ye be bought again of your vain living of (your) fathers' tradition, (knowing that not by corruptible gold, or silver, ye be redeemed, or released, from the empty and useless living of your fathers' traditions,)

19   (no) but by the precious blood as of the lamb undefouled and unspotted, Christ Jesus, (but rather, by the precious blood as of an undefiled and unspotted lamb, yea, the Messiah Jesus,)

20   that was known before the making of the world, but he is showed in the last times, for you (who was known before the creation of the world, but he was shown in these Last Times, for you)

21   that by him be faithful in God; that raised him from death [or that raised him from (the) dead], and gave to him everlasting glory, (so) that your faith and hope were in God.

22   And make ye chaste your souls in obedience of charity, in love of (the) brotherhood; of simple heart love ye together more busily (or with a sincere heart love one another more diligently).

23   *And be ye* born again, not of corruptible seed, but [of] uncorruptible (seed), by the word of (the) living God, and dwelling into without end (or and living forever).

24   For each flesh *is* (as) hay, and all the glory of it *is* as the flower of hay; the hay dried up, and his (or its) flower felled down;

25   but the word of the Lord dwelleth [into] without end (or but the word of the Lord remaineth forever). And this is the word, that is preached to you.

CHAPTER 2

1   Therefore put ye away all malice, and all guile, and feignings [or simulations], and envies, and all backbitings [or all detractions];

2   as now born young children, reasonable, without guile, covet ye (the) milk [*of full teaching*], that in it ye wax into health (or so that by it ye grow in your salvation);

3   if nevertheless ye have tasted, that the Lord is sweet.

4   And nigh ye to him, that is a living stone, and reproved of men, but chosen of God, and honoured; (And come near to him, who is a living stone, and rebuked and rejected by men, but chosen and honoured by God;)

5   and yourselves as quick stones (or and yourselves like living stones), be ye above builded into spiritual houses, and an holy priesthood, to offer spiritual sacrifices, acceptable to God by Jesus Christ.

6   For which thing the scripture saith, Lo! I shall set in Sion [or I shall put in Sion] the highest cornerstone, chosen and precious; and he that shall believe in him, shall not be confounded. (For which thing the Scripture saith, Behold, I shall put in Zion the highest cornerstone, chosen and precious; and he who shall believe in him, shall not be shamed.)

7   Therefore honour to you that believe; but to men that believe not, the stone whom the builders reproved, this is made into the head of the corner; (And so honour to you who believe; but to those who do not believe, the stone which the builders rejected, this is made into the head of the corner;)

8   and the stone of hurting, and the stone of stumbling, to them that offend to the word (or to those who stumble at the word), neither

believe *it*, in which they be set.

9 But ye *be* a chosen kin [or Forsooth ye *be* a kind (that was) chosen], a kingly priesthood, (a) holy folk, a people of purchasing, that ye tell the virtues of him, that called you from darknesses into his wonderful light, (or so that ye tell out his praises, he who called you from darkness into his wonderful light).

10 Which sometime were not a people of God, but now ye be the people of God; which had not mercy, but now ye have mercy.

11 Most dear (ones), I beseech you, as comelings, [or as guests], (or as newcomers), and pilgrims, to abstain you from fleshly desires, that fight against the soul;

12 and have ye your conversation [or your life] good among heathen men, that in that thing that they backbite of you, as of mis-doers, they behold you of good works, and glorify God in the day of visitation. (and live a good life among the Gentiles, so that in those things in which they now slander you, as mis-doers, they shall instead see your good works, and glorify God on the Day of Visitation.)

13 Be ye subject to each creature of man, for God, (or Be subject to each creation, or to each institution of man, for God); either to the king, as to him that is higher [or is more worthy] in state,

14 either to dukes, as to those that be sent of him to the vengeance of mis-doers, and to the praising of good men [or of good deeds].

15 For so is the will of God, that ye do well, and make the uncunningness, (or the unknowingness, or the ignorance) of unprudent men [or of unwise men] to be dumb (or to be silent).

16 As free men, and not as having freedom the covering of malice, but as the servants of God.

17 Honour ye all men, love ye (the) brotherhood, dread ye God (or have fearful reverence toward God), honour ye the king.

18 Servants, be ye subject in all dread to (your) lords, not only to good and to mild (ones), but also to tyrants. (Servants, be subject in all fear or with all due respect, or reverence, for your lords, not only to good and to meek ones, but also to tyrants.)

19 For this is grace, if for conscience of God any man suffereth heavinesses [or sorrows], and suffereth unjustly.

20 For what grace is it, if ye sin, and be buffeted, and suffer? But if ye do well, and suffer patiently, this is grace with God.

21 For to this thing ye be called. For also Christ suffered for us, and left (an) ensample to you, that ye follow the steps of him. (For to this ye be called. For the Messiah also suffered for us, and left an example for you, so that ye follow his steps.)

22 Which did not sin, neither guile was found in his mouth. (Who did not sin, nor was a lie ever found in his mouth, or nor did a lie ever come out of his mouth.)

23 And when he was cursed, he cursed not; when he suffered, he menaced not; but he betook himself to him, that deemed him unjustly. (And when he was cursed, he did not curse back; when he suffered, he did not threaten; but he delivered himself unto him, who judged him unjustly.)

24 And he himself bare [or suffered] our sins in his body on a tree, (so) that we be dead to sins, and live to rightwiseness, by whose wan wound ye be healed.

25 For ye were as sheep erring, but ye be now turned to the shepherd [or but ye be converted now to the shepherd], and (the) bishop (or the High Priest) of your souls.

CHAPTER 3

1 Also women be they subject to their husbands; that if any man, *that is*, (their) *husbands*, believe not to the word, by the conversation of women they (shall) be won without (any) word(s). (And women should be

subject to their husbands; so that if their husbands do not believe the word of God, by the way their women live these men shall be won without any words.)

2 And behold ye in dread your holy conversation. (And so, ye women, watch over your pure way of living, with a fear of losing it.)

3 Of whom be there not withoutforth curious adorning of hair, either doing about of gold, either adorning of clothing;

4 but that that is the hid man of (the) heart, in uncorruption, and of mild spirit, [or in (the) uncorruptibility of (a) quiet and mild spirit], which is rich in the sight of God. (but within, yea, hidden in the heart, and with a meek and a humble spirit, which is rich before God.)

5 For so sometime holy women hoping in God adorned themselves, and were subject to their own husbands.

6 As Sara(h) obeyed to Abraham, and called him lord; of whom ye be daughters well-doing, and not dreading any perturbation.

7 Also men dwell together, and by cunning, (or knowing), [or science], give ye honour to the woman's frailty, [or to her vessel], (or to her body), as to the more feeble, and as to even-heirs of grace and of life, (so) that your prayers be not hindered.

8 And in faith all of one will (or of one intention), in prayer be ye each suffering with (the) other, lovers of (the) brotherhood, merciful, mild (or humble), meek; [Forsooth in faith all of one understanding, or will, in prayer be ye compassionate, or each suffering with (the) other, lovers of (the) fraternity, merciful, mild, meek;]

9 not yielding evil for evil, neither cursing for cursing, but on the contrary blessing; for in this thing ye be called, that ye wield blessing by heritage (or so that ye can possess the blessing by inheritance).

10 For he that will love life, and see good days, constrain his tongue from evil, and his lips, that they speak not guile, [or that they

speak no guile], (or so that they do not speak lies).

11 And bow he (away) from evil, and do good; seek he peace, and perfectly follow it.

12 For the eyes of the Lord *be* on just men, and his ears on the prayers of them; but the cheer [or the face] of the Lord *is* on men that do evils.

13 And who is it that shall annoy you, if ye be (pur)suers and lovers of goodness? [And who is it that shall annoy to you, if ye shall be good (pur)suers?] (And who is it that shall harm you, if ye be followers and lovers of goodness, or if ye pursue after that which is good?)

14 But also if ye suffer anything for rightwiseness, ye be blessed; but dread ye not the dread of them (or but do not fear them), (so) that ye be not disturbed [or distroubled].

15 But hallow ye the Lord Christ in your hearts, and (for)evermore be ye ready to [*do*] satisfaction to each man asking you (for the) reason of that faith and hope that is in you, but with mildness, and dread, (But consecrate the Lord Messiah in your hearts, and always be ye ready to *give* satisfaction to each man asking you for the reason for the faith and hope that is in you, but with meekness and humility, and fearful reverence,)

16 having good conscience; that in that thing that they backbite of you, they be confounded, which challenge falsely your good conversation in Christ. (having a clear conscience; so that for that thing in which they slander you, they shall be ashamed, yea, they who defame your pure life in the Messiah.)

17 For it is better that ye do well, and suffer, if the will of God will, than doing evil. [Soothly it is better, if the will of God will, ye well-doing, to suffer, than evil-doing.] (For it is better that ye do good, and suffer, if it be God's will, than to do evil.)

18 For also Christ once died for our sins, he (the) just for (the) unjust, that he should offer to God us [or that he should offer us to God],

made dead in (the) flesh, but made quick in (the) Spirit. (For also the Messiah once died for our sins, or For the Messiah also died for our sins once and for all, he the righteous for the unrighteous, so that he could offer us to God, made dead in the flesh, but made alive in the Spirit.)

19 For which thing he came in (the) Spirit, and also to them that were (en)closed together in prison;

20 which were sometime unbelieveful, when they abided the patience of God in the days of Noe (or of Noah), when the ship [or the ark] was made, in which a few, that is to say, eight souls were made safe by water (or eight lives were saved through water).

21 And so baptism of like form maketh us safe; not the putting away of the filths of (the) flesh, but the asking of a good conscience in God, by the again-rising of our Lord Jesus Christ, (And so a baptism of like form saveth us; not the putting away of the filths of the flesh, but the asking by a good conscience to God, through the resurrection of our Lord Jesus Christ,)

22 that is in the right half of God, and swalloweth death, that we should be made heirs of everlasting life, (or who is at the right hand, or on the right side, of God, and swalloweth death, so that we can be made heirs of eternal life). He went into heaven, and angels, and powers, and virtues (or authorities) be made subject to him.

CHAPTER 4

1 Therefore for Christ suffered in (the) flesh (or And so because the Messiah suffered in the flesh), be ye also armed by the same thinking; for he that suffered in (the) flesh ceased from sins,

2 that that is left now of (the) time in (the) flesh live not now to the desires of men, but to the will of God.

3 For the time that is passed is enough to the will of (the) heathen men to be ended, which walked in lecheries, and lusts, in much drinking of wine, in unmeasurable [or oft] eatings, and drinkings, and unleaveful worshipping of maumets [or of idols]. (For the time that is passed was enough for the desires of the Gentiles to be done, or to be finished, yea, they who lived, or went, in lecheries, and lusts, in much drinking of wine, in immeasurable or oft eatings, and drinkings, and unlawful worshipping of idols.)

4 In which now they be astonied (or astonished), in which thing they wonder (about), for ye run not together (with them) into the same confusion of lechery, and (so they) blaspheme (thee), (or and so they insult thee, or they vilify thee).

5 And they shall give reason to him, that is ready to deem the quick and the dead. (But soon they shall have to give an answer to him, who is ready to judge the living and the dead.)

6 For why for this thing it is preached [or it is evangelized] also to dead men, that they be deemed by men in (the) flesh, and that they live by God in (the) Spirit.

7 For the end of all things shall nigh. Therefore be ye prudent, and wake ye in prayers; (For the end of everything shall approach or it is near. And so be prudent, and be on watch, keep praying;)

8 before all things have ye charity each to (the) other in yourselves always lasting; for charity covereth the multitude of sins. (above all, love one another always and earnestly; for love covereth a multitude of sins.)

9 Hold ye hospitality together without grudging; (Have hospitality toward one another without grumbling;)

10 each man as he hath received grace, ministering it into each other, [or ministering each to (the) other], (or serving one another), as good dispensers of the manifold grace of God.

11 If any man speaketh, *speak he* as the

words of God; if any man ministereth, as of the virtue which God ministereth; (so) that God be honoured in all things by Jesus Christ our Lord, to whom is glory and lordship into worlds of worlds. Amen. (If anyone speaketh, *speak he* with the words of God; if anyone serveth, *serve he* with the strength which God supplieth; so that God be honoured in all things by Jesus Christ our Lord, to whom is glory and lordship forever and ever. Amen.)

12   Most dear *brethren*, do not ye go in pilgrimage in fervour, that is made to you to temptation (or that is made to test you), as if any new thing befall to you;

13   but commune ye with the passions of Christ, and have ye joy, (or but share in the sufferings of the Messiah, and rejoice), (so) that also ye be glad, and have joy in the revelation of his glory.

14   If ye be despised for the name of Christ, ye shall be blessed; for that that is of the honour, and of the glory, and of the virtue of God, and the Spirit that is his, shall rest on you. (If ye be despised for the name of the Messiah, ye shall be blessed; for that that is of the honour, and of the glory, and of the power of God, and the Spirit that is his, shall rest upon you.)

15   But no man of you suffer as a manslayer, either a thief, either curser, either a desirer of other men's goods [or of other men's things];

16   but if *he suffer* as a christian man, shame he not (or be he not ashamed), but glorify he God in this name.

17   For (the) time is, that doom begin at God's house; and if *it begin* first at us, what end *shall be* of them, that believe not to the gospel? (For it is now the time that judgement begin at God's household; and if *it begin* first with us, what end *shall be* for those, who do not believe the Gospel or the Good News?)

18   And if a just man scarcely shall be saved, where shall the unfaithful man and the sinner appear?

19   Therefore and they that suffer by the will of God, betake their souls in good deeds to the faithful Maker of nought. (And so let them who suffer by God's will, deliver their souls through good deeds unto the faithful Maker of everything out of nothing.)

CHAPTER 5

1   Therefore I, an even-elder man, and a witness of Christ's passions, which also *am a* communer of that glory, that shall be showed in (the) time to come; beseech the elder men, that be among you, (And so I, a fellow elder, and a witness of the Messiah's sufferings, who also *shall* partake of, or *shall* share in, that glory, which shall be shown, or shall be revealed, in the time to come; yea, I beseech the elders, who be among you,)

2   feed ye the flock of God, that is among you, and purvey ye, not as constrained, but willfully, by God; not for love of foul winning, but willfully, (feed the flock of God, who be among you, yea, provide for them, not like someone who is compelled, but willingly, or by free will, through God; not for the love of foul gain, or for immoral profit, but willingly, or by free will,)

3   neither as having lordship in the clergy, but (so) that ye be made (an) ensample to the flock, of (free) will [or by intent].

4   And when the prince of shepherds shall appear, ye shall receive the crown of glory, that may never fade (or that can never fade).

5   Also, ye young men, be ye subject to elder men, and all show ye together meekness (or and all of you show humility and humbleness before them); for the Lord withstandeth proud men, but he giveth grace to meek men.

6   Therefore be ye meeked under the mighty hand of God, that he raise you in the time [or in the day] of visitation, (And so be humble under the mighty hand of God, so that he can raise

you up at the Time of Visitation, or on the Day of Visitation,)

7 and cast ye all your busyness into him, for to him is (the) care of you. (and throw all your concerns onto him, for he careth for you.)

8 Be ye sober, and wake ye, (or Be resolute, and be on watch), for your adversary, the devil, as a roaring lion goeth about, seeking whom he shall devour.

9 Whom against-stand ye, strong in the faith, witting that the same passion is made to that brotherhood of you, that is in the world. (Yea, he whom you must stand against, or whom you must withstand, being strong in the faith, and knowing that your brothers, who be in the world, experience the same suffering.)

10 And God of all grace, that called you into his everlasting glory, you suffering a little [in Christ Jesus], (or though you do suffer now for a short time in the Messiah Jesus), he shall

perform, and shall confirm, and shall make firm.

11 To him *be* glory and lordship, into worlds of worlds (or forever and ever). Amen.

12 By Silvanus, [a] faithful brother to you as I deem, I wrote shortly; beseeching, and witnessing that this is the very grace of God, in which ye stand. (I have written this short letter by Silvanus, a faithful brother of yours whom I trust; beseeching, and testifying that this is the true grace of God, in which ye should stand.)

13 The church that is gathered in Babylon, and Marcus, my son, greeteth you well. (The church that is gathered in Babylon, and my son Mark, send you hearty greetings.)

14 Greet ye well together in holy kiss. Grace *be* to you all that be in Christ. Amen. (Give hearty greetings to one another with a holy kiss. Grace *be* to all of you who be in the Messiah. Amen.) †

2ND PETER

CHAPTER 1

1   Simon Peter, (a) servant and (an) apostle of Jesus Christ, to them that have taken with us the even-faith (or to those who have received the same faith as us), in the rightwiseness of our God and Saviour Jesus Christ,

2   grace and peace be [full-]filled to you, by the knowing of our Lord Jesus Christ.

3   How all things of his god-like virtue, that be to life and piety, be given to us, by the knowing of him, that called us for his own glory and virtue. (How all the things of his godly or his divine power, which be for life and piety, be given to us, through the knowledge of him, who called us to share in his own glory and power.)

4   By whom he gave to us most precious promises; that by these things ye shall be made fellows of God's kind (or of God's kin), and flee the corruption of that covetousness, that is in the world.

5   And bring ye in all busyness, and minister in your faith (with) virtue, and in virtue cunning, (or knowing), [or science], (or and with virtue knowledge);

6   in cunning, (or in knowing), [or in science], abstinence, in abstinence patience, in patience piety; (and with knowledge abstinence, with abstinence patience, with patience piety;)

7   in piety, love of (the) brotherhood, and in (the) love of (the) brotherhood charity. (with piety, love of the brotherhood, and with the love of the brotherhood kindness.)

8   For if these be with you, and overcome, [or be plenteous], they shall not make you void, (or empty and useless), neither without fruit, in the knowing of our Lord Jesus Christ.

9   But to whom these be not ready, he is blind, and gropeth with his hand, and forgetteth the purging of his old trespasses.

10   Wherefore, brethren, be ye more busy, (so) that by good works ye make your calling and choosing certain; for ye doing these things, shall not do sin any time, [or soothly ye doing these things, shall not sin any time].

11   For thus the entering into [the] everlasting kingdom of our Lord and Saviour Jesus Christ, shall be ministered to you plenteously. (And so your entrance into the eternal kingdom of our Lord and Saviour Jesus Christ, shall abundantly be afforded you.)

12   For which thing I shall begin to admonish you (for)evermore of these things; and I will, that ye be cunning (or knowing), and confirmed in this present truth. (For which thing I shall always admonish you about these things; and I desire, that ye know, or have knowledge of, and be confirmed, or established, in this truth that is present with you.)

13   Forsooth I deem justly [or Forsooth I deem (it) just], as long as I am in this tabernacle, to raise you in admonishing; (For I judge it just or appropriate, for as long as I am in this body, to remind you of these things;)

14   and I *am* certain, that the putting away [or the putting off] of my tabernacle is swift, by this that our Lord Jesus Christ hath showed to me.

15   But I shall give busyness, that oft after my death ye have mind of these things. (But I shall make every effort now, so that after my death ye shall often remember these things.)

16   For we not (pur)suing unwise tales (or For we not following unwise tales), have made known to you the virtue (or the power) and the before-knowing [or the prescience] of our Lord Jesus Christ; but we were made beholders of his greatness.

17   For he took of God the Father honour and glory, by such manner voice slid down to him from the great glory, This is my (be)loved Son, in whom I have pleased to me; hear ye him. (For he received honour and glory from God

the Father, when that voice came down to him from the Great Glory, saying, This is my beloved Son, in whom I am pleased; listen to him.)

18   And we heard this voice brought from heaven, when we were with him in the holy hill (or when we were with him on the Mount of Transfiguration).

19   And we have a firmer word of prophecy, to which ye giving attention do well, as to a lantern that giveth light in a dark place, till the day begin to give light, and the day star spring in your hearts.

20   And first understand ye this thing, that each prophecy of scripture is not made by proper [or by (one's) own] interpretation;

21   for prophecy was not brought any time by man's will, but the holy men of God inspired with the Holy Ghost spake. (for prophecy was not brought forth at any time by man's will, but rather, the saints of God, or God's people, inspired by the Holy Spirit spoke it forth.)

CHAPTER 2

1   But also false prophets were in the people, as in you shall be masters liars, (or who be lying teachers, or false teachers), that shall bring in sects of perdition; and they deny that Lord that bought them, and bring on themselves hasty perdition [or damnation].

2   And many shall (pur)sue their lecheries, by whom the way of truth shall be blasphemed; (And many shall follow their lusts, by whom the Way of Truth shall be blasphemed;)

3   and they shall make merchandise of you in covetousness by feigned words. To whom doom (or judgement) now a while ago ceaseth not, and the perdition of them nappeth not.

4   For if God spared not (the) angels sinning, but betook them to be tormented, and to be drawn down with bonds of hell into hell, to be kept into doom (or to be kept unto the Day of Judgement);

5   and spared not the first world, but kept Noe (or Noah), the eighth man, the before-goer of rightwiseness, and brought in the great flood [or the deluge] to the world of unfaithful men;

6   and he drove (down) into powder the cities of (the) men of Sodom and of (the) men of Gomorrha (or of Gomorrah), and condemned (them) by turning (them) upside-down, and put them the ensample of them that were to doing evil, [or were doing unpiously], (or and made them an example for those who were doing evil);

7   and delivered the just Lot, oppressed of the wrong, and of the lecherous conversation of cursed men; (and saved Lot, a good man, who was oppressed by all the wrong-doing, and by the lecherous living of cursed men;)

8   for in sight and hearing he was just, and dwelled amongst them that from day into day tormented with wicked works a just soul.

9   For the Lord knoweth how to deliver pious men from temptation, and keep wicked men into the day of doom, to be tormented; (For the Lord knoweth how to deliver pious men from testing, and to keep, or to reserve, the wicked under torment, unto the Day of Judgement;)

10   but more them that walk after the flesh, in coveting of uncleanness, and despise lordshipping, and be bold, pleasing themselves, and dread not to bring in sects, blaspheming, (or and fear not to bring in blaspheming sects);

11   where angels, when they be more in strength and virtue (or power), bear not the execrable doom [or the cursed judgement] against them(selves).

12   But these *be* as unreasonable beasts, kindly, (or by kind, or naturally), into taking, and into death, blaspheming in these things that they know not, and shall perish in their corruption,

13   and receive the hire (or the wages) of unrightwiseness. And they guess delights of defouling and of wem, to be (the) likings of the

day, (or And they think that the delights of defilement, and of spot, or of blemish, to be the pleasures of the day), flowing in their feasts with delights, doing lechery with you,

14　and have eyes full of adultery, and unceasing trespass, deceiving unsteadfast souls, and have the heart exercised to covetousness; the sons of cursing,

15　that forsake the right way, and erred, (pur)suing the way of Balaam of Bosor, which loved the hire of wickedness. (who forsake the right way, and erred, following the way of Balaam of Bosor, who loved the wages, or the recompense, for doing wickedness.)

16　But he had reproving [or correction] of (or for) his madness; a dumb beast under yoke, that spake with (the) voice of (a) man, that forbade the unwisdom of the prophet.

17　These be wells without water, and mists driven with whirlwinds [or and clouds driven with whirling winds], to whom the thick mist of darknesses is reserved.

18　And they speak in (the) pride of vanity, and deceive in (the) desires of (the) flesh of lechery them, that escape a little. Which live in error,

19　and promise freedom [or liberty] to them, when they be (the) servants of corruption. For of whom any man is overcome, of him also he is (their) servant.

20　For if men forsake the uncleannesses of the world, by the knowing of our Lord and Saviour Jesus Christ, and again be [en]wrapped in these, and be overcome, the latter things be made to them worse than the former.

21　For it was better to them to not know the way of rightwiseness, than to turn again after the knowing, from that holy commandment that was betaken to them. (For it would have been better for them to have never known the way of righteousness, than to turn away after knowing it, yea, from that holy commandment that was delivered to them.)

22　For that very proverb befelled to them,

The hound (re)turned again to his vomit, *or casting* (up), and a sow *is* washed in wallowing in fen [or in clay]. (This proverb hath proven true for them, A dog returneth to its vomit, and after a pig *hath* washed itself, it walloweth again in the mire.)

CHAPTER 3

1　Lo! ye most dearworthy brethren, I write to you this second epistle, in which I stir your clear soul by admonishing together,

2　that ye be mindful of those words (or so that ye remember those words), that I before-said of the holy prophets, and of the commandments of the holy apostles of the Lord and Saviour.

3　First know ye this thing, that in the last days deceivers [or scorners] shall come in deceit, (or with guile, and treachery), going after their own covetings,

4　saying, Where is the promise, or the coming of him? for since the fathers died [or slept], all things last from the beginning of creature (or everything is as it was from the beginning of Creation).

5　But it is hid from them willing this thing (or But it is hidden from those, or unknown to those, desiring this), that (the) heavens were before, and the earth of water was standing by (the) water, by God's word; [Soothly it is hid from them willing this thing, that (the) heavens were first, and the earth of water and by water being, *or standing*, together by God's word;]

6　by which that same world (was) cleansed, then by water perished.

7　But the heavens that now be, and the earth, be kept by the same word, and be reserved to fire into the day of doom (or and be reserved for the fire unto the Day of Judgement), and (the) perdition of wicked men.

8　But, ye most dear (ones), this one thing be not hid to you, [or be not unknown], (or let not this be hidden from you, or be unknown to you), that one day with God *is* as a thousand years, and a thousand years *be* as one day.

9 The Lord tarrieth not his promise, as some [men] guess, but he doeth patiently for you, and will not that any man perish [or not willing any to perish], but that all turn again to penance. (The Lord delayeth not his promise, as some think, but he patiently waiteth for you, and desireth not that anyone perish, but that all turn, or come to repentance.)

10 For the day of the Lord shall come as a thief, in which (the) heavens with great rush [or with (a) great fierceness] shall pass (away), and (the) elements shall be dissolved by heat, and the earth, and all the works that be in it, shall be burnt (up).

11 Therefore when all these things shall be dissolved, what manner men behooveth it you to be in holy livings and piety,

12 abiding and hieing into the coming of the day of our Lord Jesus Christ, by whom (the) heavens burning shall be dissolved, and (the) elements shall fail by (the) burning [or (from the) heat] of (the) fire.

13 Also we abide by his promises new heavens and (a) new earth, in which rightwiseness dwelleth.

14 For which thing, ye most dear (ones), abiding these things, be ye busy to be found to him in peace, unspotted and undefouled. (For which thing, ye most dear ones, awaiting these things, do your best to be found at peace with him, without fault or blemish, and undefiled.)

15 And deem ye (that the) long abiding of our Lord Jesus Christ (is) your health (or And understand well that the patience that our Lord Jesus Christ *hath with us* is our salvation), as also our most dear brother Paul wrote to you, by wisdom given to him.

16 As and in all his epistles he speaketh in them of these things; in which be some hard things to understand, which unwise [or untaught] and unstable men deprave, as also they do other scriptures, to their own perdition.

17 Therefore ye, brethren, before-witting keep yourselves, lest ye be deceived [or be over-led] by (the) error of unwise men, and fall away from your own firmness.

18 But wax ye (or grow) in the grace and the knowing of our Lord Jesus Christ and our Saviour; to him *be* glory now and into the day of everlastingness. Amen. †

1ST JOHN

CHAPTER 1

1 That thing that was from the beginning, which we heard, which we saw with our eyes, which we beheld, and our hands touched, of the word of life; (That which was from the beginning, which we heard, which we saw with our eyes, which we beheld, and our hands touched, of the Word of Life, or of the Living Word;)

2 and the life is showed. And we saw, and witness, and tell to you the everlasting life, that was with the Father, and appeared to us. (and that Life was shown. And we saw, and testify, and tell you about the Eternal Life, who was with the Father, and appeared to us.)

3 Therefore that thing, that we saw, and heard, we tell to you, (or And so that which we saw, and heard, we tell to you), (so) that also ye have fellowship with us, and our fellowship be with the Father, and with his Son Jesus Christ.

4 And we write this thing to you, that ye have joy, and that your joy be full. (And we write this to you, so that ye have joy, and that your joy be complete.)

5 And this is the telling, that we heard of him, and tell to you, that God is light, and there be no darknesses in him. (And this is the tiding, or the message, that we heard from him, and tell to you, that God is light, and there is no darkness in him.)

6 If we say, that we have fellowship with him, and we wander in darknesses (or and we walk in the darkness), we lie, and do not (have the) truth.

7 But if we walk in (the) light, as also he is in (the) light, we have fellowship together; and the blood of Jesus Christ, his Son, cleanseth us from all sin.

8 If we say, that we have no sin, we deceive ourselves, and (the) truth is not in us.

9 If we acknowledge our sins, he is faithful and just, that he forgive to us our sins, and cleanse us from all wickedness.

10 And if we say, that we have not sinned, we make him a liar, and his word is not in us.

CHAPTER 2

1 My little sons, I write to you these things, (so) that ye sin not. But if any man sinneth, we have an advocate with the Father, Jesus Christ (who is) [just],

2 and he is the forgiveness [or (the) helping] for our sins; and not only for our *sins*, but also for *the sins* of all the world.

3 And in this thing we know, that we know him, if we keep his commandments (or if we obey his commands).

4 He that saith that he knoweth God, and keepeth not his commandments, is a liar, and (the) truth is not in him. (He who saith that he knoweth God, and obeyeth not his commands, is a liar, and the truth is not in him.)

5 But the charity of God is perfect verily in him, that keepeth his word (or But the love of God is truly perfect in him, who obeyeth his word or his commands), [or Forsooth who keepeth his word, verily in him is perfect charity (or But who obeyeth his word, truly in him is perfect love)]. In this thing we know, that we be in him, if we be perfect in him.

6 He that saith, that he dwelleth in him, he oweth to walk, as he walked. (He who saith, that he remaineth in him, he ought to walk, like he walked.)

7 Most dear *brethren* (or Most dear *brothers*), I write to you, not a new commandment, but the old commandment, that ye had from the beginning. The old commandment is the word, that ye heard.

8 Again I write to you a new commandment, that is true both in him and in you; for (the) darknesses be passed (away), and very light shineth now, (or for the darkness hath

gone away, and the true light shineth now).

9 He that saith, that he is in (the) light, and hateth his brother, is in darknesses yet. (He who saith, that he is in the light, and hateth his brother, is still in darkness.)

10 He that loveth his brother, dwelleth in (the) light, (or He who loveth his brother, remaineth in the light), and (a) cause of stumbling is not in him.

11 But he that hateth his brother, is in darknesses, and wandereth in darknesses, and knoweth not whither he goeth; for darknesses have blinded his eyes. (But he who hateth his brother, is in darkness, and walketh in darkness, and knoweth not where he goeth; for the darkness hath blinded his eyes.)

12 Little sons, I write to you, that your sins be forgiven to you for (the sake of) his name. [Little sons, I write to you, for your sins be forgiven to you for his name.]

13 Fathers, I write to you, for ye have known him, that is from the beginning, (or Fathers, I write to you, because ye have known him, who is from the beginning). Young men, I write to you, for ye have overcome the wicked (one). I write to you, young children [or infants], for ye have known the Father.

14 I write to you, brethren, for ye have known him, that is from the beginning. I write to you, young men, for ye be strong, and the word of God dwelleth in you, and ye have overcome the wicked (one). (I write to you, brothers, for ye have known him, who is from the beginning. I write to you, young men, for ye be strong, and God's Word liveth in you, or and God's word remaineth in you, and ye have overcome the Wicked One.)

15 Do not ye love the world, nor those things that be in the world. If any man loveth the world, the charity of the Father is not in him. (Do not love the world, nor those things that be in the world. If anyone loveth the world, the love of the Father is not in them.)

16 For all thing that is in the world, is covetousness of (the) flesh, and covetousness of (the) eyes, and (the) pride of life, which is not of the Father, but it is of the world.

17 And the world shall pass (away), and the covetousness of it; but he that doeth the will of God, dwelleth [into] without end, (or but he who doeth God's will, remaineth forever, or liveth forever).

18 My little sons, the last hour is; and as ye have heard, that (the) antichrist cometh, now many antichrists be made; wherefore we know, that it is the last hour. (My little sons, it is the Last Hour; and as ye have heard, that the Anti-Messiah, or the False Messiah, or the Enemy of the Messiah, cometh, and that now many anti-messiahs have appeared; and so we know, that it is the Last Hour.)

19 They went forth from us, but they were not of us; for if they had been of us, they had dwelt with us; but that they be known, that they be not all of us. (They went out from us, but they were not of us; for if they had been of us, they would have remained with us; but now they be known, or but now it be known, that they be not of us.)

20 But ye have (an) anointing [or (an) unction] of the Holy Ghost, and know all things. (But ye have an anointing of the Holy Spirit, and know everything, or and know all the truth.)

21 I wrote not to you, as to men that know not the truth, but as to men that know it, and for each leasing is not of truth (or and because every lie is not of the truth).

22 Who is a liar, [no] but this that denieth that Jesus is not Christ? This is (the) antichrist, that denieth the Father, and the Son. (Who is a liar? none but he who denieth that Jesus is the Messiah. This is the Anti-Messiah, or the False Messiah, or the Enemy of the Messiah, who denieth the Father, and the Son.)

23 For each that denieth the Son, hath not the Father; but he that acknowledgeth the Son, hath also the Father.

24 That thing that ye heard at [or from] the beginning, dwell it in you; for if that thing

dwelleth in you, which ye heard at (or from) the beginning, ye shall dwell in the Son and in the Father. (That which ye heard from the beginning, let it remain in you; for if that remaineth in you, which ye have heard from the beginning, ye shall remain in the Son and in the Father.)

25 And this is the promise, that he promised to us, everlasting life, (or Eternal Life, or eternal life).

26 I wrote these things to you, of them that deceive you, (I wrote these things to you, about those who deceive you,)

27 and that the anointing which ye received of him, dwell in you. And ye have not need, that any man teach you, but as his anointing teacheth you of all things, and it is true, and it is not leasing; and as he taught you, dwell ye in him. (and so that the anointing which ye have received from him, remain in you. And ye have no need, that any man teach you, for his anointing teacheth you everything, and it is true, and it is not a lie; and so as he taught you, remain in him, or live in him.)

28 And now, ye little sons, dwell ye in him, that when he shall appear, we have trust, and be not confounded of him in his coming. (And now, ye little sons, remain in him, so that when he shall appear, we have trust, and be not ashamed of him at his coming.)

29 If ye know that he is just, know ye that also each that doeth rightwiseness, is born of him. (If ye know that he is just or is righteous, know also that each one who doeth righteousness, is his child.)

CHAPTER 3

1 See ye what manner charity the Father gave to us (or See what kind of love the Father gave us), that we be named the sons of God, and be *his sons*. For this thing the world knew not us, for it knew not him.

2 Most dear *brethren* (or Most dear *brothers*), now we be the sons of God, and yet it appeared not, what we shall be. We know, that when he shall appear, we shall be like him, for we shall see him as he is.

3 And each man that hath this hope in him, maketh himself holy, as he is holy.

4 Each man that doeth sin, doeth also wickedness, and sin is wickedness.

5 And ye know, that he appeared to do away sins, and sin is not in him.

6 Each man that dwelleth in him, sinneth not; and each that sinneth, seeth not him, neither knew him. (Each one who remaineth in him, or who liveth in him, sinneth not; and each one who sinneth, seeth not him, nor knoweth him.)

7 Little sons, (let) no man deceive you; he that doeth rightwiseness, is just, as also he is just.

8 He that doeth sin, is of the devil; for the devil sinneth from the beginning. In this thing the Son of God appeared, that he undo the works of the devil. (He who doeth sin, is of the Devil; for the Devil sinneth from the beginning. The Son of God appeared for this, yea, that he destroy the works of the Devil.)

9 Each man that is born of God, doeth not sin; for the seed of God dwelleth in him, and he may not do sin, for he is born of God. (Each one who is born of God, or who is a child of God, sinneth not; for God's seed liveth in him, and so he cannot do sin, for he is born of God or he is a child of God.)

10 In this thing the sons of God be known, and the sons of the fiend, (or By this the sons of God be known, and also the sons of the Devil). Each man that is not just, is not of God, and he that loveth not his brother [*is not of God*].

11 For this is the telling, that ye heard at the beginning, that ye love each other; (For this is the tiding, or the message, that ye heard from the beginning, that ye should love one another;)

12 not as Cain, that was of the devil, and slew his brother. And for what thing slew he him? for his works were evil, and his brother's (were) just. (not as Cain, who was of the Devil, and murdered his brother. And why did he

murder him? for his works were evil, and his brother's works were righteous.)

13 Brethren (or Brothers), do not ye wonder, if the world hateth you.

14 We know, that we be translated from death to life, for we love (the) brethren. He that loveth not, (yet) dwelleth in death. (We know, that we be transferred from death unto life, for we love the brothers. He who loveth not, remaineth yet in death, or still liveth in death.)

15 Each man that hateth his brother, is a manslayer; and ye know, that each manslayer hath not everlasting life dwelling in him. (Each one who hateth his brother, is a murderer; and ye know, that no murderer hath Eternal Life living within him, or that no murderer hath eternal life dwelling within him.)

16 In this thing we have known the charity of God, for he put his life for us, and we owe to put our lives for our brethren. (In this we have known the love of God, for he gave his life for us, and so we ought to give our lives for our brothers.)

17 He that hath the chattel [or the substance] of this world, and seeth that his brother hath need, and closeth his entrails from him, how dwelleth the charity of God in him? (or how can he say that the love of God dwelleth within him?)

18 My little sons, love we not in word, neither in tongue, but in work and truth.

19 In this thing we know, that we be of (the) truth, and in his sight we admonish our hearts.

20 For if our heart reproveth us (or For if our conscience rebuketh us), God is more than our heart, and knoweth all things.

21 Most dear *brethren*, if our heart reproveth not us, we have trust to God; (Most dear *brothers*, if our conscience rebuketh us not, then we have God's trust;)

22 and whatever we shall ask, we shall receive of him, for we keep his commandments, and we do those things that be pleasant before him. (and whatever we shall ask, we shall receive from him, for we obey his commands, and we do

those things that be pleasing before him.)

23 And this is the commandment of God, that we believe in the name of his Son Jesus Christ, and that we love each other, as he gave behest to us. (And this is God's command, that we believe in the name of his Son Jesus Christ, and that we love one another, as he commanded us.)

24 And he that keepeth his commandments, dwelleth in him, and he in him, (or And he who obeyeth his commands, remaineth in him, and he in him). And in this thing we know, that he dwelleth in us, by the Spirit, whom he gave to us.

CHAPTER 4

1 Most dear *brethren*, do not ye believe to each spirit, but prove ye the spirits, if they be of God, (or Most dear *brothers*, do not believe every spirit, but rather, test the spirits, to see if they be from God); for many false prophets went out into the world.

2 In this thing the Spirit of God is known; each spirit that acknowledgeth that Jesus Christ hath come in (the) flesh, is of God; (The Spirit of God is known by this; every spirit that acknowledgeth that Jesus Christ hath come in the flesh, is from God;)

3 and each spirit that undoeth Jesus, is not of God. And this is (of the) antichrist, of whom ye have heard, that he cometh; and right now he is in the world. (and every spirit that will not acknowledge Jesus, is not from God. Rather they be from the Anti-Messiah, or the False Messiah, or the Enemy of the Messiah, of whom ye have heard, that he cometh; and right now he is in the world.)

4 Ye, little sons, be of God, and ye have overcome him; for he that is in you is more, than he that *is* in the world, (or for he who is in you is greater, than he who *is* in the world).

5 They be of the world, therefore they speak of the world, (or and so they speak about the world), and the world heareth them.

6 We be of God; he that knoweth God, heareth us; he that is not of God, heareth not us. In this thing we know the spirit of truth, and the spirit of error.

7 Most dear *brethren*, love we together, for charity is of God; and each that loveth his brother, is born of God, and knoweth God. (Most dear *brothers*, love one another, for love is from God; and each one who loveth his brother, is born of God, or is a child of God, and knoweth God.)

8 He that loveth not, knoweth not God; for God is charity (or for God is love).

9 In this thing, the charity of God appeared in us, (or In this, the love of God appeared to us), for God sent his one begotten Son into the world, (so) that we live by him.

10 In this thing is charity, not as we had loved God, but for he first loved us, (or And this is love, not because we had loved God, but because he first loved us), and sent his Son (as the) forgiveness [or (as the) helping] for our sins.

11 Ye most dear *brethren*, if God loved us, we owe to love each other. (Ye most dear *brothers*, if God loved us, we ought to love one another.)

12 No man saw ever God; if we love together, God dwelleth in us, and the charity of him is perfect in us. (No one ever saw God; but if we love one another, God remaineth in us, and his love is perfect, or complete, in us.)

13 In this thing we know, that we dwell in him, and he in us; for of his Spirit he gave to us (or for he gave his Spirit to us).

14 And we saw, and witness (or testify), that the Father sent his Son (as the) Saviour of the world.

15 Whoever acknowledgeth, that Jesus is the Son of God, God dwelleth in him, and he in God.

16 And we have known, and believe to the charity, that God hath in us. God is charity, and he that dwelleth in charity, dwelleth in God, and God in him. (And we have known, and believe in the love, that God hath for us. God is love, and he who remaineth in love, remaineth in God, and God in him.)

17 In this thing is the perfect charity of God with us [or In this thing is the perfect charity of God in us], that we have trust in the day of doom; for as he is, also we be in this world. (In this then is the perfect love of God for us, so that we can have trust on the Day of Judgement; for as he is in this world, also we be in this world.)

18 Dread is not in charity, but perfect charity putteth out dread; for dread hath pain. But he that dreadeth, is not perfect in charity. (There is no fear in love, but perfect love putteth out fear; because fear hath pain, or fear cometh before pain. But he who feareth, is not perfect in love.)

19 Therefore love we God, for he loved us before. [Therefore love we God, for he former loved us (or for he first loved us).] (And so let us love God, for he loved us first.)

20 If any man saith, I love God, and hateth his brother, he is a liar. For he that loveth not his brother, whom he seeth, how may he love God (or how can he love God), whom he seeth not?

21 And we have this commandment of God, that he that loveth God, love also his brother.

CHAPTER 5

1 Each man that believeth that Jesus is Christ, is born of God; and each man that loveth him that (en)gendered [or that loveth him that (en)gendereth], loveth him that is born of him. (Each one who believeth that Jesus is the Messiah, is born of God or is a child of God; and each one who loveth him that begetteth, loveth him who is born of him.)

2 In this thing we know, that we love the children of God, when we love God, and do his commandments (or and obey his commands).

3 For this is the charity of God, that we keep his commandments; and his commandments be not heavy [or grievous]. (For this is the love of God, that we obey his commands; and his commands be not heavy or grievous.)

4   For all thing that is born of God, overcometh the world, (or For everyone who is born of God or who is a child of God, overcometh the world); and this is the victory that overcometh the world, our faith.

5   And who is he that overcometh the world, but he that believeth that Jesus is the Son of God?

6   This is Jesus Christ, that came by water and blood; not in water only, but in water and blood. And the Spirit is he that witnesseth, that Christ is [the] truth, (or And the Spirit is he who testifieth, that the Messiah is the truth).

7   For three be, that give witnessing in heaven, the Father, the Son [or the Word], and the Holy Ghost; and these three be one. (For there be three, who give testimony in heaven, the Father, the Son, and the Holy Spirit; and these three be one.)

8   And three be, that give witnessing in earth, (or And there be three, that give testimony on earth), the Spirit, water, and blood; and these three be one.

9   If we receive the witnessing of men, the witnessing of God is more; for this is the witnessing of God, that is more, for he witnessed of his Son. (If we accept the testimony of men, then the testimony of God is greater or is stronger; for this is the testimony of God, that is greater or is stronger, that he testified about his Son.)

10   He that believeth in the Son of God, hath the witnessing of God in him. He that believeth not to the Son, maketh him a liar; for he believeth not in the witnessing that God witnessed of his Son. (He who believeth in the Son of God, hath God's testimony in him. He who believeth not in the Son, maketh him out to be a liar; for he believeth not in the testimony that God testified about his Son.)

11   And this is the witnessing, for God gave to you everlasting life [or for God gave to us everlasting life], and this life is in his Son. (And this is the testimony, that God gave us Eternal Life, or eternal life, and this life is in his Son.)

12   He that hath the Son *of God*, hath also life; he that hath not the Son *of God*, hath not life. (He who hath the Son *of God*, hath also life; he who hath not the Son *of God*, hath not life.)

13   I write to you these things, that ye know, that ye have everlasting life, which believe in the name of God's Son. (I write these things to you, so that ye know, that ye have Eternal Life, or eternal life, ye who believe in the name of God's Son.)

14   And this is the trust which we have to God [or And this is the trust that we have in God], that whatever thing we ask after his will, he shall hear us (or he shall listen to us).

15   And we know, that he heareth us, whatever thing we [shall] ask; we know, that we have the askings, that we ask of him.

16   He that knoweth that his brother sinneth a sin not to death, ask he (for him), and life shall be given to him that sinneth not to death (or and life shall be given to him who sinneth not a deadly sin). There is a sin to death; not for it I say, that any man pray.

17   Each wickedness is sin, and there is [a] sin to death.

18   We know, that each man that is born of God, sinneth not; but the generation of God keepeth him (or but the Son of God keepeth him safe), and the wicked (one) toucheth him not.

19   We know, that we be of God, and all the world is set in evil.

20   And we know, that the Son of God came in (the) flesh, and gave to us wit, that we know him very God, and be in the very Son [Jesus] of him. This is very God, and everlasting life. (And we know, that the Son of God came in the flesh, and gave understanding to us, so that we can know him, the true God, and so that we can be in His true Son, Jesus. This is the true God, and Eternal Life, or eternal life.)

21   My little sons, keep ye you (safe) from maumets. [Little sons, keep ye you (safe) from simulacra.] (My little sons, keep away from idols or false gods.) [Amen.] †

2ND JOHN

1 The elder *man,* to the chosen lady, and to her children, which I love in truth (or whom I truly love); and not I alone, but also all men that know (the) truth;

2 for the truth that dwelleth in you, and with you shall be [into] without end. (for the sake of the truth which dwelleth within you, and shall be with you forever.)

3 Grace be with you, mercy, and (the) peace of God the Father, and of Jesus Christ, the Son of the Father, in truth and charity (or in truth and love).

4 I joyed full much, for I found (some) of thy sons going in truth, as we received commandment of the Father. (I greatly joyed, when I found some of thy sons going in the truth, as we were commanded by the Father.)

5 And now I pray thee, lady, not as writing a new commandment to thee, but that that we had from the beginning, that we love each other. (And now dear lady, I beseech thee, not as writing a new command to thee, but that which we had from the beginning, that we love one another.)

6 And this is charity, that we walk after his commandments. For this is the commandment, that as ye heard at the beginning, walk ye in him. (And this is love, that we walk, or that we live, according to his commands. For this is the command, which ye have heard from the beginning, walk or live in him.)

7 For many deceivers went out into the world, which acknowledge not that Jesus Christ hath come in (the) flesh; this is a deceiver and (the) antichrist. (For many deceivers went out into the world, who do not acknowledge that Jesus Christ hath come in the flesh; yea, such a person is a deceiver and the Anti-Messiah, or the False Messiah, or the Enemy of the Messiah.)

8 See ye yourselves, lest ye lose the things that ye have wrought, that ye receive full meed; (Watch yourselves, or Be on guard, lest ye lose the things that ye have worked for, so that ye receive your full reward;)

9 witting that each man that goeth before [or witting that each man that goeth away], and dwelleth not in the teaching of Christ, hath not God. He that dwelleth in the teaching [*of Christ*], hath both the Son and the Father. (knowing that everyone who goeth away, and remaineth not in the teaching of the Messiah, hath not God. He who remaineth in the teaching *of the Messiah,* hath both the Son and the Father.)

10 If any man cometh to you, and bringeth not this teaching, do not ye receive him into *your* house, neither say to him, Hail.

11 For he that saith to him, Hail, communeth with his evil works. Lo! I before-said to you, that ye be not confounded in the day of our Lord Jesus Christ (or Behold, I have told you this ahead of time, so that ye be not ashamed on the Day of our Lord Jesus Christ).

12 I have more things to write to you, and I would not by parchment and ink; for I hope that I shall come to you, and speak mouth to mouth, that our joy be full. (I have more things to write to you, but I will not write them with paper and ink; because I hope that I shall come to you, and then we can speak face to face, or in person, so that our joy will be complete.)

13 The sons of thy chosen sister greet thee well. The grace of God *be* with thee. Amen. (The sons of thy chosen sister send hearty greetings to thee. The grace of God *be* with thee. Amen.) †

3RD JOHN

1   The elder *man* to Gaius, most dear *brother*, whom I love in truth (or whom I truly love).

2   Most dear *brother*, of all things I make prayer, that thou enter, and fare wellfully (or fully well), as thy soul doeth wellfully (or fully well).

3   I joyed greatly, for brethren came, and bare witnessing to thy truth, as thou walkest in truth. (I greatly joyed, for the brothers came, and gave testimony about the truth of thee, or and gave testimony about thee and the truth, yea, how thou walkest in the truth.)

4   I have not more grace of these things (or I have no greater joy), than that I hear that my sons walk in (the) truth.

5   Most dear *brother*, thou doest faithfully, whatever thou workest in (the) brethren, and that into pilgrims, (Most dear *brother*, thou hast done faithfully, all that thou hast done for the brothers, who were strangers, or were visitors,)

6   which yielded witnessing to thy charity, in the sight of the church; which thou leadest forth, and doest well-worthily to God. (and they gave testimony about thy love, here in the church; yea, whom thou leadest forth, and helpest in a way worthy of God.)

7   For they went forth for his name, and took nothing of heathen men. (For they went forth for his name, and took nothing from the Gentiles.)

8   Therefore we owe to receive such, that we be even-workers of (the) truth. (And so we all ought to receive such men, so that we be fellow workers, or do our share of the work, in spreading the truth.)

9   I had written peradventure to the church, but this Diotrephes, that loveth to bear primacy, [*or*

(the) *chief places*], in them, receiveth not us. (I had written to the church, but this Diotrephes, who loveth to be in the lead of them, *or to take the chief place among them*, would not receive us, or did not welcome us.)

10   For this thing, if I shall come, I shall admonish his works, which he doeth, chiding [or chattering] against us with evil words. And as if these things suffice not to him, neither he receiveth brethren, and forbiddeth them that receive, and putteth out of the church (or And as if this did not suffice for him, he would not receive the brothers, and forbade those who had wanted to receive them, and even put them out of the church).

11   Most dear *brother*, do not thou (pur)sue (any) evil thing, but that that is (a) good thing. He that doeth well, is of God; he that doeth evil, seeth not God. (Most dear *brother*, do not follow after anything evil, but only after that which is good. He who doeth good, is of God; he who doeth evil, seeth not God.)

12   Witnessing is yielded to Demetrius of all men, and of (the) truth itself; but also we bear witnessing, and thou knowest, that our witnessing is true. (A good testimony is given about Demetrius from everyone, and even by the truth itself; and I also give good testimony about him, and thou knowest, that my testimony is true.)

13   I had many things to write to thee, but I would not write to thee by ink and pen (or but I will not write them to thee with pen and ink).

14   For I hope soon to see thee, and we shall speak mouth to mouth. Peace *be* to thee. (Your) Friends greet thee well. Greet thou well (my) friends by name. (Amen.) (Because I hope soon to see thee, and then we shall speak face to face, or in person. Peace *be* with thee. Your friends send hearty greetings to thee. Give hearty greetings to all of my friends by name. Amen.) †

JUDE

1   Judas, the servant of Jesus Christ, and brother of James, to these that be loved, that be in God the Father, and to them that be called and kept of Jesus Christ, (Judah or Jude, the servant of Jesus Christ, and the brother of James, to those who be loved, who be in God the Father, and to those who be called and kept safe by Jesus Christ,)

2   mercy, and peace, and charity be [full-]filled to you. (may mercy, and peace, and love be filled full unto you.)

3   Most dear *brethren*, I doing all busyness to write to you of your common health, had need to write to you, and pray to strive strongly for the faith that is once taken to (the) saints. (Most dear *brothers*, I making every effort to write to you about your shared salvation, had need to write to you, and beseech you to strive strongly for the faith that was given to God's people once and for all.)

4   For some unfaithful men privily entered, that sometime were before-written into this doom, and overturn the grace of our God into lechery, and deny him that is only a Lord, our Lord Jesus Christ. (For some unfaithful or unbelieving men have privately, or secretly, entered in among you, they whom long ago the judgement was written about, and who now turn the grace of our God into a license for lust, and deny him who is the only Lord, our Lord Jesus Christ.)

5   But I will admonish you once, that know all things, that Jesus saved his people from the land of Egypt, and the second time lost them that believed not. (But I will admonish you, ye who know all things, that Jesus saved his people once from the land of Egypt, but then afterward he destroyed those who did not believe.)

6   And he reserved under darkness (the) angels, that kept not their princehood, but forsook their house, into the doom of the great God (or unto the judgement of the great God), into everlasting bonds.

7   As Sodom, and Gomorrha (or and Gomorrah), and the nigh coasted cities, that in like manner did fornication, and went away after other flesh, and be made ensample(s), suffering pain of everlasting fire (or suffering the pain of eternal fire).

8   In like manner also these that defoul the flesh, and despise lordship, and blaspheme majesty. (In like manner also these people who defile the flesh, and despise authority, and blaspheme Majesty.)

9   When Michael, [the] archangel, disputed with the devil, and strove of Moses' body, he was not hardy to bring in doom of blasphemy, but said, The Lord command to thee. (When the archangel Michael disputed with the Devil, and argued over Moses' body, he was not so bold as to bring in the judgement of blasphemy, but instead said, The Lord shall command to thee!)

10   But these men blaspheme, whatever things they know not. For whatever things they know kindly as dumb beasts, in these they be corrupt, (or For whatever they know by kind, or naturally, like dumb beasts, by those things they be corrupted).

11   Woe to them that went the way of Cain, and that be shed out by (the) error of Balaam for meed, and perished in the gainsaying of Core. (Woe to those who went the way of Cain, and who were poured out by the error of Balaam while seeking reward, and who perished in rebellion like Korah.)

12   These be in their meats (or They be at their banquets), feasting together to filth, without dread feeding themselves. *These be* clouds without water, that be borne about of (the) winds (or who be carried about by the winds); harvest trees without fruit, twice dead,

drawn up by the root(s);

13   waves of the mad sea, foaming out their confusions, [or waves of the wild sea, frothing out their confusions]; erring stars, to which the tempest of darknesses is kept [into] without end, (or stars gone astray, for whom the tempest of darkness is kept forever).

14   But Enoch, the seventh from Adam, prophesied of these (or prophesied about them), and said, Lo! the Lord cometh with his holy thousands,

15   to do doom against all men, and to reprove all unfaithful men of all the works of the wickedness of them, by which they did wickedly, and of all the hard words, that wicked sinners have spoken against God. (to execute judgement against everyone, and to rebuke all the unbelievers for all the works of their wickedness, by which they did wickedly, and for all the hard words, which wicked sinners have spoken against God.)

16   These be grudgers full of (com)plaints, wandering after their desires; and the mouth of them speaketh pride, worshipping persons, because of winning. (These people be grumblers full of complaints, going after their own desires; and their mouths be full of pride, and give honour to people because of their profits, or their increases.)

17   And ye, most dear *brethren*, be mindful of the words which be before-said of [the] apostles of our Lord Jesus Christ; (And ye, most dear *brothers*, remember the words, which were earlier said by the apostles of our Lord Jesus Christ;)

18   which said to you, that in the last times there shall come beguilers [or scorners], wandering after their own desires, not in piety. (who said to you, that in the Last Days, or at the Time of the End, or the End Time(s), there shall come deceivers, or mockers, going after their own desires, and not in piety.)

19   These be, which separate themselves (or who set themselves apart), beastly men, not having (the) Spirit.

20   But ye, most dear *brethren*, above build yourselves on your most holy faith, and pray ye in the Holy Ghost, (But ye, most dear *brothers*, build yourselves up in your most holy faith, and pray in the Holy Spirit,)

21   and keep yourselves in the love of God, and abide ye the mercy of our Lord Jesus Christ into life everlasting. (and keep yourselves in the love of God, and wait for the mercy of our Lord Jesus Christ unto eternal life.)

22   And reprove ye these men that be deemed, (And rebuke those men who be judged,)

23   but save ye them, and take ye (hold of) them [or ravish them] from the fire. And do ye mercy to other men, in the dread of God, and hate ye also that defouled coat, which is fleshly. (but also save them, yea, snatch them out of the fire. And do mercy to other men, in fearful reverence for God, and hate also that defiled coat, which is your flesh.)

24   But to him that is mighty to keep you without sin, and to ordain before the sight of his glory you unwemmed, in full out joy, (But to him who is mighty to keep you without sin, and to ordain you without spot, or blemish, before the presence of his glory, with great joy,)

25   in the coming of our Lord Jesus Christ, to God alone our Saviour, by Jesus Christ our Lord, *be* glory, and magnifying, empire, and power, before all worlds, and now, and into all worlds of worlds (or and forever and ever). Amen. †

APOCALYPSE of JOHN

CHAPTER 1

1 (The) Apocalypse of Jesus Christ [or The revelation of Jesus Christ], which God gave to him to make open to his servants, which things it behooveth to be made soon. And he signified, sending by his angel to his servant John,

2 which bare witnessing to the word of God, and (to the) witnessing of Jesus Christ, in these things, whatever things he saw. (who testified to the word of God, and to the testimony of Jesus Christ, in these things, whatever he saw.)

3 Blessed *is* he that readeth, and he that heareth the words of this prophecy, and keepeth those things that be written in it; for the time is nigh. (Blessed *is* he who readeth, and he who heareth the words of this prophecy, and obeyeth those things that be written in it; for the time is near.)

4 John to the seven churches, that be in Asia, grace and peace (be) to you, of him that is, and that was, and that is to coming [or that is to come]; and of the seven spirits, that be in the sight of his throne;

5 and of Jesus Christ, that is a faithful witness (or who is a faithful witness), the first begotten of dead men [or the first begotten of (the) dead], and (the) prince of (the) kings of the earth; which loved us, and washed us from our sins in his blood,

6 and made us a kingdom, and priests to God and to his Father; to him *be* glory and empire into worlds of worlds (or to him *be*

glory and empire forever and ever). Amen.

7 Lo! he cometh with clouds, and each eye shall see him, and they that pricked him; and all the kindreds of the earth shall bewail themselves on him. Yea, Amen! (Behold, he cometh with clouds, and every eye shall see him, and they who pierced him; and all the peoples of the earth shall bewail themselves over him. Yea, Amen!)

8 I am alpha and omega, the beginning and the end, saith the Lord God, that is, and that was, and that is to coming [or that is to come], (the) almighty. (I am Alpha and Omega, the Source and the Fulfillment, saith the Lord God, who is, and who was, and who is to come, the Almighty.)

9 I, John, your brother, and partner in tribulation, and kingdom, and patience in Christ Jesus, was in an isle, that is called Patmos, for the word of God, and for the witnessing of Jesus. (I, John, your brother, and partner in suffering, and kingdom, and patience, or endurance, in the Messiah Jesus, was on an island called Patmos, because of the word of God, and because of my testimony about Jesus.)

10 I was in (the) Spirit in the Lord's day [or in the Sunday], and I heard behind me a great voice, as of a trump, (I was in the Spirit on the Lord's day, or on a Sunday, and I heard a loud voice behind me, like the sound of a trumpet,)

11 saying *to me*, Write thou in a book that thing that thou seest, and send to the seven churches that be in Asia; to Ephesus, to Smyrna, and to Pergamos (or to Pergamum), and to Thyatira, and to Sardis, and to Philadelphia, and to Laodicea.

12 And I turned, that I should see the voice that spake with me, (or And I turned, so that I could see who spoke to me); and I turned, and I saw seven candlesticks of gold,

13 and in the middle of the seven golden candlesticks one like to the Son of man, clothed with a long garment, and girded at the

teats with a golden girdle, (or and girded at the breast with a golden girdle, or and with a gold band around his chest).

14 And the head of him and his hairs were white, as white wool, and as snow; and the eyes of him as (a) flame of fire,

15 and his feet like to latten [or like the dross of gold], as in a burning chimney; and the voice of him as the voice of many waters. (and his feet were like latten, or the dross of gold, like in a furnace; and his voice was like the sound of many waters.)

16 And he had in his right hand seven stars, and a sword sharp on ever either side went out of his mouth [or and a sword sharp on both sides went out of his mouth]; and his face as the sun shineth in his virtue (or and his face shone like the sun in its strength).

17 And when I had seen him, I felled down at his feet, as dead. And he putted his right hand on me, and said, Do not thou dread (or Do not fear); I am the first and the last;

18 and I am alive, and I was dead; and lo! I am living into (the) worlds of worlds, (or and behold, I shall remain alive forever and ever), and I have the keys of death and of hell.

19 Therefore write thou which things thou hast seen, and which be, and which it behooveth to be done after these things.

20 The sacrament of the seven stars [or The mystery of (the) seven stars], which thou sawest in my right hand, and the seven golden candlesticks; the seven stars be [the] angels of the seven churches, and the seven candlesticks be [the] seven churches.

CHAPTER 2

1 And to the angel of the church of Ephesus write thou, These things saith he, that holdeth the seven stars in his right hand, which walketh in the middle [or in the midst] of the seven golden candlesticks (or who walketh in the midst of the seven gold candlesticks).

2 I know thy works, and thy travail [or thy toil], and thy patience, and that thou mayest not suffer evil men, (or I know of thy works, and thy labour, and thy endurance, and that thou cannot allow or tolerate evil men); and thou hast assayed them that say that they be apostles, and be not, and thou hast found them (to be) liars;

3 and thou hast patience (or and thou hast endured), and thou hast suffered for my name [or and thou hast sustained for my name], and failedest not.

4 But I have against thee a few things, that thou hast left thy first charity. (But I have a few things against thee, yea, that thou hast left thy first love.)

5 Therefore be thou mindful from whence thou hast fallen, and do penance, and do the first works; or else, I shall come soon to thee, and I shall remove thy candlestick from his place, [no] but thou do penance. (And so remember from where thou hast fallen, and repent, and do again the first works; or else, I shall come soon to thee, and I shall move thy candlestick from its place, unless thou repent.)

6 But thou hast this good thing, that thou hatedest the deeds of (the) Nicolaitanes (or the Nicolaitans), which also I hate.

7 He that hath ears, hear he, what the Spirit saith to the churches. To him that overcometh, I shall give to eat of the tree of life, that is in the paradise of my God.

8 And to the angel of the church of Smyrna write thou, These things saith the first and the last, that was dead, and liveth.

9 I know thy tribulation, and thy poverty, but thou art rich; and thou art blasphemed of them, that say, that they be Jews, and be not, but be the synagogue of Satan. (I know thy suffering, and thy poverty, even though thou art rich; and thou art blasphemed by those, who say, that they be Jews, and be not, but be Satan's synagogue.)

10 Dread thou nothing of these things, which

thou shalt suffer. Lo! the devil shall send some of you into prison, that ye be tempted [or that ye be proved]; and ye shall have tribulation (for) ten days. Be thou faithful to the death, and (then) I shall give to thee a crown of life. (Fear none of the things, which thou shalt suffer. Behold, the Devil shall send some of you into prison, so that ye can be tested; and ye shall suffer for ten days. But be faithful unto death, and then I shall give thee a crown of life.)

11   He that hath ears, hear he, what the Spirit saith to the churches. He that overcometh, shall not be hurt of the second death, (or He who shall overcome, shall not be hurt by the second death).

12   And to the angel of the church of Pergamos (or of Pergamum), write thou, These things saith he, that hath the sword sharp on either side [or on each side].

13   I know where thou dwellest, where the seat of Satan is (or where Satan's throne is); and thou holdest my name, and deniedest not my faith. And in those days *was* Antipas, my faithful witness, that was slain at you (or who was killed there before you), where Satan dwelleth.

14   But I have against thee a few things; for thou hast there men holding the teaching of Balaam, which taught Balac to send (a) cause of stumbling before the sons of Israel (or who taught Balak to put a cause of stumbling before the Israelites), to eat of (the) sacrifices of idols, and to do fornication;

15   so also thou hast men holding the teaching of (the) Nicolaitanes. (and thou hast men who believe and follow the teaching of the Nicolaitans.)

16   Also do thou penance (or And so repent); if anything less, I shall come soon to thee, and I shall fight with them with the sword of my mouth.

17   He that hath ears, hear he, what the Spirit saith to the churches. To him that overcometh

I shall give angel meat hid [or manna]; and I shall give to him a white stone, and in the stone a new name written, which no man knoweth, but he that taketh [*it*], (or and I shall give him a white stone, and a new name written on the stone, which no man knoweth, but he who receiveth *it*).

18   And to the angel of the church of Thyatira write thou, These things saith the Son of God, that hath eyes as (the) flame of fire, and his feet like latten, (or who hath eyes like fiery flames, and his feet be like latten, *or like the dross of gold*).

19   I know thy works, and (thy) faith, and charity (or thy love), and thy service, and thy patience, and thy last works (be) more than the former (or greater than thy first works).

20   But I have against thee a few things; for thou sufferest the woman Jezebel, which saith that she is a prophetess, (or for thou hast allowed the woman Jezebel, who saith that she is a prophetess), to teach and deceive my servants, to do lechery, and to eat of things offered to idols.

21   And I gave to her time, that she should do penance, and she would not do penance of her fornication. (And I gave her time, so that she would repent, but she would not repent of her fornication, or of her idolatry, or her immorality.)

22   And lo! I send her into a bed, and they that do lechery with her shall be in most tribulation, [no] but they do penance of her works, (And behold, I shall send her into a bed, and those who do lechery with her shall suffer greatly, unless they repent of their works.)

23   And I shall slay her sons into death, and all (the) churches shall know, that I am searching reins and hearts; and I shall give to each man of you after his works.

24   And I say to you, and to (the) others that be at Thyatira, whoever have not this teaching, and that knew not the highness of Satan, how they say, I shall not send on you another

charge (or I shall not put another burden upon you);

25 nevertheless hold ye (onto) that that ye have, till I come.

26 And to him that shall overcome, and that shall keep till into the end my works, I shall give power on folks, (And to him who shall overcome, and who shall continue doing my works unto the end, I shall give power over the nations and the peoples,)

27 and he shall govern them in an iron rod (or and he shall govern them with an iron rod); and they shall be broken (al)together, as a vessel of a potter, as also I received of (or from) my Father;

28 and I shall give to him a morrow star.

29 He that hath ears, hear he, what the Spirit saith to the churches.

CHAPTER 3

1 And to the angel of the church of Sardis write thou, These things saith he, that hath the seven spirits of God, and the seven stars. I know thy works, for thou hast a name, that thou livest, and thou art dead.

2 Be thou waking, (or Wake up, or Be on guard), and confirm thou (the) other things, that were to dying; for I find not thy works full (or finished) before my God.

3 Therefore have thou in mind, how thou receivedest, and heardest; and keep, and do penance. Therefore if thou wake not, I shall come as a night thief to thee, and thou shalt not know in what hour I shall come to thee. (And so remember, how thou hast received it, and hast heard it; and so obey it, and repent. And if thou do not wake up, or be on guard, I shall come to thee like a thief in the night, and thou shalt not know in what hour I shall come to thee.)

4 But thou hast a few names in Sardis, which have not defouled their clothes, (or But thou hast a few people in Sardis, who have not defiled their clothes); and they shall walk with me in white clothes, for they be worthy.

5 He that overcometh, shall be clothed thus with white clothes; and I shall not do away his name from the book of life, and I shall acknowledge his name before my Father, and before his angels.

6 He that hath ears, hear he, what the Spirit saith to the churches.

7 And to the angel of the church of Philadelphia write thou, These things saith the holy and (the) true (one), that hath the key of David; which openeth, and no man closeth, he closeth, and no man openeth.

8 I know thy works, and lo! I gave before thee a door opened, which no man may close; for thou hast a little virtue, and hast kept my word, and deniedest not my name. (I know thy works, and behold, I have put before thee an open door, which no one can close; for thou hast a little strength, and hast kept my word, and deniedest not my name.)

9 Lo! I shall give to thee (those) of the synagogue of Satan, which say that they be Jews (or who say that they be Jews), and be not, but lie. Lo! I shall make them, (so) that they come, and worship before thy feet; and they shall know, that I loved thee,

10 for thou keptest the word of my patience. And I shall keep thee from the hour of temptation, that is to coming into all the world [or that is to come into all the world], to tempt men that dwell in earth. (because thou hast obeyed my word and endured, or because thou hast obeyed my word to endure. And I shall keep thee from the hour of testing, that is to come into all the world, to test those who live on the earth.)

11 Lo! I come soon; hold thou that that thou hast, (so) that no man take thy crown.

12 And him that shall overcome, I shall make (him) a pillar in the temple of my God, and he shall no more go out; and I shall write on him the name of my God, and the name of the city

of my God, of the new Jerusalem, that cometh down from (the) heaven of my God, and my new name.

13 He that hath ears, hear he, what the Spirit saith to the churches.

14 And to the angel of the church of Laodicea write thou, These things saith (the) Amen, the faithful witness and (the) true (one), which is (the) beginning of God's creature(s), (or who is the beginning, or the Source, of all of God's Creation).

15 I know thy works, for neither thou art cold, neither *thou art* hot; I would (like) that thou were cold, either hot;

16 but for thou art lukewarm, and neither cold, neither hot, I shall begin to cast thee [or to vomit thee] out of my mouth.

17 For thou sayest, That I am rich, and full of goods, and have need of nothing; and thou knowest not, that thou art a wretch, and wretchful [or and wretched], and poor, and blind, and naked.

18 I counsel thee to buy of me burnt gold (or I counsel thee to buy from me gold which was refined in the fire), (so) that thou be made rich, and be clothed with white clothes, (so) that the confusion [or the shame] of thy nakedness be not seen; and anoint thine eyes with a collyrium, *that is, a medicine for* (the) *eyes, gathered of diverse herbs*, (so) that thou (can) see.

19 I reprove, and chastise whom I love; therefore (pur)sue thou *good men*, and do penance. (I rebuke, and chastise whom I love; and so pursue the *good*, and repent.)

20 Lo! I stand at the door, and knock; if any man heareth my voice, and openeth the gate to me, I shall enter to him, and sup with him, and he with me.

21 And I shall give to him that shall overcome, to sit with me in (or on) my throne, as also I overcame, and sat with my Father in (or on) his throne.

22 He that hath ears, hear he, what the Spirit saith to the churches.

CHAPTER 4

1 After these things I saw, and lo! a door was opened in heaven. And the first voice that I heard, *was* as of a trump speaking with me, and said, Ascend thou up hither, and I shall show to thee which things it behooveth to be done soon after these things. (After these things I saw, and behold, a door was opened in heaven. And the voice like a trumpet, that I had heard before, *was* speaking to me, and it said, Come up here, and I shall show thee what it behooveth to be done next.)

2 And anon I was in (the) Spirit, and lo! a seat was set in heaven, and upon the seat *one* sitting. (And at once I was in the Spirit, and behold, there was a throne in heaven, and *One* sitting upon the throne.)

3 And he that sat (there), was like the sight of a stone jasper, and to sardine; and a rainbow was in [the] compass of the seat, (or and a rainbow was all around, or encompassed, the throne), like the sight of (an) emerald.

4 And in the compass of the seat *were* four and twenty small seats; and above [or upon] the thrones four and twenty elder men sitting, covered about with white clothes, and in the heads of them golden crowns. (And all around the throne *were* twenty-four small thrones; and sitting upon those thrones were twenty-four elders, clothed in white clothes, and with gold crowns on their heads.)

5 And lightnings, and voices (or and sounds), and thunderings came out of the throne; and seven lamps burning before the throne, which be the seven spirits of God.

6 And before the seat as a sea of glass, like crystal, and in the middle of the seat, and in the compass of the seat, [were] four beasts, full of eyes before and behind. (And in front of the throne was a sea of glass, like crystal, and in the midst of the throne, and around it, *were*

four creatures, covered with eyes, in front and behind.)

7   And the first beast like a lion; and the second beast like a calf; and the third beast having a face as of a man; and the fourth beast like an eagle flying. (And the first creature was like a lion; and the second creature was like a calf; and the third creature had a face like a man; and the fourth creature was like an eagle in flight.)

8   And the four beasts had each of them six wings; and all about and within they were full of eyes; and they had not rest day and night, saying, Holy, holy, holy, the Lord God almighty, that was, and that is, and that is to coming [or and that is to come]. (And each of the four creatures had six wings; and all about, inside and out, they were covered with eyes; and they had no rest day or night, but were always saying, Holy, holy, holy, the Lord God Almighty, who was, and who is, and who is to come.)

9   And when those four beasts gave glory, and honour, and blessing to him that sat on the throne, that liveth into (the) worlds of worlds, (And when those four creatures gave glory, and honour, and blessing to Him who sat on the throne, who liveth forever and ever,)

10   the four and twenty elder men fell down before him that sat on the throne, and worshipped him that liveth into (the) worlds of worlds. And they cast their crowns before the throne, and said, (the twenty-four elders fell down before Him who sat on the throne, and worshipped Him who liveth forever and ever. And they threw their crowns before the throne, and said,)

11   Thou, Lord our God, art worthy to take glory, and honour, and virtue; for thou madest of nought all things, and for thy will those were, and be made of nought. (Thou, Lord our God, art worthy to receive glory, and honour, and power; for thou madest everything out of nothing, yea, because of thy will, they were

made out of nothing, and they be.)

CHAPTER 5

1   And I saw in the right hand of the sitter on the throne, a book written within and without, and sealed with seven seals.

2   And I saw a strong angel, preaching with a great voice (or asking with a loud voice), Who is worthy to open the book, and to undo the seals of it?

3   And none [or And no man] in heaven, neither in earth, neither under (the) earth, might open the book, neither behold it.

4   And I wept much, for none [or no man] was found worthy to open the book, neither to see it.

5   And one of the elder men said to me, Weep thou not; lo! a lion of the lineage of Juda(h), the root of David, hath overcome to open the book, and to undo the seven seals of it. (And one of the elders said to me, Weep not; behold, a lion from the tribe of Judah, the Root of David, hath overcome to open the book, and to undo its seven seals.)

6   And I saw, and lo! in the middle of the throne, and of the four beasts, and in the middle of the elder men, a lamb standing as slain, that had seven horns, and seven eyes, which be [the] seven spirits of God, sent into all the earth. (And I saw, and behold, in the midst of the throne, and of the four creatures, and of the elders, a Lamb standing there, who appeared to have been killed, and he had seven horns, and seven eyes, which be the seven spirits of God, sent into all the earth.)

7   And he came, and took of the right hand of the sitter in the throne the book. (And he came, and took the book from the right hand of Him who sat on the throne.)

8   And when he had opened the book, the four beasts and the four and twenty elder men fell down before the lamb; and had each of them harps, and golden vials full of odours,

which be the prayers of (the) saints. (And when he had opened the book, the four creatures and the twenty-four elders fell down before the Lamb; and each of them had harps, and gold basins, or gold bowls, full of incense, which be the prayers of God's people.)

9 And they sung a new song, and said, Lord our God, thou art worthy to take the book, and to open the seals of it; for thou were slain, and again-boughtest us to God in thy blood, of each lineage, and tongue, and people, and nation, (or for thou wast killed, and so thou hast redeemed us to God with thy blood, yea, from every tribe, and language, and people, and nation);

10 and madest us a kingdom, and priests to our God; and we shall reign on earth. (and madest us into a kingdom, and priests for our God; and we shall rule on the earth.)

11 And I saw, and heard the voice(s) of many angels all about the throne, and of the beasts, and of the elder men, (or And I saw, and heard the voices of many angels all about the throne, and the voices of the creatures, and of the elders). And the number of them was thousands of thousands,

12 saying with a great voice, The lamb that was slain, is worthy to take virtue, and Godhead [or and Divinity], and wisdom, and strength, and honour, and glory, and blessing. (saying with loud voices, The Lamb that was killed, is worthy to receive power, and Godhead, or Divinity, and wisdom, and strength, and honour, and glory, and blessing.)

13 And each creature that is in heaven, and *that is* on [the] earth, and under (the) earth, and the sea, and which things be in it, I heard all (of them) saying, To him that sat in the, and to the lamb throne, blessing, and honour, and glory, and power, into (the) worlds of worlds, (or To Him who sat on the throne, and to the Lamb, blessing, and honour, and glory, and power, forever and ever).

14 And the four beasts said, Amen. And the

four and twenty elder men fell down on their faces, and worshipped him that liveth into (the) worlds of worlds. (And the four creatures said, Amen. And the twenty-four elders fell down on their faces, and worshipped Him who liveth forever and ever.)

CHAPTER 6

1 And I saw, that the lamb had opened one of the seven seals. And I heard one of the four beasts saying, as a voice of thunder, Come thou, and see. (And I saw, that the Lamb had opened one of the seven seals. And I heard one of the four creatures say, with a voice like thunder, Come, and see.)

2 And I saw, and lo! a white horse; and he that sat on him had a bow, and a crown was given to him. And he went out overcoming, (so) that he should overcome.

3 And when he had opened the second seal, I heard the second beast saying, Come thou, and see. (And when he had opened the second seal, I heard the second creature say, Come, and see.)

4 And an other red horse went out; and it was given to him that sat on him [*power*], that he should take peace from the earth, and that they slay together themselves, (or so that he would take peace from the earth, so the people would kill each other); and a great sword was given to him.

5 And when he had opened the third seal, I heard the third beast saying, Come thou, and see. And lo! a black horse; and he that sat on him had a balance in his hand. (And when he had opened the third seal, I heard the third creature say, Come, and see. And behold, a black horse; and he who sat on him had a balance in his hand.)

6 And I heard as a voice in the middle of the four beasts, saying, (or And I heard a voice from the midst of the creatures say), A bilibre, *that is, a weight of two pounds*, of wheat for a

penny, and three bilibres of barley for a penny; and hurt thou not (the) wine, nor (the) oil.

7   And when he had opened the fourth seal, I heard a voice of the fourth beast saying, Come thou, and see. (And when he had opened the fourth seal, I heard the voice of the fourth creature say, Come, and see.)

8   And lo! a pale horse; and the name *was* Death to him that sat on him, and hell (pur)sued him (or and hell followed him). And power was given to him on, (or over), (the) four parts of the earth, to slay with (the) sword, and with hunger, and with death, and with beasts of the earth.

9   And when he had opened the fifth seal, I saw under the altar the souls of men slain for the word of God, and for the witnessing that they had. (And when he had opened the fifth seal, I saw under the altar the souls of men killed for the word of God, and for the testimony which they had given.)

10   And they cried with a great voice, and said, How long thou, Lord, that art holy and true, deemest [thou] not, and vengest not our blood of these that dwell in the earth? (And they cried with loud voices, and said, How long O Lord, who art holy and true, judgest not, and avengest not our blood upon those who live on the earth?)

11   And white stoles, for each soul a stole, were given to them; and it was said to them, that they should rest yet a little time, till the number of their fellows and of their brethren be fulfilled, that be to be slain, as also they [*were*].

12   And I saw, when he had opened the sixth seal, and lo! a great earth-moving was made, (and behold, there was a great earthquake); and the sun was made black, as a sackcloth of hair, and all the moon was made as blood.

13   And the stars of heaven felled down on the earth, as a fig tree sendeth his unripe figs, when it is moved of a great wind. (And the stars of the heavens fell down upon the earth, like a fig tree sendeth its unripe figs, when it is moved by a great wind.)

14   And (the) heaven(s) went away, as a book wrapped in [or enfolded]; and all the mountains and (the) isles were moved from their places.

15   And the kings of the earth, and princes, and tribunes, and rich, and strong, and each bondman, and free man, hid them(selves) in dens and (in the) stones of (the) hills.

16   And they say to (the) hills and to (the) stones, Fall ye on us, and hide ye us from the face of him that sitteth on the throne, and from the wrath of the lamb;

17   for the great day of their wrath cometh, and who shall be able to stand?

CHAPTER 7

1   After these things I saw four angels standing on the four corners of the earth, holding [the] four winds of the earth, (so) that they blew not on the earth, neither on the sea, neither on any tree.

2   And I saw another angel ascending up from the rising of the sun, that had a sign of the living God. And he cried with a great voice to the four angels, to which it was given to annoy the earth, and the sea, (And I saw another angel going up from the rising of the sun, who had the seal of the living God. And he cried with a loud voice to the four angels, to whom it was given to do great harm to the earth, and to the sea,)

3   and said, Do not ye annoy the earth, and the sea, neither [to] trees, till we mark the servants of our God in the foreheads of them. (and said, Do not harm the earth, or the sea, or the trees, until we mark the servants of our God with a seal upon their foreheads.)

4   And I heard the number of men that were marked, an hundred thousand and four and forty thousand marked, of every lineage of the sons of Israel; (And I heard that the number of

men who were sealed, were a hundred and forty-four thousand, from every tribe of the Israelites;)

5   of the lineage of Juda (or from the tribe of Judah), twelve thousand marked; of the lineage of Reuben, twelve thousand marked; of the lineage of Gad, twelve thousand marked;

6   of the lineage of Aser, twelve thousand marked; of the lineage of Nephthalim, twelve thousand marked; of the lineage of Manasses, twelve thousand marked;

7   of the lineage of Simeon, twelve thousand marked; of the lineage of Levi, twelve thousand marked; of the lineage of Issachar, twelve thousand marked;

8   of the lineage of Zabulon (or from the tribe of Zebulon), twelve thousand marked; of the lineage of Joseph, twelve thousand marked; of the lineage of Benjamin, twelve thousand marked.

9   After these things I saw a great people, whom no man might number, of all folks, and lineages (or tribes), and peoples, and languages [or and tongues], standing before the throne, in the sight of the lamb; *and they were* clothed with white stoles, and palms *were* in the hands of them.

10   And they cried with a great voice, and said, Health to our God, that sitteth on the throne, and to the lamb. (And they cried with loud voices, and said, Salvation cometh from our God, who sitteth on the throne, and from the Lamb./And they cried with loud voices, and said, Victory to our God, who sitteth on the throne, and to the Lamb.)

11   And all the angels stood all about the throne, and of the elder men, and the four beasts. And they fell down in the sight of the throne, on their faces, and worshipped God, (And all the angels stood all around the throne, and the elders, and the four creatures. And they fell down before the throne, on their faces, and worshipped God,)

12   and said, Amen! blessing, and clearness, and wisdom, and doing of thankings, and honour, and virtue, and strength to our God, into worlds of worlds. Amen. (and said, Amen! blessing, and glory, and wisdom, and giving thanks, and honour, and power, and strength to our God, forever and ever. Amen.)

13   And one of the elder men answered, and said to me, Who be these, that be clothed with white stoles? and from whence came they? (And one of the elders asked me, Who be these, who be clothed with white stoles? and where do they come from?)

14   And I said to him, My lord, thou knowest. And he said to me, These be they, that came from (the) great tribulation, and washed their stoles, and made them white in the blood of the lamb (or and made them white with the Lamb's blood).

15   Therefore they be before the throne of God, and serve to him day and night, in his temple. And he that sitteth in the throne, dwelleth on them. (And so they be before the throne of God, and serve him day and night, in his Temple. And He who sitteth on the throne, liveth among them.)

16   They shall no more hunger, neither thirst, neither [the] sun shall fall on them, nor any heat.

17   For the lamb, that is in the middle of the throne, shall govern them, and shall lead forth them to the wells of (the) waters of life [or and shall lead them forth to the wells of the waters of life]; and God shall wipe away each tear from the eyes of them. (For the Lamb, who is in the midst of the throne, shall govern them, and shall lead them forth to the springs of the water of life; and God shall wipe away every tear from their eyes.)

CHAPTER 8

1   And when he had opened the seventh seal, a silence was made in heaven [or silence was made in heaven], as half an hour (or for

half an hour).

2   And I saw seven angels standing in the sight of God, and seven trumps were given to them. (And I saw seven angels standing before God, and seven trumpets were given to them.)

3   And another angel came, and stood before the altar, and had a golden censer; and many incenses were given to him, that he should give of the prayers of all (the) saints on the golden altar (or so that he could offer them with the prayers of all of God's people on the gold altar), that is before the throne of God.

4   And the smoke of the incenses of the prayers of the holy men ascended up from the angel's hand before God. (And the smoke from the incense went up before God from the angel's hand, with the prayers of the saints or of God's people.)

5   And the angel took the censer, and filled it of the fire of the altar, and cast [it] into the earth. And thunders, and voices, and lightnings were made, and a great earth-moving. (And the angel took the censer, and filled it with fire from the altar, and threw it down onto the earth. And there was thunder, and sounds, and lightning, and a great earthquake.)

6   And the seven angels, that had the seven trumps, made them ready, that they should trump. (And the seven angels, who had the seven trumpets, made them ready, so that they could blow them.)

7   And the first angel trumped; and hail was made, and fire mingled together in blood; and it was sent into the earth. And the third part of the earth was burnt, and the third part of (the) trees was burnt, and all the green grass was burnt.

8   And the second angel trumped; and as a great hill burning with fire was cast into the sea; and the third part of the sea was made blood,

9   and the third part of (the) creature(s) was dead, that had lives in the sea, and the third

part of [the] ships perished.

10   And the third angel trumped; and a great star burning as a little (fire)brand, fell from heaven; and it fell into the third part of (the) rivers, and into the wells of waters. (And the third angel trumpeted; and a great star burning like a torch, fell from the heavens; and it fell into a third of the rivers, and into the springs of water.)

11   And the name of the star is said Wormwood. And the third part of (the) waters was made into wormwood; and many men were dead of the waters, for those were made bitter. (And the star was called Wormwood. And a third of the waters was made into wormwood; and many men died from the waters, because they were made bitter or they were poisoned.)

12   And the fourth angel trumped; and the third part of the sun was smitten (or and a third of the sun was struck), and the third part of the moon, and the third part of [the] stars, so that the third part of them was darked, and the third part of the day shined not, and also of the night.

13   And I saw, and heard the voice of an eagle flying by the middle of heaven, and saying with a great voice, Woe! woe! woe! to men that dwell in earth, of the other voices of the three angels, that shall trump after. (And I saw, and heard the voice of an eagle flying through the midst of the heavens, and saying with a loud voice, Woe! woe! woe! to the men who live on the earth, from the other soundings of the three angels, who shall trumpet next.)

CHAPTER 9

1   And the fifth angel trumped; and I saw, that a star had fallen down from (the) heaven(s) into (the) earth; and the key of the pit of deepness was given to it [or and the key of the pit of deepness is given to him].

2   And it opened the pit of deepness [or And he opened the pit of deepness], and a smoke of the pit ascended up, as the smoke of a great furnace; and the sun was darked, and the air, of the smoke of the pit, (or and the sun, and the air, were darkened from the smoke of the pit).

3   And locusts went out of the smoke of the pit into (the) earth; and power was given to them, as scorpions of the earth have power.

4   And it was commanded to them, that they should not hurt the grass of the earth, neither any green thing, neither any tree, but only (the) men, that have not the sign of God [or the mark of God] in their foreheads, (or but only those, who did not have God's seal upon their foreheads).

5   And it was given to them, that they should not slay them, but that they should be tormented (for) five months; and the tormenting of them, (was) as the tormenting of a scorpion, when he smiteth a man (or when he striketh someone).

6   And in those days men shall seek death, and they shall not find it; and they shall desire to die, and death shall flee from them.

7   And the likeness of (the) locusts *be* like horses made ready into battle; and on the heads of them as crowns like gold, and the faces of them as the faces of men.

8   And they had hairs, as the hairs of women; and the teeth of them were as the teeth of lions.

9   And they had habergeons, as iron habergeons, and the voice of their wings as the voice of (the) chariots of many horses running to battle. (And they had breastplates, like iron breastplates, and the sound of their wings was like the sound of many chariots and their horses rushing to battle.)

10   And they had tails like scorpions, and pricks were in the tails of them; and the might of them *was* to annoy men (for) five months (or and their power was to be used to harm men for five months).

11   And they had on them a king (or And they had a king over them), the angel of (the) deepness, to whom the name in Hebrew *is* Abaddon, but by Greek Apollyon, and by Latin he hath a name Exterminus, *that is, Destroyer.*

12   One woe is passed, and lo! yet come two woes.

13   After these things also the sixth angel trumped; and I heard a voice from the four corners of the golden altar (or and I heard a voice from the four corners of the gold altar), that is before the eyes of God,

14   and said to the sixth angel that had a trump, Unbind thou [the] four angels, that be bound in the great river Euphrates. (and it said to the sixth angel who had a trumpet, Unbind the four angels, who be bound at the great Euphrates River.)

15   And the four angels were unbound, which were ready into (the) hour, and day, and month, and year, to slay the third part of men.

16   And the number of the host of horsemen *was* twenty thousand times ten thousand (or And the number of the army of the horsemen *was* twenty thousand times ten thousand). And I heard the number of them.

17   And so I saw horses in vision; and they that sat on them had fiery habergeons, and of jacinth, and of brimstone, (or and those who sat upon them had fire-red breastplates, and hyacinth or blue ones, and yellow ones). And the heads of the horses were as [the] heads of lions; and fire, and smoke, and brimstone, cometh forth (out) of the mouth(s) of them.

18   Of these three plagues the third part of men was slain, of the fire, and of the smoke, and of the brimstone, that came out of the mouth(s) of them. (By these three plagues a third of mankind was killed, by the fire, and by the smoke, and by the brimstone, that came out of their mouths.)

19   For the power of the horses is in the mouth(s) of them, and in the tails of them; for the tails of them *be* like to serpents, having

heads, and in them they annoy (or and with them they do much harm).

20   And the other men, that were not slain in these plagues, neither did penance of the works of their hands, that they worshipped not devils, and simulacra of gold, and of silver, and of brass, and of stone, and of tree, which may see, neither hear, neither wander; (And the other men, who were not killed by these plagues, did not repent of the works of their hands, so that they did not worship demons, and idols of gold, and of silver, and of brass, and of stone, and of wood, which cannot see, nor hear, nor walk or go;)

21   and [they] did not penance of their manslayings, neither of their witchcrafts, neither of their fornication, neither of their thefts, *were slain*. (and they did not repent of their murders, nor of their witchcrafts, nor of their fornication or their idolatry, nor of their thefts.)

CHAPTER 10

1   And I saw another strong angel coming down from heaven, clothed with a cloud, and the rainbow on his head; and the face of him was as the sun, and the feet of him as a pillar of fire.

2   And he had in his hand a little book opened; and he set his right foot on the sea, and the left foot on the earth.

3   And he cried with a great voice, as a lion when he roareth; and when he had cried, the seven thunders spake their voices. (And he cried with a loud voice, like a lion when he roareth; and when he had cried out, the seven thunders spoke.)

4   And when the seven thunders had spoken their voices, I was to write. And I heard a voice from heaven, saying, Mark thou what things the seven thunders spake, and do not thou write them. (And when the seven thunders had spoken, I was about to write

down what they had said. But I heard a voice from heaven, saying, Seal up what the seven thunders have spoken, and do not write it down.)

5   And the angel whom I saw standing above the sea, and above the earth, lifted up his hand to heaven,

6   and swore by him that liveth into (the) worlds of worlds, that made of nought heaven, and those things that be in it, and the earth, and those things that be in it, and the sea, and those things that be in it, that time shall no more be. (and swore by Him who liveth forever and ever, who made out of nothing heaven, and those things that be in it, and the earth, and those things that be in it, and the sea, and those things that be in it, that time shall be no more.)

7   But in the days of the voice of the seventh angel (or But in the days of the sounding of the seventh angel), when he shall begin to trump, the mystery of God shall be ended [or shall be fulfilled], as he preached by his servants (the) prophets.

8   And I heard a voice from heaven again speaking with me, and saying, Go thou, and take the book, that is opened, from the hand of the angel, that standeth above the sea, and on the land, (or who standeth on the sea, and on the land).

9   And I went to the angel, and said to him, that he should give me the book. And he said to me, Take the book, and devour it; and it shall make thy womb to be bitter, but in thy mouth it shall be (as) sweet as honey.

10   And I took the book (out) of the angel's hand (or And I took the book from the hand of the angel), and devoured it, and it was in my mouth as sweet [as] honey; and when I had devoured it, my womb was bitter.

11   And he said to me, It behooveth thee again to prophesy to heathen men, and to peoples, and languages [or and tongues], and to many kings. (And he said to me, It

behooveth thee again to prophesy about or to the Gentiles, and the peoples, and the languages, and many kings.)

CHAPTER 11

1   And a reed like a rod was given to me, and it was said to me, Rise thou, and mete the temple of God, and the altar, and (the) men that worship in it. (And a reed like a measuring rod was given to me, and it was said to me, Rise, and measure the Temple of God, and the altar, and the number of those who worship in it.)

2   But cast thou out the foreyard [or the porch], that is without the temple, and mete not it; for it is given to (the) heathen men, and they shall defoul the holy city by forty months and twain. (But ignore the outer courtyard, which is outside the Temple, and do not measure it; for it was given to the Gentiles, and they shall defile the holy city for forty-two months.)

3   And I shall give to my two witnesses (or And I shall send my two witnesses), and they shall prophesy (for) a thousand days two hundred and sixty, and [they] shall be clothed with sackcloths.

4   These be two olives, and two candlesticks, (or They be the two olives, and the two candlesticks), and they stand in the sight of the Lord of the earth.

5   And if any man will annoy (or will harm) them, fire shall go out of the mouth(s) of them, and (it) shall devour their enemies. And if any [man] will hurt them, thus it behooveth him to be slain.

6   These have (the) power to close, [or to shut up], (the) heaven(s), that it rain not in the days of their prophecy; and they have power on waters, to turn them into blood; and to smite the earth with every plague, and as oft as they will. (They have the power to close up the heavens, so that it will not rain in the days of

their prophecy; and they have power over the waters, to turn them into blood; and to strike the earth with every plague, and as often as they desire.)

7   And when they shall end their witnessing, the beast that ascendeth up from (the) deepness [or from the depth], shall make battle against them, and shall overcome them, and shall slay them. (And when they shall end their testimony, the beast that goeth up from the abyss, shall make battle against them, and shall overcome them, and shall kill them.)

8   And the bodies of them shall lie in the streets of the great city, that is called ghostly Sodom, and Egypt, (or that is spiritually or symbolically called Sodom, or Egypt), where the Lord of them was crucified.

9   And some of the lineages, and of peoples, and of languages, and of heathen men, shall see the bodies of them by three days and an half; and they shall not suffer the bodies of them to be put in burials. (And some of the tribes, and of the peoples, and of the languages, and of the Gentiles, shall behold their bodies for three and a half days; and they shall not allow their bodies to be buried.)

10   And men inhabiting the earth shall have joy on them; and they shall make merry, and shall send gifts together, for these two prophets tormented them that dwell on the earth. (And all those inhabiting the earth shall rejoice over them; and they shall make merry, and shall send gifts to each other, for these two prophets tormented all who lived on the earth.)

11   And after three days and an half, the Spirit of (the) life of God entered into them; and they stood on their feet, and great dread fell on them that saw. (But after three and a half days, the breath of life from God entered into them; and they stood upon their feet, and great fear fell upon those who saw them.)

12   And they heard a great voice from heaven, saying to them, Come up hither. And they ascended [up] into heaven in a cloud, and

the enemies of them saw them. (And they heard a loud voice from heaven, saying to them, Come up here. And they went up into heaven in a cloud, and their enemies saw them.)

13 And in that hour a great earth-moving was made, and the tenth part of the city fell down; and the names of men seven thousand were slain in the earth-moving; and the others were sent into dread, and gave glory to (the) God of heaven. (And at that moment there was a great earthquake, and a tenth of the city fell down; and seven thousand men were killed in the earthquake; and the others were sent into fear or terror, and gave glory to the God of heaven.)

14 The second woe is gone, and lo! the third woe shall come soon.

15 And the seventh angel trumped, and great voices were made in heaven, and said, The realm of this world is made our Lord's, and of Christ [or and Christ's], his Son, or is made of our Lord, and of Christ, his Son; and he shall reign into worlds of worlds. Amen. (And the seventh angel blew his trumpet, and loud voices were heard in heaven, and they said, The Kingdom of this world is now our Lord's, and the Messiah's, His Son; and he shall reign forever and ever. Amen.)

16 And the four and twenty elder men, that sat in their seats in the sight of the Lord, fell on their faces, and worshipped God, (And the twenty-four elders, who sat on their thrones before the Lord, fell on their faces, and worshipped God,)

17 and said, We do thankings to thee, Lord God almighty, which art, and which were, and which art to coming [or and which art to come]; which hast taken thy great virtue, and hast reigned. (and said, We give thanks to thee, Lord God Almighty, who art, and who was, and who art to come; yea, thou hast taken thy great power, and hast reigned.)

18 And folks be wroth, and thy wrath came, and (the) time of dead men to be deemed, and to yield meed to thy servants, and prophets,

and hallows, and (those) dreading thy name, to small and to great, and to destroy them that corrupted the earth. (And the nations and the peoples were angry, and thy wrath came, and the time for the dead to be judged, and to give reward to thy servants, and thy prophets, and thy saints or thy people, and all those who have fearful reverence for thy name, yea, to small and to great, and to destroy those who corrupted the earth.)

19 And the temple of God in heaven was opened, and the ark of his testament was seen in his temple; and lightnings were made, and voices, and thunders, and earth-moving, and great hail. (And God's Temple in heaven was opened, and the Covenant Box was seen in his Temple; and there was lightning, and sounds, and thunder, and an earthquake, and great hail.)

CHAPTER 12

1 And a great sign appeared in heaven; a woman clothed with the sun, and the moon under her feet, and in the head of her a crown of twelve stars. (And a great sight appeared in the heavens; a woman who was clothed with the sun, and the moon was under her feet, and on her head was a crown of twelve stars.)

2 And she had [(a) *child*] in (her) womb, [or And she having in womb, *or being with child*], and she cried, travailing of (the) child (or in labour with the child), and is tormented, that she bear (the) child.

3 And another sign was seen in heaven; and lo! a great red dragon, that had seven heads, and ten horns, and in the heads of him seven diadems. (And another sight was seen in the heavens; and behold, a great red dragon, that had seven heads, and ten horns, and on his seven heads were seven crowns.)

4 And the tail of him drew the third part of [the] stars of (the) heaven(s), and sent them into the earth. And the dragon stood before the

woman, that was to bearing (her) child, that when she had born (her) child, he should devour her child, (or And the dragon stood before the woman, who was about to bring forth her child, so that when her child was born, he could eat her child).

5   And she bare a man child, that was to ruling all folks in an iron rod; and her son was ravished to God, and to his throne. (And she gave birth to a boy child, who would rule all the nations and all the peoples with an iron rod; and her son was snatched up unto God, and to his throne.)

6   And the woman flew into (the) wilderness, where she hath a place made ready of God (or where she hath a place prepared by God), (so) that he feed her there (for) a thousand days two hundred and sixty.

7   And a great battle was made in heaven, and Michael and his angels fought with the dragon. And the dragon fought (back), and his angels (or And the dragon and his angels fought back);

8   and they had not might [more] (than the others), neither the place of them was found (any) more in heaven. (but they did not have as much strength as Michael and the other angels, and so there was no longer any place in heaven for them.)

9   And that dragon was cast down, the great old serpent, that is called the Devil, and Satan, that deceiveth all the world; he was cast down into the earth (or he was thrown down to the earth), and his angels were sent with him.

10   And I heard a great voice in heaven, saying, Now is made health, and virtue, and (the) kingdom of our God, and the power of his Christ; for the accuser of our brethren is cast down, which accused them before the sight of our God day and night. (And I heard a loud voice in heaven, saying, Now there is made salvation or victory, and power, and the Kingdom of our God, and the power of his Messiah; for the accuser of our brothers is

thrown down, who accused them before our God day and night, or who accused them in the presence of our God day and night.)

11   And they overcame him for the blood of the lamb, and for the word of his witnessing, (or And they overcame him by the blood of the Lamb, and by the word of his testimony); and they loved not their (own) lives [or their (own) souls] till to the death.

12   Therefore, ye heavens, be ye glad, and ye that dwell in them. Woe to the earth, and to the sea; for the fiend is come down to you, and hath great wrath, witting that he hath (just a) little time. (And so, ye heavens, be glad, and ye who dwell in them. Woe to the earth, and to the sea; for the Devil hath come down to you, and he hath great anger, knowing that he hath just a little time left.)

13   And after that the dragon saw, that he was cast down into the earth, he pursued the woman, that bare the man child. (And after that the dragon saw, that he was thrown down to the earth, he pursued the woman, or he persecuted the woman, who gave birth to the boy.)

14   And two wings of a great eagle were given to the woman, (so) that she should fly [or should flee] into (the) desert, into her place, where she is fed by time, and times, and half a time, from the face of the serpent.

15   And the serpent sent out of his mouth after the woman water as a flood, that he should make her to be drawn (away) of the flood. (And the serpent sent a flood of water out of his mouth after the woman, so that he could carry her away with the flood.)

16   And the earth helped the woman, and the earth opened his mouth, and sopped up the flood (or and swallowed up the flood), that the dragon sent [out] of his mouth.

17   And the dragon was wroth against the woman, and he went to make battle with others of her seed, that keep the commandments of God, and have the

witnessing of Jesus Christ. (And the dragon raged against the woman, and he went to make battle with others of her seed, who obey God's commandments, and hold faithful to the testimony of Jesus Christ.)

18   And he stood on the gravel of the sea. (And he stood on the sand of the sea or on the seashore.)

CHAPTER 13

1   And I saw a beast ascending up (out) of the sea (or And I saw a beast going up out of the sea), having seven heads, and ten horns; and on his horns ten diadems (or ten crowns), and on his heads the names [or the name] of blasphemy.

2   And the beast whom I saw, was like a [leo]pard, and his feet as the feet of a bear, and his mouth as the mouth of a lion; and the dragon gave his virtue and great power to him (or and the dragon gave his strength and authority and great power to him).

3   And I saw one of his heads, as slain into (the) death; and the wound of his death was cured [or was healed]. And all the earth wondered after the beast.

4   And they worshipped the dragon, that gave (his) power to the beast; and they worshipped the beast, and said, Who is like to the beast, and who shall be able to fight with it?

5   And a mouth speaking great things, and blasphemies, was given to it; and power was given to it, to do two and forty months (or to reign for forty-two months).

6   And it opened his mouth into blasphemies to God, to blaspheme his name, and his tabernacle, and them that dwell in heaven. (And it opened his mouth to blaspheme God, yea, to blaspheme his name, and his Tabernacle, and those who live in heaven.)

7   And it was given to him to make battle with (the) saints, and to overcome them; and power was given to him into each lineage, and people, and language, and folk. (And it was given to him to make battle with God's people, and to overcome them; and power was given to him over every tribe, and people, and language, and nation.)

8   And all men worshipped it, that dwell in earth, whose names be not written in the book of life of the lamb, that was slain, from the beginning of the world. (And everyone shall worship it, who live on the earth, whose names be not written in the Lamb's Book of Life, from the creation of the world, yea, *the Lamb* who was killed.)

9   If any man hath ears, hear he.

10   He that leadeth into captivity, shall go into captivity; he that slayeth with (the) sword, it behooveth him to be slain with (the) sword. This is the patience and the faith of (the) saints (or This is the endurance and the faithfulness of God's people).

11   And I saw another beast ascending up from the earth, and it had two horns, like the lamb; and it spake as the dragon, (And I saw another beast going up from the earth, and it had two horns, like the Lamb; but it spoke like the dragon,)

12   and [it] did all the power of the former beast, in his sight. And it made the earth, and (the) men dwelling in it, to worship the first beast, whose wound of death was cured [or was healed].

13   And it did great signs (or great miracles), (so) that also it made fire to come down from (the) heaven(s) to the earth, in the sight of all men.

14   And it deceiveth men, that dwell in the earth (or who live on the earth), for (the) signs which be given to it to do in the sight of the beast; saying to men that dwell in earth (or saying to those who live on the earth), that they (should) make an image of the beast, that hath the wound of [a] sword, and lived.

15   And it was given to him, that he should give [a] spirit (or breath) to the image of the

beast, and that the image of the beast speak. And he shall make, that whoever honour not the image of the beast, be slain.

16   And he shall make all, small and great, rich and poor, free men and bondmen, to have a character, *either* (a) *mark*, in (or on) their right hand, either in (or on) their foreheads;

17   (so) that no man may buy, either sell, [no] but they have the character (or unless they have the mark), either the name of the beast, either the number of his name.

18   Here is wisdom; he that hath understanding, acount the number of the beast; for it is the number of man, and his number is six hundred sixty and six.

CHAPTER 14

1   And I saw, and lo! a lamb stood on the mount of Sion, [or and lo! the lamb stood on the mount Sion], and with him an hundred thousand and four and forty thousand, having his name, and the name of his Father written in their foreheads. (And I saw, and behold, the Lamb stood on Mount Zion, and with him were a hundred and forty-four thousand, having his name, and the name of his Father written on their foreheads.)

2   And I heard a voice from heaven, as the voice of many waters, and as the voice of a great thunder; and the voice which I heard, *was* as of many harpers harping in their harps. (And I heard a sound from heaven, like the sound of many waters, and like the sound of great thunder; and the sound which I heard, *was* like that of many harpers playing on their harps.)

3   And they sung as a new song before the seat of God, and before the four beasts, and the elder men. And no man might say the song, but those hundred thousand and four and forty thousand, that be bought from the earth. (And they sang a new song before God's throne, and the four creatures, and the elders. And no man

could learn the song, but those hundred and forty-four thousand, who be bought or ransomed from the earth.)

4   These it be, that be not defouled with women; for they be virgins. These (pur)sue the lamb, whither ever he shall go; these be bought of all men, the first fruits to God, and to the lamb; (These it be, who be not defiled with women; for they be virgins. They follow the Lamb, wherever he shall go; for they be ransomed from out of all of mankind, the first fruits to God, and to the Lamb;)

5   and in the mouth of them leasing is not found; for they be without wem before the throne of God. (and lies were not found in their mouths; for they be without spot or blemish before the throne of God.)

6   And I saw another angel, flying by the middle of heaven (or flying through the midst of heaven), having an everlasting gospel [or having the everlasting gospel], (so) that he should preach [or that he should evangelize] to men sitting on the earth, and on each folk, and lineage, and language, and people, (or and to every nation, and tribe, and language, and people);

7   and said with a great voice, Dread ye the Lord, and give ye to him honour, for the hour of his doom cometh; and worship ye him, that made heaven and earth, the sea, and all things that be in them, and the wells of waters. (and he said with a loud voice, Have fearful reverence for the Lord, and give him honour, for the hour of his Judgement cometh; and worship him, who made heaven and earth, the sea, and all the things that be in them, and the springs of water.)

8   And another angel (pur)sued, saying, That great [city] Babylon fell down, fell down, which gave drink to all folks of the wine of [the] wrath of her fornication. (And another angel followed, saying, That great city Babylon fell down, fell down, which made all the nations and all the peoples drink of the wrath

of the wine of her fornication.)

9 And the third angel (pur)sued them, and said with a great voice, If any man worship the beast, and the image of it, and taketh the character in his forehead, either in his hand, (And the third angel followed them, and said with a loud voice, If anyone worship the beast, and its image, and receiveth its mark on his forehead, or on his hand,)

10 this shall drink of the wine of God's wrath, that is mingled with clear wine in the cup of his wrath, and [he] shall be tormented with fire and brimstone, in the sight of [the] holy angels, and before the sight of the lamb.

11 And the smoke of their torments shall ascend up into the worlds of worlds; neither they (shall) have rest day and night, which worship the beast and his image, and if any take the character of his name. (And the smoke of their torments shall go up forever and ever; and they shall not have any rest day or night, who worship the beast and his image, and if any receive the mark of his name.)

12 Here is the patience of (the) saints, which keep the commandments of God, and the faith of Jesus. (Here is the endurance of God's people, who obey the commandments of God, and hold fast to their faithfulness in Jesus.)

13 And I heard a voice from heaven, saying to me, Write thou, Blessed *be* (the) dead men [or Blessed *be* (the) dead], that die in the Lord; from henceforth now the Spirit saith, that they rest of their travails; for the works of them (pur)sue them. (And I heard a voice from heaven, saying to me, Write, Blessed *be* the dead who die in the Lord; from henceforth now the Spirit saith, They can rest from their labours; for their works follow them.)

14 And I saw, and lo! a white cloud, and above the cloud a sitter [or and above the cloud one sitting], like the son of man, having in his head a golden crown, (or like the Son of man, having a gold crown on his head), and in his hand a sharp sickle.

15 And another angel went out of the temple, and cried with great voice to him that sat on the cloud, Send thy sickle, and reap, for the hour cometh, that it be reaped; for the corn of the earth is ripe. (And another angel went out of the Temple, and cried with a loud voice to him who sat on the cloud, Send thy sickle, and reap the harvest, for the hour cometh, that it be reaped; for the wheat of the earth is ripe.)

16 And he that sat on the cloud, sent his sickle into the earth, and reaped the earth.

17 And another angel went out of the temple, that is in heaven, and he also had a sharp sickle.

18 And another angel went out from the altar, that had power on fire; and he cried with a great voice to him that had the sharp sickle, and said, (or And another angel went out from the altar, who had power over the fire; and he cried with a loud voice to him who had the sharp sickle, and said), Send thy sharp sickle, and cut away [or cut off] the clusters of the vineyard of the earth, for the grapes of it be ripe.

19 And the angel sent his sickle into the earth, and gathered (the) grapes of the vineyard of the earth, and sent (them) into the great lake of God's wrath (or and sent them into the great winepress of God's anger).

20 And the lake was trodden without the city, and the blood went out of the lake, till to the horses' bridles, by furlongs a thousand and six hundred. (And the winepress was trodden outside the city, and the blood went out of the winepress, for a thousand and six hundred furlongs all around, yea, up to the bridles of the horses.)

CHAPTER 15

1 And I saw another sign in heaven, great and wonderful; seven angels having the seven last vengeances, for the wrath of God is ended in them. (And I saw another great and

wonderful sight in heaven; seven angels having the seven last plagues, for God's anger is ended with them.)

2   And I saw as a glassen sea mingled with fire (or And I saw a sea like glass mingled with fire), and them that overcame the beast, and his image, and the number of his name, standing above the glassen sea, having the harps of God;

3   and singing the song of Moses, the servant of God, and the song of the lamb, and said, Great and wonderful be thy works, Lord God almighty; thy ways be just and true, Lord, king of worlds. (and singing the song of Moses, the servant of God, and the song of the Lamb, and said, Great and wonderful be thy works, Lord God Almighty; thy ways be righteous and true, Lord, the King of all worlds.)

4   Lord, who shall not dread thee, and magnify thy name? for thou alone art merciful [or pious]; for all folks shall come, and worship in thy sight, for thy dooms be open(ed). (Lord, who shall not have fearful reverence for thee, and magnify thy name? for thou alone art pious or art holy; for all the nations and all the peoples shall come, and worship before thee, for thy judgements be opened.)

5   And after these things I saw, and lo! the temple of the tabernacle of witnessing was opened in heaven; (And after these things I saw, and behold, the Temple of the Tabernacle of the Testimony was opened in heaven;)

6   and seven angels having [the] seven plagues, went out of the temple, and were clothed with a stole clean and white, and were before-girded with golden girdles about the breasts (or and with gold bands around their chests).

7   And one of the four beasts gave to the seven angels seven golden vials, full of the wrath of God, that liveth into (the) worlds of worlds. (And one of the four creatures gave to the seven angels seven gold basins, or seven gold bowls, full of God's anger, who liveth

forever and ever.)

8   And the temple was filled with (the) smoke of the majesty of God, and of the virtue of him; and no man might enter into the temple, till the seven plagues of the seven angels were ended. (And the Temple was filled with smoke from the Majesty of God, and from his power; and no one could enter into the Temple, until the seven plagues of the seven angels were ended.)

CHAPTER 16

1   And I heard a great voice from heaven, saying to the seven angels, Go ye, and shed out the seven vials of God's wrath into the earth. (And I heard a loud voice from heaven, saying to the seven angels, Go, and pour out the seven basins, or the seven bowls, of God's anger upon the earth.)

2   And the first angel went, and shedded out his vial into the earth (or and poured out his bowl onto the earth); and a wound fierce and worst was made on all that had the character [or the mark] of the beast, and on them that worshipped the beast, and his image.

3   And the second angel shedded out his vial into the sea, and the blood was made, as of a dead thing; and each man living was dead in the sea. (And the second angel poured out his bowl into the sea, and it was made like blood, like from a dead thing; and each living thing in the sea died.)

4   And the third angel shedded out his vial on the rivers, and on the wells of waters, [and blood is made], (And the third angel poured out his bowl into the rivers, and into the springs of water, and they were made like blood,)

5   and said [or and I heard the angel of (the) waters saying], Just art thou, Lord, that art, and that were holy, that deemest these things; (and I heard the angel of the waters say, Thou art righteous, O holy Lord, who art, and who was, and who judgest these things;)

6   for they shedded out the blood of (the) hallows, and (the) prophets, (or for they poured out the blood of the saints, or of God's people, and of the prophets), and thou hast given to them blood to drink; for they be worthy.

7   And I heard another [angel] saying, Yea! Lord God almighty, true and just *be* thy dooms. (And I heard another angel saying, Yea! Lord God Almighty! true and righteous *be* thy judgements.)

8   And the fourth angel shedded out his vial into the sun (or And the fourth angel poured out his bowl onto the sun), and it was given to him to torment men with heat and fire.

9   And men sweltered with great heat, and blasphemed the name of (the) God having power on these plagues, neither they did penance, that they should give glory to him. (And men were parched by the great heat, and blasphemed the name of the God who had power over these plagues, but they did not repent, so that they would give him glory.)

10   And the fifth angel shedded out his vial on the seat of the beast (or And the fifth angel poured out his bowl onto the throne of the beast), and his kingdom was made dark; and they ate together their tongues for sorrow,

11   and they blasphemed (the) God of heaven, for (the) sorrows of their wounds [or for (their) sorrows and their wounds]; and they did not penance of their works (or but they did not repent of their works).

12   And the sixth angel shedded out his vial into that great river Euphrates, and dried the water of it, that [the] way were made ready to kings from the sun rising. (And the sixth angel poured out his bowl into the great Euphrates River, and dried up its water, so that a way was prepared for the kings of the east.)

13   And I saw three unclean spirits by the manner of frogs go out of the mouth of the dragon, and (out) of the mouth of the beast, and (out) of the mouth of the false prophet.

14   For they be (the) spirits of devils, making signs, [or *wonders*], and they go forth to (the) kings of all (the) earth, to gather them into [a] battle, to the great day of almighty God. (For these be the spirits of demons, making miracles, and they go forth to the kings of all the earth, to gather them for the battle, on the Great Day of Almighty God.)

15   Lo! I come, as a night thief. Blessed *is* he that waketh, and keepeth his clothes, that he wander not naked, and that they see not the filthhood of him. (Behold, I come, like a thief in the night. Blessed *is* he who watcheth, and keepeth his clothes on, so that he walk not, or go not naked, so that they do not see his nakedness.)

16   And he shall gather them into a place [or And he gathered them into a place], that is called in Hebrew Armageddon.

17   And the seventh angel shedded out his vial into the air, and a great voice went out of heaven from the throne, and said, It is done. (And the seventh angel poured out his bowl into the air, and a loud voice went out of heaven from the throne, and said, It is done.)

18   And lightnings were made, and voices, and thunders; and a great earth-moving was made, which manner never was, since men were on (the) earth, such (an) earth-moving so great. (And there were lightning, and sounds, and thunder; and there was a great earthquake, like never before, since men were on the earth, yea, such a great earthquake.)

19   And the great city was made [or was broken] into three parts, and the cities of (the) heathen men felled down; and great Babylon came into mind before God (or and the great Babylon came into God's remembrance), to give to it the cup of wine of the indignation of his wrath.

20   And each isle flew away, and (the) hills be not found.

21   And a great hail as a talent came down from heaven into men; and men blasphemed God, for the plague of hail, for it was made full

great. (And great hail like talents came down from the heavens onto men; and they blasphemed God, for the plague of hail, because it was so very great, or because it was so terribly severe.)

CHAPTER 17

1   And one of the seven angels came, that had (the) seven vials, and spake with me, and said, Come thou, I shall show to thee the damnation of the great whore, that sitteth on many waters, (And one of the seven angels came, who had the seven basins, or the seven bowls, and spoke with me, and said, Come, and I shall show thee the damnation of the great whore, who sitteth above, or by, many waters,)

2   with which kings of the earth did fornication; and they that dwell in the earth be made drunk of the wine of her lechery. (with whom the kings of the earth did fornication or idolatry; and they who live on the earth be made drunk from the wine of her lechery.)

3   And he took me [away] into (a) desert in (the) Spirit. And I saw a woman sitting on a red beast, full of names of blasphemy, having seven heads, and ten horns. (And he took me away by the Spirit to a desert. And I saw a woman sitting on a red beast, covered with blasphemous names, and which had seven heads, and ten horns.)

4   And the woman was environed with purple, and red, and over-gilded with gold, and precious stone(s), and pearls, having a golden cup in her hand (or and had a gold cup in her hand), full of (the) abominations and (the) uncleanness of her fornication.

5   And a name (was) written in the forehead of her, Mystery, Babylon the great, (the) mother of fornications, and of (the) abominations of the earth. (And a name was written on her forehead, Mystery, the great Babylon, the mother of fornications, and of the

abominations of the earth.)

6   And I saw a woman drunken of the blood of (the) saints, and of the blood of (the) martyrs of Jesus, (or And this woman I saw was made drunk from the blood of God's people, and from the blood of the martyrs for Jesus). And when I saw her, I wondered with (a) great wondering.

7   And the angel said to me, Why wonderest thou? I shall say to thee the sacrament of the woman (or I shall tell thee the secret, or the mystery, of the woman), and of the beast that beareth her, that hath seven heads and ten horns.

8   The beast which thou seest [or The beast which thou sawest], was, and is not; and she shall ascend up from [the] deepness, and she shall go into perishing. And men dwelling in earth shall wonder, whose names be not written in the book of life from the making of the world, seeing the beast, that was, and is not. (The beast which thou hast seen, was, and is not; and she shall go up from the depth, or from the abyss, and she shall go into perdition, or into destruction. And men living on the earth shall wonder, whose names be not written in the Book of Life from the beginning or the creation of the world, seeing the beast, that was, and is not.)

9   And this is the wit, (for) who that hath wisdom, (or And this is the understanding or the explanation, for he who hath wisdom). The seven heads be seven hills, on which the woman sitteth,

10   and kings seven be [or and (there) be seven kings]. Five have felled down, and one is, and another cometh not yet. And when he shall come, it behooveth him to dwell (only for) a short time.

11   And the beast that was, and is not, and she is the eighth, and is of the seven, and shall go into perishing. (And the beast that was, and is not, he is an eighth king, and yet is of the seven, and shall go into destruction, or into

perdition.)

12 And the ten horns which thou hast seen, be ten kings, that yet have not taken kingdom; but they shall take power as kings, one hour after the beast. (And the ten horns which thou hast seen, be ten kings, who have not yet received their kingdoms; but they shall receive their power as kings, one hour after the beast.)

13 These have one counsel, and shall betake their virtue and power to the beast. (They shall be of one accord, and shall deliver their authority and power to the beast.)

14 These shall fight with the lamb, and the lamb shall overcome them; for he is (the) Lord of lords, and (the) King of kings; and they that be with him, *be* called, [and] chosen, and faithful.

15 And he said to me, The waters which thou hast seen, where the whore sitteth, be peoples, and folks, and languages, (or be peoples, and nations, and tongues).

16 And the ten horns that thou hast seen in the beast, these shall [hate the fornicary woman, *or* (the) *whore*, and shall] make her desolate and naked, and shall eat the fleshes of her, and shall burn (al)together her with fire [or and shall burn her (al)together with fire].

17 For God gave into the hearts of them, that they do that that is pleasant to him, [or Soothly God gave into the hearts of them, that they do that that is pleasant before him], (and) that they give their kingdom(s) to the beast, till the words of God be ended. (For God put into their hearts, that they do what is pleasing to him, and that they give their kingdoms to the beast, until God's words be fulfilled.)

18 And the woman whom thou hast seen, is the great city, that hath kingdom on the kings of the earth (or that ruleth over the kings of the earth).

CHAPTER 18

1 And after these things I saw another angel coming down from heaven, having great power; and the earth was lightened [or was lighted] of his glory (or by his glory).

2 And he cried with a strong voice, saying, Great Babylon felled down, felled down, and is made the habitation of devils, and the keeping of each unclean spirit, and the keeping of each unclean fowl, and hateful. (And he cried with a loud voice, saying, The great Babylon fell down, fell down, and it is made the habitation of demons, and the domicile of every unclean spirit, and the home of every unclean and hateful, or loathsome, bird.)

3 For all folks drunk of the wrath of the fornication of her, and kings of the earth, and merchants of the earth, did fornication with her; and they be made rich of the virtue of [the] delights of her. (For all the nations and all the peoples have drunk of the wrath of her fornication, and the kings of the earth, and the merchants of the earth, did fornication with her; and they be made rich from the abundance of her delights.)

4 And I heard another voice of heaven, saying, My people, go ye out of it, and be ye not partners of the trespasses of it, and ye shall not receive of the wounds of it [or of the plagues of it]. (And I heard another voice from heaven, saying, My people, go out of it, and do not be made the partners of its trespasses, and then ye shall not share in its plagues, or its torments.)

5 For the sins of it came unto heaven, and the Lord had mind of the wickedness(es) of it. (For its sins came unto heaven, and the Lord remembered its wickednesses.)

6 Yield ye to it, as she yielded to you; and double ye double things, after her works; in the drink that she meddled to you, meddle or mingle ye double to her, (or of the drink which she mixed for you, mix ye double for her).

7 As much as she glorified herself, and was in delights, so much torment give ye to her, and wailing, [or weeping, *or mourning*]; for in

her heart she saith, I sit a queen, and I am not a widow, and I shall not see wailing, [or weeping, *or mourning*].

8   And therefore in one day her wounds [or her plagues] shall come, death, and mourning, and hunger; and she shall be burnt in (the) fire, for God is strong, that shall deem her, (or for God is strong, who shall judge her).

9   And the kings of the earth shall beweep, and bewail themselves on her (or and bewail themselves over her), which did fornication with her, and lived in delights, when they shall see the smoke of the burning of it;

10   standing afar, for dread of the torments of it, saying, Woe! woe! that great city Babylon, and that strong city; for in one hour thy doom cometh. (standing afar, for fear of its torments, saying, Woe! woe! that great city Babylon, and that strong city; for in one hour thy judgement cometh.)

11   And merchants of the earth shall weep on it, and mourn, for no man shall buy more the merchandise of them; (And the merchants of the earth shall weep over it, and mourn, for no one shall buy their merchandise any more;)

12   the merchandise of gold, and of silver, and of precious stone(s), and of pearl(s), and of bis, (or and of bisso, or fine linen), and of purple, and of silk, and of cotton, and of each tree thyme (or thyine), and all vessels of ivory, and all vessels of precious stone(s), and of brass, and of iron, and of marble.

13   and of cinnamon, and of sweet smelling things, and ointments, and of incense, and of wine, and of oil, and of flour, and of wheat, and of work beasts, and of sheep, and of horses, and of chariots, and of servants, and of other lives of men.

14   And thine apples of the desire of thy life, [or And thine apples, the desires of thy life], went away from thee, and all fatted things, and full clear (or truly glorious) perished [away] from thee.

15   And (the) merchants of these things shall no more find those things [or these goods]. They that be made rich of it, shall stand [a]far (off), for dread of (the) torments of it (or for fear of its torments), weeping, and mourning,

16   and saying, Woe! woe! that great city, that was clothed with bis, (or which was clothed in bisso, or fine linen), and purple, and red scarlet, and was over-gilded with gold, and precious stone(s), and margarites (or pearls),

17   for in one hour so many riches be destitute, *either done away*. And each governor, and all that sail by ship into place(s), and mariners, and they that work in the sea, stood (a)far (off),

18   and cried, seeing the place of the burning of it, saying, What [*city*] *is* like this great city?

19   And they cast powder on their heads, and cried, weeping, and mourning, and saying, Woe! woe! that great city, in which all that have ships in the sea be made rich of the prices of it; for in one hour it is desolate.

20   Heaven, and holy apostles, and prophets, make ye full out joy on it, for God hath deemed your doom on it. (Heaven, and the holy apostles, and the prophets, rejoice over it, for God hath taken vengeance upon it for you.)

21   And one strong angel took up a stone, as a great millstone, and cast (it) into the sea, and said, In this force [or In this fierceness] that great city Babylon shall be sent, and now it shall no more be found.

22   And the voice of harps (or And the sound of harps), and of men of music, and singing with pipe and trump, shall no more be heard in it. And each craftsman, and each craft, shall no more be found in it. And the voice of a millstone shall no more be heard in thee (or And the sound of a millstone shall no more be heard in thee),

23   and the light of [the] lantern shall no more shine in thee, and the voice of the husband and of the wife shall no more be heard in thee; for thy merchants were (the) princes of the earth. For in thy witchcrafts all folks erred (or For all

the nations and all the peoples went astray in thy witchcrafts).

24 And the blood of (the) prophets and of (the) saints is found in it, and of all men that be slain in (the) earth. (And the blood of the prophets and of God's people is found in it, yea, the blood of all those who were killed on the earth.)

CHAPTER 19

1 After these things I heard as a great voice of many trumps in heaven, saying, Alleluia; praising, and glory, and virtue is to our God; (After these things I heard loud voices in heaven like the sound of many trumpets, saying, Alleluia; praise, and glory, and power be to our God;)

2 for true and just be the dooms of him, which deemed the great whore, that defouled [or corrupted] the earth in her lechery, and (a)venged the blood of his servants, of the hands of her. (for true and righteous be his judgements, who judged the great whore, who corrupted the earth with her lechery, and avenged the blood of his servants, by the hands of her.)

3 And again they said, Alleluia. And the smoke of it ascendeth up, into the worlds of worlds, (or And its smoke goeth up forever and ever).

4 And the four and twenty elder men and the four beasts felled down, and worshipped God sitting on the throne, and said, Amen, Alleluia. (And the twenty-four elders and the four creatures fell down, and worshipped God sitting on the throne, and said, Amen, Alleluia.)

5 And a voice went out of the throne, and said, All the servants of our God, say ye praisings to our God, and ye that dread God, small and great. (And a voice went out from the throne, and said, All the servants of our God, say praises to our God, and ye who have fearful reverence for God, great and small.)

6 And I heard a voice [as] of a great trump, as the voice of many waters, and as the voice of great thunders, saying, Alleluia; for our Lord God almighty hath reigned. (And I heard a sound like a great trumpet, like the sound of many waters, and like the sound of loud thunder, saying, Alleluia; for our Lord God Almighty hath reigned.)

7 Joy we, and make we mirth, [or Joy we withinforth, and glad we withoutforth], and give glory to him; for the weddings of the lamb came, and the wife of him made ready herself (or and his wife-to-be made herself ready).

8 And it was given to her, that she cover her[self] with white bisso shining; for why bisso is the justifyings of (the) saints. (And it was given to her, that she cover herself with shining white linen; because fine linen is the justifyings, or the righteous deeds, of God's people.)

9 And he said to me, Write thou, Blessed be they that be called to the supper of the weddings of the lamb. And he said to me, These words of God be true.

10 And I felled down before his feet, to worship him. And he said to me, See thou, that thou do not; (for) I am a servant (along) with thee, and of thy brethren, having the witnessing of Jesus; worship thou God. For the witnessing of Jesus is the spirit of prophecy. (And I fell down before his feet, to worship him. And he said to me, See that thou do not do that; for I am a servant along with thee, and with thy brothers, bearing the testimony of Jesus; worship God. For the testimony of Jesus is the spirit of prophecy.)

11 And I saw heaven opened, and lo! a white horse, and he that sat on him was called Faithful and soothfast; and with rightwiseness he deemeth, and fighteth. (And I saw heaven opened, and behold, a white horse, and he who sat upon him was called Faithful and Truthful, or Faithful and True; and he judgeth with righteousness or justly, and fighteth with righteousness or fighteth justly.)

12 And his eyes *were* as (the) flame of fire, and in his head many diadems (or and on his head were many crowns); and he had a name written, which no man knew, but he.

13 And he was clothed in a cloth sprinkled with blood (or And he was clothed in a cloak covered with blood); and the name of him was called The Son of God [or and the name of him was called The Word of God].

14 And the hosts that be in heaven, (pur)sued him on white horses, clothed with bisso, white and clean. (And the hosts that be in heaven, followed him on white horses, and they were clothed in clean white fine linen.)

15 And a sword sharp on either side [or on each side] came forth (out) of his mouth, that with it he smite folks (or and he shall strike the nations and the peoples with it); and he shall rule them with an iron rod. And he treadeth the presser of wine of (the) strong vengeance [and] of the wrath of almighty God.

16 And he hath written in his cloth, and in the hip [or in his hem], King of kings and Lord of lords. (And he hath written on his cloak, and on his hip, or on his thigh, King of kings and Lord of lords.)

17 And I saw an angel, standing in the sun; and he cried with a great voice, and said to all birds that flew by the middle of heaven, (or and he cried with a loud voice, and said to all the birds that flew through the midst of the heavens), Come ye, and be ye gathered [together] to the great supper of God,

18 (so) that ye eat the flesh of kings, and [the] flesh of tribunes, and [the] flesh of strong men, and (the) flesh of horses, and of those that sit on them, and the flesh of all free men and of bondmen, and of small and of great.

19 And I saw the beast, and the kings of the earth, and the hosts of them gathered (or and their armies gathered), to make battle with him, that sat on the horse, and with his host.

20 And the beast was caught, and with her the false prophet, that made signs before her, (or And the beast was caught, and the false prophet with him, who made miracles before him); in which he deceived them that took the character [or the mark] of the beast, and that worshipped the image of it. These two were sent quick (or alive) into the pool of fire, burning with brimstone.

21 And the others were slain with the sword of him that sat on the horse, that cometh forth (out) of the mouth of him; and all (the) birds were [full-]filled with the flesh of them (or and all the birds were filled full with their flesh).

CHAPTER 20

1 And I saw an angel coming down from heaven, having the key of (the) deepness, (or the key of the depth, or of the abyss), and a great chain in his hand.

2 And he caught the dragon, the old serpent, that is the Devil and Satan; and he bound him by a thousand years (or and he bound him for a thousand years).

3 And he sent him into (the) deepness, and closed, and marked [or sealed] on him, that he deceive no more the folks, till a thousand years be [ful]filled, (or And he sent him into the depth, or into the abyss, and enclosed it, and sealed it over him, so that he would no longer deceive the nations and the peoples, until the thousand years were over). After these things it behooveth him to be unbound (for) a little time.

4 And I saw seats, and they sat on them, and doom was given to them. And the souls of men beheaded for the witnessing of Jesus, and for the word of God, and them that worshipped not the beast, neither the image of it, neither took the character of it in their foreheads, neither in their hands. And they lived, and reigned with Christ (for) a thousand years. (And I saw thrones, and they who sat upon them, and judgement was given to them. And I saw the souls of men beheaded for their testimony

about Jesus, and for the word of God, and those who did not worship the beast, or its image, nor received its mark on their foreheads, or on their hands. And they lived, and reigned with the Messiah for a thousand years.)

5 And (the) others of (the) dead men lived not [or The others of (the) dead lived not], till a thousand years were ended. This is the first again-rising. (And the others of the dead did not live, until the thousand years were over. This is the first resurrection.)

6 Blessed and holy *is* he, that hath part in the first again-rising. In these men the second death hath not power [or In these the second death hath no power]; but they shall be priests of God, and of Christ, and they shall reign with him a thousand years, (or but they shall be the priests of God, and of the Messiah, and they shall reign with him for a thousand years).

7 And when a thousand years shall be ended, Satan shall be unbound of his prison; (And when the thousand years shall be over, Satan shall be released from his prison;)

8 and he shall go out, and shall deceive folks, that be on (the) four corners of the earth, Gog and Magog. And he shall gather them [together] into battle, whose number is as the gravel of the sea. (and he shall go out, and shall deceive the nations and the peoples, that be on the four corners of the earth, Gog and Magog. And he shall gather them together into battle, whose number is like, or is as great as, the sand of the sea.)

9 And they ascended upon the broadness of the earth, and environed the castles of (the) saints, and the (be)loved city. And fire came down of God from heaven, and devoured them. (And they ascended upon the broadness of the earth, and encompassed the camp of God's people, and the beloved city. And fire from God came down from heaven, and devoured them.)

10 And the devil, that deceived them, was sent into the pool of fire and brimstone, where both the beast and false prophets shall be tormented day and night, into (the) worlds of worlds. Amen. (And the Devil, who had deceived them, was sent into the pool of fire and brimstone, where both the beast and the false prophet shall be tormented day and night, forever and ever. Amen.)

11 And I saw a great white throne, and one sitting on it, from whose sight (the) earth fled [or flew away], and heaven, (or from whose sight the earth, and heaven, fled or flew away); and the place is not found of them.

12 And I saw (the) dead men, great and small, standing in the sight of the throne; and (the) books were opened; and another book was opened, which is the book of life; and dead men were deemed of these things that were written in the books, after the works of them. (And I saw the dead, great and small, standing in the sight of the throne; and the books were opened; and another book was opened, which is the Book of Life; and the dead were judged by those things that were written in these books, according to their works.)

13 And the sea gave (up) his dead men, that were in it; and death and hell gave (up) their dead, that were in them. And it was deemed of each, after the works of them. (And the sea gave up its dead, who were in it; and death and hell gave up their dead, who were in them. And everyone was judged, according to their works.)

14 And hell and death were sent into the pool of fire. This is the second death.

15 And he that was not found written in the book of life, was sent into the pool of fire.

CHAPTER 21

1 And I saw (a) new heaven and (a) new earth; for the first heaven and the first earth went away, and the sea is not now (or and the sea was no more).

2   And I, John, saw the holy city Jerusalem, new, coming down from heaven, made ready of God, as a wife adorned to her husband, (or made ready by God, like a wife adorned for her husband).

3   And I heard a great voice from the throne, saying, (or And I heard a loud voice from the throne, saying), Lo! the tabernacle of God *is* with men, and he shall dwell with them; and they shall be his people, and he God with them shall be their God.

4   And God shall wipe away each tear from the eyes of them; and death shall no more be, neither mourning, neither crying, neither sorrow, (all) shall be over (or all shall be ended); which first things went away.

5   And he said, that sat in the throne, (or And he, who sat on the throne, said), Lo! I make all things new. And he said to me, Write thou, for these words be most faithful and true.

6   And he said to me, It is done; I am alpha and omega, the beginning and the end. I shall give freely of the well of quick water to him that thirtieth. (And he said to me, It is done; I am Alpha and Omega, the Source and the Fulfillment. I shall give freely from the spring of living water to anyone who thirsteth.)

7   He that shall overcome, shall wield these things, (or He who shall overcome, shall possess these things); and I shall be God to him, and he shall be (a) son to me.

8   But to fearedful men, and unbelieveful, and cursed, and man-quellers, and fornicators, and to witches, and to worshippers of idols, and to all (the) liars, the part of them shall be in the pool burning with fire and brimstone, that is the second death. (But to cowards, and to the unbelieving, or the unfaithful, and to the cursed, and to murderers, and to fornicators, and to witches, and to worshippers of idols, and to all the liars, their portion, or their lot, shall be in the pool burning with fire and brimstone, that is the second death.)

9   And one came of the seven angels, having vials full of the seven last vengeances [or the seven last plagues]. And he spake with me, and said, Come thou, and I shall show to thee the spousess, the wife of the lamb. (And one of the seven angels came, bearing seven basins, or seven bowls, full of the seven last plagues. And he spoke with me, and said, Come, and I shall show to thee the spousess, the wife of the Lamb.)

10   And he took me up in (the) Spirit into a great hill and high (or And he took me up in the Spirit onto a great high hill); and he showed to me the holy city of Jerusalem, coming down from (the) heaven of God,

11   having the clarity of God (or shining with the glory of God); and the light of it like [to] a precious stone, as the stone jasper, [and] as crystal.

12   And it had a wall great and high, having twelve gates, and in the gates of it twelve angels, and names written in, that be the names of [the] twelve lineages of the sons of Israel; (And it had a great high wall, with twelve gates, and at its gates were twelve angels, and the names written on those gates were the names of the twelve tribes of the Israelites;)

13   from the east three gates, and from the north three gates, and from the south three gates, and from the west three gates.

14   And the wall of the city had twelve foundaments, and in them, the twelve names of the twelve apostles, and of the lamb. (And the wall of the city had twelve foundations, and written on them were the twelve names of the twelve apostles of the Lamb.)

15   And he that spake with me, had a golden measure of a reed, that he should mete the city, and the gates of it, and the wall. (And he who spoke with me, had a gold measuring rod, so that he could measure the city, and its gates, and the wall.)

16   And the city was set in square; and the length of it is so much, as much as *is* the

breadth. And he meted the city with the reed, by furlongs twelve thousands, (or And he measured the city with the measuring rod, twelve thousand furlongs). And the height, and the length and the breadth of it, be even.

17 And he meted the walls of it, of an hundred and forty and four cubits, by (the) measure(ment) of man, that is, of the angel. (And he measured its walls, a hundred and forty-four cubits, according to human measurement, which the angel used.)

18 And the building of the wall thereof was of the stone jasper. And the city itself was clean gold, like [to] clean glass, (or And the city itself was made of pure gold, like clear or shining glass).

19 And the foundaments of the wall of the city *were* adorned with all precious stone(s), (or And the foundations of the city wall *were* adorned with every precious stone). The first foundament, jasper; the second, sapphire; the third, chalcedony; the fourth, emerald;

20 the fifth, sardonyx; the sixth, sardius; the seventh, chrysolyte; the eighth, beryl; the ninth, topaz; the tenth, chrysoprasus; the eleventh, jacinth (or hyacinth); the twelfth, amethyst.

21 And the twelve gates be twelve margarites, by each; and each gate was of each margarite. And the streets of the city *were* clean gold, as of glass full shining. (And the twelve gates were made out of twelve pearls; and each gate was made out of one pearl. And the city streets *were* made of pure gold, like shining glass.)

22 And I saw no temple in it, for the Lord God almighty and the lamb, is the temple of it. (And I did not see any Temple in it, for the Lord God Almighty and the Lamb be its Temple.)

23 And the city hath no need of the sun, neither [of] (the) moon, that they shine in it; for the clarity of God shall lighten it [or shall light it]; and the lamb is the lantern of it. (And the city hath no need of the sun, nor of the moon, that they shine in it; for the glory of God shall light it or shall illumine it; and the Lamb is its lantern.)

24 And folks shall walk in the light of it (or And the nations and the peoples shall walk in its light); and the kings of the earth shall bring their glory and honour into it.

25 And the gates of it shall not be closed by day; and night shall not be there.

26 And they shall bring the glory and (the) honour of folks into it. (And they shall bring the glory and the wealth of the nations and the peoples into it.)

27 Neither any man [or anything] defouled, and doing abomination and leasing, shall enter into it; [no] but they that be written in the book of life of the lamb. (And nothing defiled, and no one doing abomination and telling lies, shall enter into it; only those *whose names* be written in the Lamb's Book of Life.)

CHAPTER 22

1 And he showed to me a river of quick water, shining as crystal, coming forth of the seat of God, and of the lamb, (And he showed me a river of living water, shining like crystal, coming forth from the throne(s) of God and of the Lamb,)

2 in the middle of the street of it. And on each side of the river, the tree of life, bringing forth twelve fruits, yielding his fruit by each month; and the leaves of the tree *be* to health of folks. (in the middle of the city's street. And on each side of the river, the Tree of Life, bringing forth twelve fruits, yielding its fruit every month of the year; and the leaves of the tree *be* for the healing of the nations and the peoples.)

3 And each cursed thing shall no more be; but the seats of God and of the lamb shall be in it (or but the thrones of God and of the Lamb shall be in it). And the servants of him shall

serve him.

4 And they shall see his face, and his name [*shall be*] in their foreheads. (And they shall see his face, and his name *shall be* upon their foreheads.)

5 And (the) night shall no more be, and they shall not have (any) need to the light of a lantern, neither to (the) light of the sun; for the Lord God shall lighten them [or shall light them], and they shall reign into (the) worlds of worlds. (And the night shall be no more, and they shall not have any need for the light from a lantern, nor for the light from the sun; for the Lord God shall give them light, and they shall reign forever and ever.)

6 And he said to me, These words be most faithful and true. And the Lord God of spirits of (the) prophets sent his angel, to show to his servants, what things it behooveth to be done soon, (or And the Lord God, who inspired the prophets, sent his angel, to show his servants, what things it behooveth to be done soon).

7 And lo! I come swiftly. Blessed *is* he, that keepeth the words of prophecy of this book. (And behold, I will come quickly. Blessed *is* he, who obeyeth the words of prophecy in this book.)

8 And I *am* John, that heard and saw these things. And after that I had heard and seen (them), I felled down, to worship before the feet of the angel, that showed to me these things.

9 And he said to me, See thou, that thou do not; for I am a servant with thee, and of thy brethren, (the) prophets, and of them that keep the words of prophecy of this book; worship thou God. (And he said to me, See that thou do not do that; for I am a servant along with thee, and with thy brothers, the prophets, and with all those who obey the words of prophecy in this book; worship God.)

10 And he said to me, Sign, *or seal*, thou not the words of prophecy of this book; for the time is nigh. (And he said to me, Do not thou

seal up the words of prophecy in this book; for the time is near.)

11 He that annoyeth, annoy he yet; and he that is in filths, wax he foul yet; and a just man, be [he] justified yet; and the holy, be [he] hallowed yet. (He who harmeth, still harm; and he who is in filth, continue to grow foul; and a righteous man, still be righteous; and the holy, continue to be holy.)

12 Lo! I come soon, and my meed (is) with me, to yield to each man after his works. (Behold, I will soon come, and my reward is with me, to yield to each person after their works.)

13 I am alpha and omega, the first and the last, beginning and end. (I am Alpha and Omega, the first and the last, the Source and the Fulfillment.)

14 Blessed *be* they, that wash their stoles, (so) that the power of them be in the tree of life, and (they) enter by the gates into the city.

15 For withoutforth [*shall be shut*] (the) hounds, and witches, and unchaste men, and man-quellers, and (those) serving to idols, and each that loveth and maketh leasing. (For the hounds, and the witches, and the unchaste, and the murderers, and those who serve idols, and all those who love to tell lies, *shall be shut* outside.)

16 I, Jesus, sent mine angel, to witness to you these things in (the) churches, (or I, Jesus, sent my angel to testify to you about these things in the churches). I am the root and (the) kin of David, and the shining morrow star.

17 And the Spirit and the spousess [or the wife] say, Come thou. And he that heareth, say, Come thou; and he that thirsteth, come; and he that will, take he freely the water of life, (or and anyone who desireth, taketh freely of the water of life).

18 And I witness to each man hearing the words of prophecy of this book, if any man shall put to these things, God shall put on him the vengeances [or the plagues] written in this

book. (And I testify to everyone who heareth the words of prophecy in this book, if anyone shall add anything to these words, God shall put on him the plagues written in this book.)

19   And if any man [shall] do away of the words of the book of this prophecy, God shall take away the part of him from the book of life, and from the holy city, and from these things that be written in this book. (And if anyone shall do away with any of the words of prophecy in this book, God shall take away his portion, or his share, from the Book of Life, and from the holy city, and from these things that be written in this book.)

20   He saith, that beareth witnessing of these things, Yea, Amen. [Lo!] I come soon. Amen. Come thou, Lord Jesus. (He saith, who giveth testimony about these things, Yes, Amen. Behold, I will come soon. Amen. Come, Lord Jesus.)

21   The grace of our Lord Jesus Christ *be* with you all. Amen. †

GLOSSARY for *Wycliffe's New Testament*

For many Middle English words given below, their most obvious, modern meaning is assumed; only a supplemental, perhaps unexpected, definition is given (e.g., "and: *also*"). Commas separate variations of the same meaning; semi-colons distinguish different definitions of the same word. <u>Underlined words</u> are my replacements for "dead" or obsolete words. All other words are found in a somewhat recognizable form in the "Wycliffe Bible".

A

aback: *back, backward.*

abide: *to remain; to wait for; to endure.*

abode: (v) *remained or lived at; waited for; endured.*

above-ordaineth: *to add to.*

above-seeming: *beyond grasp or measurement, 'most excellent' (also 'over-seeming').*

abridge: *to shorten.*

accept(ed): *acceptable.*

acceptation: *favourable reception, approval, 'acceptance'.*

acception: *partiality, favour- itism, approval, 'acceptance'.*

acceptor: *one who accepts or respects preferentially, 'respecter'.*

accord: *to agree with, in concord with (also 'accordeth').*

according: (n) *an agreement.*

accursed: *cursed.*

acknowledge: (v) *to confess; to profess.*

acknowledged: (n) *friends and acquaintances, one's 'known'.*

acknowledging: (n) *'an acknowledgement'; the act of confession or profession.*

acount: *to count; to reckon (survives in 'accounting').*

adder: *viper.*

adjure: *to entreat, earnestly appeal to.*

administration: *ministry or service.*

admonish: *to reprove; to warn; to exhort.*

adorn: *to bring credit to; to add lustre to, improve the appearance of.*

adown: *down.*

afeared: *afraid.*

after: *according to.*

again-begetting: *being born again (also 'again-begotten').*

again-bought: (v) *redeemed.*

again-buy: (v) *to redeem.*

again-buyer: *redeemer.*

again-newing: *renewing.*

again-promise: *a promise.*

again-raise: (v) *to raise up; to resurrect.*

again-rise: (v) *to resurrect.*

again-rising: *resurrection.*

again-said: *'gainsaid' or 'said- again(st)', opposed, resisted, or contradicted.*

again-say: (v) *'to gainsay' or 'say-again(st)', to oppose, resist, or contradict (also 'again- sayeth').*

again-saying: (n) *'gainsaying' or 'saying-again(st)', answering back, verbally opposing, resisting, contradicting.*

against: *directly opposite; to meet (sometimes with 'to come' or 'to go').*

against-said: *see 'again-said'.*

against-say: *see 'again-say'.*

against-stand: (v) *to 'stand- against', to physically resist, withstand, or oppose.*

against-stood: *'stood-against', withstood, resisted, opposed.*

again-ward: *on the contrary; to the other side.*

alarged: *enlarged.*

alder-highest: *lit. the 'senior- highest', both 'elder' or 'oldest' highest, and 'chief' or 'most' highest (survives in 'alderman').*

alien: (n) *stranger, foreigner.*

aliened: (v) *estranged, alienated.*

alighten: *to bring to light, 'to enlighten'.*

all wise: *all ways, in all manner.*

all-gates: *always (from 'algatis' or 'allegates'; perhaps derived from the time when cities were fortified with gates as 'ways' to enter and exit; hence, 'all-gates' prefigures 'all-ways', and so 'always').*

allway/alway: *always (both words are found in the "Wycliffe Bible" and the KJV).*

ambush: (n, v) *lying in wait; treason (from 'aspies'; also 'ambushing(s)').*

amend: *to mend, put right or correct.*

amorrow: *the next day, 'tomorrow'.*

and: *also ('also' is found in the "Wycliffe Bible").*

announce: *to proclaim without allowing dissent, 'to command' (from 'denounce').*

anon: *at once, immediately, straightaway (found in the*

"Wycliffe Bible" and the KJV).

apert: (adv) *open (survives in 'aperture').*

apocalypse: *revelation.*

appareled: *attired, dressed, furnished.*

apprehend: *to grasp, seize, take hold of.*

approach: (v) *modern equivalent of 'to nigh' (also 'approacheth').*

araised: *raised or lifted up.*

architricline: *master of a feast.*

areach: (v) *to give to.*

areared: *reared or raised up.*

areckon: (v) *to reckon or take an accounting of (from 'arette'; 'reckon' is found in the "Wycliffe Bible").*

argentary: *silversmith.*

arms: *weapons.*

asides half: *in private (also 'asides hand').*

assay: (v) *to try, test, or prove.*

assign: *to appoint or ordain (from 'dispose'; 'assign' is found in the "Wycliffe Bible").*

assoiled: *absolved.*

assuage: *to alleviate.*

astrologer: *one who divines destiny by means of movement of heavenly bodies. The word in the "Later Version" is actually 'astronomer'. However, in the 17ᵀᴴ century, 'astronomer'/'astrologer' and 'astronomy'/'astrology' switched meanings and became defined as we know them today. And so, 'astrologer' is used in Wycliffe's New Testament.*

astronomer: *see 'astrologer' above (also 'astronomy').*

asunder: *into pieces or parts; separated or divided.*

attention: *from 'tent'.*

atwain: *in two; apart.*

atwo: *in two.*

aught: *any, anything, something.*

author: *originator, creator.*

avow: (n) *a solemn promise, declaration or pledge, a vow or avowal;* (v) *to make a vow.*

B

bade: *invited; ordered.*

bailiff: *an overseer of an estate, a steward (from 'bailee').*

bailiffship: *a bailiff's area of authority or responsibility (from 'bailey: the surrounding area of a castle contained within its outer walls, or its courtyard'; survives in 'bailiwick' and the 'Old Bailey', London's criminal courts).*

barbaric: (n) *barbarian.*

be busy: *to care about, or to be concerned about.*

be: *are (pl. form of verb 'to be').*

beastly: *animal nature; material (vs. spiritual).*

befall: *to happen or occur (also 'befell(ed)').*

before-goer: *one who goes or went before, a forerunner; one's superior.*

before-going: *going before.*

before-knew: *known before or known for a long time.*

before-knowing: *knowing beforehand, 'foreknowing'.*

before-ordained: *fore-ordained.*

before-ordinance of worlds: *Divine destiny.*

before-said: *said before, aforesaid, aforementioned.*

before-think: *to think before, or to have forethought.*

before-told: *foretold.*

before-witting: *to know beforehand, foreknowing.*

before-written: *written (long*

before, foreordained.

begotten: *engendered, caused to be.*

beguiled: *deceived.*

beguiler: *a deceiver.*

behest: (n) *a command (found in its obsolete meaning of 'promise' throughout the "Wycliffe Bible").*

beholden: *beheld.*

behoove: *ought, must, incumbent upon (also 'behooveth', 'behooved').*

belief: (n) *faith.*

bemourned: *mourned over.*

beneficence: *favours, good services, gifts (from 'benefice', which survives as 'a church office endowed with funds or property').*

benign: *kind, gentle, mild.*

benignity: *goodness, kindness.*

beseech: *to earnestly implore.*

beseechings: (n) *earnest requests, supplications, entreaties.*

beseem: *to be fitting or appropriate, 'becoming'.*

beseemeth to me: *seems to me.*

beset: *to harass, encircle, attack on all sides.*

besom: *broom or bundle of twigs used for sweeping.*

besought: *beseeched.*

bespat: *spat upon.*

bespit: *to spit upon.*

betake: *to deliver to, to give over to; to commit to.*

betaken: *delivered to or given to; committed to.*

bethink: *to think upon; to remember.*

bethought: *thought upon or about; remembered.*

betook: *gave over or delivered to.*

betwixt: *between.*

GLOSSARY

bewail: *to wail over.*

beweep: *to weep over.*

bezant: *precious Byzantine coin (of gold or silver) of substantial value, analogous to the British pound of the 14TH century.*

bilibre: *a weight of 2 pounds.*

bill: *a written statement.*

bis: *see bisso.*

bishopric: *office or diocese of a bishop.*

bisso: *a fine, sheer linen made of stiff, round yarns which give a crisp texture (now used for altar cloths).*

blame: *(v) to reproach, accuse.*

blessfulness: *blessedness.*

bliss: *heaven.*

blown: *puffed up, inflated.*

board: *(n) table; dinner; money-changer.*

body-like: *bodily.*

bondman: *a servant or slave (survives as 'bondsman').*

bonds: *bondage, captivity; bands.*

bound: *(n) prisoner.*

bowels: *see entrails.*

brand: *(n) torch.*

brethren: *brothers.*

brink: *edge or shore of a body of water.*

brock: *(n) a badger.*

broken: *stopped (2ND Cor. 11:10).*

bruise: *(v) to crush or pound into powder.*

buffet: *(n) a hit or strike; (v) to hit or strike.*

buffoonery: *jesting, ribaldry (from 'harlotry').*

burgher: *a citizen of a town, burgh or city.*

busily: *diligently.*

busyness: *diligence; concern, care; earnestness (also 'busynesses').*

butchery: *a slaughterhouse.*

by cause: *by reason of, 'because'.*

by compass: *all around; round about.*

by kind: *by nature, 'naturally'.*

by row: *in order.*

C

call: *from 'clepen' ('called' is found in the Wycliffe Old Testament).*

came against: *met.*

canst: *knowest (how to), 'knows'.*

captive: *(n) prisoner.*

care: *(v) to have concern for, or an interest in (something).*

cares: *(n) concerns or worries.*

carrions: *dead, putrefying flesh.*

cast: *(v) to throw.*

casting out: *(n) that which is discarded, thrown off or out.*

casting: *(n) vomit (also found as 'casting-up').*

castle(s): *town, village; fortified place, camp, fortress.*

cause: *reason for something; case; accusation.*

caution: *a pledge or obligation (to reimburse), a 'bill to pay'.*

chaffer: *(v) to trade, bargain, buy and sell.*

chalice: *a large drinking cup or goblet (survives as the Eucharist cup in which the wine is consecrated).*

chamber: *room.*

changer: *money-changer.*

changing: *money-exchange, exchanging.*

charge: *(n) burden, load; care, concern; a command; ship's cargo.*

charge: *(v) to burden or concern; to command.*

chargeable: *burdensome.*

chargeous: *burdensome (see 'in charge to').*

charity: *love.*

chattel: *personal property.*

cheer: *(n) face (from Old French).*

chide: *(v) to scold, rebuke, reproach.*

chidings: *(n) scoldings, rebukes, reproaches.*

child: *(n) a servant (pl. children: servants); (v) to give birth to.*

chimney: *fireplace, furnace, stove.*

christen: *to baptize (survives in 'naming during baptism', and, in particular, 'to baptize infants').*

cistern: *an artificial reservoir or tank for water.*

clarified: *'glorified' (see next entry).*

clarify: *(v) to make clear, free from all impurities, 'to glorify'.*

clarity: *clearness, lucidity, 'glory'.*

cleansings: *(n) refuse, that which is cleansed or removed, purgings.*

clear: *pure; clean; transparent; 'glorious'.*

clearness: *'glory'.*

cleaved: *split into parts; adhered to.*

cleaveth: *to join or adhere to.*

cloak: *a loose-fitting outer garment (from 'cloth', which the "Wycliffe Bible" also uses as the singular of 'clothes'; survives in 'man of the cloth').*

cloth: *outer garment; singular of clothes (see 'cloak' above).*

'clothes: *idiomatic abbreviation for 'swaddling clothes' (Luke 2:7 and 2:12).*

cockles: *weeds that grow among grain (also referred to as 'darnels' and 'tares').*

coffin: *basket (survives in 'coffer').*

collects: *the gathering of money from church-goers (survives in* 'collection: the weekly giving of money for church expenses').

collyrium: eye-salve.

colour: false pretence or appearance.

come against: (v) to meet.

comeling: newcomer, stranger (see '–ling' below).

comfort: to make strong or to strengthen; to exhort; to give help, hope or support.

commander: leader, master.

'common beholding place': a theatre or public auditorium.

common ward: prison.

communer: one who partakes in the Eucharist.

communing: fellowship; partaking with, or sharing; communion; communication; to empathize with.

company: crowd, multitude of people (also 'company of people', 'companies', 'companies of people').

comparison: (v) to compare (also 'comparisoned', 'comparisoning').

compass: (v) to go round; to surround.

comprehend: (v) to physically apprehend, grasp, catch, or lay hold of (this usage found in the "Wycliffe Bible" and the KJV); to understand.

compunct: (v) to feel remorse, guilt, or pity (also 'compuncted').

compunction: a sense of guilt, remorse, or regret arising from wrong-doing.

concision: division, a faction.

concourse: a crowd or throng of people.

concupiscences: lusts; any immoderate desires.

confirm: to affirm or establish;

to make firm or strong, 'to strengthen'.

confound: to confuse; to amaze or astonish; to be ashamed or put to shame.

confusion: embarrassment; disgrace, shame.

conjuration: a swearing together or conspiracy.

conjure: to adjure or solemnly appeal to.

constable: officer of the law or courts (from 'cachepollis: sheriff's officer, enforcer of the law'; perhaps distantly related to 'police').

constrain: to coerce or restrain.

continence: (n) self-restraint, moderation, chastity.

continent: (adj) self-restrained, moderate, sexually chaste.

contrition: remorse, guilt, shame.

conversation: living, or manner of life.

copious: abundant, plentiful.

cor: measure of wheat (8 bushels = 1 cor).

corn: a seed, or kernel, or grain of a cereal plant.

corn-floor: a threshing floor.

couch: a bed or enclosed sleeping space, hence 'bedchamber'.

countenance: face.

covenable: suitable, opportune, fitting, seasonable, in agreement (survives in 'covenant: (n) an agreement; (v) to agree to').

covenability: opportunity ('opportunity' is found in the "Wycliffe Bible").

covent: an assembly or gathering (later became 'convent'; survives in "Covent Gardens").

coveting(s): (n) lust, desire; greed.

covetousness: lust, desire;

greed, 'the over-hard keeping of goods' (from 'covetise').

craftsman: artisan (from 'craftiman').

cratch: a crib or rack especially for fodder; a trough or open box in a stable designed to hold feed or fodder for livestock; a manger; a stall (survives in 'crèche: a manager scene; a crib for feed'; see 'feed-trough').

creature: man; God's creation; man's creations.

crime: wrong-doing; violation of God's Law.

cruet: a small glass bottle.

culver: dove.

cure: to make well; to take care of or to have concern for something or someone.

curiously: meddlesome behaviour, 'pryingly'.

currier: one who curries or dresses tanned hides.

curse: (n) damnation.

cutting: rending.

D

damnation: eternal punishment.

darked: darkened.

darkful: dark-full, 'full of darkness'.

darnels: weeds that grow among wheat (also called 'cockles' or 'tares').

daunt: to tame; to cow.

days of profession: days of declaring or registering oneself, and so, 'a census'.

deadly: mortal.

deal: (v) to give or apportion out.

dearworthy: beloved (sometimes found as 'dearworth' in the "Wycliffe Bible").

decurion: officer commanding ten horsemen; member of a colony senate.

deem: *to judge; to condemn; to damn (also 'deemest'); to think.*

deemer: *one who discerns, 'a judge' ('judge' is found in the "Wycliffe Bible").*

deepness: *(n) bottomless pit, hell.*

deface: *to disfigure one's face.*

defame: *to slander or libel; to accuse.*

defoul: *to defile.*

defouling: *lechery.*

delayed: *deferred.*

delights: *great pleasures, luxuries (from 'delices').*

deliver: *to take or surrender to, to give over to; to release.*

delve: *to dig.*

den: *a cave; a dwelling place for animals.*

denounce: *to attack or condemn openly; to accuse (from 'defame'; 'denounce' is found in the "Wycliffe Bible").*

depart: *to leave.*

deposit: *'the thing betaken to thee', i.e., the word of the Lord.*

deprave: *(v) to corrupt or pervert (from 'shrewide'; 'deprave' is found in the "Wycliffe Bible").*

described: *to make a detailed word-picture or 'description'; to contribute information, and so, 'to participate in a census'.*

describing: *(n) a condition or situation which is 'described', and so, 'a census'.*

desert: *deserving; see 'without desert'.*

desolate: *deserted, forlorn, destitute of life, joy or comfort.*

despise: *to loathe, regard as contemptible; to disdain, scorn, or neglect.*

despisings: *(n) insults, mocking.*

despite: *(n) contempt, dishonour, insult; malice.*

despoiled: *stripped; robbed.*

despoiling: *putting off (of the body).*

determined: *resolutely or firmly decided.*

diadem: *crown.*

diligently: *carefully; industriously.*

discharge: *(v) unburden.*

discipless: *female disciple.*

discipline: *(n) teaching, learning, the state of being informed; (v) to chastise.*

discording: *conflict, strife, contention, the opposite of being in accordance.*

disdain: *(n) that which is unworthy of one's attention; (v) to scorn or feel superior to.*

dis-ease: *'not' ease, so, distress, trouble, tribulation, difficulty.*

dispensation: *distribution; exemption from obligation.*

dispenser: *administrator, steward.*

dispose: *(v) to put into proper arrangement, position, or order; to transfer to another, as by gift; to assign or ordain.*

disputations: *arguments, controversy, debate.*

dissolved: *to depart this life, to die.*

distressed: *extreme suffering or affliction (from 'noyen', which survives in 'annoy'; 'distressed' is found in the "Wycliffe Bible").*

distrouble: *troubled, disturbed (also 'distroubled', 'distroubling').*

diverseth: *is different or distinct from.*

domination: *that which is ruled over, 'dominion'.*

doom (place): *judgment seat, or 'place of judgment', often found in the market place.*

doom(s): *(n) judgment, Divine or legal; condemnation; decrees; law-suits.*

doomsman: *a judge (see 'deemer').*

drachma: *a silver coin of ancient Greece.*

draw: *to pull.*

drawn to pieces: *pulled to pieces ('to pieces' implied in the verb, 'to-drawn'); disembowelled.*

dread: *(n) fear.*

dreaded: *(v) feared.*

dread-full: *'full of dread', fear of the Lord, 'devout'.*

dress: *(v) to put into proper alignment, to make straight; to prepare for use; to direct (this usage survives in 'street address').*

drit: *dung, waste; dirt.*

dropsy: *an accumulation of fluid in body cavities.*

dross: *refuse or impurity in melted metal, 'slag'.*

drove: *(n) a herd or flock, often moving as one.*

drown: *from 'drenched'.*

duke: *nobleman, prince.*

dumb: *silent; mute.*

durst: *dare.*

'dwelling city': *a permanent home.*

E

earth-tiller: *worker of the soil, 'farmer'.*

earth-tilling: *working the soil to produce crops, 'farming'.*

easiness: *a state of ease, without difficulty.*

ecstasy: *'the losing of mind and reason, and hindering of tongue' (gloss from the "Early Version").*

eisell: *vinegar (from Old French).*

either: *or.*

embrace: *from 'biclippe'.*

enclosed: *contained (within).*

encompass: *to surround.*

end: *to become perfect.*

endeavoured: *attempted, made an effort to (from 'enforced').*

ended: *to be made perfect.*

ending: *perfection.*

endured: *made hard, hardened.*

enfatted: *made fat.*

engender: (v) *to bring about, create, produce (from 'gender').*

engolded: *gilded.*

enhance: *to raise up on high, and so, to heighten or increase, as in beauty or quality, 'to exalt'.*

enlighten: *to give light to, to make brighter; to impart new knowledge to (found only in the "Early Version").*

enmity: *deep-seated hostility.*

ensample: *example ('both 'ensample' and 'example' are found in the "Wycliffe Bible" and the KJV; 'example' is found only in the "Early Version").*

ensearch: *to search out or into.*

enstore: *to store up, enclose, or include.*

entering in: (n) *a visit;* (v) *to visit.*

entrails: *idiomatically, one's children or offspring; also, that which one feels most close to, or deeply about (the KJV uses 'bowels' in the same way).*

entries: *gates or entrances.*

entry: (n) *a visit; a way to enter, and so 'an entrance';* (v) *to visit.*

environ: *to encircle or surround (also 'environed', 'environing')*

enwrapped: *wrapped.*

enwrappeth: *wraps.*

epistle: *a letter.*

equity: *fairness, impartiality, justice.*

err: (v) *fig., to go astray, that is, to make a mistake; lit., to stray or wander or roam.*

eschew: *to avoid or shun.*

espy: *to watch, catch sight of, descry, discover; to spy (also 'espied', 'espying').*

evangel: (n) *gospel.*

evangelize: *to preach the gospel.*

even: *equal or one's equal (widespread usage including 'even-captive', 'even-disciples', 'even-elders', 'even-faith', 'even-fellow', 'even-heir', 'even-knight', 'even-labourer', 'even-lineage', 'even-prisoner', 'even-servant', even-worthy, even-worker'); evening.*

evenness: *equality.*

even-pence: *lit. 'equal pennies', the same or equal pay.*

eventide: *evening.*

ever-each: *each and every one.*

evil-at-ease: *sick; distressed.*

excellent: *exceedingly.*

except: *with the exclusion of, without, aside from, besides (from 'outakun: take out').*

excite: *to encourage.*

excusation: (n) *an excuse.*

execrable: *detestable, extremely bad.*

exemplar: *a model, pattern, example (from ('en)saumpler').*

exercitation: (n) *exercise, exertion.*

expedient: *advantageous, profitable.*

expedite: *hasten or speed (up).*

experiment: *to make a test or trial, an assay.*

expound: *to state or declare in detail; to explain or interpret.*

F

facility: *ease, easiness.*

faculties: *gifts or possessions.*

fair: *beautiful; seemly.*

faithful: *'full of faith', believing.*

famed: (v) *proclaimed, celebrated.*

family: *from 'meyne'.*

farthing: *a small British coin of bronze, worth ¼ of a penny.*

fear you: *make you have fear or to be afraid.*

fearedful: *fearful.*

feeble: *maimed, crippled; weak.*

feed-trough: *a trough or open box in a stable designed to hold feed or fodder for livestock, a 'manger' (from Old French 'cratch', which survives in 'crèche: a crib for feed, as well as a representation of the Nativity or 'manager' scene'; see 'cratch').*

feel: *to perceive; to think or judge (also 'feeled', 'feeling').*

feign: *to make a false show of or a sham.*

fell (wisdom): *wicked or deceitful.*

fen: *marsh, bog.*

fescue: *a piece of straw, a mote or a speck of dust.*

field place: *a plain.*

fiend: *a devil; the Devil.*

fiendly: *devilish.*

figure: (n) *form, pattern, example; design.*

fill: *to supply with as much as can be contained, to become full.*

filled: *completed, fulfilled; full.*

filthhood: *dirtiness, shamefulness.*

firm: *solid, stable, secure (from 'sad'; also 'firmer').*

firmness: *moral constancy.*

fleshly: *carnal.*

flew: *fled (p.t. of flee).*

flock: (n) *a group of the same type of animals, 'a herd'.*

flood: *a great body of flowing water, a stream or river; waves.*

flourish: (v) *to blossom, flower, or thrive.*

GLOSSARY

flowered: (v) *blossomed, revived.*

flume: *a narrow passageway (natural or manmade) for water, and so, 'a river'.*

flux: (n) *a flow or discharge.*

foal: *colt.*

folk(s): *nation(s).*

follily: *foolishly.*

folly: *foolishness; acting foolish.*

fond: *foolish.*

for why: *because; for this reason.*

fore-knowing: *prescience.*

forethinking: *repenting (survives in 'forethought: (re)consideration').*

foreyard: *an outer court or enclosed front yard.*

forsake: *to renounce, abandon, relinquish, 'to leave'.*

forsook: *renounced, left.*

forsooth: *'for truth', in truth, certainly.*

forswear: *to swear falsely, to commit perjury, to break an oath.*

forsworn: *those who commit perjury or give false testimony.*

'found': *to provide with food and lodging (Deeds 28:7).*

foundament: *foundation (survives in 'fundament', 'fundamental').*

frail: *physically or morally weak.*

frauded: *defrauded.*

frothing: *foaming.*

froward: *disobedient, intractable.*

fulfill: *to accomplish; to satisfy.*

full hieingly: *speedily.*

full sorry: *extremely regretful.*

full waxen: *reached adulthood, mature, fully grown.*

fuller: *one that 'fulls' or makes cloth thicker and more compact through moistening and beating.*

full-fill: *to completely fill.*

full-filled: *full.*

G

gab: *to lie or spread falsehoods (also 'gabbing'; survives as 'to prattle or chatter').*

gainsaid: *'said-against', opposed, resisted, or contradicted.*

gainsaith: (v) *to 'say-against', to oppose, resist, or contradict (also "gainsay").*

gainsayer: (n) *one who answers back, contradicts, verbally opposes or resists.*

gainsaying: (n) *'saying-against', answering back, verbally opposing or resisting, contradicting.*

garden: *from Old French; found in the "Wycliffe Bible", as well as 'ȝerde: yard/ garden'.*

garring: *(much) talking (survives in 'garrulous').*

gelding: *eunuch.*

gender: (v) *to cause to be, to beget, 'to engender' (also 'gendereth').*

generation: *offspring; creation of offspring; group of individuals born at the same time (also 'generations').*

germane: *closely related by blood or attitude, and so, a partner, comrade, or yoke-fellow.*

ghostly: *spiritual; spiritually.*

gird: *to clothe oneself; to make ready (also 'girded').*

gladded: *rejoiced, 'full out joyed'.*

glassen: *glassy.*

glory: (n) *magnificent splendour; worshipful adoration.*

glory: (v) *to take pride in; to boast or brag about.*

glossing: (n) *flattery (survives in 'gloss: a superficial or deceptive appearance').*

go against: *go to meet.*

gobbet: *piece or fragment (also 'gobbets').*

Godhead: *divinity.*

goggle-eyed: *bulging eyes, from injury or defect.*

goods: *good things.*

gospel: *'good news' or 'glad tidings', that is, the life and teaching of Jesus Christ.*

governance: *the exercise of authority.*

governor: *steersman; shipmaster; ruler, leader.*

grace: *favour or gift from God; any gift (also 'graces').*

graces: *'thanks to God'.*

graving: *carving, 'engraving'.*

great hunger: *famine.*

grees: *steps or stairway (survives in 'degrees').*

grievous: *burdensome (survives in the idiom of 'to give one grief').*

grieved: *made to feel sorrow or grief.*

grind: *to gnash (the teeth).*

grumble: (v) *to complain in a low, muttering manner (from 'grutchen'; also 'grumbled', 'grumblers', 'grumbling').*

grutch: *to grumble (survives in 'grudge' and 'grouch'; also spelled 'grucche'; also 'gructched', 'grutcher', 'grutching').*

guess: (v) *to suppose or consider; to think.*

guileful: *deceitful, treacherous.*

guiler: *deceiver (survives in 'beguiler').*

guilts: *trespasses, transgressions.*

H

habergeon: *breastplate (from 'haburion'; survives in 'haber-*

dasher').

habit: *deportment, disposition, personal custom; apparel.*

habitacle: *place of habitation (suffix survives in 'tabernacle').*

had mind: *remembered.*

haircloth: *from 'heyre'.*

half: *hand; side.*

hallow: *to make holy, to sanctify.*

hallows: (n) *saints.*

halt: (n) *the crippled or lame.*

harbour: *shelter, lodging, place of rest and refuge.*

harbourgerie: *inn or guest-chamber (from Old French; part of the sense survives in 'menagerie: an enclosure for...').*

harded: *hardened, made stubborn.*

hardeneth: *make stubborn.*

hardily: *boldly.*

hardness: *harshness, severity.*

hardy: *able to endure, tough; bold.*

harlotry: *see 'buffoonery'.*

harm: *to hurt, to wrong (from 'noyen'; survives in 'annoy'; 'harm' is found in the "Wycliffe Bible").*

harmful: *from 'noyous' (close in meaning and sound to 'noxious', but they have different roots).*

hasted: *hastened.*

haunt: *to practise habitually.*

have mind: *to remember.*

having mind: *remembering.*

heals: *healings.*

health: *salvation; healing; soundness, well-being.*

heathen: *the Gentiles (also 'heathen men').*

heaviness: *sorrow, grief (also 'heavinesses').*

heavy: *grieved, burdened, troubled (also 'heavied').*

her: *herself.*

hereof: *of this, in regard to this.*

heretofore: *before now, previously.*

heritage: *inheritance.*

hid place: *secret or private place or conference (the "Wycliffe Bible" also renders this as 'huddles', see below).*

hie: (v) *to hasten or to hurry (also 'hied').*

hieingly: *speedily, hastily.*

high priest(s): *chief priest(s).*

him: *himself; it, itself.*

hind: *a hired farm labourer, 'a hired hand'.*

hinder: (v) *to impede, hamper or delay (from 'let'; also 'hindered', from 'letted').*

hinder: *situated at the back of or rear (the verb form of hinder, 'to hold back or thwart', is not found in the "Wycliffe Bible").*

hire: (n) *payment for labour, wages; reward for service.*

hireling: (n) *he who serves for hire.*

his: *its.*

hold in mind: *to keep in mind, to remember.*

hold: (n) *a prison.*

holden: *held.*

'holding knighthood': *engaged in active military service; 'making war', and so, contextually, 'engaged in spiritual warfare'.*

holiday: *'holy day'.*

holy day: *survives in 'holiday' (but now the meaning is upside-down).*

holy letters: *the scriptures.*

home-church: *church in/at one's home.*

honest: *honourable; good; seemly, becoming, decent.*

honestly: *seemly, becomingly.*

honesty: *seemliness, decency.*

honour: (v) *to do homage to; to give glory to. In the "Wycliffe Bible", as per British usage, 'honour' and 'worship' are interchangeable; in Wycliffe's New Testament, usage follows modern conventions.*

honourable: *worthy of honour (the "Wycliffe Bible" alternates use with the British term 'worshipful').*

honouring: *doing homage to; worshipping.*

honours: (n) *gifts, tokens of respect.*

hoses: *trousers-like garment, worn by men, to cover the lower body (survives in 'hose' and 'hosiery').*

host(s): *army (armies); sacrifice(s) to God.*

hosteller: *inn keeper.*

hostelry: *inn, lodging place (survives in 'hostel').*

household: *from 'meyne' ('household' is found in the "Wycliffe Bible").*

huddles: (n) *secret or private place or conference (the "Wycliffe Bible" gives 'hid place' as an alternate rendering; survives in the modern 'to huddle', which paints a particularly expressive picture in Matt. 6:4 ff.).*

hurled: *thrown (down or against) with force or violence.*

hurting(s): *cause of sin or stumbling, obstacle to righteous living; spurning (see 'offence').*

hurtled: *to rush violently into, to collide with; to strike; to scuttle a ship.*

husbandman: *farmer, earth-tiller; master of a household.*

I

idiot: *untaught or uninstructed*

person.

idle: *lazy.*

idly believed: *ineffectively, frivolously, or vainly believed.*

idol: *an image representing a god and worshipped as divine; the object of heathen worship (the "Wycliffe Bible" uses 'idol', 'simulacrum' and 'maumet' interchangeably).*

impaired: (v) *damaged, harmed, made worse, weakened.*

impairing(s): (n) *harm, damage, worsening, weakening, injury, loss (also 'impairment').*

improbity: *persistent or continual asking, 'importunity'.*

impugned: *physically attacked or assailed.*

'in charge to': *as a charge or a burden to, so 'burdensome' (see 'chargeous').*

in compass: *all around, round about, 'to encompass'.*

in kind: *by nature.*

in mind: *to remember, a remembrance.*

in-bloweth: *to puff up or swell (with pride).*

in-blown: *puffed up or swollen (with pride).*

in-call: *to inwardly call upon, to 'invoke'.*

include: *to contain within.*

incorrupt: *not corruptible or subject to decay or ruin (also 'incorruptible', 'incorruption').*

indignations: *provocations, that which raises ire.*

indissoluble: *that which may not be dissolved or undone.*

indulgence: *tolerance (of), permission (to).*

infirmity: *physical, mental, and/or moral weakness; mortality (i.e., humanness).*

inform: *to give character to, to*

imbue or inspire; to teach, give knowledge to or instruct, and so, to 'in-form' or 'form within'; further, to 'reform' or 'restore'.

informing: (n) *making known by example or pattern; inspiring or 'in-forming' (see entry above).*

inopportune: *unsuitable, not fitting, inappropriate, out of season (from 'uncovenable').*

inputted: *placed (or put) on or in; loaded up.*

inset: *set-in or joined.*

'into the middle': *into the centre (of attention).*

inwardnesses: *that which one feels most close to or deeply about (idiomatic expression synonymous with 'entrails' and 'bowels').*

irreprehensible: *without reproof (undeserving of blame or censure).*

itching: *pleasing, tickling, arousing, stirring.*

'it happens': *from 'in happe' (survives in 'hapless').*

J

Jewess: *a female of the Jewish faith.*

Jewry: *Jewish people; the Jewish religion, that is, Judaism.*

joinings: *joints.*

jointures: *junctures, joints.*

joying: *rejoicing.*

jument: *a work or yoke-beast, 'a horse' (survives in 'jumentous').*

just: *righteous.*

justifying: *righteousness.*

justifyings: *ordinances, laws.*

K

keep: (v) *to care for, take care of.*

keeper: *guard, jailer; guardian.*

keeping: (n) *prison, hold, cage; (v) guarding, watching, custody*

of.

kept: (n) *prisoners; (v) guarded, watched; preserved.*

kids: *young goats.*

kin: *kindred, family.*

kind: *nature; type, sort; kindred; offspring or generation.*

kindled: *caused to burn, ignited.*

kindlings: *the young of a particular 'kind' or family, so 'offspring' (survives in 'kindergarten'; see '–ling' below).*

kindred: *relatives; tribes.*

knave: *boy, male child.*

knight: *a soldier (remember, this text dates from the 14TH century).*

knighthood: *warfare, combat, battle (see 'holding knighthood').*

knighthood of heaven: *host or army of heaven.*

knitches: *a number of things tied or knit together, 'a bundle' (survives in 'knitting').*

knowing: (n) *knowledge (from 'kunnyng'; 'knowing' is found in the "Wycliffe Bible").*

known: (n) *one's acquaintances.*

L

laid ambush: *laid wait.*

language(s): *a spiritual language or spiritual speaking; words of speech used by a group to communicate (e.g., 'the English language'). The "Wycliffe Bible" uses 'language(s)' and 'tongue(s)' interchangeably for both of these meanings, the context determining which definition applies. Wycliffe's New Testament follows suit. The KJV uses 'language' only for words of speech, but 'tongue(s)' for both meanings.*

languisheth: *obsessed with or*

dwelling unhealthily upon.

languishings: *sicknesses, torments.*

languor: *weakness; sickness; weariness of mind or body.*

latten: *a kind of brass hammered into thin sheets, used for making church utensils, such as candlesticks and crosses.*

lay (men): *uninstructed or untaught (from 'lewide'; survives in 'laity').*

learn: (v) *to teach.*

learned: *taught or instructed.*

leave: (n) *permission, license.*

leave: (v) *to let go, send away, dismiss.*

leaveful: *with permission or leave, 'permissible' or 'lawful' ('lawful' is found in the "Wycliffe Bible").*

leavest not: *without pause, unceasing.*

lecher: *a lewd, prurient man.*

lechery: *uncontrolled sexual activity.*

leech: *physician ('blood-letter'; one who treats with leeches).*

left: (v) *sent away, dismissed, to have let go.*

legacy: *a commission, that which one is entrusted with, authorized, or commanded to fulfill; that which has been received.*

leprous: *filled with leprosy.*

let: (v) *to hinder (!); to allow or permit.*

letted: (v) *hindered (!); allowed or permitted.*

letters: *writings, and so, 'the scriptures'; study, higher learning.*

letting: *hindering (!).*

libel: *'a little book of forsaking' or of divorcement (from Latin via Old French; survives in 'libel: a written statement which*

damages a person's reputation').

lieth: *is present with or before, or 'at hand'.*

lifelode: *alt. spelling of 'livelode' (see below).*

light: *easy; lit., not heavy, so unburdened, relieved, free from discomfort.*

lighten: *to give light or to make bright, to illumine, 'to enlighten'.*

lightened: *lit up; brought to light, 'enlightened'.*

lightening: *illumining, bringing to light, 'appearing'; making bright.*

lighter: *easier.*

'-like': *-ly, -ily (i.e., god-like or 'godly'); as a ..., or like a ... (e.g., 'beast-like', 'heathen-like', 'heaven-like', 'home-like', 'Jew-like').*

likeness: *similitude, parable, proverb.*

likings: *pleasures, enjoyments.*

lineage: *line of descent, ancestry, family, tribe, kindred.*

'-ling': *denoting a person or young animal having the quality or characteristics implied (e.g., 'comeling', 'darling or dear-ling', 'duckling', 'hireling', 'suckling', 'underling', 'youngling').*

litigious: *chiding, quarrelsome (survives in 'prone to taking legal action').*

little book: *see 'libel' above.*

little master: *teacher of young.*

livelode: *livelihood, sustenance (also spelled 'lifelode').*

living(s): (n) *conduct, way of life.*

lo!: *behold!*

loaves of proposition: *'bread of the presence (of Yahweh)'; 'shew-bread' or 'showbread'; 'loaves of the setting/putting*

forth' *(initially described in Exodus 35:13).*

loose: *to loosen or undo.*

lordship: (v) *to rule or have authority over.*

lordshipper: (n) *one who has the dominion, power and the authority, or the supremacy, of a lord; the Lord High God.*

lordshipping: *power or authority over people, 'ruling' or 'governing'.*

lose: *to destroy (active sense; 'destroy' is found in the "Wycliffe Bible").*

lost: *destroyed (active sense; survives in the sense of "the ship was lost at sea"; 'destroyed' is found in the "Wycliffe Bible").*

lot: *inheritance or fate, destiny (sometimes from 'sort').*

lot(s): *the process of deciding something by a game of chance (survives in 'lottery').*

lowed: *made low, lowered, humbled, abased.*

lying: (n) *a lie or lies (sometimes replaces 'leasing', which is also found in the KJV); reclining.*

lying-by: *to procreate.*

lying-monger: *liar ('liar' is found in the "Wycliffe Bible").*

M

mad: *crazy or insane (from 'wood'; 'mad' is found in the "Wycliffe Bible").*

madded: *made mad or insane.*

maddest: *'art mad'.*

made void: *nullified; put away or done away.*

madness: *from 'woodness' ('madness' is found in the "Wycliffe Bible").*

magistrates: *rulers of the temple.*

make merchandise: *commerce, to buy and sell.*

make mind: *to remember.*

make ready: *to prepare.*

make void: *to nullify, to do away with.*

mal-ease: *'bad' ease, disease, sickness; great discomfort.*

male-kind: *male human being.*

'man-homicide': *a murderer.*

manhood: *(hu)manhood or 'humanity'.*

manor: *a feudal domain or landed estate; a field or fields.*

man-queller: *'man-killer', so, executioner or murderer.*

manslayer: *murderer.*

mantle: *loose, sleeveless garment worn over other garments.*

Maranatha: *'in the coming of the Lord'.*

margarite(s): *pearl(s) (survives as 'Margaret').*

master: *teacher (also 'little master', 'under-master').*

masterful asker: *officer of the law court.*

maumet: *(n) idol, false god (the "Later Version" uses 'maumet' and idol interchangeably; derived from a misunderstanding of Islam).*

may: *to be able to, 'can'.*

meat: *eating; dinner, feast.*

meddle: *(v) to mix.*

medley: *a mixture.*

meed: *reward.*

meek: *(v) to humble or abase oneself (also 'meeked', 'meeking').*

menace: *(v) to threaten.*

menaces: *(n) threats (also 'menacings').*

menslayers: *murderers.*

'mercyable place': *'the propitiary' or 'mercyseat'.*

mercyseat: *the lid of the ark of the covenant, fashioned as a* throne for the Majesty of God, the Holy of Holies.

mesels: *lepers (survives in 'measles', the sickness that produces red spots on the skin).*

mete: *(v) to measure (also 'meted', 'meting').*

metretes: *liquid measurement of ancient Greece (1 metrete = 9 gallons).*

mild: *meek, gentle.*

mind: *(n) remembrance.*

mindful: *remembering.*

mined: *'undermined'.*

minister: *servant.*

ministered-under: *served under.*

ministration: *service, ministry.*

ministry: *service, providing for the needs of others.*

minutes: *small pieces of money of minuscule value, 'mites'.*

mirth: *gaiety, social merriment.*

mis-born child: *an abnormal birth; an abortion.*

misdoer: *one who does wrong.*

mis-ease: *'bad ease' or 'ill being', need, want, distress, poverty.*

mis-turn: *(v) to pervert or to turn wrong.*

mite: *small coin or sum of money; a dust speck or particle (also 'mites').*

mix: *from 'meddle' (also 'mixed').*

mixture: *from 'meddling'.*

moist: *(v) to water or 'moisten'; to wash or wet (also 'moisteth', 'moisted').*

moot hall: *judgment hall or trial court.*

morrowing: *morning.*

morrowtide: *morning.*

morsel: *small fragment of food.*

most: *mostly, most of all, especially.*

mote: *a tiny speck of dust or sand (survives in 'mite').*

much-fold: *manifold.*

must needs: *of necessity.*

must: *(n) grape wine.*

mustard seed: *from 'seneuey'.*

N

napkin: *a small piece of towelling (replaces 'sudarium' or 'sweating cloth').*

nappeth: *to nap or sleep.*

nard: *spikenard.*

natural: *from 'of kind' or 'by kind'.*

naturally: *from 'kindly'.*

nature: *from 'kind'.*

near: *nearer.*

need(s): *needed or needful, so necessary, or of necessity; want, that which is necessary for life or living.*

neediness: *deprivation, poverty; distress.*

new: *newly.*

nigh coasted: *bordering.*

nigh: *(adv) near; (v) to approach (also 'nighed', 'nighing').*

nigheth: *to approach.*

no wise: *no way.*

nobility: *nobleness, honour.*

noise: *disturbance, uproar.*

nol: *neck.*

none: *'not one' (the word 'no' before words starting with a vowel, similar to 'a'/'an' before words starting with 'h').*

not subject (to): *not under the power of; unruly, insubordinate, disobedient.*

nought: *nothing, without existence.*

nourish: *(v) to nurse or suckle an infant; to bring up or raise.*

nourished: *nursed; brought up, raised.*

nourishing: *(v) nursing.*

now born: *'newborn'.*

nurse: *(v) to suckle; to nourish.*

nursing: *suckling; nourishing.*

O

obligation: *pledge, bond, contract.*

occasion: *pretense, pretext.*

odourments: *sources of pleasing scents and odours.*

of belief: *'of faith'.*

of kind: *by nature, naturally.*

of: *from; for; by; to.*

offence: *an act of stumbling or 'sin'; a cause or occasion of sin; a stumblingstone or stumbling-block; to cause insult or make angry; synonymous with 'hurting' and 'spurning' (each use is found in the "Wycliffe Bible" and the KJV).*

offend: *to cause to stumble, sin or fall; to insult, or cause anger or resentment (both uses are found in the "Wycliffe Bible" and the KJV; sometimes from 'sclaundre', though 'offend' is found in the "Wycliffe Bible").*

office: *service or ministry.*

old men: *forefathers, those in olden times, 'elders'.*

on-putting: *putting on.*

opportune: *from 'covenable'.*

opportunity: *sometimes from 'covenably', though 'opportunity' is found in the "Wycliffe Bible".*

ordain: *to pre-destine; to appoint; to order or decree; to set in order.*

ordinance: *order or decree; conduct; founding or ordering.*

ought: *to have a moral duty, or to be obliged, to do something.*

ourself: *ourselves.*

out of belief: *out of, or without, faith; disobedient.*

out-casting: *'outcasts' or exiles; refuse, trash.*

over-cloth: *survives in 'overcoat'.*

overcome: *to conquer or triumph over, to gain mastery of; to be plenteous, to abound.*

over-go: *to go beyond, to overreach.*

'over-hard keeping of goods': *covetousness, greediness.*

overlaying: *burdening, 'pressing' or pressure, dis-ease, trouble, tribulation.*

over-led: *deceived, seduced, led away.*

over-seeming: *beyond measurement, 'most excellent' (see also 'above-seeming').*

over-thwart: *perverse, head-strong, obstinate, 'athwart'.*

over-waxeth: *grows or increases greatly.*

owe(th): *obligated to or bound to; indebted to; 'ought'.*

P

pale: *a pointed stick, stake or pole; a surrounding fence or 'palisade'.*

palsy: *paralysis.*

parings: *scraps, the part 'pared off' (survives in 'paring knife').*

part taking: *'partaking'.*

part: *(v) to divide or break into parts; to share, give or impart; to depart or leave.*

parter: *one who divides.*

parting: *(v) sharing with; dividing; difference or distinction.*

partings: *(n) that which is 'parted', divided or shared, and so, 'distributions' or even 'gifts'.*

pask: *Passover (survives in 'paschal').*

'pass we': *'surpass we'.*

pass: *(v) to depart or leave.*

passible: *able to suffer, human, mortal.*

passingly: *surpassingly.*

passion(s): *(n) suffering.*

passion: *(v) to suffer.*

pasture(s): *(n, v) from 'lesewe'.*

pasturing: *from 'leswynge'.*

peaceability: *peacefulness, calm (also 'peaceableness').*

penance: *repentance; a rite involving contrition, confession, acceptance of penalties, then absolution.*

pence: *pennies (pl. of penny).*

pens: *wings or feathers (survives in 'pinion: the wing or flight feathers of a bird' and in 'pen: a writing instrument originally derived from a feather').*

people of purchasing: *people bought or 'redeemed' by the sacrifice of Jesus Christ.*

peradventure: *perhaps, perchance.*

perdition: *eternal damnation, hell.*

perish: *to be lost; to die; to be destroyed (from the Latin, 'to go away').*

perturbation: *to disquiet or disturb greatly, to agitate; to cause confusion.*

Pharisees: *Jewish sect that emphasized strict adherence to ritual.*

physician: *a medical doctor (from 'leech: a blood-letter or one who treats with leeches').*

piety: *godliness (from 'pitee').*

pilgrim: *one who journeys, especially to some sacred place; any wanderer or wayfarer.*

pilgrimage: *long, arduous journey; metaphorically, 'the Christian walk'.*

pious: *devout, godly, reverential (from 'piteous'; also 'piously' from 'piteously').*

GLOSSARY

plaint: *complaint.*

pleasance: *pleasantness, pleasure.*

plenteouslier: *more plenteously, more plentifully.*

plowing: *from 'eringe' ('plough' as a noun is found in the "Wycliffe Bible").*

plummet: (n) *a plumb bob.*

pointel: *a stylus or writing instrument.*

poll: (v) *to shave, clip, shear, trim, or cut off the hair.*

potentate: (n) *an authority or power (from 'potestate').*

power of the prince: *authority.*

precellent: *primary and excellent.*

precept: *order; commandment.*

prelate: *ruler (survives as 'high-ranking member of the church').*

prepuce: *the foreskin; 'the uncircumcised', so the heathen or Gentiles.*

prescience: *foreknowledge.*

president: *one who 'presides' or occupies the seat of power; a governor.*

pressing: *'dis-ease', overlaying, 'pressure'.*

prevarication: *breaking of the law (survives as 'telling lies').*

pricked: *pierced.*

pricks: (n) *stings.*

primacies: *first fruits ('primacy' survives as 'the state of being first, as in rank or excellence; the office of an archbishop; the office of the Pope').*

princehood: *principality; authority to rule over.*

principat: *principality.*

private(s): *truth(s) that can be known only through Divine revelation; 'mysteries'.*

privily: *privately, secretly.*

privy: *private, secret.*

proconsul: *Roman official with authority over a province or military company; a governor.*

procurator: *Roman official who served as a provincial or financial administrator; steward of a farm (survives in 'curator').*

profession: *the act of 'professing', that is, declaring or avowing; 'a declaration'.*

proffer: *to offer.*

profiteth: *to benefit.*

progenitor: *forefather or parent.*

proper: *its or one's own, personal, particular (found in the "Wycliffe Bible" and the KJV; survives in 'property').*

propitiation: *conciliation, atoning or atonement, sacrifice (found in the "Wycliffe Bible" and the KJV).*

propitiatory: *the place of conciliation, the 'mercyseat', the throne serving the Majesty of God.*

proposition: *see 'loaves of'.*

prove: *to try or test; approve.*

proveth: *approveth.*

provisions: *supply of food, necessities for living.*

provost: *official having authority over others; a magistrate.*

prudence: *sound judgment; sagacity.*

publican: *a Roman tax collector.*

publish: *to proclaim, to make known publicly.*

purpless: *seller of purple.*

purposing: *purpose.*

pursue: *to persecute or to harass.*

purvey: *to provide provisions, necessities of life (also 'purveying').*

purveyance: *the act of purveying; that which is*

supplied (i.e., provisions), 'the means or way to survive' (1 Cor. 10:13).

put: *to lay down; laid down.*

Q

quarternion: *a military unit of four men under one's authority.*

queller (man-): *one who extinguishes by force, puts down, and so, 'an executioner'.*

querne: *hand-mill.*

quick: *living, alive.*

quicken: *to make alive, to give or restore life to (also 'quickened').*

R

rabbi: *a 'master' or teacher.*

raven: (n) *robbery; the act of pillaging and plundering;* (adj) *rapacious.*

raveners: *those who pillage, plunder, ravage, take by force.*

ravening: *ravaging.*

ravish: *to seize, to snatch, to catch.*

reach: *to give to, to reach forth or extend to.*

ready: *available, at hand.*

realm: *kingdom.*

reared: *raised.*

recapitulation: *a summary (from 'capitale'; found in the Prologue to the "Wycliffe Bible").*

reckest: *to have a care or a concern for, to heed (survives in 'reckless').*

recorded: *remembered.*

recording: *making mind of, remembering.*

rectus: *straight (from Latin).*

redeem: *to regain possession of by paying a price, to ransom; to pay off and receive back.*

reform: *to make better; to improve morally, to give up sin;*

to 'form again' or anew, to 're-form'.

regeneration: rebirth; spiritual and/or moral renewal.

reliefs: (n) fragments; scraps or leavings of food.

remission: pardon, forgiveness, delivered from debt.

remnants: from 'reliefs'.

repent: from 'forethink' ('repented' and 'repentant' are found in the "Wycliffe Bible").

replete: full, sated.

repromission: promise.

reproof: (n) rebuke, blame, reproach.

reprovable: reproachable.

reproved: rebuked.

reproves: (n) rebukes, censures.

repugn: oppose, fight (against), resist (survives in 'repugnant').

requite: to compensate or repay; to make return to (from 'quit').

riddle: (v) to sift.

rightful: righteous; just; right.

rightwise: righteous.

rightwiseness: righteousness.

ripely: readily, hastily.

rising-again: resurrection.

rivelling: wrinkle/ing ('wrinkle' is found in the "Wycliffe Bible").

river: from 'flood'.

rod: staff ('staves' is found in the "Wycliffe Bible"); a sceptre.

rubbing: from 'frotinge'.

rudder: from 'governail'.

ruddy: tinged with red, rosy.

rude: rough (texture).

rue: (v) to feel sorrow, regret, or remorse for.

ruth: (n) compassion, pity; regret.

S

sackcloth: from 'sack' or 'sak'.

sacrileger: one who commits sacrilege.

safe: saved from sin, 'salvation'; made whole.

sampler: 'exemplar' (from Old French ('en)saumpler').

satchel: a small handbag.

satisfaction: from 'aseethe' ('satisfaction' is found in the "Wycliffe Bible").

savour: (n) to understand or perceive (survives in 'savoir-faire'); odour; taste.

savoured: seasoned, made flavourful.

savourest: (v) to think upon, perceive, or to understand (also 'savoureth').

science: knowledge.

scribe: temple copyist, interpreter of scriptures.

scrip: a small bag, wallet, or purse.

seat: seat of government, and so, 'a throne'.

secureness: security.

seek: search.

seemliness: from 'honesty'.

seemly: from 'honest'.

semblance: likeness, outward appearance, countenance.

sendal: a piece of fine linen or silk.

seniors: elders.

servage: servitude, bondage.

service: ministry, office.

set: put, ordained, appointed.

shame: (v) to be ashamed of.

shamed: (v) ashamed, was ashamed of ('ashamed' is found in the "Wycliffe Bible").

shamefastness: shamefaced, showing shame or bashfulness.

shames: (n) reproofs, rebukes.

shed: to pour (out) (also 'shedded').

shewbread: unleavened bread displayed in the Jewish temple and dedicated to God (see also

'loaves of' proposition').

shined: shone (p.t. of shine; found in the "Wycliffe Bible" and the KJV).

shogged: shaken, jogged, tossed.

shortly: in few words, briefly.

showbread: see 'shewbread' above.

shrewd: depraved, wicked.

sick: weak (British usage); unwell.

sickness: weakness, frailty (British usage); illness.

siege: seat, and so, a throne (from Latin, via Old French, meaning 'to sit').

sign: token or miracle.

signal: sign.

signet: mark or seal.

silveren: made of silver (suffix survives in words like 'golden').

similitude: (n) a likeness, and so, 'a parable'.

simulacra: idols.

simulacrum: idol.

simulations: 'feignings', hypocrisies, pretence.

Sire: 'Sir', form of address to a superior.

sistren: sisters.

slack: (v) to slacken or make loose. **slake:** (v) to lessen the intensity of, 'to loosen'.

slander: (v) to injure with malicious, false utterances.

slates: plates or tiles of slate used for roofing.

slough: a bog, or a place with deep mud.

smaragdus: Greek for emerald.

smite: (v) to strike.

smiter: fighter.

snatch (up): to seize or catch (from 'ravyshe'; also 'snatched', 'snatching').

snub: to reproach or reprove.

GLOSSARY

solace: (n) *comfort in grief;* (v) *to soothe.*

solar: *loft or upper chamber (British usage; somewhat survives in 'solarium').*

soldiers: *from 'soudes' (see also 'wages').*

solds: *wages (from 'soudes').*

somewhat: *something.*

sooth: *true; truth.*

soothfast: *truthful.*

soothly: *truly.*

sopped up: *to take up by absorption, and so, figuratively, 'swallowed'.*

sore: *greatly or in high degree, intensely.*

sorry: *aggrieved; regretful.*

sort(s): *class, set, group, or type of something; kind(s); inheritance; lot.*

soul: *mind, reason; understanding; life.*

sovereign: *leader; one who exercises authority over others.*

species: *kinds or sorts (of).*

speedeth: (v) *to profit or benefit; is expedient (survives in term 'Godspeed: best wishes/good fortune' and in 'expedient' and 'expedite').*

speedful: *expedient.*

spoil: (v) *to impair or destroy the value of; to rob or to take from by force; to be stripped of (also 'spoiling').*

spot: *stain or blemish, and so, 'a sin'.*

spousals: *weddings.*

spouse: *bridegroom; a partner in marriage, male or female.*

spoused: (v) *espoused.*

spousess: *wife; bride.*

sprinkle off: *to scatter or shake off (from 'sprengen').*

spurning: *'to kick with the foot'(synonymous with 'hurting',*

'offence' and 'stumbling').

stable: *sure, firmly established, fixed, steadfast, enduring.*

stablish: *to found, 'establish'; fix, confirm (also 'stablished').*

stably: *firmly in place, fixed, not easily moved.*

state: *status, standing; condition.*

stater: *gold or silver coin of ancient Greece.*

staves: *staffs.*

stead: *place.*

steadfast: *firmly fixed in faith, constant.*

stole: *a long, narrow band of decorated cloth worn around the neck and over the shoulders; a vestment; a long, loose robe.*

stony sea: *rough, hard sea, waves hitting like rocks.*

store up: *include, enclose (from 'enstore').*

strait: *narrow.*

strand: *river.*

strength: (n) *a strengthened place, and so, 'a stronghold'.*

strife: (n) *struggle, fight.*

strive: (v) *to struggle, fight, or contend with.*

strives: (n) *contention, fighting, struggles (also 'strivings').*

strove: *struggled, fought.*

stumbling: *occasion or cause of sin or a spiritual fall, and so, 'an offence' (archaic meaning).*

sturdinesses: *indignations ('angry tempers').*

stylus: *a writing instrument used on clay or wax (from 'pointel').*

subject (to): *under the control or power of; in control or orderly.*

subjection: *the state of being brought under the power of another.*

substance(s): *goods of this world.*

suckling-frère: *foster brother.*

sudarium: *napkin; towelling; cloth used to cover the face of a corpse (pl. sudaria).*

sue: *to follow (survives in 'pursue', 'ensue'; 'follow' is found in the "Wycliffe Bible").*

suffer: *to permit or to give leave to; to endure.*

suffice: *to be enough.*

sufficence: *'sufficiency', contentment, having enough.*

suitable: *appropriate, fitting, in season, opportune (from 'covenable').*

suitably: *from 'covenably'.*

supping thing: *something to eat.*

supplement: *provision for what is lacking, 'a supply'.*

surpass: *to exceed (from 'pass').*

surpassingly: *exceedingly (from 'passingly').*

sustain: *to endure; to bear with.*

sweating cloth: *a small piece of towelling (sense survives in 'sweatshirt', 'sweater').*

sweven: *dream; vision.*

T

take keep: *take care.*

take recording: *am reminded of.*

take: (v) *to receive; to bring; to deliver or give up to; to commit or entrust; to lay hold of or seize.*

taken: *received; delivered or given up to; seized; betrayed (Luke 21:16).*

talent: *in ancient Greece, a weight or unit of gold or silver, often in coin form.*

tares: *weeds that grow among wheat (also called 'cockles' and 'darnels').*

tarry: *to linger or remain longer than expected.*

temporal: *temporary; earthly.*

termineth: *to limit;*
to determine.

testament: *a covenant.*

thankings: *thanksgiving, thanks*
(also called 'graces').

that: *that which, or that what.*

the thirsting: *those who thirst.*

the which: *who, whom; what,*
which.

them: *themselves.*

themself: *themselves.*

therefore: *for this reason.*

thereto: *to this thing.*

therf loaves: *unleavened bread.*

therf: *without souring.*

thither: *in that direction; to that*
place.

thyme (tree): *misspelling of*
thyine (tree).

tiding: *a report or information,*
news.

tillers: *those who work the soil*
to produce crops, 'farmers'.

tithes: *1/10ᵀᴴ of annual income*
given to representatives of God.

to be before: *to lead the way.*

to little charge: *'to little care*
for', and so, to neglect,
disregard or even despise.

to: *of; for.*

token(ing): *visible sign; miracle.*

tongue(s): *spiritual language or*
spiritual speaking, 'strange
language not understood';
words of speech used by
a group to communicate
(e.g., 'one's native tongue').
Wycliffe's New Testament
follows the "Wycliffe Bible",
as does the KJV, in using
'tongue(s)' for both meanings
(see 'language(s)').

took: *received; delivered or*
gave over to; seized.

'to pieces': *implied in such*
verbs as 'to-drawe', to-bruise',
'to-rente', 'to-powder'.

tother: *the next; other ('other'*
is found in the "Wycliffe Bible").

transfigure: *to change the*
outward appearance of; to
transform; to glorify.

translate: *to transform; to*
change; to carry across or
over, to pass from (one side
to the other).

translation: *change or*
transformation.

transmigration: *to migrate or*
move from one country to
another.

travail: *(n) toil or labour;*
(v) to toil or labour; to trouble.

travailest: *to trouble.*

treat: **(v)** *to handle something*
physically; to 'handle' (a topic)
with one's mind, and so to
discuss or dispute or study
(survives in 'treatise').

treated: *discussed, disputed,*
handled or dealt with (a topic).

treating: *considering,*
discussing, disputing, dealing
with (a topic).

tribune: *a magistrate.*

trow: *to believe or suppose.*

trump: *(n) trumpet.*

trumped: *trumpeted.*

trust: *(n) confidence, boldness*
(from 'trow'; 'trust' is found in
the "Wycliffe Bible").

trustily: *confidently, boldly.*

turds: *dung.*

turn again: *to return (also*
'turned again', 'turning again').

turned: *converted.*

twain: *two.*

U

unbelief: *disobedience.*

unbelieveful: *'full of unbelief',*
so not believing in; disobedient;
unbelievable.

uncharged: *discharged,*

unloaded.

unchastity: *lechery.*

uncontinence: *unrestrained*
and uncontrolled (sexual)
behaviour, 'incontinence'
(also 'uncontinent').

uncorrupt: *'incorrupt', immortal*
(also 'uncorrupted').

uncorruption: *'incorruption',*
and so immortality
(also 'uncorruptible',
'uncorruptibility').

unction: *the act of anointing*
with oil.

undeadliness: *immortality*
('immortality' is found in
the "Wycliffe Bible").

undeadly: *immortal.*

undefouled: *undefiled.*

under colour of: *false*
appearance or pretence.

under-brought in: *stealthily*
brought in.

under-delved: *under-dug,*
or dug under.

under-lay: *to submit or subject*
oneself to.

under-master: *schoolmaster,*
teacher.

under-minister: *to serve under*
(also 'under-ministering').

under-putted: *put under, laid*
down or risked (one's life).

under-sailed: *sailing with sails*
spread.

under-serving: *serving under*
or together with.

under-set: *given to the*
undercurrent or under-tow.

understand: *(v) to have mind of,*
to think, reflect or meditate
upon, to consider.

under-yoked: *made tame.*

undo: *(v) to destroy; to deny*
the truth of (1 John 4:3)
(also 'undoeth').

unequity: *wickedness, injustice,*

'iniquity'.

unfaithful: 'not full of faith', and so, unbelieving, out of the faith or belief.

unfiled: undefiled.

unfouled: 'undefouled' or undefiled.

unfruitous: unfruitful (survives in 'unfructuous').

unhaply: unluckily; unfortunately.

unhonoured: to not honour, to dishonour (also 'unhonourest').

unknow: to not know, to be ignorant of (also 'unknoweth').

unknowing: (n) 'not knowing', and so, ignorance; (adj) ignorant; (adv) ignorantly.

unknowingness: the state of 'not knowing' or ignorance ('ignorance' is found in the "Wycliffe Bible").

unlearned: untaught or uninstructed.

unleaveful: without 'leave', license or permission, so impermissible or 'unlawful'.

unlettered: without 'letters' or a degree, study or formal education.

unnarrable: unable to be told out, 'unspeakable' (survives in 'narrate: to tell or describe').

unnobility: 'ignobility', dishonour, baseness.

unnoble: 'ignoble'; dishonour; base (also 'unnobleness').

unobedience: disobedience.

unordinately: 'inordinately', out of good order, unruly, disorderly.

unpeaceable: agitated, unruly, disorderly (also 'unpeaceably').

unpiety: 'impiety', ungodliness.

unpious: 'impious'.

unpliable: unbowing.

unportable: unable to bear

or to carry.

unprudent: 'imprudent', foolish.

unquieted: disquieted (see 'unpeaceable').

unreprovable: unreproachable.

unrightwiseness: unrighteousness.

unseemly: from 'unhonest'.

unspotted: without stain or blame, so, 'sinless'.

unstable: 'moving from place to place', so, without a home (1 Cor. 4:11).

unsteadfast: weak.

unsteadfastness: weak in belief.

unwashen: unwashed.

unwemmed: unspotted, without blemish or fault, so, 'sinless'.

unwisdom: ignorance; foolishness.

unwitting: (n) 'not knowing', ignorance.

unwitty: without wit (without mind or understanding or reason), and so, unwise or foolish.

unworshippest: to dishonour (see 'unhonourest').

up-bearing: bearing up.

upbraid: to reproach severely.

us self: ourselves.

usuries: interest (usually excessive) paid on money.

utter-more: 'outer-more', utmost.

V

venge: (v) to avenge; to revenge.

vengeance: plagues (Apoc. 15:1, 21:9, 22:18); retribution.

venger: avenger; one who takes revenge.

verily: truly; indeed.

very: true.

vestments: one of the ritual garments of the clergy.

victualed: (v) provided with

'victuals' (food) and other provisions for living (from Middle French 'vitaille'; survives in 'vittles').

vinery: a vineyard.

vinolent: given to much wine, drunken.

virtue: power, strength, might; authority; moral rectitude.

virtues: mighty powers; 'works of power' or miracles; moral excellence.

voice: sound, noise.

void: empty; null.

voided: made void.

volatiles: birds; 'enfatted' feast offerings (survives in 'volatile: flighty').

volupties: pleasures or delights (of a sensual nature), lusts of life (survives in 'voluptuous').

W

wages: (n) those who are paid to serve and fight, and so, 'soldiers' (from 'soudes').

wagged: quickly moved from side to side.

wake: (v) to awaken; to be alert or to watch for; to stand watch.

waking: (n) a watch or duty period, usually 4 hours; watchful.

wallowed: rolled.

wan: pale from sickness or injury.

wander: to walk; to travel.

ward: prison, prison cell; hold for prisoners.

warded: guarded (survives in 'prison warden').

wardings: fortifications, strong-holds; prisons.

warily: cautiously, carefully.

warn: to notify, advise or admonish of possible harm; to proclaim or state without allowing dissent; to order under threat of penalty, and so, 'to command' (synonym of 'announce').

washen: *washed.*

waste: *to destroy, come to nought, consume (also 'wasteth').*

wasted: *destroyed; devastated; consumed.*

wax: *(v) to grow or to increase; to become.*

wayward: *willful, untoward, following one's own wanton or depraved inclinations.*

ween: *(v) to suppose or guess; to think.*

well: *good.*

wellfully: *'fully well', so successfully, prosperously, 'healthfully'.*

wellsomely: *successfully, prosperously, 'healthfully' (suffix survives in 'handsomely').*

wem: *spot, stain, blemish, fault, and so, 'sin' (survives in 'wen: a benign skin tumour or cyst').*

what: *why; that.*

whelps: *young dogs.*

whereof: *of or from what; of which or of whom.*

whereto: *why; to what place or end.*

which: *who, whom, whose; what.*

whichever: *whomever.*

whither: *to which or what place; where.*

Whitsuntide: *the 7ᵀᴴ Sunday after Easter, 'Pentecost'; also the week that follows 'Whitsunday'.*

who: *which.*

whole: *wholesome.*

wield: *to control or to rule; to manage.*

will: *(n) pleasure; wish, desire; mind.*

willful: *willful(ly) or willing.*

willing: *'willingly'.*

wily: *sly, cunning.*

win: *gain.*

winning: *wealth, material or financial gain.*

wintern: *(v) to dwell (in a place) during winter.*

wise: *way of doing, manner.*

wist: *knew ('wist' and 'knew' are found in the "Wycliffe Bible" and the KJV).*

wit: *(n) mind; understanding; reasoning; insight; intelligence.*

witen: *(v) we/they know ('witen' and 'know' are found in the "Wycliffe Bible" and the KJV).*

withhold: *to retain or hold back (also 'withholdeth').*

withholden: *withheld.*

withinforth: *'within', inside.*

without: *(adv) outside.*

without: *(prep) from 'outakun' or 'take out'.*

without desert: *without deserving (of special privilege).*

without discipline: *without learning, uninformed.*

withoutforth: *'without', outside.*

without letters: *without a degree or formal education.*

withstand: *to resist or oppose (also 'withstandeth').*

witless: *mindless; foolish.*

witness: *(v) to testify.*

witnessing(s): *(n) testimony, testimonies.*

wits: *minds; understanding.*

witting: *knowing.*

womb: *belly.*

won: *gained.*

wont: *habit, personal custom.*

word of belief: *'word of faith'.*

work(s) of power: *miracle(s) (from 'virtue(s)'; 'power' is found in the "Wycliffe Bible").*

worlds of worlds: *eternity, 'forever and ever' (also found in*

the "Later Version" as 'world of world' and 'world of worlds').

worlds: *for ever.*

worship: *(v) to pay homage to, to venerate; to adore or to admire excessively (in the "Wycliffe Bible", as per British usage, 'worship' and 'honour' are interchangeable; in Wycliffe's New Testament, modern usage is followed to avoid confusion).*

worshipful: *'honourable', worthy of respect (British usage).*

worthy: *of worth or value.*

worts: *herbs.*

wot: *(v) I know ('wot' and 'know' are found in the "Wycliffe Bible" and the KJV).*

wounds: *(n) affliction, 'plagues' (Luke 7:21; Apoc. 18:4, 8).*

wrath: *(n) rage, anger, indignation.*

wrathed: *angered or made angry, and so, 'provoked'.*

wrathing: *angering or making angry, and so, 'provoking', or 'a provocation'.*

wreathed: *twisted and turned (from 'writhe').*

wrenched: *violently twisted and pulled (from 'debraided'/ 'to-braided'; also 'wrenching').*

wretchednesses: *miseries.*

wroth: *furious, filled with anger.*

wrought: *worked.*

Y

yard: *enclosed piece of ground; a garden (from Old German '3erde: yard/garden'; see 'garden').*

yield: *(n) reward; (v) to give or render to; to reward.*

you: *yourselves.*

youngling: *young person.*

yourself: *yourselves.*

Endnote: Regarding the "Early Version"

The "Early Version" of the "Wycliffe Bible", hand-printed about 1382, has long been criticized by Bible historians as too literal, often unintelligible, at best a deeply-flawed 1ST attempt. In fact, much of the "Early Version" Gospels and the Apocalypse were transferred to the "Later Version" without significant change, and closely resemble the text you have read in *Wycliffe's New Testament*.

However, it is also true that when the "Early Version" is directly compared to the "Later Version", the "Early Version" is, overall, a less satisfying read. It is not so finely-tuned and contains many more italicized glosses which interrupt the flow. That is why hand-written variations of the "Later Version" became the foundation upon which the "King James Version" (KJV) was built. But, as was stated earlier, comparing all three versions side-by-side, it becomes clear that the KJV translators rejected numerous revisions made in the "Later Version", and chose instead individual words and phraseology found in one variant or another of the "Early Version". Why did they do this? Simply put, in countless passages of the "Early Version", both the poetry of the language and fidelity to the original Greek text are superior to that found in the "Later Version".

As the words contained within the square brackets in *Wycliffe's New Testament* readily demonstrate, the KJV translators repeatedly followed the "Early Version", rather than the "Later Version", in regard to prepositions ("the" in "EV" replaced by "a" in "LV"), verb forms (e.g., "saying" and "sitting" in "EV" replaced by "said" and "sat" in "LV"), and phrase order within a verse ("a/b/c" in "EV" rearranged into "b/a/c" in "LV").

But of greatest consequence are almost one hundred significant words that appear in the "Early Version", which were later copied in the KJV, but which are not found in the equivalent "Later Version" verses. Translation is an inexact science. A single word can often be rendered several ways (as the "Wycliffe" versions themselves amply demonstrate). Therefore these linguistic agreements between the "Early Version" and the KJV are meaningful. Examples include: "unction" ("anointing" in "LV"), "allegory" ("understanding" in "LV"), "mystery" ("private" in "LV"), "liberty" ("freedom" in "LV"), "captive" ("prisoner" in "LV"), "Caesar" ("emperor" in "LV"), "prize" ("reward" in "LV"), "wise men" ("astrologers" in "LV"), "veil" ("covering" in "LV"), "faith" ("unbelief" in "LV"), "concision" ("division" in "LV"), and "sand" ("gravel" in "LV"). These words, and many others, were first introduced into the English New Testament lexicon in the 1382 "Early Version" of the "Wycliffe Bible". More than two hundred years later, they were utilized again by the KJV translators.

Presented on the following page are a sampling of "Early Version" verses (limited only by space, for there are literally 1000s to choose from) which read like a 1ST draft of the KJV. Sometimes fine-tuning would be required, but often the KJV translators' 'red pencil' would scarcely be needed. Compare these verses with their counterparts in *Wycliffe's New Testament*.

Endnote: Regarding the "Early Version"

WYCLIFFE, 1382

MATTHEW

2:1,2 ...lo! kings, *or wise men*, came from the east to Jerusalem, saying, Where is he, that is born the king of Jews?

11:29 Take ye my yoke upon you, and learn ye of me, for I am mild and meek of heart; and ye shall find rest to your souls.

18:20 For where two or three shall be gathered in my name, there I am in the midst of them.

22:21 ...Therefore yield ye to Caesar those things that be Caesar's, and to God those things that be of God.

MARK

1:3 The voice of *one* crying in desert, Make ye ready the ways of the Lord, make ye his paths rightful.

1:6,7 †...and he ate locusts, and wild honey, and preached, saying,...

LUKE

4:8 ...Thou shalt worship the Lord thy God, and to him alone thou shalt serve.

4:12 It is said, Thou shalt not tempt the Lord thy God.

JOHN

3:16 Forsooth God so loved the world, that he gave his one begotten son, that each man that believeth into him, perish not, but have everlasting life.

ACTS

20:36 ...for he said, It is more blessed to give, more than to receive.

KJV, 1611

MATTHEW

2:1,2 ...behold, there came wise men from the east to Jerusalem, saying, Where is he that is born King of the Jews?

11:29 Take my yoke upon you, and learn of me; for I am meek and lowly in heart: and ye shall find rest unto your souls.

18:20 For where two or three are gathered together in my name, there am I in the midst of them.

22:21 ...Render therefore unto Caesar the things which are Caesar's; and unto God the things that are God's.

MARK

1:3 The voice of *one* crying in the wilderness, Prepare ye the way of the Lord, make his paths straight.

1:6,7 ...and he did eat locusts and wild honey; and preached, saying,...

LUKE

4:8 ...Thou shalt worship the Lord thy God, and him only shalt thou serve.

4:12 It is said, Thou shalt not tempt the Lord thy God.

JOHN

3:16 For God so loved the world, that he gave his only begotten Son, that whosoever believeth in him should not perish, but have everlasting life.

ACTS

20:36 ...how he said, It is more blessed to give than to receive.

In Conclusion

Consider these well-known phrases:

Ye be light of the world...for many be called, but few *be* chosen...
a prophet is not without honour, but in his own country...He that is not against us,
is for us...Suffer ye little children to come to me, and forbid ye them not, for of
such is the kingdom of God...how hard it is for men that trust in riches to enter in
to the kingdom of God...My God, my God, why hast thou forsaken me?...Go ye
into all the world and preach the gospel to each creature...And Mary said, Lo! the
handmaid of the Lord...ask ye, and it shall be given to you; seek ye, and ye shall
find; knock ye, and it shall be opened to you...for lo! the realm of God is within
you...Those things that be impossible **with** men, be possible **with** God...Father,
forgive them, for they **know** not what they do...In the beginning was the
word...He was in the world, and the world was made by him, and the world knew
him not...And the word was made man, and dwelled among us...Truly, truly, I say
to thee, but a man be born again, he may not see the kingdom of God...For God
loved so the world, that he gave his one begotten Son, that each man that
believeth in him perish not, but have everlasting life...I am bread of life...I am the
light of the world...ye shall know the truth, and the truth shall make you free...I
am a good shepherd...I and the Father be one...And Jesus wept...I am way, truth,
and life...As my Father loved me, I have loved you...I have overcome the
world...My kingdom is not of this world...What is truth?...For in him we live, and
move, and be...For we deem a man to be justified by faith, without works of the
law...For the wages of sin *is* death...If God *be* for us, who *is* against us?...ye be the
temple of God, and the Spirit of God dwelleth in you...If I speak with tongues of
men and of angels, and I have not charity, I am made as brass sounding, or a
cymbal tinkling...When I was a little child, I spake as a little child, I understood as
a little child, I thought as a little child...and I shall walk among them; and I shall
be God of them, and they shall be a people to me...And now live not I, but Christ
liveth in me...I have kept the faith...be ye doers of the word, and not hearers
only...as the body without spirit is dead, so also faith without works is dead...for
your adversary, the devil, as a roaring lion goeth about, seeking whom he shall
devour...that **one** day **with** God *is* as a thousand years, and a thousand years *be* as
one day...Lo! I stand at the door, and knock; if any man heareth my voice, and
openeth the gate to me, I shall enter to him, and sup with him, and he with
me...And he said to me, It is done; I am alpha and **omega**,
the beginning and the end.

In Conclusion

John Wycliffe and John Purvey wrote all of these famous words more than 600 years ago. More than two centuries later, the most beloved and revered Bible translation of all time, the "Authorized Version" or "King James Version" (KJV), was published. It contains many similar, and numerous identical, phrases. But nowhere are the brilliant contributions of Wycliffe and Purvey credited. Bible historians followed the lead of the KJV translators and denigrated and dismissed their masterful work.

These particular phrases are far from obscure. In fact, they constitute the very essence of the New Testament. After modernizing the spelling, only four replacement words – appropriate, understandable modern words substituting for obsolete, "dead" Middle English words – were needed to make all of these 14ᵀᴴ century passages fully comprehensible. (The replacement words are printed in boldface: "with", "know", and "one" are found in both their obsolete and modern forms throughout the "Later Version"; "omega" is only found in its symbolic form.) **All of the other words, in precisely the order that you see them here, are found in the "Later Version" of the "Wycliffe Bible".** Clearly, the replacement words do not create the consistency between the "Later Version" and the KJV. Even if no replacement words were utilized, the dependence of the latter upon the former would be undeniable. That is intrinsic to both.

As previously stated, translation is an inexact science. Phrases, even individual words, can be rendered numerous ways (witness the multiplicity and diversity of translations of the New Testament currently available). So when we find so many similar sentences in the KJV New Testament, it is no accident, and it is more than mere coincidence.

Simply put, based on these passages alone, one can unequivocally state that the KJV could not have been written without careful study of the "Later Version" of the "Wycliffe Bible". The foregoing 400+ pages demonstrate this point *ad infinitum*. They also provide ample evidence that the "Early Version" of the "Wycliffe Bible" was also utilized innumerable times. The word choice, word order, verb forms, phrase order, even the punctuation of the KJV New Testament, could not have been written as is, without repeated reference to *both* versions of the "Wycliffe Bible". That is the great discovery found within *Wycliffe's New Testament*. And that is the historical wrong that has now been righted.

But let us go one step further. Put aside all considerations of influence upon the KJV, and simply judge the Wycliffe New Testament on its own merits. In this regard alone, it stands as a work of genius, deserving our respect, indeed our awe. The Wycliffe New Testament is an honourable, memorable, worthy, first English vernacular translation of the New Testament. And its authors, John Wycliffe and John Purvey, have earned their standing in the pantheon of English Literature, alongside such luminaries as Chaucer, Shakespeare, Milton, Tyndale, and the translators of the King James Version of the Bible.

Bibliography

Berry, George R., *The Interlinear Literal Translation of The Greek New Testament (With the Authorized Version)*. Grand Rapids, Mich.: Zondervan Publishing House, 1971.

BibleGateway.com. [Online]. (2001). Available: http://www.biblegateway.com (September 30, 2015). Many Bible translations and a plethora of resources for Bible study. Another helpful website is: http://bibledatabase.net (September 30, 2015).

Bruce, F. F., *History of the Bible in English*, 3RD ed. New York: Oxford University Press, 1978.

Cruden, Alexander, and C. H. Irwin, A. D. Adams, and S. A. Waters, editors, *Cruden's Complete Concordance to the Bible, With Notes and Biblical Proper Names under one Alphabetical Arrangement*. Guildford and London: Lutterworth Press, 1977.

Daniell, David, *Tyndale's New Testament*. New Haven, Conn.: Yale University Press, 1989.

Davies, W. D., *Invitation to the New Testament, A Guide to Its Main Witnesses*, Anchor Books ed. Garden City, New York: Doubleday & Company, Inc., 1969.

Davis, N., D. Gray, P. Ingram, and A. Wallace-Hadrill, *A Chaucer Glossary*. New York: Oxford Clarendon Press, 1979.

Fisiak, Jacek, *A Short Grammar of Middle English, Part One: Graphemics, Phonemics and Morphemics*. London: Warszawa*PWN Polish Scientific Publishers, Oxford University Press, 1968.

Forshall, The Rev. Josiah, and Sir Frederic Madden, editors, *The Holy Bible, Containing the Old and New Testaments, With the Apocryphal Books, In the Earliest English Versions, Made from the Latin Vulgate by John Wycliffe and His Followers, Volume 4*. London: Oxford University Press, 1850.

Gehman, Henry Snyder, editor, *The New Westminster Dictionary of the Bible*. Philadelphia: The Westminster Press, 1970. A brilliant book, highly recommended for anyone studying the Bible.

Good News Bible New Testament, Today's English Version, 4TH ed. New York: American Bible Society, 1976.

The Holy Bible (King James Version). Cleveland, Oh.: World Publishing Company, n.d.

Lampe, G. W., editor, *The Cambridge History of The Bible, Volume 2*. Cambridge: Cambridge University Press, 1980.

Lindblom, J., *The Bible: A Modern Understanding*. Philadelphia: Fortress Press, 1973.

Merriam-Webster's Collegiate Dictionary, 10TH ed. Springfield, Mass.: Merriam-Webster, Inc., [Online]. (2001). Available: http://www.merriam-webster.com (September 30, 2015).

Miller, Madeleine S., and J. Lane Miller, *Harper's Bible Dictionary,* 7TH ed. New York: Harper & Row Publishers, 1961.

Morehead, Albert H., editor, *The New American Roget's College Thesaurus in Dictionary Form.* New York: New American Library, 1962.

Mossé, Fernand, *A Handbook of Middle English.* Translated by James A. Walker. Baltimore: The Johns Hopkins Press, 1952.

The New English Bible, The New Testament, 2ND ed. Oxford: Oxford University Press, Cambridge University Press, 1970.

Noble, Terence P., editor, *Wycliffe's Apocrypha.* Vancouver: Rasmussen and CreateSpace, 2014. Available: http://www.biblegateway.com, http://www.ibiblio.org, http:///www.amazon.com, and other websites (September 30, 2015).

Noble, Terence P., editor, *Wycliffe's New Testament.* Vancouver: Ward, 2001. [Online]. (2001). Available: http://www.biblegateway.com, http://www.ibiblio.org, http:///www.amazon.com, and other websites (September 30, 2015).

Noble, Terence P., editor, *Wycliffe's Old Testament.* Vancouver: Rasmussen, 2010. [Online]. (2010). Available: http://www.biblegateway.com, http://www.ibiblio.org, http:///www.amazon.com, and other websites (September 30, 2015).

The Oxford English Dictionary, 2ND ed., 20 vols. Prepared by J. A. Simpson and E. S. C. Weiner. Oxford: Clarendon Press, 1989.

Stratmann, Francis Henry, and Henry Bradley, editors, *A Middle-English Dictionary, Containing Words used by English Writers from the Twelfth to the Fifteenth Century, A New Edition Re-arranged, Revised, and Enlarged.* London: Oxford University Press, 1891.

Tortora, Phyllis G., editor, and Robert S. Merkel, consulting editor, *Fairchild's Dictionary of Textiles.* New York: Fairchild Publications, 1996.

Wegner, Paul D., *The Journey from Texts to Translations. The Origin and Development of the Bible.* Grand Rapids, Mich.: Baker Academic, A Division of Baker Book House, 1999.

Winn, Herbert E., editor, *Wyclif: Select English Writings.* London: Oxford University Press, Humphrey Milford, 1929.

yourDictoinary.com. [Online]. (2001). Available: http://www.yourdictionary.com (September 30, 2015).

Recommended Reading (Regarding Gospel Origins)

Bauscher, Rev. Glenn David, *The Original Aramaic New Testament in Plain English, with Notes and Commentary*, 6TH ed. Lulu Publishing, 2011.

Biven, David, *New Light on the Difficult Words of Jesus: Insights from His Jewish Context*. Holland, MI.: En-Gedi Resource Center, 2005.

---------, and Roy Blizzard Jr., *Understanding the Difficult Words of Jesus: New Insights from a Hebrew Perspective*, rev. ed. Shippensburg, PA.: Destiny Image, 1994.

Black, Matthew, *An Aramaic Approach to the Gospels and Acts*, 3RD ed. Oxford: Clarendon Press, 1967.

Blass, Frederich, *Philology of the Gospels*. London: Macmillan and Co., 1898. [Online]. (2012). Available: http://archive.org (September 30, 2015).

Burney, C. F., *Aramaic Origin of the Fourth Gospel*. Oxford: Oxford University Press, 1922. [Online]. 2012. Available: http://archive.org (September 30, 2015).

---------, *The Poetry of our Lord, An Examination of the Formal Elements of Hebrew Poetry in the Discourses of Jesus Christ*. Oxford: Oxford University Press, 1925.

Carrington, Philip, *The Primitive Christian Calendar*. Cambridge: Cambridge University Press, 1952.

Casey, Maurice, *Jesus of Nazareth*. London: T&T Clark International, 2010.

Edwards, James R., *The Hebrew Gospel and the Development of the Synoptic Tradition*. Grand Rapids: Wm. B. Eerdmans Publishing Co., 2009.

Gordon, Nehemia, *The Hebrew Yeshua vs. the Greek Jesus*. Arlington: Hilkiah Press, 2006.

---------, and Keith Johnson, *A Prayer to Our Father*, 2ND ed. Arlington: Hilkiah Press, 2010.

Goulder, M. D., *A Tale of Two Missions*. Norwich: Hymns Ancient and Modern Ltd. 1994.

Howard, George, *The Hebrew Gospel of Matthew*. Macon: Mercer University Press, 2005.

Lewis, Agnes Smith, *Light on the Four Gospels from the Sinai Palimpsest*. London: Williams and Norgate, 1913. [Online]. (2012). Available: http://archive.org (September 30, 2015).

---------, *Some Pages of the Four Gospels Re-Transcribed from the Sinaitic Palimpsest with a Translation of the Whole Text.* London: C.J. Clay and Sons, 1896. [Online]. (2012). Available: http://archive.org (September 30, 2015).

Lindsey, Robert Lisle, *A Hebrew Translation of the Gospel of Mark: A Greek-Hebrew Diglot with English Introduction*, 2ND ed. Jerusalem: Dugit, 1973.

---------, *Jesus, Rabbi and Lord: The Hebrew Story of Jesus Behind Our Gospels.* Oak Creek, WI: Cornerstone Publishing, 1990.

Minge, Brenton, *Jesus Spoke Hebrew: Busting the Aramaic Myth.* Brisbane: Shepherd Publications, 2001.

Spong, John Shelby, *Liberating the Gospels: Reading the Bible with Jewish Eyes.* San Francisco: HarperCollins Publishers Inc, 1996. (Highly controversial, with much here that I do not subscribe to, but also very informative and insightful.)

Torrey, C.C., *Documents of the Primitive Church.* New York: Harper & Brothers, 1941.

---------, *Our Translated Gospels.* London: Hodder & Stoughton, 1936.

Trimm, James Scott, *The Hebraic-Roots Version Scriptures, containing the Tanak and Ketuvin Netarim, translated out of the original Hebrew and Aramaic.* Republic of South Africa: Institute for Scriptural Research, 2004.

Trocmé, Etienne, *The Passion as Liturgy.* London: SCM Press Ltd. 1983.

Zimmermann, Frank, *The Aramaic Origin of the Four Gospels.* New York: KTAV, 1978

About the Author

Terry Noble attended the University of British Columbia (BA'75) and the Vancouver School of Theology. His articles have appeared in numerous magazines and newspapers. His books include *The Sculpture of Elek Imredy* (1993), *Wycliffe's New Testament* (2001), *Wycliffe's Old Testament* (2001, 2010), the revised *Wycliffe's New Testament* (2011), *Wycliffe's Bible* (2012), and *Wycliffe's Apocrypha* (2014). His interests in photography and travel have taken him to the 7 continents. Terry and Quynh live in Vancouver, Canada.